D1551454

EVANGELISM AND CHURCH GROWTH

Elmer L. Towns

Regal Books
A Division of Gospel Light
Ventura, California, U.S.A.

Published by Regal Books
A Division of Gospel Light
Ventura, California, U.S.A.
Printed in U.S.A.

Regal Books is a ministry of Gospel Light, an evangelical Christian publisher dedicated to serving the local church. We believe God's vision for Gospel Light is to provide church leaders with biblical, user-friendly materials that will help them evangelize, disciple and minister to children, youth and families.

It is our prayer that this Regal Book will help you discover biblical truth for your own life and help you meet the needs of others. May God richly bless you.

For a free catalog of resources from Regal Books/Gospel Light please contact your Christian supplier or call 1-800-4-GOSPEL.

Library of Congress Cataloging-in-Publication Data
Towns, Elmer L.
    Evangelism and church growth / Elmer L. Towns.
          p. cm.
    Includes bibliographical references and index.
    ISBN 0-8307-1742-0 (hardcover)
    1. Evangelistic work—Encyclopedias. 2. Church growth—Encyclopedias. I. Title.
    BV3790.T66 1995   95-38507
    269'.2'03—dc20   CIP

Rights for publishing this book in other languages are contracted by Gospel Literature International (GLINT). GLINT also provides technical help for the adaptation, translation and publishing of Bible study resources and books in scores of languages worldwide. For further information, contact GLINT, P.O. Box 4060, Ontario, CA 91761-1003, U.S.A., or the publisher.

1 2 3 4 5 6 7 8 9 10 11 12 13 14 15 / 02 01 00 99 98 97 96

With Appreciation to
Bob and Carol Zinngrabe
Huntington Beach, California
    The Zinngrabe Charitable Foundation made a donation for research and preparation of a course in Evangelism and the Christian Life at Liberty University, 1994.
    The educational content of this course was delivered through the Liberty University School of Lifelong Learning, through interaction with a televised lecturer, a content-driven work text and the substantive content of this encyclopedia.

Dedication

This encyclopedia is dedicated to four people whose influence has been used by God to bring multitudes to Christ in modern times. Of all those doing evangelism, only God knows who has brought the most to Christ in history and who has the greatest influence today. But these four people are generally recognized as great contemporary leaders of evangelism and their names have been synonymous with winning the lost to Christ and growing His Church.

Bill Bright founded and built Campus Crusade International, Inc. into one of the largest evangelical organizations driven by evangelism on the university campus, but his influence through it extends into all the world and every part of the Church. Of all the anointed tools of Campus Crusade, the *Jesus* film may have presented the message of Christ to more unsaved people than any other form of mass media. When Bill Bright first wrote and used "The Four Spiritual Laws," he may have given people the most-used tool in presenting Christ by personal evangelism. This author was a student at Columbia Bible College when he heard Bill Bright in the early 1950s challenge the student body to evangelize the world in our generation. Bright's message electrified the student body and this author believed Bright intended to do all he could to fulfill the challenge. Because this author also attempted to fulfill that challenge, this volume is dedicated to Bill Bright.

Dr. David (Paul) Yonggi Cho has built the largest church since Pentecost, during our lifetime, in Seoul, South Korea, consisting of a congregation of more than 600,000 souls. The size defies earthly understanding—only God could do it. But the human leader is Dr. Cho, who has used cells in homes to evangelize his Jerusalem.

Anyone who studies this giant church knows it is not external factors of church growth that has produced its fantastic influence, but it is a church committed to prayer, fasting, Spirit-anointed preaching (i.e., spiritual factors of church growth). Because of Dr. Cho's godly influence on evangelism, this book is dedicated to him.

Dr. William Franklin Graham Jr., Billy Graham, has presented the gospel to more people than any other evangelist who is now living, or has ever lived. He burst onto the scene of America's attention during the Hollywood Crusade in the late 1940s when screen stars and underworld leaders made decisions for Christ. He was among the first to effectively use media, placing his program, "Hour of Decision," on radio, television and later in films. He has held citywide crusades in every major American metropolitan area, in addition to most of the world. He preached in Russia before the Berlin Wall came down and has been a spiritual counselor to presidents and world leaders. Because the name "Billy Graham" is synonymous with mass evangelism, this encyclopedia is dedicated to him.

Dr. D. James Kennedy, pastor, Coral Ridge Presbyterian Church, Fort Lauderdale, Florida, became a leader in personal evangelism throughout the world through Evangelism Explosion, a program he originated and organized to train and develop soul winners in the local church. The credibility for Evangelism Explosion (called by many EE) came from the megachurch he built in south Florida, which became a leader in his denomination and to all in the church growth movement. Because of his contribution to personal evangelism and his preaching by television throughout America and to the world, this encyclopedia is dedicated to him.

Executive Editorial Committee

Dr. Robert Coleman
Billy Graham Center of Evangelism
Wheaton, Illinois

Dr. Lewis Drummond
Billy Graham Professor of Evangelism and
  Church Growth
Beeson Divinity School
Birmingham, Alabama

Dr. Gary Greig
Regent University
Virginia Beach, Virginia

Dr. Kent Hunter
Church Growth Center
Corunna, Indiana

Dr. Charles Kelly
Director, Center of Evangelism and Church
  Growth
New Orleans Baptist Theological Seminary
New Orleans, Louisiana

Dr. Gary McIntosh
Director of the Doctor of Ministry Program
  at Talbot School of Theology
Talbot School of Theology
La Mirada, California

Dr. Paige Patterson, President
Southeastern Baptist Theological Seminary
Wake Forest, North Carolina

Dr. Thom S. Rainer, Dean
The Billy Graham School of Missions,
Evangelism
  and Church Growth
Southern Baptist Theological Seminary
Louisville, Kentucky

Dr. Alvin L. Reid
Bailey Smith Chair of Evangelism
Southeastern Baptist Theological Seminary
Wake Forest, North Carolina

Dr. John Vaughan
Southwestern Baptist University
Bolivar, Missouri

Dr. C. Peter Wagner
Donald McGavran Chair of Missions and
  Church Growth
Fuller Theological Seminary
Pasadena, California

Introduction

My prayer for this volume is that God would use it to win people to Christ and thus carry out the Great Commission. To that end, I trust this will be a practical encyclopedia that will help pastors, ministers of outreach, youth workers, children's directors and lay evangelists. The book is also designed for those who are in the professional work of crusade evangelism, directing denominational evangelism, and any other person who is working to carry out the Great Commission. This volume also targets serious students; therefore, definitions, research and background are included to help those who need reference and resources on evangelism and church growth.

Note that in the title the word "evangelism" comes before the term "church growth." Some may question why. Technically, as the articles will explain, these two terms reflect two sides of the salvation door of entry to Christ and the Church. Dr. Donald McGavran, missionary to India and modern father of church growth, coined the phrase "church growth" in the 1950s while he was looking for a new term for evangelism. McGavran believed the term "evangelism" had lost its meaning because many being evangelized in India were learning the catechism or submitting to Christian water baptism. The people of India were converting to outward Christianity but not necessarily acquiring faith in the living Lord Jesus Christ.

McGavran said at a banquet of the North American Society for Church Growth that the term "evangelism" had picked up so much luggage, it no longer meant what the New Testament meant. McGavran explained that evangelism was an input word meaning "the church evangelizes people to get them saved." But McGavran was disillusioned with the output of evangelism (i.e., outward profession). He reasoned that when people are won to Jesus Christ and followed-up into the local churches, the result is church growth. Therefore, McGavran explained, "Why not use an output term (i.e., church growth), rather than the traditional term of input (i.e., evangelism)."

During the early 1990s, several voices are being raised against church growth. Some people see church growth as marketing, hence they have attacked church growth as being filled with novelties, non-Christian methods or advertising (i.e., "selling Jesus"). Other people have become disillusioned with the field of church growth, thinking that when they learned about church growth and applied it, their church would naturally grow. When growth did not occur, they started criticizing church growth.

Regardless of the reason, this encyclopedia takes the position that although both terms "evangelism" and "church growth" are biblical, when we return to the priority of evangelism (presenting the Lord Jesus Christ), the results of church growth will naturally take care of themselves. Hence, the term "evangelism" appears first in the title.

This encyclopedia does not include articles about evangelistic (commercial) products and programs. Also, this volume does not include notations on the thousands of nonprofit organizations that engage in all kinds of evangelism. This encyclopedia will not include them unless they are transtemporal and transcultural. This means that to be included, a program, method or organization must have endured the test of time and have been accepted worldwide.

This encyclopedia will emphasize principles of evangelism because they are transtemporal and crosscultural (i.e., a principle is eternal). These are seen explicitly or implicitly in Scripture and, therefore, we must analyze them to understand evangelism. Specifically, a method is defined as the application of a principle to culture. As such, Sunday School is considered a *method*, while reaching people for Christ and teaching them is the *principle* used in Sunday School. In the same sense, Vacation Bible School is a *method* that has reached millions of children and adults for Christ, because it used the eternal *principles* of evangelism.

The basis for choosing people to be described in this volume is their total-life influence in the cause of evangelism. Many famous people in the history of the Church are not included because their primary influence was in education or other ministries of the Church. Those included had a great influence on evangelism and church growth. Those associated with evangelism or church growth who are still living are omitted because the total influence of their ministry cannot be measured. However, some men who have made an obvious influence, but are still alive, will be included, such as Billy Graham, D. James Kennedy, David Yonggi Cho and Bill Bright.

This volume includes articles on some of the newest areas of evangelism, such as seeker services, evangelizing the boomers and busters, and modern church growth terminology such as the homogeneous unit principle and people movements. It also includes material from church history such as the First Awakening and the history of the gospel invitation. But it also includes practical material on using Sunday School enrollment to reach people for Christ and evangelism through small groups.

I want to thank the editorial review members for reading and making suggestions for this project. The only biographical sketches included in this volume are the Executive Editorial Committee and the four people to whom this volume is dedicated. It would be humanly impossible to determine and include all of the influential people in all denominations and movements in the world. Perhaps in a future edition they could be included.

Some of the Executive Editorial Committee members have contributed articles and have their names attached to the articles with their initials. These articles reflect their strengths and their orientations. I have written the unsigned articles and I take all responsibility for their strengths and weaknesses, for their omissions and oversights. Yet, the articles I have written are not solely my work. Through the years, I have worked with researchers who helped locate data and footnotes. No scholar ever stands alone, and surely I do not. Also, many of the insights are not my own.

Through the years, at several seminaries and universities, I have been the mentor for dissertations and theses. It has been my privilege to look over the shoulders of graduate students exploring new areas of study. I have grown in my understanding through the research of my students. Of all the students who have helped me, Dr. Doug Porter stands out for continual assistance. He has entered part of this encyclopedia into the computer and has worked with me on this project. The others who helped input this volume are Shelly Seager, Karla Temple and Sharon Fulcher. As mentioned before, I give the credit for this volume to others, and assume responsibility for all its weaknesses.

This encyclopedia is dedicated to "reaching the reachable" and "winning the winnable." May God use it greatly, according to its usability.

Sincerely Yours in Christ,

Elmer L. Towns
Summer 1995

Contents

A   15

A-1, A-2, A-3
Accepting Christ
Acculturation
Adaptive Deceptions
Adherents
Administration, Gift of
Adult Evangelism
Africasia
Age-Graded Sunday School
Age of Accountability
Agricola, Martin
Aidan
American Sunday School Union
Amsterdam Affirmations
Andrew
Animism
Anointed Preaching
Annual Growth Rate (AGR)
Anskar
Anthropology
Antinomianism
Archbishop's Definition of Evangelism
Archival Unit
Aristides
Arminius, Jacobus
Arrested Church Growth
Arrested Spiritual Development
Asbury, Francis
Assimilation Factors (See Culture and
    Assimilation Factors)
Atheism
Athenagoras
Atonement
Attributes (Absolute)
Attributes (Comparative)
Attributes of God
Augustine of Canterbury
Augustine of Hippo
Autopsy
Average Annual Growth Rate (AAGR)
Awakening (See Revival)
Axioms for Church Growth

B   25

Baptism, Reasons (See Believer's Baptism)
Barnabas
Barriers: Overcoming Them
Barriers to Evangelism and Church Growth:
    Definition
Barriers to Evangelism and Church Growth:
    Description
Bartholomew
Base
Baxter, Richard
Believer's Baptism
Beza, Theodore
Bible
Biblical Barriers
Biederwolf, William Edward
Billington, Dallas Franklin
Binding the Strongman
Biological Church Growth
Bishop
Body Evangelism
Body Life
Bonding People to the Church
Boniface
Boomers, Evangelism of Baby
Booth, William Bramwell
Born Again
Brainerd, David
Bridges of God
Bridging Growth
Bus Evangelism
Busters, Evangelism of Baby

C   45

C-1, C-2, C-3
Capital Fund-Raising
Carey, William
Carriers of Revival
Cats; Catalysts
Celebration
Cell
Cell and Celebration Growth

Cell Churches: Four Paradigms
Chafer, Lewis Sperry
Chalmers, Thomas
Chapman, Wilbur J.
Character Snapshots
Charter Statement (for Church Planting)
Children, Evangelism of
Cho, David (Paul) Yonggi
Christianity
Christianization by Abstraction
Chrysostom
Church: Comparison Between Old and New
    Testaments
Church: Contemporary Definition and
    Description
Church: First Reference in Scripture
Church: New Testament Explanation
Church: Theological Definition
Church: The Universal
Church: When Did It Begin?
Church Age
Church Extension
Church Growth Balance (See Church Growth
    Wheel)
Church Growth, Biblical Paradigms
Church Growth Conscience
Church Growth: Definition
Church Growth Eyes
Church Growth Justification: Should a Church
    Be Small or Large?
Church Growth Movement, Beginning of
Church Growth Movement
Church Growth Principles
Church Growth Rates
Church Growth: Social Science
Church Growth—Church-Planting Types
Church Growth Wheel
Church Membership: Biblical Basis
Church Membership: Qualifications for
    Admission
Church Planting
Church-Planting Models
City Gates
Class, Beginning a New
Class, Law of the
Class Sunday School
Classes
Classes of Workers/Leaders
Classifications of Revival

Classroom, Law of the
Clenched Fist, Law of the
Coleman, Robert
Commitment to the Land
Communicant Members
Communication: Role in Evangelism
Communion (See Lord's Supper)
Community Church Paradigms
Composite Membership
Conditions of Pain
Confession
Confluent Events
Conglomerate Congregation (See Modality)
Congregation
Congregational Structure
Conscience
Constitution: Church
Contextual Factors
Contouring Events
Conversion
Conversion Church Growth
Conversion: Doctrine of
Conviction
Corporate Sin
Covenant, Church (Suggestion for Church
    Planting)
Cross-Cultural Evangelism (See Bridging Growth)
Crusade Evangelism
Cults, Evangelizing People in
Cultural Chauvinism
Cultural Mandate
Cultural Overhang
Culture
Culture and Assimilation Factors

 D 125

Data Overlays
Data Sets
Dawn
Death, Church
Decadal Growth Rate (DGR)
Decline in Attendance
Decree of God
DeHaan, Martin R.
Demographic Study
Demon Possession: Definition
Demon Possession: Description
Demons

Denominations
Departmental Sunday School
Depravity (See Total Depravity)
Discerning the Body
Discernment, Gift of
Disciple
Discipling (See Perfecting)
Discipling a Whole Nation (DAWN)
Discipling Families
Discipling — Perfecting
Discipleship
Discipleship: Content
Discipleship Training
Discovery Questions
Doctrinal Faith (See Faith: Six Expressions)
Doubling Sunday School Class Attendance
Drummond, Lewis
Duff, Alexander

E   195

Earle, Absalom Backus
Edwards, Jonathan
Egalitarianism
Eicos Pattern
Elder
Election
Electronic Church
Elliot, Jim
Encouragers
Engel Scale
Enrollment, Sunday School Evangelism by
Equippers
Essential Elements
Eternality
Ethclass
Ethics of Church Growth
Ethne
Ethnikitis
Ethnocentricity
Eurica
Evangelical Revival (See Revival, First Great
    Awakening)
Evangelism
E-0 Evangelism
E-1 Evangelism
E-2 Evangelism
E-3 Evangelism
Evangelism: Biblical Description

Evangelism Explosion
Evangelism, Gift of
Evangelist, Local Church (See Soul Winning)
Evangelism: P-1, P-2, P-3
Evangelism: Process and Event
Evangelism, Team
Evangelism: Types of (See Evangelism, P-1,
    P-2, P-3)
Evangelist: New Testament Usage
Evangelistic Mandate
Evangelistic Myopia
Event, Evangelism
Excluded Middle
Exhortation, Gift of
Expansion Church Growth
Extension Church Growth
External Growth

F   225

Factors of Growth
Faith and Church Growth
Faith: Doctrine
Faith, Gift of
Faith Projection
Faith, Saving (See Faith: Six Expressions, and
    Believing)
Faith: Six Expressions
Family Analysis
Family of God
Fasting
Fellowship
Fellowship Circle
Fellowship Inflammation
Fellowship Saturation
Felt Need
Field Totals
Filling of the Spirit (See Fullness of the Spirit)
Finney, Charles
First Great Awakening
Fluctuating Receptivity
Fog
Folding
Follow-Up Gap
Forgiveness of Sins Committed Before the Cross
Four Spiritual Laws
Fourth World
Fox, George
FRANS

CONTENTS

Frelinghuysen, Theodore
Friend Day
Friendship Evangelism
Front-Door Evangelism
Fuller, Charles
Fullness of the Spirit
Fundamentals of the Faith

G   245

Gardiner, Allen
Ghost-Town Disease
Gift Assimilation
Gift Confidence
Gift Gravitation
Gift Ignorance
Gift Imitation
Gift Intrusion
Gift Manipulation
Gift Mix
Giving, Gift of
Goal Setting
God
Gordon, Adoniram Judson
Gospel: Definition
Gospel: Description
Grace
Graham, William (Billy) Franklin, Jr.
Graphs of Growth
Great Awakening
Great Commission
Gregory the Great
Gregory the Illuminator
Gregory, Thaumaturgus
Greig, Gary
Grid Mapping
Ground-Level Spiritual Warfare
Growth, Measuring
Growth, Traditional Laws of Sunday School
Gutzlaff, Karl

H   257

Haldane Brothers
Ham, Mordecai
Harvest Principle
Harvest Theology
Heart
Heart Language

Helpers
Hidden People
High Places
History of Evangelism: Survey
Holiness
Holy Spirit: His Working
Homesteaders
Homogeneous Unit (See People Movement)
Homogeneous Unit and People Movements
Homogeneous Unit: Biblical
Homogeneous Unit Church
Homogeneous Unit Principle
Homogeneous Unit Principle: Application
Houts Questionnaire
Hubmaier, Balthasar
Hunter, Kent
Huss, John
Hutter, Jacob
Hyde, John
Hypercooperativism
Hypothesis of the 10 Percent

I   273

Ideological Export Center
Illumination
Image of God
Incarnation
Indwelling of the Spirit
Inerrancy
Inspiration
Intercession
Intercessors
Intercessory Prayer
Intercessory Unity
Internal Church Growth
Inverted Discipleship
Irving, Edward

J   279

Jackson, Sheldon
Jehovah
John of Antioch (See Chrysostom)
John of Monte Corvino
Jones, Robert Reynolds
Jones, Samuel Porter
Judson, Adoniram
Justification

K   283

Kelly, Charles S., Jr.
Kennedy, D. James
Kenosis
Kerygma
Kinship Circle
Koinonitis
Korean Pentecost
Krapf, J. Ludwig

L   285

Latfricasia (See Africasia)
Law of God (Natural)
Leadership Classes
Leadership Descriptions
Leadership, Gift of
Leadership Training
Left-End Peoples
Ley Lines
Life-saving Station; Illustration of Church
    Purpose
Lifestyle Evangelism
Livingstone, David
Lord's Supper
Loyola, Ignatius
Lull, Ramon
Luther, Martin

M   291

Makemie, Francis
Manchurian Revival (1906)
Mandate for Evangelism
Marsden, Samuel
Martin, T. T.
Martyn, Henry
Mass Evangelism
Mass Movement
Masses
Mastering the Bible (See Discipleship: Content,
    Become Grounded on the Word of God)
Mayhew Family
McCheyne, Robert Murny
McIntosh, Gary
McGavran, Donald A.
Media Evangelism (See Saturation Evangelism)
Melting-Pot Theory

Membership, Church
Memcon
Mercy, Gift of
Methodius
Methods, Evangelistic
Meyer, Frederick Brotherton
Mills, Samuel John
Ministry
Ministry, Gift of Helps
Missiology
Mission
Mission Structures
Missions Education for a Church
Mobile Unit
Modality
Model Church Approach
Modernity
Moffat, Robert
Moody, Dwight L.
Moravian Revival
Morrison, Henry Clay
Morrison, Robert
Mosaic
Motivation for Evangelism and Church Growth
Motives for Evangelism
Mott, John
Multicongregational Model
Multi-Individual Decision
Multiracial or Multiethnic Church
Music, Evangelistic

N   307

Nathaniel
Natural Revelation
Near-Neighbor Evangelism
Neesima, Joseph Hardy
Networking Evangelism
Nevius, John L.
New Measures
Nominality
Nongrowth Excuses

O   309

Oikos Evangelism
Old Age (See Ghost-Town Disease)
Omnipotence
Omnipresence

Omniscience
One-by-One Conversion
One Hundred Barrier to Sunday School
    Growth
One Room Sunday School (See Class Sunday
    School)
OPS
Ordinances
Organic Growth
Organization
Organization and Church Growth
ORGS
Outpouring of the Holy Spirit (See Revival,
    Awakening, First Great Awakening)

P   313

Panta ta Ethne
Parallelism
Participatory Activities
Pastoral Leadership Transition
Pastoral Ministry Paradigms
Pathology of Church Growth
Paton, John Gibson
Patrick
Patterson, Paige
Paxon, Stephen
Pentecost, Day of
People Approach
People Blindness
People Flow
People Group
People Movement (See Homogeneous Unit and
    People Movement)
People Vision
Perfecting
Personal Sin
Persuasion Evangelism
Philip the Evangelist
Philosophy of Ministry
Pietism
Pilgrimages of Repentance
Pioneers
Planned Parenthood
Plateauing
Plutschau, Henry
Post-Denominational Churches
Power Encounter
Power Evangelism

Power in Evangelism (See Anointed Preaching
    and Filling of the Spirit)
Power Points
Pragmatism
Prayer Expeditions
Prayer Journeys
Prayer Revival of 1857-1858
Prayerwalking
Predestinate
Presence Evangelism (See Evangelism, P-1,
    P-2, P-3)
Priesthood of Believers
Primary Sources
Principalities and Powers
Priorities
Problem of the 9.5
Proclamation Evangelism (See Evangelism, P-1,
    P-2, P-3)
Prophecy, Gift of
Propitiation: Definition
Propitiation: Description
Prospect
Providing Additional Space
Pyramid Principle

Q   329

Qualitative Growth
Quantitative Growth
Quesnel, Pasquier
Quid Pro Quo Contract

R   329

Rader, Paul
Raikes, Robert
Raineer, Thom S.
Ramabai, Pandita
Reaching People for Christ
Receptivity
Receptivity: How to Cultivate
Receptive-Responsive People (See Prospect)
Reconciliation
Redemption: Doctrine
Redemption and Lift
Redemptive Gift
Reid, Alvin L.
Regeneration
Relationship Evangelism

Remnant Theology
Renewing Allegiances
Repentance
Resistance-Receptivity Axis
Resurrection of Christ
Retardation, Mental
Revelation
Reversion
Revival (See Awakening, First Great Awakening)
Ricci, Matteo
Right-End Peoples
Ripe Fields
Roberts, Evan
Robinson, Reuben
Roll Padding
Roll Purging
Romans Road
Rules of Interpretation

S   345

Salvation: Definition
Salvation, Plan of
Sanctification
Sanctification Gap
Sanctification: Practical
Sanctification: Prospective
Satellite Principle
Saturation Evangelism
Savonarola, Girolamo
Schmidt, George
Schwartz, Christian Frederick
Scofield, Cyrus Ingersoll
Scudder, John
Search Theology
Secondary Sources
Second Great Awakening
Seeker Services
Senility
Setting Personal Goals in Evangelism
Seven Touches, Law of (See Evangelism:
    Process and Event)
Sheep Stealing
Shepherding
Shepherding, Gift of
Shields, Thomas Todhunter
Showing Mercy, Gift of
Side-Door Evangelism
Signs and Wonders: Biblical Overview

Signs and Wonders: Definition
Signs and Wonders Movement
Simons, Menno
Simpson, Albert Benjamin
Sin
Sin of Commission
Sin (Imputed)
Sin (Omission)
Sin (Personal)
Sin Nature
Single-Cell Church (See Cell Churches: Four
    Paradigms
Small Sunday Schools
Social Action
Social Bondage Sites
Social Service
Sociological Strangulation
Sociological Tissue Rejection
Sodality
Soil Testing
Soul
Soul Winning (See Evangelist, Local Church,
    and Discipleship: Content)
Sovereignty of God and Church Growth (Also
    see Church Growth: Social Science)
Span and Control, Law of
Special Revelation
Speer, Robert E.
Spiritual Gift, Biblical Definition
Spiritual Gift Inventory
Spiritual Gifts
Spiritual Mapping
Spiritual Quest Sites
Spiritual Territoriality
Spiritual Strongholds
Spiritual Warfare
Spontaneous Growth
Spurgeon, Charles Hadden
St. John's Syndrome
Stained-Glass Barrier
Stair-Stepping
Static Churches
Strategic-Level Spiritual Warfare
Stew Pot
Stewardship Campaign
Stewardship, Five "Pockets"
Strategy
Strategy to Reach One's Friends
Studd, Charles T.

Sunday, Billy
Sunday School
Superaggressive Evangelism (See Saturation
    Evangelism)
Superchurch
Sympathizers
Synagogue: Relationship to the Church
Systematic Theology

T   383

Taylor, James Hudson
Teaching, Gift of
Tennent, Gilbert
Tennent, William, Jr.
Territorial Spirits
Tertullian, Quintus Florens
Testimony Evangelism
Third Wave Movement (See Signs and Wonders)
Thomas
Thomson, James
Three Battlegrounds
Three Hearings, Law of (See Seven Touches)
Three Priorities
Torrey, Reuben Archer
Total Depravity
Tour Questions
Towns, Elmer L.
Tradition Bearers
Transfer Church Growth
Trotter, Melvin Ernest
Truett, George W.
Twentieth-Century Awakening
Two-Humped Camel, Law of
Two Hundred Barrier
Tyndale, William
Types of Church Growth, or Worship Types

U   395

Universalism
Unreached People Group
Urbana Conference

V   399

Vacation Bible School
Vaughan, John
Virgin Birth

Visitation Program
Vital Signs of a Healthy Church

W   403

Wagner, C. Peter
Waagner-Modified Houts Questionnaire (See
    Houts Questionnaire)
Waldo, Peter
Warfare Prayer
Web Movements
Welsh Revival
Wesleyan Revival (See Great Awakening)
Wesley, John
Whitefield, George
White Flight (See *Ethnikitis*)
Wilfred
Williams, George
Williams, John
Willibrord
Winnable People
Winning, Soul
Wordless Book
Word of God
World Rulers of Darkness
Worldview
Worship Service
Worship Service: Beginning Another
Worship Service Paradigms (See Types of
    Worship Service)
Wycliffe, John

X   415

Xavier, Francis

Y   415

Youth Evangelism

Z   419

Zeisberger, David
Zelotes, Simon
Zero Growth
Ziegenbalg, Bartholomew
Zinzendorf, Count Nicolaus Ludwig, von
Zwemer, Samuel M.
Zwingli, Huldreich

A-1, A-2, A-3 See CULTURE AND ASSIMILATION FACTORS.

ACCEPTING CHRIST
An expression describing the act of becoming a Christian based on the biblical expression "received him" (Luke 8:40, *KJV*; 10:38, *KJV*; 15:27; 19:6; John 1:12; 4:45; 6:21). Some synonyms are "conversion," "becoming saved," "regeneration," "repented to salvation," "revived" and "born again."

How to Accept Christ as Savior
The expression "accepting Christ" is used by evangelical Christians to describe the means by which a person becomes a Christian. Many people understand they are sinners and alienated from God. They also know God loves them enough to send Jesus to die for their sins, but just knowing all this is not enough. People must respond to what they know and receive Jesus into their lives.

Jesus described Himself as being on the outside of our lives, seeking to come into our lives (Rev. 3:20). He pictures Himself as knocking on the door to our lives, waiting for our responses. Although Jesus is capable of doing so, He chooses not to force His way into our lives. The only way He can come in is in response to our invitation.

When people knock on our doors at home, we can ignore them, tell them to go away or invite them inside. Each of us has the same options when Jesus begins knocking on the door of our lives. We can ignore Him, reject His offer of eternal life as a part of His family, or invite Him in. The following prayer can be used to invite Jesus into our lives.

Dear Lord Jesus, thank You for loving me enough to die for my sins. Please forgive me for my sins and save me as You promised to do. I repent of my sins. I now receive You as my Lord and Savior. Come into my life and forgive my sins. Enable me by Your grace to live for You. Amen.

The words used to accept Christ are the means by which people express their desire for God. Those who sincerely welcome Christ on His terms are accepted by Him as they accept Him.

ACCULTURATION
The process by which a person changes his or her culture and orientation and adapts to the new situations, accepts some innovations and modifies its system through contact with other societies. A person who does not go through acculturation will experience cultural disequilibration.

ADAPTIVE DECEPTIONS
Deceptive schemes adopted by the enemy to replace earlier strategies whose beguiling powers have waned. These new deceptions may be viewed either as necessary course corrections or as upgrades to the adversary's product line. — GOJR

ADHERENTS
The unbaptized members of a declared Christian community in which many individuals are baptized believers and deeply interested in Christianity.

ADMINISTRATION, GIFT OF
One of the task-oriented gifts of the Holy Spirit. The supernatural ability to manage human, physical and financial resources through the management functions of planning, organizing, leading and controlling.

In a church or Christian organization, a person with this gift can lead an organization or program of outreach or evangelism in an effective manner because of his or her ability.

The strengths of this gift include (1) the ability to see the overall picture and think of long-range objectives; (2) the ability to delegate tasks to other people; (3) task orientation rather than person or need orientation; (4) the ability to counsel and motivate others regarding the task and; (5) tending not to be a perfectionist, but rather judging tasks by objectives.

The weaknesses of this gift include (1) appearing to want to get out of work because the person delegates; (2) appearing insensitive to people and inflexible in God's work because of being committed to long-range goals; and (3) being perceived as a glorified bureaucrat.

The person with this gift needs to avoid the danger of (1) becoming power-hungry; (2) using people to accomplish goals (manipulation); or (3) lowering standards to use anyone (in spite of character flaws or doctrinal errors) to get a job done.

References: Ted W. Engstrom, *Your Gift of Administration: How to Discover and Use It* (Nashville: Thomas Nelson Publishers, 1983); Douglas Porter, *How to Develop and Use the Gift of Administration* (Lynchburg, Va.: Church Growth Institute, 1994).

ADULT EVANGELISM

When God began the human race, He made adults. Although the Bible clearly shows God's interest in children, the great programs center around men and women. A small Samuel answered God's voice in the Temple and David defeated Goliath as a shepherd lad. But leadership in both Old and New Testaments rested with adults. Our Lord trained adult leaders who shaped the course of the world. Today, the divine imperative is for men and women, whose lives have been changed by the Lord, to reach lost adults for Christ.

Adult Needs

Relationship with God. Needs demand attention. Some are felt needs: for example, affection, self-respect, peer approval, independence and commitment. Often adults can be reached through their felt needs. Adults will listen to the claims of Christ when they realize God is interested in their problems. The acceptance of the gospel makes a difference in people's reaction to pressures. Although people are usually aware of felt needs, underneath is the spiritual need of which they may not be aware.

Adults need Christ and a proper relationship with Him. The adult should be guided into a meaningful understanding and appreciation of the teachings, life and sacrifice of the Lord Jesus Christ. The adult should have an opportunity to accept Christ as Savior from sin, and the experience of commitment to Christ as Lord. The adult must also have a knowledge and an experience of the person and work of the Holy Spirit as teacher, guide and source of power.

Recognition of failure. Life may have regrets for adults. Certain goals set early in life have not been attained. A feeling of guilt may be present because they have not done the best for their children. Their consciences could be troubled because of wrongs they have never rectified. Because of these failures, the adult may have an attitude of defeat, bitterness and cynicism.

Failures point up human frailty. They provide opportunity to guide people humbly to seek God. God allows some failures in order to reveal that He is faithful and just to forgive both the present and the past (1 John 1:9). Failures ultimately prove God's mercy. No one can relive the past. But God can forgive the past and people can take care of the present and future by settling a transaction with God for salvation.

Strength for the future. "As for man, his days are like grass; as a flower of the field, so he flourishes. For the wind passes over it, and it is gone, and its place remembers it no more" (Ps. 103:15,16). People know the brevity of life. They are here to live for a few short years. During these years, people are constantly faced with tomorrow. Decisions are made that will affect tomorrow. "Where will my employment take me?" "What will be the result of my latest opportunity of advancement?" "How will my children turn out?" All of people's problems force them to think of consequences.

The Bible deals with the past, present and future. Christ will forgive the past when a person places faith in Him. The Bible provides many specific examples of how to face the present world. The adult must be led into the Bible for his answers. Biblical teaching about the future, its rewards and punishment in connection with life after death must be clearly taught.

As the Bible is taught, more than factual presentation is needed. Teaching must be for decision, because people's dilemma demands an answer. To the unsaved the emphasis is now.

Salvation must be secured now in order to be secure after this life.

Adult World Environment

Adulthood usually comprises a span of 50 years or more. The cultural environment in which adults live needs to be appraised because it contains both assets and liabilities. The pressure is heavy upon adults. If we are to interest and reach adults, we must understand them and their world.

Mobility. Mobility has accelerated recently all over the world. It has become a threat to the stability of the home, the family and, ultimately, the church. Mobility results in people living in a community without becoming neighbors, and without getting closely involved. As a result, people have fewer personal roots in community life. Because the church often is a community institution, it suffers.

The effect of expressways has also contributed to the tremendous movements of population. From one perspective, the expressway appears to be a "divisive force rather than a new dimension in church planning."[1] Church members who move a distance away can within a few minutes drive back to their home church. This trend has serious implications for the pastor and the church, for it is difficult for the member to assume leadership and to regularly attend church functions. The member is faced with the task of traveling the distance several times a week to attend church. The distance and the radius of his parish also presents a significant problem to the pastor who desires an efficient and consistent program of visitation among the church members. He is forced to decide between evangelistic visitation in the immediate neighborhood of the church and visitation distant from the church where some of the members live.

Anonymity. Impersonal interdependence seems characteristic everywhere. We depend upon others to help us yet we seldom form deep relationships with these many people. Time won't permit it. This condition contributes to the depersonalization of people in society. People live lonesomely together.

In many places, adults have been reduced to numbers. As a result, adults lose their names and identities as dynamic human beings in their relationships with others. Hence, the cry that "adults are more than impersonal function, they need to be elevated [and respected] for who they are as well as what they can do."[2] The depersonalization of people is another reason for the church to be active in reaching people with the gospel. The friendly, adult Bible-study group can be the advance guard for evangelism in the church.

Spiraling knowledge. Increased knowledge is both an asset and a liability. It is an asset because adults know more today than in the past. It has helped them to advance in all areas of life. It has helped alleviate the ills of humanity. Aspects of knowledge extend from the minutest spaces or parts of the atom to the farthest reaches of the universe. Humans are learning, discovering, classifying and recording new information at a phenomenal rate. As new information is found, discovery of still newer knowledge is facilitated. So the increase of knowledge poses a threat to individual adults because they must keep learning if they are to keep up with the world around them. Keeping current with respect to new knowledge both intellectually and skillfully is difficult.

Reaching Adults Is Important

Increasing numbers. Throughout the world, the number of adults is constantly increasing. Medical advances in science have helped to prolong the life span of adults as never before, and the large youth population will soon become adults. As a result, the adult population is growing today.

Strategic positions. Adults occupy key and strategic functions in homes, business, political and religious life. For this reason, evangelism of adults should be emphasized. More adults should be integrated into Bible study groups.

Church support. Adults are the principle source of leaders for the local church. The financial support for the entire church program comes from adults. Where there is good adult support, the church evangelistic program is bound to succeed and, conversely, where there is little adult support, the work limps along and often ultimately fails.

Adults also determine the attendance in other

divisions of the church. If adults come, they will bring their children, whereas, if children come alone, only part of the family is reached. Adults also will take responsibility for leadership and financial support. As a result, they become the backbone of the church, not only in number, but in leadership, experience and potentialities.

Barriers to Evangelism

Formed habits. Because many adults have crystallized their habits, it is hard for them to establish new habit patterns. However, human nature is essentially modifiable and adults can learn. Every normal human being is a changing creature. This change continues during the lifetime of the person. Adults adjust to new, different and even difficult situations. Conversion causes a change within the inner being of the person, which results in a change of action, words and way of life.

Hardened hearts. Most adults are not hardened to the call of the gospel. Christ evangelized adults. He won men and women, and their lives were changed. Christ's claim came with force and impact upon mature, intelligent men and women. The apostle Paul devoted his time in declaring the gospel message to the adult world in Europe and Asia. Adults need God's forgiveness, comfort and guidance. This is equally true of young and older adults.

Those who are attending church when they are establishing their families (25-35 years of age) will probably continue attending church through retirement. Therefore, emphasis at the young-adult level will pay lasting dividends. Young adults are the least-reached group in the church. The young adult has struggled for freedom from his family ties during his teen years and now must form new ties. This struggle in forming new ties represents a lonely and individualistic period of life.

This should challenge each church leader to reach young adults. The message comes loud and clear. Reach them, win them, teach them—they are the church of tomorrow.

Older adults often turn to religion and spiritual things. They have time to reflect on the past and on the future. Their interest in material things is replaced by a growing concern for spiritual things. The senior citizen can be reached and will respond to the gospel. "The elderly individual is often more open to the message of the church than he has ever been before."[3]

Hesitancy to attend. Many adults have never attended church and are not familiar with the people, the program or procedures in a church. Adults fear this new venture because it can cause them embarrassment and a feeling of insecurity. Thus, friendly men and women who serve as greeters can help visitors feel more comfortable in a church setting.

Adults must be reached for Christ, and can be, through a church's educational program. Understanding adults and their unique problems, planning an attractive program for them and providing good teaching will open many ways to evangelize and make Christ known.

References: [1]Lyle E. Schaller, *Planning for Protestantism in Urban America* (Nashville: Abingdon Press, 1965), p. 64. [2]Gibson Winter, *The Suburban Captivity of the Churches* (New York: Macmillan Co., 1962), p. 24. [3]Robert M. Gray and David O. Moberg, *The Church and the Older Person* (Grand Rapids: Wm. B. Eerdmans Publishing Co., 1962), p. 37.

AFRICASIA

A term developed by Donald McGavran to identify peoples living in Africa, Asia and Latin America (i.e., the Third World). Later changed to LATFRICASIA.

AGE-GRADED SUNDAY SCHOOL

A Sunday School that has an average attendance of up to 1,000-1,200, so named because of its organizational structure, which adds a department for each age in the school grades and a department of adults with class divisions for each five-year span (e.g., ladies ages 25 to 29). The upper limits of an age-graded Sunday School represent the third danger-level plateau in a growing Sunday School.

AGE OF ACCOUNTABILITY

The age of accountability is that point in the development of children (physical, mental, social, psychological and spiritual) where they realize their personal accountability for sin and are able to respond to salvation based on their emerging personal responsibility.

Most Christians are assured that babies who die will be in heaven. This conviction is generally based on the belief of David, that he would someday go to the place where his dead infant had gone (2 Sam. 12:23). How this is possible is completely open to speculation. Edgar Mullins suggests, "Infants dying in infancy are changed in so far as they inherit a natural bias toward sin. But how this change is wrought by the Spirit is needless to inquire, since there is no light available on the subject beyond our speculations."[1] One possibility is suggested by Augustus Strong:

Since there is no evidence that children dying in infancy are regenerated prior to death, either with or without the use of external means, it seems most probable that the work of regeneration may be performed by the Spirit in connection with the infant soul's first view of Christ in the other world. As the remains of natural depravity in the Christian are eradicated, not by death, but at death, through the sign of Christ and union with Him, so the first moment of consciousness for the infant may be coincident with a view of Christ the Saviour which accomplishes the entire sanctification of its nature.[2]

Christians generally have believed that those who die before the age of accountability are not saved in the same sense of experiencing salvation as Christians do, but they are safe, meaning God has protected and will protect them according to His own nature. This means that God could not condemn, without an opportunity to respond, an unborn baby or child who dies before the age of accountability, because that would be inconsistent with God's nature.

Some traditions practice infant baptism. In these traditions, the emphasis in baptism is not on what the believer does, but what God does. This, in their view, parallels the initiation rite reflected in Israel: circumcision. Traditions that practice infant baptism often have a response

mechanism. Sometimes it is called "confirmation." This serves as a rite of entry into adult membership of the church in most of these traditions and reflects an age of accountability among them.

References: [1]Edgar Young Mullins, *The Christian Religion in Its Doctrinal Expression* (Philadelphia: Roger Williams Press, 1917), p. 383. [2]Augustus Hopkins Strong, *Systematic Theology: A Compendium Designed for the Use of Theological Students* (Grand Rapids: Fleming H. Revell Company, 1970), p. 663.

AGRICOLA, MARTIN (1486–1556)

Martin Agricola was the primary influence in establishing the Protestant reformation in Finland. Illiteracy was so high in Finland, Agricola had to first teach the Finnish people how to read before they could read his books and those by other reformers. He was, however, successful in his task and by 1520 the Finnish people and their leaders had adopted Lutheranism as their state religion.

AIDAN (d. 651)

Aidan was sent to Northumbria in response to a request for a bishop from Iona by King Oswald. In 634, he became the bishop of Northumbria and established his headquarters on the Island of Lindisfarne. He built a monastery on the "holy island," which became a significant center of evangelism. Aidan himself also traveled widely through the kingdom evangelizing the people, edifying the saints, addressing social concerns, training and ordaining local priests.

AMERICAN SUNDAY SCHOOL UNION (1824–1970)

The American Sunday School Union (ASSU) was the primary agency for the foundation and development of the American Sunday School. Founded in 1824, the ASSU was primarily a lay movement committed to using the Sunday School to teach Americans moral and democratic values. The threefold purpose of the Union was to (1) organize Sunday School leaders; (2) publish religious literature for Sunday School; and (3) develop new Sunday Schools in unreached population centers.

As early as 1832, the ASSU organized America's first national Sunday School convention. They published the first widely used Sunday School lessons and a 100-volume Sunday School library for children. Their best known missionary thrust was the Mississippi Valley Enterprise launched in 1830. In time, this thrust led to establishing more than 3,000 new Sunday Schools.

Following the War between the States, the rise of Sunday School conventions and denominational involvement in Sunday School weakened the influence of the ASSU. The Union continued its ministry, primarily in rural communities, but lacked the successes of its early history. In 1970, the ASSU changed its name to the American Missionary Society to reflect its new focus in working primarily with multicultural and ethnic groups to form new churches.

AMSTERDAM AFFIRMATIONS

A document developed in 1983 and adopted by itinerate evangelists outlining an ethical code for those involved in itinerate evangelistic ministry.

Reference: Billy Graham, *A Biblical Standard for Evangelists.*

ANDREW

A native of Galilee born in Bethsaida, Andrew holds the distinction of being the first-called disciple. Three events recorded in the Gospels describe Andrew in the context of bringing people to Jesus (John 1:40-42; 6:8,9; 12:20-22). Early church tradition describes Andrew bringing the gospel to the Synthians north of the Black Sea. Tradition holds he was crucified in Greece by order of the proconsul Aegeates on an X-shaped cross. "Saint Andrew's Cross" is featured prominently on the flag of Scotland.

The major contribution of Andrew to the cause of evangelism was introducing Simon Peter to Christ, who later became the chief spokesman for the gospel on the Day of Pentecost.

Andrew is viewed as the patron saint of

Greece, Russia and Scotland by Christians in those countries.

ANIMISM

The belief that all natural elements, such as mountains, rivers, trees, thunder, fire, stars, animals and human beings are endowed with, and likened to, a pervasive and conscious spiritual life force. —GOJR

ANNUAL GROWTH RATE (AGR)

A statistic showing the rate of a church's membership growth, using data from two consecutive years.

How to Determine Your AGR

To determine the annual growth rate of your church, substitute the appropriate data into the following equation: this year's membership – last year's membership ÷ last year's membership x 100 = AGR. The AGR is read as a percent of annual growth.
References: See AVERAGE ANNUAL GROWTH RATE (AAGR); DECADAL GROWTH RATE (DGR)

ANOINTED PREACHING

Preaching is anointed when the proclamation of the gospel has God's power to (1) transform lives; (2) bring people to Christ; (3) free people from immoral habits; (4) bring people into intimate fellowship with God; (5) transform lives to be like Christ; (6) work in ministry to the needs of hearers; (7) initiate revival (which is God's pouring Himself on His people); (8) and above all to bring glory to God. When there is anointed preaching, people respond to Christian service, find their spiritual gifts, give money to the cause of Christ and feel the presence of Christ.

ANSKAR (801–865)

A native Saxon from Flanders, Anskar began his mission in 826 at the request of the Danish King Harold and urging of Louis the Pious. He traveled widely throughout Scandinavia with other missionaries and had limited success in evangelism. He began the work, bringing Christianity to the Scandinavian nations.

ANTHROPOLOGY

One of the behavioral sciences that describes the origin of how people innovate, how they govern themselves, what restraints they set up for society and how they think.

ANTINOMIANISM

The belief system that maintains that Christians are freed from the moral law by the dispensation of grace. In a social context, it is the rejection of established morality. (Lit. means "against law" and is often indicative of a flagrant lifestyle.)

ARCHBISHOP'S DEFINITION OF EVANGELISM

A 1918 statement by the Anglican Archbishops' Committee defining evangelism as follows: "to evangelize is to so present Christ Jesus in the power of the Holy Spirit, that men and women shall come to put their trust in God through Him, to accept Him as their Savior, and serve Him as their king in the fellowship of His church."

Reference: See PERSUASION EVANGELISM.

ARCHIVAL UNIT

A spiritual mapping-team cell that is skilled in culling information from secondary sources. An archival unit will typically devote significant time to research in libraries and community archives. —GOJR

ARISTIDES (Second Century)

Aristides, a Christian philosopher in Athens, wrote an apology to Emperor Antonius Pius about 140 in which he compared Christian, Chaldean, Greek, Egyptian and Jewish worship forms. A complete Syriac version of this work was discovered in the Monastery of Saint Catherine at Mount Sinai in 1889.

ARMINIUS, JACOBUS (1560–1609)

Educated at Leyden and Geneva, Jacobus Arminius was a student of Bez, trained in the Calvinism of Reformed Theology. In 1603, he became professor of theology at Leyden. His attempt to modify Calvinism to prevent God from being viewed as the author of sin and to recognize the evolution of people was opposed by his colleague Francis Gomar and other Calvinists. Arminius called for a national synod to discuss the issue but died before the 1618 synod at Dortmund.

Arminius laid the theological foundation of Arminian theology, a theological view adopted by most holiness groups, including such outreach-oriented movements as the Methodist movement and the Salvation Army. Arminian theology emphasizes human responsibility in the conversion process and is viewed by some as a strong motive for evangelistic efforts.

ARRESTED CHURCH GROWTH

Arrested Church Growth is one of the causes that keeps a church from growing. It is called pathology of church growth caused by (1) excessive feeling of "family" spirit within the church and feelings of irritation toward "outsiders"; (2) undue attention toward "Christian perfection"; and (3) "bad air" generated by self-centered bickering in the congregation.

ARRESTED SPIRITUAL DEVELOPMENT

A pathology of church growth resulting when church members cease growing adequately in their relationship with God and one another. Because internal growth in grace is foundational to external or numerical church growth, a church characterized by a lack of prayer, the practice and tolerance of sin, a de-emphasis on the Scriptures, a neglect of vision and a lack of compassion for others, will soon cease experiencing numerical growth.

How to Overcome Arrested Spiritual Development

To overcome arrested spiritual development, steps should be taken to address neglected spiritual factors of church growth and to re-establish an adequate foundation upon which the church may experience renewed growth. The church may conduct a stewardship campaign to teach church members biblical stewardship of time, talents and treasures. The pastor of a church in this condition should address known cases of unconfessed sin among members personally and, if necessary, publicly. The church may also be organized to pray for the resolution of church problems and needs of the community. Many churches find a growth-oriented campaign, such as Friend Day, is effective in motivating church members to reach out beyond themselves to the lost in their sphere of influence. Also, a church should be creative in establishing new times, meetings and ministry forms for its ministry of prayer and intercession. If the traditional prayer meeting has lost its vitality, perhaps a series of early morning prayer meetings before members go to work will revitalize the church. Other churches may choose to organize a network of prayer cells meeting in homes, offices and other places throughout the week. Bible study is another means to overcome arrested spiritual development.

Reference: Elmer L. Towns, *154 Steps to Revitalize Your Sunday School and Keep Your Church Growing* (Wheaton, Ill.: Victor Books, 1988), p. 37.

ASBURY, FRANCIS (1745–1816)

Born into a Methodist home near Birmingham, England, Francis Asbury was himself converted at age 13 and began preaching three years later. Early on, John Wesley recognized Asbury's preaching ability and appointed him as an itinerant preacher. In 1772, Wesley appointed Asbury as his "general assistant" in charge of Methodist work in America. In 1784, Wesley appointed Asbury and Rev. Thomas Coke as bishops of the Methodist church in the United States, a position accepted by Asbury only after ratification by the Methodist conference. In his role as Bishop Asbury, he led in establishing new settlements on the American frontier, traveling 6,000 miles to preach 300 to 500 sermons annually. He became the organizer, dominant leader and driving force in the early growth of the Methodist Episcopal Church.

ASSIMILATION FACTORS See CULTURE AND ASSIMILATION FACTORS.

ATHEISM

The belief system that denies the existence of God.

ATHENAGORAS (Second Century)

Athenagoras was an Athenian professor who was converted through reading the Scriptures. In 177, he wrote "Supplication for the Christians" in which he defended Christians against charges of atheism, incest and cannibalism and appealed to the emperor for clemency for Christians. Much of this work is devoted to demonstrating the inadequacies of pagan deities.

ATONEMENT

(The root meaning in English, "at-one-ment," i.e., the bringing together of two who have been enemies into a relationship of peace.) The blood of Christ cleanses the sinner from sin's defilement. The term includes substitution, redemption, propitiation and reconciliation. The atonement of Christ is substitutionary in nature. On the cross of calvary, God placed our sins upon Christ and accepted Him in our place, thereby making it possible for God and people to be at peace.

ATTRIBUTES (ABSOLUTE)

The inherent qualities that only God possesses, such as omniscience, omnipresence and omnipotence.

ATTRIBUTES (COMPARATIVE)

Those attributes of God in which human abilities are reflected in God's divine nature (i.e., holiness, love and goodness).

ATTRIBUTES OF GOD

Those inherent virtues or qualities that manifest God's nature. We do not know the number of attributes, but they are usually classified as comparative and absolute.

AUGUSTINE OF CANTERBURY (d. 604/605)

He was a missionary sent to England by Pope Gregory the Great and was the first Archbishop of Canterbury.

Frustrated with the failure of the British bishops to work for the conversion of pagans, Pope Gregory the Great commissioned a group of monks under the leadership of Augustine as missionaries to England (596). Landing on the coast of the Kingdom of Kent in the spring of 597, Augustine began his outreach in the capital, Canterbury. The king was among thousands baptized as a result of this mission. He continued to work closely with Gregory and extended his influence and that of the Roman church throughout England.

Augustine established a Benedictine monastery in Canterbury, which became a prototype for others established throughout England. Also, he introduced and established the diocesan system to the English church with archbishops at Canterbury and York.

AUGUSTINE OF HIPPO (354–430)

Early church father whose concept of a church within a church may be the first mention of small-group ministry in church history.

AUTOPSY

The study of a dead church for the purpose of determining factors leading to its demise in hopes of preventing a similar fate in other churches.

AVERAGE ANNUAL GROWTH RATE (AAGR)

A statistic showing the rate of membership growth in a church over a period of years.

How to Determine Your AAGR

To determine the average annual growth rate of your church, substitute the appropriate data into the following equation: this year's membership – your first year's (base) membership ÷ your base membership ÷ number of years being examined x 100 = AAGR. The AAGR is read as a percent of annual growth.

References: See ANNUAL GROWTH RATE (AGR); DECADAL GROWTH RATE (DGR).

AWAKENING

The result of an outpouring of the Holy Spirit in a community in which significant numbers of saved persons are "revived" to begin again to live for God, and the unsaved experience conviction of sins and are "awakened" to their need for Christ and salvation. This term is sometimes confused with "revival."

Reference: See REVIVAL.

AXIOMS FOR CHURCH GROWTH

Four widely accepted preconditions for growth in a church are usually stated as follows: (1) The pastor must want the church to grow and be willing to pay the price. (2) The people must want the church to grow and be willing to pay the price. (3) The church must agree that the goal of evangelism is to make disciples. (4) The church must not have a "terminal illness."

Reference: See PATHOLOGY OF CHURCH GROWTH.

B

BAPTISM: REASONS

On many of the mission fields of the world, profession of faith is a relatively insignificant event in the life of candidates until they submit to baptism. Opposition usually begins when candidates identify with a Christian church. Despite the problems involved in being baptized, thousands obey the Scriptures and are baptized. In contrast, in North America where religious and personal liberties are protected by law, some are not eager to acknowledge the authority of the Bible in the area of baptism. Every Christian should submit to baptism and identify with Christ for several reasons.

Baptism is the first step of obedience. Every Christian should be baptized immediately after being saved, because baptism is not optional, it is commanded. There is no record in the New Testament of an unbaptized believer who, given the chance, refused to follow God's plan. On the Day of Pentecost, Peter confirmed that baptism is a natural result of conversion. He cried out, "Repent, and be baptized every one of you in the name of Jesus Christ for the remission of sins, and ye shall receive the gift of the Holy Ghost" (Acts 2:38, *KJV*). Those who believed the gospel had to demonstrate it by the public act of baptism. Baptism did not save because the Scriptures bear out, "Then they that gladly received his word were baptized" (Acts 2:41, *KJV*). Receiving the Word of God was the cause that brought salvation; baptism was a result of their faith. That day, 3,000 people received the Word of God and were baptized. They acted immediately.

Baptism follows the example of Christ. The ordeal of God becoming flesh is called the humiliation (Phil. 2:8). Although Jesus was King, He did not demand royal treatment, but came as a servant (Phil. 2:7). John was baptizing in the river of Jordan for the repentance of sin. Jesus could not repent from sin for He knew no sin. Five times in the New Testament we are told that the Son of God was sinless (John 18:38; 2 Cor. 5:21; Heb. 4:15; 1 Pet. 2:22; 1 John 3:5). John the Baptist was reluctant to baptize Jesus, for he said, "I

have need to be baptized of thee, and comest thou to me?" (Matt. 3:14, *KJV*). Yet, Jesus was baptized to identify with the remnant of Israel. These were the ones He came to save. Second, Jesus was baptized to fulfill all righteousness. "And Jesus answering said unto him, Suffer it to be so now: for thus it becometh us to fulfil all righteousness. Then he suffered him" (Matt. 3:15, *KJV*). Here, Jesus was revealing Himself as the predicted Messiah in the Old Testament, the One coming to bring righteousness to His people. Next, Jesus was baptized to publicly announce the beginning of His ministry. Up until this time, He had not preached or performed miracles. His baptism launched His ministry.

Baptism follows the example of the early Christians. Soul winners in the New Testament put into practice getting new converts baptized. Everyone who accepted Christ was baptized: 3,000 on the Day of Pentecost, Paul, Cornelius and his household, the Ethiopian eunuch, new believers in Samaria, Lydia, the Philippian jailor and many others. Their example should motivate every young Christian to be baptized. Because every new convert in the New Testament who could be baptized was baptized, why should anyone put it off today?

Baptism is a testimony to the world that the candidate professes salvation. All a person has to do to become a Christian is believe and receive Christ. After reading the Word of God, a person can believe in Jesus Christ and become a child of God. A person does not have to be baptized for salvation and does not have to confess publicly to be saved. Therefore, a person can be a secret believer, but should not be. If a new Christian is obedient, he or she will be baptized, thus giving a testimony to salvation (Rom. 10:9).

The public confession of baptism may strengthen a new believer, thus, the person should be baptized as quickly as possible, for it is also being obedient to Scripture. Also, the new convert makes a commitment that he or she is going to follow Jesus Christ. Now the unsaved community expects the person to live like a Christian, and the Christian community will encourage him or her. God has strengthened many young Christians because they have honestly obeyed Him through baptism. Many have won spiritual battles sooner than they could have otherwise because they took this first obedient stand for Christ.

Baptism is a good conscience before God. Baptism is simply obedience to Jesus Christ. The hymn writer concludes, "Trust and obey, for there's no other way to be happy in Jesus." The candidate fulfills the requirement of his or her conscience, that which he or she knows to do. "The like figure whereunto even baptism doth also now save us (not the putting away of the filth of flesh, but the answer of a good conscience toward God)" (1 Pet. 3:21, *KJV*). When the candidate has been baptized, he or she has done all that God has required. His or her conscience is at peace. Therefore, to be happy and confident in the Christian life, the candidate should submit to baptism.

Baptism is usually entrance into a local church. Many churches treat baptism as entrance into fellowship with a local church. However, not all churches agree with this position. Some will baptize a person and not require him or her to join the church, and/or will receive the person into the church without water baptism.

In some traditions, particularly those practicing infant baptism, confirmation is entrance into the local church.

BARNABAS

Barnabas was part of the first missionary team sent out from Antioch to Cyprus and Galatia.

Originally known as Joses, Barnabas is better known by the name ascribed to him by the apostles because of his sacrificial ministry of encouragement (Acts 4:36,37). His name stands for "son of encouragement," and it was his encouraging efforts (probably the spiritual gift of exhortation) that won him that name. He was the human instrumental in introducing Saul of Tarsus to the apostolic circle (Acts 9:27), appointing him as a teacher in Antioch (Acts 11:25,26) and later accompanied him on the first missionary journey (Acts 13:2). He broke with Paul as the two made plans for a second missionary journey and argued about taking John Mark with them (Acts 15:37-39). Various attempts have been made to identify Barnabas with the

rich young ruler, one of the 70 disciples sent out by Jesus, and the author of Hebrews. A nonbiblical Epistle of Barnabas has been defended by some as authentic. Most of the church traditions surrounding the later life of Barnabas describe his ministry and martyrdom on Cyprus.

Barnabas's primary contributions to evangelism involved his discipling ministry. He appears to have had a significant influence on Paul, who to this date is viewed as the prototype of the career missionary. He also had a significant influence on Mark, the author of the second Gospel. Historically, Mark is usually the first portion of Scripture translated and distributed by Bible translators.

Reference: William Steuart McBirnie, *The Search for the Twelve Apostles* (Wheaton, Ill.: Tyndale House Publishers, 1973).

BARRIERS: OVERCOMING THEM

The first step in overcoming barriers is to identify them. The Christian has the responsibility to make that step. Paul said, "I have become all things to all men, that I might by all means save some" (1 Cor. 9:22).

In treating any physical sickness, the first step is always diagnosis. This process may require days as well as weeks of testing, but it is essential to proper treatment. Viruses are treated differently from bacteria, and even among viruses, one particular drug may be more effective than another. So it is with the barriers to evangelism. It is needful to identify the classification of the barrier (E-0, E-1, E-2 or E-3).

Remember, people are all different from each other, and the barriers standing in the way of each also differ. The key is to identify the specific barrier, and then tear it down. If it is a barrier the prospect has erected in his or her own mind, the evangelizer has to take the initiative and cross the barriers. If the barrier is in the church, again, the evangelizer must take the initiative to change it.

A person may not have erected the barriers, but must remove them. People should not let their fears keep them from being witnesses. The task begins with gaining victory over fears. Jesus said the world, the flesh and the devil

(John 17:5-26) should not be taken out of the world, but the world should be insulated against itself. Jesus' petition was, "You should keep them from the evil one" (John 17:15). Victory is available to the believer by walking in the Spirit rather than in the flesh. "Yet in all these things we are more than conquerors through Him who loved us" (Rom. 8:37). For the believer, the key to victory over fear is faith in God and His promises.

Once Christians have overcome their own fears, they are free to begin tearing away the fears of the unsaved. This is done by establishing redemptive friendships. This exposes the unsaved to Christians, the Christian lifestyle and the joys of the Christian life. In Luke 14:12,13, Jesus suggested that when believers give a dinner they should not invite only friends and relatives, because they will only feel obligated to return their hospitality. Instead, he said to invite the poor, maimed, lame and blind. (This means those who are rejected by others.) When these people begin to see that Christians are people much like themselves, the stained-glass barrier begins to dissolve.

Christians must not be judgmental. Christ alone is the righteous judge, and Paul indicated that He will judge His own servants (1 Cor. 4). Christians have the task of accepting the unsaved as they are and win them to themselves, so that they can lead the unsaved to a saving knowledge of Jesus Christ. Once the unsaved have become new creations in Christ (2 Cor. 5:17), the Holy Spirit will work through the Word of God to bring about the needed changes in their conducts and lifestyles.

BARRIERS TO EVANGELISM AND CHURCH GROWTH: DEFINITION

"People like to become Christians without crossing racial, linguistic or class barriers." Perhaps no other single statement captures the heart of effective evangelism strategy advocated by those in the Church Growth Movement as this often repeated statement by the movement's patriarch, Donald A. McGavran. The research of McGavran and others suggests people are more likely to be responsive to the gospel when

they are receptive to the messenger bringing them the gospel. The reverse is also true. These same people are most likely to resist conversion when many barriers need to be overcome in the conversion process.

McGavran's statement does not mean that those from outside a person's race or linguistic group cannot evangelize them, but rather it is a descriptive statement. God made humans as social creatures, and barriers that interfere with social relationships may have a profound spiritual influence on them. If our churches are going to grow, we need to remove as many barriers as possible to make it easier for people to become Christians.

A study of the words *panta ta ethne* "all the nations" (Matt. 28:19), in the context of all Scripture, clearly shows that God's intention for evangelistic strategy is a "people group" approach, that is, an approach of evangelistic methods that is "people group" sensitive. This is God's way of looking at the world. It is one of the key designs of world evangelization and the standard approach for most of all missionaries today. It is the basis of world mapping and strategic thinking everywhere.

The Church Growth Movement generally marks its beginnings with the 1955 publication of McGavran's *The Bridges of God*.[1] In that book, McGavran outlined his thesis that the most effective evangelism takes place in the context of existing social networks in a society that overcame existing barriers.

George G. Hunter III explains:

In every land and tribe and language and culture in which the faith has spread, the social networks composed of the relatives and friends of caring credible believers have made up *The Bridges of God*. The faith is not usually spread between strangers, but between persons who know and trust each other. The social networks of the body of believers provide opportunity for a "web movement" of the Christian faith.[2]

Identifying Evangelism Barriers
One key to effective evangelism is to remove the barriers that keep people from the gospel. Of

course, some barriers can never be removed (i.e., the offense of the cross, and the message of salvation is an intricate part of the gospel). The barriers that can be removed are secondary and are not related directly to the root of Christianity. Grace is also a barrier to some for they want to do good works to be saved and resist being saved by grace alone (Eph. 2:8,9). Repentance of sin is yet another nonnegotiable barrier between the sinner and salvation.

The more barriers that are put between a person and Christ, the more difficult it is to win the person to Christ. "E-0 Evangelism" is a term used to designate the evangelism of those who are already in the church. This would include the children of adults affiliated with the church as well as adult members and adherents who have never been born again.

BARRIERS TO EVANGELISM

E-0 Evangelism — Conversion of Church Members

E-1 Evangelism — Stained-Glass Barrier

E-2 Evangelism — Class/Cultural Barriers

E-3 Evangelism — Linguistic Barriers

The E-1 Barrier has been called "The Stained-Glass Barrier." Church-growth writers speak of E-1 Evangelism as evangelism that overcomes the stained-glass barrier. The word "stained glass" is a symbolic word for those things that stand between those on the outside of the church and getting them inside to hear the gospel. These barriers make it difficult for a person to attend a church, or to continue to attend. The stained-glass barrier includes such things as poor location, inadequate parking and unkept or poorly maintained facilities. Stained-glass barriers also include perceptions, such as a person's dislike for a denomination's name or what a person knows about a particular name.

Cultural and class barriers also hinder the evangelistic outreach of some churches. E-2 Evangelism is that which overcomes cultural and class barriers. From this barrier comes a principle that recognizes members of certain cultures may not wish to attend a church that is predominantly made up of members of another culture. Although the church must be the church of the open door and willing to admit all, usually members of a culture distinct to that of the members of the church will not feel comfortable becoming a part of the church. Related to cultural barriers are also class barriers. The difference in classes may not be money, but rather the values people bring with their money. The music of a church often presents a barrier to those of another class. Just as members of one class do not usually like the "long-hair" music of another class, so some classes often fail to appreciate the twang of country music.

Sometimes culture is defined by money. In fact, sometimes it's not race. In actuality, it is never simply just one thing, but usually a cluster of things that would include not only values, but also education, lifestyle, socioeconomic level, dress, worldview, hopes and dreams—a cluster of issues that are obviously closely related for most people. (For example, a person who has a better education usually earns more money, has a different worldview and so forth.) The cluster of these things makes up a culture or a people group. Consequently, you could have blacks, Hispanics, Anglos and Asians living in an apartment complex in a place such as Los Angeles and they all drive BMWs, live fast-paced lives, have a party atmosphere, are upper management and live in a no-pets, no-kids world. They are one homogenous unit, or people group, although racially and visually they appear to be extremely different from each other. However, to a great extent they share all of the cluster of things previously mentioned.

Linguistic barriers are perhaps the most obvious barriers to evangelism. E-3 Evangelism is that which overcomes language barriers. People like to hear God speak in their heart language (the language in which they think) even when they themselves speak a second language. The wonderful truth of the Incarnation in which God demonstrates His love to them is the greatest heart language of all.

Al Henson began the Lighthouse Baptist Church in Nashville, Tennessee, intent on reaching greater Nashville with the gospel. When he learned many Laotians were moving to his city, he sent his people into the streets to reach them with the gospel. Soon he had a service where about 200 Laotians were attending. A layman preached to them and a Laotian translated the gospel into their mother tongue. When they learned English, Henson cancelled the Laotian service and brought them into his English service. But only about 50 people made the transition. By beginning the Laotian service again, he was able to continue reaching Laotians with the gospel. He learned that although the Laotians could speak English, they preferred to hear God speak their "heart language." The First Baptist Church of Los Angeles, California, has adapted its ministry to reach the various ethnic groups in its community and has five separate linguistic groups meeting on one church campus.

Building Bridges, Removing Fences

According to McGavran's normative statement concerning conversion, "People like to become Christians without crossing racial, linguistic, or class barriers." This means the key to the most effective evangelism is to build bridges over the barriers or remove the fences that separate the church from those they seek to reach. But in any attempt to "market" the gospel, it should always be remembered that the gospel that sells best may not be the gospel that saves. Still, Christians should make an effort to remove the fences that separate the unsaved community from the gospel without changing the message of salvation in Christ.

The church can take several steps to build bridges over the barriers between themselves and the lost. First, it can study its own unique church subculture and that of its community to find areas of commonality. These areas of commonality are the basis on which redemptive bridges can and should be built to the unsaved within the church's sphere of influence.

Second, in the process of this undertaking, it may be that certain practices within the church may be viewed as barriers that are nonessential and can be adapted to better meet the needs of the community (e.g., the pastor wearing robes, collars or uniforms, the choice of musical instruments used in the church, peeling paint in the church auditorium). Other practices may be viewed as important denominational distinctives that could be observed in services other than that

which is likely to attract the unsaved (e.g., practices such as breaking bread, foot-washing and speaking in tongues). Still other practices may be viewed as essential to the church, but could be explained in more contemporary terms to the unsaved through a visitor's bulletin (e.g., congregational singing and the sermon).

Third, churches can remove fences by identifying those whom they are most likely to reach and strengthening the relationships that already exist between the unsaved and the church. Research into evangelism and church growth suggests most people come to faith in Christ as the result of the witness of a Christian in a close personal relationship (e.g., friend or relative). Recognizing this, churches can overcome barriers to evangelism by reaching people through existing social networks.

Ultimately, a church may determine the fences are too high or too many to remove between themselves and some lost people in its community. Perhaps the best way to reach these people is for those who are the most burdened for them to cross the fence themselves and establish a new church distinct to the unreached people's culture. Beginning a new church for a distinct racial, ethnic or linguistic group should not be done out of a motive of racism or desire to keep the church segregated, but rather out of a realization that a Spanish-speaking church will be more effective in reaching Latinos than an English-speaking church.

References: [1]Donald A. McGavran, *The Bridges of God* (New York: Friendship Press, 1955). [2]George G. Hunter III, "The Bridges of Contagious Evangelism," eds. C. Peter Wagner, Win Arn, and Elmer Towns, *Church Growth: State of the Art* (Wheaton, Ill.: Tyndale House Publishers, 1989), p. 71. "The People Group Approach to World Evangelism" *Global Church Growth* (January/February/March 1990) no. 1, XXVII. See E-0/E-1/E-2/E-3 EVANGELISM.

BARRIERS TO EVANGELISM AND CHURCH GROWTH: DESCRIPTION

Back in the early 1960s, somewhere along Highway 301 in central Florida, an American buffalo ranch was open to the public. The buffalo were restrained only by a chicken-wire fence. When asked about the seeming lack of security, the attendant responded, "Those animals weigh a ton and can run 60 miles per hour." (That isn't altogether true, but it is what he said.) "They could run right through any fence we put up, so one kind of a fence is as good as any." The buffalo were effectively restrained, not by force but by conditioning.

Like a chicken-wire fence, the barriers to evangelism have two sides. The wire fence served both to keep the buffalo in and the people out. The barriers to evangelism serve to keep Christians separated from the unsaved, and the unsaved separated from Christians. The barriers can be equally difficult to cross from either side.

One of the first principles of evangelism deals with barriers or hindrances that keep people from getting saved. Barriers are both spiritual and natural. Some barriers grow out of the nature of the gospel message. The message of "repentance" (Acts 2:38) is a barrier to those who do not want to give up their sin. Their sin may involve an act, place or person that he or she has difficulty giving up. Also, the message of the Cross is foolish (1 Cor. 1:18), or an offense (Gal. 5:11). The instinct of natural humans is to save themselves, or to perform good works. So the conditions of grace (Eph. 2:8,9) become a barrier to salvation. These barriers are spiritual in nature and there is no way to remove them, nor can a person water down the implication of the message.

Some natural barriers are constructed by the church. Some churches create barriers by their bad breath, poor grammar or adding the importance of church membership to the message of salvation.

Some unsaved people have created barriers by their prejudice against people from certain denominations, races, sections of the country or language presentation. Many barriers are created to effective evangelism, and most of them are far less obvious than race, language and ethnic differences, but their effect is no less real. People do not like to cross barriers of any kind.

Children are conditioned from infancy not to cross barriers such as the playroom floor or the street in front of their home. Infants are placed in playpens. Toddlers and small children are held back by doors and fences. Young people and adults are restrained by the written and unwritten rules and regulations of family, society and government.

At some point, emotional conditioning becomes so strong that the reality of the barriers is unimportant. Whether real or imagined, if barriers are perceived to exist, the effect is the same.

Barriers are erected from both sides. A security chain-link fence will often have three or four strands of barbed wire around the top. If the fence is intended to keep intruders out, the barbed wire will usually be tilted outward. If it is intended to keep occupants in, the barbed wire will tilt inward.

Some churches have symbolic chain-link fences surrounding their churches, seemingly to keep people away. The barriers to evangelism can be thought of as fences that have barbed wire tilted in both directions. They make it difficult for the unsaved people to cross into the family of God, they also make it difficult for the Christian to cross out to the unsaved.

Failure to admit the existence of barriers, and overcome them, is devastating the cause of evangelism. If barriers are not removed, money and time is wasted in getting out the gospel, and those involved in the task become frustrated and discouraged by their failure to get results.

Dr. Ralph D. Winter has established four helpful classifications for the barriers to evangelism.

E-0	Internal Barrier
E-1	Stained-Glass Barrier
E-2	Class and Cultural Barrier
E-3	Language Barrier

E-0 stands for evangelism that is carried on among people who are already church attenders. The "0" represents those already in the church, so they have no barriers to cross. The "E" Evangelism means the people in the church need to be evangelized. This includes evangelizing unsaved church members, the children born to church members, children and young people brought in by bus and any other unsaved people who might be attending the church.

E-1 is evangelism that crossed the stained-glass barrier (i.e., the church building becomes a barrier to getting people saved). E-1 evangelism is carried on outside the local church setting, but it does not cross any linguistic, ethnic or cultural barriers. This would be near-neighbor evangelism, reaching those people who do not attend church.

E-2 evangelism crosses cultural or class barriers. E-2 evangelism reaches out to people who are separated by ethnic, cultural and class barriers.

E-3 evangelism crosses the linguistic barrier. This is usually thought of as foreign missions because the missionary who goes to another country has to learn another language or dialect. The cultural barriers and language barriers also exist in the United States. Because the principles of reaching people in foreign countries are the same that are used in some places in the United States, E-3 is now usually called cross-cultural missions.

BARTHOLOMEW

One of the 12 disciples.

Bartholomew is generally identified with Nathanael, who was first introduced to Jesus by Philip (John 1:45). The name Bartholomew means "son of Tolmai," causing some to conclude he was a descendent of David through Maacah or descendent of one of the Egyptian Ptolomies. Early Church traditions describe Bartholomew as being instrumental in bringing the gospel to the Armenians of Persia.

References: William Barclay, *The Master's Men* (Nashville: Abingdon, 1976); Leslie B. Flynn, *The Twelve* (Wheaton, Ill.: Victor Books, 1985); William Steuart McBirnie, *The Search for the Twelve Apostles* (Wheaton, Ill.: Tyndale House Publishers, 1973).

BASE

The average attendance in the weekly worship service(s). This base attendance is foundational to both planning church growth and measuring the effectiveness of church-growth plans after they are implemented.

How to Determine Your Base
To determine your base attendance, use the following formula: the total recorded attendance in your morning worship service over the past year ÷ 52 = base (average weekly attendance over the past year).

Reference: Elmer L. Towns, *154 Steps to Revitalize Your Sunday School and Keep Your Church Growing* (Wheaton, Ill.: Victor Books, 1988), p. 110.

BAXTER, RICHARD (1615-1691)

A prominent Puritan reformer during the English Commonwealth, who pastored at Keddeminster for many years. He refused to accept a bishopric under the Restoration and was thereafter banned from preaching. His refusal to accept the ban resulted in fines and imprisonment. Of his many works, his best known is *The Reformed Pastor.* He also wrote *Saints' Everlasting Rest*, a book about the Christian life and prayer. He is the one who said, "Preach as a dying man, to dying men."

BELIEVER'S BAPTISM

Baptism means a lot of different things to a lot of different people today. Although some churches baptize infants, this article examines the view of other churches that baptize only after a profession of faith has been made. They believe the Early Church Christians recognized baptism as the first step of obedience in their new lives in Christ. It was the means by which they publicly told others of the change that had taken place in their lives when they repented of their sins and placed their faith in Christ for salvation. It was assumed everyone who became a Christian would want to be baptized as quickly as possible.

What Does It Mean to Be Baptized?
Some faith communities teach that baptism is a means of grace, a way God makes people right with Him.

When Christians are baptized, they use this symbol to describe salvation that has already taken place in their lives. This is something that happens when we trust Christ as Savior, but needs to be implemented in our lives each day (Rom. 6:11).

But baptism is more than a statement of what has occurred. It is also a statement of our personal commitment to obey God. At His baptism, Jesus said, "Permit it to be so now, for thus it is fitting for us to fulfill all righteousness" (Matt. 3:15). Jesus' willingness to be obedient in baptism demonstrated His commitment to obeying God in other areas of His life.

When Christians express their commitment to God in baptism, they are also expressing their commitment to their church. The Bible describes Christians as "baptized into one body" (1 Cor. 12:13), referring to the baptism of the Holy Spirit by which all Christians are united in Christ. The Bible also uses the expression "body of Christ" to describe the local church (1 Cor. 12:27). Therefore, when Christians are baptized in/by water as a testimony of what has taken place in their lives, they usually join a local church, expressing their desires to serve as healthy members of the Body.

There is a fourth aspect to the statement we make when we are baptized. Baptism is also a statement of faith in our future with Christ for eternity (Rom. 6:4). In His resurrection, Jesus was victorious over death and the grave. He shares that victory with Christians today (1 Cor. 15:57). That hope is one of the primary motivating factors in the Christian life (1 Cor. 15:58).

Who Should Be Baptized?
In the Early Church, everyone who received Christ as Savior was baptized at the earliest convenience. On the Day of Pentecost, Peter called on people to "repent, and let every one of you be baptized" (Acts 2:38). When an Ethiopian convert asked Philip what was needed to be baptized, Philip responded, "If you believe with all your heart, you may" (Acts 8:37). Jesus called people to be converted by turning to God from their sins (repentance) and believing the gospel (Mark 1:15). Therefore, only Christians, and every Christian, should be baptized. That's why certain evangelical churches use the expression "believer's baptism" to describe this ordinance.

Why Be Baptized?
Baptism is the first step of obedience in a person's new life in Christ. In the Early Church, people were baptized and joined a church immediately after becoming Christians (Acts 2:41). They took that first step of obedience because they were eager to begin walking in their new lives in Christ. Typically, Christians who hesitate and delay being baptized tend to hesitate throughout their Christian lives and are slow to obey God in other areas.

Baptism is described as "the answer of a good conscience toward God" (1 Pet. 3:21). People tend to have a problem with their consciences when they try to excuse themselves from doing what they know God wants them to do (Rom. 2:15). Christian maturity involves having a good conscience (1 Tim. 1:5). When Christians hesitate in obeying God by not being baptized, they struggle with their consciences. But when the same Christians obey God and are baptized, their consciences are at peace and they are taking important steps toward maturity.

God never intended Christians to live Christian lives in isolation from others. Christians need one another to be all God wants them to become (Heb. 10:24,25). That's why Jesus established the Church (Matt. 16:18). The sooner Christians are baptized and become part of a church family, the sooner they experience the support of others in the church as they help them live Christian lives.

Why Be Baptized Again?
The New Testament describes an occasion when 12 men who were baptized prior to receiving Christ as Savior were baptized again after becoming Christians (Acts 19:1-5). They recognized their former baptism represented something other than that emphasized in believer's baptism. As much as they appreciated their faith heritage, they were baptized again as an expression of their faith in Christ as Savior.

Some churches practice a tradition of baptizing children shortly after they are born. Their response to salvation is not to be baptized again, but confirmation, which basically represents a public testimony, confirming what they believe

God accomplished for them as reflected in their baptism and their response to His grace at that time.

Where Should I Be Baptized?

Although the Bible consistently emphasizes the need for people to follow the example of Christ in baptism, it never identifies the place where a person should be baptized. Each of us needs to ask God individually where He wants us to be baptized.

Baptism is closely associated with both salvation and church membership. As people consider where to be baptized, they usually want to identify with the churches that were instrumental in their coming to faith in Christ. As a result, they normally decide to be baptized in the churches they plan to join.

BEZA, THEODORE (1519–1605)

The principle reformer in the generation following John Calvin.

Born in Vexelay, Burgundy into an aristocratic family, Theodore Beza was educated under Melchoir Wolmar, who had also been John Calvin's teacher. At age 20, Beza rejected his family's plans for a career in law and moved to Paris to pursue a literary career as a poet. Following a serious illness in his late 20s, Beza identified with the Reformers and moved to Geneva. In Geneva, he developed into a famous scholar and teacher and began traveling widely to advance the reform cause. Following the death of Calvin, Beza was elected as his successor.

Among Beza's contributions to the Reformed Church was his work in producing the Geneva Psalter and translating it into French.

Reference: H. M. Baird, *Theodore Beza, the Counsellor of the French Reformation* (New York: G. P. Putman's Sons, 1899).

BIBLE

God's revelation of Himself to man, that is inspired by the Holy Spirit, accurate in every word, inerrant in content, canonized in 66 books and preserved as God's Word for everyone.

BIBLICAL BARRIERS

Barriers to church growth that are intrinsic to the gospel and, therefore, cannot be removed without radically changing the evangelical message. These include (1) the offense of the Cross; (2) opposition to repent of sins and turn from them; (3) opposition to confess Christ before others and be baptized; and (4) opposition to grace by those who want to do good works for salvation.

BIEDERWOLF, WILLIAM EDWARD (1867–1939)

International evangelist.

William Biederwolf, converted at age 20, was educated in France, Germany and at Princeton. Following his ordination at age 30, he served three years as a pastor and a year as an army chaplain before beginning a 35-year career as an international evangelist. During this time, he established a leper home in Korea (1920) and the Winona Lake Assembly in Winona Lake, Indiana (1923). Following his years in evangelism, Biederwolf returned to the pastorate and extended his influence through writing.

Reference: Elmer L. Towns, *The Christian Hall of Fame* (Grand Rapids: Baker Book House, 1975), p. 186.

BILLINGTON, DALLAS FRANKLIN (1903–1972)

Pastor of the world's largest Sunday School.

Born in a log house in western Kentucky and raised in a devout Christian home, Dallas Franklin Billington was 21 years old when he was converted in a tent meeting in Paducah, Kentucky. In 1927, during a serious illness of his infant son, Billington yielded to God's call to preach. In June 1934, he was invited to organize a group of people into a Baptist church in Akron, Ohio. Beginning with 13 people in an elementary school and an offering of $1.18, for the next 38 years the Akron Baptist Temple grew to more than 16,000 members and had physical assets valued at several million dollars. Billington died of a heart attack on August 26, 1972.

Billington's Akron Baptist Temple claims to be the first church to evangelize by installing its own television studio. Its radio, television and missionary outreach extended its ministry worldwide. In 1968, the Akron Baptist Temple was recognized by *Christian Life* magazine as the world's largest Sunday School, an honor it held throughout the remainder of Billington's life.

References: Dallas F. Billington, *God Is Real* (New York: David McKay Co., 1962); Elmer L. Towns, *The Ten Largest Sunday Schools and What Makes Them Grow* (Grand Rapids: Baker Book House, 1969), pp. 15-24.

BINDING THE STRONGMAN

Neutralizing the deceptive hold or control that demonic powers have over given human subjects so that the latter are able to freely reconsider divine propositional truths. —GOJR

BIOLOGICAL CHURCH GROWTH

Numerical church growth resulting from those born into Christian families who affiliate with the church.

BISHOP

A title for the pastor or elder of the church. (Lit. overseer, and applies to the administrative responsibilities of the pastor.)

Reference: See PASTORAL MINISTRY PARADIGMS.

BODY EVANGELISM

A perspective that emphasizes the outreach by a local church (in contrast to interdenominational outreach or cooperative evangelism by many churches). The goal of evangelism is to make disciples and incorporate them into the local Body (i.e., a local church). The result leads to growth in church membership, church attendance and church offerings (i.e., those measurements that relate to a local church).

Reference: See HISTORY OF EVANGELISM.

BODY LIFE

The clustering of Christians together in a shared intimacy to achieve growth by all members of the Body working together and building up one another.

References: Gene A. Getz, *Sharpening the Focus of the Church* (Chicago: Moody Press, 1974); Robert C. Girard, *Brethren, Hang Loose* (Grand Rapids: Zondervan Publishing House, 1972); Lawrence O. Richards, *A New Face for the Church* (Grand Rapids: Zondervan Publishing House, 1970); Ray C. Stedman, *Body Life* (Ventura, Calif.: Regal Books, 1972).

BONDING PEOPLE TO THE CHURCH

The process of bonding (assimilating or churching) newcomers into the church is commonly referred to as postevangelism, but it is actually a part of the biblical and holistic process of disciple-making. After someone comes to know Christ, it is imperative to get that person assimilated into a local fellowship. Throughout the New Testament, those who were saved became active members of an existing local church, or local churches were formed and they became active in them.

A holistic approach to evangelism requires that provision be made for the new Christian's normal growth and development. This normal growth and development requires that the new Christian become settled in, or bonded, to, a local church. That is where the new Christian will be introduced to the ministry of the Word of God that will result in spiritual growth (1 Pet. 2:2), victory over sin (Ps. 119:9-11), answered prayer (John 15:7), growth in character (1 Cor. 3:23) and strengthened faith (Rom. 10:17). The local church is also where the new Christian will be able to grow through fellowship with other Christians (Heb. 10:25).

When the local church fails in the bonding process, and the new Christian stops attending church regularly (or is out of the church completely), the growth and development process is handicapped.

Bonding is essential to the task of closing the

back door of the church. Nothing is more frustrating than spending time and effort to win people to Christ and then watching them become unfaithful, join another local church or drop out of church completely. But that is exactly what happens when the task of bonding is not taken seriously. New Christians drift from one Sunday School class to another, and from one social group to another, trying to find a place where they are made to feel as though they are a vital and needed part of the church. If such a place is not found, they become discouraged and stop searching. In time, they either become casual church members, move to another church or just drop out of church.

Bonding is a biblical pattern. The first church, the one started in Jerusalem on the Day of Pentecost, grew more rapidly than any church since that time. Yet those early Christians were able to keep the back door effectively closed. Why? The reason is simple. New Christians were bonded to the church. Their felt needs were met by the church (Acts 2:44), and they were made to feel a part of the church family (Acts 2:42). Those who were already members were willing and eager to make room for the newcomers (Acts 2:47).

It is often assumed that new Christians and new members are bonded to the church when they formally join. In practice, nothing could be further from the truth. If such an assumption is made, the back door will always swing wide open. The key to the bonding process is *not* church membership, but church ownership. Newcomers are bonded to the church only when they begin to think of the church in terms of "my church," and that only happens when they begin to feel as though they are a vital part of the church as a whole or some group or organization within the church.

Networking Evangelistic Strategy for Local Churches

When people visit the church on a Sunday morning (usually the most common time to make a first visit to a new church), they should be immediately followed up in accordance with the laws of the three hearings and seven touches. The most important immediate concern of the church should be to get that visitor back the second and third time. To do this, the visitor should be contacted seven times before the next Sunday.

Seven Touches

The first of these seven contacts, or touches, is Sunday afternoon. The pastor or teacher should phone the visitors and thank them for visiting the church. The phone call should establish three things. First, callers should offer to help the family in any way they can. Second, the caller will want to mention the special "Friendship Packet" the church has prepared for them and that someone would like to deliver the packet to their home. This packet includes a Bible, Christian literature for children, a cassette tape of church music, a sermon by the pastor that describes the goals of the church that year, literature about various church ministries and a book on the Christian life. Third, the visitors should be told that the church secretary will phone for an appointment to bring the packet to the home.

The next of the seven touches occurs Sunday evening. The pastor or Sunday School teacher should write a letter covering much of what was said during the phone call.

Suggest a time for the visit to their home during the phone call and/or follow-up letter, which can later be confirmed by the secretary. Because it is important to win the winnable while they are winnable and reach the reachable while they are reachable, many churches find Tuesday evening a good time for this second call. When suggesting a time, the callers should be approximate so as to have liberty to stay longer or leave earlier on other visits they may make that evening. The callers might suggest they could drop by around 7:00 P.M. on Tuesday evening.

After the Tuesday evening phone call, the caller should write a letter to the prospect confirming the time of the visit. (Although some letters arrive after the visit because of delays in postal service, it is part of the accumulative effect of follow-up.) Again, the caller should express interest in being of service to the family and assure them they are welcome to visit the church services as often as they can.

On Wednesday or Thursday evening, someone from the church, or the Sunday School class in which they would be involved, should visit them. Ideally, this visit should be by the teacher, but if several people need a follow-up visit, it is better that another class officer or member make the visit rather than putting it off several weeks until the teacher can make the call.

During this visit, the teacher should tell the prospects about the class and how they could fit into the class. The teacher will also want to be familiar with the rest of the church program that might be of interest to others in the family (e.g., children's and youth ministries). The primary reason for visiting the home is to present Jesus Christ to the people. Beyond this, the pastor/teacher should be alert to the needs in the home and share the gospel with the prospects if the opportunity arises.

The pastor/teacher should immediately take the time to write a letter to the prospect, outlining the next spiritual step they should take. After the visit, the pastor/teacher should know if the people need to accept Christ, rededicate themselves, join the church or whatever. The letter should clearly outline what is expected. The letter should also thank the people for letting him or her visit and again extend the invitation to visit the appropriate Sunday School class that Sunday.

An informal follow-up with a phone call on Saturday inviting the prospect to the Sunday School class or service the next day provides the finishing touches to a week of following up a receptive responsive person. By the end of the week, the casual visitors have met several people from the church and recognize the church is interested in them. Unless there is some particular reason for not visiting again, it is likely the visitors will return to the church where they know they are welcome and accepted the following week.

Skyline Wesleyan Church in San Diego, California, grew from 800 to more than 3,000 attenders in six years (1984-1990), implementing this program of networking people into the church. Although church growth is very complex, this is one factor to explain its growth. During the same period, the church grew from one to three morning services.

Infrastructure is important in bonding people to a local church. The use of cell or fellowship groups will contribute to bonding.

Reference: Kent Hunter, *Foundations for Church Growth: Biblical Basics for Church Growth* (Corunna, Ind.: Church Growth Center 1994), chap. 9.

BONIFACE (680-754)

First missionary to the Teutonic tribes of Germany.

Born near Exeter, England, and named Winfrid, Boniface first expressed the desire to become a monk in early childhood. He was trained in monasteries near Exeter and Winchester. In 716, he left England as a missionary to the Frisians, a mission that was aborted about 18 months later. In 718, Boniface obtained Papal approval for a mission to Germany. His success in this mission is in part attributed to a unique power encounter with the Norse god Thor. In Geismar, near Hesse, Boniface began cutting down an oak that was sacred to Thor. Before he finished the job, a strong wind blew the tree over, causing it to break into four parts. The pagans who witnessed this event became convinced of the power of the Christian faith and built a chapel to Saint Peter out of the wood of that tree. Boniface was later instrumental in establishing the church in Bavaria.

Reference: G. W. Robinson, *The Life of St. Boniface by Willibald* (Harvard: University Press, 1916).

BOOMERS, EVANGELISM OF BABY

Today, a subculture within American society is becoming more receptive to the gospel—the baby boomers—those born between 1946 and 1964. For some time, many boomers remained outside the evangelical church. In recent years, however, church growth statistics indicate many boomers are returning to the church in record numbers. By using the principles of cross-cultural evangelism, existing evangelical churches can effectively reach these young and middle-aged adults.

An effective ministry to boomers will adopt a specific strategy to reach this group, based upon certain eternal principles. At some point in the developmental phase of that ministry strategy, the church needs to understand what it is the boomer is looking for in a church, and then determine the best way it can respond to the demand of its market. Just as a businessman must understand his market to be successful and operate with a profit, so the church must understand the boomers if it is going to be effective in reaching them for Christ.

What Is the Boomer Looking for in the Church?

Research into the attitudes of boomers that influence their choice of a church suggests seven things they want in a church. When these seven things are present, they will commit themselves to its ministry both financially and to some degree through involvement in some aspect of ministry or service in the church. When these are absent in a church, so are boomers. The church that will be effective in reaching the boomer in the 1990s, and on into the twenty-first century, needs to consider what is important to the boomer.

First, the church that is most attractive to boomers is the church that is functional in its approach to their faith. They will commit themselves to things that will help them function in life. They differ from their parents in that they will not attend church meetings because of (1) tradition, (2) guilt, or (3) because someone expects them to attend. They want their Christianity to work in the marketplace. They are looking for functional sermons that will help them cope with the problems of life and living.

Second, boomers are concerned with excellence in form. They want things to be as perfect as they see on television. They want their church to use the latest tools to do a job (e.g., personal computers, fax machine, seminars, overheads and VCRs). They believe they can't use yesterday's tools in today's ministry to meet the challenge of tomorrow. Boomers know that using the right tools is more efficient and they don't want their churches to waste their time. They will serve in the churches, but they want their churches to use them for their strengths.

Third, boomers will commit to churches that

are characterized by "team ministry" (this phrase can mean a multiple pastoral staff or lay ministers who have various spiritual gifts). Boomers respond to a new style of leadership. They want a church that provides opportunities such as (1) shared goal setting, (2) shared problem solving and (3) shared decision making. The business model for boomers is "corporate management," which is also identified by such terms as "the management team" or "shared leadership." Their parents worked or managed in isolation from others, but networking is important to boomers.

Fourth, boomers are looking for churches that are both innovative and conservative. Boomers are antitraditional, but they are also conservative and institutional. Boomers are generally perceived as being anti-institutional because they were involved in the protests of the 1960s. This conclusion is based on a misunderstanding of what boomers were attempting to do during those years of unrest. They were not against the institutions themselves, but against their hypocrisy and abuses. Boomers are in favor of the five basic institutions of society including (1) the family, (2) the church, (3) good government, (4) schools and (5) business. This tendency in boomers means the church that reaches boomers runs the risk of having valued traditions of the church challenged if they are not perceived to have value in themselves nor have a functional purpose.

Fifth, the church that reaches the boomer is the church that is businesslike without becoming a business. Boomers want to be part of a successful church that meets their needs with quality ministry. They want to accomplish goals. They want form (dress, tools, job descriptions [what must I do?] and job objectives [what must I accomplish?]). Again, this is one of the areas in which boomers differ from their parents. The motto of their parents was, "Do the best you can with what you have." In contrast, boomers believe, "A job worth doing is worth doing right." Their parents worked for the sake of work and worked out of habit, viewing their work as a means to an end. Boomers work hard, some think even harder than their parents, but they do it for different reasons. They are more likely to take pride in both process (their work) and product (their goal).

To be businesslike means the church must commit itself unreservedly to the pursuit of excellence in every aspect of its ministry. This does not mean the church must be perfect, for that will never happen prior to the rapture of the church. It does mean the church will strive to be the best it can be.

Sixth, churches that reach boomers are relational in their outreach strategy. Boomers consider relationships to be important. Their music reflects the intimacies of relationships. Boomers tend to have a series of deep relationships with members of the opposite sex before marriage. Relationship is an imperative factor in seeking a marriage partner. Also, boomers tend to have more difficulty with broken relationships than do their parents. For the boomer, the quality of life is measured by relationships.

Churches can respond to this boomer attitude by offering Bible study along with fellowship. Boomers will respond to learning biblical principles in settings that foster group relationships and will apply the principles in other relationships. Their parents learned in isolation. This is one reason the cell-group movement is more popular with boomers, and in boomer churches, than with the parents of boomers and in older more traditional churches.

Seventh, boomers are looking for experienced-based churches to attend. Although the school of psychology known as "experiential" tends to be anti-Christian, an effects-based philosophy of life and ministry does not have to be anti-Christian. Every church must remain an island in that it remains different from the world. But the church should adopt a philosophy of being experiential in that it encourages its people to experience their Christianity and apply the principles of biblical doctrine to their lifestyles.

Boomers want to experience their Christianity. They want to love, laugh, talk, pray together, share with, and care about, others. They will reject correct doctrine if it is presented with manipulating methods, but will accept it when they understand how it can influence their lives positively. They expect Christian experience to grow out of the essentials (the fundamentals). They are more tolerant for deviation in secondary doctrine issues than for deviation in lifestyle issues. This means church leaders should teach doctrine from the perspective of how to live.

How Does the Church Respond?

How should the church respond to these expectations of the boomers? First, it should not seek to indiscriminately copy their world. The gospel that sells best is not always the gospel that saves. The workable principles that are discovered in a market survey may not be eternal truth, only public opinion. Although public opinion is important to know in making decisions concerning the emphasis of a church's ministry, that ministry must be based on the eternal principle of the Word of God.

The church can respond to boomer expectations by applying cross-cultural principles in developing a strategy to reach the boomer for Christ. Just as the gospel must be communicated "cross-culturally" to reach and win the Chinese, so the gospel must be communicated "cross-culturally" to the boomer. Dr. Donald McGavran, the father of the Church Growth Movement, taught, "every person wants to become a Christian without crossing racial, linguistic or cultural barriers."

This means the pastor and church that reach the boomer should be aware of the barriers of their culture and correctly interpret them. The boomers are relatively sophisticated in their knowledge of films, music, drama, performers, art and the topics presented on talk shows. An uninformed and nonrational, negative attitude toward their culture will alienate them, but if their culture is correctly interpreted, it will be easier to reach them. The boomer culture contains some evil, as do all cultures, but much of it is neutral, and some of it is good. Knowing the difference is one key to ministering to boomers.

Churches that want to be effective in reaching the boomer for Christ need to create a ministry based on biblical objectives. "Thus saith the Lord" is still true, although it may read slightly different in the new Bible translations used by the boomer. God did not say, "Thus saith the Lord until the boomer comes." This means the church needs to give boomers biblical principles to live by and base church strategy on Scripture, not tradition. The leader should continue to communicate God's standard of perfection for living and ministering.

The church can do other things to help the boomer—things that reflect this balance of remaining strongly committed to the unchanging eternal principles and adapting them to their culture. Church leaders should involve boomers in ministry, but do so by giving careful consideration to their spiritual gifts. Also, they should help boomers correctly interpret the Bible for themselves. When planning church programs, remember boomers respond to feelings, thinking and doing. It is important to build transparent Christianity into every church program.

The purpose of this article has been to illustrate the process by which a Bible-based data-driven strategy to reach the boomer may be developed in cross-cultural evangelism. To be effective in cross-cultural evangelism, the leader needs a thorough understanding of both the gospel and the culture targeted for evangelism. Only then can bridges be built that will transcend cultural presuppositions and effectively communicate the gospel that is beyond cultural limitations.

What a Church Should Know to Reach Boomers

Just as a missionary cannot effectively minister to the Chinese without understanding the culture, values and language of the Chinese, so a church must understand boomers to develop an effective cross-cultural strategy to reach America's largest demographic group. The sheer numbers of boomers make them unique. Nine months after the end of World War II, 233,454 babies were born, more than at any other time period in American history. The explosion in fertility continued for 18 years, until 1964. This bulge in the demographic graph of births has been described by sociologists as "a pig in a python."

Baby boomers went into the adolescent subculture being different from teenagers of previous generations. Usually, young people are assimilated into adult culture as they grow older and society goes on. Baby boomers, however, have remained a distinct subculture. Rather than becoming like adults, the reverse has happened. The older male drives a sports car to keep his youthful image. America has become a nation ruled from the bottom, or controlled by her young.

The negative influences of the boomers are: (1) they tend to be antitraditional, (2) they are narcissistic, (3) they are weak in personal separation from worldly activities, (4) they tend to be so pragmatic that they reject absolute standards, (5) they are geared to change for the sake of change and (6) they tend to be materialistic.

The positive influences the boomers are bringing to the church are: (1) honesty and transparency, (2) efficiency in ministry, (3) caring and relational with people, (4) functional Christianity, (5) less guilt-ridden motivation and (6) equipping ministry for every church lay member.

Newspaper articles report that boomers are more conservative than previously thought; they are returning to the church. A 1989 Gallup Poll indicated 76 percent of all new American church members are between the ages of 18 and 36. Those churches that ignore the baby boomer have realistically cut off 76 percent of their potential market outreach.

Those churches that refuse to reach the baby boomer will become hibernating churches. Those that effectively reach them will be churches that influence culture.

What Type of Ministry Effectively Reaches Baby Boomers?

Churches that target and effectively reach baby boomers are growing through reaching young and middle-age adults. One boomer pastor claims that to reach the baby boomer a church must have (1) a synthesizer, (2) a young-adult Sunday School class for them, and (3) practical sermons on parenting, spouse relationships and financial management.

References: Mike Bellah, *Baby Boom Believers: Why We Think We Need It All and How to Survive When We Don't Get It* (Wheaton, Ill.: Tyndale House Publishers, 1988); Hans Finzel, *Help! I'm a Baby Boomer* (Wheaton, Ill.: Victor Books, 1989); Landon Y. Jones, *Great Expectations: America and the Baby Boom Generation* (New York: Ballantine Books, 1980); Elmer L. Towns, *An Inside Look at 10 of Today's Most Innovative Churches* (Ventura, Calif.: Regal Books, 1990).

BOOTH, WILLIAM BRAMWELL (1829-1912)

Founder of the Salvation Army.

At age 15, William Booth was converted and began preaching within the Methodist movement. He broke with the movement nine years later and became an independent evangelist. In 1864, Booth moved to London to begin the Christian Mission in London slums. This mission became the Salvation Army in 1878. As the name suggests, the Salvation Army was organized like a military unit, complete with ranks and uniforms. General Booth directed his army of Christian workers in a wide variety of Christian relief missions as part of his worldwide evangelistic strategies. The Salvation Army continues to be influential in many parts of the world today, especially in the area of social work.

Booth's major contributions to evangelism included a renewed emphasis on urban evangelism (especially the inner-city slums), using creative means to reach people (bands and open air preaching) and integrating social ministries and evangelism on an unprecedented scale.

References: William Booth, *In Darkest England and the Way Out* (London: International Headquarters of the Salvation Army, 1890); St. John Ervine, *God's Soldier: General William Booth* (London: William Heinemann, 1934).

BORN AGAIN

New life from above. A person needs a spiritual rebirth because he or she is spiritually dead. At conversion, the indwelling presence of Jesus Christ comes into the person's life (a synonym for regeneration.)

Reference: See REGENERATION.

BRAINERD, DAVID (1718-1747)

Missionary to the native people of America.

Born April 20, 1718, in Haddam, Connecticut, David Brainerd became convinced of God's call upon him to preach the gospel to native Americans. He studied three years at Yale until

ill health forced him to return home to complete his studies privately. In 1743, he turned down two pastorates to begin his work among the native people of America. Physical hardships affected his fragile health, and in 1747 Brainerd died in the home of Jonathan Edwards at age 29. He was at the time engaged to be married to the daughter of Edwards.

Brainerd's greatest contribution to evangelism has been his widely published diary. William Carey, Robert McCheyne and Henry Martyn are among many missionaries who have read the journal and been influenced to give their lives to the cause of world evangelism. Also, Jonathan Edwards, John Wesley and Oswald Smith are among those revivalists who have been so influenced by Brainerd's diary as to publish an edition of it during an era of revival.

Reference: Jonathan Edwards, *The Life and Diary of David Brainerd* (Chicago: Moody Press, 1949).

BRIDGES OF GOD

Intimate and natural relationships through which the gospel can spread most unhindered. Also, the title of the book by Donald McGavran that first suggested the embryonic principles of church growth.

Reference: See WEB MOVEMENTS.

BRIDGING GROWTH

The increase of a church's membership through cross-cultural church planting in a local church context, represented in two degrees: first degree (E-2 evangelism)—in cultures somewhat different from the base church; second degree (E-3 evangelism)—in cultures significantly different from the base church.

BUS EVANGELISM

An evangelistic strategy that usually involves establishing a network of bus routes by a local church to transport prospects to Sunday School and/or church services. Some identify bus evangelism as transporting people to evangelistic meetings or other church meetings, but the popular term usually refers to Sunday School and church. An effective bus ministry is characterized by committed ministry personnel who visit prospects along the bus route and have a view to secure the prospects' commitment to ride the bus the following Sunday. The ultimate goal of bus evangelism is to evangelize the riders and those in their immediate social network (e.g., friends and family members).

During the 1970s, a significant increase in the costs of gasoline, insurance and maintenance on the vehicles resulted in a decline in the number of churches using bus evangelism and the number of buses used by churches committed to this evangelistic model.

How to Use Buses in Evangelism

Every church should consider having at least one church bus as a part of its total evangelistic outreach. Bus evangelism helps churches focus their soul-winning outreach, resulting in a renewal of enthusiasm for the churches as children come to personal faith in Christ as Savior.

Those opposed to busing tend to focus on the negative aspects of this ministry (i.e., costs involved in transporting people to church, damage and/or inconvenience caused by pranks by bused kids). "Where no oxen are, the trough is clean; but much increase comes by the strength of an ox" (Prov. 14:4). This proverb reminds us that every situation has both assets and liabilities. Churches that have effective bus ministries have learned to look beyond the problems and rejoice in those who come to Christ through this outreach.

Bus evangelism can also be used to reach families for Christ. After the child who rides the bus is won to Christ, the church workers can use that leverage to reach the child's parents. Through side-door evangelism, families are brought into the church.

References: Wally Beebe, *All About the Bus Ministry* (Murfreesboro, Tenn.: Sword of the Lord, 1970); Jack Hyles, *Church Bus Handbook* (Hammond, Ind.: Hyles-Anderson Publishers, 1971); Elmer L. Towns, *World's Largest Sunday School* (Nashville: Thomas Nelson Inc., 1974); Jim Vineyard, *The Program on the Bus* (Hammond, Ind.: First Baptist Church of Hammond, 1976).

BUSTERS, EVANGELISM OF BABY

When busters join a crowd with a Walkman plugged into their ears, they don't relate, talk or interact. They listen to music by themselves and remain isolated in the midst of the crowd. To understand the "Isolated Generation," compare the way various generations danced.

The first generation, "Depression Kids," listened to the Big Band sound and hugged and squeezed one another on the dance floor. Dancing was relationship and they whispered into one another's ears as they suggestively held each other in their arms. The Depression Kids idolized Fred Astair and Ginger Rogers for their perfect grace and flair that represented two people in perfect harmony.

Then came their kids, the baby boomers. They listened to Dick Clark and "The American Bandstand." They did the twist, the swim and many other dances whereby two couples danced together but seldom touched. Boomers did not have the intimacy, relationship or interpersonal involvement in their dance routine.

The boomer generation is now followed by the busters who dance alone. They idolize Michael Jackson and Madonna, who dance by themselves; no one else is on stage. Their idols are the perfect expression of the Isolated Generation.

The busters are children of divorce. Many grew up in isolation, perhaps without the intimacy of a father and a mother in the nuclear family. They thought they were alone in this world and found it hard to dream by not having anyone with whom to share their intimate thoughts.

The Devalued Generation. The very fact that fewer children were born during the baby bust generation implies that babies were not valued as highly as before. But notice other things that crept onto center stage during their childhoods. First came *Roe vs. Wade* (1973), resulting in rampant abortion, the ultimate act against devalued children. Because children were no longer valued as in the past, America slaughtered more than 3 million fetuses a year.

The busters have also been the target of an

explosion in child abuse. Some people believe child abuse was going on for years, but not reported by and to the police; others think that family restraints were lifted by changing family values. Adults took their hostilities out on their children; surely suggesting children were devalued in adults' thinking. Many parents did not want children (e.g., birth control by using the pill or by other means). When many of the busters finally went off to college, many parents said to them, "Don't come back." In many homes, the busters were not wanted because of parent midlife divorce. Busters were children left to work out their own problems; they could not go to Mom and Dad to talk about it.

Another factor that produced the Devalued Generation is the nature of their parents—the baby boomers. Boomers have been called the "Me Generation," which meant they were proud, egotistical or, at best, self-centered. Those people who are too concerned about themselves don't have time to give of themselves to their children, which devalues the children's relationship to their parents and their self-perception.

The Self-Proclaimed Generation. The baby busters grew up with parents who told them, "You are important," but many of the parents denied by actions the words that came out of their mouths. They were too busy with their own pilgrimages in their lives. As a result, the busters believed they were important, but did not see importance coming from other people. Because healthy ego development comes from proper self-recognition, they had to beat their own drums. Busters are characterized by "self-proclamation" or to express it another way, they are "self-absorbed."

The Lengthened Adolescent Generation. One obvious thing about the still emerging baby buster generation—they are slow to grow up. They seem to grow into maturity later than previous generations, which means they take on the roles and responsibilities of adulthood later than their parents or grandparents did.

Adolescence is a transition between childhood and adulthood. Generally, adolescence is a protected time when children are allowed to find themselves, develop some maturity, choose vocations, choose partners and learn how to make their ways in the world. Traditionally, adolescence has been called by sociologists a time of "passages" or the "season of the soul" when the personality ripens into maturity.

Historically, adolescence has lasted from ages 13 to 17 or 18—at least it took that long for the Depression Kids. In her 1986 article entitled "The Postponed Generation," Susan Littwin indicated that adolescence now lasts from ages 11 to 28. Adolescence has been lengthened on both ends of the age continuum. Kids enter adolescence earlier and leave it much later. Whereas the first generation took four or five years to make the transition to adulthood, it takes the buster 15 to 17 years.

First the boomers lengthened adolescence on the front end, entering it earlier because of their general sexual freedom and the sexual revolution they introduced to the world.

Now the buster is lengthening adolescence on the exit end. They are refusing to grow up. Like Peter Pan, they seem to desire perpetual adolescence (i.e., freedom to make mistakes, goof off and mess around), all without consequence. Disturbingly, busters come out of adolescence about 10 years later than did their parents. What we see are young people in their 20s who have all the characteristics of a teenager. We are not talking physical characteristics, but their emotional outlook and commitment to handle the pressures of life.

The postponed generation knows more because of television, has experienced more in the realm of sex, has traveled farther, yet usually does not accept responsibility and usually cannot act upon what they know.

At one point in time, a clear line existed between adolescence and adulthood; it was when a person left high school, joined the military or graduated from college. In other eras, it was when a person got married or got that first job. But now, a baby buster can work for five years and still live like an adolescent at home, or can earn a Ph.D., marry and still not accept the responsibilities of adulthood.

What are some results of postponed adolescence? They marry later, are not in a hurry to get through college, but will reduce academic loads and change majors. If and when they graduate, they will switch jobs, switch mates, change apartments, make short-term commitments to sports teams, duck responsibilities and float from one hobby to another, or from one singles bar to another.

The Noncommitted Generation. Busters seem overwhelmed by life. Because they know more, have experienced more from the multitude of television advertisements, media information, and the possibilities of travel, work and an open-ended life, they seldom know how to handle any of it. So they don't commit to anything. The busters believe they must try everything before making a decision. They live life in a consumer's market. They leave their options open. Rather than buying a computer, they shop around but do not make a commitment because next year the model may be cheaper and have more options. Because they live in a changing world, they do not commit to the present because it may be out of date tomorrow.

The buster shops for a car phone but puts off buying one for 90 days, when the price drops from $800 to $150. This is the way the buster learns to get along in life. The buster often doesn't make a deep commitment to a partner because a better prospect might come along. The buster does not make a deep commitment to a job; a better offer might come along when a head hunter phones with an attractive offer. The buster does not make a deep commitment to anything because everything is transitory.

The Unfocused Generation. The busters have difficulty focusing on anything for a long time period. Their lives are like news stories presented on the evening news. Everything is instant, an instant war, an instant crisis, an instant political drama. For 15 minutes, busters give rapt attention to earth-shaking danger, then back to pizza or the football game.

Some believe television has produced more dysfunctionalism than anyone is willing to admit. The way television makes people experience information and feelings is the way they relate to others and to their culture. Television presents news in nice "bit-size" 30-second modules of time. So busters drift through life unconnected to their previous or their future experiences. They are dysfunctional.

Television never moves to closure on anything. The soaps never end, they just keep on going. When baby busters get wrapped up in the famine of Africa, before they know it, it is no longer a news item. Suddenly it's Grenada, then herpes, then the nuclear freeze. Before long, the flow of news makes it difficult for them to commit to any issue, so life becomes an existence of nonissues. They are the nonfocused generation.

The Unisex Generation. The busters are the first generation who are the products of America's growing unisex orientation to life. Unisex is a movement toward the center; both boys and girls wear jeans, T-shirts and have the same hair length. Outward adornings are not the issue; it is crossing the ontological bridge between the sexes that becomes the issue. The boy-girl relationship seems to contain no mystery. Buster children have grown up being taught sex education. They have seen nude pictures, can identify the human plumbing fixtures, know what they are expected to do in copulation and can explain it by properly identifying the organs. But they don't know the mystery of the sexual relationship. Marriage often contains a contractual agreement. They have not experienced what Jesus described, "the two shall become one flesh" (Matt. 19:5).

The growth of women's rights has resulted in both men and women performing all the roles for an airline company: pilots, computer operators, luggage handlers and mechanics. This in itself is not wrong because in many of these tasks previously relegated to men, women are observably better. The issue is that in the middle of America's social struggle to correct a historic wrong, busters seem to be swimming in a stream where they can't find bottom.

The Anomaly Generation. Anomaly means a person is hot and cold at the same time, or happy and sad, or depressed and vibrant. Anomaly means both extremes exist without coming to a middle synthesis. The busters are the anomaly generation, at least to their parents and grandparents. They wear a $500 suit and sneakers to work. They want to be comfortable, yet present a good image. They wear shoes without socks. They drink a diet cold drink for breakfast rather than the traditional coffee. The anomaly buster

Christians wear T-shirts displaying rebellious slogans, or silk-screened ads for beer, not caring about the antichurch implications for their parents or grandparents.

Busters are tolerant of change, expect change and embrace change with affection. They can take change in stride because they are nontraditional. But their parents—the baby boomers—and their grandparents—the Depression Kids—look at moral situations through the eyes of tradition. Their parents interpret by the standards of consistency, and when things are not consistent, they get uptight. But busters don't agree. They hold contradictory beliefs and have no trouble with them. They may not believe in losing their salvation (eternal security), but they attend Pentecostal churches that say they can lose their salvation. They may speak in tongues, yet attend Bible churches that preach against sign gifts.

The buster generation says contradictory things, which does not bother them because consistency is not a rule of thumb. Their view of Christianity contains choices similar to a cafeteria, so they load up their trays with a little Mexican food, Southern black-eyed peas, Italian pasta and a bottle of beer, which may or may not be opposed by their pastors. The anomaly buster quips, "What's the big deal?"

The First Atheistic Generation. The buster generation is a product of Madalyn O'Hair, who persuaded the Supreme Court of the United States to kick the Word of God, recognition of God and the symbols of God out of public schools. So buster children were reared without knowledge or training of an absolute deity, either Jewish, Catholic or Protestant. Supposedly, they were reared in a neutral environment that gave no reference to God. They were supposed to be reared free of all moral restraints and choices. But that is not the way it happened. Because nature abhors a vacuum, anti-God forces rushed in under the guise of neutrality, and public schools became humanistic and atheistic. The result is not just, "no God," but "anti-God." What do they think about God? Their orientation is secular, humanistic, and they will not allow the church to run their moral lives.

The busters do not get their theological views from the church or organized religion, rather they get their views about God from films and music. As a result, they have a watered-down view of God, the church and ministers. Their pluralistic viewpoints of life make them antidoctrinal and antiorthodox. Yet they are not theologically liberal, but are against the liberalism of the mainline churches. Busters believe in supernaturalism because in the movies they see demons and supernatural events. They have seen the realism of The *Exorcist* and the surrealism of *Ghostbusters*.

C-1, C-2, C-3 See CULTURE AND ASSIMILATION FACTORS.

CAPITAL FUND-RAISING

As a church grows, it must provide expanded facilities to accommodate its growth. The high costs often involved in church construction prompts most churches to engage in some sort of capital fund-raising program to raise funds to build or renovate facilities. Several principles need to be considered before launching a capital fund-raising program: (1) Before beginning a building program, determine the giving potential of church members. (2) A building program is an incentive for many to give half again as much as previously. (3) Keep the congregation fully informed of the needs and progress. (4) It is easier to raise money for a building than for missions, staff or for any other purpose. Therefore, make sure the giving level for missions and for current expenses is up where it should be before beginning a building fund drive. (5) A church normally begins to develop a building program in response to needs. But the amount of money available often determines the final size and nature of the building. (6) During the first building fund drive, anticipate several large cash gifts. (7) It is easiest to raise money for a building under construction, harder to raise money to pay off a mortgage. The older the building, the harder it is to raise money; therefore, keep the mortgage term as short as possible. (8) Do not bind the hands of the future decision makers of the church by building more than can be paid off in about five years.

CAREY, WILLIAM (1761–1834)

Born into a poor family in Northamptonshire, England, William Carey began working at an early age as a shoemaker's assistant. The long hours of work did not diminish Carey's desire to learn, and by age 20 he had mastered Dutch, French, Greek, Latin and Hebrew. By age 22, he had joined a Baptist church and had begun preaching on the theme of evangelism. His desire to see Baptists involved in world evangelism resulted in his raising the issue at a ministerial meeting at Northampton. He was opposed by the moderator who believed God would convert the heathen if He so willed without human intervention. Undaunted by this early rejection, Carey published *An Inquiry Into the Obligation of Christians to Use Means for the Conversion of the Heathen,* which became the basis for Baptist missions in India. He helped organize the English Baptist Missionary Society and became one of its first missionaries.

As a missionary to India, Carey established an indigenous church, the Serampore College to train Indian workers, and translated the Bible into 44 languages and dialects. From India, he continued to encourage others to become involved in the cause of world evangelism. His influence was instrumental in founding the London Missionary Society of the Congregationalists (1795). He also had a significant influence of early American missionaries Adoniram Judson and Luther Rice.

Most church historians look to William Carey as the beginning of the modern missionary movement. He not only had an effective ministry as a missionary in India, but was also instrumental in promoting the cause of missions across denominational lines.

CARRIERS OF REVIVAL

The phrase "carriers of revival" has been coined to describe the means by which the spirit of revival may be transferred from one place to another. At least three kinds of carriers may be identified and utilized to create a desire for revival. These include (CR-1) people who have themselves experienced revival, (CR-2) authentic accounts of revival experiences and (CR-3) anointed literature that uniquely motivates others to begin working toward revival.

CATS; CATALYSTS

People who are equipped to make something happen and who can get new projects started (i.e., the entrepreneur in ministry).

References: See OPS; ORGS.

CELEBRATION

The gathering of the church collective in its function of worship and praise to God; the sum total of worshipers' response to God. Also used to describe the quality of contemporary worship in contrast to other worship styles.

CELL

The foundational unit of a church's infrastructure, sometimes called a kinship circle. A cell is a small group of approximately 8 to 12 believers functioning in a manner to establish spiritual accountability and provide intimacy in fellowship. A cell most frequently meets on a weekday rather than Sunday, and meets in a location outside the church building (i.e., not meeting in an institutional setting contributes to its strength). Most cells have a secondary function such as Bible study, prayer, training, fellowship and support.

Some cells (technical) meet outside the church building (see previous paragraph). Some in the church use the term "cell" (descriptively) when referring to small groups such as teaching cells (Sunday School classes), service cells (women's missionary groups), administrative cells (official committees) and so forth.

As we study the pattern of church growth in the Early Church, church life appears to have contained two aspects. First, the cell, which was the smaller group meeting together (i.e., for fellowship [cf. Acts 4:32]). Second, the celebration, which was a gathering of the cells in a larger group for some corporate activity (cf. Acts 5:14).

The existence of cells and celebration as part of church life are evident in the New Testament apart from the church in Jerusalem. The church in the city of Corinth was apparently composed of several Gentile cells (cf. Rom. 16:4) and several Jewish cells (cf. Rom. 16:16). It is significant that in writing to the Romans from Corinth, the apostle Paul sends greetings from "the whole church" in Corinth (Rom. 16:23).

Cells can provide the infrastructure (technical and descriptive cells) needed to build a larger church. Most people will be bonded to a cell group in the church before they will become a part of a larger ministry. But there must also be a place for celebration. The two are complementary, not contradictory. What is learned in cells is expressed in celebration. What is gained in celebration should strengthen the cell experience.

Cells have been called many things through the years. Zinzendorf and the Moravians spoke of their choirs. Wesley and the early Methodists had their class meetings. The Southern Baptist Convention has traditionally called cells adult Sunday School classes.

One of the primary analogies for the church in the New Testament is that of the body (cf. 1 Cor. 12:27,28). This being the case, we need to understand the church in terms of both cells and celebration, or fellowship groups and congregations. Just as the human body grows by the division of cells, so the church grows by the division of cells. The secret of church growth is adding ministries, adding ministers and adding places of ministry. We must add classes, teachers, and expand our base for growth. If the physical cell grows without division in the human body, it becomes cancer. The same sort of cancer happens in the Body of Christ.

How to Use Cells to Encourage Church Growth

To reach adults effectively, churches must create classes that are structured for adults (age-graded classes). Many churches begin this growth strategy by grading adults into classes for each decade of chronological age (i.e., 20s, 30s, 40s and so on). But open classes must also be created. Structure is like a skeleton that gives strength to the Body, and the open class is like the heart that gives feeling to the Body. Although we must organize adult classes according to the principles of age grading to effect a structure that best meets the unique needs of adults at various times during their maturing process, we must not forget the Auditorium Bible Class, which is open to everyone.

In starting new, open Bible classes, the thinking is psychographic rather than demographic. Many churches have begun open classes for single adults, single again (divorced persons), newly married, college, single parents, young married couples, expecting couples, young couples, business and professional women, senior saints, teacher training, new members, choir, widows, the hearing impaired and mentally retarded. These classes complement the traditional Auditorium Bible Class and separate classes for men and women.

CELL AND CELEBRATION GROWTH

The church is an assembly of professing believers in whom Christ dwells under the discipline of the Word of God organized to carry out the Great Commission, to administer the ordinances and reflect spiritual gifts. By this definition, the church is both an organism and an organization. One of the primary analogies for the church in the New Testament is that of the body (cf. 1 Cor. 12:27,28). This being the case, the church gets its life from cells. Just as the physical body grows by the division of cells, so the local church grows by the division of cells.

The author visited Dr. David Yonggi Cho, pastor of the largest church in the world, the Full Gospel Church of Seoul, Korea, in 1978. He explained the nature of church growth in South Korea and compared it to Americans building churches. In 1978, his church had 160,000 people in attendance and he would have had to build facilities four times the size of the University of California, Los Angeles (UCLA) to house them all. UCLA had 40,000 students, one fourth of the 160,000 people in Cho's church. Cho went on to explain that if he built a church campus that large, it would curtail growth because they could not afford it and if they built a campus that large, they couldn't afford to build for continued growth.

Dr. Cho explained that his church grew by cell groups in homes during the week. He explained the physical body as an analogy for the church Body. He explained where cells originate: "The life of the man in his seed (sperm) joins to the life of the woman in her egg and produces a cell."

Cho held his fingers so they almost touched and said, "The cell is so small the human cannot see it with the natural eye. But all the characteristics of the new baby," he smiled, "are in this cell, whether blonde hair, black hair or," looking at me, "bald."

"If the cell grows, it is diseased and is discharged," he explained. "The fertilization process must start again; the cell divides into two cells and the two cells are identical. You cannot tell which began first. Then each of the two cells divide, making four cells. They divide into eight cells. The physical body grows by the division."

The church—the local Body of Christ—also grows by the division of cells or classes and departments. Cho was right about Korean church growth; growth came as he divided his home Bible study cells for growth.

For many years, authorities failed to understand just how large the Early Church was. It was assumed there were no church buildings because believers met primarily in home cell groups. Recent findings, however, suggest this may not have been the case. In his book, *The Large Church*, John Vaughan refers to three synagogues in the Near East that could seat as many as 10,000 people. Although at times the church met in homes (cells), it is also evident they met in large gathering places such as the Temple (cf. Acts 2:46) or in the large synagogue.

CELL CHURCHES: FOUR PARADIGMS

When churches are examined from a church-growth perspective, four basic kinds of churches demand a distinct kind of leadership. These include the single-cell, the multi-cell, the multi-congregation, and the stretched-cell church. Because of the character of these churches, the pastor's role varies in each kind of church. Some pastors have been frustrated in their ministry because they had a leadership style appropriate for one kind of ministry but found themselves involved in another kind of ministry. It is important for the pastor-leader to understand the nature of these four kinds of churches and the unique role of the pastor in each situation.

The Single-Cell Church

The average church in the United States has an attendance of 87 people on a typical Sunday morning. This suggests the typical church in America is a single-cell church. It has been described as the American Family Church because it is usually made up of about five extended families. It is the kind of church where everyone knows everyone, everyone relates to everyone, and everyone waits on everyone before anyone will do anything. The strength of this church is found in these bonding relationships. It is virtually impossible to destroy a single-cell church.

But this church is not without its weaknesses. Perhaps the most obvious from a pastoral perspective is that the pastor's authority to determine the direction of the church is almost inconsequential. The pastor is really never a part of the church family and is unique in that he or she is the obvious outsider. The pastor of the single-cell church is like the owner/operator of a small family business—he or she does everything, but doesn't get the profits.

The Multi-Cell Church
The second kind of church is called the multi-cell church. This refers to a church that has a group of cells within the church. This kind of a church has sometimes been called the departmental Sunday School, or the middle-size church.

Churches that move from being a single-cell church to a multiple-cell church usually do so by incorporating new cells into the existing ministry. One of the simplest ways of doing this is to create cells by offering adults multiple options in Bible study through new adult Bible classes. Sometimes new cells are created by hiring a functional specialist to build a new ministry for which he has a particular burden (e.g., bus ministry, church choir). A third way to introduce new cells into an existing single-cell church is to begin special ministries (e.g., hearing-impaired ministry, ministry to singles, drug rehabilitation). Yet another means by which this goal is accomplished is by offering multiple options in worship (e.g., a second morning service).

The pastor of a multi-cell church has a different role from that of the single-cell church. This pastor must be a manager, primarily responsible for managing money, people, resources and time. To some degree, the continued growth of this church is dependent upon the pastor's ability to grow as a manager. At some point, the Peter

Principle often takes effect—the pastor-manager rises to his or her level of incompetence.

The Multi-Congregational Church
The third kind of church is the multi-congregation church. This is also called the mega-church, or the super-church characterized by multiple ministers, multiple ministries and multiple places of ministry. This kind of church is a fairly recent phenomenon.

The pastor of these super-churches is an executive pastor, not just a manager. As such, the pastor may have many managers working for him. Although the management styles of these pastors may vary, one constant is that the big churches are not controlled churches. The larger the church becomes, the less control is exerted by the pastor. The reverse also is true. The more control exerted by the pastor, the smaller the church.

The function of the executive pastor is to give general direction to the ministry and to evaluate its progress. This means the executive pastor leads by making decisions, and by casting vision. C. Peter Wagner suggests this pastor may be likened to the rancher who runs a sheep farm but hires shepherds to care for the sheep.

The Stretched-Cell Church
These first three kinds of churches are norms in the historic experience of a growing church. The fourth kind of church is somewhat deviant from the norm and perhaps the most difficult of the four. The stretched-cell church is the church in which the pastor has a direct line of communication to each of the members and the church may vary in size from about 150 to 1,400. This is the church where the maxim, "Everything rises or falls on the pastor" is perhaps most true. The pastor is the key to growth and generally has an episcopal form of church government. Many times, he may also be the bonding agent that holds this church together.

The role of this pastor-leader is similar to that of the proprietor/owner who has employees working with him rather than for him. He tends not to operate on principles and does not have proper employee/employer relationships. This kind of church tends to not have effectively used job descriptions and objectives governing the ministry. Often there is little accountability because there is little responsibility.

The stretched-cell church is a single-cell church that failed to develop new cells as it continued to grow. Because of the inherent weaknesses of the infrastructure of this kind of church, the pastor should take steps to begin new cells and correct the management problems that characterize the church. Just as the single-cell church is virtually indestructible, it is extremely difficult to continue to sustain growth in a stretched-cell church.

CHAFER, LEWIS SPERRY (1871–1952)

Born on February 27, 1871, at Rock Creek, Ohio, Lewis Sperry Chafer graduated from Oberlin College in 1892 and was ordained to the Presbyterian ministry in 1900. He traveled widely as an evangelist and gospel singer, then later as a Bible teacher. Becoming convinced of a need for a theological seminary that emphasized the expository preaching and teaching of the Bible, Chafer contacted other prominent Bible teachers and began the Dallas Theological Seminary in the fall of 1924. He served as the school's first president until his death on August 22, 1952.

In addition to Chafer's personal evangelistic ministry, he also helped advance the cause of world evangelism through his teaching ministry at Dallas and his many books that have become standard works in their fields. Directly through his books and lectures and indirectly through graduates of Dallas Seminary, Chafer may have trained more dispensational evangelists than any other man of his generation.

Chafer also earned a reputation as a leading systematic theologian. His eight-volume *Systematic Theology* is still viewed as a standard evangelical theology textbook.

CHALMERS, THOMAS (1780–1847)

Thomas Chalmers came from a large family and developed an extensive knowledge of mathematics and science prior to his ordination as a minister in the Church of Scotland. He was already a popular preacher and scholar when at about age 30 he was converted and became a leader of the revival among Scottish Presbyterians. From 1815 to 1823, Chalmers pastored two successive parishes in Glasgow. From there, he held chairs first in Saint Andrews and later in Edinburgh. In 1831-1832, Chalmers served as moderator of the Presbyterian Church. When the split about the Free Church issue divided Scottish Presbyterians, Chalmers led about a third of the churches out of the state church to form the Free Church. This group represented the primary evangelistic and missionary emphasis among Scottish Presbyterians.

Thomas Chalmers' greatest contributions to the cause of evangelism included his work as a leader in the Scottish revival and the Free Church.

CHAPMAN, WILBUR J. (1859–1918)

Wilbur Chapman was one of several citywide evangelists who experienced unusual success during the late nineteenth and early twentieth centuries. Born in Richmond, Indiana, the Presbyterian Chapman was influenced by D. L. Moody and was later a mentor to Billy Sunday.

Chapman was mostly a pastor of Presbyterian churches that were ignited with evangelistic zeal under his leadership. For a time he was also a denominational leader in evangelism. However, it is for his itinerant evangelism that led to powerful citywide campaigns in the United States, Great Britain, Australia and other locales that Chapman is best remembered. He was also a founder of the Winona Lake Bible Conference at Winona Lake, Indiana, in 1885. His elaborate preparation prior to speaking at a city was emulated by others, including Billy Graham. —ALR

Reference: Ford C. Oltman, *J. Wilbur Chapman: A Biography* (New York: Doubleday, Page & Company, 1970).

CHARACTER SNAPSHOTS

Reassessment of a community's spiritual status in the aftermath of important historical decisions and/or events. —GOJR

CHARTER STATEMENT

A statement of intent and commitment signed by charter members when organizing a new church.

Sample Charter Statement
In the year of our Lord, (*Date of Charter Service*)

We, the undersigned, relying on the guidance of the Holy Spirit and by signing our names hereto do agree and covenant with the Lord Jesus Christ and with one another that we do constitute ourselves as Charter Members of the (*your church name here*) of (*your city, state*).

Further, we, the undersigned, each declare and confess our faith wholly in the Lord Jesus Christ for salvation by the experience of the new birth that we have been scripturally baptized and therefore are qualified to become Charter Members.

Also, we, the undersigned, do believe in those great distinctive principles for which born-again Christians have ever stood, namely:

1. The preeminence of Christ as our Divine Lord and Master.
2. The supreme authority of the Bible and its sufficiency as our only rule of faith and practice.
3. The right of private interpretation and the competency of the individual soul in direct approach to God.
4. The absolute separation of Church and State.
5. The regenerate church membership.
6. The beautiful symbolic ordinance of believer's baptism and the Lord's Supper in obedience to the command of Christ.
7. The complete independence of the local church and its interdependence in associated fellowship with other churches.
8. The solemn obligation of majority rule, guaranteeing equal rights to all and special privileges to none.
9. A worldwide program of missionary fervor and evangelism in obedience to the final command of the Lord Jesus Christ.
10. The personal, imminent, premillennial return of the Lord Jesus Christ.

And, we, the undersigned, accept the doctrines of the Articles of Faith included herein; and, accept the duties of the Church Covenant included herein; we assemble ourselves together as the (*your church name here*), and adopt as our plan of outreach, government and service the bylaws included herein.

Reference: Adopted from *The New Hampshire Confession of Faith*, 1832.

CHILDREN, EVANGELISM OF

Children can be converted and come to Jesus Christ. Jesus said, "Let the little children come to Me, and do not forbid them; for of such is the kingdom of God" (Luke 18:16). Those who love children as Jesus did will bring them to the Savior.

A child is capable of accepting Christ or rejecting Him. Children, like adults who do not know Christ, naturally choose evil and turn from God. It is not easy for them to disregard the many influences that clamor for their attention. As these attractions are recognized, the importance of evangelism becomes more apparent.

When the disciples discouraged people from bringing children to Jesus, He rebuked them and encouraged children to come (Mark 10:14). Matthew 18:1-14 emphasizes the evangelism of children. Children are given as examples of humility (v. 4). They are not to be offended (v. 7) or despised (v. 10). It is also the will of the Father that they should not perish (v. 14).

The young child who is won to the Lord has a total life potential to be used in God's service. Not only is a soul saved, but also a life of service to God and people is conserved. Gypsy Smith said in regard to the salvation of children, "You save an old man you save a unit but save a boy and you have a multiplication table."[1]

Another evangelist was asked how many people received Christ in a meeting. "Three and a half," was his reply.

"Oh, you mean three adults and one child," was the response.

"No, three children and one adult. For the child has his whole life before him, the adult only has half a life left."

Often the question is raised, "At what age is a child able to accept Jesus as Savior?" This varies from child to child and from tradition to tradition. The Word of God teaches that children can learn about God, Jesus Christ and other foundational truths while young. "That from childhood you have known the Holy Scriptures, which are able to make you wise for salvation through faith which is in Christ Jesus" (2 Tim. 3:15). Many Christians teach that children reach the "age of accountability" (i.e., the earliest age when children can be converted) when they are old enough to realize they are sinners. At that point, they are also old enough to be converted.

Thus, children should be exposed to the message of God's Word, and taught that God is love. They should be taught that by nature people turn away from God. They should be taught that God is holy and cannot accept sinful things. By such teachings, the children are being nurtured to respond to the claims of Christ during their youth.

Some influences that prepare a child to know Jesus are worship periods, Bible reading, conversations about spiritual things, prayer and singing Christian songs both at church and at home. The radiant and godly life of the parent or teacher also exerts an influence.

The best time to share the Lord with a child is when he or she is prepared by the Holy Spirit. Pray that the Holy Spirit will make the child's heart ready to respond to the gospel. An alertness to the time when a child becomes conscious of sin and feels a need to come to the Lord should characterize every Christian. A child's decision should be recognized even though he or she previously made one.

Grouping for Evangelism

Church educational programs are often graded by ages so that students' needs are similar and better teaching results. Evangelism is another good reason for age grouping. Evangelistic emphasis can be more effective when geared to those of the same age group.

The cradle roll (birth-two) provides an organized outreach of the Sunday School into homes that have new babies. Each year, many parents in a community can be reached with the gospel through an organized cradle-roll program. The experience of new life in a home warms the hearts of parents and creates an excellent opportunity to reach them because they may be ready for the gospel. When parents are won to Christ, their children will also be won to Christ.

Gear the nursery (ages two-three) to evangelism. This department has a ministry to the child. The child learns that the church is God's house, God loves the child, the Bible tells him/her of God, and he/she is to love God. These are tremendous concepts that can be learned early in life and they prepare the child for a salvation experience. The nursery department has a further evangelistic contribution. Many fathers and mothers will attend a Sunday School or church that has facilities for its children. They are more likely to respond to the gospel when they can listen to a sermon without the interruptions of a small child.

Kindergartners (ages four-five) are at an important age. Some people believe they are too young to be converted. Others believe that kindergarten children can know they do wrong and that when a person realizes he or she sins, he or she is old enough to receive Christ. The teacher must be careful to be led of the Spirit in personally dealing with children about salvation. Don't minimize the response of small children. A display of faith by the small child is great in God's sight. Because some children come from Bible-teaching homes, they are aware of God. Others have no concept of God in their lives. All are old enough to love God, pray to God and, in their own way, serve God.

Primary children (ages six-eight) are old enough to place their faith in Christ. They realize that they have sinned and often are ready to respond to the gospel. Small children find it easy and natural to trust Jesus as Savior. For those who do not experience conversion at this time, the primary years can be a time to lay vital groundwork that will lead to a knowledge and conviction of sin and ultimately to personal acceptance of Jesus Christ.

Many people believe that junior age (ages 9-11) is the best age for evangelism. Surely most of them have an awareness of accountability and recognize a need to respond to the gospel. This is when many traditions that practice infant baptism provide instruction, culminating in an opportunity for individuals to respond to what they believe God has done in baptism, by confirming that baptismal act—often called confirmation. The Sunday School teacher must present an evangelistic challenge to the junior if he or she is to fulfill one of the greatest responsibilities of teaching this age group. The teacher should guard against prematurely pushing children into church membership or baptism. The children may need considerable instruction, not being fully aware of the meaning of some of the obligations nor prepared for the responsibilities.

Presenting the Gospel

Presenting the gospel to children takes prayerful preparation and thoughtful expression. Children should not be expected to apply to their hearts a truth the teacher has not applied to his or her own life.

In presenting the gospel to children, language must be simple and on the child's level. Theological or biblical words should not be taken for granted but explained plainly. Many Sunday School manuals provide a glossary of terms graded to the understanding of the child. Unclear terms often must be explained many times. Some words or expressions that are difficult for children are the following: sin, everlasting life, saved, died for our sins, received or accept Christ as Savior, sinner, forgiveness, God's love. The fundamental facts that explain the gospel include: (1) God loves you (John 3:16); (2) all have sinned (Rom. 3:23); (3) Christ died to pay for your sin (1 Cor. 15:3); (4) believe Christ died for your sin (John 1:12); and (5) when you believe, you receive everlasting life (Rom. 6:23).

The underlying motive and universal language a child understands is love. When a teacher faces the class or an individual student, the nonverbal language must say, "I love you." The teacher's looks, actions, attitudes and words must radiate love from the Lord. A knowledge of child psychology is helpful to be a successful worker with children but there is no substitute for love.

Public Invitations

Some dangers can be involved in giving a public invitation to children. Children are taught to be obedient to parents, so they may do what the "adult up front" asks of them. As a result, a decision to accept Christ may not be a spiritual reality. Children are also influenced by others; they express a desire to be converted because their friends are doing so. They have tender hearts. Stories that play on the emotions may cause them to make an outward response, especially stories of danger, death or loss of parents. The teacher must be careful that decisions for Christ made by children are properly motivated and are centered in faith in Christ.

When talking with children who respond in a general evangelistic meeting, it is necessary to determine the basis of their faith. Faith must be in Jesus Christ. Children can have a subjective faith that comes from desire, but is not based on Christ. Although this is not saving faith, it can provide an opportunity to make clear that trust must be in Christ.

An open invitation in a children's meeting is sometimes given simply because the leader is hesitant to talk personally with children about Christ. When a general invitation is given, carefully plan to personally explain salvation to each child who responds.

If a public invitation must be given because the group is large and time does not permit a personal interview with all, children can be prepared by having them bow their heads and close their eyes. This can help assure a reverent atmosphere. The invitation should not be too easy nor too difficult. If it has no meaning to the child, he or she might respond without a change of heart. If the invitation is too difficult, the timid child might be discouraged.

Decisions should not be forced upon children. A child's reticence may be because he or she does not understand what is said, or the child may not be ready at that moment. It is not necessary to wait until the end of a lesson to extend an invitation. Occasionally, a teacher might pause in the middle of the lesson and invite children to accept the Lord Jesus Christ. The guidance of the Holy Spirit is available to those who seek and will follow it. A teacher should never permit the amount of lesson material to prevent him or her from taking the necessary time to present an invitation to accept Christ. Lessons are taught to change lives, not just to communicate content.

Using the Hand to Explain the Gospel

Many methods and Scripture verses may be used when leading a child to the Lord. The following method uses John 3:16 as a basis for explaining the way of salvation. John 3:16 contains five simple divisions, which are as follows: (1) For God so loved, (2) the world, (3) that he gave His only begotten Son, (4) that whosoever believes in Him, (5) should not perish but have everlasting life. A simple plan is to let every finger on the hand represent one part of God's great plan for salvation.[2]

In the beginning of God's plan is His love, so the thumb can stand for God's love. God created all things. He made the beautiful flowers and trees, the birds and bees buzzing in the trees, the animals and grass all around. The sun, the moon and stars were also made by God. And God made each boy, girl, man and woman. He loves each one.

The index finger can represent the world. Children call this finger the "pointer." Each child is one of the people in the world. The teacher should be specific and personal at this point. The child does not belong to God because he or she is a sinner. He or she is separated from God because of sin in the heart. God is holy and cannot look at sin. "For all have sinned and fall short of the glory of God" (Rom. 3:23). This sin must be forgiven before a child can become a child of God.

The middle finger (tall man) can stand for the Son, the Lord Jesus Christ. Jesus is God's Son. God sent His Son to die on the cross for people's sins. Christ had no sin, but He paid for sin on the cross. Man deserves to die, but Jesus died instead. But He did not stay dead. He rose again from the dead after three days. He showed Himself to His friends and they were glad. Jesus is now alive. He is in heaven. He talks to the heavenly Father about believers. He is waiting for each child to make Him his or her friend and Savior.

The ring finger can stand for the sinner who receives Jesus Christ. When a person receives Jesus Christ as Savior, he or she is saved. He or she must believe that Jesus died in his or her place and trust Him to forgive. A brief prayer can be, "Dear Lord Jesus, I know I am a sinner. I now believe in you and accept you as my Savior. Forgive my sins and make me your own."

Finally, the little finger can stand for the assurance that God has given eternal life. Using John 3:16 or Romans 6:23, a child who has received Christ can be shown that he or she now has eternal life, not because the teacher said so, but because God's Word says so. This eternal life is a gift from God not because the child prayed for it, but God gave it in response to his or her faith.

After a child has asked Christ to come into his or her life, a prayer of thanksgiving for salvation should be offered audibly by both child and evangelist. Encourage the student to tell someone of his or her decision as soon as possible. If the child accepted Christ privately in church, let him or her tell the pastor or class. If public invitations are given in church, it is good to encourage the child to go forward and confess that Christ is his or her Savior. Make sure the child shares the experience with his or her parents. If the parents are not Christians, the teacher may go home with the child or call during the week to help explain what has happened.

Guide the child in spiritual growth, encouraging and praying with him or her. The child should be enrolled in church activities and introduced to mature Christians in the church who can be an encouragement in the child's Christian walk. This added Christian fellowship will strengthen the child's Christian life.

References: [1]Cited by David M. Dawson, *More Power in Soul Winning* (Grand Rapids: Zondervan Publishing House, 1947), p. 58. [2]Walter H. Werner, "How to Lead a Child to Christ," *Guidelines for Christian Parents* (Lincoln, Nebr.: Good News Broadcasting Assn., Inc., 1967), pp. 12-16. Clifford Ingle, ed. *Children and Conversion* (Nashville: Broadman Press, 1975). Marjorie Soderholm, *Explaining Salvation to Children* (Minneapolis: Free Church Publications, 1979).

CHO, DAVID (PAUL) YONGGI

David (Paul) Yonggi Cho has built the largest

single church yet reported by church historians. The source of the growth has been by cell ministry in the homes of believers throughout Seoul, South Korea. The church had more than 60,000 weekly cell meetings and a membership of more than 700,000 believers when this volume was written in 1995. The church auditorium, seating more than 25,000, has multiple services each Sunday.

David Yonggi Cho graduated from Bible school on March 15, 1958, and started a small tent church on a small parcel of land next to the Bulkwang-dong cemetery in Seodaimoon-ku, Seoul, Korea. This was the beginning of what is now the largest church in the world: Yoido Full Gospel Church, which as of this writing has more than 700,000 members.

For the first worship service in the tent church, Pastors Cho, Ja-shil Choi and her three children were the only ones who attended. Although young Cho was battling tuberculosis, he had to spend more than two hours riding buses to lead the Wednesday worship services, and the all-night and early morning prayer meetings also taxed his strength.

In September 1959, a heavy rain came through the tent onto the podium and soaked the rice bags that had been spread on the dirt floor on which the congregation sat. Unexpectedly and miraculously, the tent filled with people. Rain-soaked people took out their Bibles and song-books they had held close to their bodies to keep dry. Pastor Cho was moved at this sight. That night, he preached a stirring sermon titled, "Jesus Who Comes with the Storm."

Cho told the audience, "Even when we do not see the proof and cannot touch anything during our suffering and painful days, if we overcome it with faith, we can meet Jesus who comes with the storm and high waves." Then he cried out, saying, "Let's say 'Amen' when we believe that Jesus is here with us in the tent, which is shaking from the wind." The congregation clapped loudly and responded with a hearty amen.

Cho went into military service on January 30, 1961, and after seven months of service received a medical discharge as a result of a serious hernia operation. On September 1, 1961, a few days after his discharge, he held a tent church crusade in Seodaimoon Rotary, the place where a circus group had performed.

The Holy Spirit then led Pastor Cho to establish another church at that same location. On October 15, 1961, the first worship service in the Seodaimoon arena was held. Pastor Cho's preaching grew more powerful day by day. Where once he had been a reluctant person, he now had the anointing of the Holy Spirit, and his messages were profound and meaningful to the attenders. The church membership in the tent church increased, and the church prospered in many ways.

In November 1961, the Seodaimoon Revival Center building was completed. A nucleus from the original tent church helped to pioneer the Revival Center at Seodaimoon. The number of attenders at the Revival Center increased to 300 people; every week 20 to 30 members were added to the Revival Center.

On April 20, 1962, Pastor Cho was ordained as a pastor. On May 13 of that year, the Full Gospel Revival Center was renamed the Full Gospel Central Church. By this time the membership had grown to more than 500.

Dr. John Hurston, American missionary from the Assembly of God, had a significant role in guiding the development of the church.

By 1964, the pioneer church at Seodaimoon had grown to a membership of 3,000. The home-cell system was organized and the church grew stronger and prospered financially.

On March 1, 1965, Pastor Cho married Sung-Hae-Kim, the daughter of his copastor Ja-shil Choi. This marriage was the result of Pastor Cho's 10 years of prayer for a suitable wife. The prayers of his copastor—his mother-in-law—also helped put Cho and Sung-Hae-Kim together. About 3,000 church members attended the marriage ceremony.

As the church increased in its membership, the church building at Seodaimoon could no longer accommodate all the people. One elder of the church recommended a site on Yoido Island to expand the church facilities. At that time, Yoido was merely an island of sand and was being used as an airport. The island was considered a wilderness because it had no bridge between it and the mainland.

The city was planning a future development for Yoido, however, so this sounded promising to Cho. At first, the congregation strongly opposed the idea of moving to the island. They questioned how many members would go way out to Yoido for worship services because transportation was a big problem. They feared that the church might lose all its members and have to start from scratch on Yoido. Nevertheless, they purchased the land and Cho moved the church to Yoido. The cost of construction, however, was enormous.

The first worship service at Yoido Full Gospel Church was held on August 19, 1973. One month later, the tenth World Pentecostal Conference, with 50,000 members participating, including 5,000 foreigners, was held in the new Yoido Church sanctuary and at Hyochang Stadium. On September 23, a touching dedication ceremony of the newly constructed Yoido Church was held with 18,000 people participating.

Church membership reached 200,144 at the end of November, 1981, up from 100,000 two years earlier. At the 200,000 Membership Celebration, Pastor Cho admonished the pastors "to remember that this growth was not by human efforts but by God who uses the church which is faithful to Him."

CHRISTIANITY

A belief system based on a person's relationship to God that has at its heart the life, death and resurrection of Jesus Christ. A belief system based on the triune God, the death of Christ and that God has revealed Himself only in the Scriptures known as the Old and New Testaments.

CHRISTIANIZATION BY ABSTRACTION

A widely held approach to evangelism in which converts are extracted from their social setting at conversion. This one-by-one method of spreading the gospel usually results in slow growth of the church.

CHRYSOSTOM (c. 345–407)

One of the fathers of the Eastern Church and widely recognized as one of the greatest preachers of the Eastern Church.

Born into an aristocratic family in Antioch (Syria), John of Antioch was educated in the Greek classics and rhetoric. He practiced law until his baptism in 368 at which time he became a monk. Ordained in 386, he began preaching in Antioch. In 398, he was made a Patriarch of Constantinople. He was banished from that ministry six months later after offending the Empress Eudoxia in one of his sermons. He died in exile in 407. Shortly after his death, he was nicknamed "Chrysostom," which means "golden-mouthed." The name reflects his reputation as an able orator. About 640 of his sermons are still extant, most of which are based on the Epistles of Paul.

CHURCH: COMPARISON BETWEEN OLD AND NEW TESTAMENTS

The Church is a New Testament doctrine and the word "church" never appears in the Old Testament, although lessons and principles of the Church that became revealed in the New Testament are concealed in the Old Testament. This present dispensation is called the "times of the Gentile," and the inclusion of the Gentile into God's plan is different from God's dealing with non-Jews in the Old Testament.

Basic distinctions exist between the Old and New Testament. In the Old Testament, the people of God are the Jews, also called Hebrews (i.e., a national ethnic entity), while in the New Testament, the people of God are gathered from every ethnic background into a new community—Jews and Gentiles—into the Church.

In the Old Testament, we find the emphasis was on being born a Jew, a physical descendant of Abraham. The identifiable covenant sign was a physical sign: circumcision. The New Testament assembly involves being born again: a spiritual birth. The identifiable sign in the New Testament is baptism.

In the Old Testament, the symbols of redemption were located in the Tabernacle (Temple), priesthood and offering; all were located at one place—Jerusalem. The New Testament symbols in the Church can be administered any place the Church gathers (i.e., the Lord's Table and baptism).

CHURCH: CONTEMPORARY DEFINITION AND DESCRIPTION

Christianity contains many forms of expression: the varieties of denominations, systems of theology, modes of worship, styles of church polity, schools of evangelism and architecture of church buildings. Along with this diverse expression of Christianity is the influence of the interdenominational movement, the charismatic movement, the electric church, the Bible college movement, the Christian school movement and the variety of evangelical media (Christian magazines, books, radio stations, television stations, film companies and so on). Out of this milieu comes an ever-growing chorus to interpret all this to the world.

We live in a church age of sociological research where many people base church ministry on the findings of surveys, median scores and case studies. These findings have their place, but this article assumes that the only true model for the Church is found in the pages of the New Testament. The student must study the New Testament to determine, first, the nature of the Church and, second, the principles of evangelism. After an ecclesiology is grounded in the Word of God, the findings of sociological research can be applied to these principles for the outworking of ministry.

This article assumes that the Church has life and spirit because it is the Body of Jesus Christ (1 Cor. 12:27; Eph. 4:15,16) and that its founder and head is Jesus Christ who gives it authority and vitality. As such, the Church is an organism and an organization. The Church is an organism that elevates it above the business and social organizations of our day. It is also an organization and as such must carry out its ministry in an age of business management and administration.

The media seem to have little respect for the contemporary Church, portraying it as weak and anemic. The young person who watches a church service in the movies or reads about a religious ceremony in the newspaper gets the impression the Church is filled with either the elderly or hypocrisy. The problem is that the young people who are either "anti-Church" or have rejected the Church do not see it as a dynamic organization that is responsible for changing society and lives. The average young person usually hears of the hypocrisy of those who call themselves Christians or the bureaucracy of those who serve in the church for the wrong reasons. As a result, many young people reject the Church, not without some justification. Many churches are guilty of the abuse that is hurled on it by today's youth.

Young people who reject the contemporary Church, however, would like its founder, Jesus Christ. He was as antibureaucratic as they are. He condemned the religious sham of His age as young people condemn the religious sham of their day. Jesus was antibureaucratic in both His teachings and in His life. In every sense of the word, Jesus was a revolutionary. But the problem is that the revolution Jesus began against the dead religion of His day ultimately becomes the standard for the spiritual institutions of our day. In many cases, the Church has become as dead as the organization against which Jesus revolted.

Christianity began with the man Jesus Christ. Jesus, the eternal Word of God, became flesh. It was in His physical body that Jesus at times was hungry, worked and became tired, and as all other humans, grew to full manhood. While in this physical body, Jesus was limited by its humanity. But on the other side, Jesus was also God and as such had the power of deity and possessed all of God's attributes. As the Son of God, Jesus did not sin, but the threat of death awaited Him as it does all other humans. In His unique physical body that was both divine and human, Jesus died, was buried and on the third day His physical body arose from the dead. Finally, the physical body of Jesus Christ ascended into heaven and today He is at the right hand of God the Father.

The physical body of Jesus Christ is the same one with which every Christian is identified on calvary. In the baptism of the Holy Spirit, the believer is baptized (placed into) the death of Jesus Christ (1 Cor. 12:13; Rom. 6:4-6). This action is also called the vicarious substitutionary death of Jesus Christ. In this body we died with

Him, were buried with Him and were raised on the third day (Rom. 6:4,5).

Now the Church is called His Body (1 Cor. 12:27), sometimes called the local church. As such, the visible church is subject to the limitations of humanity but is very much divine in its supernatural authority and spiritual power. Just as Jesus Christ in the human body was the God-man, so the Church is both an organism and an organization.

The Church of Jesus Christ should be anti-institutional, antiestablishment and revolutionary. That is because the Church is God's institution to challenge the sinful ways of humans, especially those that represent a human's attempts to substitute for the provision of God. As such, the Church should be those Christians who are on the cutting edge of society. However, the Church, as an institution established by God, is sometimes more institutional and bureaucratic than dynamic and life giving.

The fact that our youth misunderstand the Church is reflective of the problem the Church faces today. The outward Church is a misunderstood institution. It is diverse in appearance, conflicting in purpose and often ineffective in ministry.

The Sunday morning church service varies from street to street and town to town. One church reminds a person of an eighteenth-century ritual, while across town a person enters a "mod" church service that is freewheeling and contemporary.

Some churches meet in humble frame buildings on dirt streets, others are cathedrals that have soaring spires and magnificent stained-glass windows. Some churches are the "do it yourself" variety and have lay preachers and simple religious forms. Other churches are traditional America mainline Protestant churches. Some emerging groups emphasize "body life" and *koinonia* fellowship.

Religious intensity varies from apathy in the traditional mainline denominational churches to the revivalistic fervor in some fundamentalist churches. The not-so-traditional ethnic sect (Mennonite) values family tradition; and the ritualistic, liturgical cathedral demands reverence from its worshipers. Those who worship in

structured, loose-knit living room churches center their religious expression around *koinonia*, while the emotional Pentecostal churches involve its members in charismatic worship; the mystical deeper life churches demand meditation and reflective worship. The only thing we know for sure is that churches are different from one another.

American churches present many images to the worshipers. Some churches appear to follow the New England Puritan tradition: a few hymns, some praying and finally a sermon. Other churches resemble a schoolroom. The sermon-lecture is filled with references to the original text; many in the congregation take notes, while the pastor-teacher may use an overhead projector to help deliver the sermon. Moving on to the next church we may find the sermon sounding like a political address at a rally. The next church visited may give the atmosphere of a group-dynamics therapy session where the minister is the psychiatrist.

The differences in the churches are deeper than doctrinal distinctives of denominations. Cultural and social differences also affect the way people worship God. The varied expressions in churches and denominations are necessary because people are different from each other. God has planned variety in His Church, yet, every New Testament Church has similar characteristics because it is a reflection of the same Jesus Christ. Actually, all can agree with Paul, who said, "There is one body and one Spirit, just as you were called in one hope of your calling; one Lord, one faith, one baptism; one God and Father of all, who is above all, and through all, and in you all" (Eph. 4:4-6).

CHURCH: FIRST REFERENCE IN SCRIPTURE

The law of first reference concerning the Church gives insight into evangelistic outreach (i.e., the first reference to any doctrine in Scripture usually contains the embryonic truth of its development. God introduces a subject in microscopic form and explains it fuller at a later time). "And I also say unto you that you are Peter, and on this rock I will build My church, and the gates of

Hades shall not prevail against it" (Matt. 16:18). Note the following from the first mention of the word "church."

The Church was introduced by divine revelation. Jesus told Peter that his insight concerning Christ as the Son of the living God came from the Father. Peter did not think up his ideas about Christ or the Church. "Jesus answered and said to him, 'Blessed are you, Simon Bar-Jonah, for flesh and blood has not revealed this to you, but My Father who is in heaven" (Matt. 16:17).

The Church was initiated by Jesus Christ. When Jesus said He would build the Church, it was in response to Peter's declaration of the deity of Christ. "You are the Christ, the son of the living God" (Matt. 16:16). When Christ was now properly recognized, the topic of the Church was introduced, for this is the vehicle for His future manifestation.

The Church introduced was predicted as future. Jesus stated, "I will" (future tense) "build," (lit. Greek) "be building" My church.

The Church belongs to Christ. He said, "I will build My church." It would be owned by Christ as a peculiar possession.

If we are puzzled about the use of "building" with the word *ekklesia,* it will be helpful to check 1 Peter 2:5. Peter, the very one to whom Jesus is here speaking, writing to the Christians in the five Roman provinces in Asia (1 Pet. 1:1), says: "You are being built up a spiritual house." It is difficult to resist the impression that Peter is recalling the words of Jesus to him. Further on (2:9) he speaks of believers as an elect race, a royal priesthood, a holy nation, showing beyond controversy that Peter's use of building a spiritual house is general, not local. This undoubtedly is the picture in the mind of Christ here in Matthew 16:18.

The Church (ekklesia) is a group of "called out ones." The word *ekklesia* comes from *ek,* the Greek preposition out, and *kaleo,* the Greek verb "to call." Hence, the Church is composed of those who are called out. This has a twofold meaning: (1) the people are called out from the world and their previous ungodly lifestyle; (2) they are called together for a purpose. This purpose is fellowship, education, worship and service.

The word "church" has four separate interpretations. The term "church," *ekklesia,* appears in the singular in Matthew 16:18 and raises some difficulty in interpretation. Some interpretations are the following:

1. Christ was referring to one Church (i.e., the Roman Catholic church and its system).
2. Christ was referring to the Universal Church, composed of all true believers. In essence, He would build up that assembly composed of every true believer in the Church Age, regardless of church affiliation.
3. Christ was referring to a church (i.e., He would build up one local church at a time, each separate from the others) implying the independent nature of local churches. Christ would build a church in one area, then another. Those who hold this view are rejecting the Roman Catholic and the Universal Church view.
4. Christ was emphasizing "My church," indicating that He would build His kind of an assembly as opposed to other kinds of churches that were false.

The first mention of Church introduces the embryonic teaching that will be elaborated throughout the New Testament. The Church is uniquely the possession of the Savior. He will build it through His Word as He calls individuals into His fellowship. Once a person is incorporated into the Church, that person belongs to Jesus Christ. The Church can never be disassociated from the deity of Jesus Christ, and when its members are responsive to Him, it will be victorious.

CHURCH: NEW TESTAMENT EXPLANATION

The word "church" first appears in Matthew 16:18 when Jesus says, "I will build My church." The term "church" comes from ekklesia, which is a combination of *ek* (the preposition out) and *kaleo* (the word for "to call.") Hence, Church in its original meaning is "called out ones." People are called to follow Christ and called from the world of self and rebellion.

When the word "church" was introduced by Christ, it took on a specific Christian context so that the *ekklesia* of Jesus was quite different from the ekklesia of the Jews or the secular *ekklesia*. Further, Jesus took a generic word that meant to assemble and gave it a technical sense to mean a Christian assembly—both physical and spiritual unity. Earl Radmacher notes, "Concerning this development it has been observed that the meanings do not shade off into one another in abrupt, sudden changes, but in gradual, almost imperceptible growth."[1]

The word "church" can be used in a general, nontechnical way in Scripture. It can mean an assembly of people that is a gathering of folks— "the assembly" (Acts 19:32). This was simply a gathering or an assembly of people. The term "church" also refers to the nation Israel because Israel was gathered as a church is meant to be gathered. It does not mean Israel has the same doctrine as the technical Church (Acts 7:38; Heb. 2:12).

In Greece, the word *ekklesia* had a political meaning, never a religious meaning. In Athens, for example, the *ekklesia* was the regularly summoned assembly of all the citizens, that is, of those who had the freedom of the city. All the inhabitants of the city did not have this right; full citizens formed only a small minority. At the call of the herald, the citizens came out of their homes, separated themselves from the rest of the inhabitants of the city, and assembled in a place agreed upon to discuss city affairs, such as the nomination of magistrates, officers, governors of the city, military operations and so on. Each convocation began with prayer and sacrifice. The word *ekklesia* is used by Luke in this sense: "In the lawful assembly" (Acts 19:39).[2]

Remember, similarity does not mean identity. God works in parallel ways in the Old and New Testaments. In both testaments, God is gathering His people together; however, the aim and catalyst of each assembly is different.

When a general word is used in a special way, it becomes technical. As such, the word "church" was a deliberate choice by Christ. He chose the common word for assembly and gave it technical content or theological meaning. "The assembly" to which He referred was to be His assembly.

Because the New Testament writers were verbally inspired (i.e., borne along by the Holy Spirit) they initially used the word "assembly" without an explanation. Paul later began to define it with new meaning and purpose. He gave it the interpretation that came to him by revelation from God.

Technically, our English word "church," like the German word *kirche*, stems from the Byzantine Greek form *kuriez*, meaning "belonging to the Lord." These words come from the Greek word *ekklesia*, which means "to assemble."[3]

Technical Use of the New Testament Word

The Church is His body. The word "church" is sometimes used to refer to the physical body of Christ that died on calvary. But as referred to later, the body is also a reference to a local church (1 Cor. 12:27,28), and for a reference to those in heaven who are identified as dwelling "in Him." The reference to the Church carries a twofold meaning, revealing that the Church is an organism that has divinelike properties. This implies that the Church is more than an organization similar to worldly organizations although comprised of the saved. The spiritual application is reflected by the phrase "in Christ" (1 Cor. 12:12ff; Eph. 1:22; 5:23,29; Col. 1:24; 2:19).

The body of Christ represents Paul's maturest reflections on the subject. The body-concept is applied by Paul to the Church and sheds much light on the nature of the Church as he understood it.

The Church is an unassembled assembly. This is a reference to those in a local assembly when they are not meeting together. In Acts 8:3, Saul did not enter into the assembly while it was meeting, but into houses of Christians who belonged to the assembly (cf. Acts 9:31; 14:17).

The Church is an assembled assembly. Technically, when the saved are assembled, they are a unique assembly in God's sight. Note Matthew 18:17 and especially 1 Corinthians 14:4,23.

The Church may refer to an assembly that teaches the doctrine of Christ or lives by His standards. Certain assemblies are called "church" but in fact are not recognized by Jesus Christ because its aims, nature and catalyst do not fit the New Testament criteria. In Revelation 3:14-19, Christ uses the term "church," although this group of people had denied the foundational makeup of a church.

The word "church" refers to more than one church. The plural uses of ekklesia in Acts 9:31 obviously refer to many local churches. It is also used in Galatians 1:2 to refer to several local churches in Galatia.

References: [1]Earl D. Radmacher, *What the Church Is All About* (Chicago: Moody Press, 1978), p.368. [2]Alfred Kuen, *I Will Build My Church* (Chicago: Moody Press, 1971), p.46. [3]Ibid.

CHURCH: THEOLOGICAL DEFINITION

The biblical definition of a church is established by correctly interpreting Scripture (see article CHURCH: FIRST REFERENCE IN SCRIP-TURE, and CHURCH: NEW TESTAMENT DEFINITION AND EXPLANATION) and then assimilating the biblical teaching into a complete theological system. This article gives six aspects of a theological definition of the Church.

1. A church is an assembly of professing believers. The first criterion for a New Testament Church is an assembly of those who have their faith in Jesus Christ (Rom. 10:9), as an outward evidence to an inward reality of having their sins forgiven. On the Day of Pentecost, those who believed were immediately baptized and added to the Church. "Then those who gladly received his word were baptized; and that day about three thousand souls were added to them" (Acts 2:41).

Not all who make an outward confession of faith actually possess eternal life. There will be some in the church who are not saved, as was the case in New Testament times (Acts 8:13-23). However, all should be accepted into the church upon their profession of faith. The church is an assembly of professing believers. It seems no matter how carefully the church examines individuals (Acts 8:5-25; 18:24-28), some gain access into the fellowship, only to be questioned at a later time.

2. The unique presence of Jesus Christ dwells in a church. Christ is the light of the world (John 8:12), and the primary purpose of the Church is to hold up the light in a dark world (Phil. 2:15,16). The Church does more than possess a light: it is a light, expressly a corporate group of lights—"you shine as lights" (Phil. 2:15). Therefore, the Church is an organism and its light and life is Jesus Christ. He dwells in the midst of His people. "For where two or three are gathered together in My name, I am there in the midst of them" (Matt. 18:20). Yet Christ does more than indwell a church; He *is* the Church. It is His Body and He is its life.

Christ walked through the seven churches in the book of Revelation and commended them for their good works (Rev. 2:3) and rebuked them for their sin and false doctrine (Rev. 2:4). When Christ rebuked the churches in the book of Revelation, He threatened to take away their candlestick (Rev. 2:5, *KJV*), which would have been removing His presence from the people. When Christ is removed from a New Testament Church, it is similar to the *shekinah* cloud leaving the Old Testament Temple. If a group of people does not have Jesus Christ dwelling in its midst, it is no longer a New Testament Church, no matter what name it uses above the church door.

3. A church is under the discipline of the Word of God. One of the first religious exercises of the New Testament Church after the Day of Pentecost was that "they continued steadfastly in the apostles' doctrine" (Acts 2:42). Doctrinal commitment is essential for a New Testament Church. There is a unique union between Christ and the Bible for both are the Word of God.

When an organizational problem arose in the Early Church, the apostles realized they had to place a priority on their time, and that they should be giving themselves to the Word of God (Acts 6:4). A local church must place itself under the authority of God by placing itself under the discipline of the Word of God.

The minister gives positive proclamation of the Word of God. This is positive discipline, thus leading to correct life and belief. When the minister rebukes a congregation for its sins, this is negative discipline, just as a parent rebukes a child for going too near the fire. The purpose of discipline by the Word of God is the positive and negative correction of the New Testament Church. When an assembly of people removed themselves from the authority of the Word of God, they no longer met the criteria of being a New Testament Church.

4. A church is organized to carry out the Great Commission. The Early Church "did not cease teaching and preaching Jesus as the Christ" (Acts 5:42). Because everyone outside of Christ was lost, the Church believed that everyone must be presented with the gospel. The persecutors could say, "You have filled Jerusalem with your doctrine" (Acts 5:28). The early disciples were carrying out the Great Commission.

5. A church administers the ordinances/sacraments (some traditions call these sacred acts through which God gives His grace). Most believers participate in the ordinances of the church: baptism and the Lord's Table. These are to be celebrated by the church when it assembles together.

6. A church reflects the spiritual gifts. Not every group of Christians is destined to grow into a church. If it becomes a New Testament Church, however, spiritual gifts will emerge. This process begins when God raises up leadership to bring the church into existence. These leaders minister through their "spiritual gifts" (Rom. 12; 1 Cor. 12; Eph. 4). God gives gifted men to a church, and when these leaders appear, it is an indication that God wants the people to organize into a New Testament Church. "God has appointed these in the church: first apostles, second prophets, third teachers" (1 Cor. 12:28).

"And He Himself gave some to be apostles, some prophets, some evangelists, and some pastors and teachers" (Eph. 4:11). Paul wrote to the church at Corinth to "covet earnestly the best gifts" (1 Cor. 12:31, *KJV*). The word "covet" is plural, implying that a church must desire spiritual gifts. Hence, if a church has no spiritual gifts, we can imply it is not a church or has not obeyed the admonition to seek gifted leaders to carry out its aim.

CHURCH: THE UNIVERSAL

Although the concept of an invisible or universal Church is probably believed by many, historically, the idea was first articulated by Augustine in *City of God*. It is also called the triumphant

Church, the true Church, the Body of Christ or the glorified Church. Most theologians have held to some form of a nonlocal church in their teachings, attempting to deal with the description of the Church as a mystery (Eph. 3:1-10) or a Body (1 Cor. 12:12-23). Some believe the Church is made up of true believers in the midst of professing believers. Others believe it is the organic aspect of the local organization. Still others believe it is composed of all true believers in this dispensation regardless of local church membership.

Perhaps the most profound influence of the doctrine grew out of the teaching of J. N. Darby, which was basically dispensational in nature and popularized by *The Scofield Reference Bible*. As such, the universal Church would be defined:

The Universal Church is that group composed of all true believers in this present dispensation (Pentecost to Rapture) permanently united by the baptism of Holy Spirit into vital spiritual union with all believers of this age thus forming His mystical body.[1]

The universal Church emphasizes the unity of believers, and the positional nature of each believer as he or she stands perfect in Jesus Christ.

One of the key verses to explain the universal Church is 1 Corinthians 12:13: "For by one spirit we were all baptized into one body—whether Jews or Greeks, whether slaves or free—and have all been made to drink into one Spirit." The believer is baptized or "placed" into the Body of Christ, which is pictured as the universal Church. This spiritual union happens at salvation and is the positional basis by which God deals with the believer.

Reference: [1]Elmer L. Towns, *Theology for Today* (Dubuque, Iowa: Kendall Hunt Publishing Co., 1994), p. 635.

CHURCH: WHEN DID IT BEGIN?

Ever since the current attention to church growth, the issue of church growth and the Old Testament has gained more attention because the

Church Growth Movement bases its objective on the Great Commission (Matt. 28:19,20). Although this article does not address the issue of the Kingdom, the Old Testament mandate and other related issues, it does concern itself with the issue of when the Church began.

Many viewpoints are considered in trying to determine when the Church began. Each of these views grew out of a system of theology, and in some way complement the ideas that gave it life.

A. The Church began with the saints in the Old Testament. This view is common among covenant or reformed theologians. In this position, some believe the Church was established when the promise was given to Abraham (cf. Rom. 4). Others believe the Church was established with the promise of the covenant of grace. They generally say that the Church originated in the Garden of Eden immediately after the Fall of humans, when God promised a Savior and humans accepted that promise in faith.

B. The Church began with the ministry of John the Baptist. In this view, it is noted that John's baptism is said to be given from heaven and because Jesus sought baptism by a baptizer, our Lord gave this position credibility. John began baptizing and pointing people to the coming Christ; hence, they view that John the Baptist was the starting point of the Church.

C. The Church began with the public ministry of Jesus Christ. This view interprets Matthew 10 where Jesus called His disciples to Him. This event is viewed as the beginning of the Church because the word "church" means to "call together" or to be in "assembly." Also, those who follow this view note that the followers of Jesus were called "disciples" before this point and "apostles" afterward. Therefore, sending forth the 12 apostles is the beginning point of the Church.

D. The Church began somewhere in the book of Acts (chaps. 8,13,28) as an eighth dispensation. This is the hyperdispensational view of O'Hare and Bullinger. They teach that a Jewish church existed in the book of Acts immediately after the resurrection of Christ. The test of fellowship in the seventh dispensation (the Jewish church) is water baptism. Thus, water baptism is seen as not being required in the age of grace.

E. The Church began on the Day of Pentecost. This is the view of most dispensationalists. It is represented by Lewis Sperry Chafer in his *Systematic Theology.*[1]

1. There must be a death.
2. There must be a Resurrection.
3. There must be an Ascension. This would be God's seal on Christ's work.
4. There must be an advent of the Holy Spirit. Until these four events take place, there is no Church. Therefore, Acts 2 is the beginning of the Church.

Peter, although chosen of God to be the chief spokesman at Pentecost, did not understand that Spirit baptism had begun on that day. It was not until some time later, when there was visible evidence of the Spirit baptizing new believers at the house of Cornelius, that he realized this work of Spirit baptism had actually begun on the Day of Pentecost. Notice carefully his words of explanation to the Jewish brethren after his return to Jerusalem:

"And as I began to speak, the Holy Spirit fell upon them, as upon us at the beginning. Then I remembered the word of the Lord, how He said, 'John indeed baptized with water, but you shall be baptized with the Holy Spirit.' If therefore God gave them the same gift as He gave us when we believed on the Lord Jesus Christ, who was I that I could withstand God?" (Acts 11:15-17).

What happened to Cornelius was the same as what happened at Pentecost (the beginning) and was the same as the gift of the Spirit. Peter identifies himself with the gift of the Spirit in the words "as He gave us." He did not mean that he had received the baptism and gift of the Spirit on Pentecost, for that would be contradictory to the words of Jesus in John 14:17: "He dwells with you and will be in you." Rather, Peter was identifying himself as one of the group upon whom the Spirit came on the Day of Pentecost.

Spirit baptism marks the beginning of the Church. In 1 Corinthians 12:12,13, Paul writes that the Body of Christ, the Church, is formed as the Spirit baptized individuals into the Body, and into union with Christ. This is one of the primary identifications of the Church as distinct from the people of God in Old Testament times. Because the Church is formed by Spirit baptism, and Spirit baptism began at Pentecost, the Church began at Pentecost.

F. The Church began at calvary when Christ provided salvation. Because calvary is the focal point between the Old and New Testaments and between law and grace, the Church was introduced at the initiation of grace. The Church is called His Body and because He provided salvation by the death of His body on the Cross, the Church came into existence then. Also, Christians were placed by Spirit baptism into that body, so that initiated the Church.

Jesus states, "I will [future tense] build My church" (Matt. 16:18), indicating that the Church would be established in the future. Later, the Bible declares (Acts 2:41,47) that on the Day of Pentecost the people were added (past tense) to the Church that was already in existence. Hence, the Church must have been established after the events of Matthew 16 and before Acts 2. The obvious event between these points of limitation is the death of Christ.

The Church is built upon the apostles and prophets (Eph. 2:20) and Jesus Christ is the chief cornerstone. The reference to the cornerstone is the work Jesus did on calvary (1 Cor. 3:11).

The Church is called a mystery (Eph. 3:1-10), which is "the dispensation of the grace of God" (v. 2). This mystery was not made known in previous generations. It is now revealed (v. 5). The basis of the mystery is the work of redemption that made Jew and Gentile one (v. 6). Because this was accomplished at calvary, the Church was embryonically conceived then.

Reference: [1]Lewis Sperry Chafer, *Systematic Theology* (Dallas: Dallas Seminary Press, 1948).

CHURCH AGE

The period of time (dispensation) that stretches from the advent of the Holy Spirit to the rapture (a synonym for the age of grace.)

CHURCH EXTENSION

Church growth through a strategy of planting new churches. This is sometimes described as expansion growth (within the same culture) and extension growth (beyond the same culture) and sometimes called bridging growth when it is beyond the same culture. This has two subdivisions, one for close cross-cultural efforts and another one for when it's a longer distance between cultures.

CHURCH GROWTH BALANCE
See Church Growth Wheel

CHURCH GROWTH, BIBLICAL PARADIGMS

One way the Church is described in the New Testament is through the use of seven pictures or symbolic images. Each of these pictures tends to emphasize certain eternal truths about the nature, purpose and function of the Church. These pictures were not haphazardly included by human authors as purely idiomatic expressions of the culture of that day. Rather, they are divinely inspired and included to represent important issues. Each image speaks to a different way life is found in the Church. Each image portrays the Church from a different perspective. Each image implies certain principles of church growth.

PICTURE	CENTRAL TRUTH
Body	Unity
Building	Indwelling
Bride	Intimacy
Flock	Provision
Garden (Vine)	Union
Family	Identity
Priesthood	Service

1. The Body of Christ. The picture of the body is one of the most often used analogies of the Church. The Bible presents Christ as the head, and the body is the Church. The members of His body are to grow up in all aspects "into Him who is the head" (Eph. 4:15). In the husband-wife relationship, "Christ is head of the church; and He is the Savior of the body" (Eph. 5:23). Christ is to be placed first in all things because "He is the head of the body, the church" (Col. 1:18). Paul's sufferings for the Colossian Christians was done on behalf of Christ's body, "which is the church" (Col. 1:24). Christ is also the source and supplier of all growth to the body (Col. 2:19). Christians are a part of the body and part of one another (Rom. 12:5; 1 Cor. 12:12-31).

Biologically, a body comes into existence when the seed or sperm joins an egg and forms a cell. In that embryonic cell are the components that will fashion the body as it is fully developed. The sex, hair color and thousands of other features are inherent in that first cell. The body grows by the division of cells, and when two cells emerge, it is impossible to determine which was the original. When a local church is formed, believers are joined together into one unified body that should function in harmony. The Bible uses the analogy of a body for the Church to reveal the inherent life with a church and its intended unity.

Robert Saucy gives six aspects or principles of how the head (Christ) relates to the body (Church): (1) unity, (2) diversity, (3) mutuality, (4) sovereign leadership, (5) the source of life, and (6) the sustenance of life.[1]

Every church and every Christian should give Christ first place in everything! The reason for His priority is: (1) He produced all things for Himself (Col. 1:16); (2) He preceded all things (v. 17); (3) He preserves all things (v. 17); and (4) He purposes to be first in all things (v. 18).

As the head controls our lives, so Christ must be given preeminence. The head always gives direction to the body, so Christians must be willing to receive His orders. Both quantitative and qualitative growth in the Church comes from obedience to the head, Jesus Christ.

The church in Corinth did not follow Christ. Christians were no longer a body united, but members divided! But if each member of His body, beginning with pastors, would acknowledge the lordship of Christ and depend upon His presence, the resulting unity would produce growth. Robert Saucy explains the results of unity:

The apostle (Paul) begins his discussion of gifts with the Corinthian church by placing all of the pneumatic gifts under one Lord and Spirit (1 Cor. 12:3-5). Therefore, there must be no schism in the body (12:25 ff.) caused by a disorderly display of gifts (1 Cor. 14:33). All of the gifted members are under the same Head and are part of the same body, and such members in a normal body do not oppose each other, thus tearing the body apart.[2]

If a body is healthy, all of its parts will function properly. Disease and sickness often strike the areas of greatest weakness, and when that happens, the entire body is disabled (1 Cor. 12:26). Disease could be overt or covert sin by the members or by the body acting as a whole. Just as disease comes from without the body, so there are problems that weaken or destroy the body from sociological or internal problems.

In his references to Colossians 2:19 and Ephesians 4:15,16, Saucy remarks: "The body grows through the supply of energy distributed to each part through the Head. As each member, receiving his gift of grace contributes to the whole, the body grows."[3] Gary Inrig notes:

The truth is that the Body of Christ is designed to teach us that we need one another and that we must care for one another. To the world we must show ourselves one in Christ, united in love and a shared life. Such a unity is not uniformity or conformity. It is rather a Spirit-given sense of our mutual needs and the recognition that our diversity is both God-given and essential to maturity and health. 'Unity, diversity, interdependence.' This is not to be just the motto of the local congregation, but its experience under God.[4]

When the Word of God uses the term "the body of Christ," it is important to note whether it means a figure of speech or the term is used literally. First, if the Church is literally the body of Christ, it makes the local assembly equal to Christ. This raises the question of Roman Catholicism beliefs, for the Roman church makes their church equal with Christ Himself.

Saucy notes, "The heart of the Roman Catholic doctrine of salutary and authoritative church rest on the literal interpretation which defines the church or the body of Christ Himself."[5] The figurative view implies the local church is only similar to Christ's body and has no organic connection.

A third view might be suggested. Just as Christ indwells the believer, so He indwells His Church. And just as the life of the Church depends upon the indwelling Christ, so the Church is an organism (in addition to being an organization) because Christ indwells His Church. This might be titled a mystical indwelling, not in the sense of a sixth-sense mysticism, but rather a biblical mysticism that is based on objective revelation—the Word of God.

In the mystical sense, each church is a Body of Christ because Christ dwells in His Church. No church is spoken of as a finger or eye, nor do we speak of a church as part of the body of Christ (members of the body are always individuals, not churches). Nor is there any reference in Scripture that one body (a denomination) is made up of many churches. The Bible implies that the body is Christ, and that a body is a church.

In summarizing the Church as the body of Christ, Earl Radmacher brings the purpose of the body into clear perspective.

It is clear that the source of all—both unity and nourishment—is Christ Himself. The channels of the communication, however, are the different members of the body of Christ, in their relation one to another.[6]

2. The Temple of God. The expressions "temple of God" and "building of God" are word pictures that present the Church as a place for the dwelling of God. Our bodies are also referred to as buildings and houses (2 Cor. 5:1) in which God dwells (1 Cor. 3:16).

Today, God's building is the Church, which is also pictured as a growing edifice (Eph. 2:21). The illustration of the Church as a growing building is similar to the analogy of the growing body, which is "built up" with spiritual gifts

(1 Cor. 14:12; Eph. 4:12, 16). Some have seen spiritual gifts as mortar that joins the "living stones" (1 Pet. 2:5) together in the building. These bricks or living stones are carefully "joined together" by the Holy Spirit (Eph. 2:21).

The building exalts Christ as His indwelling presence is seen in the individual believer and through the corporate building (the Church). Paul warned the Corinthians that their individual bodies are the temples of God (1 Cor. 6:19,20). Homer Kent writes:

Each convert, whether he be Jew or Gentile, adds to the growth of the structure, and this structure is no less a holy temple for God dwells within it. If the Jewish temple at Jerusalem suggested Paul's figure, it is important to note that he chose the word that denoted the sanctuary proper, rather than one that described the outer courts and buildings. It was this inner sanctuary which was regarded as God's dwelling place.[7]

A building is constructed to house a tenant, and the analogy of the building is to present the truth that it is to house the Lord! Lewis Chafer writes, "Israel had a building in which God was pleased to dwell. The Church is a building in which God is pleased to dwell."[8]

A building contains three sections: first the foundation, second the cornerstone, and third the building blocks or stones. Every building begins with the foundation. The foundation must be Jesus Christ alone (1 Cor. 3:11). Paul had determined that he would preach "Jesus Christ and Him crucified" (1 Cor. 2:2), who is the foundation.

Another important biblical issue concerning the building is the role of human builders and how they built. In Ephesians 2:20, Paul indicates that the apostles and prophets were builders of the Church. This text refers to the apostles and prophets as laying the original foundation for the Church, but how did they do it?

The apostles and prophets did establish many local churches, but is this what is meant? Their church-planting activity was probably an application of Ephesians 2:20, but more was meant.

They were the human instruments that established the Church in general. Paul was the church planter at Corinth "as a wise master builder I have laid the foundation" (1 Cor. 3:10). Saucy explains that "the apostle has laid the foundation by teaching the doctrines of Christ and bringing men into a relationship with him who is the only foundation that is laid. The church is not built upon a man or creed but upon the person of the living Christ."[9] But there is a greater sense of being the foundation of the Church.

The apostles and prophets were the foundation in the sense that they established the faith in the basic tenets of Christian doctrine, not on their own, of course. They received revelatory truth, (1) directly from Christ, (2) by the Holy Spirit (John 14:26), (3) they were the human instruments of inspiration (2 Pet. 1:21) and (4) were the leaders of the Church, where doctrine and policy were received and recognized.

In addition to the apostles who laid the original foundation, many contemporary builders are needed. In 1 Corinthians 3:10-15, Paul indicates that many builders are involved: "But let each one take heed how he builds on it....Now if anyone builds on this foundation"; and the phrase "each [everyone's] one's work" is repeated four times. Everyone who is a "living stone" in the building can also be a builder of the building.

Paul urged the Corinthians to build a permanent church and to do it right. After the foundation is firmly settled, the rows of bricks or stones are then laid. The foundation determines the rest of the building. The Lord Jesus is also the cornerstone. R. C. H. Lenski affirms the importance of this stone, which is:

...set at the corner of a wall so that its outer angle becomes important. This importance is ideal; we may say symbolic: the angle of the cornerstone governs all the lines and all the other angles of the building. This one stone is thus laid with special, sometimes with elaborate ceremonies. It supports the building no more than does any other stone. Its entire significance is to be found in its one outer angle. Its size is immaterial and certainly need not be immense. It is

thus also placed at the most important corner, in or on the top tier of the foundation, so as to be seen by all.[10]

As the entire building is determined by the cornerstone, so the building is set by Christ the stone. "This is the 'stone which was rejected by you builders, which has become the chief cornerstone'" (Acts 4:11).

The building material for the local church referred to by Paul in 1 Corinthians 3:12 includes gold, silver, precious stones or wood, hay and stubble. This material is none other than believers. If believers properly allow the cornerstone to set the course for their lifestyles, the results are quality. In 1 Corinthians 3:9, Paul refers to a building of God. James Boyer explains:

Certainly the context makes the primary application to people. They (the materials) represent persons being built into the church. This is not to be understood, however, as a mere adding of another brick to the wall by getting another convert to Christ. Remember, these people are "living stones." They themselves grow, so that the temple grows and is edified as its people grow. Thus, the minister's work is twofold: He builds (1) by getting new people into the building, and (2) by getting those in the building to increase in stature and maturity.[11]

The people are the work (1 Cor. 9:1), and the building of God has no value unless it centers on people. Because believers are the building, it is not biblical to use people to build a church, but rather to use the church to build believers. When the main concern of the building is quality people, it will bring glory to God. Gene Getz summarizes:

"Be careful how you build!" warned Paul. A church can be weak or immature—constructed of wood, hay, and stubble. Or it can be strong and mature—composed of gold, silver and precious stones (1 Cor. 3:10-15). If it is immature, it reflects impatience, jealousy, strife, divisions, pride, arrogance, and unbecoming behavior. If it is mature, it reflects a growing love, a unity of faith, and a steadfast hope.[12]

3. The Bride of Christ. The Church is also described as the bride of Christ. "Come, I will show you the bride, the Lamb's wife" (Rev. 21:9). "For I am jealous for you with godly jealousy. For I have betrothed you to one husband, that I may present you as a chaste virgin to Christ" (2 Cor. 11:2). The picture of a bride is also used to describe the Church in Ephesians 5:23-32. Radmacher describes those who make up the bride of Christ as "the church, the bride of Christ, includes all those who have put their faith in Christ in this age of grace which had its beginning at Pentecost and will continue until the Bridegroom comes to receive His bride unto himself to consummate the marriage."[13]

It is said, "We are unable to love someone else until we first realize that someone loves us." Paul illustrates the love of Christ for His Church by using an illustration of a husband's love for a wife. Christ loves His Church first and far more than anything known in human relationships.

The major teaching of the picture of the bride and groom is its demonstration of Christ's limitless love. When Christians fail to live by His standards, it is concluded that they do not love Him. The root problem is that they fail to realize how much He loves them. Scripture is clear: Christ loves Christians in spite of themselves, and not because of what they do, or how they show their love to Him. Because Christ is God, He is love (John 3:16).

For Christians to believe and accept His love requires faith. Accordingly, Christ loves them and in the process cleanses and perfects them. As Paul prayed for the Ephesian church, so Christians should pray for others that they "may be able to comprehend with all the saints what is the width and length and depth and height—to know the love of Christ which passes knowledge" (Eph. 3:18,19).

The apostle John reinforces this principle: "We love Him because He first loved us" (1 John 4:19). People usually respond to those who refuse to stop loving them. The issue, however, is the kind of love people will show to Him.

Christ the Lord desires subjection to Him in every area. Because the Church is totally dependent upon Him for life and purpose, every believer should be totally dependent upon Him for the same reasons. Saucy reinforces this: "The life of the church in each member is to be arranged under the headship of Christ. Their authority and leadership are found in Him. His thoughts and attitudes must be theirs."[14]

Just as human marriage involves intimacy, so the heavenly picture reflects an intimate relationship between Christ and His Church. Paul notes, "We are members of His body, of His flesh and of His bones" (Eph. 5:30).

4. The Flock of God. The flock of God is one of the most practical illustrations of Christ and the Church. Paul told the Ephesian church elders, "Therefore take heed to yourselves and to all the flock, among which the Holy Spirit has made you overseers, to shepherd the church of God which He purchased with His own blood" (Acts 20:28). Peter also used this picture when he instructed the elders, "Shepherd the flock of God which is among you, serving as overseers, not by constraint but willingly, not for dishonest gain but eagerly; nor as being lords over those entrusted to you, but being examples to the flock" (1 Pet. 5:2, 3).

Jesus used the flock and the shepherd to illustrate the relationship between Himself and His followers. He observed, "And other sheep I have which are not of this fold; them also I must bring, and they will hear My voice; and there will be one flock and one shepherd" (John 10:16). Saucy notes:

It is important to note the distinction between "fold" and "flock" which is blurred in the Authorized Version. "Fold" denotes an outward organization and refers to Israel, some of whom were Christ's sheep but some who were not because they did not believe. "Flock" speaks of the inner unity of the sheep, "created in and by Jesus."[15]

Christ is "the Chief Shepherd" who will reward His faithful undershepherds when He appears (1 Pet. 5:4). The human undershepherds of the flock are the pastors. Christ told Peter, "Tend My sheep" (John 21:16). The church or sheep belong to Christ. Pastors work for Him and in the place of Him, and will someday answer to Him concerning the sheep given to their care (Heb. 13:17).

The illustration of people as sheep may not be flattering, but it is true. The Word of God consistently refers to the Church as a flock of sheep who need food, protection and direction. Radmacher notes, "Long lists of specific items could doubtless be listed at this point, but it seems that they could all be summarized under provision, particularly the provision of spiritual food."[16]

Before feeding or providing for the flock, the undershepherd must find lost sheep. This is the role of evangelism or church growth. According to Donald A. McGavran:

> God wants countable lost persons found. The shepherd with ninety-nine lost sheep who finds one and stays at home feeding or caring for it should not expect commendation. God will not be pleased by the excuse that His servant is doing something "more spiritual" than searching for strayed sheep. Nothing is more spiritual than the actual reconciliation of the lost to God.[17]

The Great Commission is fulfilled by finding sheep (making disciples), folding sheep (baptizing) and feeding sheep (teaching). *Finding* results in bringing the lost one into the flock. No one can deny that when lost sheep are added to the flock, church growth occurs (Luke 15:1-7). *Folding* is following the biblical example of the Church in Acts by adding to the Body. "Those who gladly received his word were baptized; and that day about three thousand souls were added to them" (Acts 2:41). *Feeding* results in qualitative teaching of the sheep. Paul reminded the Ephesian elders, "For I have not shunned to declare to you the whole counsel of God" (Acts 20:27). Paul urged them to protect the flock as he had done to them. "Therefore watch, and remember that for three years I did not cease to warn everyone night and day with tears" (Acts 20:31).

Finally, Paul commended his sheep "to God and to the word of His grace, which is able to build you up and give you an inheritance among all those who are sanctified" (Acts 20:32). The undershepherd must know where to find the food, regularly supply it for his flock, or lead them to where it is located, causing his sheep to grow.

The shepherd's role of protection and discipline is also important. The rod and the staff were used by the shepherd to protect his flock (Ps. 23:4). Saucy writes:

> The staff was a long, crooked stick used for pulling back straying sheep, while the rod was a stout piece of wood about three feet long with a lump on the end; it was used as a weapon against wild beasts and robbers. It was also the practice of some shepherds to lay down across the opening of the fold during the night so that their bodies became literally the protecting door.[18]

The shepherd is no longer armed with the staff or the rod but with the faithful Word, which "is profitable for doctrine, for reproof, for correction, for instruction in righteousness" (2 Tim. 3:16). The Church must have undershepherds who tend the sheep. Peter writes, "For you were like sheep going astray, but have now returned to the Shepherd and Overseer of your souls" (1 Pet. 2:25). Isaiah also says, "All we like sheep have gone astray; we have turned, every one, to his own way" (Isa. 53:6).

For the sheep to know the shepherd's provision and protection, yet not follow, is to disobey Scripture. The illustration of the sheep and the shepherd tells us that every Christian should be involved in a church and follow the undershepherd. Saucy notes:

> Essentially, the sheep can provide nothing for itself and can only prosper as it follows the direction of the shepherd. Its only obligation is to submit to his leading and authority. Thus the church is directed as the flock of God to submit to His authority and that of the chief Shepherd. Because this direction is communicated through the Word and the ministry of the undershep-

herds which God has placed in the church, members are exhorted to "obey them that have the rule over [literally, lead] you, and submit yourselves" (Heb. 13:17, *KJV*). As even the leaders of the church are sheep, they also are obligated to submit ultimately to the chief Shepherd.[19]

5. The Garden of God. The garden of God is a collective phrase of several organic illustrations found in the New Testament, including vine (John 15:1-8), planting (1 Cor. 3:6-8) and husbandry (1 Cor. 3:9, *KJV*). A. R. Tippett notes, "The teaching of Jesus was charged with expectation of growth."[20] He classifies the teachings into various types of imagery and refers to fields "white already to harvest" (John 4:35, *KJV*) and the mustard seed parable (Matt. 13:31, 32), as well as other examples.[21]

A garden is a cultivated plot of ground where weeds and rocks are removed, seed is sown and crops are harvested. In 1 Corinthians 3:6-9, the Church is described as a cultivated field. In John 15, the Christians are pictured as branches, and Christ is portrayed as the life-giving vine.

The church at Corinth had a schism in its leadership. To answer this problem, Paul taught that ministers are servants, co-laborers and fellow workers with God. According to Paul, each laborer had a special ministry, but God was the one giving life (1 Cor. 3:6). When two or more "farmers" or pastors are working a garden, one planting and the other watering, they should be viewed as a team, although each will be rewarded individually. "Now he who plants and he who waters are one, and each one will receive his own reward according to his own labor" (1 Cor. 3:8). All farmers are working together for one purpose—the harvest.

The Scriptures teach the Christian's dependence upon Christ, who is the only source of life and growth, and this is pictured by the vine and the branches portrayed in John 15. Two central issues need to be considered. One is the cause of growth, and the other is the product or fruit of growth.

Jesus commanded Christians to abide in Him because it is impossible for them to produce fruit apart from Him. "Abide in Me, and I in you. As the branch cannot bear fruit of itself, unless it abides in the vine, neither can you, unless you abide in Me" (John 15:4). C. I. Scofield explains "abiding," noting:

To abide in Christ is, on the one hand, to have no known sin unjudged and unconfessed, no interest into which He is not brought, no life which He cannot share. On the other hand, the abiding one takes all burdens to Him, and draws all wisdom, life and strength from Him. It is not unceasing consciousness of these things, and of Him, but that nothing is allowed in the life which separates from Him.[22]

To abide in Christ is to act on His indwelling presence, experiencing a vital faith walk with Jesus day by day, and to faithfully obey the Word of God. When the Christian is not abiding in Christ, the resulting productivity of the vine's potential is reduced from what it could be.

The best way to know whether a person is abiding in Christ is to obey His words (John 15:7). Christ further explains that abiding in His love is keeping His commandments (John 15:10). In order to produce fruit, a healthy church must demonstrate love one to another, which is another result of abiding in Him (John 15:12).

Although both the vine (Christ) and branches (Christians) make up the Church and are intimately related, the fruit-producing power flows only one way, from the vine to the branches. Chafer summarizes the results as "pruning (v. 2), prayer effectual (v. 7), joy celestial (v. 11), and fruit perpetual (v. 16)."[23]

The purpose of the garden of God is to bear fruit. Christ reminded His disciples, "You did not choose Me, but I chose you and appointed you that you should go and bear fruit, and that your fruit should remain" (John 15:16). The central purpose of every Christian's life is to produce fruit because a fruitless branch denies the purpose of its existence.

What is the fruit? First, it is winning souls. Christians should be active in evangelism. But there is a second meaning; this fruit (singular) is best described by the fruit (plural) that the Holy

Spirit produces (Gal. 5:22,23). Basically, it is the life of Christ flowing through the branches, producing the nine qualities (fruit of the Spirit) cited by Paul. This union is life. It is "Christ in you, the hope of glory" (Col. 1:27). The Christian character bearing fruit in and through the branches causes others to be drawn to the Savior. Love, joy, peace, patience, kindness, goodness, faithfulness, gentleness and self-control (fruit of the Spirit) will attract others to Christ and then produce fruit by winning souls.

After referring to His Father as the vinedresser, Christ explained that the Father prunes the branches that they may bear more fruit (John 15:2). The word "prune" means "cleanse," signifying a purging process of anything that may reduce or prevent additional fruit. Every fruitbearing Christian can expand his or her field of effectiveness and become more fruitful. Saucy comments:

Again the pertinency of this particular metaphor is seen in the fact than no tree requires such extensive pruning as that of the vine, and yet it is the characteristic of the vine, that even though it is severely cut back, it does not die but grows again.[24]

Donald Grey Barnhouse cites an amazing example of this lasting potential fruitfulness:

In Hampton Court near London, there is a grapevine under glass; it is about 1,000 years old and has but one root which is at least two feet thick. Some of the branches are 200 feet long. Because of skillful cutting and pruning, the vine produces several tons of grapes each year. Even though some of the smaller branches are 200 feet from the main stem, they bear much fruit because they are joined to the vine and allow the life of the vine to flow through them.[25]

Pruning, cleansing or disciplining in a believer's life is loving discipline from the Father (Prov. 3:11, 12) and ultimately leads to additional fruit bearing. "For they indeed for a few days chastened us as seemed best to them, but He for our profit, that we may be partakers of His holiness.

Now no chastening seems to be joyful for the present, but grievous; nevertheless, afterward it yields the peaceable fruit of righteousness to those who have been trained by it" (Heb. 12:10,11).

The Father (the vinedresser) does the pruning. Hollis Green urges churchmen to think of the Church as a living organism similar to a tree or a vine. Although pruning primarily refers to the life of Christians, Green applies the principle of pruning to policies, programs and organizational structures of the Church that may be diseased or not as productive as they should be. Green explains:

Fruit bearing always takes place on new growth. It is this aspect of administration that should be the primary concern of churchmen. The fruit bearing apparatus must be kept in operation. New growth in the fruit bearing area also produces foliage. Foliage has a direct relationship to the food supply and the healing of wounds caused by pruning. In horticulture it is suggested that the pruning should take place as close to the main branch as possible so the growth tissues surrounding the wound may form new tissues to heal the wound. Since food moves down through the stems and comes from leaves above the wound, the wound must be in position near this food supply if healing is to occur. The implication here is one of distance. Pruning must be done close to the foliage and food-moving mechanism if the plant is to survive.

Arbitrary and indiscriminate pruning at a distance from the main branch leaves a stump because the healing of the wound cannot occur. When church leaders prune or tamper with the fruit bearing mechanism of the church, it must be done with due caution and careful planning. The ultimate objective of repairing the wound and nurturing the whole body into a productive unity must be considered.

Where churchmen do not have the courage to prune, disease gnaws at the fruit bearing areas, and the process of strangulation cuts off the flow of life to the superstructure. Without the courage to prune, it is only a matter of time until fruit bearing stops and the slow but sure process of death destroys the foliage, the superstructure and even the roots. The tree may stand but it is dead. There is no shade for the weary traveler and no fruit for the hungry. The structure is there, the organization is there, but the life is gone. This is the sad plight of many churches.[26]

6. The Family of God. This picture of the Church incorporates several phrases or terms that depict it as saints, sanctified ones, elect, members of Christ, believers, disciples, Christians, and the term that closely reflects the family, brethren and children. To the Ephesian Christians, Paul emphasized that both Jews and Gentiles became a part of God's family "household," (Eph. 2:19). In fact, Christians experience an entirely new family relationship different from anything previously experienced.

For He Himself is our peace, who has made both one, and has broken down the middle wall of division between us, having abolished in His flesh the enmity, that is, the law of commandments contained in ordinances, so as to create in Himself one new man from the two, thus making peace, and that He might reconcile them both to God in one body through the cross, thereby putting to death the enmity (Eph. 2:14-16).

John describes believers as children: "But as many as received Him, to them He gave the right to become children of God, even to those who believe in His name" (John 1:12). Because of this family relationship, Paul said, "God has sent forth the Spirit of His Son into your hearts, crying out, 'Abba, Father!'" (Gal. 4:6). W. E. Vine states that according to the Gemara (a rabbinical commentary):

Slaves were forbidden to address the head of the family by this title. "Abba" is the word framed by the lips of infants, and betokens unreasoning trust; "father" expresses an intelligent apprehension of the relationship.

The two together express the love and intelligent confidence of the child.[27]

As a result of believing in Jesus Christ, Jews and Gentiles entered the family of God. People who had no relationship to each other were now members of a household, the Church. They were brothers and sisters, loving, helping, encouraging, teaching and sharing with one another. Just as the human family demands order and direction, unity and oneness, so the Church has the same demands. Every believer, once he or she becomes a part of the household of God, has full family privileges.

Paul indicated that a man must manage his family as a qualification for New Testament church leadership (1 Tim. 3:4,5,12). Paul's main intent is not programs or concern for the building itself, but giving leadership to the family so each person would grow and fulfill God's plan for his or her life.

7. The Priesthood. In the Old Testament, a man was set aside to the office of priesthood. In the New Testament, all believers are priests, and they need no one to mediate to God for them. All believers have access to Christ who mediates for them (1 Tim. 2:5). Peter notes that Christians are "a royal priesthood" (1 Pet. 2:9).

In the Old Testament, only the high priest could stand in the holy of holies. The word for priest was *cohen,* which means to stand. The thick veil that separated people from God was broken down by Christ so the believers could enter the "Holiest" through Christ (Heb. 10:19-21).

The priests performed three functions: (1) sacrifice, (2) witness and (3) intercession. The New Testament believer carries out these three functions.

First, believers do not sacrifice animals on an altar because Christ has ended the ritualistic sacrifice, but believers sacrifice themselves as a "living sacrifice" (Rom. 12:1) by their holy lives and service. Paul implied this when he said he was "poured out as a drink offering" (Phil. 2:17). The Christian is then obliged to "continually offer the sacrifice of praise to God, that is, the fruit of our lips, giving thanks to His name" (Heb. 13:15).

Second, the Old Testament priest was called the "messenger of the Lord" because the people were told to hear the law of God from him (Mal. 2:7; Deut. 33:10). When Christians share the gospel, they are carrying out this role of the priest.

The third function of the priest was intercession. Granted, Christ is the intercessor for the Church, but believers are also to intercede, based on (1) the example of Christians interceding in the New Testament, (2) the exhortation to Christians to pray and (3) the nature of the Church as a channel between God and the lost.

Remember, the emphasis is not on individual priests, but each Christian is a member of a priesthood having position and authority. This privilege comes because Christians are in Jesus Christ, members of His Body, and "bone of His bone."

The implications of understanding the pictures and metaphors of the Church are important. In each case, the Church is illustrated as a living organism. Even in the example of the building, the church is composed of "living stones."

These biblical pictures remind us that the Church is not a building occasionally inhabited by people. Rather, the Church is a gathering of believers who have the living Christ indwelling them individually and corporately.

These pictures do not view the Church as a place of business and action. These illustrations reveal that the Church has life in relationship to its Lord (organism) and the outgrowth of that life is seen in its practices (organization).

References: [1]Robert L. Saucy, *The Church in God's Program* (Chicago: Moody Press, 1972). [2]Ibid, p. 26. [3]Ibid, p. 32. [4]Gary Inrig, *Life in His Body* (Wheaton, Ill.: Harold Shaw, 1975), pp. 36, 37. [5]Saucy, *The Church in God's Program*. [6]Earl D. Radmacher, *The Nature of the Church* (Portland, Oreg.: Western Baptist Press, 1972), p. 240. [7]Homer A. Kent Jr., *Ephesians: The Glory of the Church* (Chicago: Moody Press, 1971), p. 48. [8]Lewis Sperry Chafer, *Systematic Theology*, Vol. 4 (Dallas: Dallas Seminary Press, 1948), p. 64. [9]Saucy, *The Church in God's Program*, pp. 33, 34. [10]R. C. H. Lenski, *The Interpretation of St. Paul's First and Second Epistles to the Corinthians* (Columbus, Ohio: The Wartburg Press, 1946), p. 455. [11]James L. Boyer, *For a World Like Ours* (Winona Lake, Ind.: BMH Books, 1971), p. 61. [12]Gene A. Getz, *Sharpening the Focus of the Church* (Chicago: Moody Press, 1974), p. 61. [13]Radmacher, *The Nature of the Church*, p. 246. [14]Saucy, *The Church in*

God's Program, p. 46. [15]Ibid. [16]Radmacher, *The Nature of the Church*, p. 246. [17]Donald A. McGavran, *Understanding Church Growth* (Grand Rapids: William B. Eerdmans, 1970), p. 41. [18]Saucy, *The Church in God's Program*, p. 52. [19]Ibid, p. 53. [20]A. R. Tippett, *Church Growth and the Word of God* (Grand Rapids: William B. Eerdmans, 1970), p. 13. [21]Ibid. [22]C. I. Scofield, *The Scofield Reference Bible* (New York: Oxford University Press), pp. 1136, 1137. [23]Chafer, *Systematic Theology*, pp. 60, 61. [24]Saucy, *The Church in God's Program*, p. 52. [25]Donald Grey Barnhouse, "Chain of Glory," *Eternity* 2, no. 17 (March 1958). [26]Hollis L. Green, *Why Churches Die* (Minneapolis: Bethany Fellowship, 1972), pp. 201, 202. [27]W. E. Vine, *An Expository Dictionary of New Testament Words* (London, England: Oliphants, Ltd., 1940), p. 9.

CHURCH GROWTH CONSCIENCE

The conviction that both internal and external church growth is fundamental to God's will for His Church.

CHURCH GROWTH: DEFINITION

The science that investigates the nature, function and health of Christian churches as they relate specifically to the effective implementation of God's Commission to "make disciples of all nations [peoples]" (Matt. 28:19). Church growth is simultaneously a theological conviction and an applied science, striving to combine the eternal principles of God's Word with the best insights of contemporary social and behavioral sciences, employing as its initial frame of reference the foundational work done by Donald McGavran and his colleagues.

CHURCH GROWTH EYES

An orientation that recognizes growth potential and applies appropriate strategies to effect maximum numerical church growth.

CHURCH GROWTH JUSTIFICATION: SHOULD A CHURCH BE SMALL OR LARGE?

During the last 25 years, the world has seen a significant increase in the number of large churches. When the author wrote *The Ten Largest Sunday Schools*, only eight churches in the United States had an average attendance of more than 2,000. Today, 14 churches in the city of Seoul, South Korea, average ten thousand or more attending each week. Weekly attendance at one of these churches has reached 675,000, when its satellite campuses are counted.

The large church is not unique to our age. It is reported that 6,000 people lined up outside the Metropolitan Tabernacle in London, England, to hear Charles Haddon Spurgeon preach a century ago. There is evidence that many of the principal early churches in the first few centuries were significantly larger than formerly believed by church historians. But the explosive growth of many churches in the last 25 years has raised a question concerning how large a church should be.

Why a Church Could Be Small

Some people perceive the large church as not being a church at all. Their argument for small churches tends to emphasize several preconceptions concerning the nature and function of the church. *First,* they claim the churches of the New Testament were small enough to meet in homes of Christians. *Second,* they claim a church should be a small group based on Bible study and fellowship. They view the church as a place where Christians are reinforced through intimate relationships and prepared to go into the world to witness. *Third,* they value the small church as a place where people get to know their pastor and are fed spiritually. *Fourth,* they believe a city can be better reached with the gospel by establishing many churches in various sections of a city rather than by building a large church that has a citywide ministry. *Fifth,* they argue that the cost involved in building and maintaining a large church campus is not as cost effective as would be the case in a small church.

Those who argue that a church should be small tend to have a view of the church that naturally limits growth. As a church grows, it changes character. It moves from being a single-cell church to being a multi-cell church and eventually a multi-congregational church. Students of church growth have noted that the life of a

church has several natural growth plateaus. These plateaus occur about the time the morning worship reaches 200, 500, 2,000 and 5,000 people attending each week. The first three figures are the approximate upper limits of growth in the class Sunday School, the departmental Sunday School and the closely graded Sunday School. To continue growing beyond these natural limits, the church experiences a significant change in its character. Another significant change in the character of a church apparently occurs as the church breaks through the 5,000 weekly attendance growth plateau.

Recognizing the change in the character of churches in each of these phases of church growth helps explain some of the tension of the large church versus the small church. A study done by students at Trinity Evangelical Divinity School, Deerfield, Illinois, revealed that the average church member was on a speaking basis (called people by their first names) with 60 people, whether the church had 60, 600 or 1,000 members. Therefore, it is questionable to accuse the large church of being impersonal. The average person will speak to approximately 60 people no matter what the size of the church.

Why a Church Could Be Large

Just as reasons are offered for a small church, so advocates of the large church also have reasons for their commitment. They recognize that most churches begin as small churches, but healthy growth results in small churches becoming large churches. Here are several reasons why these advocates believe a church should be large.

1. The large church is biblical. The first church, the church at Jerusalem, was a large church. Jesus told His disciples "not to depart from Jerusalem, but to wait for the Promise of the Father" (Acts 1:4), which was the outpouring of the Holy Spirit. He promised they would "receive power when the Holy Spirit has come upon you; and you shall be witnesses to Me in Jerusalem, and in all Judea and Samaria, and to the end of the earth" (v. 8). The spiritual power for growth came from God and expansion was inevitable.

That embryonic church met for prayer in the Upper Room and numbered "about a hundred and twenty" (v. 15). When Peter preached on the Day of Pentecost, "that day about three thousand souls were added to them" (2:41). The church continued to grow as "the Lord added to the church daily those who were being saved" (v. 47). Later, "the number of the men came to be about five thousand" (4:4). Then, "believers were increasingly added to the Lord, multitudes of both men and women" (5:14).

The church at Jerusalem was accused by the apostles' enemies of having "filled Jerusalem with your doctrine" (v. 28). Despite opposition to their ministry, "daily in the temple, and in every house, they did not cease teaching and preaching Jesus as the Christ" (v. 42). As a result, the church continued to experience growth. The Bible describes this continued growth by using the expressions "the number of the disciples was multiplying" (6:1), and "the number of the disciples multiplied greatly in Jerusalem" (v. 7). This church apparently reached at least 50 percent of its city for Christ.

2. A church can be large because of the biblical mandate of evangelism. Most large churches are based on evangelism. This is one of the reasons they are large. The task is to reach and win as many people as possible. The marching orders for a New Testament Church are found in Matthew 28:19, "Go therefore and make disciples of all the nations." This task is not done until every person is reached with the gospel. Growing churches are usually evangelizing churches.

Although some small churches are effective in reaching their neighborhoods, many are not getting the job of evangelism done. In many communities, the large churches help the small churches do a better job of evangelizing by encouraging them and motivating them to grow. This serves as a pattern of excellence to small churches.

3. Large churches can reach large metropolitan areas. No longer do we see just the small-neighborhood, geographic-parish church. We see both the megachurch and the small church. Eighty-five percent of American life is located in sprawling metropolitan areas. These areas seem to be expanding faster than churches can be built to minister to each new suburb. Anonymity seems to plague the large city, where people are lost in

apartment buildings and suburbia alike. The large church can reach the large city, where the small church cannot.

First, many large churches have the commitment to evangelize the city in every way possible. *Second,* the large church has the people power to visit every home or attempt to reach every area. *Third,* the large church has the finances to purchase media time and space to influence a city. *Fourth,* the large church has the status to feature special meetings that attract large crowds. *Finally,* the large church can look at the metropolitan area in a sensitive way that targets people groups with evangelistic activities that are specifically suited to their heart language and felt needs.

The increasing urbanization of the world is presenting new challenges to the Church of Jesus Christ. More than half the world now lives in urban centers of 100,000 people or more. Land values in these centers are usually much higher than the traditional church lots in smaller centers. The cost of buying land, erecting a building, and maintaining a basic ministry is prohibitive in many cities for a church that has fewer than 300 active members. Denominations that do not understand this reality and adapt to a more urban ministry philosophy are failing to establish churches in world-class cities today.

The principle of a strong witness reaching an area is biblical. Paul went to Ephesus and from that metropolitan area reached Asia Minor. "And this continued for two years, so that all who dwelt in Asia heard the word of the Lord Jesus, both Jews and Greeks" (Acts 19:10). Paul apparently did not visit every rural hamlet, and yet they heard the gospel. Many rural churches are closing their doors, yet God is not leaving Himself without a witness. A family may drive as far to church as they drive to work or for groceries. Mobility is a way of life in America. The large church in the metropolitan area can minister to families 30 and 50 miles away.

4. The large church attracts the respect of many of the unsaved. Big shopping centers, big corporations and big business have provided jobs and prosperity for the nation. The consolidation of many small public school districts has provided America with a more efficient educational system. Just as the businesses, schools and athletic events that are big draw the greatest attention from the public, so the large church attracts the respect of the unsaved.

5. The large church can give a well-rounded ministry to the total needs of Christians. The pastor of a small church lacks the staff to help him promote, organize, visit, counsel, preach, finance, teach, administer and look after the flock. The pastor is a jack-of-all-trades, but master of none. A large church is able to attract a variety of ministry specialists who can better meet the particular needs of people. Together, the pastoral team of a large church provides better pastoral service to its congregation than could the single pastor of a small church.

The concept of multiple services is a practical application of spiritual gifts. "Each one has his own gift from God" (1 Cor. 7:7). God has given different abilities to each person. One pastor is gifted to preach (12:28), another to counsel (Rom. 12:8) and another to administer (1 Cor. 12:28). These gifted pastors are then led to a church where they exercise their gifts for the glory of God. The large church allows many gifted people to use their talents and, in the final analysis, each member can receive more and thus grow more.

6. A big church can be the conscience of the city. The large church has a citywide influence because of its size. When a small community church speaks out on an issue, the city usually ignores the church. But the large church can act as the conscience of the city council.

7. The large church replaces the need for denominations. The large church can have the enlarged ministry that is often relegated to denominations. When all ministry is kept under the control of a local church, it stays in the hands of the people who pay the bills. Some pastors of large churches believe a centralized denomination is unbiblical, but the extended ministry carried on by a large local church is biblical.

The denominational church has historically provided many services to the small church, such as financing, homes for orphans and senior citizens, literature, counsel, centralized programming and advertising. The large church, however, can provide all of the services for itself and does not run the risk of encouraging "institution-alization" or "centralization" of authority.

The large church can be a teaching and training center for other churches and pastors. A few have suggested that ministerial training bypass the academic seminary and be done in large churches by apprenticeship.

8. The large church is more efficient. When many people carry the financial burden of ministry, the result in the long run is efficiency. Just as a large business can cut the price of products because of its high volume of sales, so the per capita cost of a large church can be reduced while still maintaining a higher standard of excellence in ministry. This enables the large church to give more money to missions than a smaller church can.

9. A large church is more effective in church planting and missions. The large church has the people and other resources necessary to begin new congregations and to help ensure a healthy birth. Some contemporary models of urban church planting advise beginning a new church with a congregation large enough to support a pastoral team (i.e., a church of at least a hundred people and at least two pastors). A small church of 150 people cannot afford to commission two-thirds of its congregation to begin a new church without seriously hindering its own ministry. But a church of two thousand could start several churches and quickly replace these seed members with new growth. In his study of the world's 20 largest churches, Dr. John Vaughan noted that 7 of these large churches had planted in excess of 1,400 new churches.[1]

Large churches are also able to utilize creative approaches to missions, thus involving more people in active missionary service. Again, the pastor of a small church usually cannot mobilize a team from the church to travel to another culture for an extended time period to be involved in missionary activity. But large churches often have a minister of missions who may lead several groups from the large church on ministry tours in other cultures regularly throughout the year.

Reference: [1]John H. Vaughan, "Trends Among the World's Twenty Largest Churches," in *Church Growth: State of the Art*, ed. C. Peter Wagner with Win Arn and Elmer L. Towns (Wheaton, Ill.: Tyndale House Publishers, 1989), p. 133.

CHURCH GROWTH MOVEMENT, BEGINNING OF

The church growth movement began in the heart and vision of its modern-day founder, Dr. Donald McGavran. In the 1950s as a missionary in India, McGavran saw an inept attempt of the Christian church to evangelize the lost. Slowly, McGavran formed several hypotheses that with time proved to be the stones of what was to become the modern church growth movement. In an address to the banquet of the North American Society of Church Growth, McGavran stated that he saw the name "evangelism" confused with catechism classes, baptism, and/or church membership. McGavran believed these good attempts all were necessary and had their places, but they were not evangelism. To McGavran, evangelism was an *input term*, meaning first the lost should be evangelized (i.e., "gospelized"), and when that was done, they would be baptized and brought into the Church. As a result, church growth occurred. McGavran rationalized: Why not use the term "church growth" as an *output term* to give new meaning to the movement of evangelism. Hence, he used the term "church growth" synonymously with evangelism, but to him the name "church growth" meant more than just getting people saved.

In time, church growth has evolved into three definitions. First, many people see church growth as growth in numbers (i.e., the growth of the church). By this, church growth is an increase in attendance, offerings, baptisms and membership. Hence, the very nature of the church growth movement was concerned with those observable, countable, repeatable phenomena that could be measured.

The second meaning to the term is that church growth is church planting. McGavran saw the difficulty in carrying out the Great Commission, *matheteusate pauta ta ethne*, reaching across class and cultural barriers to evangelize new groups of people. He reasoned that when new churches were planted, churches in new ethnic areas overcome the barriers to evangelism that he experienced as a Westerner trying to evangelize in other countries. In new churches, those in the ethnic church would evangelize their own people.

Hence, the Church of Jesus Christ would grow by planting new churches.

The third aspect of church growth is seen in its scientific base of research (i.e., church growth is a discipline that takes its place under systematic theology). In this third definition, McGavran would point us to a "Bible-based ministry that was data driven in strategy." By this, McGavran wanted us to discover those principles that were most successful and effective in evangelizing new people groups. This third aspect of church growth applied the scientific method of research that was used by all disciplines to determine principles and methods of evangelism.

As such, researchers (1) began with a problem that focused their inquiry; (2) gathered all of the data possible, beginning with the Word of God, but also examining society and culture; (3) established a hypothesis, which is a suggested principle that solved the problem of how to do evangelism and church growth; (4) tested the proposed principle (law) to see if it is biblical, valid and effective; (5) established new laws of evangelism and church growth.

In a magazine article in *Christianity Today*, the founders of the church growth movement were criticized for their desire to give "cute" names to the new principles they found, such as "The Law of Three Hearings" or "The Homogeneous Principle."

Dr. McGavran isolates five key events that have contributed immeasurably to the expansion of the movement. The five episodes include: (1) in 1961 establishing the Institute of Church Growth on the campus of Northwest Christian College (Eugene, Oregon) to develop students knowledgeable in growth concepts; (2) publication of Church Growth Bulletin in 1964; (3) relocating the Institute of Church Growth from the campus in Eugene (1961) to Fuller Seminary at Pasadena (1965); (4) establishing the William Carey Library (1969) for mass publication and circulation of church growth books; and (5) creation of the Institute for American Church Growth in 1973 by Dr. McGavran and Dr. Win Arn.

On June 16-20, 1969, McGavran conducted a historic gathering of church growth leadership in the first Annual Church Growth Colloquium at the Emmanuel School of Religion, Milligan College, Tennessee. This four-day conference included such topics as "The Scientifically Measurable Factors of Church Growth," "Why Churches Stop Growing" and "How to Activate Churches."

Also in that year (1969), I wrote *The Ten Largest Sunday Schools and What Made Them Grow* (Baker Book House), a volume that C. Peter Wagner has called the first American church growth volume because I applied the scientific principle of social research to determine church growth principles. As I approached this project, I was doing graduate work at Garrett Theological Seminary (Evanston, Illinois), and was examining the influence of sociology on the Church. The work of Ernst Troeltsch, The Social Teaching of the Church, motivated me to develop "The Sociological Cycles of Church Growth and Death," examining the Church as a social institution, not just a theological Body. I realized that the 10 largest churches could be examined for workable principles, and if applied to other churches, they too could grow. Therefore, I visited 10 churches, interviewed the pastor and staff and tried to determine the dynamics that made them grow. I developed a lengthy questionnaire and compared the findings, trying to find causes for growth.

The most important chapter in the book was not the description of each of the 10 churches, but chapter 13, which explained the sociological method of research based on *Methods of Research* by Carter V. Good and Douglas E. Scates.

One of the principles I found in these 10 churches was the use of Sunday School busing as an evangelistic tool. Certain churches followed a movement into evangelistic bus outreach and they grew proportionately. The principle of pastoral leadership was also noted as the principle of building a superaggressive church. This was the first book to identify and examine the megachurches.

The year 1972 was pivotal for Fuller Theological Seminary: Dr. Donald McGavran and Dr. C. Peter Wagner instituted the Fuller Evangelistic Association Department of Church Growth to apply church growth methodology to American churches.

The Institute for American Church Growth

was founded by Dr. Win Arn and Dr. McGavran in 1973 to provide information and research on North American church growth. Win Arn produced 27 films and had served as director of religious education for a denomination. He used color films, books, seminars, workshops, audiotapes and curriculum to spread the good news of church growth. The Institute for American Church Growth, according to James H. Montgomery, reached nearly 30,000 key lay leaders and pastors representing 4,000 local congregations to give momentum to the movement.

When the Church Growth Movement was growing during the 1970s, it was not without its critics. Most criticism pointed out the stress on numerical growth, proselytism, priority of the church over interdenominational agencies, priority of evangelism over ministry, emphasis on removing barriers that prohibited evangelism, pragmatism versus scriptural authority, and manipulation and/or unbiblical motivation. Also, some criticized the Homogeneous Unit principle as cultural exclusivism in the Church, viewing it as a racial membership policy rather than understanding it as an evangelistic outreach strategy.

In 1973, J. Robertson McQuilkin wrote *Measuring the Church Growth Movement: How Biblical Is It?* (Moody Press), and reduced the multitude of church growth principles to five areas: (1) numerical growth, (2) focus of receptivity, (3) people movements, (4) use of science as a tool and (5) right method guarantees large response.

In his book, McQuilkin categorized the five principles of church growth into three classifications: (1) biblical mandate, (2) biblical principles and (3) extrabiblical principles.

CLASSIFICATION
1. Biblical Mandate (Commanded in Scripture)
2. Biblical Principles (Implied in Scripture)
3. Extrabiblical Principles

PRINCIPLE
1. Importance of Numerical Growth
2. Focus on Receptive Groups
3. People Movements
4. Science, a Valid Tool
5. Right Method Guarantees Large Response

In the mid 1970s, C. Peter Wagner, in "Church Growth: More Than a Man, a Magazine, a School, a Book" *(Christianity Today)*, listed what he believes are six irreducible presuppositions on which church growth was founded. He noted that those who disagreed with the church growth movement invariably disagreed with one of these six principles. These principles are: (1) nongrowth displeases God; (2) numerical growth of a church is a priority with God and focuses on new disciples rather than decisions; (3) disciples are tangible, identifiable, countable people who increase the Church numerically; (4) limited time, money and resources demand that the Church develop a strategy based on results; (5) social and behavioral sciences are valuable tools in measuring and encouraging church growth; and (6) research is essential for maximum growth.

In *Christianity Today*, Wagner repeated the premise that nongrowth is a disease, it is abnormal in the Church and is displeasing to God. In his optimistic outlook, he felt nongrowth among churches was correctable.

The almost immediate acceptance of church growth by the majority of American churches came from the ministry and writings of C. Peter Wagner from his influential platform as professor at Fuller Theological Seminary. After communicating his findings to the students at Fuller, many became leaders of denominations, mission boards, or were nationals who returned to their homes around the world to influence their churches with church growth principles. As such, Fuller Theological Seminary became the dominant influence of the church growth movement. John Vaughn coined the phrase, "The Fuller Factor," which was a combination of Fuller Theological Seminary, the Institute for American Church Growth and the Charles E. Fuller Evangelistic Association.

CHURCH GROWTH MOVEMENT

A designation describing those pastors, denominational executives, missionaries, professors and other Christian leaders who allow their ministries to be influenced by the principles of church growth developed by Donald McGavran and others involved in church growth research.

CHURCH GROWTH PRINCIPLES

Expressions of truth that, when consistently applied, affect significant growth in local churches and/or groups of churches.

CHURCH GROWTH RATES

How to Evaluate a Church's Growth Rate

The following table has been developed by the School of World Mission at Fuller Theological Seminary, Pasadena, California, as a basis for evaluating a church's growth rate. These growth rates are based on decadal composite membership measurements in the United States and Canada:

25% per decade (2.3% AAGR*) —biological growth only: minimal

50% per decade (4.1% AAGR)—fair

100% per decade (7.2% AAGR)—good

200% per decade (11.6% AAGR)—excellent

300% per decade (14.9% AAGR)—outstanding

500% per decade (19.6% AAGR)—incredible

*AAGR = Average Annual Growth Rate

References: See AVERAGE ANNUAL GROWTH RATE; DECADAL GROWTH RATE.

CHURCH GROWTH: SOCIAL SCIENCE

In the past 20 years, the Church Growth Movement has received public recognition for several reasons. *First*, superchurches have emerged on the scene and become influential in determining and applying church growth strategy. *Second*, a growing interest is occurring in the science and practice of church planting. *Third*, growing churches are experiencing more exposure by the media in general than two decades ago. At the same time, the Church Growth Movement has become a discipline, and it has become more sophisticated as it uses both theological and sociological research to examine churches to determine principles of growth.

Church Growth is a behavioral science. As such, it follows the scientific method of inquiry, as do the other natural sciences (i.e., psychology, sociology and so on). The scientific method involves five steps. *First*, data must be gathered by the Church Growth researcher. This involves finding all of the facts about one source of church growth, or all the facts about the lack of church growth. *Second*, the data are examined for causes and effects. At this point, the researcher determines if when the facts are repeated, they will bring about the same results in growth. If they do result in growth, it leads to the *third* step, where the researcher suggests a hypothesis. This is a suggested principle or law that causes church growth. (The word "hypothesis" comes from *hypo*, meaning "to propose," and *thesis* meaning "an unproven law.") The *fourth* step is to test the suggested law to see if it is functional, workable and produces the same results in all situations. When the results are consistent, the *fifth* step leads to establishing the results as a law or principle that God will bless evangelism and church growth, or when the law is broken, will cause a church to plateau or deteriorate.

What Constitutes "Church Growth"?

The term "church growth" has several connotations. *First*, it is generally associated with churches that grow—both internally and externally—and as such, Church Growth has a generic meaning that began with the growth of the first church in Jerusalem. *Second*, the term "church growth" is associated with evangelism and/or missionary enterprises that imply outreach to the lost and their incorporation into a church, hence causing local church growth. Fifteen years ago, C. Peter Wagner defined Church Growth as "all that is involved in bringing men and women who do not

have a personal relationship with Jesus Christ into fellowship with Him and into responsible church membership."[1] This definition seems to define evangelism, but it is too broad for Church Growth because of the phrase "all that is involved," which could include the areas of Christian education, pastoral theology, missiology or other disciplines.

The *third* definition of Church Growth adds the aspect of research and limits the things included in its scope. In a later definition Wagner writes:

Church Growth is the science which investigates the planting, multiplication, function and health of Christian churches as they relate specifically to the effective implementation of God's commission to "make disciples of all peoples" (Matt. 28:19, 20). Church Growth strives to combine the eternal theological principles of God's Word concerning the expansion of the church with the best insights of contemporary social and behavioral sciences, employing as its initial frame of reference, the foundational work done by Donald McGavran.[2]

Wagner notes the following aspects of a definition of church growth: (1) It is scientific in nature, (2) its scope is Christian churches, (3) it is related to the implementation of the Great Commission, (4) it combines eternal theological principles with insights from contemporary social and behavioral sciences and (5) its initial frame of reference is Donald McGavran.

Some have agreed with Wagner's definition, but questioned the reference to one person as its source. One of Wagner's former students, John Vaughan, research professor in Church Growth at Southwest Baptist University in Bolivar, Missouri, states that Southern Baptists have been guided by the objectives of the Great Commission, have followed principles derived from research and have enjoyed success in church growth. However, although the Southern Baptists and other groups understood and employed with varying degrees of efficiency the principles of church growth, it was not until the general growth of scientific technology after World War II that Church Growth became recognized in some quarters as a discipline. Although Donald McGavran has probably had a greater influence than any other person in drawing attention to the modern Church Growth Movement, he said "Church Growth is much bigger than Pasadena."[3] Therefore, an explicit definition of Church Growth should not be attached to one person, but to the principles Wagner advocated, without neglecting the indispensable influence of McGavran on the movement. The following is suggested because it is more explicit in definition and recognizes the universality of the movement:

Church Growth is that science that investigates the planting, multiplication, growth, function, health and death of churches. It strives to apply the biblical and social principles in its gathering, analysis, displaying and defending of the facts involved in implementing the Great Commission.

The heart of the Church Growth Movement involves research into growth to establish principles that will guide others in the harvest. J. F. Engel and H. W. Norton indicate that the harvest is not going well in certain fields because cutting blades are missing from the evangelistic instruments. They write, "The cutting blades of any Christian organization are the research-based, Spirit-led strategy to reach people with the Good News and to build them in the faith."[4] Many church workers are diligent in evangelism, but their churches are not growing. They are not seeing souls saved, baptized and added to their churches. The reasons for nongrowth are not mystical nor are they subjective. Reasons for nongrowth are usually discernible. Some workers are not properly applying the correct principles that would bring in a greater harvest. Principles and strategy based on research is one of the indispensable facts of the modern Church Growth Movement. J. Robertson McQuilkin indicates five indispensable principles in the modern Church Growth movement, and the fourth on his list is "science as a valid tool of outreach." He concludes, "The Church Growth

Movement would change completely in character if any of the five basic presuppositions were omitted."[5] Wagner lists six elements as an irreducible minimum of Church Growth. Number six is that "research is essential for maximum growth."[6]

Incorporating the Full Mosaic of Church Growth

If a church desires to experience effective church growth, it must develop strategies that will overcome the barriers to church growth and enable it to experience growth. A church can experience several kinds of growth, and most "growing churches" are experiencing some of each kind.

The first is *internal growth*, which is qualitative growth—growth in the Word of God, the Lord, Christ, grace and/or spiritual maturity. This is also called "spiritual factors of church growth."

The second kind of growth is *external growth*, *numerical growth*. Numerical growth deals with growth in attendance, membership, offerings, baptisms, enrollment and so on. This growth relates to data that are observable, measurable and countable. Those who strive for numerical growth without also seeking spiritual growth are limiting the effectiveness of their ministries.

A third kind of growth is *biological growth*. As church members have babies, the children swell the attendance figures of the church.

A fourth kind of church growth is *conversion growth*. This is sometimes called "making sheep." Evangelism is winning people to Christ and His Church. If a church is effectively reaching its community with the gospel, this will also result in numerical increase in the church.

Transfer growth is the fifth kind of church growth experienced by many churches. Some object to this kind of growth, calling it sheep stealing, but others realize that mobility is increasingly becoming a part of Western society and prefer to call this kind of growth "finding lost sheep." It is estimated that approximately 20 percent of all Americans move every year. The adjustments involved in a major move make people more open to changes, including a change in attitude toward a church or denomination. If a church is serious about reaching people, it should have a strategy for reaching Christians who are moving into their community.

Expansion growth is yet another kind of growth experienced by many churches. This sixth kind of growth results in beginning another church like themselves. Rather than build new facilities, many churches have opted to begin a mission Sunday School or church in another part of town or a nearby community. They expand their ministry into the same kind of community.

The seventh kind of growth is *extension growth*. This means a church begins a new ministry in its facilities that is geared at reaching another culture or ethnic group moving into the community. In communities experiencing changes in ethnic character, churches are developing strategies that produce both kinds of growth.

Church Growth and the Theological Method

Although Church Growth is a social science because it influences the ministry of a church, it must also be considered under the broad area of theology—specifically as a part of ecclesiology, the doctrine of the Church. Lewis S. Chafer described systematic theology as "the collecting, scientifically arranging, comparing, exhibiting and defending of all facts from any and every source concerning God and His works."[7]

Mixing scientific research with theological research in Church Growth, however, raises several problems. *First*, it is possible for some researchers to examine by social research and reject a principle of Church Growth that may be explicitly taught in Scripture. This happens when a correct principle is wrongly applied in a local church. *Second*, it is possible to examine and identify by social research a principle of Church Growth that is causing church growth, and yet that principle may not be biblical (it may even be antibiblical) in its expression. *Third*, it is possible to accept or reject a biblical Church Growth principle because a person's sociological data are faulty or incomplete. *Fourth*, it is possible to accept or reject a Church Growth principle based on sociological observation alone (growth statistics), while the church that is growing in numbers does not meet the criteria of the New Testament in doctrine or practice.

The Church Growth Movement must recognize the following principles to remain on track:

1. The Word of God is the ultimate standard of faith and practice, and no principle of Church Growth that contradicts Scripture, even if it produces numerical growth, is a biblical Church Growth principle.

2. The Scriptures have not given a systematic presentation of Church Growth principles, but rather have given the Great Commission, described the principles and circumstances of growing churches, given solutions to church problems and dealt with various aspects of ministry that produce growth. From these data, Church Growth principles can be scientifically determined and then applied to various churches.

3. Where the Scriptures are silent, it is possible to gather data from natural revelation to determine or verify Church Growth principles. These principles, however, must be consistent with models, commands and principles that are explicitly found in Scripture.

4. There is a difference in basing Church Growth principles on those that are explicit in Scripture and basing them on those that are implied from Scripture. The Church Growth researcher should recognize the absolute nature of explicit principles, but when principles are only implied should seek more data, test it through correspondence to other Scripture, test it through internal consistency, and then wait for confirmation through scientific research.

5. Where Scripture is silent, scientific research can determine Church Growth principles. These, however, must be in harmony with those explicit principles previously established.

6. Theological and Church Growth research are not two mutually distinct methods of research that lead to separate sets of principles, Church Growth then being forced to harmonize its findings with theology. Rather, both theology and Church Growth grow out of the same orientation to research, and harmonizing should be integrated in the total process.

7. Church Growth research and principles are not addenda to theological methods and principles but are at the heart of theology and its methods.

Once the Church Growth researcher has identified principles, he or she must be careful to distinguish between them and techniques or programs. The focus of the research is to establish principles, not programs. Dan Baumann warns, "Mark it well—much is not transferable from one setting to another. Programs are not absolutes; biblical principles are. Take care to distinguish one from the other."[8]

When viewing Church Growth, remember the following:

1. Techniques and programs are not the same as biblical principles. Although a technique or program may accomplish a biblical result because it contains some biblical principles, techniques and programs are not absolute truths.

2. Techniques and programs may be used effectively by certain people at certain times in certain circumstances, but will not be equally effective overall.

3. Principles alone are biblical; they transcend programs and techniques.

4. Programs and techniques tend to change with time and culture.

5. Programs and techniques may be effective in one contemporary setting but not in the next.

6. Some programs seem to be effective when used in a specific time frame, but with changing circumstances they become ineffective. The program, although effective because it applies biblical principles, becomes less effective when circumstances change. Principles do not change, but the way principles are applied must change. Therefore, the church worker must be grounded in biblical principles and yet be flexible to determine what program and technique will best solve his or her problem and cause his or her church to grow. McGavran suggests, "Analytical tools are available for pastors and concerned laypeople to determine whether their own churches have desirable growth patterns."[9]

Biblical principles will lead to Church Growth strategy that is a total approach or tool for carrying out the Great Commission. Church Growth strategy is based on three things: (1) the biblical objective of the Church, which is the Great Commission; (2) applying the biblical principles of Church Growth; and (3) identifying a biblical paradigm to evaluate the effectiveness of Church Growth.

References: [1]C. Peter Wagner, *Your Church Can Grow* (Ventura, Calif.: Regal Books, 1976), p. 12. [2]C. Peter Wagner, printed class notes, Church Growth I (MN 705), "Church Growth Eyes," p. 6. Wagner also used this definition in his inaugural address when he was installed as the Donald A. McGavran Chair of Church Growth at Fuller Theological Seminary on November 6, 1984. [3]E. Towns, J. Vaughan and D. Seifert, *The Complete Book of Church Growth* (Wheaton, Ill.: Tyndale House Publishers, 1982), p. 105. [4]J. F. Engel and H. W. Norton, *What's Gone Wrong with the Harvest? A Communication Strategy for the Church and World Evangelism* (Grand Rapids: Zondervan Publishing House, 1975), p. 14. [5]J. R. McQuilkin, *Measuring the Church Growth Movement* (Chicago: Moody Press, 1973), pp. 73-76. The five principles are: (1) importance of numerical growth, (2) focus on receptive people, (3) people movements, (4) science as a valid tool, and (5) right method guarantees large responses. [6]C. Peter Wagner, "Church Growth: More Than a Man, a Magazine, a School, a Book," *Christianity Today* 18, no. 5 (December 7, 1973): 11, 12, 14. The six principles are: (1) nongrowth displeases God; (2) numerical growth of a church is a priority with God; (3) disciples are tangible, identifiable, countable people; (4) limited time, money and resources require strategy based on results; (5) social and behavioral sciences are valid tools in encouraging and measuring church growth; and (6) research is essential for maximum growth. [7]Lewis S. Chafer, *Systematic Theology* Vol. 1 (Dallas: Dallas Theological Seminary, 1947), p. 4. [8]Dan Baumann, *All Originality Makes a Dull Church* (Ventura, Calif.: Vision House, 1976), p. 23. [9]Donald McGavran, *Understanding Church Growth* (Grand Rapids: William B. Eerdmans, 1970), p. 162.

CHURCH GROWTH— CHURCH -PLANTING TYPES

(1) Expansion—growth of the local congregation by evangelizing non-Christians within its ministry area. (2) Extension—growth of the church by establishing daughter churches within the same general homogeneous group. (3) Bridging—growth of the church by establishing churches in different cultural areas, which also have two subdivisions, one for close cross-cultural efforts, and another for when it's a longer distance between cultures.

CHURCH GROWTH WHEEL

"Growth" is a dynamic word. Church growth is a dynamic concept. When a New Testament Church is planted, it is expected to grow just as parents expect their baby to grow. Every pastor called to a new congregation expects results in the ministry, and expects to see people won to the Lord and Christians to grow in spiritual stature. This is church growth.

Because church growth is the natural result of a healthy ministry, it is fitting that we define church growth.

First, growth means numerical growth. The purpose of the Church is to carry out the Great Commission: winning the lost to Jesus Christ

(Matt. 28:19,20). When this is done, the congregation will automatically expand. Because of evangelism, the church in Jerusalem grew in numbers (Acts 1:15; 2:41; 4:4; 5:14; 6:1,7), suggesting that all churches should be growing numerically.

The second area of growth deals with spiritual maturity, called "spiritual factors of church growth." A church should grow in grace, that is, in the total development of its spiritual life. Just as an individual grows in character, so the church grows in spiritual strength. As people within the church yield themselves to God, they grow in spiritual power. As people acquire more Bible knowledge, they grow in maturity. As people pray and commune with God, they grow in inner character.

Christians make two false assumptions regarding church growth. First, some believe that if the church is growing in spiritual character, an automatic expansion in numbers will result, and that quality will lead to quantity. This is not necessarily so. The second false assumption, a reversal of the first, is that churches that are growing in numbers automatically are growing in biblical maturity. It is possible for a numerically growing church to be superficial. It is also possible for a stagnant congregation to have people who are growing in grace and truth. Both congregations are growing, but neither reflect the full intention of God.

The diagram of the Church Growth Wheel at the beginning of this article focuses on church growth. The inner circle indicates the priority of growth—spiritual factors. The outer circle indicates the human or numerical aspects of growth. Some pastors focus all of their attention on spiritual factors such as prayer, Bible teaching and holiness, but neglect organization, outreach and wise administration. Other churches focus all their attention on programs, leadership, outreach and attendance campaigns, but neglect the spiritual dynamics.

A. Outreach as a Factor in Church Growth

Spiritual Factors in Outreach

Some churches seem to naturally grow in num-

bers and are reaching the community. These churches do not have organized visitation nor do they use promotional campaigns. Yet, visitors come to their services, new members join their ranks, offerings climb and enrollment indicators go up. God has a plan for growing churches. This plan is found in the Word of God. Growing churches in the book of Acts were characterized by the following spiritual factors:

1. Churches grow when they have New Testament aims. The aim of the church is to go and "make disciples" of all peoples (Matt. 28:19). The Early Church practiced soul winning, going to every house in Jerusalem (Acts 5:42). Paul went to every home in Ephesus (Acts 20:20) and reached every person in the city (Acts 20:31). God expects a church to grow.

2. Churches grow best when they offer effective Bible teaching programs. The Great Commission summarizes the aims of the local church and is the last command Jesus gave before returning to heaven. This is the strategy of the church that includes preaching and teaching (Sunday School and church):

Go therefore and make disciples of all the nations [people groups], baptizing them in the name of the Father and of the Son and of the Holy Spirit, teaching them to observe all things that I have commanded you; and lo, I am with you always, even to the end of the age (Matt. 28:19,20).

The Great Commission is one command, but contains three aspects: evangelism, baptism and teaching. Christians cannot choose which aspect of the Great Commission they will obey. A person disobeys the whole command in disobeying part of it. If workers emphasize teaching but neglect evangelism, they are not carrying out the Great Commission.

The aspect of the Great Commission found in the word "teaching" (v. 20), is better translated "disciple." Christians are commanded to disciple (evangelize) all nations [people groups]. Implied in the word "disciple" is reaching the lost, communicating the gospel to them and leading them to Jesus Christ. When Christians are discipling (evangelizing), they are helping members follow

Jesus Christ and His commands. Therefore, evangelism involves more than presenting the gospel to the unsaved or sharing salvation with them. Believers should allow the Holy Spirit to work through them to persuade the unsaved to become Christians and to follow Jesus Christ.

There is no success in the Lord's work without successors. God wants more than large crowds; God wants disciples of Jesus.

Another thrust of the Great Commission is to baptize the new convert after salvation. When new Christians are baptized, they are identified with Christ in His death, burial and resurrected life (Rom. 6:4,5). When New Testament believers were baptized, they were also added to the church (Acts 2:41, 47). Just as baptism reflects a Christian being placed in Jesus, so baptism demonstrates being placed in the local Body of Christ. Therefore, when Christ commanded the disciples to go and "baptize," He was commanding to go and "church" people (i.e., get them identified with a local church).

The third aspect of the Great Commission is education. The Church is given the responsibility of carrying out the example of Jesus the Teacher. Jesus spent time with His disciples. The Sermon on the Mount begins with the observation, "His disciples came to Him. Then He opened His mouth and taught them" (Matt. 5:1,2). After Jesus taught the disciples and the multitudes, we find this explanation: "He taught them as one having authority, and not as the scribes" (Matt. 7:29). The content of Christian education is suggested in the Great Commission, "Teaching them to observe all things that I have commanded you" (Matt. 28:20).

3. Churches grow when they aim to carry out the Great Commission (Matt. 28:18-20). Churches are to make disciples of as many people in the world as possible (Matt. 28:19): (a) by showing compassion to the needs of people, (b) by having a vision of what God can do for the lost, (c) by bringing the lost to hear the gospel, (d) by sharing their Christian experience with the lost, (e) by communicating the gospel to all people and (f) by persuading the lost to accept the gospel.

Second, churches are to identify each Christian with a local church (Matt. 28:19):

(a) by having each Christian learn from the teachings of the Scriptures, (b) by using the total abilities of each Christian for God's purpose, (c) by encouraging fellowship among Christians so they may strengthen each other, (d) by producing corporate worship and motivating Christians to private devotions, (e) by becoming the focus for an organized outreach into the community and (f) by administering the church ordinances/sacraments.

Third, churches are to teach each Christian to be obedient to the Scriptures (Matt. 28:20): (a) by communicating the content of the Word of God, (b) by training each Christian to use his or her skills to carry out God's plan for life, (c) by inculcating Christian values and attitudes in all believers, (d) by motivating Christians to live a godly life as called for in the Scriptures and (e) by supporting the aims and sanctity of the family.

4. Churches grow by personal soul winning. Philip won the Ethiopian eunuch; Peter preached to Cornelius; Paul witnessed to Sergius Paulus. Churches grew through winning souls to Christ. Evangelism means communicating the gospel in an understandable manner, then persuading the person to accept Christ.

5. Churches grow by a program of evangelism. Evangelism results from an organized program. The city of Jerusalem was filled and every house received the gospel (Acts 5:42). This was the result of a systematic, comprehensive coverage of the city. In other words, the apostles had a master plan to reach Jerusalem. Today, some people suggest that evangelism should be spontaneous, and argue against revival meetings, Sunday School growth campaigns, visitation programs or Sunday School busing.

A master program of outreach, however, is necessary for New Testament evangelism: (a) because the church is an organization (plus organism) with a specific goal (i.e., to reach its Jerusalem); (b) because of the evidence of a program in churches in the book of Acts; (c) because the average Christian does not win souls unless motivated, and goals, requirements, examples and programs will motivate him; and (d) because the Lord is a God of order and rationality. The universe is governed by laws, the spiritual world is governed by laws and the church should have

organization, procedure and goals commensu-
rate with the laws of God.

6. Churches grow through biblical revival. When the
church is in a general state of revival, God bless-
es its outreach. "If My people who are called by
My name will humble themselves, and pray and
seek My face, and turn from their wicked ways,
then I will hear from heaven, and will forgive
their sin and heal their land" (2 Chron. 7:14).

*7. Churches grow through public preaching and
teaching.* In the twentieth century, an emphasis is
placed on home Bible studies. Evangelistic
preaching has been de-emphasized. The Early
Church, however, believed in preaching in the
open as well as house-to-house (Acts 2:14-38;
3:12-26; 5:42; 20:20). The Bible is a dynamic
book (Heb. 4:12) and it changes lives. New
Christians (2 Cor. 5:17) will attract the interest
and attendance of the unsaved. When the Bible
is properly preached, the unsaved will want to
attend church and hear its message.

8. Churches grow by prayer and biblical conviction.
We do not usually think of prayer as a principle
of outreach, at least in a casual manner. A praying church, however, is a growing church.

Here are four basic prayer concerns:

a. Pray that the lost will be convicted.
b. Pray that God will use the preaching of the
   Word to accomplish His purpose.
c. Pray for spiritual growth and revival.
d. Pray for changed lives.

As a result of answered prayer, outsiders will
come into the church, producing growth.

Natural Factors in Outreach

God's program for the church to communicate
the gospel does not break the natural laws of
communication. People must know the message
that is presented. Therefore, use the various
branches of media to communicate your message: newspapers, radio, TV, magazines and so
on. The natural principles of church growth as
well as the spiritual factors of outreach stem from
God.

1. Growing churches project an aggressive image. A
pastor must determine the kind of church he or
she believes will best communicate to the com-

munity. This will establish an image, which may
be defined as "the sum total of the impressions
that a church wants to make on the community."
Churches may be known as busing churches,
youth churches, foreign mission churches or
Bible-teaching churches. When new to a community, a pastor should have a clear statement of
aims and objectives, and should know what
needs to be accomplished. These aims will determine the church's image and vision statement.
The pastor will communicate this image to the
entire community.

*2. Growing churches determine what clientele they can
reach.* Many "publics" surround a congregation. A
clientele is a natural grouping of people who have
one factor in common. The church can reach
these people through this common interest.

First, the church must identify this grouping of
people, determine their needs and adapt advertising to reach them with the gospel. Factors that
help determine a church's clientele are: (a) the
friends of regular attenders, (b) the relatives, (c)
neighbors who would not be called their friends,
(d) neighbors to the church, (e) those living in
the community who are unchurched, (f) unsaved
people in other churches, (g) visitors who drive a
distance to the church and (h) new residents to
the community.

In addition to the above clientele, each of the
areas can be further broken down into: new couples; singles, including the divorced; servicemen;
middle-aged couples; senior citizens; and college
students.

No single advertising campaign can reach
every kind of clientele. The church must appeal
to the needs of each group it wants to reach.
Then the church must communicate to each that
it is able to meet their needs by its program of
ministry.

*3. Growing churches determine to reach every person
in the community.* When the gospel is presented to
many people, a larger crowd will be likely to
attend the church. This is a principle of sowing
and reaping.

Never be satisfied when only one person
comes for salvation. Rejoice with those who are
saved, but keep seeking others. And don't be discouraged. Some soul winners lose their zeal
when their young converts drop out of church.

Although there are many variables, the more fully a person is committed to Jesus Christ at the moment of salvation, the more will be the likelihood of follow-through in the Christian life. Therefore, preach repentance. Let a new convert know the obligations to the church in witnessing, attendance, tithing, Christian service, baptism, visitation and prayer meetings.

The secondary motive that often causes a person to make a decision for salvation results in a primary action. Some go to church because they are lonely, others to satisfy parents, others attend because it is the thing to do, or to make business contacts. Some commit their lives to Jesus because they want to please their wives. If they sincerely receive Christ, however, they receive eternal life. This principle reveals that people may go to church for secondary reasons, but when the gospel is preached, their primary needs of salvation are usually met.

Even though a church determines to reach every person in its community, depending on its size and homogeneous makeup, it may not be able to reach every group of people. Sometimes it is necessary and more productive for daughter churches to target a particular people group.

4. Growing churches use every effective advertising medium possible. The following attitudes toward advertising will make a Sunday School outreach successful:

Advertise in keeping with the church's "image."

Make the advertising personal to each separate clientele. A general poster or announcement to everyone is not as effective as a "personal announcement" regarding a specific need of a small clientele.

Use advertising to lead to personal contacts. People may not go to church because of impersonal advertising; they go because of a human contact.

Remember, advertising begins at home. In a small church situation, spend most of the time and money to reach the officers, the teachers and the pupils. When these are convinced of the program, they will bring in the outsiders. Advertising is like waves from a splash in a pond; the waves are highest near the splash. Therefore, concentrate advertising on those who are close to home.

Advertising should get everyone involved. If a church wants to draw 500 people to attend Sunday School, it needs to try to get 500 people "in" on the special push. This involves contests, delegated work or other techniques to get people involved.

Advertise by: (a) personal testimonies, (b) personal invitations, (c) skits, (d) phoning, (e) distributing handbills and (f) writing letters.

Every church resource should be used to advertise special campaigns: (a) church-planning calendar, (b) church bulletins, (c) church newspaper, (d) pastor's newsletter, (e) church bulletin boards, (f) announcements, (g) posters and (h) announcements on church radio broadcasts.

Advertise through direct mail. God's people should make their advertisements neat, attractive and informative. Most important, use them. Try church newspapers, letters, postcards and handwritten letters. Photocopies and/or hastily written newspapers have been used effectively by many groups or "movements."

Advertise through communication media: (a) purchased advertisements and press releases in newspapers; (b) radio church programs, community service programs; (c) community bulletin boards; (d) bumper stickers; (e) billboards; (f) posters in store windows; and (g) church announcement boards.

Effective advertising takes place when people hear the message again and again. Many churches that send a mailing will send it to 10,000 people once rather than to 2,000 people five times. They actually end up with less response because they neglect the key principle of saturation (i.e., making sure the recipients know your message).

5. Growing churches set goals to grow. Set attendance goals. Usually a church will not grow unless it aims to grow. First, set long-range attendance goals for a period of years. Next, set a yearly goal. A goal will keep the vision lifted and create a challenge for the people.

B. Organization as a Factor of Church Growth

Most people who want to build a New Testament Church give attention to the spiritual-growth principles in the Word of God, but neglect the natural factors of good organization and techniques. These principles built on "common sense" cannot be ignored in building a New Testament Church. The natural and spiritual factors fit hand in glove. It is possible to get numerical growth by using circuses or Bozo the Clown. This is not "biblical," although the end result has been salvation of souls. Leaders in each church will have to prayerfully consider the "means to the end."

Spiritual Factors of Organization

1. Churches grow when they meet the biblical qualifications for a church. Not every group calling itself a church is in fact a church. Many organizations go by the generic term "church," yet do not meet New Testament criteria. The following principles describe a New Testament Church: (a) a church is a group of believers (Acts 2:41; Rom. 6:3-6); (b) a church has the presence of Jesus Christ in its midst (Rev. 1:13,20; 2:1,5); (c) a church places itself under the authority of the Word of God (Acts 2:42,43; 1 Tim. 3:15); (d) a church is organized to carry out the Great Commission (Matt. 28:19,20; Acts 5:42—6; (e) a church administers the ordinances/sacraments; and (f) a church manifests the spiritual gifts of leadership and service (Acts 11:22-26).

2. Churches grow when their leaders are truly called and led of God. Dr. Lee Robertson says, "Everything rises and falls on leadership." The greatest factor in church growth is the leader. The pastor must assume the biblical position of leadership within the flock (Acts 20:28): (a) the pastor leads by example (1 Pet. 5:3), (b) the pastor leads by preaching (Heb. 13:7), (c) the pastor leads by watch care (Acts 20:29-31) and (d) the pastor leads by wise decision making (1 Pet. 5:2).

3. Churches grow when laypeople are in their proper places of responsibility. Committees, councils and boards are biblical means of organization. Some fast-growing churches have neglected committees. These churches have strong pastors who make all of the decisions, and although this may be effective, it has liabilities. The church becomes only as stable as the personality of its leader. Only a few leaders are talented enough to become the organizational personification of a church.

A pastor of a growing church needs assistance from the congregation. Laypeople can and should help the pastor in the leadership of the church by serving in organizations such as the finance committee, the board of Christian education, building committee, Sunday School council and so on.

Some biblical examples of organization include the following: The 12 tribes of Israel were organized around the Tabernacle. Jesus fed the 5,000 after they were organized into groups of 50. A committee of 7 (deacons) was organized to look after the material needs of widows. Paul organized the churches in Asia Minor.

The Church was commanded to produce the results of organization: "Let all things be done decently and in order" (1 Cor. 14:40).

The nature of the church demands organization. The church is people, each one working to carry out the Great Commission, not watching from the pews while the pastor performs the ministry. A good pastor leads all the congregation into Christian service. The best way to get everyone involved is through an organized program. When a congregation organizes itself for service, it is carrying out the purpose for which the Church was constituted.

Natural Factors of Organization

The Southern Baptists built the largest Protestant denomination in America by organizing their evangelistic outreach through pastored leadership.

1. Growing churches allow the pastor to exercise leadership. These congregations allow their pastors to lead. If a pastor goes in a direction and the people do not follow, he or she is not a leader. Or, if the pastor runs beyond the people's ability to follow, he or she is not a leader. It must be remembered that the pastor is a leader, not a dictator. There are dangers in a pastor-dominated church, but there are also dangers in a board-dominated church. Dictatorial abuses abound by both pastors and decision-making boards. Neither can be successful without the cooperation of the other.

2. Growing churches have workers who assist the pastor through service, prayer and encouragement.

3. Growing churches are organized to meet the needs of the congregation. Never organize a committee or agency before it is needed. When the organization is no longer serving the needs of its members, disband it.

4. Growing churches employ qualified people to carry the work forward. Committees do not get jobs done—people do. Too often committees are regarded as personalities. In fact, a committee is only the sum total of its people. The following principles will help solve this point of irritation: (a) never give a job to a committee that can be done by one person; (b) never allow productive people to be tied up in committee work that hinders their leadership or efficiency; (c) committee work is most effective for gathering opinions, policy decisions and input from the masses; (d) a person may learn leadership by effectively serving on a committee; (e) excessive committees bog down a church in bureaucracy; and (f) the gifted person should be exposed to a great number of people in the largest variety of ministries to accomplish the greatest good for the total church.

This last principle applies to both organization and teaching. The most gifted man might be the Sunday School superintendent and the most gifted woman may teach a large class. People should be used according to their abilities. Find the key people and use them.

5. Growing churches can pinpoint their needs to best solve problems. The sharper the aim of an organization, the more it can accomplish. Considering this principle, students should be grouped by age in Sunday School for efficient teaching.

6. Growing churches get more people involved in the organization and administration of the Sunday School than the average church. Traditionally, the Sunday School has attempted to get 1 worker for every group of 10 students. This law is still effective when kept in balance with the law of the master teacher. The gifted teacher should be allowed to instruct large classes, but needs many assistants to take care of follow-up, visitation, keeping records and counseling. The master teacher is most effective as a "lecturer." It is impossible, however, for the teacher to be a pastor-counselor of a large class; many under-shepherds are needed.

7. Growing churches build loyalty to the organization. We live in a changing society where people

have few loyalties. The one characteristic of change is that it rearranges priorities and disassociates the past.

8. Growing churches are measured by attendance, financial support and member involvement. A church is healthy when people attend, give money and involve themselves in its programs. Therefore, a growing church ought to incorporate: (a) an active program to foster consistent attendance, (b) an active program to attract new attenders, (c) excellent curriculum content to bolster attendance and (d) external stimulation to encourage attendance.

Many people have accused churches of "grabbing money." As a result, some leaders feel "unspiritual" when they talk about money. The opposite is true. When leaders do not mention stewardship, they are not obeying God (Mal. 3:10,11). The average American church attender donates $12.50 a year to a church (Source: Barna Research Group, 1993). Therefore, a church ought to: (a) teach stewardship in its curriculum, (b) provide an organizational program for its members to give, (c) motivate everyone to give and (d) keep careful records of all income.

9. Growing churches construct buildings and educational space to reflect the purpose of the Sunday School. The traditional laws of Sunday School growth indicate there must be 10 square feet per pupil. Because the laws also hold there should be only 10 pupils per class, classrooms contained approximately 100 square feet. These classes were ideal for small-group discussion. The trend today is to build classrooms the approximate size of public schoolrooms. These larger rooms can: (a) expand attendance; (b) provide more motivation to pupils; and (c) provide space for a larger, more impersonal group where they can listen to the Word of God. Many adults would rather not visit a small class. The Sunday School should have rooms constructed for efficient class instruction.

10. Growing churches use their buildings as a major means of publicity. Many people choose a church for its physical facilities.

   a. The church should have visibility in the community. It should be located on a major thoroughfare. The building should be placed on the property so it can be seen by people passing by. Its prominence in the community will determine the likelihood of attendance.

b. Visitors tend to frequent a church that is convenient and easily accessible.

c. Exposure to the masses is also important. The church should be located near a shopping center, business district, high school or some other place where people can easily see the building. The rule of thumb for attracting shoppers is that a store should be seen by the family on their way to work and school in the morning, then again in the evening as they return home. The same rule holds for attracting prospective church members.

11. Growing churches have expandable, convertible and interchangeable educational space. A church should get maximum use of its educational space.

a. Rooms should be constructed so they can be expanded when a class grows in size.

b. Next, rooms should be convertible. When the adult class expands from 50 to 100, the students should be able to use the facilities with very little remodeling.

c. Finally, space should be interchangeable for various activities. When a gymnasium is built, it should be useable for recreation, education and banquets, if necessary. Multipurpose facilities can better serve the congregation, and they cost less.

12. Growing churches are reflected by expansion of buildings. If a church never builds or adds to its present facilities, it communicates to the community that it is not growing. Therefore, a pastor is counseled to build a little every few years rather than to initiate a massive construction project every 15 years.

13. Growing churches economize on building use. The traditional Sunday School had a "three chair" philosophy. The child was provided a chair and space for the traditional opening exercises. This took approximately 20 minutes. This space had to be heated, cleaned, insured and painted. After opening exercises, the child was

sent to a second chair in a small classroom. This space had the same overhead costs as the first. Finally, the child was sent to the sanctuary where a third chair was provided, although this was a pew. Hence, within a three-hour period, the house of God had provided three chairs for the child. This is no longer thought to be a wise use of space.

C. Leadership as a Factor of Church Growth

The leader is the length and shadow of the work he or she builds for God. New Testament growth does not come from Madison Avenue public relations moguls, but begins with the leader who is called of God. In finding biblical leadership, the following criteria must be observed:

Spiritual Factors of Leadership

1. Growing churches have a leader "called" of God. People can be assured they are called of God when they meet the following criteria:

a. Have a burden to serve God. The word "burden" was used of the Old Testament prophet Ezekiel (Ezek. 12:10).

b. Have a desire to serve God. This is a consuming desire that encompasses all of their perspectives (Phil. 3:10-14).

c. Have fruit in their lives and service (John 15:16).

2. Growing churches have effective leaders who display biblical spirituality. A person who is used of God must be filled with the Spirit (Eph. 5:18). To be filled with the Spirit is to be controlled by the Holy Spirit. God can then put His power through that leader to build a church or to teach a class. Being filled with the Spirit leads to soul winning (Acts 2:1-4), answers to prayer (Acts 4:31), joy (Acts 13:52) and fruitfulness (Gal. 5:22,23). To be filled with the Spirit, the church leader must (a) be separated from all known sin, (b) yield all conscious endeavors to God, (c) seek the leadership of God in all areas of service and (d) trust God to work through his or her service to accomplish the results of the Spirit.

3. Growing churches see the power of God work through their leaders. Securing the empowering of the Holy Spirit requires no formula. It comes as a leader is yielded to God and exerts every energy in prayer. The leader must be mature and dedicate every ability to serve God. To secure spiritual power, the leader must meet all of the qualifications in the Word of God.

4. Growing churches share the vision of their leaders. Just as the Old Testament prophet was called a seer (1 Sam. 9:9), so the biblical leader must see first, see farthest and see most. The leader must have a vision of what God is going to do with the church, and must have a vision of growth. Then the leader must inspire the congregation.

5. Growing churches have leaders who have several spiritual gifts (Rom. 12:3-8; 1 Cor. 12:1-27; Eph. 4:7-13). A person with a spiritual gift can accomplish spiritual results through the effective use of that gift.

  a. People who have spiritual gifts are relative in their abilities to accomplish results. Some people who have the gift of teaching are more effective than others.
  b. Some people have more gifts than others.
  c. The person who has a large number of gifts is able to accomplish more for God than those who have fewer gifts. This accomplishment can be measured in quantity or quality (the person can produce a depth of spirituality in the followers and/or a large numerical following).
  d. A leader's faithful use of gifts will result in the growth of abilities. The leader either accumulates more abilities, or those he or she already has become more effective.
  e. When a leader faithfully uses his or her gifts, others will come alongside (a team effort) who have dominant gifts not manifest in the leader, to help build the Body of Christ.

6. Growing churches have leaders who aggressively obey the commands of Christian service. Some leaders are called of God, have spiritual gifts and have yielded themselves to God, but they are not effective in their Christian service. They have not been seeking places to serve God. Those who aggressively seek to carry out the New Testament commands concerning service are

those who experience the power of God in their lives. The Bible tells us to have a vision (Prov. 29:18, *KJV*), aggressively reach the lost (Luke 14:23) and preach to as many people as possible (Mark 16:15). Those leaders who actively seek out and obey commands in the Bible are those who have more blessings of God upon their ministries.

7. Growing churches are the result of the faith of their leaders. Faith is usually considered an intangible quality. Like love, if you have it, you know it. Most people go through life exercising many acts of "faith" every day. We have faith in chairs to hold us, or faith in an airplane to get us to our destinations. Biblical faith is centered in Jesus Christ. (a) When people are knowledgeable about Jesus Christ, they can trust Him more. (b) A successful act in trusting God for small things leads to greater spheres of faith. (c) Biblical faith is not wishfully hoping God will bless our endeavors. (d) The closer our projects are to the will of God, the more effective our faith will be in trusting God for His blessing upon them. (e) If a service project fails, it is not the leader's lack of faith. Either the project or the service was not in keeping with the will of God.

8. Growing churches have leaders who are mature. Spiritual maturity is not an overnight acquisition. Maturity grows through time, successful service and accumulated experiences. Some Sunday School teachers do not have 20 years of experience; rather, they have one year of experience repeated 20 times. Those teachers have not grown in maturity. Every time people trust God and receive answers to their prayers, they grow in their abilities to trust God for bigger things. The same holds true for their spiritual gifts. Every time people stretch their abilities to their ultimate, their abilities grow in future potential uses. Thus, maturity is acquired as people walk with God and serve Him for many years. All things being equal, the young person just out of Bible college cannot build a great church as quickly as the seasoned pastor.

9. Growing churches are built by leaders who have resolute determination. This means they must never give up. When they commit themselves to building churches, they are not open to calls from other congregations. They feel the burden of

God to reach communities. Therefore, these leaders stay in one place and build their churches. When they meet obstacles, they overcome them and continue to build.

Natural Factors of Leadership

Leadership has been defined as helping people accomplish the goals of the New Testament Church. Therefore, a leader who builds a great church will help people accomplish the goals of that church.

1. Growing churches employ gifted workers to accomplish the most for God. Every person should be used in the church. Those who can accomplish the most, however, should be used in strategic places of leadership. The outstanding person, through aggressive outreach, can produce numerical growth. The gifted teacher should be exposed to the maximum number of people in the largest variety of learning experiences to accomplish the greatest influence in people's lives. This teacher is usually mature, spiritual and trained. This teacher can lead students into greater knowledge of the Scriptures and their lives can become more Christlike.

2. Growing churches realize that effective leadership produces a multiplication of their ministries (2 Tim. 2:2). When leaders properly carry out their duties, they accomplish two results. First, the work of God prospers. Second, new workers are trained for the ministry. As the leader performs tasks, (a) others are inspired to serve, (b) those that are reached grow and want to help in the ministry and (c) the ministry duplicates itself in the people.

3. Growing churches spawn leadership abilities through "hot poker" approaches. Just as heat transfers from the coals to the poker, so the qualities and attitudes of effective leadership are assimilated. A recruit should spend time with an experienced leader to (a) gain self-confidence, (b) develop a proper leadership attitude, (c) keep from immature mistakes, (d) acquire a vision of potential production and (e) understand the overall strategy of the ministry.

The best methods for developing "hot poker" leaders are (a) by a teaching internship, (b) by bringing great educators to the church and (c) by taking the staff to seminars, conventions and training sessions outside the church.

4. Growing churches improve leadership abilities through formal training sessions. A growing Sunday School should plan a training program. This is effective through (a) a weekly Sunday School teachers meeting, (b) a specified training class, (c) placing assistants under the master teacher and (d) providing literature *that will increase leadership ability.*

5. Growing churches effectively use leadership by providing a consistent, constant interaction between workers. No worker can be expected to keep performing at a high level without constant motivation, evaluation and reward. Most fast-growing Sunday Schools have a weekly Sunday School teachers' meeting. Workers are reminded of their tasks and motivated to better service. Those who have performed well are rewarded. This face-to-face encounter between leader and worker is a necessity for constant growth.

6. Growing churches give direction to Sunday Schools through written standards. When the standards are written, the leaders extend their ministries beyond their oral communications. Written standards give (a) direction for growth, (b) a basis for solving problems, (c) cohesiveness to the staff, (d) a basis for determining why the church is or is not growing and (e) practical help to another person when the leader leaves the scene.

7. Growing churches have leaders who know and apply the laws of leadership. The eight laws of leadership include (a) the law of dreams and vision, (b) the law of rewards, (c) the law of credibility, (d) the law of communication, (e) the law of accountability, (f) the law of motivation, (g) the law of problem solving and (h) the law of decision making.

D. Discipleship as a Factor of Church Growth

No work is effective for God unless the people are willing to follow God and the leader He has placed to look after them. Jesus said, "And whoever does not bear his cross and come after Me cannot be My disciple" (Luke 14:27). The effectiveness of the church is measured to the degree by which the people follow the Lord.

Spiritual Factors of Discipleship

1. Growing churches are characterized by people who

love God. Although this is an intangible factor, a person's love will be a motivator to endure hardships, ride on a bus eight hours to visit on a Saturday, stay up and pray all night, or endure any other hardship for the cross of Christ.

2. Growing churches are characterized by people who have commitments and/or yieldedness. To be disciples of Christ, people must yield themselves to do God's will. This involves (a) a total commitment of conscious endeavors and (b) daily yielding of self to God.

3. Growing churches are characterized by people who pray. The effective disciple spends time (a) worshiping God (John 9:31), (b) fellowshipping with God, (c) asking for power (Luke 11:13) and (d) praising God.

4. Growing churches are characterized by people who know and live by the Word of God. A disciple must continue in the Word of God (John 8:31).

5. Growing churches are characterized by biblical fellowship among its members. A disciple must want to fellowship with other disciples. True disciples spend time with other disciples so that they might grow through fellowship.

Natural Factors of Discipleship

1. Growing churches reach people as and where they are. We cannot expect a person from a lower economic level to attend a church that performs highbrow music. The person from the housing project cannot "feel affinity" with people who have a another value system. God will reach certain people through a renewal kind of church, while others will be reached through a rational Bible study. This principle reflects Genesis 1, "like produces like."

2. Growing churches spend time and money on those who will respond most readily. Jesus taught His disciples that if they were not received in a town, they should shake the dust off their sandals (Luke 9:5). By this, Jesus implied that they should spend time on those who would respond to the message. Therefore, a church should invest most of its energy on those who will attend rather than on those who won't. This does not mean, however, that we should neglect any segment of the population.

3. Growing churches have more people making professions of faith, hence they have more who can become dis-ciples. The criticism often is heard that fast-growing churches need a backdoor revival. Many people are receiving Christ, yet not everyone continues to grow in faith. However, it is important not to criticize the churches where many people make decisions to follow Christ. Two points should be made. First, every person who can possibly be reached should be saved. Second, those who are saved need to grow in Christ. This is called "discipling." Emphasizing only discipleship, however, is not the purpose of the church, although the church that has the most professions of faith is most likely to be effective in discipleship.

4. Growing churches involve new Christians in service. God wants new Christians baptized so they will feel the obligation of carrying out their new commitments. The outward confession of baptism can be a stimulus to motivate the young Christian to faithfulness. When a person receives Christ, the church congregation should be told immediately. The congregation's expectations also motivate the new Christian into service for the Lord.

5. Growing churches stress salvation of the whole person. Salvation involves intellect, emotion and will. For people to be saved, they must know the gospel content, feel the conviction of sin and the love of God, then respond by acts of their wills. This is called "believing." Because the end product determines the process, plan to appeal to the intellect, emotions, and will of the person. The person needs to know the content of the gospel, so communicate Bible content. The person must feel hatred for sin as well as love for God. Singing songs to stir emotions and using humor, testimonies and pithy sayings are excellent activities to motivate people to accept God. Salvation involves a decision of the will, so people also need to be immersed in the Word of God.

6. Growing churches have disciples that assume the attitudes and practices of their leaders. If the people in the churches are not soul winners, it is often because pastors are ineffective in their outreaches. When the people do not sacrifice, it is usually because of their pastor's attitude. Jeremiah the prophet said, "Like priest, like people," meaning pastors are the length and shadow of the church. Pastors cannot get the people in the congregation to do what they themselves are not willing to do.

7. Growing churches realize the power of informed disciples. The effectiveness of church workers is in direct proportion to their education. Some workers are not successful because they have not been trained. Others fail because they have enough education, but don't know the right things (their theology is wrong). Therefore, the leader must reinforce the primacy of the church; this is the cornerstone of Christian education. The leader must also reinforce the primacy of the church's methods; the disciple must be convinced that the method used is the most effective to reach a lost world. The leader must continually reinforce loyalty to the cause. The rededication service is effective for growth. It is helpful for church workers to come to the altar and renew their pledges for church growth.

8. Growing churches realize the power of motivated workers. Fast-growing churches have been built on the shoulders of motivated workers. Therefore, the leader must make the following assumptions: (a) People do not naturally want to serve God, because they are sinners. (b) Because everyone has a gift (ability to serve God), everyone should be serving God. (c) Therefore, the leader should motivate everyone to serve God. To magnify the motivated worker does not lessen an emphasis on the trained worker, for God uses both. But the worker who is trained and motivated is the most effective disciple of all.

References: Elmer Towns, *The Complete Book of Church Growth* (Wheaton, Ill.: Tyndale House Publishers, 1981); Elmer Towns, *The Successful Sunday School and Teacher's Guidebook* (Carol Stream, Ill.: Creation House, 1975), pp. 198-213.

CHURCH MEMBERSHIP: BIBLICAL BASIS

The idea of belonging to a church is assumed in the New Testament. Every person who was a Christian was part of a fellowship with other Christians in the locality. No one was left to live or minister independently, nor did Christians become a rule unto themselves. John Donne said "no man is an island," and that description is true of a Christian.

Saints (disciples) in the New Testament were numbered, which seems to be equivalent to adding to a membership roll (Acts 1:15; 4:4; 6:1,7,). When people were saved and/or baptized they were added to the church (Acts 2:41,47; 5:14; 11:26). The result of growth is that the church multiplied (Acts 6:1,7), which implies that both a count of the total number and a means of ascertaining new members was recorded. This gives a biblical base for the practice of a church keeping a record of its members.

The apostles had an inclusive number of 11 (Acts 1:26) or 12 in its membership (Acts 2:14). Having a set number of leaders in the church gives credibility to keeping a record and numbering its members.

Some churches do not keep a formal church membership record, and traditionally the question is asked, Is church membership biblical? Those who do not keep a membership record also have an unwritten standard for those who are considered "insiders." They know who is a part of the group and how the church makes decisions.

Access to church membership is decided by congregational approval. It is sometimes decided by the members, the official board, the membership committee or by the pastor. The Roman believers were exhorted, "Receive one who is weak in the faith" (Rom. 14:1).

CHURCH MEMBERSHIP: QUALIFICATIONS FOR ADMISSION

Four conditions are usually considered in receiving a person into church membership: (1) belief, (2) baptism, (3) doctrine and (4) morals. But the Bible explicitly teaches only two: belief and baptism. Nothing is found in Scripture about new members needing to meet doctrinal and moral requirements, although these qualifications are implied. The question arises: Should anyone be allowed into the church upon profession of faith and baptism? For example, should a known prostitute be given church membership the minute she professes salvation? How about a known alcoholic? Should these people prove themselves before being accepted into church fellowship?

Profession of Faith for Church Membership

A church should have a goal to accept only regenerate members. Those who are received into the local church Body must first be born again before they are accepted into the Body of Christ, who died for them. The unregenerate are always welcome in church to visit, listen or attend, but not to become church members. It is impossible, however, to assess humanly who truly possesses eternal life. Therefore, the Early Church required a candidate to "confess...the Lord Jesus" (Rom. 10:9), which is also called public profession of faith. Those who truly have Christ in their hearts will desire to confess it with their mouths (Rom. 10:9,10). The opposite is not always true, however; some confess with their mouths but do not believe in their hearts.

As a result, some are accepted into church membership and are found not to be Christians at a later time. The problem with profession of faith also faced the church in apostolic times. "Examine yourselves as to whether you are in the faith" (2 Cor. 13:5). Hebrews 6:1-9 seems to describe those who profess but are not really saved. Another passage, 1 John 2:19, describes some who were included in the church upon their profession of faith; however, they left the assembly, revealing they were never really saved.

The question is often raised whether a church should accept a new convert into church membership, or whether it should wait to make sure the person will continue in the profession. Some people make professions of faith without actually possessing salvation; therefore, some churches withhold membership until young Christians have proven themselves. Those who hold this position argue that Paul was not given immediate recognition/fellowship by the church in Jerusalem, but was only accepted after Barnabas vouched for him (Acts 9:26-28).

On the other side of the issue, there is a strong argument to receive new believers into church membership immediately. Paul told the Romans, "Receive one who is weak in the faith" (Rom. 14:1), implying that the new believer who is weak in the faith will benefit from church fellowship/membership. Paul argues that if Christ received the weak into His body, should not the local church receive them into its body (Rom. 15:7)? Further, it is noted that the purpose of church membership is to strengthen Christians through fellowship, not to impose a "trial" period to improve him- or herself for membership. After all, every Christian is a sinner saved by grace who will be strengthened by fellowship.

Water Baptism for Church Membership

The Bible implies that believers were accepted into fellowship upon baptism in water after their conversions. In reverse, the Bible gives no illustration of a believer who was not connected to a fellowship, nor does it give any illustration of believers who were unbaptized. In only one place was baptism deferred, and that is the case of the thief on the cross. His willingness to receive Christ, however, indicates that he would have been baptized if given the opportunity. The Bible gives no example of baptism being withheld so a person could prove him- or herself, or so a church could further examine a candidate. An argument from silence suggests water baptism precedes church membership. Just as Spirit baptism identifies us in Christ's body in death, burial and resurrection, so water baptism identifies us with the local body, which is a New Testament Church. This argument of symbolism is a major reason to require water baptism before church membership.

Doctrinal Fellowship for Church Membership

First: How much doctrine does a person need to know to be a church member? And second; How much of the doctrinal statement shall a person agree with before becoming a church member? Can a person disagree in minor areas and still fellowship with a community of believers?

Regarding the first question: If a church accepts new Christians as members who are baptized immediately upon their professions of faith, they probably have a minimum knowledge of doctrine. Therefore, that church cannot require a new member to have complete knowledge of the doctrinal position of the church. The candidate for church membership should know basic doctrines of Christianity that surround salvation. This would include the authority of Scripture, the deity of Christ, the death and resurrection of Christ (the gospel). The basis of church membership should include the essentials of Christianity.

After a young convert is accepted into church fellowship, it is the responsibility of a church to see that the person is taught the church's doctrine. Doctrine is essential for a balanced life in a church; without it, the church will be unbalanced.

What about disagreement with some aspect of a church's doctrinal statement? How much conformity is necessary for church membership? Luke suggests, "those things which are most surely believed among us" (Luke 1:1, *KJV*). Christian truth is known in the Scriptures as "sound doctrine." Paul notes, "Holding fast the faithful word as he has been taught, that he may be able, by sound doctrine, both to exhort and to convict those who contradict" (Titus 1:9).

Sometimes doctrine is referred to as "the faith." "If indeed you continue in the faith, grounded and steadfast, and are not moved away from the hope of the gospel which you heard," (Col. 1:23).

"Beloved, while I was very diligent to write to you concerning our common salvation, I found it necessary to write to you exhorting you to contend earnestly for the faith which was once for all delivered to the saints" (Jude 3).

The basis of good sound doctrine was the whole body of revealed truth contained in the Scriptures. Therefore, Paul said, "All Scripture...is profitable for doctrine" (2 Tim. 3:16). But in the days of Acts 2, the New Testament had not yet been written and doctrine had to be transmitted orally by the apostles. For this reason it is called the "apostles' doctrine." Those who were "added" to the church (Acts 2:41) continued in the "apostles' doctrine" (Acts 2:42).

Anyone who denies "the doctrine of Christ," meaning His deity, His Sonship, His virgin birth, His atoning death and His resurrection, is not a Christian. "Whoever denies the Son does not have the Father either; he who acknowledges the Son has the Father also" (1 John 2:23). Therefore, any who deny the fundamental doctrine of Christ are denied church fellowship because they have not met the criteria for being Christians.

If a new convert held a heretical doctrine that would later be a condition to cast him or her out of church fellowship, however, that denial would be a condition to not give the person the "right hand of fellowship" in the first place. Note the following exhortation by Paul. "A man that is an heretick after the first and second admonition reject" (Titus 3:10, *KJV*). Some were also put out of the church "which some having put away concerning faith have made shipwreck: Of whom is Hymenaeus and Alexander; whom I have delivered unto Satan, that they may learn not to blaspheme" (1 Tim. 1:19,20, *KJV*). Most new converts are ignorant of some doctrines and should not be rejected. But if a new convert comes out of a cult, that person should demonstrate yieldedness to accept the authority of Scripture in his or her doctrine and life before being accepted into church fellowship.

Moral Standards for Church Membership

The basis for receiving church members is explained in Romans 14:1-4. Paul makes it clear that the church is not a body limited to mature saints only. Paul opens membership to include, "Receive one who is weak in the faith" (Rom. 14:1). Paul does not mean ignorance of the creed (statement of faith), but one who has difficulty trusting God for victory in his or her life. Paul is not saying to receive the one who is weak in reliance for justification (chap. 4), for that would be accepting those who doubt their salvation. The weak Christian Paul wanted to accept into fellowship had a problem with sanctification, or the problem of separation (eating meat) in his day. "Let not him who eats despise him who does not eat" (14:3). (Auton prose labeto makes noneating a condition by which he is received).

Paul exhorts, "Who are you to judge another's servant?" (v. 4). He asks if we have the right to judge the servant of God. "Receive" (v. 1) is to welcome into fellowship—not to criticize, but to build up. So the church should accept a person on his or her profession of faith. We cannot determine a person's spirituality; again, only Christ is the judge (v. 10).

Therefore, everyone Christ has received into salvation we ought to be willing to receive as brothers and sisters and church members. At the end of the section about the brother who had problems, Paul states, "Therefore receive one another, just as Christ also received us, to the glory of God" (15:7).

A new Christian is accepted into church membership upon his or her profession of faith, and a profession of repentance. The person testifies that he or she has turned from sin to Jesus Christ. Faith and repentance cannot be separated. This does not assume that the young Christian is perfect or that the person has cleaned up every bad habit. Therefore, we can ask: What sin should be purged and what sin should be allowed in the new Christian? This question helps us to remember that no Christian, no matter how mature, is sinless.

Any sin that is a cause for church discipline would be a sin that could exclude a new Christian from church membership. This could alleviate discipline-prone people from entering the church. Examples might be excluding people who are living in open immorality, unmarried couples living together or an owner of a porno store.

CHURCH PLANTING

Church planting is an approach to evangelism and church growth that sets as its primary goal the establishment of new churches as the primary means of reaching a specific community and/or people group.

Biblical Foundations for Church Planting

Most people recognize that the Great Commission commands Christians to evangelize unsaved people. Few people realize the implied method of carrying out this commission. The Great Commission implies that church planting is the primary method to evangelize the world. To reach unsaved people in every culture of the world, a church must be established in every culture to communicate the gospel and nurture those who are saved. In a simplistic observation, one of the reasons so much foreign missions work is fruitless is because great effort is spent on winning people to Christ apart from identifying them with a New Testament church. All methods of evangelism have their places: radio

evangelism, television evangelism, medical evangelism, mass evangelism, personal evangelism, educational evangelism and presence evangelism. But God's primary method of evangelizing a new community is by planting a New Testament church to reach the area with the gospel.

Many people are ignorant of the role of church planting in evangelism. Others dissent because they do not really understand God's program of evangelism. They have never understood the role of church planting in the Great Commission. A careful study of the Great Commission reveals the complex and divergent nature under which the command was given and the difficult task Jesus wanted accomplished.

The Great Commission was given five different times in separate locations. On each occasion, the Lord added to the previous command, and the reader must see the total picture to understand the full implication of the Great Commission.

The Great Commission was initially given on the afternoon of the Resurrection to 10 disciples. Jesus said, "As the Father has sent Me, I also send you" (John 20:21). Jesus was simply giving His perplexed disciples a commission to represent Him. On this occasion, the message, destination and task were not given to the disciples. Perhaps they were not ready to receive it.

A week later in the Upper Room, Thomas was present, now totaling 11 disciples. Jesus told them, "Go into all the world and preach the gospel to every creature" (Mark 16:15). Two aspects were added to the commission. First, they were not just to minister to Israel, but also to the world. Second, they were to preach the gospel to every person in the world.

The next time the Great Commission was repeated was at least two weeks later. The disciples were no longer in Jerusalem, but on a mountain in Galilee approximately one hundred miles away. Jesus assumed they would eventually obey, for He used the participle "as you are going" (Matt. 28:19, literal translation). This is based on the previous command to go and preach the gospel to every person. Here, Jesus added two additional aspects to the Great Commission. First, they were to disciple (imperative), which involves a command to get results. Second, they were to center on nations, *ethne,* "people groups." This concern with social groups has vast implications, on which we will focus later.

The fourth time the Lord repeated the Great Commission (Luke 24:46-48), He stated that the gospel message must include repentance and belief. The last reiteration was given the same day at the Ascension. This included the power of the Holy Spirit to indwell them and also the geographic scope: "Jerusalem...Judea and Samaria, and to the ends of the earth" (Acts 1:8).

The fifth time our Lord repeated the Great Commission, He was on the Mount of Olives, immediately before the Ascension. Here He included geographical development (i.e., Jerusalem, Judea, Samaria and the world).

Strategy in Matthew 28:19,20

When Jesus gave the Great Commission in Matthew 28:19,20, He included a strategy. The Church is to go to many nations or groups of people and evangelize them. This is best done by planting indigenous churches in which people can be saved, baptized and continually discipled in the Word of God. Having this in mind, Vergil Gerber concludes, "The ultimate evangelistic goal in the New Testament, therefore, is twofold: (1) to make responsible, reproducing Christians, (2) to make responsible, reproducing congregations."[1]

Matthew 28:19,20 states: "Go therefore and make disciples of all the nations [people groups], baptizing them in the name of the Father and of the Son and of the Holy Spirit, teaching them to observe all things that I have commanded you." This Great Commission includes church planting for the following reasons:

1. To "make disciples of" people in all nations is best fulfilled by an indigenous church in every culture.

THE GREAT COMMISSION					
	WHERE	WHEN	TO WHOM	WHAT	KEY
John 20:21	Upper Room, Jerusalem	Resurrection Day	10 disciples	I am sending you	Commission
Mark 16:15	Upper Room, Jerusalem	One week later	11 disciples	Go to all the world, preach to every person	Recipients
Matthew 28:19,20	Mountain in Galilee	At least two weeks later	11 disciples 500 brethren	Disciple all "peoples," then baptize and teach	Strategy
Luke 24:46-48	Jerusalem	Fortieth Day	11 disciples	Preach repentance and forgiveness of sins, based on resurrection of Christ	Content
Acts 1:8	Mount of Olives	Fortieth Day	11 disciples	Jerusalem to uttermost parts of earth	Geography

2. "Baptizing" identifies a new believer with Christ and with the church. Baptizing was the result of planting a church to carry on this process.

3. The focus of discipling is *ethne*—"nations"—which has three meanings: (1) ethnic groups, or people groups (cultural groups), (2) Gentiles and (3) nations. In each case, the target is not individuals but groups of people. The best means of evangelizing a group of people is through a ministering assembly of saved people—the church.

4. "Teaching them to observe all things that I have commanded you" means instructing believers to obey the words of Christ (including the Great Commission). This command was carried out in the New Testament church by teaching "the apostles' doctrine" (Acts 2:42). The continual teaching in the church became the basis of the church's growth and fellowship. When new areas were evangelized, the result was new churches that had new believers who had to be taught the words of Christ.

5. By illustration, the New Testament records stories of believers going everywhere establishing churches (9:31). Wherever the gospel was successfully presented, a church sprang into existence.

Beginning with the great dispersion of the Jerusalem believers (8:1), the disciples successfully multiplied congregations and planted additional churches. "New congregations were planted in every pagan center of the then-known world in less than four decades."[2] As the believers were scattered, so was the seed of the gospel that would take root in various national soils. In Acts 9:31 a geographic broadening had occurred, so believers were described in "churches throughout all Judea, Galilee, and Samaria" as directed in Acts 1:8. Based on the understanding of the 11 disciples and the success that resulted from their obedience, it is evident that planting local churches throughout the world is God's plan.

The dynamic church-planting efforts of the apostle Paul, Barnabas, Silas, Timothy, and others who were all early disciples verifies the concept of local church expansion to which Jesus Christ is committed. Surely they would have done no less than He commanded and no more than He empowered.

6. By analogy, each produces after its own kind, so a church sends out missionaries who will plant churches like those that sent them. Paul David notes:

From the day God said to Adam and Eve, "Be fruitful, multiply, replenish the earth," multiplication has been the secret of the growth of the human race, until this geometric progression has reached the staggering proportions of a population explosion.

Even when we grasp the simple fact that multiplication is the secret of the growth of the church, we need to ask—a multiplication of what? Not committees, not high offices, not even individual believers as such. We must apply our secret at the level of the local church. To start rapid growth by multiplication, we must encourage our own local church (be we pastor, layman, or missionary) to reproduce itself in another part of the city or in a neighboring town or village.[3]

Paul Engel and Wilbert Norton believe that one believer winning another is not enough. They state, "It is a demonstrated principle of church growth that Christianity gains in a society only to the extent that the number of existing churches is multiplied. Multiplication of new congregations of believers, then, is the normal and expected output of a healthy body."[4]

Several authors, including Weld, McGavran, Michael Green, Roland Allen and others, refer to the strategy that the apostle Paul used in his church-planting endeavors. The apostle Paul concentrated his efforts on cities, which were centers of communication, transportation and commerce. Paul planned to evangelize these areas by planting churches. He would often go to the synagogue and seek first to win his Jewish countrymen (Acts 13:5, Salamis; Acts 13:14, Pisidian Antioch; Acts 14:1, Iconium; Acts 17:1, Thessalonica; Acts 18:1,4, Corinth). Paul gained a hearing with the Jews who attended the synagogues, and later continued with the Gentile God-fearers who also had heard of him and his message. As Scripture indicates, before Paul reached Thessalonica, he had been practicing his plan for starting churches to the point where Acts 17:2 records, "Then Paul, *as his custom was*, went in to them, and for three Sabbaths reasoned with them from the Scriptures" (emphasis added).

Referring to the rapid and wide expansion of the Early Church, Roland Allen emphasizes "spontaneous expansion," although he does explain the issue of organization as well.

> The Church expanded simply by organizing these little groups of early disciples as they were converted, handing on to them the organization which she had received from her first founders. It was itself a unity composed for a multitude of little churches, any one of which could propagate itself, and consequently the reception of any new group of Christians was a simple matter. By a simple act the new group was brought into the unity of the Church, and equipped, as its predecessors had been equipped, not only with all the spiritual power and authority necessary for its own life as an organized unity, but also with all the authority needed to repeat the same process whenever one of its members might convert men in any new village or town.[5]

Donald McGavran, whose concern and interest was clearly multiplying new churches, believed the sequence of the Great Commission to "make disciples of all nations" precedes "teaching them to observe all things." McGavran argued:

> Only churches that exist can be perfected. Only babies who have been born can be educated. Only where practicing Christians form sizable minorities of their societies can they expect their presence seriously to influence the social, economic, and political structures. The Church must, indeed, "teach them all things," but first she must have at least some Christians and some congregations.[6]

Because the purpose of the Great Commission is finalized when a New Testament Church is planted, those church planters who establish a church are not doing something that is spectacular or overwhelmingly unique. They are simply carrying out the command of Jesus Christ. Church planters should not be thought of as divisive (sapping strength from existing churches) or selfish (wanting to control a church so they plant their own) nor independent (unwilling to take an existing pulpit). They should be thought of as those who are employing the most biblical methods to reach the developing areas of the world.

References: [1]Vergil Gerber, *God's Way to Keep a Church Going and Growing* (Ventura, Calif.: Regal Books, 1973), p. 18. [2]Ibid, p. 17. [3]Paul David, "Church Multiplication," *Church Growth Bulletin* 2, no. 1 (September 1965): 92. [4]James F. Engel and H. Wilbert Norton, *What's Gone Wrong with the Harvest? A Communication Strategy for the Church and World Evangelism* (Grand Rapids: Zondervan Publishing Company, 1975), pp. 143, 144. [5]Roland Allen, *The Spontaneous Expansion of the Church* (Grand Rapids: William B. Eerdmans, 1962), p. 143. [6]Donald A. McGavran, *Understanding Church Growth* (Grand Rapids: William B. Eerdmans, 1976), p. 359. Charles L. Chaney, *Church Planting at the End of the Twentieth Century* (Wheaton, Ill.: Tyndale House Publishers, Inc., 1986). See EXTENSION CHURCH GROWTH.

CHURCH-PLANTING MODELS

A new church can be established in at least six ways. Neighborhoods, people and church planters all differ from each other, hence, various methods can be employed to start a church. Each method works well in certain circumstances.

First, some churches start other churches by using a mother church approach. A mother church plants a daughter church when the congregation commissions a nucleus of seed members and sends them to another section of town to begin a new church.

A second method is to plant churches by first establishing a mission Sunday School or a preaching point. When attendance at the extension location grows sufficiently, it is then organized as a New Testament church.

A Bible study group is the third method of beginning a church. As people study the Word and are nurtured in the Scriptures, they sense a growing burden to organize into a New Testament church.

The fourth method of church planting is through local associations. This is a variation of the mother church model, but rather than one church contributing to the nucleus of seed members, several churches in an association of churches contribute members.

The fifth method used in getting a church started is through church splits. Church splits are often emotionally painful experiences for those who experience them, but they do result in new churches. In his study of church growth among Latin American Pentecostal churches, C. Peter Wagner concluded this was the means by which most new churches were started.

The sixth method of church planting centers around the pioneer church planter. This approach commissions an individual pastor or ministry team to a new community to find prospects, win souls and start a new church. The success of the new church depends upon the stature and influence of its pastor in this model.

Mother-daughter church planting. When the author organizes a new church, he normally gives the congregation several prayer goals. One challenge is that God would call some young person in the church to enter the ministry. This is in keeping with God's plan of reproduction. In the first chapter of Genesis, we read that plants and animals reproduce after their kind, each producing its unique fruit. Fruit bearing is a universal principle. The fruit of an oak is the acorn that gives birth to another oak. The fruit of a peach tree is a peach and its seed, which will produce another peach tree.

A technique of church planting grows out of the reproduction principle. It is each church producing another one. Just as a mother gives birth to a child, so a mother church gives birth to a new church.

Several denominational leaders urge their churches to take a more active part in church planting by the reproduction method. This is accomplished when the mother church commissions several families to start a new "daughter" church, usually in an area nearby that needs evangelizing. When this model is employed, the mother church often pays the church-planting pastor's salary and provides needed office space. Also, the members of the daughter church tend to utilize special services provided by the mother church until they can provide these services for themselves (e.g., a place to baptize, special children's programs, special music and so on).

The first step in starting a church this way is normally taken by the mother church. A survey of church families is done to determine where clusters of families may live. Next, a survey is conducted to determine the needy area for a new church. In connection with this survey, possible meeting places and church sites are also considered. It is advisable that a report be made to the mother church at this point and approval be given to take further action.

The strength of mothering a new church is that the outreach comes from the Christians of a church. After all, they are the church, and when they are willing to sacrifice themselves for the new church, it will have a better opportunity for success. The weakness is the failure of a person (church planter) who has the vision and burden to go to an area to bring the new church into being.

The group that goes out from the mother church would normally include a cross section of the church's membership. If mature Christians remain in the mother church, the new church will struggle with leadership if it depends on those won to Christ in the new area. On the other hand, if too many mature Christians leave, it could hinder the continued ministry of the mother church.

The new church group generally keeps its membership in the mother church until the new church is chartered. This way they have all the advantages of church membership. When people are saved in the new church, they become members of the mother church until the members are officially broken off into the daughter church. This sometimes solves the problem of people who are reluctant to join a new church for its lack of stability and permanence.

Often this method of church planting not only reaches the new area, it also serves to revive the mother church and to train its members. Most mother churches testify that the space left by those who transfer to the daughter church is soon filled by new members. Thus, two churches experience the benefits of this method and no one loses.

Advocates of this approach advise pastors that starting daughter churches should be a part of the long-range plan for every church's evangelism and missions program. Keeping this in mind, the area in which new churches are to be planted can be prepared several years in advance. A church may conduct a vacation Bible school or operate a Sunday School bus in the area. Also, Christians in the area may be organized for home Bible studies and/or prayer meetings.

Several churches in the decaying inner city have moved to the suburbs by this method. Instead of moving in one giant leap, the old church began a daughter church in a new area. Gradually, as the members moved to the suburbs, the daughter church got stronger. The pastor of the mother church alternated his preaching schedule to minister with more frequency to the daughter church. The mother church took on more ethnic/social ministry to those in its changing neighborhood. Although this illustration is not the same as reaching a new area by church planting, it follows many of the same principles.

Several problems confront this method of church planting, most of which relate to the mother church. Although most churches will agree to start a church in two or three years, they are sometimes reluctant to give up their tithing members when the specific starting date arrives. Also, some churches are unwilling to give their assets to the infant congregation. A third problem with the mother church is provincialism. Many churches fail to see the need to start a church on the other side of town. They may argue that the mother church would remain empty if several families started a new church, but normally the reverse is true. Both churches experience growth in attendance almost immediately.

A final problem involves the mentality of certain big churches. The mother church thinks it can better minister to the people by having better preaching, music, programs, services and so on.

The larger church wants to continue to grow and sees the daughter church as a threat to its progress.

This approach to church planting, however, is achieving results in many established cities. These are successful among those unlikely to attend the storefront mission in the poor part of town. Also, these churches are able to achieve a degree of financial stability after erecting attractive buildings within a few years. In large cities, where land and building prices prohibit building a large campus ministry, or a multicultural neighborhood hinders the growth of the church, the objectives of the church may be best accomplished through daughter churches. Many city churches have begun ethnic daughter churches, giving the daughter church use of their facilities for a Sunday afternoon service until the new church can build or buy its own facilities.

Mission Sunday School church planting. Using a mission Sunday School to plant a church is not a new technique. More than 61,000 Sunday Schools were established by Sunday School missionaries employed by the American Sunday School Union between 1829 and 1879 in a campaign called the Mississippi Valley Enterprise. Many of these Sunday Schools evolved into Methodist churches because of their evangelistic fire that covered the nation. A Sunday School mission is usually an evangelistic outreach where children and adults are brought together to be taught the Word of God in a systematic manner. The Sunday School mission is usually staffed by Christians from a nearby church, and the expenses (e.g., rent, printed materials and travel) are paid by the sponsoring church. If and when property is purchased, it is owned by the sponsoring church. The difference between a mission Sunday School and mothering a new church is that the mission Sunday School was not begun with the purpose of being an independent church.

Some large churches extend their ministries into other parts of the city or nearby communities by establishing missions. In some cases, these missions are established with the realization that they may never become established churches. Sometimes the population is too small in a rural community to support a church. In other areas, the population may be too transient, poor or uneducated to develop indigenous leadership. The people in the area need a ministry, but do not have enough stability to support a church and meet the obligation of supporting a pastor.

Leadership for these missions may come from

uing influence in the neighborhoods of the students and are identified as gospel assemblies by the lost people in their communities. A mission Sunday School has more stability than does a bus route. But Sunday School busing cannot be ruled out. Those who are transported to a larger

LOCAL CHURCH	MISSION SUNDAY SCHOOL
1. Self-Supporting Controls income and purchasing. 2. Self-Propagating Can reproduce itself. 3. Self-Governing Able to direct itself and is not controlled by outside influences.	1. Depends on sponsoring church. Property owned by sponsoring church. Offerings go to central treasury. 2. Ministry is led by Christians from sponsoring church. Mission people help in ministry. 3. Decisions for ministry and organization made by sponsoring church.

a variety of sources. Students preparing for ministry may serve these missions as part of their Christian service requirements. Some larger churches use their staff to preach in these mission churches. Some pastors train their laypeople for "pastoral ministry" in church missions.

Many churches are developing mission

church will usually be exposed to better and more extensive ministry.

Extension missions may be the wave of the future in establishing new churches and/or extending the ministry of larger churches. Several societal factors will contribute to the increased use of this approach.

EXTENSION MISSIONS	
Advantages 1. Stability through outside leadership. 2. Outside financing pays for what the mission could not otherwise afford. 3. Represents an effective tool to reach areas of a city for the church. 4. May be a biblical method.	Disadvantages 1. Members of the mission often do not accept responsibility for the work. 2. Many missions never become churches. 3. The nature of a mission keeps it from becoming self-supporting, self-governing and self-propagating. 4. The mission is often run by a board not involved in the work.

Sunday Schools in lieu of extensive bus routes. As busing has become increasingly expensive, workers also realize it is difficult to have a continuing influence on people who are transported a great distance from their neighborhoods. At the same time, mission Sunday Schools have contin-

First, advanced principles of administration and supervision will make it possible for a large church to give better guidance and support to outlying groups. Second, improved promotion in areas of Christian radio programs, telephone, mailings, advertising and printing will make it easier for the sponsoring church to communicate its "heart" and the direction for ministry to its outreach groups. Third, improved transportation will provide cars, buses, roads and mass transit to get gospel teams out to the areas away from the sponsoring church and to bring the masses back for special meetings. Fourth, money is available to finance the teams and to provide the facilities for outreach into surrounding communities. The fifth reason involves improved understanding of the role of the church and enlightened techniques of how churches are getting the job done. When pastors know what others are doing and how they get it done, they will follow their examples.

Pastors who want to build evangelistic churches are finding that there appear to be natural plateaus beyond which the church will not grow. These pastors are using extension works to reach new areas, extend their influence and continue their growth.

Some questions tend to be raised about this approach to church extension/planting. Is it consistent with the biblical teaching of local church autonomy? In Korea and South America, some churches have extension missions that themselves have more than 1,000 members. Is this consistent with biblical models of the Church?

The church at Jerusalem began with 120 men in the Upper Room (Acts 1:15) and later grew to approximately 5,000 men, plus wives and children. Then the numbers continued to grow larger. Josephus estimates that half of Jerusalem became Christians (about 100,000 believers). Common sense suggests they would gather in smaller groups for prayer, study and fellowship (Acts 12). They are called a multitude (singular). Later they are described as multitudes (plural). Some think they were divided into groups or multitudes for efficiency. Later, we know of the existence of house churches (Rom. 16:5; Phil. 1:2). This model may have also been utilized in Jerusalem.

Some have taught that the two Epistles to the Thessalonians were written to two separate sections of the church in that city. Paul's habit was to go and preach in the synagogue. Some synagogues were Christianized and at least one group in Thessalonica was predominantly Gentile (cf.

Rom. 16:4). The other Epistle may have been written to a separate Christianized synagogue that was more Jewish in nature. Hence, one church, but two gatherings in one city.

When Paul wrote the Epistle to the Romans, he addressed it "to all who are in Rome, beloved of God" (Rom. 1:7). He did not address it to the church at Rome, perhaps because more than one church was located there, or several assemblies of one church (i.e., the house-church motif, Rom. 16:5, 10,11,14,15).

The biblical argument for the geographical extended church is tentative, yet strong enough to forbid ruling out the idea of a church having several campus sites in one city. The growth of the Jerusalem/Judea church implies a church reaching a large geographic area, perhaps through extension missions. The Great Commission calling on the Church to make disciples of *pante ta ethne* may best be fulfilled by establishing ethnic missions. The use of both singular and plural forms of the word multitude(s) may suggest several large groups under one banner, as in the extension mission model. Smaller groups such as house churches may also have been extension missions. The existence of groups of Christians in Rome, Corinth and other places, along with such expressions as the Churches of Christ (i.e., Messianic Synagogues) and the Churches of the Gentiles (i.e., predominantly Gentile churches), may suggest the existence of socioeconomic or culturally based extension missions. Also, the term "elder" is plural in the New Testament, whereas the term "bishop" is singular. Many elders may have been responsible for extension ministries under the supervision of one bishop.

Bible study church planting. Many new churches have started from Bible study groups. A new church comes into existence through this means in several ways. First, church planters may go into an area and begin a Bible study in their homes or in neutral locations. Their long-range goal is to begin churches, but their immediate goals are to gather a nucleus of people, win them to the Lord and nurture them in the Word of God. In essence, Bible studies are halfway houses to churches. When the Bible studies are large enough, the church planters turn them into churches.

In the second case, a Bible study grows because it is meeting the needs of those who attend. Because of its natural attraction to people and the ministry to them, they call a pastor when they are large enough. Unlike the first illustration, they never intend to be a church. It just happens.

Some churches have strategically placed Bible study groups in certain neighborhoods to evangelize them. They were not begun by a church planter, nor are they intended to nurture Christians. They are usually led by a layperson who has a strong evangelistic thrust. They are accompanied by visitation, prayer for specific unsaved people and an ultimate desire to get them into the main church.

Beginning a church through a Bible study can have some liabilities. Sometimes the church planter is so cautious that he trusts his "flesh" and is afraid to be publicly committed to a new church. This lack of faith hinders the blessing of God. Also, the "first seed reference" principle determines that a church will grow in the way it was planted. If it is not planted with vision, it will not grow with vision. The Great Commission also implies that a church be planted, converts be baptized and then taught all things (Matt. 28:19,20). A Bible study usually teaches Bible content only, and neglects to teach the new convert the obligations of service in the church.

The home Bible-study group is a recent phenomenon in our nation. They may be known as cell-groups, the living-room church or the underground church. The home Bible study is an evangelistic technique that takes advantage of Americans' desire for dialogue and sharing. In a society of anonymity, people desire to share their problems and insight regarding the Word of God. Some are brought to a knowledge of Jesus Christ; others strengthened in their Christian lives. But most Bible study groups lack three qualities that have excluded them from becoming an aggressive New Testament Church.

First, a Bible study group usually lacks a leader committed to founding a church. The genius of a Bible study group is interaction — each person sharing insight from the Bible. Discussion, not a sermon, is the catalyst that makes it successful. Sometimes those in a Bible study group come from a variety of churches. At other times, group members may come from an unchurched background. Usually a dominant leader destroys the inherent nature of a Bible study.

Second, Bible study groups tend to lack commitment to church ordinances. The ordinances/sacraments of baptism and the Lord's Supper belong to the local church. Individuals should

STARTING A CHURCH FROM A BIBLE STUDY GROUP

Advantages	Disadvantages
1. Churches are started.	1. Slow process.
2. Converts are committed to the Bible.	2. Many Bible studies never become churches.
3. Trained leadership can be produced for the new church by laypeople who are involved in the Bible study.	3. A certain lack of faith by the leaders. They do not outwardly commit themselves to start a church.
4. Stability (financial and spiritual) can be built into the church.	4. Often Bible studies lack direction and evolve into doctrinal error.
5. Cases of church failure are eliminated.	5. People are attracted to a Bible study because of a doctrinal tangent.
6. No temporary meeting facilities are needed, as the Bible study meets in homes.	

not practice these ordinances, nor should a Bible study group, until it is constituted as a New Testament church. Even though a pastor gathers people to study the Bible, they should not practice the ordinances apart from a New Testament Church. When a group of Christians organize themselves according to the New Testament, they will want to obey the two commands that are foundational to the two church ordinances (Matt. 28:19; 1 Cor. 11:23-26). Because these are commands of our Lord, the Christian who does not join a church that observes the ordinances cannot be in the perfect will of God.

Finally, a Bible study group does not have an obligation to corporate ecclesia (the embryonic church) through mutual fellowship, attendance, financial support and numerical growth. Many people attend a Bible study group because of the personal enrichment they receive. Although this is a valid contribution to the cause of Christ, would these same Christians have experienced greater spiritual growth had they been more involved in a church where they accepted the responsibilities for ministry? When people accept the obligations of membership in a New Testament Church, they must financially support the group, understand its doctrines, support its services and be involved in Christian service through that church. People become better Christians by placing themselves under the disciplines of a church.

Denominational efforts to plant churches. In recent years, many pastors have seen value in cooperating to start new churches. To a greater or lesser degree, one purpose of a denomination is to start churches. In most established denominations, it is a matter of relying upon the home missions department to provide leadership in church planting.

The impetus for church planting in many denominations does not originate through existing local churches, but rather through a central agency. The members of the denomination's home missions committee usually represent ecclesiastical authority to plant new churches.

The work of church planting through denominations cannot be overlooked. In many respects, church planting by denominations is an asset. First, denominations maintain colleges and seminaries where men and women are trained, resulting in increased personnel to pastor existing churches and to plant new churches. Also, church loyalties to a denomination make raising money for church planting somewhat easier. Many groups have special funds to finance new churches at little or no interest. When a group of laypeople desire to begin a new church, they will often contact a denomination well known to them, thus providing a loyal group with which the church planters can build. Also, many land developers will negotiate church sites with major denominations before a community is planned, resulting in ideal community sites for the new church.

Church associations tend to stress administrative efficiency above grass-roots participation. Although a denomination attempts good stewardship of resources, a resultant side effect is often a decreased zeal and vision of the church. The independent pastor must have faith to supply financial needs and will depend on independent sources for them. The denominational church planter will also need faith to develop the new church, but will look to denominational help for financial resources.

Most denominations have a systematic strategy by which they start their churches. Of course, every church is different, but the general principles usually apply. When a denomination begins an outreach in a new town or section of a city, the following steps are usually followed: (1) select a missions committee, (2) select an area for a new work, (3) prepare sponsoring churches, (4) cultivate the field, (5) begin a mission fellowship, (6) organize a mission chapel, (7) arrange financing, (8) provide facilities, (9) organize the church.

The growth of a new church started by a denomination usually occurs in three phases. First, the mission fellowship is established. This will usually take on the form of a home Bible study or cottage prayer meeting. When an interested group is gathered, a missionary chapel is formed. The members of this chapel will be the charter members of the church. At this point, the church planter will raise money for the new church from sponsoring churches in the denominations. Also, the church planter will secure facilities for the new church to conduct its services. Plans will be made for the church to enter its third phase when the chapel is constituted into a church. Many denominations encourage the new church to call a recognition council so area churches affiliated with the denomination will be able to share in organizing the new church.

Planting a church from a split. Many new churches are started from a church split. As obnoxious as a church split may appear, at times God leads a group of people to leave their church and plant a new one. Certain advantages in beginning a new church with a group of people who have left another church include: (1) the church has a financial commitment, (2) the new church has a core of people, (3) the new church has committed and mature Christians, (4) the new group is closely knit around a cause and (5) emotional commitment results in loyalty. Starting a church from a split also has disadvantages, including: (1) inheriting a poor reputation in the community, (2) bitterness that may hinder the ministry, (3) churches being established for reasons other than evangelism, (4) inheriting problem people who will cause problems later and (5) strong opposition from the former church.

Can a congregation be split in a proper manner and bring glory to God? Because many Christians are opposed to church splits, they respond, "no!" Fights, arguments, court cases, name calling, ugly scenes and adverse news coverage that tend to accompany church splits do not help the cause of Christ. Most church splits arise over personality rather than doctrine. Because people often do not get along, they find an issue about which to split.

In spite of all the unfortunate church splits, God has used many of them to His glory. People have been brought to salvation who would not have been reached otherwise. Communities have been evangelized, colleges built, missionaries sent out and money raised that would never have come from a complacent, dead church.

The one basis on which churches should split is the "candlestick" (Rev. 1:20; 2:1,5, *KJV*). When a church is in danger of losing its existence, it should take measures that will return the candlestick to its original brilliance. It is the duty of the whole church to (1) preserve unity, (2) maintain correct doctrine, (3) practice holy living, (4) elect leaders to carry out the church's purpose and (5) exercise discipline. Each member is responsible for making sure the candlestick burns brightly. When it does not, the members should take biblical steps to put the church in order. If they cannot correct the problem, should they stay and submit, or leave? This is a difficult decision to make. If God removes His blessing from a church, it is time for the zealous believer to leave and affiliate with a church God is blessing. If no such church exists in the community, it may be time to begin a new church from the believing remnant within a dying church.

When a church split does occur, certain steps should be taken to minimize the negative fallout. First, keep issues centered on doctrine, not personality. Second, the motive to start a new church should be to fulfill the Great Commission. Also, a church split should follow the biblical pattern of dealing with grievances. Work hard at keeping your motives pure. Finally, do not win the battle and lose the war. Beware of earning a negative reputation that will hinder your ministry in the years to come.

The pioneering church planter. The sixth method of church planting is the pioneering method. This method depends upon the church planters who rise to the challenges of starting churches from scratch. This approach requires unique kinds of people who would start new churches. These people must be willing to swing hammers and negotiate loans. They must promote in the pulpits and advertise in the newspapers. They must preach, counsel, rebuke and teach the Bible. Pioneers must be able to do it all, for they usually begin with little if any help. They lead people to Christ, nurture them in the Scriptures, train them in service and inspire them to spiritual greatness.

These church planters are like self-made businesspeople. They are rugged individualists. In time, however, they change their role and self-perception. As others who have the gifts of leadership arise in their congregations, the roles of the pastors/pioneers change. They must share their work with deacons, work through superintendents, and work within the organizational structure they have established. They release authority to others without losing their influence as leaders.

Those who go out to begin new churches face insurmountable odds with limited resources in unlikely circumstances. They are motivated by the "impossible dream" and must accomplish the "unperformable task."

Choosing a Church-Planting Model

Although the Great Commission provides an indisputable biblical basis for church planting, it does not answer several crucial questions, including: (1) who should be directly involved in this aspect of evangelism and church growth and (2) how these new churches can be most effectively established. The silence of Scripture in speaking directly to these issues, together with the apparent use of various church-planting strategies by the apostles suggests the absence of a specific "best way" to start churches. Rather, certain church-planting models appear to be most effective in specific situations.

Several factors need to be considered in developing or adopting a particular model to establish a church in a community. These factors include: (1) the extent of denominational involvement in the project, (2) the community (target group) in which the new church is being established, (3) the nucleus of seed members for the new church and (4) other unique conditions that characterize the new church (i.e., denominational distinctives, a church split, significant conversion in a pagan community and so on). This article proposes to look at these factors as conditions to be considered in selecting church-planting models.

Extent of denominational involvement. Churches are started with varying degrees of denominational involvement. In some situations, the national director of church planting might target a significant city or several cities as places to begin new churches. This might also be done by the state director of evangelism or church planting. Usually, when the initiative to begin a new church originates at this level, the new church can be assured of better administration and funding than might otherwise be realized.

Most large denominations have an organizational structure that includes regional associations. Sometimes these associations are composed of all the churches in several counties. When many churches are located in an urban area, the churches in that city or some part of a city may form their own associations. Church planting is sometimes viewed as a function of the denomination. When denominations begin churches, various member churches may contribute funds and seed members to begin a new church. When a denomination begins a new church, it is likely to enjoy the support of other churches in the denomination and new members may be able to take advantage of services of a more specialized nature offered by the more established sponsoring churches (e.g., counseling services, Christian schools and so on).

The next level at which churches may be established is the local church level. Sometimes, churches started by a local church are unintentional (i.e., the result of friction within the church leading to a split). But many churches plan to start new churches in other parts of their community as a means of improving their evangelistic effectiveness. These new churches may be started to reach a distinct ethnic group not being reached by the mother church or to have a greater influence in a part of the city most distant from the church campus. Some churches that have voted to relocate to the suburbs have maintained their downtown property to begin an inner-city church.

Next, churches may begin at a grass-roots level, having little or no denominational involvement. These churches generally come into being by one of two ways. First, a church-planting pastor may become burdened for a town, claim it for Christ, move in and begin a church. Second, a group of families may move as a result of job transfers or for some other reason into a town that does not have a church where they can feel comfortable. In both cases, the impetus for starting the new church is at the very grass-roots level of the denomination.

Does it make any difference who starts a church? Sometimes a person's understanding of ecclesiology may influence the way that question is asked, but the question is asked in this context to determine the advantages of starting churches at various levels within a denomination. As noted on the following chart, an inverse relationship between administrative effectiveness and evangelistic zeal in starting churches appears to be present at various levels. Often, the more significant the involvement of the denomination in initiating a church-planting project, the better that new church is administered and funded. But projects begun by "head office" often lack "buy in" by individual church members. Churches begun at the grass-roots level of the denomination often realize a greater commitment to the church by the congregation, which generally translates into a greater willingness to become actively involved in the project.

Community types and church-planting models. A

grated multicultural churches will excel in reaching their communities. In contrast, if a particular ethnic group is dominant in a target community, serious consideration should be given to beginning an ethnic church.

This principle is obvious to most people when discussed in the context of race, ethnicity or language. But it is just as important in the context of economic status. Unionized factory workers tend to feel uncomfortable in churches where most members are doctors, lawyers and bankers. Likewise, corporate officers tend not to attend churches in mobile home parks. This is another aspect of a community's influence on the charac-

EVALUATING CHURCH-PLANTING EFFORTS INITIATED BY...	
National Denomination	BETTER ADMINISTRATION
State Convention	
Local Association	
Local Church	
Grass-roots Movement	GREATER COMMITMENT

second factor to be considered in selecting a church-planting model is the community in which the church is being established. Another article in this book discusses in greater detail the 12 basic community-church types as identified by Douglas Walwrath (See COMMUNITY CHURCH-GROWTH PARADIGMS). The Walwrath typologies suggest churches located in certain types of communities tend to be certain types of churches. Church planters need to recognize the limitations placed upon their church by the social structure of the target community.

The Walwrath church types are not the only aspect of the community to be considered in starting a church. The cultural and ethnic mosaic represented within the target community will also affect the character of the new church. According to the homogeneous unit principle, people like to become Christians without crossing cultural, racial or linguistic barriers. Few well-integrated multicultural communities are in existence in the world; therefore, few well-inte-

ter of a church and the church-planting model that should be utilized to establish new churches.

Nucleus of seed members in a new church. A third factor to consider in selecting a church-planting model is the unique character and gifting of any seed members that may form the nucleus of a new church. When a church begins with a nucleus of seed members, it already has an embryonic character. Also, the seed members, individually or corporately, may have preconceived ideas of how the church should be started. This will undoubtedly influence the church-planting model chosen to begin the new church.

The biblical teaching concerning spiritual gifts suggests several important principles to be considered in choosing a church-planting model. First, all Christians are uniquely gifted for ministry (1 Pet. 4:10). Second, God expects all Christians to use their giftedness in ministry (Rom. 12:6). Third, God has given every church all the gifts it needs to accomplish the ministry He wants that church to accomplish (1 Cor. 1:7).

Fourth, as a church uses the gifts it has in ministry, it will acquire other gifts, perhaps through those added to the church through evangelism or through the growth of giftedness in individual members (1 Cor. 12:31).

A person's spiritual gift may be viewed as an indicator of God's will for that Christian regarding ministry. So also the unique gift mix of a nucleus of seed members may be an indicator of the kind of ministry God intends for that church. By implication, this will also influence the church-planting model used to establish the church.

Other unique factors in determining a church-planting model. Other unique factors may also influence the choice of a particular church-planting model. A particular view of successionism held by some denominations may restrict the number of church-planting models that might be considered valid. Other denominations may have views about ordination that restrict who can begin a new church. In many older denominations, church-planting policies may have developed by precedent that have the weight of denominational distinctives. Innovative church-planting strategies may be rejected because they are viewed as inconsistent with the former practice of the denomination.

Perhaps the most effective means of church planting utilized by evangelical churches involves church splits. Nobody would advocate splitting churches to establish new ones, but in practice, church splits do occur. When they do happen, new churches are often started. The nature of a church split brings certain conditions into a new church that will influence the way it is begun. Often churches that begin as a result of a church split are characterized by an imbalance in their ministry, at least initially, while the church adjusts to its new status.

Yet another factor in church planting may be a significant number of conversions. In the early years of many new churches, the conversions of certain people are remembered as turning points in the ministry. The first conversion builds enthusiasm for greater evangelistic outreach. A similar response may be registered in a church when a rebellious teen or unsaved spouse is converted. Sometimes the conversion of a person who has a significant reputation in the community can mark a turning point in a church's ministry.

New churches can begin in a variety of ways. Specific church-planting strategies should not be viewed as superior or inferior, but rather as options that are most effective in certain situations. When choosing a particular strategy or church-planting model to begin a new church, the factors discussed in this article need to be considered. Only as all the data is gathered can a wise decision be made concerning the church-planting model that is likely to be most effective.

CITY GATES

Centers of political influence and authority. The place where new policies and official practices enter a community. —GOJR

CLASS, BEGINNING A NEW

The first step in beginning a new class is to find and recruit a teacher. Remember, you are looking for more than a person with teaching skills. You are looking for someone to lead the class. A spirit-filled Sunday School teacher can revitalize a class and ultimately a church.

The second step in beginning a new class is to get some seed members to help the new teacher get the class started. Sometimes seed members come from dividing a class. Do not divide a class too often because this tends to discourage members who rebuild their class only to be divided again. It is difficult to begin a new class with just a teacher. The teacher who goes into an empty room can become discouraged and quit. The teacher, however, who has a core of people to help build the class is less likely to get discouraged.

The biggest problem for some churches in beginning a new class is finding a room for the class. This problem is not insurmountable, even if you are already using the pastor's study and several halls and Sunday School buses in the parking lot. More and more Sunday School classes are meeting off campus than ever before. Classes are meeting in homes, schools, restaurants and many other nontraditional settings.

To begin new classes, leaders need to get others in the church to accept their existence. Expansion begins by accepting the goals and contributions of new classes, and then supporting them. If the new class is an open class, other teachers may view it as a threat to take away their members and to compete in recruiting potential members.

Next, expand the new class by appointing class officers to help in reaching others with the gospel. Finally, the ushers, secretaries and other administrators in the Sunday School will need to know of the existence of the new class and how it fits into the scheme of things.

Ultimately, beginning a new class will involve recruiting new people. The only way to build a church is through reaching new members, and many strategies and steps are involved in accomplishing that goal.

CLASS, LAW OF THE (SUNDAY SCHOOL CLASS)

The law of the class is one of the traditional laws of Sunday School growth, which states that one teaching center should be available for every 10 students. This does not mean one classroom, because three or more teaching centers may use the same room, especially among the smaller children's departments that use the activity teaching centers. The law of the class is a general statement that applies to the total Sunday School. Some adult classes will include 15 to 25 students; other children's classes will consist of 4 or 5 students.

CLASS SUNDAY SCHOOL

A Sunday School that has an average attendance of up to 100-150, so named because of its organizational structure based on individual classes and the tendency of these Sunday Schools to meet in a single room for opening exercises or opening worship.

CLASSES

Ruling bodies over the masses, distinguished by differences in income, language, housing, health, religion, authority and power.

Reference: See MASSES.

CLASSES OF WORKERS/LEADERS See LEADERSHIP CLASSES

CLASSIFICATIONS OF REVIVAL

The six major classifications of revival based on the apparent causal factors of that revival include: (R-1) revivals that may be a response to the discovery, comprehension and application of a particular doctrine; (R-2) revivals that may be led by a charismatic leader; (R-3) revivals that may be a response to a problematic condition; (R-4) revivals that may be a response to a revived core of believers; (R-5) revivals that may be attributed to interventional prayer; and (R-6) revivals that may be a response to "signs and wonders."

CLASSROOM, LAW OF THE

Educational space must be available for growth. Growing Sunday Schools must have classrooms if they continue to grow. But Christian educators differ in their conclusions regarding how much room must be available for Sunday School growth. The traditional laws call for 10 square feet for each student. Those who conduct an activity-centered Sunday School, however, must have 25 square feet for each pupil. The available space and building will to some degree dictate the approach to Sunday School teaching.

CLENCHED FIST, LAW OF THE

The law of the clenched fist is built on the law that pressure builds the body. That's why runners put pressure on their legs and lungs, to strengthen their bodies for the race. Weight lifters do the same thing. They pump iron (i.e., put pressure on their bodies to build them up).

Spiritual pressure (i.e., discipline) also builds the Body of Christ. A vision of reaching people puts pressure on church members. A goal of placing a Bible in every home in the area is pressure. A Sunday School campaign puts pressure on all to be included.

A person can keep the fist taut only so long, then the muscles give. Likewise, leaders can put pressure on their workers for only a short time. Just as when runners put too much pressure on their bodies, it can cause strokes; too much pressure on the Body of Christ builds up resentment or resignation in workers.

Too much exercise can lead to a heart attack or stroke in the physical body. In the spiritual body, it can lead to discouragement or other more serious problems that become counterproductive in the cause of Christ.

COLEMAN, ROBERT

Robert E. Coleman is Director of the School of World Mission and Evangelism, and Professor of Evangelism at Trinity Evangelical Divinity School in Deerfield, Illinois. He also directs the Institute of Evangelism at the Billy Graham Center in Wheaton, Illinois, and serves as dean of the International Schools of Evangelism.

Dr. Coleman is a founding member of the Lausanne Committee for World Evangelization, and a past president of the Academy for Evangelism in Theological Education. He is a graduate of Southwestern University, Asbury Theological Seminary, Princeton Theological Seminary, and received the Ph.D. from the University of Iowa.

Hundreds of articles and 21 books have come from his pen, including *The Master Plan of Evangelism* (Baker Book House, 1963; rev. ed. 1993; 2 million copies of this book have been sold), *Songs of Heaven* (Fleming H. Revell, 1980), *The Spark That Ignites* (World Wide Publications, 1989) and *The Coming World Revival* (Crossway Books, 1995). Translations of one or more of his books are published, or are in the process of publication, in more than 90 languages, and English editions alone approach 5 million copies in print.

COMMITMENT TO THE LAND

A position expounded by Rev. Bob Beckett, which maintains that personal commitment to a particular territory or community invariably precedes the release of spiritual insight into that community.—GOJR

COMMUNICANT MEMBERS

The nucleus or core of the church membership roll; those members who principally finance and support the church's ongoing ministry. They participate in the Lord's Supper or "communion."

COMMUNICATION: THE ROLE IN EVANGELISM

Evangelism is communicating the gospel to people at their point of greatest need (i.e., salvation).

The word "communicate" actually means "to have in common." When we communicate with a friend, the two of us have something in common.

God communicated to humans in many ways, but the greatest way was through Jesus Christ. Christianity is a relationship between God and humans, based on the life, death and resurrection of His Son Jesus Christ.

Every person who is saved has a living relationship to God.

Christians are expected to reach out in relationships to others. All people are potentially loners, but they can reach out of their shells for meaningful relationships when they have a full understanding of the relationship between God and themselves.

The Word of God is the basis of people's communication with God. The Bible is the communication of the gospel to people at their points of need. The gospel must be communicated so that people can understand it; its message must also be modeled in the lifestyle of a Christian. Thus, the seeker has a role-model with which to identify and may be motivated to receive Jesus Christ as Savior.

COMMUNION See LORD'S SUPPER

COMMUNITY CHURCH PARADIGMS

Church growth is related to various factors, not

the least of which is the makeup or character of the community in which the church is located. The church and people within that church form self-perceptions based on the location of the church. The nature of the community will also have an effect on the evangelistic strategy of the church. Social changes in the past 25 years have had an influence on both the growth and death of churches. Each community has its own unique strengths and weaknesses that influence the kind of churches located in that community. Unfortunately, pastors tend to transfer "ministry types" from their previous experiences, rather than adapting their ministry to their new church type. An understanding of church types will give direction in developing unique ministry strategies for various church types.

Effective pastor-leaders need to understand church growth from various perspectives. First, they need to know the eternal principles of the Word of God upon which all growth is based. Principles are eternal while methods change from culture to culture. Methods are the adaptation of eternal principles to changing cultures. Therefore, pastor-leaders also need to understand psychology, history and sociology if they are to understand how to apply the eternal principles of the Word of God to the specific communities in which they are located.

According to Douglas A. Walrath, a sociologist, a dozen distinct types of churches are in existence. These churches are located in various kinds of communities and have a variety of clientele they are seeking to serve. The following is a brief summary of what has become known as the Walrath Church Types.

Downtown Church
The downtown church is located in a business area away from residential development. Often it is the leading church in its denomination and crosses several socioeconomic lines. Characteristically, it does not have a high level of fellowship and is not growing. It is suffering from St. John's Syndrome and has become a monument to what once was. It usually has no parking and no neighborhood. This church is usually a liturgical church or an evangelistic church. It is usually pastored by someone gifted in shepherding

and helps, although it is sometimes led by a teacher or preacher.

Inner-City Church
The inner-city church is located in an area marked by institutional decay and deteriorating housing. Most of the homes in the area are owned by absentee landlords and rented to those experiencing social problems such as family breakup, drug abuse and unemployment. These problems mean that the people have a limited income and move often to escape creditors. The community is characterized by a spirit of resignation and residents have no real loyalty to the area. This church is usually suffering from what I call ethnikitis and people blindness. It is typically a sectarian storefront church and growth is difficult. The ministry of this church tends to be need oriented. Often it is a liturgical or shepherding church led by a pastor characterized as a bishop, shepherd servant and/or messenger.

Metropolitan Church
The metropolitan church draws from the total city and contains members from various socioeconomic groups in the city. The ministry tends to be led by a charismatic leader and a staff. It is well advertised and located near a major transportation route. It has a family ministry but is not neighborhood oriented. This church must give attention to leadership and communication to its clientele to continue to grow. It is need oriented and has a well-rounded program based on specific objectives. Members are very loyal to their church. This church is often characterized as an evangelistic church, renewal congregation or evangelical Bible church.

During the past 25 years, we have seen an explosion in the number of metropolitan churches in America. When the first list of the 100 largest churches in America was printed in 1967, only 97 churches in America averaged more than 1,000 in attendance. Today, thousands of churches are that large. They are largely the result of improved transportation and communications in our society. They tend to be led by a pastor who may be characterized as a bishop, teacher and/or messenger.

Outer-Urban Neighborhood

The outer-urban neighborhood church is located in a residential area that has many multifamily dwellings. Residents tend to be older and/or belong to distinct ethnic groups. The church is located near mass transportation and the neighborhood provides the usual conveniences. This church is afflicted with ethnikitis and is experiencing financial problems. The church membership crosses class lines. The church needs to expand its facilities but cannot afford the needed space. It is moving from a family-oriented church to a staff-led church. Many of these churches are single-cell churches having multicell aspirations. All kinds of ministries and philosophies of ministry are represented in this type of church.

City Suburban Church

The city suburban church is located in a mature suburban community that had formerly been affluent and is still considered prestigious. The church is breaking down as a homogeneous unit and is living on its former glory. It suffers from Ethnikitis and class conflict. It has begun to develop an emphasis on special groups within the church. Once again, all kinds of ministries and philosophies of ministry are represented in this type of church.

Suburban Church

The suburban church is located around the city in communities characterized by shopping centers, business centers, industrial parks and transportation routes that make transportation in the community more convenient. Communities tend to be made up of a single socioeconomic class. This is a church that can easily experience growth because it is a homogeneous unit. It tends to be a family-oriented church and should make use of both front- and side-door evangelism. The church may suffer from sociological strangulation. Each of the various church types and ministry philosophies may be represented in this church type.

Detached Suburban Church

The detached suburb is a middle to upper middle-class planned urban development set away from the city. These are sometimes called bedroom communities and are usually inhabited by younger to middle-age adults and their families. The church in this community has a high potential for growth because it is a homogeneous unit and land is available. The church tends to be future oriented and grows through networking evangelism. This kind of church may also have a problem with sociological strangulation. This church may represent each of the ministries and philosophies of pastoral ministry discussed in earlier articles.

Fringe Village Church

The fringe village was originally an independent town that has become overrun by city people seeking to escape the pace of city life. New residents tend not to attend the old churches and help them grow, but attend new churches. This kind of church tends to be a single-cell, family-oriented church and is experiencing difficulty in the area of growth.

Fringe Settlement Church

The fringe settlement is an area that lacks proper zoning bylaws and planned development. The community includes a mix of various kinds of housing, businesses, ethnic groupings and economic classes. Growth in the church tends to be unpredictable and based on the leadership of the church. These churches tend to be liturgical, congregational or Baptist, renewal or evangelistic churches.

Independent Town Church

The independent town is an older community that has limited newer development, but does not have restrictive zoning policies. The town is characterized by little mobility, settled values and longtime relationships. Because of this, the growth prospects for the church are unpredictable. Growth tends to be based on leadership. The church is a family- and fellowship-oriented institution. These churches tend to be liturgical, congregational or Baptist, evangelistic, renewal or Bible churches.

Rural Village Church

This is a region that has no zoning, few services

and no mobility among the residents. The village church tends to be family oriented and is unlikely to be a multi-cell church. Growth is unpredictable. Growth is dependent upon the dynamics of the leader, but the kind of leaders that could produce growth tend to gravitate to the larger population centers. These churches tend to be liturgical, congregational or Baptist and renewal congregations. The pastor of these churches tends to be a shepherd, preacher, teacher or servant.

Rural Settlement Church

The rural settlement tends to be a lot like the

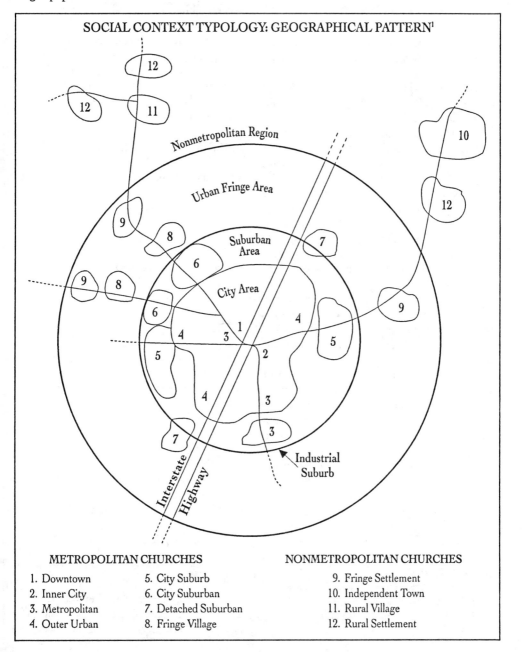

SOCIAL CONTEXT TYPOLOGY: GEOGRAPHICAL PATTERN[1]

METROPOLITAN CHURCHES		NONMETROPOLITAN CHURCHES	
1. Downtown	5. City Suburb	9. Fringe Settlement	
2. Inner City	6. City Suburban	10. Independent Town	
3. Metropolitan	7. Detached Suburban	11. Rural Village	
4. Outer Urban	8. Fringe Village	12. Rural Settlement	

rural village but has less to offer in terms of services and has a lower standard of housing. The prognosis for this church is much the same as that of the village church. Often this church has a bivocational pastor or is one of several churches pastored by the same pastor. The pastor is often a shepherd or servant.

Summary and Conclusions
Growth can occur any place, anytime and in any circumstances. A pastor must know the possibilities and principles for growth in each church typology to develop an effective program of evangelism and ministry. All pastors have subconscious "church typologies" that influence their values, expectations and ministries. When pastors minister in churches that correspond to their subconscious expectations, they can have successful growth.

The problem is that many pastors assume the leadership of churches that are different from their subconscious expectations and previous experiences. When this occurs, they experience culture shocks. If they are accepted by the churches, even though recognized as outsiders, they can adapt and cause growth. If they are perceived as outsiders and are rejected, growth will be difficult, if not impossible. That rejection will be felt by both the pastors and their families. The conflict will reflect the pioneer-settler struggle in church growth.

A knowledge of the science of church growth will help pastors overcome barriers to growth. Because growth is both spiritual and natural, their spiritual ministries can become the basis for numerical growth. Before pastors accept pastorates of church types that are different from their experiences, they should study that particular church typology, consider its effects on their families, and consider their own track records. Only then do they have the basis to make intelligent decisions in these matters.

Reference: [1]Chart adapted by the author from "Social Change and Local Churches, 1951-75" by Douglas A. Walrath in *Understanding Church Growth and Decline, 1950-1978*, ed. by Dean R. Huge and David A. Roozen.

COMPOSITE MEMBERSHIP
A statistic used by church-growth researchers to represent a comprehensive view of church health and growth.

How to Determine Your Composite Membership
To determine your church's composite membership, use the following equation: Church membership at end of year + average Sunday School attendance over 52 Sundays + average Sunday worship attendance over 52 Sundays ÷ 3 = _____. The final answer is read directly as the composite membership figure.

CONDITIONS OF PAIN
A primary form of social bondage that involves suffering associated with injustice, poverty, violence and disease. — GOJR

CONFESSION
The new Christian publicly acknowledges salvation, or a Christian acknowledges error or sin to God.

CONFLUENT EVENTS
External historical influences such as immigration, war and natural disasters that flow into and profoundly affect the life of a community. — GOJR

CONGLOMERATE CONGREGATION
A multicultural local church characterized by a membership representing various ethnic, linguistic and educational backgrounds.

Reference: See HOMOGENEOUS UNIT.

CONGREGATION
A secondary grouping within the infrastructure of a local church sometimes called a fellowship group or fellowship circle. A congregation represents a

group of approximately 35 to 80 (some expand it from 40 to 120) believers who have a primary social function of fellowship and the secondary functions of Bible study and Christian growth.

CONGREGATIONAL STRUCTURE
See MODALITY.

CONSCIENCE

The inner agent that makes a person aware of the morality of his or her desires or actions.

CONSTITUTION, CHURCH

The constitution is a foundational governing document of a church and its related ministries. The provisions of some church constitutions are necessarily restrictive and tend to hinder church growth. Others fail to provide the necessary checks and balances to encourage good administration in a growing church.

Sample Church Constitution

PREAMBLE
We, the members of *(your church name here)*, in orderly manner do hereby establish the following principles by which we mutually agree to be governed in the affairs of our church.

ARTICLE I – NAME
This church shall be known as the *(your church name here)* of *(your city, state)*.

ARTICLE II – PURPOSE
This church shall have as its purpose the evangelism of the lost, the promotion of the historic Christian faith, the worship of God, the education of its members, friends and their families, and such other purposes as are specified in the Holy Bible for a New Testament Church.

ARTICLE III – STATEMENT OF FAITH
This church holds the following Statement of Faith as being a summary of Christian doctrine whose authority consists only in its agreement with the Word of God.

(insert here your denominational doctrinal statement or a statement reflecting your doctrinal views)

ARTICLE IV – COVENANT
(insert here your church covenant - see article on COVENANT)

ARTICLE V – CHURCH MEMBERSHIP
The membership of this church shall consist of persons who have accepted Jesus Christ as personal Savior and have been baptized by immersion into this church or a church of like faith and order. The membership reserves the exclusive right to determine who shall be a member. New members may be accepted by vote of the membership when requesting membership in any of the following ways:

1. By profession of faith and baptism.
2. By letter from a church of like faith and order.
3. By statement of faith, having been scripturally baptized by another church of like faith and order.
4. By restoration.

Membership can be terminated by:

1. Death
2. Dismission to a church of like-faith and order.
3. Discipline
4. The request of the members.

ARTICLE VI – CHURCH OFFICERS
1. Pastor:
The pastor is the undershepherd of Jesus Christ, the leader of the church, and is primarily responsible to Christ for the work of the church. The pastor is the chief executive and administrative officer of the church in spiritual and physical matters. The pastor is to be called to the church to serve indefinitely.

When the church comes to be without a pastor, the deacons will serve as a pulpit committee to seek out a new pastor. They shall prayerfully search until agreed on one candidate to recommend to the church. The church will be given the opportunity to vote within one week of the (name of church board) recommendations to call the candidate as pastor. A two-thirds majority vote is required to call a pastor.

The pastor may be removed from office at a special business meeting of the congregation called by the (name of church board) where reasons for removal would be presented, and would be allowed to answer the accusations, and a vote would be taken. The pastor should be notified of the meeting and of the charges to be brought against him or her before notice of the meeting is given to the congregation. A two-thirds majority vote would be required to remove the pastor. This step should be taken very carefully and prayerfully.

2. Church Staff:

The pastor may bring in such staff as he or she feels are necessary to assist in providing for the church. The staff will be employed at a salary agreed on by the (name of appropriate committee) and will work under the direct supervision of the pastor, or indirectly under him or her and directly under the supervision of a staff member appointed by the pastor.

3. Deacons:

(Name of church board) is to advise and assist the pastor in the spiritual interests of the church; seek out, visit and minister to the physical, moral and spiritual needs of the sick, aged and other necessities among the membership; review the church membership at least once a year and inquire about the regularity and faithfulness of the members in attendance and support of the church; serve at the Lord's Supper Table; and be zealous to guard and promote a spirit of unity and peace within the church. Deacons will act as a sounding board between the congregation and the pastor and shall discuss matters of importance to the church.

Deacons are to meet the spiritual qualifications given in 1 Timothy 3:8-13 and Acts 6:1-6.

The first (name of members of church board) will be recommended to the church by the pastor; thereafter the deacons shall recommend to the church names of those to be added. The church shall vote on each name presented.

4. Trustees:

The trustees will hold in trust the church property, serve as a financial advisory committee for the pastor and maintain the church insurance program. Trustees have no power to buy, sell, mortgage, lease or transfer any property without a specific vote of the church authorizing each action. They shall sign legal papers as needed and directed by the church. They shall be elected by the church to serve an indefinite term of office.

5. Treasurer:

The treasurer shall see that accurate records are maintained for all receipts, disbursements and individual contributions. The treasurer will be one of the cosigners on the checks. The budget shall be prepared under the supervision of the pastor with assistance from the treasurer and a financial committee if elected. The budget is then approved by the congregation at the annual meeting. The treasurer is responsible for investing the funds for the ministry of the church. All disbursements are to be made according to the budget as approved by the church. The treasurer is to provide a monthly financial report to the church. The treasurer is to be appointed by the pastor subject to approval by the (name of church board) and trustees.

6. Others:

Other officers of the church and/or its related ministries may be elected or appointed as they are needed.

7. Standards for Leaders:

All elected or appointed leaders of this church and/or any of its related ministries shall be saved, active members of the church and in agreement with the doctrinal position of the church, tithers, soul winners, loyal to the pastor and living a separated Christian life.

ARTICLE VII – CHURCH MEETINGS
1. For Worship and Study:

The church shall conduct regular services on

Sundays as well as a midweek meeting, and meetings of organizations as needed. Special meetings such as revivals, conferences and music programs will also be held from time to time as the pastor sees a need.

2. For Business:
The church shall meet for an annual business meeting. At this meeting, officers shall report to the church the activities of the previous year, new officers shall be elected, and any other business shall be presented to the church. In addition, special meetings may be called by the pastor and/or (name of church board) by giving seven days' notice to the church. The purpose of the special meeting must be announced. A majority of those present and qualified to vote may conduct any church business.

ARTICLE VIII — CHURCH GOVERNMENT
Each member of the church will have an equal voice in its government, exercised through a vote at regularly called business meetings. If the church is without a pastor, the chairman of the board will serve as moderator. The church will vote on the pastor, the chairman of the deacons and trustees; establishment or modification of major policies; the buying, selling or mortgaging of church properties; and the annual church budget. Meetings are to be conducted in accordance with Robert's Rules of Order. Matters of lesser importance will be handled by the pastor and staff, deacons and trustees within their prescribed responsibilities.

ARTICLE IX - RELATION TO OTHER CHURCHES
This church shall be fully autonomous in the government of its own affairs, exercising and retaining sole and complete control of all property that shall be held in its name by the trustees. Fellowship and cooperation will be sought with all true believers and congregations, but control of this church and/or its property will never be surrendered.

ARTICLE X - CHURCH FINANCES
The fiscal year shall be from January 1 through December 31. The members shall be expected to give their tithes and offerings through this church. The treasurer shall keep proper records, including a record of individual contributions. A budget shall be prepared by the pastor and trustees and approved by the church. Special offerings may be requested with the approval of the pastor and/or the trustees.

ARTICLE XI - DISSOLUTION
No part of the property or other buildings of this church shall ever inure to the benefit of any donor, member or officer of the church or any individual. If for any reason the church is dissolved, all assets shall be distributed equally to organizations selected by the church and recognized as charitable in nature by the Internal Revenue Service.

ARTICLE XII - AMENDMENTS TO CONSTITUTION
This constitution may be amended by a two-thirds majority vote of members present at a called business meeting announced for that purpose.

CONTEXTUAL FACTORS
National or local forces operating externally to the church and influencing it. Sociological factors of growth beyond the control of the church.

Reference: See INSTITUTIONAL FACTORS.

CONTOURING EVENTS
Internal historical events such as elections and town meetings that determine the direction of community character and policy. —GOJR

CONVERSION
A voluntary and instantaneous transformation in the personality of the sinner in which he or she turns from sin (repentance) and exercises saving faith in God. Genuine conversions have several distinctive marks. First, conversion involves a change in the personality of the sinner

and therefore should be evident to others who recognize that change. Second, conversion is voluntary and cannot be coerced against the will of the individual being converted. Third, conversions are instantaneous in that normally a point of conversion occurs within a broader conversion process in which a decision is made that effects a change. Fourth, conversion is an individual experience rather than a corporate experience. Where large numbers of people are converted in a people movement, those conversions represent individual decisions to repent and have faith in God although those several decisions may be made interdependently. Finally, conversion has both a positive and a negative element. Conversion is a positive experience in that it involves the exercise of saving faith. Conversion is a negative experience in that it involves repentance of sin and its various expressions in a person's life.

Individual conversion means evangelizing one person at a time in individual counseling time. Multi-individual conversion involves many people participating in the act, although each individual makes up his or her mind, debates with others and decides to either accept or reject Christianity. Mutually interdependent conversions occur when all those making the decision are intimately known to each other and take the step in view of what the other is going to do.

References: James Douglas John Porter, "An Analysis of Evangelical Revivals with Suggestions for Encouraging and Maximizing the Effects of an Outpouring of the Holy Spirit in Evangelism" (D. Min. Dissertation, Liberty Baptist Seminary, 1991), pp. 137-173; Elmer L. Towns, *What the Faith Is All About* (Wheaton, Ill.: Tyndale House Publishers, 1983), pp. 291-296.

CONVERSION CHURCH GROWTH

A measured numerical increase in church attendance and/or membership resulting from effective evangelistic efforts that result in unsaved members of the community being converted to faith in Christ and incorporated into the life of the church.

CONVERSION: DOCTRINE OF

The religious experience the Bible describes as conversion results in a change in the lifestyle of the convert. As a young woman was attempting to join Charles Spurgeon's church in London one day, she was asked, "What makes you think you have become a Christian?"

Not understanding the related Bible doctrines of conversion and regeneration, she simply responded, "Because now I sweep under the doormat!"

During the Welsh Revival among the coal miners of that land, the change in the lives of the men was so dramatic that the animals in the mines refused to obey them. The miners had formerly cursed and abused them to make them work. The animals were not trained to respond to kind language. Similar to the caterpillar emerging from a cocoon as a beautiful butterfly, so the person who experiences conversion emerges a "new creation" (2 Cor. 5:17).

People have various ideas about conversion. Fortunately, we are not bound to the ideas and opinions of others. The Bible describes the doctrine of conversion and what can be expected, and gives detailed examples of how people come to know God in the Scriptures.

The apostle Paul described the conversion experience of the Romans: "You obeyed from the heart that form of doctrine to which you were delivered" (Rom. 6:17). Conversion does not involve just learning a catechism or knowing the doctrine of Christ. It embraces that total person, which means conversion is related to all three powers of a person: the intellect, the emotions and the will. A person must know certain things to experience conversion, but a knowledge of these facts alone will not save him or her. Although conversion involves the emotions, it is far more than an emotional experience. Conversion is not complete until an act of the will has occurred, but an act of the will is not enough to save if it is done in ignorance or without a heart desire.

The intellect. The conversion of a person to Christ is different from a conversion to another religion or commercial product. Though many have tried, conversion cannot be passed off as a mere psychological phenomenon.

To be saved, a person must know the gospel. There is only one gospel (Gal. 1:9), but it contains two sides of the same truth. Just as a door has two sides, so the gospel is propositional and personal truth. The gospel is propositional truth, which means its formula is accurate. The gospel is the account of Christ's death for our sins and His burial, and His resurrection from the dead on the third day (1 Cor. 15:1-4). Only Jesus could provide for our salvation. "But God demonstrates His own love toward us, in that while we were still sinners, Christ died for us" (Rom. 5:8).

A second aspect of this gospel is personal truth. When Paul came to Corinth to preach his gospel he "determined not to know anything among you except Jesus Christ and Him crucified" (1 Cor. 2:2). The gospel is not complete in its presentation until it focuses attention on the person of Christ. Jesus said, "As Moses lifted up the serpent in the wilderness, even so must the Son of Man be lifted up, that whoever believes in Him should not perish but have eternal life" (John 3:14,15). If a person does not trust in Christ, that person is not saved. It is important that we know both the content (doctrine) and the person (Jesus Christ) of the gospel to be converted.

The emotions. Many religious groups place too much emphasis on a person's emotions and create what is known as a "psychological conversion" to their particular religious sect. In reaction to this, some conservative Christians have attempted to deny their emotions completely. Neither emphasis is correct. God made humans complete with an emotional capacity. If kept in proper perspective, emotions lead to a sound conversion. The abuse of emotions by some radicals should not cause us to abandon that which is good. A person will be emotionally affected by his or her conversion by either a cause or an effect experience.

The apostle Paul rejoiced "not that you were made sorry, but that your sorrow led to repentance. For you were made sorry in a godly manner,...For godly sorrow produces repentance leading to salvation, not to be regretted; but the sorrow of the world produces death" (2 Cor. 7:9,10). Paul recognized two kinds of emotional

reactions to the gospel: "godly sorrow" and "sorrow of the world." "Godly sorrow" has a place in our lives that leads to further spiritual insight. The "sorrow of the world" is remorse for getting caught, not sorrow for the act committed.

Sometimes God will allow a person to experience guilt so the forgiveness of sin can be understood and appreciated. Often God must use people's emotions to cause them to respond to the gospel. On other occasions, God will use people's emotional reactions so He can better deal with them after salvation. When Philip preached the gospel in Samaria and many people were saved, the Bible records "there was great joy in that city" (Acts 8:8). The apostle Paul expected his converts to continue to respond emotionally to God. He told the Philippians, "Rejoice in the Lord always. Again I will say, rejoice!" (Phil. 4:4). It is all right to get excited about our relationship with Christ.

Each person has a different way of expressing emotions, depending upon age, sex, background and a host of other unique experiences that make us who we are. Sometimes we tend to think the person who shouts and jumps for joy or a person who cries loudly is more emotionally involved in a situation than the person who sits apparently oblivious to what is happening around him or her. A person is not more or less saved depending upon the volume of emotional outburst, but when converted, it will affect the person's emotions.

The will. God created humans with wills to choose to respond or reject the work of God in their lives. Even then, the Lord works within the individual and, "no one can say that Jesus is Lord except by the Holy Spirit" (1 Cor. 12:3). To be converted, people must respond. This does not mean they save themselves. "For by grace you have been saved through faith, and that not of yourselves; it is the gift of God, not of works, lest anyone should boast" (Eph. 2:8,9). Although "Salvation is of the Lord" (Jon. 2:9) and we do not earn our salvation, God does tell us to receive it (John 1:12).

When Christians are baptized, they are illustrating a twofold symbol. First, it is a symbol of redemption, how Christ died for their sins, was buried, and on the third day rose again from the dead (Rom. 6:4; 1 Cor. 5:1-4). Second, baptism is a symbol of regeneration. Candidates being baptized are saying they have personally trusted Christ as Savior and a supernatural change has taken place in their lives (Gal. 2:20).

God is in the life-changing business. He takes the broken pieces of our lives and makes new vessels. Someone has said God takes the canvas of our lives when the colors are running and blurring, then paints a masterpiece. As powerful as God is, He chooses to limit His power to what the Christian will allow Him to do.

CONVICTION

The Holy Spirit works in sinners' hearts to make them aware of their sin, that Jesus is God's standard of righteousness, and that Christ's death on the cross paid the judgment for sin.

CORPORATE SIN

Group rebellion against God's law and purposes that typically results in corollary injury to a particular person or group. The offending collective may be a family, clan, tribe, neighborhood, city, nation or church.—GOJR

COVENANT, CHURCH

A statement of mutual commitment to work together toward achieving a common goal. A document used by churches to express their commitment to one another and the ministry of their church.

Sample Church Covenant

As a bond of unity among us, *(your church name here)* accepts for its members the following covenant.

Having been led by the Holy Spirit to receive the Lord Jesus Christ as our Savior and on profession of our faith in Him, having been baptized in the name of the Father, and of the Son, and of the Holy Spirit, we do now most solemnly and joyfully enter into covenant with one another as one Body in Christ.

We promise that we will watch over and counsel one another in the spirit of brotherly love, that we will remember one another in our prayers, and that we will aid each other in sickness and distress.

We further agree, by the aid of the Holy Spirit, to walk together in Christian love; to strive for the advancement of this church in knowledge, holiness and comfort; to promote its prosperity and spirituality; to sustain its worship, ordinances, discipline and doctrines; to give it a sacred pre-eminence over all institutions of human origin; and to contribute cheerfully and regularly to the support of the ministry, the expenses of the church, the relief of the poor and the spread of the gospel through all nations.

We further covenant to maintain family and private devotions; to religiously educate our children; to seek the salvation of our kindred and acquaintances; to live carefully in this present world; to be just in our dealings, faithful in our engagements and exemplary in our deportment; to avoid all tattling, backbiting and excessive anger; to abstain from everything that will cause our brother or sister to stumble or that will bring reproach upon the cause of Christ; and to strive to grow in the grace and knowledge of our Lord and Savior, that amidst evil and good report we will humbly and earnestly seek to live to the honor and glory of Him who loved us and gave Himself for us.

We moreover engage that when we remove from this place we will, as soon as possible, unite with some other church where we can carry out the spirit of this covenant and the principles of God's Word.

Reference: *Getting a Church Started* (Lynchburg, Va.: Church Growth Institute, 1985), appendix.

CROSS-CULTURAL EVANGELISM

A strategy of evangelism that communicates the gospel to peoples characterized as having significant cultural, racial, social or linguistic differences from those of the evangelist.

The expression that is widely used to describe

contemporary missionary work is "cross-cultural evangelism." Originally, this phrase was coined to describe evangelism that crossed cultural, ethnic and linguistic barriers. More recently, however, the term has been used to identify evangelistic activities that target reaching specific subcultures (i.e., people groups that may or may not fit into a former understanding of a distinct culture). For instance, an American missionary who lives among an unreached tribe in the South American jungle attempting to translate the Bible into a tribal language is engaged in cross-cultural evangelism. But in a broader understanding, the successful Chinese-American businessperson who travels to a Navajo Indian reservation to help establish a church in their mutual state is also engaged in cross-cultural evangelism.

The American melting pot contains many distinct cultures and subcultures. Some of these groups are described as "unreached people groups." This term designates those groups that have a distinct culture in which no Christian church is established. The hippies who gathered in California during the 1960s were a distinct subculture within American society and they could have been described as an unreached people group until the Jesus People became popular. To reach the flower children, this largely evangelical group used a strategy that was foreign to many established evangelical groups. They were successful only to the extent that they took the eternal principles of God and adapted them to the specific culture of their target group.

Reference: See BRIDGING GROWTH.

CRUSADE EVANGELISM

A strategy of evangelism designed to reach the masses through the dynamic public ministry of an effective evangelist. Normally, an evangelistic crusade is composed of a series of meetings in which the evangelist proclaims the gospel and urges listeners to respond during a public invitation. Follow-up of those converted is normally conducted by the sponsoring church or churches. It is a "Billy Graham" approach to evangelism.

CULTS, EVANGELIZING PEOPLE IN

Recent decades have witnessed a plethora of quasi-Christian cults. Specific insights can aid in the personal witness of a believer to someone ensnared in a cult. Cults are effective in luring people because of the cult's authoritarianism (many people will take any answer as long as it is given with authority), their use of such personal terms as "family, brother or sister," their idealism and their emphasis on experience.

A cult is usually a religious group within the broad spectrum of Christianity, and has has one or a few doctrinal tenets that are considered unorthodox or spurious when compared with historic Christianity. It tends to keep its members inclusive in fellowship and exclude others who reject its unique standards.

The following are some general principles to assist a Christian's witness to a cultist:

- Know what you believe—a Christian grounded in the basic tenets of Christianity will be much more effective in explaining the distinctives of the faith.
- Know what they believe—particularly if you have opportunities to share with several persons in one cult or to develop a long-term relationship with one person. Knowing what they believe will help you (a) accurately describe their views, (b) demonstrate your interest in them by studying their beliefs, (c) point out differences between Christianity and their beliefs.

Specific guidelines include the following:

- Treat people as courteously as possible—do not attack them.
- Try not to argue, but do try to dominate the conversation.
- Share your own experience of conversion—many people in cults come from nominal Christian backgrounds and are simply looking for a real living faith.
- Do not attack their leaders initially—after all, if people began to share their beliefs with you by attacking Jesus, you probably would not be interested in their messages.

When a relationship is established, however, do show the superiority of Christ over any other religious figure.

- Clearly explain the gospel, especially emphasizing sin and the need of a Savior.
- End any witness experience with prayer.
- Finally, pray without ceasing. People involved in cults can and are reached for Christ, but it generally takes time, genuine concern and much prayer.

Paul's sermon on Mars Hill in Acts 17 is considered by many to be a good example to use in witnessing to persons in cults or other religions.

1. Paul approached his audience as people genuinely seek God (Acts 17:22,23a). The *King James Version* translates the term meaning "religious" as "superstitious." Paul is actually acknowledging the religious commitment of the people.
2. After this courteous acknowledgment, Paul then suggested the ineffectiveness of their search (vv. 23b-28). Note that he was familiar with their views.
3. Paul then moved to the gospel and clearly proclaimed the resurrection of Jesus (vv. 29-31).—ALR

CULTURAL CHAUVINISM

The attitude of some people that those of another culture would be better off if they abandoned their cultural traditions and were assimilated into the dominant culture. It is a form of racism.

CULTURAL MANDATE

The biblical foundation for Christian ministry that is primarily concerned with meeting the social needs of people, expressed in the injunction to love your neighbor as yourself.

CULTURAL OVERHANG

The tendency to impose aspects of personal cultural expression of his or her faith upon people of another culture. The extent to which the cross-cultural missionary is unable to totally shed his or her original culture.

CULTURE

The learned set of values and behavior patterns that are mutually understood and accepted by a significantly large social group.

CULTURE AND ASSIMILATION FACTORS

Two sets of symbols measuring rates and degrees of assimilation of minority groups living in nations that have an open society allowing cultural mobility. The relative rate of assimilation is indicated by A-1, A-2 and A-3, A-1 being the slowest assimilators and A-3 the most rapid. The relative degree of assimilation is indicated by C-1, C-2 and C-3, C-1 being least assimilation (nuclear ethnics) and C-3 being virtually complete assimilation into the second (usually dominant) culture.

DATA OVERLAYS

Information display sets that are superimposed on maps or time lines for the purpose of analysis. —GOJR

DATA SETS

A grouping of related information. Data sets represent a specific part of, or perspective on, a larger problem or entity. In spiritual mapping research, useful data sets may include such things as community crime statistics and/or spiritual quest sites. —GOJR

DAWN See DISCIPLING A WHOLE NATION

DEATH, CHURCH

The opposite of biological church growth. A decline in membership associated with the death of members. The church dies when it ceases to minister and conduct services.

DECADAL GROWTH RATE (DGR)

The net increase in church membership and/or attendance over a 10-year period. This statistic is usually expressed as a percentage of decadal growth.

How to Determine Your Decadal Growth Rate

To calculate your decadal growth rate, gather statistical data for the beginning and end of a 10-year period and insert that data into the following formula: the later membership/attendance figure, minus the earlier membership/attendance figure x 100 = DGR. Your DGR is expressed as a percentage of decadal growth.

DECLINE IN ATTENDANCE

The opposite of numerical church growth is declining attendance. Sometimes church attendance declines because of factors beyond the control of the church. The first of these is the death of members/attenders. Next, when an area mine or factory closes, church members move to other communities to find work. Even in good economic times, church members may be transferred to other communities. Periodic declines in attendance may be the norm in churches that have a large white-collar or military population. But other declines in attendance are the direct result of conditions over which a church has significant control. Based on his study of America's fastest growing churches, the author suggests the following observations.

Neglected evangelism. Consistently growing churches place a high priority on evangelism, often defining their mission in the context of the Great Commission. Those churches usually have an aggressive evangelistic approach. Some, like the Southern Baptists, do much of their evangelism through the Sunday School. The Southern Baptists built the largest Protestant denomination on the premise that "The Sunday School is the evangelistic arm of the church." Some newer charismatic and seeker-driven churches are building their attendance through the worship service. They bring people to Christ through the worship experience. When the goal of evangelism is neglected, attendance decline usually follows.

Inadequate facilities. Every church building has its own limits to the number of people it can service. Just as a quart of water will not fit into a pint jar, 200 people cannot fit into a facility designed for 100. Growing attendance continually needs more space, and if the leadership lacks vision and stops adding needed space, attendance levels off. Few churches can maintain attendance beyond 85 percent of their building capacity. As attendance approaches that growth limit, church leaders need to determine how to provide more space.

The failure of a church to provide adequate facilities may be reflected in the quality of facilities provided. People work in offices and factories that are constantly redecorated to help ensure a positive workplace environment. Likewise, students study in clean freshly painted and well-lighted school classrooms. In contrast, they are invited to churches where Bible study groups meet in damp basements that have blistering paint on the walls, underequipped kitchens and dimly-lit furnace rooms. Even when a church provides space for growth, this kind of space is inadequate to reach those living in our Western society as we begin the twenty-first century.

Quality emphasis over quantity. More than a century ago, Charles Haddon Spurgeon observed, "The minister that will not emphasize numbers will not have them." Some church leaders believe that if we have a quality ministry, we will attract great crowds. Quality does not produce quantity any more than quantity produces quality. A growing church is usually characterized by an emphasis on both quality and quantity. The pursuit of excellence need not interfere with pursuing people for Christ.

Inadequate administration. Dr. Lee Roberson built one of America's largest churches on the principle that "Everything rises or falls on leadership." Few churches will ever experience sustained growth beyond the leadership ability of their leaders. The traditional laws of Sunday School growth used by the Southern Baptists to build their churches are essentially laws to manage and administer growth.

Reference: Hollis L. Green, *Why Churches Die* (Minneapolis: Bethany Fellowship, 1972).

DECREE OF GOD

God's plan by which He created, controls, sustains and takes responsibility for His creation and His creatures, including their salvation, nurturing, rewarding and/or punishing within the predetermined limits of His nature.

DEHAAN, MARTIN R. (1891–1965)

Pioneer in Christian radio.

Born in Zeeland, Michigan, M. R. DeHaan graduated from Hope College in Holland, Michigan, and the University of Illinois College of Medicine and began practicing medicine in western Michigan. During a period of illness, DeHaan sensed God's call to preach the gospel.

He gave up his medical practice and studied at Western Theological Seminary in Holland, Michigan. Upon graduation, he pastored two churches in Grand Rapids, both of which experienced significant growth. In 1938, he began broadcasting his Bible teaching on a 50-watt station. He saw his Radio Bible Class grow to include more than 600 stations worldwide. While developing his radio ministry, he traveled widely as a Bible conference speaker and also wrote 25 books. DeHaan died on December 15, 1965.

DeHaan's greatest contribution to evangelism was through his Radio Bible Class. In addition to pioneering the use of radio, DeHaan's ministry has produced literature that is used by Christians in many countries.

DEMOGRAPHIC STUDY

A study of population statistics and census data in a particular community or region with a view of defining the unique character of the target groups. Specific data normally considered include data relating to births, deaths, people groups (i.e., ethnic or minority groups), age groups, geographic location, income distribution, education and population shifts. Understanding the demographics of your community will influence the character of your church.

The following information suggests steps in conducting four kinds of demographic studies that may give you insight into your church and community.

How to Do a Demographic Study of Your Church

Church leaders need to understand the demographics of their church both to plan effective ministries and to evaluate the effectiveness of their church in reaching their communities. Several steps should be taken to collect all the relevant data and gain an accurate picture of your church.

Begin with a copy of your church's current membership list. Some churches may have a phone list that includes both members and adherents. Identify the specific ministry involvement of each person and list the number of tasks being done by them by their names (i.e., 0, 1, 2...). On the basis of this data, attempt to answer the following questions:

1. What can be concluded about the commitment level of your members?
2. Which members could be considered in a high-risk group as potential candidates of ministry burnout?
3. What training should be offered to provide equipped workers who could release overworked members from some responsibilities?
4. What support systems are in place for those actively involved in specific ministries?

Next, compile a list of all ministries affiliated with your church. Identify the target group, ministry emphasis, number of workers, number of people being serviced by that ministry, sources of income, time and space utilized in the church facilities, budgeted costs for the current year and specific ministry achievements in their area of emphasis. On the basis of this data, attempt to answer the following questions:

1. Which ministries are duplicating efforts by seeking to accomplish the same thing among the same group?
2. Which ministries have ceased to be effective in accomplishing their goals?
3. Which ministries are working to achieve goals perceived to be inconsistent with the declared direction of the church?
4. Which ministries exist without a clear sense of direction?
5. Which ministries appear highly successful in achieving their stated objectives?
6. Which groups in the church appear to be largely neglected by existing church ministries?
7. Based on the ministry emphasis of these ministries, what is the present ministry emphasis of your church?

Two more steps must be completed before concluding your demographic study of your church. First, attempt to list all existing ministries on a one-page chart that identifies both formal and informal lines of communication. This chart pictures the quality of communication between ministry leaders in your church. Second, prepare a master calendar for a typical month in your church year, listing every event conducted by each ministry. This chart pictures the schedule of a committed and involved family in your church. Using this information, attempt to answer the following questions:

1. How much time are families expected to invest in attending church functions?
2. How effectively are present facilities being utilized?
3. Does this schedule help or hinder families in other areas of responsibility (e.g., building a healthy family life, making contact with unsaved neighbors, fulfilling civic responsibilities)?
4. How could this schedule be streamlined to make room for other ministries or free up time for families heavily involved in church life?

How to Do a Demographic Study of Your Community

Church leaders also need to understand the demographics of their communities to plan effective strategies for reaching them for Christ. Several steps should be taken to collect all the relevant data and to gain an accurate picture of your community.

As you begin this demographic study, write a brief description of your target community. This description may define your community as a geographic region (e.g., those living within a certain distance of the church campus) or as a distinct people group (e.g., the Hispanic community living within the city limits). Then use the following questions as a guide to determine the kind of data you intend to gather. (Remember, modern Americans tend to measure distance in driving time rather than in actual miles. In metropolitan areas, research reveals the average person travels 12½ minutes to church, but in rural areas the driving time is longer.)

1. What identifiable people groups live within the community?

2. What felt needs are characteristic of each of these groups?
3. Which of these groups are most responsive to the gospel?
4. Which of these groups are being effectively evangelized by other evangelical churches?
5. Which of these groups are not being effectively evangelized?
6. Which of these groups are already represented in the church?

When you have determined what you are looking for, several existing reports may contain the data you need. Your community library should have a copy of the most recent census data on your community. Local chambers of commerce, business development agencies and political parties also conduct research and issue reports that may be helpful.

Having this new insight into your community, take time to walk or drive through your target community on a Saturday or Sunday afternoon. In addition to helping you collect new data, this exercise may help you understand the raw data in the context of a people-oriented ministry. Take a fresh look at your community, using the following questions as an observation guide.

1. What kinds of homes do people live in (e.g., condos, single family dwellings, apartments)? What kinds of cars are parked in their driveways? How is the property maintained? What does this suggest about the economic status of the community?
2. Where do the families who have young children live? Look for swings, bikes, toys in the yard and children playing in a community park.
3. What kind of families do you see (e.g., nuclear families, extended families, single-parent families, adults without children)?
4. What visible minorities live in the community? What languages are families speaking as they talk to each other? This will give you insight into various people groups that may be defined by ethnic backgrounds.
5. How old is the community? How old are the buildings? How old are the people living in the buildings? What evidence is there

of decay, renewal and/or growth in the community?

Use the following questions as a guide to arrive at specific conclusions:

1. Is the city growing, stable or declining in size?
2. From where do the people living in your city come? Are significant groups moving from the city to the country? Are they moving from another state to your community? Have they emigrated from another country to your community?
3. What mother tongues are spoken in your community? Is a significant group speaking a language other than that in which you minister? Remember, although first-generation immigrants may have learned English, they are usually more reachable if spoken to in their mother tongue.
4. What information have you collected about the character of families in your community? How many nonfamily households live in your community? What is the rate of divorce? How many single-parent families live in your community? What is the average number of people per household?
5. What is the economic status of your community? Rather than looking for an average income, break down the number of people in each income group. If possible, identify the average income for each neighborhood in your community. Where do they work? How many people are unemployed or on some form of government assistance? How many people are self-employed? What kind of jobs do people in your community perform (e.g., factory work, office work, service industry)? How long are their commutes to work? What days do they work? (Looking for those who cannot attend Sunday services.)

How to Measure Ministry Perceptions in Your Church

Some demographic studies are designed to collect more subjective data about the way your church is perceived. This research could be conducted to determine what groups within and outside your church think about it. The key to conducting this research is developing and using an instrument that accurately measures ministry perception.

In developing your survey instrument, begin by determining what aspects of your church's ministry you wish to research (e.g., worship, fellowship, youth ministry). Then prepare a questionnaire listing several statements that may or may not accurately describe aspects of each ministry area. People should be invited to rate the accuracy of each statement on a scale of one to five (e.g., [1] I strongly disagree, [2] I disagree, [3] Sometimes/occasionally, [4] I agree, [5] I strongly agree).

Your survey should include a place where people can identify themselves as a member of a specific demographic group in your church. This part of the survey would ask the respondent to identify his/her (1) sex, (2) age range, (3) educational background, (4) years of involvement as a Christian and/or church member and (5) level of commitment to the church (e.g., number of church services attended in a typical month, level of involvement in ministry, percentage of income given to the church).

When developing a survey to measure ministry perception, you may wish to include one or two open-ended questions, allowing the respondent to freely express himself or herself. Sample questions include: (1) The one thing I really like about our church is..., and (2) I would really like to see us do something about....

When you have completed your survey, test it among a select group. Some churches use their lay leadership team or pastoral staff as the test group. This enables you to work the bugs out of your survey before conducting a major research project. Also, this may provide important data to compare ministry perceptions of those involved in church leadership with other members of the church.

Churches may conduct a survey in at least four ways to measure ministry perception within the congregation. First, some churches will take time during a morning service to have everyone present complete the survey. Second, some churches conduct the survey through a tele-phone poll of families on the church phone list. Third, churches may elect to mail the survey to each home on their mailing list, asking them to bring the completed survey to church the following Sunday. Finally, some churches conduct a random sampling, having people interview those attending a morning service as they are arriving or leaving. Each of these approaches has its own unique strengths and weaknesses.

Churches should realize that a random sampling can give acceptable information on which to draw conclusions. Many churches think they must ask everyone a question about everything, but very little research is done in this world that way. A random sampling of 5 percent to 10 percent may be accurate. In small churches and/or small groups, however, a larger sampling is probably necessary to reflect a "pool of data" large enough to draw accurate results.

After the data has been collected, use the following questions to evaluate your findings:

1. Is there a significant difference in ministry perception between church staff, lay leaders and the congregational body?
2. Is there a significant difference in ministry perception between the men and women of the church?
3. Is there a significant difference in ministry perception between various age groups in the church?
4. Is there an apparent relationship between a person's giving rate and ministry perception?
5. Is there a relationship between the length of time people have been saved or involved in the church and their perception of the ministry?
6. Is there a difference in ministry perception among people of various educational backgrounds?
7. Is there an apparent relationship between the level of people's involvement in the church and their ministry perception?

How to Measure Ministry Perceptions in Your Community

In addition to measuring the self-perception of your church, you will want to know what people in your community think about your church. The way people in the community perceive your church will influence the way they respond when invited to a church function. If a negative reputation exists in town, steps need to be taken to change that reputation before significant evangelistic success will be realized.

To measure your community's perception of your church, design a questionnaire of 6 to 10 questions. These questions should guide people to tell you what they honestly think and/or feel about your church. The following list reflects the kind of questions normally included in this kind of survey.

1. Have you ever heard of *(your church name)*?
2. Do you know where *(your church name)* is located?
3. In five words or less, how would you describe *(your church name)*?
4. Are you attending or are you a member of a church?
5. If you were looking for a church home in our community, what sort of things would you want most in the church?
6. Why do you think some people in our community choose not to attend church services?
7. What kind of services do you think churches should offer to the community?
8. What kind of services could a church offer that would be most beneficial to you and your family?
9. How interested would you be in a life-oriented Bible study with other adults in the community?
10. If you could tell the pastor of *(your church name)* one thing, what would it be?

(Harvest Search, Church Growth Center, Corunna, Indiana, does this kind of research by telephone and by questionnaire both in churches and in communities.)

When this survey has been designed and field tested, you are ready to begin collecting data. Normally, a church will involve many people conducting surveys in a short time period. These surveyors should be trained to conduct door-to-door interviews in a professional manner. Among other things, be certain surveyors understand the importance of recording all the data neatly. They must also avoid the impulse to correct misconceptions people might have about their church. Although the purpose of this survey is to collect data, surveyors should be sensitive to those who demonstrate a sincere interest in the church. They may offer to have someone contact the person to answer any questions he or she may have about the church. Regardless of the interest level indicated by a person being interviewed, surveyors should always conclude their interview with an expression of thanks.

Normally, churches will assign specific surveyors to specific blocks or neighborhoods within a target community. You may wish to have people surveying at various times of the day (i.e., mornings, afternoons, evenings). Remember, a random survey will produce the data you seek. You may survey only one side of a street, or you may survey every other block or every other house. In extremely large areas, you may survey only one or two houses in each block.

When the data is collected, attempt to summarize what the community is saying and how strongly it is saying it. Resist the temptation to discount data that is offensive, inaccurate or inconsistent with your church's perception of itself. Remember, this is what your community believes to be true about your church. It may be wrong, but it may also not be wrong. Data collected through this kind of survey may be one way God tries to tell His Church something it needs to hear (Rev. 3:17,18).

References: Eddie Gibbs, "Measurement and Meaning" in *I Believe in Church Growth* (Grand Rapids: William B. Eerdmans Publishing Company, 1982); Roy Pointer, "Laying a Foundation for Growth" in *How Do Churches Grow* (Bromley, Kent: MARC Europe, 1984); Elmer L. Towns, *Vision Day* (Lynchburg, Va.: Church Growth Institute, 1994).

DEMONS

Fallen angels who rebelled against God and were cast out of the presence of God. Beings who are the emissaries of Satan to carry out his diabolical plans. They possess tremendous intellectual ability, and are reprobate and evil, having no opportunity of repentance or salvation.

DEMON POSSESSION

(Lit. demonized). The culmination of a volitional rejection of God and a volitional yielding to Satan and his demons. It occurs when God permits demons to embody a person and control the mind or body.

DESCRIPTION OF DEMON POSSESSION

The ultimate activity of demons in or with individuals is popularly referred to as demon possession. However, this phrase does not occur in the original language; it is *daimonizomai*, which is properly translated "demonized."

Demon possession, as we understand it, occurs when God permits demons to possess a person and control the mind or body. It is a culmination of a volitional rejection of God and a volitional acceptance of Satan and his demons.

Demon possession is the opposite of the filling of the Spirit. Just as some Christians are more effective when filled with the Holy Spirit, so some unbelievers have greater demonic power as a result of their demonic possessions. The same word is used of the Holy Spirit's control in Ephesians 5:18 as in Satan's control of Ananias and Sapphira in Acts 5:3. Demon possession and demon activity are more commonly recognized among heathen societies. However, there is increasing evidence of demonic activity in Western society because of many reasons, one of them being the waning of Christian influence. As this nation turns from God and more people worship Satan and demons, there will be more evidence of demon activity in our society.

Another reason for increasing evidence of demonic activity is the growth of interest in the supernatural, which is a reflection of people's interest in the occult, New Age religion and the growing interest in Christianity of "touching" the supernatural God. Maybe the growing spiritual warfare is a direct result of Satan's response to the growing effectiveness and strategic efforts of the Christian Church as promoted by the Church Growth Movement. As Christian workers effectively evangelize, no doubt Satan could accelerate the warfare.

An unbeliever who ventures deeper into the spiritual realm, seeking for greater possession by demons, will undoubtedly begin to emit certain characteristics that are manifested in demonized people. John Nevius, a Christian missionary for many years in China, recounts firsthand contacts with the rampant evil forces behind an ancient pagan culture. Through working with the Chinese, Nevius became acutely aware of demonic strongholds and predominant characteristics of demonized people. Nevius assigns the following characteristics to demon possessed individuals.[1]

1. The supposed demoniac at the time of "possession" passes into an abnormal state, the character of which varies indefinitely, being marked by depression and melancholy; or vacancy and stupidity amounting sometimes almost to idiocy, or the person may become ecstatic, or ferocious and malignant.

2. During transition from the normal to the abnormal state, the subject is often thrown into paroxysms, more or less violent, during which the person sometimes falls senseless to the ground or sometimes foams at the mouth, presenting symptoms similar to those of epilepsy or hysteria.

3. The intervals between these attacks vary indefinitely from hours to months. During these intervals, the physical and mental condition of the subject may be healthy and normal in every respect. The duration of the abnormal states varies from a few minutes to several days. The attacks are sometimes mild, and sometimes violent. If frequent and violent, the physical health suffers.

4. During the transition period, the subject often retains more or less normal consciousness. The violence of the paroxysms is increased if the subject struggles against and endeavors to repress the abnormal symptoms. When yielding to them, the violence of the paroxysms abates or ceases altogether.

5. When normal consciousness is restored after one of these attacks, the subject is entirely ignorant of everything that has passed during that state.

6. The most striking characteristic of these cases is that the subject evidences another personality, and the normal personality, for the time being, is partially or wholly dormant.

7. The new personality presents traits of character utterly different from those that really belong to the subject in a normal state, and this change of character is with rare exceptions in the direction of moral obliquity and impurity.

8. A differentiating mark of demonomania, intimately connected with the assumption of the new personality, is that with the change of personality there is a complete change of moral character.

9. Many people while "demon possessed" give evidence of knowledge that cannot be accounted for in ordinary ways. They often appear to know of the Lord Jesus Christ as a divine person and show an aversion to and fear of Him. They sometimes converse in foreign languages of which, in their normal state, they are entirely ignorant.

10. Often, in connection with "demon possessions," rappings and noises are heard in places where no physical cause for them can be found; and tables, chairs, crockery and the like are moved about without, as far as can be discovered, any application of physical force—exactly as we are told is the case among spiritualists.

Drawing from his experiences in China, Nevius was able to develop a system that categorized demonized people into one of four different stages. Based upon the nature and extent of the characteristics employed by a demon-possessed person, Nevius could determine how severely a person was possessed. Nevius concluded that no one became demonized suddenly. Rather, demon possession represented a gradual process that was marked clearly by stages of development.

First, the initial stage of demon influence may be called "obsession." It is the stage of the first approach, and the introductory or tentative efforts of the demon. In this stage, cases are often unpronounced in their character, leaving it difficult to determine whether they are to be classed with demon-possession, idiocy, lunacy or epilepsy. In many cases of demon possession, this stage is wanting, the second stage being the first.

The second stage is marked by a struggle for possession in which the unwilling subject resists, sometimes successfully, but generally pines away until the person yields an involuntary subjection to the demon's will. This may be called the transition stage or the crisis. It is of comparatively short duration.

The third stage may be designated, with regard to the subject, as that of subjection and subserviency, and with regard to the demon, development. The condition of the subject is healthy and normal most of the time. The subject is peaceful and quiet except in the paroxysm that occurs in passing from the normal to the abnormal state. This state may continue for years.

In the fourth stage, the demonized subject has developed capabilities for use and is willing to be used. The subject is the trained, accustomed, voluntary slave of the demon. The subject is called "Wu-Po," "woman sorcerer"; in the language of the Old Testament (according to the particular line of The subject's development and use), a "witch," "soothsayer" or "necromancer"; in modern English phrase, a "developed medium."[2]

References: [1]John Nevius, *Demon Possession* (Grand Rapids: Kregel Publications, 1973), pp. 142-145. [2]Ibid., pp. 285-286.

DENOMINATIONS

"Connectionalism" is the historical term for the way churches united in fellowship or organic unity. The modern phrase is "denominations." There are more than 250 denominations in the United States, some large, such as the Southern Baptist Convention with 15 million members in 1994; others small, such as the Two-Seeds-in-the-Spirit Predestinarian Baptist, with 201 members in 16 churches.

Definition of a Denomination

Obviously, the word "denomination" does not come from Scripture, nor is the idea of a denomination explicitly taught therein. It is surely implied, however. The existence of denominations is a fact of Christianity; therefore, how they fit into God's plan must be examined. But to understand them, they must be defined.

A denomination is a group of churches that have similar doctrinal beliefs, similar traditions and backgrounds, share the same goals in ministry, desire fellowship to encourage one another and have organically bound themselves together to establish corporately what they believe cannot be wrought separately.[1]

This description of a denomination becomes much more inclusive than some religious bodies are willing to admit. Some who are denominations deny that label, while others accept it willingly.

Some denominations are much more centralized, while others appear to be a confederacy or an unorganized fellowship. The longer a denomination exists, the more supervision and control of the church grows within the system; hence, it becomes a tight denomination. At the same time, newly emerging denominations have no organic connection, but are held together by fellowship because their churches have similar purposes. These denominations do not require a yearly report of attendance and budgets, nor do they have officials or a district superintendent to supervise the business of the churches. There is little centralized direction, hence little control of the individual churches. These are called "loose denominations."

Sources of denominations. Some see the seeds of denominationalism early in the book of Acts. Two great churches evolved, each a little different from the other. First, there was a Jewish church in Jerusalem; its members met on Solomon's porch, they had all things in common and banded together to saturate the Holy City with the gospel. We read of these Christians, "daily in the temple, and in every house, they ceased not to teach and preach Jesus Christ" (Acts 5:42, *KJV*). The Jerusalem church grew and was numbered in the thousands (Acts 2:41; 4:4; 6:1,7).

Next, a great church evolved to the north—a Gentile church in Antioch. Its members were the first to be called "Christians." The church had spiritually gifted leaders—Barnabas and Paul. We read of this Gentile church that "many people were added to the Lord" (Acts 11:24). They assembled themselves together and taught many people throughout Antioch. The Gentile church was more world-missions minded than was the Jewish church, and sent Paul and Barnabas out as the first missionaries (Acts 13:1-3).

The seeds of dissension were inherent in the nature of these two churches and reflected in the controversy at the Council at Jerusalem. The first issue to divide Christendom was circumcision, the Jewish church demanding "Unless you are circumcised according to the custom of Moses, you cannot be saved" (Acts 15:1). The Gentile churches held views similar to the conclusions of the Council—circumcision was not necessary.

The leaders of the churches, including Peter, Paul, James and others, were called to Jerusalem for a conference. The problem was stated and leaders were given opportunity to state their opinions. After a lengthy discussion a group consensus was reached: "Then it pleased the apostles and elders, with the whole church" (v. 22). The group had to work out their differences for continued fellowship. "It seemed good to us, being assembled with one accord" (v. 25). The problem among individual churches was solved, giving a biblical basis for church meetings (councils, committees or conferences) to solve their problems.

The conclusion was: "For it seemed good to the Holy Spirit, and to us, to lay upon you no greater burden than these necessary things: that you abstain from things offered to idols, from blood, from things strangled, and from immorality. If you keep yourselves from these, you will do well. Farewell" (vv. 28,29). Although the churches met for a decision, there was no pressure from an authoritarian head or lordship over an individual church. At the core of the Jerusalem Council was a recognition of the importance of the local church, rather than a doctrine of denominationalism—each church was autonomous.

These two great churches were both blessed of God, yet differed in their interpretation of the Christian life. Whereas later denominations differed about doctrine, these agreed to exist and minister through their separate ways, yet stay in fellowship.

God never intended denominationalism to grow into its present splintered forms, so that in one city more than 100 separate denominational churches are found. Yet, although God's primary purpose was not the establishment of denominations, if they believe in the essentials, practice a godly life and attempt to carry out the Great Commission, the gospel can have some effect through their ministries. In some cases, the message can go farther and deeper because churches exist with different emphases and practices.

Later in the book of Acts, the Christians in Jerusalem were experiencing a famine. Paul took up an offering from the Corinthian Christians to help them in this matter (Acts 21:26). Once again there was no control or central treasury. One church simply provided help for another.

The book of Acts ends with a number of individual churches, each having fellowship with the other, yet no centralized superstructure emerges. Luke wrote the book of Acts, yet it is unfinished, indicating that the church that had begun should continue in its original form. At the apostle's death, the only common denominator among the churches was salvation predicted in the Old Testament and fulfilled in the Person of Jesus Christ, who was dead yet now lived at the right hand of God the Father. Churches seemed to recognize one another, receive gifts from one another, and transfer members from one to another. An attitude of love characterized Christians as churches helped one another in their service to Jesus Christ.

The New Testament ends with churches independent of each other, different in focus and unique in problems. Yet they fellowshipped with one another and were interrelated in communication and mutual support.

History of the Development of Denominations

After the postapostolic age, the Church began to express its beliefs and practices on paper. The living fellowship of the Church was reflected in creeds and statements of expectation. *The Didache* and other doctrinal creeds inevitably appeared. Intellectual conformity to the emerging creeds was the way a Christian expressed the heart's dedication. The creed makers fought life-and-death struggles in those early days concerning the essentials of Christianity. Eventually, Christians had to fight theological battles for all major church doctrines. People who did not conform were threatened with excommunication. Personal infidelity was equally penalized. The Church grew within the Greek-intellectual milieu. Some of the greatest scholars of this time were within the Church, rather than outside its walls.

During the fourth century, Christianity was announced as the official religion of the Roman Empire. When the hordes of barbarians demolished the outward forms of the already decayed empire, the only remaining nucleus of social order was the preachers of the gospel who garbed themselves with simple apparel and proclaimed faith in a living God. Church control over society grew; denominationalism was never considered.

In the decades after the apostles' ministry, a centralization of authority began to arise. The office of bishop (elder or pastor) began to grow in authority. Bishops no longer gave leadership to only one church; their authority extended over several churches within a geographical area. Bishops began to ordain men into the ministry and control the financial affairs of the churches. Each city had its own bishop supervising the work of smaller surrounding churches. Usually the greater the city the greater the bishop's authority. Because Rome was the capital of the civilized world, the bishop in Rome became a leading ecclesiastical figure. As individual cities fell to the invading Huns, their bishops and churches were also destroyed. Rome was the last city to hold out against the invaders, hence Rome was the last city to have an ecclesiastical leader.

When the Roman Empire and its civilization fell, however, the Church retreated into its monasteries. Although this seclusion enabled it to endure, it became stagnant. Ignorance prevailed, and Europe entered a period that some characterize as the Dark Ages. The Church, which held the lamp of knowledge, saw the light flicker through superstitions, tradition and the addition of works to the grace that had been preached by the apostles.

The Church became a church-state, political-religious institution, and was the only organization able to compete with the times. There was unity in Christian profession and practice because the individual's life was closely controlled by the Church's authority. A Christian's belief was born out of deep conviction to God and duty to the Church. The problem with such a structure was that the sins of the clergy were hidden from the public and the weaknesses of the organization were not seen by the laymen. No successful criticism could revive the church. Because all religious organizations created by fallible human beings are destined to destruction, the Church began to decay. It hid the light of the gospel under a bushel and sent the world into a millennium of darkness.

The first major split in the Church came in the twelfth century, which divided East and West into the Roman Catholic church, centered in Rome, and the Greek Orthodox church centered in Constantinople.

It was inevitable that the conscience and human reason should revolt from the intolerable claims of papal absolutism. The reformers personified that revolt and gave rise to the Reformation churches. Two widely accepted church systems were evident—Catholicism and Protestantism. (Even during this time, however, there was always a Remnant Church, without notoriety or political influence.) Because of the Reformation, doctrines that had been undiscovered, forgotten or ignored now were discovered, declared and defended. People's consciences and reason gave them access to the Word of God. People had the light, and rebelled against the darkness. People had no problem with the glare of Truth; it was the shadows that gave them trouble.

These questionable areas were unimportant in the early days of the Reformation; people were glorying in their newfound liberty of the gospel. But divisions were inevitable. People disagreed on minor points, and the minor doctrines became major.

Sin has always been humankind's problem. Sin blinds people's understanding (1 Cor. 2:14; 2 Cor. 4:3,4), so they cannot fully and correctly know God. Sin brings on religious pride that leads to doctrinal arrogance, causing good people to disagree and divide regarding theological distinctives. Also, sin influences humankind's motives, so that they will recruit and train disciples to perpetuate their doctrinal beliefs. Usually what is a doctrinal tangent in the founders of a movement becomes heresy in their spiritual grandchildren because they hold the doctrines more vehemently and have less understanding.

Surely God cannot sanction false doctrine. Baptism by sprinkling and immersion cannot both be right; therefore, one must be wrong. Yet God seems to use sincere people on both sides of the issue. God does not always withhold His blessing from people for some false teaching, but when a church preaches the gospel, God uses them to the extent that they have the truth and seek His blessing on their ministries. At the same time, some churches have the truth, but are dead. These churches accomplish little for eternity because they neglect spiritual power and disobey the truth they have.

God works in this doctrinal milieu; therefore, He works through various denominations, although they may not be in the perfect will of God. Although He could never condone false teaching, God appears to bless churches in spite of some false doctrine if they are faithful to the essentials of the faith and seek His blessing on their ministries. Therefore, denominations exist within the permissive will of God. He condescends to use the frail creations of religious organizations.

Other causes brought about the explosive growth of denominations in America. The pluralistic society of America gave rise to denominations, as no other nation since Pentecost has experienced. A careful study of church history will show that five or six church types usually developed within a country, but no nation has spawned hundreds of denominations as has the United States of America. After all is said and done, Christianity can only be divided into five or six major camps, each reflecting a different doctrinal statement and each reflecting its own organization. But the strong individualism found in this new frontier country gave rise to a diversity of denominations. Also, economic freedom, freedom to travel and the lack of competition from a "state church" produced an environment in which a person could begin a church or start a denomination.

Americans glorify their heroes. The invincible person against overwhelming odds brings an unbelievable victory. Americans admire strong biblical individualism and firm convictions. Thus, Americans have produced the person of God. This person has a Bible in hand and in faith walks into a town and does the work of God. The frontier preacher establishes a church and gathers a congregation around biblical leadership. The stronger the leader, the larger the following. Thus, great people build great churches. But the movement did not stop there. Strong leaders gathered several others around their cause—thus building a denomination.

Community stability mitigates against the growth of denominations. When families grow and die in the same community, it is difficult to get them to change church membership, much less establish new churches. Children tend to join the same church their parents and grandparents attend. When a family moves to a new town, however, the tendency is to lose moral restrictions and, with it, to drop church loyalties. Americans attend the church of their choice, which is usually the most convenient in the neighborhood or the one in which the pastor's ministry meets their needs. It is thus possible for aggressive denominations to build new churches and increase membership. Lethargic denominations tend to lose members. Americans want to go "where the action is," therefore, they attend the church that has life or an aggressive outreach. A mobile nation makes possible the growth of denominations, and because the United States is one of the most mobile nations in history, we can expect to find a greater number of denominations in our nation than in any other since Pentecost.

Reference: [1]Elmer Towns, *Is the Day of the Denominations Dead?* (Nashville: Thomas Nelson, Inc., 1973).

DEPARTMENTAL SUNDAY SCHOOL

A Sunday School having an average attendance up to 250–300 in which everything is organized around the departmental structure.

DEPRAVITY See TOTAL DEPRAVITY

DISCERNING THE BODY

An accurate and objective view of a local church or a denomination based on gathered data and systematic analysis of that data concerning the church and/or denomination and its individual members. The phrase comes from Paul's instructions about the proper way to partake of the Lord's Supper in 1 Corinthians 11:29.

DISCERNMENT, GIFT OF

One of the enabling gifts of the Holy Spirit. A God-given ability to distinguish between truth and error.

Reference: Larry Gilbert, *Team Ministry* (Lynchburg, Va: Church Growth Institute, 1987).

DISCIPLE

A Christian who follows Jesus Christ as Savior and Lord, is growing in the grace and knowledge of Him and is a responsible member of His Body.

DISCIPLING

Bringing people to a personal relationship with Jesus Christ. A more refined classification follows: D-1: Turning a non-Christian society for the first time to Christ. D-2: Turning any individual from nonfaith to faith in Christ and incorporation into a church. D-3: Teaching an existing Christian as much of the truths of the Bible as possible, helping him or her grow in grace.

Reference: See PERFECTING.

DISCIPLING A WHOLE NATION (DAWN)

An evangelism strategy that coordinates the resources of many churches and encourages the use of various evangelism strategies to effectively plant a church in every people group (i.e., ethnic group), evangelize an entire nation or significantly large region. The plan is the vision and driving force of James Montgomery.

How to Develop a Regional Evangelistic Strategy

As the evangelical church approaches the conclusion of the second millennium of the Christian era, there is once again a renewed interest in evangelism. By approaching evangelism as an ongoing involvement that builds over the years, it is anticipated that positive progress can be made toward more effective evangelism.

One of the most obvious evidences of this renewed interest in world evangelism is the proliferation of plans to completely evangelize the world by the end of this present decade. Ralph Winter has identified what he has called "The A.D. 2000 Movement." This international movement to evangelize the world by the year 2000 represents the concern of several separate groups who have independently set a goal to evangelize the world by that date. Indeed, at least 78 megaplans are in place by various denominations, missions and parachurch ministries to completely evangelize the world by the year 2000.

Around the world, another parallel movement has begun to spring up and has a goal of "Discipling A Whole Nation" (DAWN). These strategies tend to represent the efforts of evangelicals to evangelize every person within their nation. By evangelizing the nation, organizers usually mean to give each person an opportunity to hear, understand and respond to the gospel. This would be a P-2 Proclamation Evangelism view of evangelism, although the actual strategy developed in many of these plans assumes a P-3 Persuasion Evangelism approach to evangelism. At present, many DAWN strategies target the date 2000 as a completion date.

The process by which a DAWN strategy is prepared and implemented varies from nation to nation. Some countries, such as the Philippines and Canada, have well-defined goal statements and strategies involving several evangelical groups. In other countries, especial-

ly those in which a single evangelical group is particularly dominant, DAWN strategies tend to be tied to the progress of a particular mission or denomination. In other nations, DAWN strategies do not yet exist. This is particularly true in many Moslem nations and other places where a strong evangelical church has not yet been established.

One of the first steps in this process involves taking inventory. Because most evangelicals in many nations tend not to collect and report statistics regularly, this is often a major undertaking. Census data in many nations fails to distinguish evangelicals from other Protestant or Christian groups. These figures need to be collected through various evangelical denominations, schools and other affiliations. Even when this data is gathered, often independent evangelical churches need to be polled for the information being sought. In many cases, those responsible for gathering data have published a preliminary report that includes annual or periodic updates as their database is expanded.

Once evangelical leaders know where they are, they can then determine where they are going. As noted, the goal of discipling a whole nation tends to be somewhat vague. Just what does it mean to "disciple"? Even when the goal is expressed in terms of giving every person in the nation an opportunity to hear, understand and respond to the gospel, how is it determined when that goal has been accomplished? When the Evangelical Fellowship of Canada (EFC) adopted its DAWN strategy—Vision 2000—it set a goal of having one evangelical church for every 2,000 people in the country. Specific research was conducted on the basis of census data and projections to determine the specific number of churches needed in each community to accomplish that goal. In larger centers that have a significant ethnic population, the number of new churches needed for each ethnic group was also identified. It was deemed inadvisable to establish new churches for groups already well churched when significant and identifiable ethnic minorities remained unchurched.

Since the Day of Pentecost, more than 700 attempts to completely evangelize the world within a certain time period have been recorded.

Most of these visions quickly fizzled and faded because the dream of the visionary was not communicated to the wider population, and a practical strategy by which that goal could be accomplished was not developed. To encourage greater buy-in to a national evangelism strategy, interfaith leaders have attempted to work through existing institutions wherever possible.

In the Canadian model, the EFC has elected not to establish a centralized evangelism department, but rather to serve as a networking and consultation agency to existing evangelical denominations. In keeping with the unique governing policies of its particular denominations, each denominational group has likewise attempted to communicate the DAWN vision to its existing churches. In churches committed to congregational government, strategies have been developed to encourage congregational buy-in to the process. In some cases, individual evangelism strategies have been developed by church members or small groups as part of the national DAWN strategy.

Few evangelicals committed to the Great Commission, which calls us to disciple "all nations," can be opposed to developing a national evangelism strategy. Some concerns, however, need to be raised. In the past, evangelical leaders have apparently developed evangelism strategies in lieu of doing evangelism. Also, in some cases it has been suggested that the work put into a DAWN strategy, such as Evangelism in Depth, actually took away from existing strategies that proved effective in evangelism. The third concern sometimes raised may be expressed in the question: What happens in 2001? If evangelicals in Canada are effective in establishing one church for every 2,000 people in their country, will 2001 mark a continuation or decline in new church starts?

When developing a DAWN strategy, evangelical leaders would do well to determine what is currently being done that appears effective in reaching people for Christ. In some cases, significant progress in evangelism could be made by building on existing strengths even if more ambitious evangelistic crusades or other similar projects are to be neglected. The overriding concern in developing a DAWN strategy should be the conversion of the lost rather than the increased

activity of the saved. Ideally, a balance could be struck that mobilizes the saved more effectively in reaching the lost.

A DAWN strategy is effective only as it is implemented. This means great care should be taken in the developmental phase to encourage widespread grassroots input and thus support for the strategy. The best DAWN strategies utilize many ways to reach people for Christ and leave the door open for developing alternative evangelism strategies. The real test of the effectiveness of a DAWN strategy is its success in mobilizing an unevangelizing Christian into the ministry of evangelism.

DISCIPLING FAMILIES

A small group of approximately 6 to 20 members having a primary purpose of training group members in discipleship and providing friendship activities for them.

DISCIPLING—PERFECTING

The two stages in the process of Christianization. Discipling refers to bringing a person or group to commitment to Christ, while perfecting has special reference to nurturing them in their faith, thus bringing about significant ethical change. Some traditions refer to this as the sanctification process.

DISCIPLESHIP

Wallace Acorn, in his 1974 New York University Ph.D. dissertation entitled "The Biblical Concept of Discipleship as Education for Ministry," came to the following 10 conclusions or principles by which discipleship is effective as a tool for educating people for ministry.

The principle of dual commitment. Discipleship is basically a personal commitment to God in intimate spiritual discipleship to Christ by both a noviced and mastered minister who are bound to a divine call to the ministry in further commitment to each other; the former momentarily submitting to the immediate discipline of the latter and exercising discipline within the context of his or her life and ministry.

MECHANICAL LAYOUT OF
EPHESIANS 4:11-16

(American Standard Version, 1901, public domain.)

Verse	
11	......And He gave
	some (to be) apostles;
	and some, prophets;
	and some, evangelists;
	and some, pastors and teachers;
12	....................for the perfecting of the saints,
	unto the work of ministering,
	unto the building up of the body of Christ:
13	....................till we all attain
	unto the unity
	of the faith,
	and of the knowledge of the Son of God,
	unto a full grown man,
	unto the measure of the stature of the fullness of Christ:
14	....................that we may be no longer children
	tossed to and fro and
	carried about with every wind of doctrine,
	by the sleight of men,
	in craftiness,
	after the wiles of error;
15	....................but speaking truth
	in love, may grow up
	in all things
	unto him
	who is the head,
	(even) Christ;
16	....from whom the body
	fitly framed
	and knit together
	through that
	which every joint
	supplieth, according
	to the working in
	(due) measure of
	each several part,
	maketh the increase
	of the body unto
	the building up
	of itself in love.

The principle of direct observation. The disciple is given and led to use the opportunity to observe closely the master's practice of his or her ministry so that he or she becomes empirically familiar with the goals to be achieved, the problems encountered and the methods employed in terms of experience with concrete reality.

The principle of theoretical understanding. The disciple is led to abstract from observed experiences a conceptual understanding of the practicing of the ministry. In so doing, he or she is able to formulate an understanding of the theory of which the practice is an implementation and upon which he or she can predicate his or her own practice of ministry in the same or different situation and under the same or different conditions.

The principle of personal involvement and shared ministry. The disciple is ultimately involved and strongly identified with the person of his or her mentor, who has opened himself or herself as an example and who performs his or her ministry by sharing it with his or her disciple, who learns by experiencing ministry. This is both possible and necessary because ministry is itself a pastoral discipleship.

The principle of proportionate opportunity or graduated levels. The disciple is immediately given opportunities to perform some ministry (often beginning with simple and menial tasks, and encouragingly led to progress to the next performance level) in a graduated sequence, each demanding increased knowledge and skill but offering greater opportunity. He or she is retained on each level until he or she has learned what is necessary to progress, but is fully entrusted with greater responsibility and authority as he or she becomes capable—so that he or she is always learning by productive ministry proportionate to his or her ability and constantly encouraged toward full ministry by the experience of achievement along the way.

The principle of increasing sufficiency. The master enhances his or her disciple's personal commitment to God and professional mastery by fostering an increasing ability to relate directly to God and minister out of his or her own professional resources. The disciple is able to depend upon his or her master as he or she needs, but becomes independent as he or she is able—until he or she

has mastered both himself or herself and his or her ministry; while spiritual discipleship to Christ continues, educational discipleship to the master is promptly to be fulfilled.

The principle of subsidiary mastership. Both for the instruction of junior disciples and the growth of a senior disciple, the master shares his or her mastership with the latter until each has experienced learning from the relationship.

The principle of control and evaluation. The master prepares the field and orients the disciple to ministry shared, supervises the exercise by protection in the field and correction of the performance and contemplates deficiencies and gives a critique of the experience so that the field has experienced ministry and the disciple has learning.

The principle of successorship and continuity. In the disciple's engagement in his or her own ministry, he or she conceives that ministry in terms of a theory which is essentially the same as that which he or she learned from his or her master. His or her practice of ministry is essentially a duplication of the practices observed in and shared with his or her master, so that the field experiences a continuity of ministry and recognizes the disciple as the successor of the master. Educational discipleship having been accomplished, he or she continues spiritual discipleship to Christ as the essence of both his or her life and ministry.

The principle of discipleship perpetuity. Now a disciple only of Christ and master of ministry, the former disciple exercises his or her spiritual discipleship by accepting responsibility for his or her own disciples, becoming a master of disciples, and so transmits the traditional theory and practice of ministry to still another generation and perpetuates the ministry.

DISCIPLESHIP: CONTENT

The following 10 sections are suggestions of the content that should be taught to a young Christian. It is also the material that would be taught to a follow-up or new Christian class.

Lesson 1—What You Did to Become a Christian

During World War II, Joel Orthendahl knelt in

the bottom of a foxhole. When the Germans advanced, he was scared. Remembering verses from the Bible his grandmother had read to him, he received Christ as his Savior and now testifies that he was saved at that moment. It took several years before he began to walk with God, but ultimately he became a preacher.

James Mastin sat in New Testament Baptist Church, Miami, Florida, with a number of other junior boys. The Sunday School teacher asked him if he wanted to go forward to receive Christ during a church service. Embarrassed, he did so—not because he had volunteered, but because he had been taught to respond to adults. Although it was at the prodding of an adult, young James sincerely received the Lord; he, too, became a minister and now pastors Central Baptist Church, Milwaukee, Wisconsin.

Florence Smith described herself as being on the bottom rung of the ladder of society. She drank incessantly in her trailer in the backwoods of Virginia. She contemplated suicide and went as far as to take a pistol to a small gravel pit where she planned to commit the deed. There she decided to give God a chance. For two or three weeks she listened to every radio preacher she could find and did everything they all commanded. She repeated the "Sinner's prayer," but knew in her heart she was not saved.

Finally, she went to a nearby church that preached the gospel. During the invitation, she started to walk forward and later testified, "God saved me as I turned from the pew to walk down the aisle." Although she again repeated the Sinner's Prayer at the altar, she testified that God saved her at the moment she responded and began walking forward. An act of faith did it for Florence Smith.

Ruth Jeane Forbes received the Lord when she came home from Sunday School, where they had talked about having a "dirty" heart. She wanted Jesus to clean her heart, and as a five-year-old, she knelt by her mother's knee and received Christ as her Savior. She grew up to live for Christ.

Every one of these stories is different. Each person's experience is different, and the story of how you were saved may be different yet. Some are saved after a person talks with them; others are saved when they are alone. Some listen to a sermon; others have not heard a sermon in years. Some are embarrassed; others are afraid. Florence Smith prayed the right words, but it didn't work for her at the time. Yet God does not save people differently. Why, then, are our experiences different? What are the ingredients of salvation?

The Way of Salvation

Salvation is as simple as a relationship with Jesus Christ; you put your faith in Him. The Bible says, "Look...and be saved" (Isa. 45:22). Look and live. When you look to Him to answer your sin problem, you live for eternity. Yet, the theologians have made salvation complicated.

Not every church member will go to heaven; yet most have declared they believe in God. "Many will say to me in that day, Lord, Lord, have we not...in thy name...done many wonderful works? And then will I profess unto them, I never knew you: depart from me, ye that work iniquity" (Matt. 7:22,23, *KJV*). Obviously, some people who think they are going to heaven will not make it. They know the "religious" answers, but that is not enough.

Salvation is pictured as a road; you take steps along this road to get to heaven. Jesus said, "Enter ye in at the strait gate: for wide is the gate, and broad is the way, that leadeth to destruction, and many there be which go in thereat: Because strait is the gate, and narrow is the way, which leadeth unto life, and few there be that find it" (vv. 13,14, *KJV*).

In the book of Acts, early Christianity was referred to as "the Way" (9:2). It is the way to God. In approaching God, you must take four steps; you need no more, and can take no less.

1. Know your need. People do not turn to God until they feel a need for Him. And this compulsion is not felt until they realize that their paths will lead to destruction. God says, "For all have sinned and fall short of the glory of God" (Rom. 3:23). The word "all" includes every human of all ages.

A minister once tried to convince a small boy he was a sinner, but the boy would not admit it.

"Have you ever lied to Mommy?" the preacher asked. The boy shook his head no.

"Have you ever taken anything that didn't belong to you, or fought with your brother or sister?" Again the boy shook his head no.

"He's sinning to you now," observed his older brother.

You see, the older brother knew his little brother was guilty of these actions. The Bible says we *all* have sinned. People will never turn to God until they first realize they are sinners.

2. Know your punishment. In our society, we usually don't worry about people who break the law until they hurt someone else. But God's laws are different. God said, "For the wages of sin is death, but the gift of God is eternal life in Christ Jesus our Lord" (6:23). Here "sin" refers to both the condition of being separated from God, and the act of rebellion against God. God punishes both our sinful condition and our offenses. Because you have sinned, the wages of your sin is death.

When you break a speed law, you don't get caught for every offense. But if you speed through a radar trap, unless you are a good talker, you pay the fine. You never escape God's radar, for He catches every offense, and the penalty is death.

"Even for one sin?" a woman asked at the church altar. The soul winner showed her, "For whoever shall keep the whole law, and yet stumble in one point, he is guilty of all" (Jas. 2:10). One sin makes you a sinner.

"The wages of sin is death" (Rom. 6:23a). You get wages for your work; wages are what you have coming to you. This verse shows that you have death or hell coming because you have sinned. In contrast, "the gift of God is eternal life" (6:23b). The gift is free and undeserved; it is not wages. You get death for your sins, yet God gives you life as a gift.

3. Know the gospel. "But God commendeth his love toward us, in that, while we were yet sinners, Christ died for us" (5:8, *KJV*). The word "commendeth" means "to give." God has given His Son to die for our sins. This is the gospel. Gospel means "good news," and the greatest news ever is that God saves us.

The gospel has two aspects: *propositional truth* and *personal truth.* Propositional truth reflects the truth on paper—it is written in our doctrinal statements. This is the gospel that is God's plan of salvation. Paul defined it: "I declare unto you the gospel which I preached unto you, which also ye have received, and wherein ye stand; By which also ye are saved,...that Christ died for our sins according to the scriptures; and that he was buried, and that he rose again the third day according to the scriptures" (1 Cor. 15:1-4, *KJV*). The gospel explains the death, burial and resurrection of Jesus Christ. He died for us.

4. Respond to the gospel. The gospel is more than propositional truth; it is personal truth. This means truth exists in a person—the person Jesus Christ. When you receive this truth, you do more than give mental assent to His death, burial and resurrection. You receive Christ as your Savior. The gospel becomes personal when you invite Christ into your life. "But as many as received Him [Christ], to them He gave the right to become children of God" (John 1:12).

Some have a correct doctrinal statement, but if they do not have the person Jesus Christ in their hearts, they are wrong—dead wrong. Others claim to know Jesus as a person; yet, when their experience is not backed up with correct doctrine, they, too, are wrong. Belief in Jesus Christ is finding the way that leads to heaven. When you find it, you must do something about it. "If you confess with your mouth the Lord Jesus and believe in your heart that God has raised Him from the dead, you will be saved" (Rom. 10:9). You respond by belief in the heart and confession of the mouth.

Salvation—a Total Experience

Belief is not head knowledge only. It involves a total response to God. When you get on a jetliner, you don't place only one leg on the plane and then fly to another city. You must respond completely by placing yourself wholly in the plane. Salvation is the same total experience. You must put your complete trust in Jesus Christ, trusting Him to take you to heaven. This involves your intellect, emotion and will.

1. Using the intellect is the first step of experience. A person must know God's plan of salvation before it can be accepted. Just as you cannot communicate to another person apart from understanding, God follows the same law: God cannot communicate with you unless you understand His plan of salvation.

Knowledge involves awareness and understanding, but knowledge does not convert the soul. Jesus illustrates this point: "Not everyone who says to Me, 'Lord, Lord,' shall enter the kingdom of heaven, but he who does the will of My Father in heaven" (Matt. 7:21). These people had knowledge, but it did little good. Jesus said, "I never knew you" (v. 23), even though they had head knowledge of the Lord.

2. The stirring of emotions is the second step of experience. Humans are emotional beings. They feel deeply about many issues. We cannot neglect the part emotion plays in conversion, although not everyone will express it openly. Some clap their hands and sing for joy. Others weep and agonize. On the other hand, some are converted without any outward display of emotions.

A man in Roanoke, Virginia, confessed to his wife that he had committed adultery. In a blind rage, she ripped the curtains from the window, broke all the dishes and announced she was suing for divorce. The next Sunday morning, the couple attended church and, during the invitation, he went forward, crying like a brokenhearted lover. A few minutes later, she followed him to the altar. After the service was over, those who stood nearby were embarrassed by their hugs and kisses. Theirs was an emotional salvation—emotional both before and after receiving Christ.

A minister visited in the home of a certified public accountant (CPA). After analyzing the gospel, the CPA received the Lord. Later the minister confessed, "I didn't think he was converted because he didn't show any feelings." Yet the CPA has gone on to become one of the greatest workers in his church.

What place do emotions have in conversion? We should never judge a person's seriousness by the tears shed at the altar. The ruler Felix trembled, but told Paul, "Go away for now; when I have a convenient time, I will call for you" (Acts 24:25). His emotions were stirred, just as some who come to the altar and weep yet never are saved. We cannot judge the sincerity of a person by the outward display of emotions. The country preacher said it eloquently: "The toot of the car's

horn doesn't tell you how much gas is in the tank." Merely because a person does not cry or show joy doesn't mean a lack of sincerity. Many people keep their emotions to themselves, yet they feel deeply.

Just as knowledge alone cannot save, so religious emotionalism will not get a person to heaven. God uses emotions to motivate people to seek relief. Some are terrified of judgment and seek salvation. Others are overwhelmed with love. Other emotions that might make a person seek salvation are guilt, gratitude, pressure and uncertainty. Emotions, like repentance, are an outward manifestation of an inner work of God. After being saved, the person might experience feelings of relief, joy or tears of happiness.

3. The response of the will is the third step of experience. People can do nothing to save themselves—Jesus Christ has done it all. But people must respond with their inner beings: They must accept salvation.

Faith is believing in Jesus Christ. You know what the Bible says He did for you on the cross, and you accept it. Your feelings are stirred by the convicting work of the Holy Spirit and you respond by an act of the will. You have expressed biblical faith.

When a person's will responds in belief, it is an act of obedience to God. "Yet you obeyed from the heart that form of doctrine to which you were delivered" (Rom. 6:17). The will must say yes to God.

Repentance is necessary for salvation, but repentance does not save a person. Like the bus ticket that states "This half good for passage, not good if detached," salvation is good for passage to heaven, but salvation is not salvation if detached from repentance. The second half of the bus ticket reads, "Not good for passage; keep in your possession until arriving at destination." This ticket stub represents repentance: Not good for passage to heaven; keep doing good works until you get to your destination.

Eternal life does not begin with repentance, for these are dead works that cannot merit salvation before God. Eternal life begins when Christ comes into your heart. The Bible gives life. When you hear the preaching of the gospel,

God's Word stirs the heart.

Conviction that stirs the spirit to respond to God begins with the Scriptures: "For the word of God is living and powerful,...and is a discerner of the thoughts and intents of the heart" (Heb. 4:12). The Word of God lays bare the sin that is hidden in the thoughts of a person. Our sin is never hidden from God, but the Bible convicts us by illuminating the mind, showing us our sinfulness.

Conviction begins deep in the mind and moves to consciousness. A person becomes aware of having offended God. The effect is that the person cries, trembles or becomes reflective. Sad stories or persuasive arguments will not bring conviction. It comes from the Word of God by the Holy Spirit. The Holy Spirit convicts you of sin (John 16:8) because you had not believed in Jesus Christ (v. 9). He also performed the same work of conviction in your heart concerning righteousness and judgment (vv. 8-10).

Tears will not convince God of your sincerity, nor will your smile convince others that you have an inner peace. The stirring of the emotions is a necessary concomitant of salvation, not salvation itself. You must respond.

Your mind knows the facts of the gospel and your emotions motivated you, but your will must respond. Paul describes this: "You have obeyed from the heart that form of doctrine" (Rom. 6:17). Other descriptions are used to show this response: receiving Christ, accepting the Lord, asking Christ into your heart and placing your trust in Him. These statements mean a person has made a volitional act of the will in turning his or her life over to Jesus Christ.

A young minister was dealing for the first time with a seeker at the church altar. As they were kneeling, he told the person to pray, "Dear Jesus, come into my heart." When they got up, the soul winner thought of an extra prayer. They returned to the altar, where he instructed the seeker to pray, "Dear Jesus, forgive me of my sins." Then, as they returned to the first pew, he thought of a third prayer, "Dear Jesus, take me to heaven." Actually, people are saved by using any one of these three prayers. God is not as interested in the words of your mouth as He is in the attitude of your heart.

So to be truly saved, you must know the content of the gospel, respond with your emotions and make a decision of your will to turn your life over to Christ.

Lesson 2—What God Did to Save You

What does it take to get a person ready for heaven? If you listen to the message of various churches, you will hear them tell you: be baptized, come to Bible classes, go forward, take communion and/or quit smoking cigarettes. None of these instructions will forgive your sins. You must allow God to meet you in a real way if you want to go to heaven.

A nine-year-old boy visited the Buffalo Avenue Baptist Church in Tampa, Florida. When the teacher picked up the attendance book, he asked the boy's name.

"Bobby Gray."

"Are you saved?" the teacher asked the scared boy.

"No."

"Do you want to become a Christian?" the teacher asked. When the boy said yes, the teacher pulled his chair next to Bobby's and read the plan of salvation. The other boys listened.

"Let's get on our knees and you accept Christ," the gentle teacher instructed. All the boys in the class knelt on the rough concrete. They heard Bobby Gray pray, repeating the prayer directed by the teacher: "Dear Jesus, please come into my heart and save me. I am sorry for my sin; forgive me and make me ready for heaven."

Some might question if the nine-year-old boy could be changed for eternity by that short prayer. The teacher told me the story and confessed, "That was the first person I ever led to the Lord. It was so simple and unemotional that I wondered if the boy was really saved."

There is no doubt in anyone's mind today, because that boy became Dr. Bob Gray, pastor of Trinity Baptist Church in Jacksonville, Florida, the tenth largest church in the United States.

Bobby Gray came to the Lord, but behind the scenes God was working to save him. First, God worked in his heart; and second, God worked at calvary. God follows this same pattern for everyone who is saved.

God Works in the Heart

1. God motivated someone to give you the gospel. Hearing the gospel is important because the Bible promises that "faith comes by hearing, and hearing by the word of God" (Rom. 10:17). You may have heard the gospel from one person or from many persons. You may have heard it in a sermon, Bible study or from a soul winner. You may have heard it once or many times. Paul wrote, "How beautiful are the feet of those who preach the gospel of peace, who bring glad tidings of good things!" (v. 15).

Are you thankful for those who were concerned enough about you to tell you of God's plan of salvation? The gospel is the good news that Jesus died for your sins (1 Cor. 15:1-3). But just hearing the gospel is not enough to save a person. Some have a false security, thinking they have salvation just because they have heard about it. Jesus said, "Hearing you will hear and shall not understand" (Matt. 13:14). Hearing is only the first step.

2. God planted the Bible as a seed in your heart. God has a tool for your salvation; it is the Bible. "Having been born again,...through the word of God which lives and abides forever" (1 Pet. 1:23). Because the Bible produces salvation, it is more than a record of sacred history. The Bible is a living book (Heb. 4:12). When the Bible was planted in your heart, it grew like a seed and sprouted into life. The Bible produces eternal life.

How can the Bible give life? The answer is found in the way the Word of God was written. Its origin and content are not like any other book. The Bible is inspired (2 Tim. 3:16), meaning it was written by God. The Holy Spirit breathed life into its authors who wrote the Word of God so that their words came directly from God, not from man. Because God is life, when His Word is planted into our hearts, it produces life.

A second step in the life-giving properties of the Bible has a unique message. It says that people have sinned against God and will be punished for their rebellion. But the Bible does not end with that dismal picture. It announces that Jesus Christ has died for the sins of the world, and those who believe in Him will not perish but

have everlasting life (John. 3:16,36). When you believe God's message, you gain eternal life. Just as life begins with birth, so eternal life begins when you are born again.

Some alcoholics have read the Bible and sobered up permanently because they were born again. Rebellious teenagers have heard the Bible in youth rallies and learned submission because they were born again. Small children have memorized Scripture in Sunday School and lived their entire lives for God because they were born again.

The Word of God is likened to seed in Mark 4:14. It grows when planted in the human heart. The seed germinates under the soil before breaking into the sunlight. The Bible has the same effect in our hearts. Some are converted immediately upon hearing the Word of God. Others hear the Bible many hours before they are converted. But in the time prior to their conversions, the Bible is working in their hearts. It gives knowledge of sin, producing guilt and conviction (John 16:7-11). Sometimes conviction is manifested with tears (2 Cor. 7:9,10); at other times people respond silently.

3. God brought conviction for your sins. God is continually seeking out those who should be saved and calling them to Himself. He uses the Holy Spirit to bring people to Christ. God brings a person to salvation by convicting him or her of sin. This draws or motivates the sinner to Christ. "No one can come to Me," Jesus said, "unless the Father who sent Me draws him" (John 6:44). Conviction makes a person uneasy about personal sin.

When conviction hits one person, he or she may be sorry for cursing. The next person is afraid of going to hell. A third will feel ashamed to stand in the presence of a holy God. The Holy Spirit reveals sin in the heart in the same way an inspector crawls in a dark, dirty engine room with a flashlight looking for trouble.

The Holy Spirit and sin conflict like boxers in the ring. Both struggle for mastery of your heart. Some people will quit going to church to get away from the unpleasant feeling of conviction. Conviction unsettles the personality.

The body struggles with a high fever or nasal congestion when it has a virus; only rest will cure the common cold. Just so, the soul struggles under conviction and only the rest of salvation will cure its problem. The time you were under conviction may have been very difficult, but it was a blessing because it brought you to the place of repentance.

Jesus said we are born of the water and of the Spirit (John 3:5). Water is a picture of the Word of God (Eph. 5:26), the instrument of salvation. The Holy Spirit is the agent that works in the heart to produce the born-again experience. The Holy Spirit works in our hearts before conversion to bring conviction. He works through the Word of God that has been planted in the heart. The seeker may read the Bible. At other times, a soul winner or preacher will give the seeker the Word of God.

However it is done, the Holy Spirit illuminates the mind to understand the Bible. Understanding brings conviction. God puts pressure on the person to respond to Jesus Christ. Even when a person is searching for God, it is the Holy Spirit who is seeking that person. As the mountaineer said, "I chased the Lord till He caught me."

There are nine important, formative months after conception before a baby is born. But the final act of birth is equally important. The time of birth is recorded by the hospital. Even though the baby has been in the process of life for nine months, the segment of time in which the birth occurs is vital. It is the final product that is important. If the baby is not born healthy, nine months of preparation were futile.

Nine months are not necessary for a person's spiritual conversion. It may happen quickly the first time a person hears the gospel or it may be stretched out over a lengthy time. Some people run from God for years, even decades. Some hear the gospel in their teen years, but aren't saved until adulthood. But even when they were running from God, the Scriptures and the Holy Spirit were at work in their hearts. The Bible is called a fire that burns in the heart (Jer. 20:9), and the Holy Spirit is pictured as one who strives with humankind (Gen. 6:3).

Just as a baby is born at a specific hour in a designated place, so is conversion. You do not grow into salvation. You must make a decision for Christ at some point in time.

On the Day of Pentecost in Acts 2, approxi-

mately 3,000 people believed and were baptized. That was the day of their spiritual birth. The Philippian jailer was told in the middle of the night, "Believe on the Lord Jesus Christ, and you will be saved" (Acts 16:31). That night he became a Christian and was baptized.

You are born again when you ask Jesus Christ to come into your heart. "But as many as received Him [Jesus], to them He gave the right to become children of God,...who were born, not of blood, nor of the will of the flesh, nor of the will of man, but of God" (John 1:12,13).

We have discussed what God did in your heart; this is only half of the picture. The first half is people centered; the second half is what Christ accomplished for you.

What God Did at Calvary

God gave His only begotten Son to die on the cross of calvary in your place because of your sin. In dying, Christ simultaneously accomplished many things on the cross for us. All of these are applied instantaneously the moment we are saved. This once-for-all act of history is the basis for our salvation experience. Don't ever let Satan convince you otherwise.

1. God cleansed you of all your sins by the blood of Christ. Hebrews 9:22 tells us that "without shedding of blood there is no remission [of sin]." The life of a creature is in its blood (Deut. 12:23). When Jesus shed His blood, He gave His life. He gave Himself as a substitute for sin. Jesus became a man in order to have a body that could be offered as the only worthy sacrifice for the sins of humankind. He was born without sin and lived without sin. He was perfect. We were sinners—failures in God's sight.

God accepted Christ's blood for our sins. If you are caught speeding, you have to pay a fine. Your money is the price for breaking the law. You are free to leave the judge's courtroom because the price was paid. The blood of Christ is the price that forgives your sin (1 Pet. 1:18,19). Now you can leave God's courtroom a free person.

2. You were justified and made perfect before God. Before you were saved, you were alienated from God. You may have been an average citizen without filthy habits. Or you may have committed every crime in the book. But no person, no matter how good or bad, can reach God without help. The United States is not legally responsible for citizens of another nation because they belong to another government. When aliens become United States citizens, they can claim the benefits guaranteed under our Constitution and Bill of Rights. Likewise, as an alien, you could not claim the benefits of heaven. But when you put your faith in Christ, God changed your citizenship. Now you belong to a new nation: you have a new King. This is the act of justification.

Paul wrote, "Therefore having been justified by faith, we have peace with God through our Lord Jesus Christ." He went on to write, "For if when we were enemies we were reconciled to God through the death of His Son, much more, having been reconciled, we shall be saved by His life" (Rom. 5:1,10).

When you are justified, God declares you righteous, just as if you had never sinned. When a man goes to prison, his record shows he is a criminal; his confinement shows he is a criminal. A pardon gets him out of prison and forgives his crime, but his record shows he is an ex-con.

In a similar picture, the forgiveness of sins gets a person out of hell, but that person would still be an ex-sinner were it not for justification. This makes the record perfect, and then the person is no longer an ex-sinner, but made just-as-if-the-person-had-never-sinned. The sinner becomes as perfect as God's Son. Justification equips a person for heaven as though he or she had never sinned once.

Now that you are saved, you want to learn how to live the successful Christian life. That is now possible because God has adjusted your record in heaven to appear as if you have never sinned. Try to live according to your record.

3. God made you His child. All people are "children of God" by creation, but that is not good enough for claiming salvation. The Bible claims we were also children of Satan (John. 8:44) and of disobedience (Eph. 2:2). We could not rightfully pray, "Our Father in heaven" (Matt. 6:9) without salvation.

Salvation is described as being born again (John. 3:7). You were born into God's family. You became a child of God by receiving Jesus Christ as your Savior. "But as many as received Him, to them He gave the right to become children of God" (John 1:12). Perhaps you went forward to the altar; there you prayed, "Come into my heart and save me." If you were sincere, you became a child of God; now you can call God your Father.

In one sense, God is the Lord to be reverenced because He judges sin and demands righteousness. The Bible says God is a consuming fire (Heb. 12:29). You should never take your relationship with God lightly. But on the other hand, you can be intimate with God because He is your heavenly Father. Just as a child runs into a father's arms, you can go to God in prayer. He will never turn you away. When Christ came into your heart, you became worthy to approach God. You have His nature (2 Pet. 1:4); you belong to Him.

4. God gave you a new nature, which means you have a new life. Paul referred to sinners as being "dead in trespasses and sins" (Eph. 2:1). He knew sinners were alive physically, mentally and emotionally, but they were dead spiritually. Your spirit, which is capable of knowing God, was dormant and inoperative until it was made alive in Christ. "Therefore, if one is in Christ, he is a new creation: old things have passed away; behold, all things have become new" (2 Cor. 5:17). Only after the new birth can a person grow spiritually.

The new nature opens many wonderful vistas to you. Before you were saved, you probably didn't want to pray, listen to sermons or win souls. Before you were saved you might have craved drink, evil friends and enjoyed evil thoughts.

Now you should experience a "flip-flop" in attitude. You should have new friends. Things about the church you previously thought were silly should become meaningful. You should want to pray and study the Bible. You should become embarrassed by your temper and uncontrolled desires. Your new nature should change your life.

To be a successful Christian, you must let the new nature control you. You are to "put off, concerning your former conduct, the old man" (Eph. 4:22). Don't allow the things that controlled you before salvation to control you now. At the same time, you are to "put on the new man which was created according to God, in true righteousness" (v. 24). God has given you a new nature; you are responsible to let it direct you toward success.

5. God put His seal of ownership on you through the ministry of the Holy Spirit. When you become a Christian, you no longer belong to yourself; you belong to God. Ephesians 1:13 says that "having believed, you were sealed with the holy Spirit of promise." Ephesians 1:14 goes on to say that the presence of the Holy Spirit in the believer "is the guarantee of our inheritance until the redemption of the purchased possession, to the praise of His glory."

God has marked us with His seal. Ford automobiles have a "Ford" trademark stamped into the engine block. In the same way, God stamps His children. The same idea is continued in 2 Corinthians 1:22, which states that God "has sealed us and given us the Spirit in our hearts."

The Evidence God Expects

The salvation experience is not the end of God's dealings with you, but the beginning of a whole new relationship. Christians are expected to "grow in the grace and knowledge of our Lord and Savior Jesus Christ" (2 Pet. 3:18). Here are some of the things for which Christians are responsible.

1. Restitution. If you wronged other people before you were saved, you ought to go to them and make things right. Making restitution may be impossible in some cases if you don't know how to contact these people or if they have died, but if possible, restitution should be made.

Acts of restitution should be done quietly and without publicity. This can be a wonderful way to testify to what Christ has done for you. It may involve humbling and embarrassing situations, but don't let this discourage you. If people you offended will not forgive you, you just have to leave their situations with God and go on from there.

Perhaps the best biblical example of a believer making restitution is that of little Zacchaeus in Jericho. Jesus invited Himself to the home of this hated tax collector. Evidently Jesus had a great influence on Zacchaeus because he said, "Look, Lord, I give half my goods to the poor;

and if I have taken anything from anyone by false accusation, I restore fourfold." Jesus was so impressed by his promise that He observed, "Today salvation has come to this house" (Luke 19:8,9).

2. Identifying with Christ. A new convert should try to live as much like Christ as possible. Several things are involved.

The convert should be baptized immediately—an outward act showing an inner change. In the Early Church, baptism took place as soon after conversion as possible. Baptism is your identification with Christ in His death, burial and resurrection, and your identification with a local church through being placed into the local Body of Christ.

You should attend all the services of your church to fellowship with other Christians for mutual encouragement and service. "And let us consider one another in order to stir up [or stimulate] love and good works, not forsaking the assembling of ourselves together, as is the manner of some, but exhorting one another, and so much the more as you see the Day [of Christ's return] approaching" (Heb. 10:24,25).

You should tell someone immediately that you are saved. Then follow the example of Christ in telling others the goods news of salvation. Jesus said, "Therefore whoever confesses Me before men, him I will also confess before My Father who is in heaven" (Matt. 10:32).

You should be willing to share in the sufferings of Christ. There may be persecution now that you are saved. Realizing that Jesus had suffered to make salvation possible for all people, Paul felt he had a responsibility to fulfill his own share of suffering in getting the gospel message out to lost humankind (Col. 1:24,25). He was also willing to suffer for Jesus if it meant he could know the same kind of power in his life that Christ had experienced when He was raised from the grave (Phil. 3:10,11).

You should do everything possible to provide for spiritual growth. This includes prayer, Bible reading and study.

3. Keeping yourself separated from the world system. "Do not be unequally yoked together with unbelievers. For what fellowship has righteousness with lawlessness? And what communion has light with darkness?...Therefore 'Come out from among them and be separate,' says the Lord. 'Do not touch what is unclean, and I will receive you. I will be a Father to you, and you shall be My sons and daughters, says the Lord Almighty'" (2 Cor. 6:14,17,18).

Now that you are a born-again believer, it is a good idea to remind yourself often of what Christ did for you at calvary. If doubts come and you question your feelings about salvation, recall the fact that Christ died for you. Accept that atonement and realize you were made a new creation in Him (Rom. 5:17). Satan will try to defeat you, but you need not be ignorant of his devices (2 Cor. 2:11). Nothing can separate you from God and His love (Rom. 8:35-39).

Lesson 3—Be Sure of Your Salvation

One of the first obstacles you will face in your Christian life is doubts. You may have many doubts, but none is as demoralizing as doubting your salvation.

The Experience of Doubting

Jim Carlson was a Christian businessman in Atlanta, Georgia. He sat across the desk from his pastor and with difficulty said, "I'm not sure God loves me. The Lord did not hear my prayer." His wife had died of cancer, leaving him with two daughters.

"I asked God to heal her and He didn't," continued the young salesman. "When she suffered, I asked God to take her and He didn't do that immediately." Jim explained that he was $45,000 in debt because of a $300-a-day hospital bill, in addition to doctor's fees. He didn't have money for a baby-sitter and had filed for bankruptcy.

"How can God do this to me?" was his question.

If ever a man's works demonstrated his salvation, Jim Carlson's had. He had taught Sunday School, read the Bible to his family and conducted family prayers. He was respected at the office for his Christian testimony. But now he was confused. Difficult circumstances had clouded his relationship with God. But Jim rebounded and served God once again.

You may have doubts about your salvation when you pray and the heavens seem shut up. Circumstances may one day make you doubt you are a Christian, even though you are presently confident of the fact. This article is written to give reasons for the assurance of your salvation.

Sometimes Christians have doubts when their circumstances are not nearly as spectacular as Jim's. A middle-age housewife came forward during an invitation to confess her sin of depression. "How can I be a Christian and stay so miserable?" she asked. She doubted her salvation because of her depression. (Depression is not always a sin; it can come as a result of chemical or physical imbalance and be beyond the control of the patient.)

A teenage boy stood chatting with some friends. Someone told a story and when the punch line came, it was dirty. The teenage boy laughed, but inwardly he thought, *Christians shouldn't laugh at dirty stories. Am I really a Christian?*

When riding his motorcycle down the street, another young man saw a girl sunbathing in a bikini on her front lawn. He looked two or three times, then thought to himself, *I shouldn't be doing this. Am I a Christian?* He doubted his salvation because of temptation.

Others have doubts because they are ignorant of the Scriptures. An unchurched mother was invited to a Bible study where she began learning the Word of God. Many of her questions were answered. Later she attended an evangelistic service, went forward during the invitation and had a deep experience with Christ. Her life was turned around.

All the way home she sang the hymns she had learned. She threw her arms around her husband, saying, "Honey, I got saved!" She gathered the family and told them the thrilling story. A week later she broke her leg on the steps. Her housework piled up, the kids fought when they took care of the chores and she got discouraged. The height of her salvation became the depth of despondency. *Was it real?* she wondered. She had let her emotions prop up her Christian life to the point where she depended on them.

Others have doubts for another reason. After I spoke at the Philadelphia Sunday School Convention, I gave an invitation for teachers to come forward and dedicate themselves to double their class attendance. A middle-aged lady had come to the civic center meeting by mistake. But she felt a need and came forward at the end of my message.

"Something is wrong with my spiritual life," she kept telling me. She had come forward previously during a giant crusade in the same arena.

"Did you ask Christ to come into your heart?" I asked.

She answered, "Yes." But she was not praying or reading her Bible, nor had she attended church.

"I don't even want to," she answered. "I thought going forward was just emotion, so I dismissed it from my mind until tonight. I choked up just like I did two years ago."

After talking with her for 30 minutes, I determined she had not been saved. I realized she had only voiced a few words the previous time. She prayed the Sinner's Prayer, then we talked about how she should grow spiritually. Later I received a letter telling me: "I feel it all the time."

This lady had doubted because she was not saved. Too many people depend on their *feeling* saved and not on the basis of their actual salvation. They want to add to their salvation experience their ability to "stick it out" as a requirement for getting to heaven. And when they fail, as they surely will at times, they believe they have to get saved again almost every time there is a revival meeting.

What these people need is assurance of salvation, the knowledge that as believers they are saved—absolutely, perfectly, eternally saved. There is no such thing as partly saved and partly lost, partly justified and partly guilty, partly alive and partly dead, partly born of God and partly not. You become a believer through the experience of salvation based on the finished work of Christ on the cross for you—your salvation is secure throughout all eternity.

Your condition may be similar to this woman's; you may have nagging doubts about your spiritual condition. You may have doubts about your salvation, and when you compare your circumstances to the checklist that follows, you may realize you are lost. This thought is not intended to unsettle you, but to help you discover the truth about your spiritual condition.

The Basis of Your Assurance

"Nothing is sure in life but death and taxes," the saying goes. But that is not true. You can be sure of your salvation. Just as you are sure that you will go down when falling from a tree, you can know that God has saved your soul. Just as you know that a fire is hot, you can know that you have eternal life. This is called the assurance of salvation. It is the opposite of doubt and it is based on scriptural fact.

1. Assurance of salvation comes because you have Christ in your heart. First John 5:12 states clearly, "He who has the Son has life." Jesus Christ came into your heart when you invited Him in. If you have the Savior, you are saved. Christ says in Revelation 3:20, "Behold, I stand at the door and knock. If anyone hears My voice and opens the door, I will come in." With His entrance comes eternal life. "Christ in you, the hope of glory" (Col. 1:27).

I started attending revival services when I was a 17-year-old teenager. The pastor realized I didn't know I was unsaved. I was trusting in my church membership. I was not convinced I needed to be saved.

The pastor took me on a hospital visit. "Go lead everyone in that ward to Christ," he said. I began handing out tracts.

An elderly man asked me, "How do you get to heaven?" The only answer I could give was an erroneous one I had been taught.

"Believe in Christ and do the best you can," I told the old gentleman.

"I don't think you are correct," the man replied. "You might not have salvation, either."

The seed of concern was planted in my heart. It grew after I went to a church prayer meeting where people gave testimonies of having Christ in their hearts. I returned home and knelt by my bed and prayed, "Lord, I don't think I have ever done it before, but I want Christ in my heart now." I experienced salvation when Christ came into my heart.

2. Assurance of salvation comes from the witness of the Word of God. "He who believes on the Son of God has the witness in himself" (1 John 5:10). *Has* means you have salvation—now. It does not say, "He who belongs to a church." It is not a question of who is right, but of what the Bible says. "And this is the testimony: that God has given us eternal life, and this life is in His Son" (v. 11).

Whereas the first reason dealt with experience, this proof of salvation is based on the facts of the Bible. If you have received Christ, you should not have doubts about your salvation because God promised to save those who trust in Him. If you want assurance, first study the Bible promises of salvation, then claim them. God never goes back on His promises, so the promises provide anchors that hold the believer fast.

Certain verses in the Bible make the offer of salvation crystal clear. These should remove any doubts you have about your relationship with God. "For God so loved the world that He gave His only begotten Son, that whoever believes in Him should not perish but have everlasting life" (John 3:16). "Believe on the Lord Jesus Christ, and you will be saved, you and your household" (Acts 16:31). "If you confess with your mouth the Lord Jesus and believe in your heart that God has raised Him from the dead, you will be saved" (Rom. 10:9). Assurance is based on accepting these promises and acting on them.

Paul had much to say about assurance. He wrote that the gospel came to believers "in power, and in the Holy Spirit, and in much assurance" (1 Thess. 1:5). Paul told believers that he was "confident of this very thing, that He who has begun a good work in you will complete it until the day of Jesus Christ" (Phil. 1:6). Paul's own personal testimony was, "I know whom I have believed and am persuaded that He is able to keep what I have committed to Him until that Day" (2 Tim. 1:12).

The writer of Hebrews expressed his desire that believers enjoy full assurance of their hope to the end (Heb. 6:11). He rejoiced in the fact that Christ had opened the way for people to approach God, "Having a High Priest over the house of God, let us draw near with a true heart in full assurance of faith" (Heb. 10:21,22).

The apostle John said believers could assure themselves of a right relationship with God by keeping His commandments (1 John 2:3; 3:22). He said believers can know they have eternal life by studying scriptural truths (5:13).

Jude said that believers are preserved in Christ (Jude 1), that God is able to keep them from falling and will receive them into His presence as if they were faultless because of their identification with their Savior (vv. 24,25). The promises of God guarantee our security. The Bible asks, "Who shall separate us from the love of Christ?" (Rom. 8:35). The answer is obvious—no one, and nothing.

3. Assurance of salvation comes because God answers your prayers. The Lord has promised to answer the prayers of His children. "If you ask anything in My name, I will do it" (John 14:14). Of course, there are conditions to prayer, but when you meet these conditions, God will answer your prayers.

On the other hand, God has stated that He will not answer the prayers of the unsaved. "Behold, the Lord's hand is not shortened, that it cannot save; nor His ear heavy, that it cannot hear. But your iniquities have separated you from your God; and your sins have hidden His face from you, so that He will not hear" (Isa. 59:1,2; see also Matt. 7:7,8; John 9:31; 14:14; 15:7; 1 John 5:14,15). "If I regard iniquity in my heart, the Lord will not hear" (Ps. 66:18). The only prayer God can answer for the unsaved is "God be merciful to me, a sinner, and save me for Jesus' sake."

"Now this is the confidence that we have in Him, that if we ask anything according to His will, He hears us. And if we know that He hear us, whatever we ask, we know that we have the petitions that we have asked of Him" (1 John 5:14,15).

4. Assurance of salvation comes if you understand the Bible. John promises, "And we know that the Son of God has come and has given us an understanding" (v. 20). An inner understanding of the Bible is proof that you are a Christian. Why? Because unsaved people are blinded to spiritual truths. "But the natural man does not receive the things of the Spirit of God" (1 Cor. 2:14). This is again described by Paul as "having their understanding darkened" (Eph. 4:18).

Just as blind people cannot see the world about them, unsaved people are blind to God's Word. They cannot understand the message of the Bible. They know the meaning of words and the plot of the story, but the spiritual message of redemption is withheld from them.

Before you were saved, the Holy Spirit convicted you of sin, righteousness and judgment (John 16:9-11). The word "convict" means to cause to see; the Holy Spirit made you see or understand God's plan of redemption. This was the work of God in your heart, bringing you to salvation. Those who rejected the Word were further blinded. Now, if you have a desire to read the Bible and understand God's message, you are saved. This does not mean you could pass a test in biblical knowledge, but that you understand the plan of salvation.

5. Assurance of salvation comes when you want to keep His commandments. God's commandments are based on His nature; they are what He wants us to do. The natural man has a sinful nature and doesn't want to follow God. When you were unsaved, you did not want to do God's will. After you received Christ, however, a desire came to do God's will (2 Cor. 5:17), even if you didn't always follow your desire.

A young father put off receiving Christ for several months. The pastor went by to talk with him on several occasions, but the father always said, "Later." Finally, he told the pastor that he came from a family that always drank beer and wine with their meals. "When I go back home for a family reunion, I know I'll drink alcohol with them."

The pastor showed him the victory that was promised in Jesus Christ, and the young father was saved. A year later, he came to the altar one Sunday morning, crying. He wouldn't let anyone deal with him but the pastor.

"I have been drinking with some buddies. I must not be saved." The pastor prayed for wisdom in handling the situation.

"Do you remember drinking on Christmas right before that day you came to the altar?" the pastor asked.

"Yes," the man said. The pastor pointed out that the young man did not feel convicted at the time, and did not show any emotional upheaval or tears.

"Why are you crying about your drinking now?" the pastor asked. The father saw the point. Christ lived in his heart, so he could no longer go back to his old habits without offending Jesus Christ.

Assurance of salvation comes when you realize you have new desires. "We know that whoever is born of God does not sin; but he who has been born of God keeps himself, and the wicked one does not touch him" (1 John 5:18). This sounds like a contradiction of 1 John 1:8, "If we say that we have no sin, we deceive ourselves, and the truth is not in us." One verse says a Christian will sin; the other says a Christian will not sin. What is the answer?

The second verse indicates the Christian still has a sinful nature. First John 1:10 states, "If we say that we have not sinned, we make Him a liar, and His word is not in us." The verse "Whoever is born of God does not sin" (1 John. 5:18) describes the Christian's new nature. Your new nature cannot sin; it wants to do the will of God.

"Whoever is born of God does not sin" has been used wrongly to attempt to prove sinless perfection. The original language indicates "does not sin" means "does not sin continually." The Christian will not continue in sin (live there habitually). God puts the desire within the Christian to live above sin.

A missionary to China told the story of a servant girl who worked in their home. Before the girl became a Christian, the missionary could not trust the girl because she stole articles around the home. It was necessary to search her before she left each day.

After she accepted Christ, the girl took a $20 gold piece while dusting one day; but she came back in the middle of the night to return the stolen money. Her new nature had made her miserable in her sin. If you are miserable in your sin, it is evidence of salvation.

Some go forward in church and make an open profession of faith, but there is no work of God in the heart. It is only an outward display. You can take a pig from the mud, scrub it and paste on lamb's wool so that it gives the appearance of being a sheep, but when you turn the pig out to pasture, it will return to the mud with the pigs rather than eat grass with the sheep. It is the pig's nature. The Christian is different—now you have a new nature. You might sin, but you won't like it.

6. Assurance of salvation comes when you love the brethren. "We know that we have passed from death to life, because we love the brethren. He who does not love his brother abides in death" (1 John 3:14). Love manifests itself first in fellowship. When you are born again, you want to be around other Christians. Because God is Father to both you and other Christians, there is a common bond among you.

Love manifests itself in a burden for other Christians. When you see a Christian sin and it bothers you, that is a sign you are saved. When you see a Christian who has a need and you want to help the person, that also is a sign you are saved. When you see a victorious Christian and you want to live like that person, rejoice, for your name is written in the Lamb's Book of Life.

A minister recently went to a mission church to preach at a prayer meeting. The host pastor and his wife prepared a steak dinner with all the trimmings, including apple pie for dessert.

The crowd was small—only 26 people were present. The love offering for the guest preacher came to $26. When the visiting preacher discovered the financial pressures in the mission church and that the pastor only had a can of beans left in the cupboard, he gave him the $26. Both gave evidence of the fellowship of salvation—the mission pastor and his wife because they gave all except a can of beans, and the visiting pastor because he gave all in return.

Love for other Christians is proof of your salvation—but becoming angry at another believer does not prove you are not saved. Paul and Barnabas got angry at each other. Some Christians may inflict wrong on you and you might lose your temper; this should not make you doubt your salvation.

If you like to fellowship with Christians at church, you are probably saved. If the people you love most in this world are Christians, you are probably saved. If they are not, you ought to ask yourself why.

Love is giving yourself to the one you love. When you give yourself to a group of Christians (the assembled church) and together you give yourselves to the Great Commission, you should have confidence that you are saved.

7. *Assurance of salvation comes when you have the inner witness of the Holy Spirit.* When you became a Christian, the Holy Spirit came into your heart to create a new nature within you (Rom. 5:5), and to seal you until the final day of redemption (Eph. 1:13,14). The Holy Spirit dwells in every Christian. One clue that a man is not saved is that he doesn't have the Holy Spirit (Rom. 8:9).

The indwelling Holy Spirit witnesses that you are saved. He does not communicate through the ears or eyes. He communicates from His heart to your heart. "The Spirit Himself bears witness with our spirit that we are children of God" (v. 16). This is innate knowledge, knowledge that doesn't need proof. Some young Christians, when asked how they know they are saved, reply, "I just know." They may not be educated or articulate, but they know they are saved. This is the witness of the Holy Spirit.

Several New Testament references show the Holy Spirit gives assurance. The Holy Spirit in our hearts gives us assurance of sonship: "Because you are sons, God has sent forth the Spirit of His Son into your hearts, crying out, 'Abba, Father!'" (Gal. 4:6). The Aramaic term *Abba* and the Greek term *Pater* are both used here. This means God is an intimate Father (papa).

The apostle John said, "By this we know that He abides in us, by the Spirit whom He has given us" (1 John 3:24). He combined the concepts of the witness of the Spirit and belief in God's Word in 5:10: "He who believes in the Son of God has the witness in himself; he who does not believe God has made Him a liar, because he has not believed the testimony that God has given of His Son."

The inner presence of the Holy Spirit gives the desire to live a clean life. If you want to live a godly life, you are probably saved. Writing to believers, Paul said, "But now having been free from sin, and having become slaves of God, you have your fruit to holiness, and the end, everlasting life" (Rom. 6:22).

The best-known reference regarding the grace produced in the believer by the Holy Spirit is Galatians 5:22,23: "But the fruit of the Spirit is love, joy, peace, longsuffering, kindness, goodness, faithfulness, gentleness, self-control. Against such there is no law." If you are loving, joyful, peaceful, meek and self-controlled, you will be fulfilling what the Holy Spirit desires for you. If you desire righteousness, you are probably saved.

Some Christians backslide; they don't desire a pure life. They don't portray what Paul wrote: "The fruit of the Spirit is [manifested] in all goodness, righteousness, and truth" (Eph. 5:9). We can't say the sinning saint is not saved. The Bible teaches that children of God will sin, even though they shouldn't; and God has provided His way for the sinning Christians to be cleansed of their sins. Read 1 John 1:5-10 and realize that the apostle is writing to believers. But if Christians do not follow this way of confessing their sins to God and ask to be forgiven, God will chasten them.

The writer of Hebrews said divine discipline is administered to God's children. "Now no chastening seems joyful for the present, but grievous; nevertheless, afterward it yields the peaceable fruit of righteousness to those who have been trained by it" (Heb. 12:11). If you have sinned and you realize you are suffering because of it, it is a sign that you are saved. If you get away with your sin, you might not be a child of God.

Summary

In summary, then, those are the ways to know if you have been truly saved. You are saved if you believe God's Word and have applied the promises of salvation to yourself, have the witness of the Spirit that you are a child of God and demonstrate the fruit of the Spirit in your life.

Don't let the enemy rob you of your assurance of salvation, for God gave you these promises to hold you fast. It is a tragic thing for believers to lack assurance; their spiritual lives will stagnate. Doubt keeps them from the Bible, prayer, witnessing and the desire to live for God. But once we become absolutely sure of our relationship to the Lord, our relationships with people will improve.

The Rewards of Assurance

The following are three of the main blessings you will enjoy from assurance.

1. Your fear of being eternally lost is gone. It is a terrible thing to constantly wonder whether your future destiny is heaven or the lake of fire. Those lacking assurance are likely to become so discouraged that they give up and begin to backslide. Or, they may become legalists, thinking that by rigid adherence to a multitude of rules and regulations, they can satisfy God and ultimately be saved. Such actions are unfortunate and unnecessary.

2. The assurance of your salvation will build your confidence in God. When you read your Bible, you can accept and believe all its passages. When you pray, you can come to the throne of grace and find the help every believer has a right to expect from a loving and bountiful heavenly Father. The time you once spent worrying about your position in Christ can now be devoted to service for Christ.

3. When you are sure of your salvation, you will be able to witness to others better. You can tell others that you have no doubt about having had your sins forgiven and you know where you will spend eternity. An invitation to another to accept Christ as personal Savior must be backed up by the conviction that you yourself think it is worthwhile.

Your search for assurance must find its conclusion in God. First, His Word provides the basis of salvation. Second, His Spirit provides the inner witness that speaks to your spirit. Finally, the fact of a changed life convinces you of salvation. Remember, the changed life is not self-improvement; righteousness cannot be earned or self-induced. Your new nature must be imparted by God—it will give assurance to those who put their faith in God and His Son, Jesus Christ.

Lesson 4—Become Grounded on the Word of God

As a Christian, the most indispensable instrument for your life is the Bible. You can't be a growing Christian without it.

The Bible Teaches Christians How to Live

The first time Harold Shickley attended church he went forward and received Christ. The only things he knew about Christianity were the things he had heard on radio and television at Christmas and Easter.

"I don't know much about God," Harold told his pastor.

Harold was given a Bible and told to start reading it.

"The Bible will keep you from sin, or sin will keep you from the Bible," his pastor told him.

"I don't understand it," he later told his pastor. As a matter of fact, he didn't understand much that happened the evening he was saved because it was his first time in a church. But he knew in his heart something had happened to him.

Because Harold wasn't grounded in the principles of the faith, he continued hanging around with his drinking buddies. At first he went to church, but gradually he lost the desire and drifted away.

"Why did you give up?" the pastor asked when they met in a convenience market.

"I just couldn't hold out," he replied.

"I'll help you grow in your faith," the pastor promised.

The defeated Harold agreed to "try" the Christian life again. This time the pastor showed him how to study the Bible. Harold began reading the Gospel of John. Staying up late at night, he devoured the pages of Scripture; like a hungry man, he couldn't get enough. As the Bible changed his desires, his drinking buddies lost interest in him and he in them. The lesson was hard for Harold to learn, but the Word of God will keep a person from sin.

1. You are protected from sin by the Word of God. "Your word have I hidden in my heart, that I might not sin against You" (Ps. 119:11). The Bible keeps you from sin by its instructional power. It teaches the correct way of life. "Your word is a lamp to my feet and a light to my path" (Ps. 119:105). Arnold Toynbee, a historian, noted, "It pierces through the intellect and plays directly upon the heart."

The Scriptures are similar to a vaccination protecting you by cleansing your conscience (John 15:3); giving you joy (Jer. 15:16); correcting wrong teaching that would allow deviation (2 Tim. 3:16); and producing a hedge against sin in your life (Heb. 4:12).

2. You grow in faith by the Word of God. Five times the Bible refers to Christians as "babes" or "children," and each time the answer to immaturity is found in the Bible (1 Cor. 3:1-3; 4:14-21; Eph. 4:14; Heb. 5:11-14; 1 Pet. 2:2). When you received Christ as Savior, you were born into God's family. Now you must grow as a child of God.

Nothing is wrong with babies; in fact, they are delightful. As a young father, I was the first to arrive at the maternity ward each evening with a camera to take pictures of Debbie. We kept a scrapbook that listed a record of her pounds, inches and vital statistics. I bragged to Richard Strauss that my daughter would outgrow his son, who was born at approximately the same time. If she had never grown, my expectations would have been destroyed.

Growth is the natural process of the foods we eat working in our bodies. If we eat the right things, we'll grow. A Christian must eat the right spiritual food to grow spiritually. Jeremiah noted, "Your words were found, and I ate them, and Your word was to me the joy and rejoicing of My heart" (Jer. 15:16).

A man of God once told me that every reference to spiritual growth was connected with knowing and obeying the Bible, and he was right. If you don't eat properly, you will get sick eventually; and if you neglect the Word of God, you'll dry up spiritually like a shriveled raisin. The Bible is milk for the spirit (1 Pet. 2:2), meat for the growing Christian (Heb. 5:12-14), bread for the hungry (John 6:51) and honey for satisfaction (Ps. 19:10).

3. You hear the voice of God through the Word of God. The Bible brings peace when your heart is troubled. For many years, the Gideons have placed Bibles in hotel rooms. Their files are filled with stories of people who were contemplating suicide, divorce or an act of violence, but picking up the Bible, turned to the guide "When in Trouble" and found that the Word of God gave them encouragement and hope. Christians hear the Bible with the ears of their hearts. God speaks to them through the Scriptures. Chiang Kai-shek testified, "The Bible is the voice of the Holy Spirit."

But what about the unsaved? What is their response to the Bible? First, the Scriptures work in a person's heart to bring conviction. Paul describes Timothy's salvation: "And that from childhood you have known the Holy Scriptures, which are able to make you wise for salvation through faith which is in Christ Jesus" (2 Tim.

3:15). Many children, like young Timothy, grow up in Christian homes, but Scripture is what brings them to Christ.

Martha Towns received Christ because she memorized the Word of God. She had her devotions "religiously" each night and never became involved in sin. Her brother, Elmer Towns, believed she had not experienced salvation. He typed 100 verses on 3-x-5-inch cards, and promised her a new *Scofield Reference Bible* when she could repeat them perfectly. As she quoted each verse, he instructed her in the verse's meaning. Halfway through the project, she went to camp. Phoning long distance, Martha told of conviction that led to salvation because an evangelist quoted the verses she had been learning.

God's Word does more than speak to the innocent. It reaches the hardened heart, too. Two men struck up a conversation at an evangelistic crusade. Before the service both were critical of the evangelist's methods, but the speaker kept repeating the phrase "The Bible says." At the invitation, one man said to the other, "I don't know about you, but I'm going forward to get saved." The other hesitated a moment, then reached into his coat and replied, "Here's your wallet; I took it. I'll go with you."

4. The Word of God will set you free. There is no such thing as absolute freedom, although we hear many people today claim it. Everyone, saved and unsaved, is responsible to God. As a lost person you accepted Christ and fulfilled that responsibility to God. Now you must learn what God wants you to do and what He prohibits. The Bible is a guidebook containing both positive and negative principles that God expects you to follow. If you saturate yourself with scriptural principles, you will be able to live within His framework.

You become like Jesus Christ as you study the Bible. Paul tells us, "We all, with unveiled face, beholding as in a mirror the glory of the Lord, are being transformed into the same image from glory to glory" (2 Cor. 3:18). This verse illustrates the truth by describing a person standing in front of a mirror, which is God's Word. In the mirror, the person doesn't see his or her image, but a reflection of Jesus Christ. The more the person studies the mirror (the Bible), the more that person becomes like Jesus Christ.

Some habits will disappear immediately after conversion. Others will linger. The Bible is your source of strength for overcoming all habits. As God's Word becomes a part of your thinking, you in turn will think like God and overcome bad habits.

How to Study the Bible

1. Study the Bible itself. The Christians in Berea were called "noble" because "they received the word with all readiness of mind, and searched the scriptures" (Acts 17:11, *KJV*). Don't study books about the Bible first. These books have their value, of course, but books are what men think about the Bible. Let the Holy Spirit speak directly to you. He can do it when you study the Scriptures.

A young college student asked Dwight L. Moody's advice about his life's work after seminary. "Don't go into business. Your father's wealthy and you have more money than you'll need. Devote your life to teaching the English Bible."

"I don't know it," was the astonished young man's reply.

"Don't you go to a religious college where they have professors to teach you the Bible?"

"Yes, that is true. But I have listened to one professor lecture for six months and we still haven't determined who wrote the first five books of the Bible."

Moody told the young man, "Study the Bible on your own; master its contents." The young man took his advice and became one of the greatest Bible teachers of his day. You, too, should begin studying the Bible so you can master its contents.

2. Study the Bible diligently. When you study the Bible, don't just casually read it, but drink in every word. Remember the Berean Christians who "searched the scriptures." The word "searched" means investigated, inquired, sifted or scrutinized.

Pay attention to every word because God placed every word there for a reason. Have a dictionary handy and look up the important words. Acquire *The Scofield Reference Bible* and study the words in the reference column or in the subject index at the back of the Bible.

Try to remember everything you read. If your mind wanders, practice concentrating. You'll soon be able to concentrate on every verse.

"Tell me in one word how to study the Bible," a man once asked R. A. Torrey.

"That's not easy, but if I could use only one word it would be 'thoughtfully.'"

The Berean Christians "searched the scriptures daily, whether those things were so" (17:11, KJV). They were not satisfied just to read the Bible; they wanted to know if the things Paul preached were accurate. We make a big mistake when we fit our church's view into the verses we read in the Bible.

3. *Study the entire Bible.* The Bereans studied "daily." On Easter Sunday afternoon, two disciples were walking to Emmaus. Jesus joined them. "And beginning at Moses and all the Prophets, He expounded to them in all the Scriptures the things concerning Himself" (Luke 24:27). In this short hike to Emmaus, Jesus covered the first five books of the Bible (Moses) through the last 17 books (all the prophets). Jesus evidently had studied all the Scriptures. The fact that He taught it to His disciples shows He wants us to know it all, too.

Dr. Ash Moore, a missionary for 50 years, started teaching the book of Hebrews. It raised so many questions regarding the ceremonial law that he began teaching the book of Leviticus; but still the questions came. He decided to go back to Genesis and start with the foundation of Scripture.

If you have never read through the Bible, begin doing so now. Start with Genesis. If you don't understand some things, don't get discouraged. Theodore Epp, speaker of "Back to the Bible" radio broadcast, once said, "I had to read through the Bible 10 times before I really understood it."

G. Campbell Morgan said one could read through the Bible at the pulpit rate in 60 hours. A banker challenged his statement.

"Well, sir, the proof lies with you," responded Morgan.

The banker returned to tell Morgan he was wrong. "I did it in 40 hours."

"I said the *pulpit* rate," the wise Morgan said, stroking his white beard. "You can't trust a banker's rate."

Some study a pet book such as John, Romans, Daniel or Revelation. Some study only pet subjects such as healing, dispensationalism or the Second Coming. But the entire Bible is the Word of God, so we ought to study all of it.

4. *Study the Bible systematically.* The word "daily" also meant that the Bereans studied the Bible in a systematic order. Jesus must have studied the Bible as He taught it—systematically. "Beginning at Moses and all the Prophets, He expounded to them in all the Scriptures the things concerning Himself" (Luke 24:27). In your study, select a subject and follow it through. Take one word and look up every reference to that word in a concordance.

As you begin studying a book, read through it to the end. One minister became a great doctrinal preacher, in spite of the fact that he never went to college. When asked where he had learned his doctrine, he answered, "What I know I've learned, one subject at a time, one book at a time." He went on to explain, "When I began studying a topic, I stayed with it until I got to the conclusion."

Read through the Bible. Then go back and read each New Testament book through in one sitting. Finally, read the entire New Testament through in one weekend.

5. *Study the Bible as the Word of God that demands complete obedience to every command that applies to you.* God will keep all the promises in the Bible. The Bereans studied the Bible to determine "whether those things were so." They found out, "All the promises of God in Him are yes, and in Him Amen" (2 Cor. 1:20). God will keep all His promises because "It is impossible for God to lie" (Heb. 6:18). When you study, you must trust God without reservation, doubt or anxiety. The promises God made regarding His coming again to earth, He will keep. You cannot spiritualize these as His coming into your life. God will keep His promises, as He said—not as you want them fulfilled.

When the Bible promises something, believe it. When the feeble mind can't comprehend it, believe it. "In hope of eternal life which God, who cannot lie, promised before time began" (Titus 1:2).

While pastoring in Dallas, Texas, I was doing

some carpenter work in the back of the auditorium. Gradually I felt self-conscious and turned around to see a small boy watching me. His presence changed my actions. When you study the Bible, visualize Christ standing there, speaking to you. The Bible will come alive as His presence changes your actions.

After I was engaged, my fiancée and I were separated for three summers. At the college mail call, I didn't dare read her letters in front of others. I'd go to my room, take out her picture and read the letter in privacy, pouring over every word. When you study the Bible, find a private place and picture Christ standing nearby.

7. Study the Bible in an attitude of prayer and yieldedness. "With all readiness of mind" means to yield in our minds to believe what the Bible teaches. When I was a college freshman, questions about the Bible assignment were mimeographed for us. At the top of the page were the instructions: "Pray for the illumination of the Holy Spirit as you study."

From this class, I learned a lifelong habit of praying before I study the Bible. Just as I ask God to bless the food before I eat, I ask God to bless me before I study the Word. I usually pray something like this: "Lord, help me to see things in the Bible I've never seen before, and make me understand the difficult passages. Help me to retain as much as possible. Now, I'm completely dependent upon You in this study."

If you have difficulty in Bible study, tell Jesus. If your mind is dull, if you can't concentrate, if you can't remember, if you get sleepy, tell Jesus.

Steps in Bible Study

Take Christianity seriously. Set aside a time to hear, read, study and memorize the Word of God, and to meditate on it. Five words are stepping stones to mastering the Bible.

1. Hear. The first step is to listen to the Bible because "Faith comes by hearing" (Rom. 10:17). Listen to the Bible as it is read at church and in Sunday School. Pay attention to the Word of God as it is taught and preached.

But be careful how you listen to the Bible. Jesus told the story of the parable of the sower, explaining that the various soils represented the different ways people listen to Scripture. Some

seeds fell by the wayside and were consumed by birds. This represented people who heard the gospel, but allowed Satan to snatch it away before it could take root.

Some seeds fell on stony places without much soil. Because the seed could not put down roots, it withered under the hot sun. This represented people who heard the Bible, but did not take the gospel seriously. They wilted under the heat of persecution.

Some seeds fell among thorns and germinated, but were choked out. This represented people who heard the gospel, but let the cares of this world keep them from responding to it.

Finally, some seeds fell on good soil and eventually produced a harvest. This represented people who heard the gospel, believed and applied it. After this parable, Jesus noted, "Hearing they do not hear, nor do they understand" (Matt. 13:13). We should listen sincerely with our hearts and with our heads.

2. Read. Paul counseled Timothy to read the Word: "Till I come, give attention to reading, to exhortation, to doctrine" (1 Tim. 4:13). The great revival under Nehemiah broke out because "they read distinctly from the book, in the Law of God; and they gave the sense, and helped them to understand the reading" (Neh. 8:8). Notice that they didn't just read; they understood. Let the Son of God illumine your reading. The Bible without the Son is like a sundial lit by the moon.

Read the Bible daily. Don't leave Bible reading up to your inclination; don't wait until you are ready to study the Bible. Some days you won't feel like reading Scripture. You will have to discipline yourself if you are to grow in Bible knowledge. General Douglas MacArthur claimed, "Believe me, sir, never a night goes by, be I ever so tired, but I read the Word of God before I go to bed." Develop a daily Bible reading plan. You can read the entire Bible in one year if you read four chapters a day.

A veteran Christian who had long walked with God confessed, "When praying, I am talking to God; when reading the Scripture, He is talking to me. And I'm better off when *He* does most of the talking."

Great Christians were once characterized by much prayer, more Bible and total surrender.

3. *Study.* Paul exhorted Timothy, "Study to shew thyself approved unto God, a workman that needeth not to be ashamed, rightly dividing the word of truth" (2 Tim. 2:15, *KJV*). Two facts are seen in this verse. First, you are to study the Bible by giving it your best. Second, you are to divide the Bible, which means slice into it. We personally do our slicing (study) by answering questions.

As a young Christian, you are similar to those who are in the first grade. You don't know the material, nor how to study. An effective plan is to begin with a basic Bible study book, one that has questions that will make you think your way through each verse. This guide will give you a systematic approach to personal study. Reading will give breadth; study will give depth.

The first question to ask yourself is: What does this passage say? In other words, you are concerned with the facts in the passage. These are often easier to understand in narrative and doctrinal passages than they are in prophetic and poetic passages because they are less likely to be expressed in symbolic terms.

After you have studied the Bible, it is helpful to have Bible study tools, such as a good reference Bible, an exhaustive concordance, a Bible dictionary and a Bible commentary or two on hand for unraveling difficult verses. Other valuable helps are a Bible handbook, an atlas, word-study books and a harmony of the Gospels.

You must remember that the books of the Bible were written long ago and describe concepts and customs that are often foreign to our own culture. Until you understand what God was saying through the various men who wrote the Bible, you will have difficulty interpreting its facts. Everything in the Bible should be taken as literally true except in cases where it is obvious that figurative or symbolic language is being used. Even then, symbols, similes and metaphors have a literal interpretation. Never interpret words apart from their literal meaning.

The second question we should ask ourselves about a passage of the Bible is: What does this passage mean? In other words, you are concerned about the principle underlying the facts. This is not too difficult to determine in narrative passages. Four kinds of stories are presented in

the Bible: problem, search, journey and character change. Each has a climax, a time when the problem is solved, the search is ended, the destination is reached or the character of a person changes for good or bad. The main principle is usually found at the climax.

For example, the story of the prodigal son, as recorded in Luke 15:11-32, can be reduced to the principle that a loving father forgives a repentant son. Discovering this principle in that passage gives us an eternal truth we can use today, for our heavenly Father forgives us when we repent, too.

Finding the main principle in a doctrinal, prophetic or poetic passage demands that we look carefully for the main idea in that passage. It may have something to do with people, places, times, things or events. Sometimes certain terms indicate a summary or conclusion, such as "therefore," "so then" or "wherefore."

It may take considerable time to determine the principle in a passage of Scripture, but if we are patient and depend on the Holy Spirit to reveal it to us, we will find it. A grasp of facts may be primarily a mental thing, but gaining spiritual insights requires something more. Discernment is a special gift from the Lord and it cannot be rushed or forced.

The third question we should ask ourselves about a passage of the Bible is, What does this passage mean to me? In other words, we are to be concerned about the applications of the principle of the passage to our lives.

Applications are suggested to us in a variety of ways. Sometimes you will hear the principles applied from pastors, evangelists, teachers and others to whose ministry you listen. Sometimes you will hear them from other students in your classes. You may hear them in conversations with other believers. You may discover them in real-life experiences as you go along from day to day. Sometimes you will read about them in good Christian books or periodicals. Some applications are simply the voice of the Holy Spirit speaking directly to your heart. Whatever the sources of your applications, they become real only if you use them.

The inductive method of Bible study recognizes that learning moves in stages. The intellect analyzes the facts of God's Word as it tries to understand them clearly. The emotions respond to the principle drawn out of the facts of a passage and stimulate a person to change. The willpower takes the principle and applies it to a person's life so that changes are made. The order cannot be reversed, for God has made people so they operate in this particular way.

We might compare the process to driving. The automobile represents the Bible. The fuel that gives it power is the Holy Spirit. The owner gets in, turns the key of a yielded will and off the owner goes.

4. Memorize. The next step in Bible study is learning it by heart. The psalmist declared, "Your word I have hidden in my heart, that I might not sin against You" (Ps. 119:11). You will want to memorize portions of Scripture for a variety of reasons. When Jesus was tempted in the wilderness, He quoted Scripture. If you have the Bible in your heart, you too can quote the Scriptures in a moment of trial.

When Philip, a deacon, wanted to witness to the Ethiopian in the chariot, he knew Isaiah 53 and used it to lead the eunuch to salvation. Besides using Scripture to combat temptation and as a soul-winning tool, God's Word will guide you into God's will by helping you make difficult decisions.

Memorize Scripture by first underlining the verse in your Bible. Mark the verse so it will stand out the next time you study the passage. Next, write or type the verse on a small card. Carry it with you for review in your free time.

Plan a systematic way to review the verses you have already memorized. Without reviewing, you can't remember the exact words; you may even forget the entire verse. But you will grow in the process of applying diligent effort to master the verse and its meaning.

"Why should I memorize?" someone asked. "The Bible runs through my mind like a sieve."

The Bible is like water. At least it keeps the sieve clean.

The Navigators organization was born when Dawson Trotman challenged men to memorize large numbers of Scripture texts. The organization was especially effective during World War II. One sailor left his packet of verses lying

around and Trotman picked it up to see if the owner could repeat them all.

When he stumbled repeatedly over familiar verses, Trotman said, "That is why the Lord hasn't saved the 240 men on your ship. You do not take the Bible seriously." When you memorize Scripture, you show God you mean business.

5. Meditate. The Bible commands us to meditate on its words (Ps. 119:15). This means thinking about Scripture all the time in your mind. When you wash the dishes, cut the grass or wait for your wife or husband, meditate on Bible verses you have memorized.

Meditation involves repeating the words in your mind again and again. It's similar to an old cow in the field, chewing the cud, getting all the goodness she can out of every bite.

The psalmist indicated that the growing Christian is like the growing tree, prospering because of meditation. "Blessed is the man who walks not in the counsel of the ungodly, nor stands in the path of sinners, nor sits in the seat of the scornful; but his delight is in the law of the Lord, and in His law he meditates day and night" (Ps. 1:1,2). The psalmist continues, "He shall be like a tree planted by the rivers of water, that brings forth its fruit in its season" (v. 3).

You should meditate on the Bible because it is a message from God. Because each word has significance and none is there by error, you should meditate on every word. You can spend a lifetime studying the Bible and never exhaust its depth.

Lesson 5—Make Prayer a Regular Part of Your Life

A man met a former high school friend recently on the streets of Savannah, Georgia. In school he thought she was pretty, but they had been only casual friends. After reminiscing about old friends, she asked, "Why didn't you ever ask me for a date?"

"I didn't think I was good enough," he explained. "You dated the football heroes and fellows with the fancy cars. I didn't think girls cared about me because I was going to be a preacher."

She shook her head in amazement. "I wanted to date you *because* you were going to be a preacher." She told how she had walked by his house hoping he would come out the door. As they talked, he remembered the words of Scripture, "You have not because you ask not." He could have dated the girl, but didn't ask. Many Christians miss the things God has for them because they don't ask.

Prayer is asking and getting answers from God. Every Christian is invited to go directly to the Father in heaven: "Ask, and it will be given to you; seek, and you will find; knock, and it will be opened to you" (Matt. 7:7). Jesus told us, "If you ask anything in My name, I will do it" (John 14:14). "If you abide in Me,...you will ask what you desire, and it shall be done for you" (15:7). "If we ask anything according to His will, He hears us" (1 John 5:14). "You do not have because you do not ask" (Jas. 4:2).

Prayer is not just asking; it's confession, adoration, thanksgiving and fellowship with God. Some people don't ask for anything, while others ask all the time. They treat God as if He were a Santa Claus. To them, prayer is just wishing. We must learn the true nature of prayer.

The Nature of Prayer

1. Prayer is talking with your heavenly Father. A father talks to his baby long before the child talks back. Our heavenly Father did that for us in the Bible. He wrote a message to us long before we were saved. Now we talk back in prayer. God hears our prayers because we are His children.

During the Civil War, a little girl tried to get into the White House to see President Lincoln. She wanted a pardon for her father. When she was turned away, she stood crying on the street. Lincoln's son saw her and asked the problem. He took her past the guard where she asked Lincoln to free her dad.

"Any father who raised a little girl like you must be a good man," Lincoln said in pardoning the father.

When we are Christians, we are related to God through His Son. Jesus takes us past the barriers of heaven so we can get answers to our requests. To get answers to prayer, sonship is necessary. The New Testament emphasizes this truth, "Now we know that God does not hear sinners; but if anyone is a worshiper of God and does His will, He hears him" (John 9:31). You must become a child of God and know He is your heavenly Father to get answers to your requests.

If you never talked to your friends, nor they to you, it would be a strange kind of friendship. So it is with the believer who never talks with God. It is not only people who desire fellowship with God; God desires fellowship with them.

2. Prayer is the basis of a successful Christian life. If your next-door neighbor who is a doctor asked you to call him when you got sick, but you nevertheless lived in sickness, it would be your fault. Your neighbor could help you if you asked him, just as God could answer your prayers if you asked Him.

A man traveled to London, but he had little cash so he skipped breakfast and dinner at the hotel where he stayed. When he received his bill, it also included the meals. When he tried to reduce the bill because he didn't eat, the manager said, "It's your fault; the room included meals and the food was on the table." When we fail to take advantage of the life-sustaining resource of prayer, it's no one's fault but our own.

God wants you to claim "the victory that has overcome the world" (1 John 5:4). You obtain the victory by prayer. God promises that He is "able to do exceedingly abundantly above all that we ask or think" (Eph. 3:20). You tap into this power by prayer. Prayer is the doorway to a successful Christian life. Many pray without becoming triumphant Christians, but no one is triumphant who has not prayed.

Successful Christians experience release from tension when they pray; they find relief from problems. Although prayer is much more than a psychological release from anxiety, it certainly does perform that function. Life is wonderful when you cast your cares upon God. Realizing He cares for you will give you grace to endure trials and eventually give you deliverance from them.

Prayer motivates to success. Waiting in His presence settles you so you can review your life. Your goals become crystal clear. The power needed to reach these goals successfully is bestowed on the supplicant. Creative answers to your problems are found in prayer, as are new ways to serve the Lord. Prayer shuts out the world. Spiritual discernment is found in the quiet place with God.

Prayer will bring about needed changes in your life. Some things will never happen unless you pray. God is sovereign and His will is always done, but it is your responsibility to make petitions known to Him. It is part of His plan that certain things do not take place until His servants have prayed.

3. Lack of prayer can be considered sin by the Lord. If you don't pray, it means you don't trust God or you don't believe God can answer your request. When our churches don't win souls, it means the people haven't prayed. "Therefore, to him who knows to do good, and does not do it, to him it is sin" (Jas. 4:17). Believers should not be found guilty of prayerlessness.

Samuel was upset when the Israelites demanded he give them a king, but he still promised to pray for them. His sense of responsibility for their spiritual care was so great that he said, "Far be it from me that I should sin against the Lord in ceasing to pray for you; but I will teach you the good and the right way" (1 Sam. 12:23). This is evidently one of those "sins of omission" referred to in James 4:17.

The Steps of Prayer

Prayer is similar to the cry of a small child in the night. The psalmist described prayer in these terms: "Pour out your heart before Him" (Ps. 62:8). You can pray anytime, anyplace, under any condition. But some requests by God's children are more effective than others. Over the long stretch, you will want to do more than just cry out. You will want to make your time with God as effective as possible. The following suggestions will help.

1. Address your prayer to the Father. Remember, you are praying to God in heaven. When Jesus was on earth, He followed this formula: He prayed, "Our Father" (Matt. 6:9). Some address their prayers to Jesus or the Holy Spirit. This is not wrong; however, the Bible teaches us to pray to the Father. When Jesus was on earth, He reminded His disciples, "And in that day you will ask Me nothing" (John 16:23).

Sometimes people cry at the altar, "Jesus, Jesus, Jesus, Jesus, Jesus." God understands their hearts' desires and answers their cries. But follow God's pattern and you will get God's

blessing. Noah followed the blueprint and his ark floated. Moses followed the blueprint in building the Tabernacle and God's presence filled the sanctuary. If you follow God's blueprint in prayer, He will answer your requests.

2. Begin your prayer with adoration. In the Lord's Prayer, Jesus began by magnifying the Father: "Hallowed be Your name" (Matt. 6:9). As you worship God, you recognize His ability to grant your request.

The Psalms are filled with praise. "We give thanks to You, O God, we give thanks! For Your wondrous works declare that Your name is near" (75:1). Praise is adoration, and God wants His people to magnify Him. "Oh, magnify the Lord with me" (34:3). When we use a magnifying glass, the print doesn't get larger; our perception is enlarged. Our praise doesn't change God, for He is unchangeable. When we magnify God, our spiritual perception is enlarged. We have more faith with which to get answers to our prayers.

3. Prayer should include thanksgiving. Paul gave us direction relative to our lives: "In everything by prayer and supplication, with thanksgiving" (Phil. 4:6). When you give thanks, you bring salvation into the present tense.

Include in your prayer praise to God for what He has done for you. Thank Him for your salvation, for your home, for your family, for your church and for using you. Everyone has something for which to be grateful. When you recognize what God has done in the past, you have a basis for expecting future answers to prayer.

4. You must confess your sin. Because we are always sinners (1 John 1:8), we must always ask God to forgive us of our sins. Include in your prayer confession of your sins to God and a request for forgiveness. You can't be in an offensive position with someone and get that person to give you something. David said, "I acknowledged my sin to You, and my iniquity I have not hidden. I said, 'I will confess my transgressions to the Lord,' and You forgave the iniquity of my sin'" (Ps. 32:5). The best-known biblical prayer of confession is probably found in Psalm 51. Read it the next time your sin keeps you from praying.

If you owe your doctor a bill you refuse to pay, be careful about getting sick. He might not treat you. Or you might be embarrassed and have to apologize, "I'm sorry I haven't paid you. I will pay you, but please help my son." Likewise, you may have to tell God, "I'm sorry for my sin; please help me." Live clean; you never know when you may desperately need to pray.

To the believer in fellowship with God, He says, "Call to Me, and I will answer you, and show you great and mighty things, which you do not know" (Jer. 33:3).

Jesus suggested the model for intercession: "And forgive us our debts, as we forgive our debtors" (Matt. 6:12). We must clean up our lives before we can pray. We must confess every time we pray because we are sinners even after we pray. The Bible teaches, "If we say that we have no sin, we deceive ourselves" (1 John 1:8).

5. Make reconciliation with others. Because prayer is talking with a Holy God, you must forgive others as you ask God to cleanse you. Jesus said, "For if you forgive men their trespasses, your heavenly Father will also forgive you" (Matt. 6:14). This may require reconciliation with someone who has offended you in some way (vv. 23,24).

6. Pray for your personal needs. Jesus taught us to pray, "Give us this day our daily bread" (v. 11). Paul said, "Be anxious for nothing, but in everything by prayer and supplication, with thanksgiving, let your requests be made known to God; and the peace of God, which surpasses all understanding, will guard your hearts and minds through Christ Jesus" (Phil. 4:6,7). This is the privilege extended to believers, and they ought to take advantage of it every day.

Curtis Hutson delivered mail for his livelihood and also pastored the Forrest Hills Baptist Church in Decatur, Georgia. By faith, he resigned the post office position, and began working for the church—for only $75 a month. His house payments alone were $92 a month.

In a couple of months the bills mounted, so he piled them on the kitchen table. At 2:00 A.M. he and his wife, on their knees, prayed, "God, if I have to go back to the post office, You'll be embarrassed."

At this same time, another couple awoke, talked about their pastor, got out of bed, and brought a check to the pastor's house in the mid-

dle of the night. It was for the exact amount of the bills on the table.

7. Prayer should include intercession for the needs of others. Paul said, "Brethren, my heart's desire and prayer to God for Israel is that they may be saved" (Rom. 10:1). Paul usually reminded those to whom he wrote that he was praying for them (Rom. 1:9; Phil. 1:4; Col. 1:3; 1 Thess. 1:2).

Only a selfish people would pray for themselves only. It is unlikely God would honor the requests people make for their own needs alone.

8. Conclude your prayers in Jesus' name. He instructed us, "If you ask anything in My name, I will do it" (John 14:14).

How can sinners come into the presence of a Holy God? We cannot come in of ourselves; we must stand dressed in the righteousness of Jesus Christ, "that we might become the righteousness of God in Him" (2 Cor. 5:21). When we stand before God the Father in His Son, we have all the perfection and purity of Jesus Christ. This is because of His shed blood on calvary. We add Christ's name at the end of the prayer because in using the proper conclusion we recognize we are in Him, and He is our advocate who always "lives to make intercession" for us (Heb. 7:25).

We should not feel obligated to include all of these things in every prayer we offer to God, for at times we just express one thought. However, the eight elements described are important to structured prayers, such as those we hear in a public worship service or those we pray in our own private devotions.

The Basis of Answered Prayer

But I ask and my prayers are never answered, you might say. Maybe something is choking off the answers. Perhaps a sin pointed out here will flash in your mind. If so, do something about it so you can receive answers to your prayers. Remember, God answers prayers in three different time frames: first, He gives an answer, second He says "no" and third, He says "wait."

1. Your prayers are answered when you obey God. God is our heavenly Father and He loves His children. We can go to Him just as children do who ask things of their earthly father.

A little boy often went to see his dad at the hardware store, and each time he asked for a nickel to buy a cold drink from the machine in the supply room. When Dad was angry at his son, he didn't get the nickel. So the little boy was careful to stay on Dad's good side when he wanted a cold drink.

"And whatever we ask we receive of Him, because we keep His commandments and do those things that are pleasing in His sight" (1 John 3:22). Note that we get "whatever we ask" when we keep His commandments and please God.

A teenage son asked to borrow his father's car for a date. He thought the family car was more luxurious than his own car.

"No!" was the answer. "The other day I asked you to wash it and sweep out the sand, but you didn't have time." Within 30 minutes, the boy was back to tell his father the car was clean and asked again to borrow it.

Christians who disobey God don't have the freedom to pray to their heavenly Father and get the answers they seek without first seeking forgiveness.

The Bible tells us the prayers of the righteous are effective. We are never righteous by our own efforts; our righteousness is imputed by Jesus Christ. There is a sense in which we are righteous, however, for the word "righteous" also means "doing right." If we want our prayers answered, we must do right by paying our bills, not cursing, going to church, tithing, witnessing and doing all the other things we know are right.

"Confess your trespasses to one another, and pray for one another, that you may be healed. The effective, fervent prayer of a righteous man avails much" (Jas. 5:16). The phrase "avails much" means "makes tremendous things available." When you are right with God, your prayers make the greatest things in the world available.

2. Your prayers are answered when you get rid of known sin. The Bible teaches that our sins make it impossible for God to hear us. "If I regard iniquity in my heart, the Lord will not hear" (Ps. 66:18). Iniquity is sin—doing the exact opposite of God's will. If God tells us not to take His name in vain and we do, how can we ask Him to answer our prayers?

Another verse says we plug up God's ears with sin. "Behold, the Lord's hand is not shortened,

that it cannot save; nor His ear heavy, that it cannot hear. But your iniquities have separated you from your God; and your sins have hidden His face from you, so that He will not hear" (Isa. 59:1,2). God has the ability to help us and His ears can hear us, but our sins make it impossible.

Robert was a mischievous boy. When his mother was angry, he hid in his favorite hiding place—a dark closet—where she couldn't see or hear him. When Robert was hiding was not the time to ask his mother for money to go to the store for ice cream. If you have sin in your life, get rid of it, then present your petition to God. When sin blocks your communication with God, He is not obligated to hear you. However, in grace He may answer. Then out of love to God, we should repent and ask His forgiveness.

3. Your prayers are answered when you abide in Christ. Jesus promised, "If you abide in Me, and My words abide in you, you will ask what you desire, and it shall be done for you" (John 15:7). The word "abide" means to join yourself to God without any obstruction. It does not mean to hang onto God. When a branch is just hanging onto the vine, it usually withers. But when the branch is growing from the vine, it prospers and produces fruit.

Just as the branch allows the life-giving sap to flow through it, Christians who abide in Christ and His Word as a part of their lives allow the Holy Spirit to control them.

We allow important people to do most of the talking and we ask them only pertinent questions. Likewise, when we allow God to speak to our hearts through the Bible, we are prepared to make the right requests.

4. Your prayers are answered when you ask according to His will. God has a will that is His desire for us. It is God's will that we pray for the things He wants us to have.

I used to always looked forward to a visit from my Uncle Herman, who usually brought candy. But I had to ask for it. Sometimes I had to rummage through his pockets to find the candy. It gave Uncle Herman as much happiness to give me the candy as it did for me to find it. "Now this is the confidence that we have in Him, that if we ask anything according to His will, He hears us. And if we know that He hears us, whatever we ask, we know that we have the petitions that we have asked of Him" (1 John 5:14,15).

Once I prayed outside God's will. When I was going through Bible college, I prayed for money. A hole-in-one contest was being held at a nearby golf course. Every person who could hit the ball into the cup would receive a prize of $200. I prayed that God would help me make a hole-in-one. I knelt on the golf tee and asked God to guide my swing. None of the balls went into the cup.

This was not God's way of providing for my financial needs. There was an element of gambling in the contest. Also, I used to enjoy playing golf and wanted some glory for achieving a hole-in-one.

How can you know if the things you ask are His will? Certain things are obviously God's will, such as people being saved. God wants everyone to be saved (2 Pet. 3:9). It is not God's nature to frustrate His children; however, we may have to go through several doors or stages of prayer to arrive at an answer to prayer. God tests our sincerity. We need to go through each open door as it appears. It may take awhile to receive an answer to prayer, but we should pray with confidence. Our heavenly Father doesn't play games with us, hiding His will in the same way Easter eggs are hidden, and hoping we will find it.

5. Your prayers are answered when you ask in faith. Faith is to expect an answer. As a schoolboy, I sent off coupons for magic rings, code books and other trinkets. Every day I'd ask the mailman, "Did it come today?"

"Not today," the postman would say. "Maybe tomorrow." I'd get so excited I could hardly wait for the postman to come.

When we pray, we have to believe the answer is coming. "Therefore I say to you, whatever things you ask when you pray, believe that you receive them, and you will have them" (Mark 11:24). The sincerity of our faith determines the answers we receive. "He who comes to God must believe that He is, and that He is a rewarder of those who diligently seek Him" (Heb. 11:6).

When I was a child, I asked my mother for a quarter to go downtown. Twenty-five cents paid for the streetcar, popcorn and a cold drink. I never asked for a dollar because I knew she wouldn't give it to me. I asked for what I thought she would give me—25 cents. "But let him ask in faith, with no doubting, for he who doubts is like a wave of the sea driven and tossed by the wind" (Jas. 1:6).

It's obvious that some of us need more faith, not more time in prayer. Therefore, we ask, How do we get more faith? One way is to pray for it. Faith is sending off the coupon, then going to the mailbox every day looking for the answer. Expect answers from God. Build yourself a spiritual mailbox. "I got a reply this morning," you can tell your friends.

6. Your prayers are answered when your motives are right. When we come to God in prayer, our desires must be pure. The Bible tells us that we sometimes do not get answers because of our lusts (selfish desires). "You ask, and do not receive, because you ask amiss, that you may spend it on your pleasures" (4:3).

After I was saved, I immediately began praying for a car. I had been poor all my life. "Dear God, give me a car," I prayed sincerely, then added, "If you give me a car, I'll pick up people and take them to church." I was bargaining with God. God, however, looked through the words and saw my selfish desire. I wanted a car to take girls on dates and to impress the boys. God didn't give me the request.

Years later, I became a pastor and still didn't have a car. I made my pastoral calls on a bicycle. In God's time, the members of the church collected money and bought a car for me. When your motives are right and you are willing to do anything to accomplish God's will, God will give you a car or whatever you need—in His own time.

7. Your prayers are answered when you live peaceably with your mate. Some husbands and wives fight. The Bible commands husbands and wives to live together peacefully so that their prayers can be answered. "Likewise you husbands, dwell with them with understanding, giving honor to the wife, as to the weaker vessel, and as being heirs together of the grace of life, that your prayers may not be hindered" (1 Pet. 3:7). When a husband argues constantly with his wife, how can the children see Christ in the father? If the father and mother then pray for their child to be saved, their arguments have made it impossible for their prayers to be heard.

Practical Helps for Prayer

Giving practical helps for prayer is similar to telling a child how to ask a father for things. Some children, however, don't get their requests because they ask in the wrong way. Here are some right ways to pray.

1. Make a prayer list. This is an itemized list of things you need from God. Sometimes these may be "wants," but should represent our needs. Some people place the items on one side of a sheet of paper and leave the other side blank to record the answers.

A prayer list gives you discipline in praying. A prayer list will challenge you to keep praying until you finish your obligations. A prayer list adds incentive to your faith. You'll be encouraged when you look at the answers to your prayers. It will provoke you to greater prayer.

2. Find a private place. A regular place for private prayer is necessary. Jesus was disgusted with the hypocritical ways of the religious leaders of His day, those who loved to pray on street corners and in synagogues to receive the praise of men. Therefore, He taught His followers to find a private "closet" where they could be alone with the Lord (Matt. 6.5,6, KJV).

It is not always easy to find a secluded spot for prayer, but we can generally work it out. Although we know we can pray anywhere, something about associating a particular activity with a particular place is helpful.

Perhaps your "closet" could be your bedroom or the den after the children have gone to school. Some businessmen pray in their private offices. You must find the place that is the best for you. However, you can pray in the crowded waiting room of an airline terminal. You can pray with your eyes open as you drive on the expressway. But a quiet place is better. You won't be distracted or embarrassed. Two lovers will talk anywhere they can, just to be together, but they would rather talk in private.

3. Make a regular schedule. Try to schedule the same time each day for prayer. If you wait until you have time, it will never happen. You must make time to commune with God. Then, don't pray because you are required to do it, but pray because you need it and desire it. Prayer is more than a few seconds of grace before the meal.

Because prayer gives us our greatest victory and is our greatest strength, we should give it our serious consideration and the best time of the day.

Jesus said people "always ought to pray" (Luke 18:1), and Paul said to "pray without ceasing" (1 Thess. 5:17), suggesting that prayer at anytime is appropriate. This is true, of course, but something about associating a particular time with prayer is helpful in maintaining the habit.

4. The posture of prayer. Some believers are convinced they must kneel to pray, thus showing their humility and contrition before God. They take their example from Paul, who said, "I bow my knees to the Father of our Lord Jesus Christ" (Eph. 3:14). However, in the Bible we can find examples of people who prayed while standing (Jer. 18:20), sitting (2 Sam. 7:18) or lying prostrate (Matt. 26:39), while some prayed with their hands lifted upward (1 Kings 8:22; Ps. 28:2; 1 Tim. 2:8).

The important thing is not the position of the body, but the condition of the heart. Christians today usually bow their heads to show reverence and close their eyes to shut out distractions while praying, but we ought not to become legalistic about these things.

5. Study Bible prayers. You will get your greatest answers to prayer when you pray as did the men of Scripture. When Moses prayed, Israel prevailed in battle. When Daniel prayed, the lions' mouths were stopped. When Elijah prayed, it didn't rain for three and a half years. When you follow the successful ingredients of the prayers of godly men, you are more likely to have success than if you create your own prayer patterns.

After you get up off your knees, put your prayers to work. The old saint reminded us, "The best place to pray for potatoes is at the end of a potato hoe."

Lesson 6—Why You Should Be Related to a Church

My brother, Richard, had not been baptized. He was saved but didn't want to join a Baptist church. My arguments about baptism by immersion never convinced him fully until he heard me preach a sermon on the subject: "Why a church should be growing." I pointed out that growing churches are obeying the Scriptures and people are being baptized.

As a result, Richard came forward and was baptized, explaining, "My former church wasn't getting people saved so it must not be right." The presence of God bringing people to Christ in a growing church convinced him to be baptized.

A lady came forward after I preached in a church in Kansas City, Kansas, telling me she wanted rededication. I asked if her membership was in that church.

"No," she whispered, "I promised Mama I would stay in her church." I explained to her that the book of Acts gives illustrations of people taking letters of introduction from their home churches to their new residences.

Then I asked, "Did it ever occur to you that you may have backslidden because your membership was not in a church that could watch over you?"

Why You Should Join a Church

We are moving fast into the "unchurch" age of Christianity. Some think they can stay home on Sunday morning and watch church on television and they have fulfilled their obligations to God. Others attend a home Bible class, while many do not go to church at all but claim to be Christians. It is difficult to see how a Christian can be spiritual without belonging to a local church.

In recent years, we have heard arguments against being connected to an organized church. Cell groups meeting in people's homes become substitutes for regular churches. And as good as Christian television might be, none can take the place of a church.

How can an adequate program of instruction for various age groups be provided without a church? How can worship be given a prominent place in a community without a church? How can an expanded sense of fellowship among believers be promoted without a church? How can effective Christian service projects be coordinated without a church?

It is difficult to maintain your spirituality without the support and fellowship of a local body of believers. Many, such as those in nursing homes or prisons, are growing spiritually without the

benefit of organized services, of course, but it makes the road between here and heaven mighty lonely.

1. Church membership fulfills the symbol of baptism. Every person is a sinner and deserves death. But Christ died on calvary to take the place of every sinner. He died that the sinner might not die, but have eternal life. When Christ hung on calvary, God took the believing sinner and placed the sinner into Jesus Christ. Technically, this is called the vicarious, substitutionary atonement. It means that when Christ died, the sinner died. Paul witnessed to this identification: "I have been crucified with Christ; it is no longer I who live, but Christ lives in me" (Gal. 2:20).

To become a Christian, all the sinner has to do is believe on Jesus Christ (Acts 16:31). After salvation, the first step of obedience is baptism. When new Christians are baptized, they testify to the world that they have died with Christ. Baptism is also a picture of the new life we received from Christ.

When you are baptized, you become a member of a local church. The Bible describes the Church as the Body of Christ, "the church, which is His body" (Eph. 1:22,23). Just as you were identified with Christ on calvary for salvation, you fulfill this truth by identifying with His local body, the church. This is done by baptism.

2. Church membership places you under the ministry of the Word of God. Christians should be in the Lord's house every week so they can learn the Word of God. One of the primary purposes of the Church is to teach the Scriptures. Immediately upon the first manifestation of the church after the Day of Pentecost, the people put themselves under doctrine (Acts 2:42). The Early Church taught more often than just on Sunday: "And *daily* in the temple, and in every house, they did not cease teaching and preaching Jesus as the Christ" (Acts 5:42, italics mine). You ought to be in church so you can be under the ministry of the Word of God.

Knowledge of the Bible will cause you to grow (1 Pet. 2:2), to abstain from sin (Ps. 119:105), to have your prayers answered (John 15:5), to be like Christ (1 Cor. 3:23) and to strengthen your faith (Rom. 10:13). Those who don't study the Bible sometimes backslide and corrupt those about them. Because it is mandatory to study the Word of God, and because the church is God's instrument for teaching it, a Christian ought to be a faithful attending member of a church.

3. Church membership helps you grow through fellowship. God's Word commands that we not forsake "the assembling of ourselves together" (Heb. 10:25). God did not choose the word "together" in this verse by mere chance. When Christians come together, a mutual interaction occurs—a give-and-take relationship. This does not mean that Christians give up their doctrines or convictions. Fellowship is not necessarily consensus, which is like water seeking its lowest level. Rather, when Christians have give-and-take, they give to one another and take something back in return. This is fellowship. Christians grow through fellowship.

Some churches may announce "We will have fellowship after the evening service," where Christians drink coffee and chat. This activity is enjoyable, but biblical fellowship is much deeper than making small talk and having refreshments.

Fellowship involves revealing yourself to other people as you really are. First, you confess that you are a sinner. Second, you confess your need of reliance upon God to work out all things in your life. Third, you confess that you cannot live for God by yourself. Fourth, you confess a need for the way of life found in the local church. You become like those with whom you fellowship.

Concerning fellowship, John wrote, "If we walk in the light as He is in the light, we have fellowship one with another, and the blood of Jesus Christ His Son cleanses us from all sin" (1 John 1:7). This verse teaches that as a Christian you should attempt to do the very best you can to keep the commandments of God. This is walking in the light, whereby you follow the example of Jesus Christ who is the light of the world (John 8:12).

When you walk in the light, you have fellowship with other children of God. If they are conscientiously serving Jesus Christ, they also will be involved in a church where fellowship is experienced. A conscious endeavor to serve Christ means that as a Christian you will submit yourself to God and to one another. Yieldedness to God is the basis of fellowship with one another. The blood of Jesus Christ covers those who are

fellowshipping together. Fellowship is not the basis for forgiving sin, but people who experience fellowship have followed the New Testament requirements by confessing their sins (1 John 1:9); hence, the blood has cleansed you and you are forgiven.

It has been said, "You can't be a Christian alone," meaning that a person cannot grow in the Christian life without getting along with other people. God is not looking for the hermit to "come apart from the world" by climbing a pole. God is looking for believers to work out their faith in relationship to others.

4. Church membership is taught by the example of the Early Church. Those who attempt to live for Christ outside the local church deny the example set for them in Scripture. As you examine the pages of the New Testament, you find Christians joining with other Christians to hear the Word of God (Acts 2:42; 5:42; 19:9,10). They also fellowshipped together (Acts 2:42), and they joined their hearts together in prayer (Acts 4:24). The local church was a launching pad for evangelism; they went out together to win lost people to Jesus Christ (Acts 5:42; 20:20,31). In Acts, you will not find occasions of Christians going it alone. Wherever Paul went, he organized Christians into churches (Acts 15:41).

Before they were saved, the Jews brought their money to the Temple. The early Christians brought their money to the church. They laid it at the apostles' feet (Acts 4:34,35). The apostles used this money to provide for widows (Acts 6:1). They also gave to needy saints (Acts 11:29,30) and to carry out the work of evangelism (Phil. 4:18). The early Christians were loyal in their financial giving to the church. Some gave all they had (Acts 2:45), while others gave according to their ability (Acts 11:29).

5. Church membership is taught by the principles of "God's place" for worship in the Old Testament. God has always had a place for corporate worship, although illustrations of people individually worshiping God in various places and circumstances can be found.

First, the Tabernacle was God's place for centralized worship and He cautioned His people that they should not worship at other than the designated place (Deut. 12:2-4,11). Later, God's place for worship was the Temple in Jerusalem. Whenever people got away from God's place, they began worshiping as they pleased. The principle of "God's place" does not tie salvation to sacrificing the blood of animals in the Old Testament. It became a man-made religion when people began worshiping God at a place that was contrary to God's commandment.

Just as God required His people to assemble for corporate worship in a certain spot in the Old Testament, so He has a place for corporate worship in the New Testament. This place is the church. This does not, of course, exclude individual worship, for in both Testaments, people have access to God at any time and any place.

The three characteristics of God's corporate place of worship are seen in Deuteronomy 12:1-32. First, God required His people to assemble for worship where He promised to meet with them (vv. 4,5). God's presence in the Tabernacle and later in the Temple was an invitation for His people to assemble. Second, God's place was located where the symbols of redemption were celebrated (vv. 13,14). In the Old Testament, these symbols were the blood sacrifice and the furniture of the Tabernacle. Third, the people were commanded to assemble for worship where they would find God's name (v. 11).

In the New Testament, the local church meets the three requirements mentioned in Deuteronomy for God's place. First, the church has God's presence. Remember, a church is not a building, but an assembly of people. God has promised to be with them when they are assembled together (Matt. 18:20; Acts 4:31; Heb. 10:25). The church is called a candlestick (Rev. 1:20; 2:1,5) and the candle is a symbol of Jesus, the light of the world (John 8:12). Christ is the light in the midst of the church, so a local church has the presence of God there in a unique way.

Second, today's symbols of redemption are the Lord's Table and baptism, whereas the symbols of redemption in the Old Testament were the sacrifice and the furniture in the Tabernacle. Baptism and the Lord's Table are local church ordinances. Christians are required to assemble where these symbols are celebrated.

Third, God's people are called to minister in the church. God calls His servants (John 15:16) and gives them gifts (Rom. 12:3-8), then gives these gifted people the church (Eph. 4:7-13). Because God's people serve in the church, Christians should gather themselves under their ministry.

God has promised to dwell with His children anywhere (Deut. 33:27); but more important, when they serve Him, God has promised to be with them (Matt. 28:20). Believers may drop to their knees by their beds and be enveloped in the love of God. God has promised, "I will never leave you, nor forsake you" (Heb. 13:5).

Some extremists claim God's presence dwells only in the church. This is not so. Personal Christianity demands the presence of Christ in every believer (Gal. 2:20; Eph. 3:17); however, His special presence is in the local church. This demands both private and corporate access to God. Private Christianity alone is unbalanced religion. To be a successful Christian, you must worship both by yourself and with the church corporate.

Belong Where You Live

Recently, a middle-aged school teacher walked down the aisle during the invitational hymn, saying, "I've been praying about it a long time; I want to put my membership here where I live."

The pastor looked at her in mute surprise. Finally he said, "You've been coming here for 10 years. I thought you were a member."

Many Christians have their church membership somewhere other than where they live. Some leave their church memberships in the churches where their parents are located. Others, wanting to get away from God, leave their church memberships where they are.

Belong-where-you-live is a New Testament practice. Apollos was eloquent in the Scriptures. The church-where-he-had-been wrote a letter to the church-where-he-was-going recommending him (Acts 18:27). And he immediately became involved in the new church's ministry (v. 28).

Why should you transfer your church membership when you move?

1. For spiritual discipline. When you join a church, you take on its obligations, which involve purity of life, service, faithfulness in attending services and belief in the fundamentals of the faith. You place yourself under the teaching and preaching of the Word of God. In the past, the church's practice and belief was called church discipline. If Christians did not discipline themselves, they were disciplined by the congregation. By positive discipline of teaching and preaching as well as negative discipline (correction), Christians were encouraged to live for God.

When you move to a new community, you should place yourself under the discipline of a local church. In "Come Thou Fount of Every Blessing," Robert Robinson, the hymn writer, noted: "Prone to wander, Lord, I feel it." Because all people have a tendency to drift away from God, they need a group of people to encourage them to faithfulness. Church membership should be like food to strengthen the weak, salve to heal the oppressed, a conscience to smite the tempted and a mother's love to encourage the child.

2. For the influence of your testimony. The very act of aligning yourself with a group of fundamental believers is an announcement to your new community that you plan to serve Jesus Christ.

"Why can't we wait awhile to make sure that we have the right church?" is often heard. Some like to "shop around." But you don't find a local church the way you shop for a lawn mower. When Christians move to new cities, they should purchase homes in suburbs where gospel-preaching churches are located. Because Christians believe the spiritual development of their families are more important than anything else, they should never locate their families in areas that have no gospel-preaching churches.

Many people purchase a home for status, convenience or business reasons only. But a Christian should locate near a fundamental church or plan to start a fundamental church if none is available. If a family is not strong enough to start a church, their relocation may be outside the will of God. It is never God's will for a Christian to be placed in circumstances where spiritual life will decay. Perhaps a Christian will have to give up the business promotion that is associated with moving, or even resign from the company.

Why join another church as expediently as possible? You are a light for God. A candle gives off light immediately on being lit, not sometime later. Also, the closer you move to the candle, the brighter the light. Because Christians want their testimonies to be brightest in their home communities, they should join churches as soon as they find Bible-believing churches with which they feel comfortable.

3. For more effective service. Christians who belong to a church are able to accomplish more for God. You can invite people to "your" church with enthusiasm and authority. Paul told the Colossians, "And whatever you do, do it heartily, as to the Lord" (Col. 3:23). To be a wholehearted soul winner, you should be an enthusiastic church member.

"To attach soul winning to church membership sounds narrow," someone might criticize. Yet, this is a biblical teaching. First, everyone is lost without Christ, so every Christian is commanded to be a soul winner (Matt. 28:19a). Christ commands every person to be baptized (v. 19b); therefore, soul winners ought to have their converts baptized. Because baptism places a person into the local body (Rom. 6:3, 4; Eph. 1:22, 23), every soul winner ought to be a church member to be an example of what others are expected to be. Just as you have to have measles to spread them, every person ought to be enthusiastic about the local church so he or she can encourage others.

Many Christians want to teach Sunday School, work a bus route, sponsor youth organizations or serve in some other place in the new church. If you have a gift for service, you ought to be using it for Jesus Christ. Most New Testament churches will not allow people to serve until they are members. Although some may believe it is narrow to expect a person to be a church member before serving, that position can be considered for good reasons. When a person makes a commitment to the membership of a local church, the congregation receives a commitment regarding the person's belief, life and loyalty.

Therefore, you should prepare yourself for Christian service by moving your membership to the new church. You moved your dog, kitchen table, bank account and mailing address so you can live in the new town. Why not move your church membership for the same reason?

Lesson 7—Victory over Sin
Is Promised You

When we were in high school, my buddy Art Winn and I went squirrel hunting. As we were walking in the bottom of a 12-foot drainage ditch, the ditch suddenly forked into two different directions. Art took the right branch and planned to meet me about a mile away. After he left, it began to rain, and I crawled under the overhanging root system of an oak tree, which gave me a cavelike protection.

I lay in the dry leaves for several minutes before realizing how cold I was. Pulling some leaves together, I made a fire. In the light of the flames, I saw a black snake. Although I knew it was nonpoisonous, I scrambled out of my small cave. I enjoyed the cave until the light revealed the snake; then I wouldn't go back even to get out of the rain.

The same thing happened in my Christian life. I was comfortable with sins in my life until the light of Christ revealed them. Then I had to change, and I can't enjoy going back to the old ways.

Learn How to Deal with Sin

If you are a new Christian, you might have questions regarding right and wrong. Some things you enjoyed before you were saved may now make you uncomfortable.

In the following material, we will try to stay away from pronouncements by naming sins, unless they are called sin in the Bible. Rather, principles will be laid down from the Word of God by which each Christian can determine what is wrong for the child of God.

1. Do what God directs. The Westminster Confession of Faith asks the question, "What is sin?" The first part of the answer is, "Sin is any want of conformity..." Anything that does not conform to God's Word is sin.

When a mother says to her son, "Go to the store and get bread," what should her reaction be when he disobeys? When she finds him playing baseball on the corner, she can't be happy. He has disobeyed his mother (Eph. 6:1) and if he continues, a serious flaw will develop in his character.

Certain commandments are easy to obey, meaning there is no question about what the Christian should do. You are to tithe (Mal. 3:10), attend church (Heb. 10:25), confess your sins (1 John 1:9) and love other Christians (John 13:34). The same can be said for reading your Bible, praying and watching for the Lord's second coming.

We may think the sin of omission is not as great as the sin of hardheaded disobedience. When a father asks his 12-year-old boy to wash the car and he forgets, it doesn't seem to be as bad as when his twin brother throws mud at the car. The father is displeased with both sons, and he deals with each offense differently. But he can't overlook the one who didn't wash the car. The Scriptures teach, "Therefore, to him who knows to do good and does not do it, to him it is sin" (Jas. 4:17).

2. Do not do what God says is wrong. The Ten Commandments are all negative warnings, beginning, "You shall not..." You sin when you go against God's commandments. God says it is wrong to kill, lie, steal, commit adultery and have idols in your life (Exod. 20:3-17).

The commands of God are not grievous; He did not take away the fun things. Some have mistakenly thought, *All the pleasure is gone now that I am a Christian.* God is not a mean father who keeps His children locked in a closet all day. Jesus said, "I have come that they may have life, and that they may have it more abundantly" (John 10:10).

Like a wise father, God knows some things will harm His children. What parents would allow their children to play near a busy highway or in a field filled with snakes? When God says no, don't rebel or see how close you can get to the edge. Try to see why God said no. When you understand the purpose of God, you can obey with enthusiasm.

3. Obey your conscience. Your conscience is a moral regulator that flashes information to the brain. It tells you what it thinks is right and wrong. It is like the thermostat upstairs that starts the furnace in the basement when things get chilly. When your conscience tells you something is wrong, it is a sin to go against it. At birth, the conscience is pure, reflecting the image of God in which you were made. The conscience tells a person it is wrong to murder, steal and lie.

You have the moral law of God branded in your heart. God recognized the moral law that He has implanted within a person, and you sin when you violate your conscience.

A certain father was an alcoholic. The son saw the misery his father caused his mother. As a child, the son had to do without because the father drank so heavily. No one knows if alcoholism is communicated by influence or physical succession or both. The son always had a fear of alcohol because of his childhood experience with his father.

The son once refused communion because real wine was served. He would not eat meat cooked in liquor in any form, even though the alcohol was burned off. His conscience told him if he got one taste, he might become an alcoholic. Some may think the son is narrow, but he did not want to go against his conscience. "Therefore, to him who knows to do good and does not do it, to him it is sin" (Jas. 4:17).

Although it is a sin to ignore your conscience, some will tell you, "Let your conscience be your guide." This is bad advice. Your conscience cannot always be trusted. Your conscience can be "educated" not to feel the wrongness of some situations, and then your spiritual life will suffer.

The conscience can be "seared": "Having their own conscience seared with a hot iron" (1 Tim. 4:2). This pictures a hot poker burning a scar on the skin. The conscience is seared when one goes against its instructions continually.

Note the following guidelines regarding the conscience. First, everything your conscience tells you to do may not be right. Some people think it is allowable to steal or lie under certain conditions. Second, your conscience won't tell you everything that is wrong. The conscience depends on the training it has received. Some people commit adultery, not realizing what God has said about sexual purity.

Third, it is wrong for you to go against your conscience even when others disagree with you. Many Christians eat flaming steaks marinated in liquor and they may get no more alcohol than when others eat them charcoal broiled. Marinated steaks may be acceptable to them, but for others it is wrong because it would be going against the conscience.

Follow your conscience to a certain extent, but pray that God will enlighten it daily. Don't let your conscience be the final deciding factor in what you do for God.

4. Do not harbor impure thoughts. We live in a "girl watchers" age. Men enjoy thumbing through *Playboy* or walking the beaches to look at the bikinis. A lot of wives know this and say, "It's all right to window shop; just don't touch."

Sinful thoughts involve more than sex; the whole issue of lust is involved. Some men dream of money and the lust of "things" consumes their minds. Some women watch soap operas and the lust of illicit happiness eats them up.

You are supposed to have a clean mind (2 Cor. 10:4,5; 11:3); therefore, you shouldn't listen to filthy stories. Jesus said, "Whoever looks at a woman to lust for her has already committed adultery with her in his heart" (Matt. 5:28). Therefore, you shouldn't allow filthy thoughts to pollute your mind. This doesn't mean you won't be tempted with impure imaginations. A great evangelist once explained, "You can't be responsible for birds flying over your head, but it is your fault if they lodge in your hair."

As a man "thinks in his heart, so is he" (Prov. 23:7). Before Eve sinned by eating the forbidden fruit, she lusted in her mind. "But I fear, lest somehow, as the serpent deceived Eve by his craftiness, so your minds may be corrupted from the simplicity that is in Christ" (2 Cor. 11:3). The first step toward sin is usually our minds thinking about the act. Paul tells us we should "meditate on these things" (Phil. 4:8) that uplift.

5. Do not defile your body. Some people have the attitude, *It's my soul that lives forever, so I can ignore the body.* As a result, they overfeed their already fat bodies, stink them up like tobacco barns or pickle them in alcohol. You cannot separate your body from your soul until death. The way you treat your body reflects your attitude toward spiritual things and vice versa.

The little child stamps his feet and insists, "I can do what I want!" Yet, the parent knows that if the child plays under the water heater he could receive a permanent scar. A teen sat brooding and depressed because he was not able to serve the Lord as a minister. He began smoking pot to experience blackouts so he would not have to face the pressure and tension. This made the depression deeper, which brought on more, and the cycle continued. In a final fit of depression, he committed suicide. The sin of taking his life began with the first sin of drug abuse.

6. Do not link yourself with those who will cause you to stumble. Your friends are important, for they help to determine your outlook on life. Therefore, the Bible warns, "Do not be unequally yoked together with unbelievers" (2 Cor. 6:14). This doesn't mean we should not work at the same store with a non-Christian nor join the same club. It does mean you should not link yourself with an unsaved person in marriage or in any other way wherein his or her decisions will determine your Christian life.

The Bible teaches, "Come out from among them and be separate, says the Lord. Do not touch what is unclean, and I will receive you. I will be a Father to you, and you shall be My sons and daughters" (vv. 17,18). Don't get involved with people who will pull you down.

7. Do not influence others adversely. When Cain killed Abel, he asked, "Am I my brother's keeper?" (Gen. 4:9). Many have repeated that question, implying they are not responsible for others. However, John Donne states, "No man is an island." We live in a human community where every action is influenced by and has an impact on others.

The Bible uses the phrase "stumbling block" to teach that it is sin to harm others by our influence. Paul warns, "Beware lest somehow this liberty of yours become a stumbling block to those who are weak" (1 Cor. 8:9).

In many New Testament villages, the meat sold in butcher shops had first been sacrificed to idols. New Christians who had previously worshiped idols refused to eat the meat because it was a compromise of their convictions. A few Christians, however, thought hamburger was hamburger, ignoring the convictions of the other Christians.

Paul counseled: "Neither if we eat are we the better, nor, if we do not eat are we the worse" (v. 8). Paul, however, saw that it was wrong if other people were tempted to go against their consciences by what he ate, so he affirmed, "If food makes my brother stumble, I will never again eat meat" (1 Cor. 8:13). The Christian cannot do questionable things that may make others stumble into sin.

Many believe dancing is an artistic form, reflecting coordination, style and rhythm. Some Christians, however, have been ensnared by lust through the power of suggestion, touch, a rhythmic beat and tempting words. It comes down to a question of morality. Can Christians who enjoy dancing purposely cause others for whom Christ died to stumble?

Recently, a man's car began to sputter and lose its power. His mechanic checked the spark plugs, fuel pump and distributor; still he couldn't find the problem. Finally, the mechanic's boss told him to blow out the fuel line. A little bit of trash was causing the problem. There was not enough grit to fill a quarter of a teaspoon, yet it was enough to make the car lose its power.

Sin is like trash in the fuel line. It makes you lose power to do the will of God and you fall into bad habits. Sin makes you irritable and keeps you from doing what you know is right.

8. Avoid temptation. All Christians are tempted to sin. When you are plagued with temptation, don't think something is wrong. Paul notes, "No temptation has overtaken you except such as is common to man" (10:13). As a matter of fact, if you are not tempted by sin, you are probably not doing much for God. To be victorious over temptation, avoid what you know to be temptation to you. The truly born-again person should not sin willfully.

When you yield to temptation, and it is possible that you will, you should be grieved that you have disappointed God, but don't let sin destroy your walk with Him. Apply God's prescription for restoring fellowship with Him: "If we confess our sins, He is faithful and just to forgive us our sins and to cleanse us from all unrighteousness" (1 John 1:9). Confession means to agree with God about our sins. We agree that sin is terrible and will destroy our Christian testimony. "He who covers his sins will not prosper" (Prov. 28:13). But notice the last part of that verse, "but whoever confesses and forsakes them will have mercy."

Learn to Live a Righteous Life

A teenage girl stood on the ledge of a burning

building. The fireman on the hook and ladder couldn't get any closer to her than a handclasp. He said, "You grab my arm, and I'll grab you—jump and trust me."

Victory over sin has the same two ingredients. You must leave sin and jump into God's arms. You can't keep rocking in a chair and praying for God to take away the dizziness you get from rocking. You must leave the rocking chair. God expects believers to live separated *from* sin and separated *unto* righteousness. It is not enough that you quit sinning; you must live a holy life. This is sometimes called the victorious Christian life. It is the basis of living the successful Christian life.

The following practical reasons for living a righteous life have grown out of the experiences of God's people. God gives us general principles we must apply to real-life situations.

1. You are living righteously when your new nature controls your life. Paul said, "Therefore if any one is in Christ, he is a new creation: old things have passed away; behold, all things have become new" (2 Cor. 5:17). This new nature is like the sap that runs in the dormant tree each spring. The new life pushes off the dead leaves.

Your old habits are like old leaves. A program to reform yourself is not enough. Counting to 10 when you get angry is not God's way of victory. You have a new nature; let it flow. But that's hard because you still have your old sinful nature.

Your distaste for the things of the world will grow as you acquire a taste for spiritual things. Your taste for some habits will change immediately, while others will take longer periods of adjustment.

Although I wasn't yet a Christian, I regularly attended a Sunday evening youth meeting as a junior boy. On several occasions, we had a consecration service designed to purify our lives. We wrote our sins on small slips of paper and deposited them into a metal dish. After prayer, a candle ignited the paper and my sins were supposedly purified by fire.

I always wrote "cursing" on my paper; and, after trying not to curse for a few days, I always went back to using filthy speech. On one occasion, I stood in front a a campfire and publicly told my friends I would quit cursing.

Two weeks later, as I was opening a bundle of papers to deliver on my news route, the wire broke and I gashed my knuckle. I cursed. My friend Art Winn made fun of my empty promise. I couldn't keep my mouth clean before I was saved, but I can say to the glory of God that I have never cursed since. This does not mean I am perfect, of course, only that I have victory over that sin.

2. You live righteously when you show gratitude to God for what Christ has done for you. Paul wrote, "And whatever you do in word or deed, do all in the name of the Lord Jesus, giving thanks to God the Father through Him" (Col. 3:17).

You dishonor Christ if you continue to live in your old sinful habits. The Bible calls people in an unsaved state "children of disobedience" (Eph. 2:2, *KJV*). If you cannot thank Christ for something you do, you had better avoid it. Let your appreciation to God for what He has done for you guide your actions.

3. You live righteously by protecting yourself and your loved ones from the dangers and miseries that sin breeds. A professor was rushed to the hospital with stomach cramps, but tests revealed nothing. A month later, the entire family went to the emergency room with the same symptoms. Again they could find nothing.

A friend with whom they had gone to Mexico phoned a warning to them. They had both bought pottery that was not properly kiln dried, and had made hot chocolate in the pots. The lead paint on the pots was melting into the hot chocolate, causing sickness.

Although improperly fired pottery is not a sin, the same principle applies. Your sin may affect your family. You may not be offended by some of the "new" movies, but your teenage children may be eaten up with passion.

We can't get every evil influence out of our lives, of course, because we live in an evil world. But separating ourselves from sinful practices whenever possible works toward godliness. When interceding for believers, Jesus prayed, "I do not pray that You should take them out of the world, but that You should keep them from the evil one" (John 17:15).

4. You live righteously by maintaining a strong testimony for Christ. After I was saved, I worried about some of my friends. *How can I keep myself clean?* I thought. I told one high school buddy I was sorry for the things we had done together before my salvation. He never came around me again.

A few days ago, I talked with a college student who said he could beat me at pool. He wanted me to go to a "recreation room" to play a game, explaining, "It's not called a poolroom anymore."

"I can't do that," I said. "If anyone sees me bending over a pool table, what will that person think of me as a minister?"

The Bible demands, "Abstain from every form of evil" (1 Thess. 5:22). Paul said, "I wrote to you in my epistle not to keep company with sexually immoral people. Yet I certainly did not mean with the sexually immoral people of this world, or with the covetous, or extortioners, or idolaters, since then you would need to go out of the world. But now I have written to you not to keep company with anyone named a brother, who is a fornicator, or covetous, or an idolater, or a reviler, or a drunkard, or an extortioner—not even to eat with such a person" (1 Cor. 5:9-11).

Believers have to maintain contact with sinners and backsliders to be witnesses to them, but intimate association with them is discouraged. I would go into a "recreation room" to witness for Christ, but not for pleasure. I would go into a bar to witness, but not to drink even a soft drink.

5. You live righteously when your life has priorities. If you have only a limited time for reading, do not spend it all on secular novels or magazines. Jesus said, "Seek first the kingdom of God" (Matt. 6:33). The first priority in your life is spiritual maturity. Read Christian books and magazines that will enrich your life. Spend time with your Bible. This doesn't mean you shouldn't read the newspapers or other necessary items. Matthew 6:33 continues, "All these things shall be added to you." The principle is that you should use your time, money and energy to achieve spiritual growth.

You should not support evil enterprises. Satan offers many pleasures and evil habits to people and takes their money, time and energy to pay for them. Christians certainly ought not to be guilty of supporting any of them. A boycott of evil things is one of the most powerful ways we can show our protest against their existence and influence.

6. You live righteously by preparing yourself for heaven. There will be no evil in heaven, so separation from evil here on earth gives us a foretaste of heaven.

The young girl stops dating other boys the minute she falls in love with her future husband. She doesn't wait until the wedding ceremony; she prepares herself to live with one man by spending time with him. You should get ready to spend all eternity with the bridegroom—Jesus Christ. If you don't like the thought of loving Him only, maybe you are not a child of God.

Paul said that if we will think about "whatever things are true,...noble,...just,...pure,...lovely,...of good report,...if there is any virtue...anything praiseworthy,—meditate on these things" (Phil. 4:8,9). We need Him to be with us until the day we go to be with Him.

Separation from this life means entrance into heaven with God and Christ. "For our conversation [citizenship] is in heaven; from whence also we look for the Saviour, the Lord Jesus Christ" (Phil. 3:20, *KJV*). Until that day comes, however, determine to live a pure life. Paul said, "I pray God your whole spirit and soul and body be preserved blameless unto the coming of our Lord Jesus Christ" (1 Thess. 5:23, *KJV*).

Make Victory the Goal of Living

One time when I was preaching to a small congregation in northern Ontario, Canada, I saw a great moving of the Spirit; 27 out of a congregation of approximately 85 persons came forward, most of them for salvation.

"I've got a hideous sin in my life," one of the church leaders confessed to me at the altar. All sin is hideous in God's sight, but by human judgments, I didn't think his sin was all that terrible.

"I must have victory," he said, pouring out his soul to God. His sincerity and agony moved me. Never had I seen a man who wanted victory over a habit more than this Sunday School teacher and soul winner did.

Do you crave spiritual victory? Maybe your honest search for God's deliverance will bring revival to your church as this man's yieldedness triggered the Spirit's movement among the unsaved. I wish every Christian wanted victory over sin as this man did. Perhaps some don't want it because they don't know what victory is and what it can do for them. Christians can experience victory in many areas of their lives.

1. Victory over spiritual laziness. At times, you just don't want to read the Bible. Yet you know you should. You are spiritually lazy. What should you do? You should do right. Read your Bible. The same thing happens with prayer. You are spiritually lazy and you say, "I don't want to pray, but I'm supposed to pray so I will." Leave your lazy nature and go to the prayer closet and force yourself to pray. Spiritual victory is getting your lazy nature to obey your spiritual nature.

2. Victory over materialism. When you follow the commands of God, He will supply your needs: money, clothes or food. We are all familiar with Psalm 23:1: "The Lord is my shepherd; I shall not want" [for anything I need]. David also wrote, "I have been young, and now am old; yet I have not seen the righteous forsaken, nor his descendants begging bread" (37:25). Paul said, "My God shall supply all your need according to His riches in glory by Christ Jesus" (Phil. 4:19).

One of the reasons we bow our heads at the beginning of a meal and give thanks is because God provides our needs. A few people are rich and have no needs. Most everyone else has needs of all kinds; and Christians look to God to supply them. We should, therefore, bow our heads and ask God for money, food, clothes or shelter.

3. Victory over ignorance. When God offered King Solomon whatever he wanted, Solomon asked for wisdom, and God gave it to him (1 Kings 3:5-12). In Isaiah 55:8,9 we read that God's thoughts and ways are as high above a person's as the heavens are above the earth; yet in Psalm 32:8 we hear God's promise to humankind, "I will instruct you and teach you in the way you should go; I will guide you with My eye."

In the Old Testament, God taught people through visions, dreams, angels, seers, prophets, priests and various agencies. In the New Testament, God sent His Son to teach people; and on His return to heaven, Christ sent the Holy Spirit to guide us into all truth (John 16:13). God gave us His Word by inspiration of

the Holy Spirit (2 Pet. 1:21), and we are instructed in doctrine and the way of living righteously by reading and studying it. "All Scripture is given by inspiration of God, and is profitable for doctrine, for reproof, for correction, for instruction in righteousness; that the man of God may be complete, thoroughly equipped for every good work" (2 Tim. 3:16,17).

Lesson 8—Knowing God's Will for Your Life

God has a purpose for your life. You cannot be a successful Christian if you miss His plan. The plan of God is usually called "the will of God." When a father tells his son, "Go to the store," that is the father's will.

God has a place for you to live, a person for you to marry and a job for you to do. The will of God concerns these large decisions. But what about small decisions?

A zealous college freshman stood in a department store considering two shirts. He had money for only one shirt. "Which shirt is the will of God for me?" he asked his friend, who laughed at him. Is God's plan so specific that it includes what color shirts we buy?

Not all decisions Christians make are in the will of God. A missionary returned home from the field in broken health. He had worked so diligently that he had not eaten or slept properly; yet, friends said it was the will of God for him to come home. Can we blame God when we break the laws of nutrition and call the consequences the will of God?

Two high school boys wanted to preach the gospel and win souls. They went to the slums, rented a house and called it a church. They nailed up a church sign and visited the neighbors; yet the experiment lasted only one month. They were sincere and worked hard, but they failed. They thought they were in the will of God. Can we force our decisions on God and call them His will? Obviously, God would not call high school boys to start a church.

Learning About God's Will

You can look to Jesus as your example in finding the will of God. His entire life was dedicated completely to the Father's will. He once said,

"My food is to do the will of Him who sent Me" (John 4:34). Again, He prayed, "Not My will, but Yours, be done" (Luke 22:42). Doing the will of God is simply doing what God wants you to do. When Jesus taught us to pray, "Your will be done," it means we will do what God expects.

1. God's will is knowable. The psalmist said, "The humble He guides in justice, and the humble He teaches His way" (Ps. 25:9). Every person can find God's will. Everyone! Not just full-time preachers, but everyone. Even the little boy in the first grade should be taught that God wants him to develop his abilities and grow as Jesus did.

God expects us to know and do His will. Paul exhorted, "Do not be unwise, but understand what the will of the Lord is" (Eph. 5:17). Two facts arise from this verse: first, the will of God can be understood; and second, those who do not know the will of God are not wise. Some search for the will of God as though they were looking through a ring of keys by using the trial-and-error method. But God does not hide His will in the same way a miser hides money.

2. God shows His will to those who will do it. The week's groceries won't hop off the grocery shelves and place themselves onto the table. Before you can eat, you must get a job and work diligently; then you use your earnings to purchase groceries. And after you get your food to the house, it must be prepared. Laziness is inconsistent with God's will.

The will of God will not be forced on the unyielded Christian. God's will is revealed only to those who wholly desire it. We have to be sure that our wills, hearts, affections and desires are wholly surrendered to Him.

The student who wants to write the best term paper spends endless hours in the library researching material. In the same way, the Christian who wants the perfect will of God must search for it with wholeheartedly. Paul noted, "I beseech you therefore, brethren, by the mercies of God, that you present your bodies a living sacrifice,...that you may prove what is that good and acceptable and perfect will of God" (Rom. 12:1,2). The word "present" means to give. The father who gives a bicycle to his young boy has yielded it for his son's use. You must yield your life to find the will of God and be available for His use.

Almost every man in the world has driven a nail with his shoe. When his wife asks him to hang a picture, he looks for the nearest thing at hand because he doesn't want to go to the basement for a hammer. Then he drives the nail with his shoe because it's available. God doesn't walk only through the universities looking for the polished hammer who has an earned Ph.D. God is looking for available people. Any person who is willing to do anything can be used of God. Dwight L. Moody had an eighth-grade education, but he shook America with one hand and Great Britain with the other because he was willing to do anything God wanted him to do.

3. God's will is good for us. Some young people will not surrender to God because they think they will be miserable if they do. A girl remembers being embarrassed in speech class and resists becoming a missionary. A boy makes fun of a preacher and later is afraid to work on the Sunday School buses, thinking people will mock him.

In Romans 12:1,2, just quoted, Paul reminds us that the will of God is *good*. We don't have to prove to God that His will is good. He knows that. We must prove it to ourselves. We prove God's will by yielding ourselves to Him and following His revealed will.

When Paul's friends feared for his life but could not persuade him to stay away from Jerusalem, they said, "The will of the Lord be done," (Acts 21:14), and they left the matter in God's hands. That is all we can do sometimes, and that is enough in such situations. If God's will is done, the right thing will be done.

4. God's will is expressed in His laws. A missionary pilot was told by the Canadian aviation authorities that a storm was coming. Yet, he had an important meeting two hours away: The missions council was placing all missionaries for the coming three years. He took off anyway, and was killed in a snowstorm.

At his funeral, the prayer was prayed, "Lord, we don't understand Your will; we only accept it." Many asked why God took him. That was a wrong question. God directs some activities and permits others. God did not direct the missionary's death. The missionary broke the laws of aviation and of nature.

You cannot go contrary to the laws of God (whether in Scripture or nature) and not suffer consequences. A man falling out of a tree can't pray for God to keep him from breaking a leg. He must yield to the consequences and ask God to work through the circumstances.

The will of God should not be a dumping ground for personal failures. The missionary who had broken the laws of health and nutrition suffered the consequences. The missionary pilot had broken the laws of nature and suffered the consequences. God could have performed one of two miracles (the supernatural transcending of the laws of nature). He could have caused the plane to ride out the snowstorm, or He could have raised the pilot from the dead. Some thought God should have guided him through the storm, but none expected him to be raised from the dead.

When you seek the will of God for your life, don't expect Him to go against His laws. God works through His laws (sowing and reaping, working for money, tithing) to perform His will. Some have asked for God to supernaturally provide money, but they haven't worked, nor have they tithed. Maybe this is why God has not answered their prayers.

The Holy Spirit will guide you into the will of God when the Bible is not specific. "For as many as are led by the Spirit of God, these are sons of God" (Rom. 8:14). The Holy Spirit can lead through your desires. If you are yielded, what you want to do may be God's will for you. "Delight yourself also in the Lord, and He shall give you the desires of your heart" (Ps. 37:4). Then the Holy Spirit gives us power to make our desires a realization.

5. *God's will is personal.* He is interested in all your ordinary personal activities. Don't be afraid to say, "Lord, I'll do Your will whatever it is." He will not put you on the wrong airplane or make you marry the wrong person when you are willing to follow His direction. He won't even let you starve or go without a place to sleep. His will concerns your vacations, business trips or a spin to the shopping center. These fall within the larger context of God's will for your life. Paul said he

hoped to go to Rome by the will of God (Rom. 1:10; cf. 15:32). He said he would go to Corinth "shortly, if the Lord wills" (1 Cor. 4:19).

James spelled out God's will regarding the details of life in no uncertain terms when he said:

Come now, you who say, "Today or tomorrow we will go to such and such a city, spend a year there, buy and sell, and make a profit"; whereas you do not know what will happen tomorrow. For what is your life? It is even a vapor that appears for a little time and then vanishes away. Instead you ought to say, "If the Lord wills, we shall live and do this or that" (Jas. 4:13-15).

6. *God's will is that we be successful.* God never planned for you to fail. He wants us to overcome temptation (1 Cor. 10:13) and to overcome the world (1 John 5:4). When we are victorious, we endure. "And the world is passing away, and the lust of it; but he who does the will of God abides forever" (1 John 2:17).

Defeated Christians cannot be in God's will. They are living in the flesh. We should overcome our foibles and problems. The basis for victory is the death of Christ. Paul said that Christ "gave Himself for our sins, that He might deliver us from this present evil age, according to the will of our God and Father" (Gal. 1:4).

Making Decisions in God's Will

As a new Christian, you will want to do God's will. You will be faced with many decisions. Some of these will be difficult to make. You will want to make the right choice, but the alternatives are not always easy.

When you were a child, you did the will of your parents. Sometimes you didn't understand why you should do what they wanted, but you did it anyway. At other times, you did know what they wanted.

Some people have a difficult time making decisions because they are confused about God's will. Other people seem always to make the right choices. Why? Because they know the principles for finding God's will for their lives. The following principles will help you make wise decisions as a Christian.

1. Commit yourself to doing God's will. A phrase was lettered on a large poster in the dining room at a camp: THE LORD HAS A PLAN FOR YOU. God spoke to a young man who was working at the camp through that poster and convinced him He had something for him. The young man began to actively seek God's plan for his life.

The first step in knowing God's will is to seek it with all your heart. God speaks to servants who aggressively seek to know His will: "If any man willeth to do his will, he shall know" (John 7:17, KJV—paraphrased from *The Scofield Reference Bible* note).

You must actively turn your will over to God and decide to do His will before He will show it to you. You can't pray, "Lord, what is your will so I can think it over?" You can't bargain with God as Jacob did. Some don't know God's will because they are not ready to do it. God knows their hearts, so He doesn't waste energy showing them what He knows they will not do.

Total commitment involves presenting your whole self—body, soul and spirit—to God, and He will show you what is His good, and acceptable, and perfect will of God (Rom. 12:1,2).

2. Look for God's will in the Bible. The Word of God is the most vital element in finding the will of God. Read your Bible and saturate yourself with its principles. Those who know the Bible will usually experience the leadership of God in their lives. A wise grandfather once observed, "A Bible that is falling apart usually belongs to a person who isn't." It is never the slave's job to guess what the master wants done. It is the master's job to speak, and the servant's job to obey. If you do not know the Bible, you will guess at God's will.

You will find that the vast majority of problems that Christians have concerning the will of God are answered in the Word of God. Some things we shouldn't even pray about because we often use prayer as a crutch to explain our unwillingness to obey. We shouldn't pray about whether it is God's will for us to tithe or to be baptized. We should do it because it is the will of God as expressed in the Word of God. It would be ridiculous to pray whether it is God's will to take something that belongs to another. The Holy Spirit will never lead us contrary to the Word of God. He is its author and cannot deny Himself or contradict His Word.

3. Pray for guidance in knowing God's will. Many Christians want to tell the Lord how to solve their personal problems. But it is better to let Him decide how best to handle our problems, then sit back and let Him work. God's will does not operate when our will is getting in the way.

The daughter of a minister lost her contact lens on a shag carpet in the family room. The family members got down on their knees but could not find it. When the preacher realized it would cost $30 to replace the lens, he offered a $10 reward. Still they couldn't find it. The next morning the minister's wife prayed, "Jesus, You know where that lens is; lead me to it." As she prayed, the middle cushion on the couch came to her mind. When she looked under it, the lens was there.

4. Make sure your motives are pure in seeking God's will. Jesus noted, "The light of the body is the eye: if therefore thine eye be single, thy whole body shall be full of light" (Matt. 6:22, KJV). The word "single" means to look only one way. We must have an eye single for the glory of God. When self becomes involved, our eyes become blurry, and we miss the glory of God. God won't hear our prayers when we harbor secret impure motives.

In a recent Miss America pageant, a contestant was asked what she wanted to achieve. "I'd like to be happy, that's all." The will of God was never that you be happy, but rather that you be holy. The Constitution guarantees you the right to happiness, but those who seek it never find it. Nothing is wrong with being happy, but happiness is a by-product of holiness. As a goal unto itself, it doesn't work.

John Wesley said of his early Methodists, "I'm not sure they understand love. They come to church to enjoy their religion rather than to get holiness." God wants us to enjoy our religion, but that is never our aim; being faithful is our duty, and enjoyment results from doing our duty.

5. Do what you know is right. God gave you certain mental equipment to use, and surely He expects you to employ your mind under the guidance of the Holy Spirit to figure out most routine problems on your own. If the mind is being constantly upgraded by renewing, we should have an easier time doing God's will. "But be transformed by the renewing of your mind, that you may prove what is that good and acceptable and perfect will of God" (Rom. 12:2). Simply put, the will of God is doing what you know is right.

6. Face your own thoughts, strengths and weaknesses realistically. It is God's will that you work in your areas of strength rather than in your areas of weakness. If you cannot sing well enough to be a soloist, join a choir. If you aren't good enough for that, and you still love music, learn to play an instrument. Don't waste time and people's patience by trying to develop a career in an area of weakness. Put your time and energy on something you can do successfully.

7. You must have peace about your decisions. Paul said, "Let the peace of God rule in your hearts" (Col. 3:15). To claim to know God's will about something and yet be wracked by inner turmoil about that decision is ridiculous. The peace of God floods the heart and mind of a believer once God's will is revealed, and it passes all human understanding (Phil. 4:7). It may be that God wants you to do something extremely difficult or dangerous; yet, His peace will be given to you as you face it.

If God has led you to your present position, don't change to two new churches within the same week. A minister was wracked with indecision about where to serve. The more he prayed, the more anxious he became. He set Saturday midnight as a deadline to make the decision, but he grew more perplexed as the deadline approached. The decision was clear; both alternatives were wrong, and he stayed where he was. If you are not absolutely confident of a change, stay where you have peace.

A Christian once said, "Every time I'm nervous about a decision and do it anyway, it is usually the wrong decision." Paul tells us to always act out of confidence or faith: "Whatever is not from faith is sin" (Rom. 14:23).

8. Seek spiritual counsel from godly people. Godly people don't necessarily have to be your pastor or the pastor's wife, although you might go to them first. You can go to anyone who walks close to the Lord and has learned how to let God guide

his or her life. Talking about decisions and praying with that person can give new insight to handling problems. "Where there is no counsel, the people fall; but in the multitude of counselors there is safety" (Prov. 11:14).

9. Study circumstances to see whether doors are open or closed. It seems foolish to pound on closed doors and overlook the fact that open doors are available; yet, many believers do just that. The open doors may also lead to difficulties, but if it is God's will to go through them, that is the way to go. Paul said, "A great and effective door has opened to me, and there are many adversaries" (1 Cor. 16:9).

Opportunities are tied to the will of God. Many good things may come into your life; these may be the will of God. Although a college scholarship may be God's provision for one young person's education, being born to well-to-do parents may be God's provision for another student. Still another student may have to work his or her way through college and, in the process, learn the lesson of sacrifice. Each opportunity comes from God.

Watch for opportunities, though; not all may be God's will. Not every opportunity, no matter how attractive, may be good for you—and God's will is always good for you. Our desires might influence our understanding of God's will. For instance, a marriage proposal is not God's will if the young man will pull the young lady away from God. Test opportunities first according to the Scriptures.

10. Do not move forward until you know you are obeying the Bible. When you follow God's leadership, you know where you are going. The phrase "blind faith" is often misapplied. To make a decision because you are frustrated is not faith. Neither is it faith to step off on your own inclination.

Faith is obedience to the Word of God, and you should never be blind in your knowledge of the Bible. You must have your eyes open to your circumstances as well as to God's Word. Your mind must understand the consequences. God doesn't lead out of a vacuum; He leads out of full knowledge.

A Bible college student refused to work for a living. He maintained he must live by faith. His wife left him to seek help elsewhere because their baby was starving. His was not faith, but stupidity. The Bible specifically states that if a man will not work, neither shall he eat. It also says for a man to provide for his household.

Wait for God's will. Sometimes the more haste we make, the less speed we generate. Those who wait on God lose no time.

11. Judge decisions by an eternal perspective. Christians have eternity in their eyes. They judge every opportunity by God's scale. The will of God will never shortchange you. It is not God's will for you to be ignorant when you can get an education. It is not God's will for a church to step backward when it can reach out to the lost.

God is more concerned about your character than He is about your circumstances. At times, God will give you an easy time—rejoice. At other times, He will lead you through deep waters—still rejoice. It is God's will that you become like His Son. "And do not be conformed to this world, but be transformed by the renewing of your mind, that you may prove what is that good and acceptable and perfect will of God" (Rom. 12:2).

12. Be flexible about past decisions you have made regarding the will of God. Too many believers have the idea that once God shows them His will, they must never change. The opposite may be true in some cases; for the will of God is not time frozen, but cumulative. It builds up layer upon layer in the lives of most Christians.

The longer you follow the leading of the Lord, the more sensitive you will become to His will. You'll have more success in life. You'll find your life beautiful. You'll find yourself in constant conversation with the Lord. For instance, when you are witnessing to someone, and that person presents an argument, you may pray, "Lord, show me how to answer this person."

A friend of mine who gets up while it is still dark prays, "Lord, show me the light switch." Then he remarks to whoever is within hearing distance, "If you laugh at my praying for small things, you deserve a stubbed toe."

These are 12 ways to find God's will. John Wesley, the English evangelist, said that knowing God's will is a combination of Scripture, reason and experience. I hope these points have underscored that opinion.

Missing God's Will

Before leaving this important subject, we want to deal briefly with the problem of missing the will of God. It may be that in some situations, God's best for a person can slip by, but then be recaptured. In other situations, the opportunity may be lost forever.

1. The unsaved who miss God's will. Let's first think of the sinners who learn that it is God's will to be saved but they resist the convicting power of the Holy Spirit and remain outside of Christ. Unless they get to the place where they no longer feel the claims of Christ, they can still be salvaged. Their lives may be disastrous, but if they yield to Christ, even in their dying moments, they can be saved for all eternity.

2. Believers who resist God's will. Then let's think of the believers who discover God's will for them in some areas of their lives, but who resist the Spirit's leading and remain outside of God's will on those matters. One danger is that they will backslide and get out of fellowship with God. Another is that they will let their opportunities go by and never find them again.

A young girl was called to be a missionary, but rebelled. Much later in life, she yielded and God gave her a son who surrendered to go to the mission field. The second joy was great, but only heaven's records will show what she missed by not going herself.

If you think you have missed an important decision in God's will for you, you can have cleansing and forgiveness. God can still use you. It is never too late to do God's will. Pray much. Yield completely. God will accept your best for the rest of your life, regardless of what you might have to sacrifice to obtain it.

Lesson 9—Getting God's Power for Service

When I was 19 years old, I pastored the Westminster Presbyterian Church in Savannah, Georgia. Starting with 8 ladies and a handful of children, the church grew to an attendance of more than 100 attending Sunday School.

Two blocks away, another church conducted a noisy meeting every Friday evening. They could be heard two blocks away. One afternoon, four men from that church came to visit me. "We've come to pray with you and help you get the Holy

Ghost," the spokesman said. They flattered me, saying the hand of God was upon my life. "You can be greater than Billy Graham," they told me, "if you get the baptism of the Holy Ghost." Being an uninformed Christian, I couldn't dispute them on an intellectual level. I wanted everything God had for me, yet I know in my heart that they had nothing I needed.

Over a period of years, I have studied carefully the Scriptures regarding the filling of the Holy Spirit. The Holy Spirit fills His servants to win souls and to serve Him. Speaking in tongues is neither an evidence nor a qualification for the filling of the Spirit. Yet Paul exhorts the believers, "And be not drunk with wine, wherein is excess; but be filled with the Spirit" (Eph. 5:18, *KJV*). Because God commanded Christians to be filled with the Spirit, everyone should seek it. But many Christians are confused and fearful about the filling; they are afraid to seek it.

Ephesians 5:18 says it is wrong to get drunk, which is being controlled by the "spirits in the bottle." When a man is drunk, the "spirits from the bottle" control his walk, his talk and his eyesight. When a man is filled with the Holy Spirit, he is controlled by the Holy Spirit. Therefore, his walk, his talk and sight should be controlled by the Holy Spirit.

When Dr. A. J. Gordon was filled with the Spirit, he prayed, "Be thorough with me, Lord...be thorough." He wanted God to point out every small flaw that prevented a godly walk. Gordon built a great church because he wanted the Holy Spirit to influence every part of his life.

Dwight L. Moody was walking the streets of New York when he felt an urgent need for prayer. Borrowing a room from a friend, he prayed for two days lest the power of God should smite him dead. Dwight L. Moody was filled with the Spirit and shook two continents for God because the Holy Spirit completely controlled him.

When Christmas Evans sought the filling of the Holy Spirit, he wrote a 13-point covenant with God. Evans told God what he would do if filled by the Spirit. Because of his sincerity, Evans was filled with power, and revival came to all of Wales.

Curtis Hutson once said, "I wanted the full-

ness of the Holy Spirit more than I wanted to live." As a result, Hutson was able to influence many lives through his preaching.

When you read of the experiences of great men, be encouraged. What God has done for them, He can do for you. But be careful; don't let the experiences of others be your guide. When you seek the filling of the Holy Spirit, don't attempt to imitate their experiences, such as writing a covenant or praying for two days. Follow the principles of Scripture.

The Holy Spirit's Power in You

The Holy Spirit is the power you need to live for God. The Holy Spirit will make you holy and spiritual. He will give you the ability to overcome a nasty temper or depression. He will help you win souls. The Bible is very clear on the teaching of the Holy Spirit. Study it carefully.

1. The Holy Spirit indwells every believer. When you were saved, the Holy Spirit came into your life. Most people picture salvation as asking Christ to come into their lives, but at salvation, the Father and the Spirit also enter the heart. As a result, the Holy Spirit dwells in every believer. "And because you are sons, God has sent forth the Spirit of His Son into your hearts, crying out, 'Abba, Father!'" (Gal. 4:6). Actually, the Scriptures teach, "Now if anyone does not have the Spirit of Christ, he is not His" (Rom. 8:9). If you don't have the Holy Spirit, you are not saved.

When the Christians at Corinth sinned, Paul did not threaten them by saying, "If you sin, you will lose your salvation." When Paul saw sin in the lives of Christians, he was shocked. "What? know ye not that your body is the temple of the Holy Ghost which is in you, which ye have of God?" (1 Cor. 6:19, *KJV*). His message was, "Quit sinning because you have the Holy Spirit." He indwells all believers, no matter how carnal.

The evidence that people have the Holy Spirit living in them is seen in their actions. For the fruit of the Spirit—the results of having the Holy Spirit in us is "love, joy, peace, longsuffering, kindness, goodness, faithfulness, gentleness, self-control" (Gal. 5:22,23).

2. The Holy Spirit will never leave you. Jesus promised to send us the Holy Spirit: "I will pray the Father, and He will give you another Helper, that He may abide with you forever" (John 14:16). The word "forever" is applied to individual Christians. Paul repeats this truth when he tells the Ephesians to quit sinning because it irritates the Holy Spirit: "And do not grieve the Holy Spirit of God, by whom you were sealed for the day of redemption" (Eph. 4:30).

Obviously, you cannot lose your salvation because of sin; the Holy Spirit will dwell in you until the second coming of Christ: "You were sealed with the Holy Spirit of promise, who is the guarantee of our inheritance until the redemption of the purchased possession" (1:13,14). Your iniquity, however, grieves the Holy Spirit.

Once a friend mentioned that he was seeking the Holy Spirit. "I've fasted, tarried and thirsted according to the Bible. Why can't I get the Holy Spirit?" he asked. The sincerity of his question was evident.

I told him, "The Holy Spirit is in you and He will not leave you. The Holy Spirit is a Person who wants to control your life more than you want the flesh to control you. You've already got Him in your heart; now yield to Him so you can realize the potential that is yours."

The Holy Spirit is like the full tank of fuel in an automobile, just waiting to be ignited. But somewhere between the tank and the engine some trash may have infiltrated the fuel line. To blame the Holy Spirit for our empty lives is like blaming the full tank of gas in a car because the engine won't run. We have the fuel of the Holy Spirit in our hearts; now let's allow Him to work so we can get going for God.

3. The Holy Spirit is a Person, not a substance. Many Christians treat the Holy Spirit like a substance that can be poured into a glass. The Holy Spirit is a Person. Also, some treat the Holy Spirit like a ubiquitous spirit, such as the spirit of communism or the spirit of Americanism; but the Holy Spirit is a Person.

When Ananias and Sapphira sinned, Peter charged them, "You have not lied to men but to God" (Acts 5:4). The Holy Spirit was called "He" when Christ prophesied, "He will glorify Me, for He will take of what is Mine, and declare it to you" (John 16:14). When the Holy Spirit comes into our lives, we have a new Person within us.

Recently I was in a room, when a congressman entered. All conversation immediately silenced, and we rose. Men walked over and shook the congressman's hand; others stood and watched him. The power of the congressman's personality dominated the room. In the same way, the power of the Holy Spirit should dominate our lives. We could have ignored the congressman and gone on with our conversation, but he was so important that we couldn't. In the same way, Christians can ignore the influence of the Holy Spirit, but it grieves Him (1 Thess. 5:19), and He should be so important in our lives that we couldn't ignore His leading.

How to Be Filled with the Spirit
We are never commanded in the Bible to be indwelt or sealed or baptized with the Spirit—these are all gifts from God to the believer at the moment of salvation. We are commanded, however, to be filled with the Spirit (Eph. 5:18). To be filled with the Spirit means for believers to allow the Spirit who lives in them to control their lives. This is a matter of continuous surrender of the believer's life to the Spirit's control.

The first step to Spirit power is desire. You begin by wanting to be filled with the Spirit. God will not force His Spirit on you or anyone else. Just as the old adage maintains that "You can lead a horse to water, but you can't make him drink," the same is true of the Christian. The filling of the Spirit will not be forced upon you.

1. Thirsting. When you desire the filling of the Spirit, it is the same as thirsting. Jesus described the process: "If anyone thirsts, let him come to me and drink. This He spoke concerning the Spirit, whom those believing in Him would receive" (John 7:37,39).

2. Yielding. This is the surrendering of the will to the Spirit. When a young girl receives a proposal of marriage, she says yes if she wants the man. But that initial yes doesn't guarantee marital happiness. The couple must work at it. Both she and her husband must daily submit to the demands of marriage.

The yes of submission to God's will must be followed by a daily yes to Christ, who keeps you in the center of God's will. The child of God prays, "Today I give myself to You to be what

You want, to go where You lead, and to speak what You command."

Once you have prayed this prayer, you can expect Satan to mock and tempt you. It is one thing to surrender, but another to stay surrendered. Satan will say, "You didn't mean it," or "Things are going so poorly that God has forgotten about you." You may have gone to the altar and surrendered to God, yet after you left the church, you slipped into sin again. It is not God's fault that you slipped into sin. Don't blame Him. The initial surrendering is only the beginning of the surrendered life. You must make up your mind to always do God's will.

You need to keep an attitude of surrender. When I go downtown, I don't have to make a decision every time I come to a stop light; I just stop. I know that if I run a red light, it is dangerous, or I might get a ticket. Stopping at the red light has become an attitude of life for me.

The surrendered life takes the same approach to sin. Every time you face temptation, don't debate the merits of drunkenness, stealing, adultery or whatever sin the temptation may involve. When you first say yes to God, you make up your mind that you will serve Him. Now, when temptations come, rely on that attitude. Don't entertain evil desires. Obey God's traffic signals found in the Scriptures. Stopping at the signal is another way of daily saying yes to God and letting the Holy Spirit stay in control.

3. Asking. If you want God's power, you must ask for it. Jesus spoke the parable of the pleading neighbor who came at night when his friend was in bed. Jesus commands us to "ask, and it will be given to you; seek, and you will find; knock, and it will be opened to you" (Luke 11:9). Then Jesus explains for what we should pray: "How much more will your heavenly Father give the Holy Spirit to those who ask Him!" (v. 13).

If you are defeated, ask God to give you victory. If you have never won a soul to Christ, ask God to fill you with the Spirit so you can serve Him with power.

Some go forward during the invitational hymn at a church meeting. They yield at the altar and ask God to fill them with the Holy Spirit. Others might bow their heads as they study their Sunday School lessons and pray, "God, fill me

with the Holy Spirit so I can teach this lesson as you would teach it." Still other Christians might kneel beside their beds during devotions and ask for power to overcome explosive tempers.

A variety of circumstances may be present in the filling of the Holy Spirit, but the only power is in His Person. Various methods can be used in seeking the Holy Spirit, but only one pattern is given in Scripture to receive it. Don't seek the experience; ask for the filling of the Person of the Holy Spirit, and God will answer your prayer.

Using Your Gifts in God's Service

All Christians should be serving God according to the spiritual gifts they have been given at the time of their new birth. Paul tells us, "Each one has his own gift from God" (1 Cor. 7:7). And Peter repeats the same truth: "As each one has received a gift, minister it to one another" (1 Pet. 4:10).

"If I could sing the way she can, I'd serve the Lord," is an often-heard excuse. People envy the gifts of others, yet have little concept of their own gifts. Many would like to play beautiful instrumental offertories in church, yet they are not willing to practice three hours a day for years.

"Preaching is not my gift," a young high school boy told his Sunday School teacher.

The teacher replied, "You should not preach unless you are called." The boy had no desire in his heart to be a minister.

Yet, the pastor announced from the pulpit, "Everybody ought to be able to preach." Which one is right? The confusion about spiritual gifts abounds, yet Paul exhorts, "Now concerning spiritual gifts, brethren, I do not want you to be ignorant" (1 Cor. 12:1).

A spiritual gift is a Spirit-given ability to serve God. In the Bible, three composite lists of these gifts are given: Romans 12:6-8, 1 Corinthians 12:28-30 and Ephesians 4:11.

Beginning in Matthew 25:14, Jesus tells the parable of the talents. One servant was given five talents, another two and the last was given one. These talents were given "to each according to his own ability" (v. 15). A talent, which was a measure of silver, represented a man's ability. We don't all have the same abilities or spiritual gifts.

In the parable, the man who used his talents

faithfully received other talents. Perhaps you have three talents: teaching, giving money and administration; or you could have more than three talents. God expects you to do the very best you can with the talents you have.

Every talent gets different results. Paul places them in order, noting, "God has appointed these in the church: first apostles, second prophets, third teachers" (1 Cor. 12:28). The fact that the gifts are numbered means that some are more important (or more effective) than others.

The natural question you may ask is, "How can I find my spiritual gift?"

1. Your gifts are the work of the Holy Spirit through you. A spiritual gift may be a natural ability with the Holy Spirit working through it. Paul describes a spiritual gift as "the manifestation of the Spirit" (v. 7).

A young lady may sing beautifully and use all the training that a rich natural voice displays, yet have no spiritual effect on the hearers. The next young lady might have a simple voice and little training, yet when she sings, the Holy Spirit draws people closer to Christ. The first girl does not have a spiritual gift, whereas the second one does.

Your spiritual gifts are manifested when you are filled with the Spirit (Eph. 5:17,18), allowing the Holy Spirit to work through you. Those who are filled have separated themselves from sin and yielded their lives for service.

2. You were given embryonic gifts when you were saved. Many things happened in your life when you received Jesus Christ. One of them was that the Holy Spirit came into your life to give you abilities to serve God. The giving of gifts is associated with salvation. "When He [Christ] ascended on high, He led captivity captive, and gave gifts to men" (Eph. 4:8). This verse is tied in with the resurrection—the point of victory over death. In that victory, Christ gave abilities to His followers so that they, in turn, could be victorious in service.

At the moment of your salvation, gifts were placed in your heart, although they were not fully developed.

A pastor looking out on a group of teenagers doesn't know which one will be a missionary, doctor, accountant or housewife. They all have different gifts for potential service. Some will

find God's will and serve Christ effectively; others will choke out their spiritual strength. Because you have spiritual gifts, pray for the wisdom to develop them.

3. You find your spiritual gifts by seeking them. The Bible teaches that your gifts grow as you seek them. "But earnestly desire the best gifts" (1 Cor. 12:31). God would not give you what is impossible; He gives the ability and the option to seek greater power and usability.

The first step in being used of God is to volunteer for service. This is more than surrendering to His will; you must actively seek His blessing on your service. A missionary once told God, "I'm going to the mission field unless you run a train over me to stop me." The missionary had set his face to serve God abroad, and would do so unless God stopped him.

On the other hand, Dr. Curtis Hutson, evangelist and former pastor of Forrest Hill Baptist Church, Decatur, Georgia, had a different kind of prayer: "God, I believe You are calling me. If You are, keep the urge growing. If not, let it die away."

Curtis was a layman, preaching on weekends and delivering mail on Route 41 in Decatur, when he read that Dr. Jack Hyles had baptized more than 500 people. Hutson decided to go hear Hyles preach.

At that service, Hutson decided to build a church in Georgia as big as Dr. Hyles had built in Hammond, Indiana. Hutson's church grew from an attendance of approximately 50 people to more than 3,000 weekly.

Your success in God's service begins with your dreams. You may never build a great church, but you can be used of God. The secret is desire. What do you want to accomplish for God? You may never do all you dream, but you will never do more than you dream.

Some go through life and never win a soul. Others never teach a Sunday School class. Some will stand before God having little in their hands. This does not mean God has overlooked them by not giving them abilities. God will use Christians to the degree they place themselves at the disposal of the Divine. The choice is with you, not God. If you will meet God's qualifications, you can win great battles.

You may consider yourself too small, but you can win battles, in the same way David defeated Goliath. You may consider yourself too old, but you can be influential, as was 80-year-old Moses, who brought Egypt to its knees. You may consider yourself too insecure, but God's power can anoint you as it did Gideon, the youngest son from the least family of the smallest tribe. Gideon set 130,000 Midianites to rout with 300 men.

4. Your abilities are developed under the influence of the Bible. The Word of God is the greatest treasure on earth. It is more valuable than preachers, churches or Sunday School buses, for without the Bible, there is no Christianity. If you want to be used of God, you must love the thing that is the basis for Christianity. The Bible reveals God's heart; and the more you know God's heart, the better your preparation to serve Him. You find your ability to serve God in the Scriptures.

Some love to hear sermons; others love to read them. Some love to listen to teachers; others love to read devotional books. But a love for the Bible is imperative in the Christian life.

One great preacher testified that as a teen, "I read the Bible at camp, at home in my room and in study hall at school. I read it sitting on a rock by the lake and sitting on my bed." His love for the Word of God has given him power in his preaching.

If you are going to be used of God, you must love the Bible, for he who loves the Word of God loves God Himself. Dr. C. I. Scofield preached at the funeral of D. L. Moody and noted, "God used D. L. Moody because he believed the Bible, and he believed God blessed the Bible." Moody's sermons were filled with the Bible, and God used those sermons to save scores of people.

5. You develop your gifts by taking the opportunities at hand. The Bible teaches, "Whatever your hand finds to do, do it with your might" (Eccles. 9:10). We are to give instant obedience to service, especially when the opportunity arises. If in an emergency a Sunday School teacher is needed, do the best job you can. Don't ask, "Is my gift teaching?" When someone is needed to help set up chairs at the church, don't ask, "Is this my gift?"

Obviously, this principle can't be applied in every instance. If the pianist is not at church, you can't play without ability. The same goes for singing a solo. But then, people won't ask you to do what they know you are unable to do.

Faithfulness in a small capacity leads to a promotion in God's sight. Jerry Falwell preached to millions on the Old Time Gospel Television Network, yet he began as a student at Baptist Bible College, Springfield, Missouri, by teaching one fourth-grade boy at High Street Baptist Church. He faced the usual discouragements, but his faithful ministry to that one boy enabled Falwell to build the class up to 53 students before the year had ended.

If you want an opportunity to preach to millions, develop your ability by preaching to a handful.

Lesson 10—Winning Others to Christ

A little boy in Sunday School asked, "How can Jesus fit into my heart? He's so big." The boy's small imagination knew that Christ was large because Christ was God.

While the teacher was trying to decide how to reply, again the small boy blurted out, "He must spill over!"

Out of the mouths of children comes wisdom. The boy was wrong about the physical size of Christ, but he was truthful about the results of salvation. The new Christian spills over with the love of Christ out of gratitude. The following section analyzes the "overflow" that is the Christian's responsibility to show others.

Two emphases in evangelism are important; you should try to follow both. The first is witnessing—called sharing Christ with others. The second is personal evangelism—called soul winning.

Bill Adams came to know Christ when his foreman talked to him. Bill wanted to be a witness, so each Sunday morning with Bibles in hand, he and his family drove to church. At work, he used his sense of humor to let the other guys know he didn't appreciate filthy jokes. He told his relatives how he found Christ. Adams wanted his testimony to be an influence on others and it was. Bill is a witness who shares with others what he has seen, heard and experienced.

When people take the witness stands in court, they are not allowed to give their opinions or hearsay evidence. Witnesses only share what they have experienced. Peter and John gave a witness before the Jewish Council: "For we cannot but speak the things which we have seen and heard" (Acts 4:20). Witnessing is the first step in reaching others.

Dave Stonfield was a ministerial student who had a burden for the lost, concerned because they were on their way to hell. In chapel, he asked for prayer as he went home during the holidays. He had a list of four people he wanted to win to Christ. Dave phoned and made an appointment with each person, then tried to lead them to Christ. Stonfield is a soul winner.

Learn How to Reach Others

The following are some helpful suggestions in doing evangelism. It should be mentioned, of course, that human beings are complicated creatures and not every technique is going to be workable in every situation.

1. Try to rid your mind of all feelings of superiority toward sinners. As you pray about reaching your friends, ask the Lord to make you constantly aware that you are only a sinner saved by grace. Try also to rid your mind of a feeling of sentimental pity, for this will result in a patronizing attitude. Just plan to meet people as they are to share the good news.

2. Determine that you are going to be courteous and tactful in your dealings with those to whom you witness. People sometimes are offended when they think you don't accept them as they are. They may resent the fact that you talk to them about sin, sorrow for sin, repentance and seeking forgiveness because they think they are good as they are. They might get irritated. Some won't even talk to you.

Regardless of what happens, you have to keep calm and not lash back. If you are too aggressive, you may lose them altogether. Dallas Billington, pastor of Akron [Ohio] Baptist Temple, told me, "Don't pick green fruit." We can push for a decision too soon. What can't be said today might find a hearing another day. You cannot force anyone into the Kingdom. The Holy Spirit must be allowed to handle the timing.

3. Try to find out how much the person knows about the Bible, church life and Christian living. You have to begin where you find people. If they are atheists

or agnostics, you may discover they have only fragmented and perhaps garbled understandings of such things. If they are Jews, you might be able to meet on common ground as far as the Old Testament is concerned and go from there. If they are Roman Catholics, you may have some beliefs in common although you may differ on the basic issue of salvation. If they are members of one of the false cults, you may have to have some knowledge of its teachings. The same will be true if they are liberal Protestants.

4. Make sure any show of interest on the part of the unsaved person is not misinterpreted. Some people will be friendly and courteous to the extent that you may conclude they are ready to make decisions for Christ, but they may not be ready to do that yet. Their eternal destiny is more important than what they think of you. If the Spirit of God impresses on you that a person is ready to yield to Christ, then press for a decision. Review what you have said about being saved, so you are sure the person understands what is involved, then pray with him or her.

5. Present the entire gospel to the person because it is the power of God unto salvation.

6. Be sure to follow through on a new convert. You led this new convert to Christ, so it is your responsibility to follow up on the person. Just as a baby is helpless, this babe in Christ needs your love, guidance and protection. In the Great Commission, we are commanded to "make disciples" (Matt. 28:19)—to teach those who are saved in the ways of their new lives. We are told to baptize them, thus providing outward signs of inward changes, letting the world know they have entered into new ways of their lives.

Help anchor these new converts firmly to the Scriptures, being sure they have the witness of the Spirit that they are children of God. Discuss with them the fruits of the Spirit expected in the life of believers. Show them that in obedience to Christ's command, they should be baptized and taken into church membership. Assure them of your willingness to continue to help them in their spiritual growth as Christians.

DISCIPLESHIP TRAINING

Growing churches are characterized by people

who know and live by the Word of God. Disciples must continue in the Word of God (John 8:31). They recognize and emphasize the importance of the Bible in the Christian life, beginning with salvation. Salvation involves the intellect, emotions and will. People who are saved know the Gospel content, feel the conviction of sin and the love of God and respond by an act of their wills. Because they must know the content of the Gospel, growing churches must develop a strategy for teaching the Bible.

Some churches have made the mistake of viewing Bible study and evangelism as two mutually exclusive functions. This has resulted in two problems. First, some churches use Bible study to excuse their lack of evangelistic involvement with its resulting church growth. John R. Rice commented on this tendency when he wrote:

The first aim of every preacher called of God should be to win souls. A minister may say, as an alibi for his powerlessness and fruitlessness: "I am called to be a teaching pastor. My ministry is to the church. I must feed the flock of God." But that, I insist, is an alibi for outright disobedience to the plain command of God. The Great Commission is still binding on preachers. The Gospel is to be preached to every creature. We are to teach those already converted to go win others.[1]

A second problem arising out of this dichotomy of evangelism and Bible study is the tendency to use one's emphasis on evangelism as an excuse for neglecting Bible study. Gary Inrig addresses this issue:

It should also be noted that the main business of assembly life is the equipping and edification of believers. Unfortunately, many churches have focused so strongly upon evangelism that believers have become starved, and church life has become anemic.[2]

The ministries of evangelism and teaching the Bible are two aspects of a healthy ministry. Any ministry model that calls for one at the exclusion of the other is defective at its very core. Each has

its place in the life of a church. According to Gene Getz:

The church therefore exists to carry out two functions—evangelism (to make disciples) and edification (to teach them). These two functions in turn answer two questions: first, Why does the church exist in the world? and second, Why does the church exist as a gathered community?[3]

Discipleship Training and Church Growth

Growing churches realize the power of an educated disciple. The effectiveness of a worker is in direct proportion to his or her education. Some workers are unsuccessful because they have not been trained. Others fail because they have enough education but they do not know the right things (their theology is wrong). Therefore, the leader must reinforce the primacy of the Church. This is the cornerstone of Christian education. The leader also must reinforce the primacy of the Church's methods and continued loyalty to the cause of Christ. All this is accomplished through a systematic Bible teaching ministry.

Training church members for ministry is an important part of church ministry. According to Melvin Hodges:

Every local church should be considered a seedbed that produces Christian workers. In order to attain this, it is necessary that the pastor have a deep desire to develop leadership in his church....The ideal workers' training program includes a strong activity program in the local church, coupled with specialized training in systematic Bible teaching such as is available in a Bible institute. The church in each country should develop a broadbased training program.[4]

As important as discipleship training is, it is not a substitute for evangelism. As important as evangelism is, it is not a substitute for discipleship training. Donald McGavran noted:

Church growth follows where the lost are not merely found but restored to normal life in the fold—though it may be a life they have never consciously known. Faithfulness in "folding and feeding"—which unfortunately has come to be called by such a dry, superficial term as follow-up—is essential to lasting church expansion.[5]

Faithfulness in proclamation and finding is not enough. Faithful aftercare must be considered. Among the found, also, there must be fidelity in feeding on the Word.

Implementing Discipleship Training into a Church

If God wants His people to engage in Bible study, He wants His leaders to organize and motivate His people for Bible study. This means a church should have a plan that organizes the Bible teaching and Bible study ministries of the church, and the pastor and others should provide motivation to encourage people to study the Bible.

Every church should have a variety of Bible study opportunities for adults, understanding that not all people will take advantage of the same opportunities. Some may prefer to study the Bible in a traditional age-graded class, whereas others would rather belong to a class that has something other than age in common. Still others prefer belonging to a large Auditorium Bible Class, or may wish to study more formally in a church-related Bible Institute.

Adult education has become a way of life in recent years, and the church needs to take advantage of this opportunity in providing courses, seminars, lectures and other Bible study opportunities for those who wish to study the Scriptures. Many churches have found that Bible studies on such themes as marriage, training children or financial management have been sufficiently need oriented to attract non-Christians who might otherwise not be interested in Bible study, but are effectively reached for Christ because a church organized opportunities for Bible study.

In organizing a variety of Bible study opportunities, some attempt should be made to coordinate various efforts and gain maximum results. In a large church, a pastor may be responsible for this organization, just as a children's pastor or youth pastor might organize the educational ministries of the age group for which he or she is responsible. In a small church, this can be accomplished through the board of Christian education and the use of a master calendar in the church office. This will help avoid conflicts in programming and reduce unnecessary duplication of efforts.

People must not only have an opportunity to study the Bible, they must also be motivated to take advantage of those opportunities. The best way to motivate people is to convince them that a certain course of action will meet a perceived need, or they must be challenged with a dream. Pastors have been successful in using both of these methods to engage people in meaningful Bible study.

Pastors of growing churches preach from the same Bible as pastors of churches not experiencing growth, but they are often more successful in convincing their listeners of the relevance of their message to the listener's life. If given the choice, the average church goer would probably rather hear a message on the topic "How to Live the Successful Christian Life" than a message on the topic "The Meaning of Baptism in Romans 6," even though both messages may be based on the same passage and may have largely the same outline. People are motivated to study the Bible when they are convinced it will help them in a perceived area of need. The wise pastor will translate the systematic theology he learned in seminary into a lifestyle theology he can teach in the pulpit.

Bible study should also be promoted as a challenge. A young couple preparing for marriage can be challenged to study what the Bible says about relationships, finances, the home and other marriage-related topics on the basis that they want their marriage to be the best it can be. Similarly, new parents may be challenged to complete studies related to parenthood as they dream of being the best parents they can be. One pastor used to challenge his people at the annual watch-night service to become authorities on some book, character or chapter of the Bible that year.

In recent years, a growing interest and adoption of the practice of expository Bible preaching has been occurring. The popularity of this approach is largely because of the example of a number of leading pastors such as W. A. Criswell and the influence of schools such as Dallas

Theological Seminary. Today, many of the leading pastors who have large congregations and radio and/or television ministries use this approach to preaching almost exclusively.

Other pastors vary their preaching topics more widely, but are systematic in their Bible teaching. They plan the church year with special emphasis during campaigns and conferences such as church growth campaigns, stewardship campaigns, missionary conventions, prophecy and deeper life conferences. Other pastors rely on the use of curriculum plans in their Sunday Schools to ensure that systematic programs of Bible teaching are in place in their churches. In liturgical traditions, pastors often preach and teach according to a "lectionary," which is a list of Scripture that follows the historic church calendar year. This helps to assure a systematic coverage of Bible truths. As pastors and Sunday School teachers teach the Scriptures in this way, they help their people grow internally through Bible study. In turn, this leads to external growth as others come to have their needs met in this way.

References: [1]John R. Rice, *Why Our Churches Do Not Win Souls* (Murfreesboro, Tenn.: Sword of the Lord Publishers, 1966), p. 67. [2]Gary Inrig, *Life in His Body* (Wheaton, Ill.: Harold Shaw Publishers, 1975), p. 44. [3]Gene Getz, *Sharpening the Focus of the Church* (Chicago: Moody Press, 1974), p. 22. [4]Melvin L. Hodges, *A Guide to Church Planting* (Chicago: Moody Press, 1973), pp. 76, 77. [5]Cited in Elmer L. Towns, *What the Faith Is All About* (Wheaton, Ill.: Tyndale House Publishers, Inc., 1983).

DISCOVERY QUESTIONS

An initial set of questions used by spiritual mapping teams to focus their research. These questions are subdivided under headings related to the status of Christianity, prevailing social bondages, worldviews and allegiances, spiritual opposition, the evolution of current circumstances and the potential for spiritual breakthroughs.—GOJR

DOCTRINAL FAITH

A statement of faith or a written confession of

what a person believes concerning the person of God and Scripture.

DOUBLING SUNDAY SCHOOL ATTENDANCE

The following principles can be used by Sunday Schools to encourage growth.

1. Set an overall goal. Goal setting works. A junior class in the Florence (South Carolina) Baptist Temple hung a large sheet of paper from one wall to another, then had each of the 26 boys write his name on it and sign "52" by his autograph. In that way, each student reinforced the class goal of 52. The entire Sunday School set a goal of 1,225. Posters were put on walls, bulletin boards and doors. Every poster announced the goal of 1,225, but each differently—in German, Spanish, Greek, upper- and lower-case letters, Gothic and Roman numbers.

2. Set a goal for prospects. For your class to double, attempt to get twice as many prospects as your average attendance. This means that each member should suggest two names for the prospect list.

An adult class at a church in Salem, Virginia, distributed blank cards to members and asked them to submit names of friends they would like to see in the class. After two weeks of listing names, the goal still was not reached. Three ladies were therefore delegated to phone members of the class and write down the names they suggested. They worked until 100 new names were gathered.

To have a growing Sunday School class, put as much emphasis on finding prospects as on recruiting them.

3. Assign prospect responsibility. Many growing classes type the names of all prospects on sheets of paper, then distribute photocopies in the class, assigning prospects to be contacted before the next week. The Calvary Baptist Church in Ypsilanti, Michigan, printed a motto above its visitation board—People Expect What You Inspect. Many of the members work in the automobile assembly plants in Detroit where they are taught by General Motors that people work according to how closely the foreman supervises them. The same rule applies to Sunday School.

Thus, give all class members prospects to contact, then check up the following Sunday to see if they have made the contacts.

4. *Phone every prospect.* During a campaign, phone every prospect on your list—every week. Extend to each a friendly welcome, giving the time, place and lesson topic.

5. *Send mail to every prospect.* During a campaign, mail a postcard or letter to every prospect, inviting him or her to Sunday School. A housewife can write a personal note to 30 prospective students in two hours. A first-class letter to 20 prospects costs less than $10—and eternal benefits will result.

6. *Visit every prospect.* Visitation puts the Go in Gospel, carrying the message to every person. After you have phoned every prospect, a visit to the home will convince him or her of your love. In fact, visit every prospect every week during an attendance campaign.

7. *Start a class newsletter.* During your campaign, start a one-page (or larger) class newsletter. The junior class at the Crestwicke Baptist Church, Guelph, Ontario, Canada, distributed an eight-page paper, "The Roadrunner," to every junior. Because it is a large class, the teachers spend time writing articles about juniors who have recently committed their lives to Jesus Christ. The paper also includes crossword puzzles, homework, stories and news about the attendance campaign. The attendance motto and logo also are printed there, reminding the kids of their attendance goals.

The average Sunday School teacher who has fewer than 10 pupils cannot publish a newsletter every week, but can do it at least twice during each attendance campaign. A newsletter is not hard to prepare. If you've never issued one, simply write a one-page letter giving the news of the class. Then type the letter in two columns to make it look like a newspaper, and put a headline across the top. Fill the newsletter with the names of students, their accomplishments and what you expect to do for God.

8. *Name your class.* Bill Newton called the fourth-grade boys class at the Thomas Road Baptist Church, Lynchburg, Virginia, "The Treehouse Gang." A massive cardboard tree, which included a door, was used at the entrance of the room. Two more large trees reaching from ceiling to floor covered the inside walls. Later, a stockade was put in the hall surrounding the doors. Bill Newton started his class in September. His goal was to average 54 before the year was out. With his enthusiasm, ingenuity and determination, Newton pushed the average attendance to 94.

9. *Post attendance.* A junior boys class at the First Baptist Church, Hammond, Indiana, called their campaign "Spring Training." A massive score chart marked hits, runs and errors so that students could follow their progress each week. The class was divided into two sides, and at the beginning of each class they "batted around," adding up visitors, attendance and Bibles.

Because pupils tend to value those things that are important to teachers, make sure to keep careful attendance records. This tells each student it's his or her duty to be in class every Sunday. The extra visual encouragement of some kind of a wall chart gives added motivation.

10. *Get a motto.* The high school class at the Bible Baptist Church, Savannah, Georgia, planned a "Fat Is Beautiful" campaign. Instead of awarding stars or rockets, or putting names on the wall, they weighed in each week. The teams began with an equal total weight. Visitors tipped the scales for the winners, while absentees dragged the losers down.

11. *Get a logo.* The Indianapolis (Indiana) Baptist Temple celebrated its twenty-fifth anniversary in 1975. A huge silver seal bearing the motto—The 25th Year of Redemption—hung all year in the auditorium. Under the motto was their goal: 2,500 Souls Won to Christ in 1975. The entire seal was their logo. They had it fashioned into small silver seals that they affixed to envelopes and letterheads. It was also printed on all the literature of the church.

12. *Distribute buttons.* Dr. Bob Gray, Trinity Baptist Church, Jacksonville, Florida, set a Florida record of more than 5,000 in Sunday School on the church's twenty-fifth anniversary. Each person was given a button ahead of time that was worded—I Am One of 5,000—to remind him or her to be faithful in attendance.

13. *Stretch their faith.* The First Baptist Church, West Hollywood, Florida, planned to beat the

Jacksonville record and have the largest Sunday School in the history of Florida. To do so, attendance had to double from 2,700 to 5,400. In a three-day workers' conference, their faith was stretched.

On the first night of the conference, all workers were pinned with a "5,000+" button and asked to pray for 5,000+ every time they ate a meal during the next week. Because most people eat three meals a day, every person would pray 21 times for 5,000+. Pastor Verle Ackerman called it "Fast or Pray," reminding his people that if they didn't pray for 5,000, they should not eat.

The second night, each worker signed a card to pledge, "I will work for 5,000+."

On the third night, every teacher made a numerical commitment of a goal for his or her class on 5,000+ Sunday.

When the tally was completed, they had pledged to reach 5,400. Later they reached 5,427, the largest Sunday School in the history of Florida.

14. Choose a good day. Don't plan a Sunday School campaign for Labor Day weekend, or during the Fourth of July holiday when a dip in attendance is natural. One minister tried to have his largest attendance on Labor Day weekend and the Sunday after Easter, claiming, "Anybody can get a crowd on Easter; I want to build an attendance to show our people love God." Unfortunately, he missed the whole purpose of an attendance campaign. A high attendance should do more than demonstrate the loyalty of the faithful. It should bring visitors, electrify everyone when the attendance is doubled, and bring men, women and children to a saving faith in Jesus Christ. So plan for Sunday School growth when the best results are possible. Then you will be a good steward of your time, energy and money. Plan to grow on those days when attendance can be largest.

15. Remember the clenched fist. Just as pressure builds the physical body, so pressure builds up the spiritual Body of Christ. A challenge is given members to build up a class by goals, vision and campaigns. But a person can keep the fist taut only so long. Then the muscles give out.

Likewise, a Sunday School class can respond to a challenge for expansion for only a short time. Therefore, growing Sunday Schools plan two attendance campaigns for six or seven weeks each spring and fall. They work as hard as they can during a campaign to find prospects, excite students, phone, write and visit. The attendance drive is relaxed during the Christmas holidays, and again during the summer.

16. Get a running start. Before jumping a creek, a boy runs faster if he has to jump farther. In Sunday School, the larger the goal, the longer it takes to build up the follower's expectation. Plan a six- or seven-week fall campaign, having the high Sunday as the last day. Don't read this article and plan to double your class next week. Pray to double, plan to double and promote to double. But remember this: Teachers can't lead if the classes won't follow, and pupils won't work to double their classes unless their teachers take the time to convince them it can be done.

17. Plan a high day. Plan a high-attendance Sunday on the last Sunday of your campaign. Some criticize this, saying that it only attracts a crowd and makes small-class teaching impossible. However, the "high day" really is only a return to the old-fashioned rally day, where all pupils assembled in the auditorium to "rally" enthusiasm for Sunday School. Most teachers need to break lethargy and infuse the pupils with expectation. A "double day" convinces the pupils it can be done again and again, until the class is permanently doubled.

18. Pray. God answers the prayers of those who ask for their ministries to be enlarged, but prayers alone cannot build Sunday Schools. God will not do what He has commanded *us* to do. *We* are to go and reach people. Classes grow when teachers are busy visiting, phoning, mailing and praying all week.

19. Feed them the Word. People go to restaurants where they get good food, then they tell their friends. Books are sold by word of mouth. The satisfied customer is still the best salesperson for any product. The basis for growing Sunday School classes is still good Bible teaching that causes students to bring their friends. The Bible must be made interesting, captivating and relevant.

20. Try supersaturation. The disciples went everywhere preaching the Word, reaching people by all means. A Sunday School teacher should use every technique to excite pupils about coming to Sunday School. Extra promotion, contests and taking pupils to a ball game show that a teacher cares. Extra preparation, visitation and prayer will get results. The work of God is still spelled W-O-R-K. Any class will grow in direct proportion to the energies expended by the teacher.

DRUMMOND, LEWIS

Dr. Lewis Drummond, the Billy Graham Professor of Evangelism at Beeson Divinity School (Samford University), Birmingham, Alabama, is one of the best known and most influential professors in the Southern Baptist Convention. The Lewis A. Drummond Center for Evangelism and Church Growth on the campus of Southeastern Baptist Theological Seminary, Wake Forest, North Carolina, is named because of his successful ministry as president of that institution. He has been the associate evangelist with Billy Graham in Europe, served on the faculty of the Billy Graham School of Evangelism, preached to the Southern Baptist Convention, 1992, and served as the president of the Louisville Baptist Pastors Conference.

Drummond received his B.A. degree from Samford University, 1950, B.D. and Th.M. degrees from Southwestern Baptist Theological Seminary, 1955, and Ph.D. in philosophy from King's College, University of London, 1963. He has done post-doctoral studies at Oxford University and Spurgeon's Theological College, both in England.

Drummond pastored churches in Columbiana, Alabama; Fort Worth, Texas; Granbury, Texas; Birmingham, Alabama; and Louisville, Kentucky (the largest and most significant church in Kentucky, having 3,500 members).

Perhaps Drummond's most significant educational post was as the Billy Graham Professor of Evangelism and Director of the Billy Graham Center, Southern Baptist Theological Seminary, Louisville, Kentucky, 1973-1988. After that, he was president of Southeastern Baptist Theological Seminary and then became the Billy Graham Professor of Evangelism and Church Growth at Beeson Divinity School where he is presently located. He also taught at Spurgeon's Theological College in London, England.

Drummond's first significant book was *Evangelism: The Counter-Revolution* (Marshall, Morgan and Scott Publishers, 1972), which was also translated into several languages. In 1976, *Christianity Today* said his book *What the Bible Says*, also published by Marshall, Morgan and Scott Publishers, was the best book on Systematic Theology that year. He has written three significant biographies: *Charles E. Finney, the Birth of Modern Evangelism* (Hodder and Stoughton Publishers, 1982); *The Prince of Preachers, the Life and Ministry of Charles E. Spurgeon* (Kregel Press, 1992); and *Bertha Smith: Woman of Revival* (Broadman & Holman Publishers, 1996). In addition, he has been published in the recognized reference journals such as the *Scottish Journal of Theology, The Baptist Theological Quarterly, Journal of the Victorian Institute, Baptist Historical Journal* and *Christian History.*

Because of Drummond's outstanding contribution to evangelism, he has been invited to address more than a dozen seminaries in the area of evangelism, as well as in more than a dozen colleges.

DUFF, ALEXANDER (1806–1878)

Presbyterian missionary to India.

Alexander Duff, the first missionary of the Presbyterian Church in Scotland, was primarily engaged in Christian education. He theorized that providing Indians with a thoroughly Christian education would undermine the grip Hinduism had on the people of India. He was instrumental in extending educational ministries beyond the elementary grades. Duff's greatest contribution to evangelism was in establishing a prototype for Presbyterian missionaries who followed him and in advocating the cause of missions among Presbyterians in his native Scotland.

Reference: William Paton, *Alexander Duff: Pioneer of Missionary Education* (New York: George H. Doran Co., 1953).

E

EARLE, ABSALOM BACKUS (1812–1895)

Born in Charlton, New York, Absalom Backus Earle was converted at age 16 and began preaching two years later. At age 21, he was ordained as a Baptist pastor in Amsterdam, New York. Five years later, he left the pastoral ministry to devote the next 58 years of his life to conducting evangelistic meetings across the United States and Canada. It is estimated that he conducted 39,330 services, traveled 370,000 miles, had 160,000 recorded decisions for Christ in his meetings, and influenced 400 men to enter the ministry.

Earle's ministry had a significant role in Atlantic Canada during the mid-nineteenth century "Layman's Prayer Revival." He often emphasized future punishment in his preaching, believing it to be most effective in drawing people to salvation. More than 20,000 of his converts came in response to a single sermon based on the unpardonable sin. Earl died at his home in Newton, Massachusetts, on March 30, 1895, at the age of 83.

References: Absalom Backus Earle, *Bringing in the Sheaves, Abiding Peace, Rest of Faith, The Human Will, The Work of an Evangelist, Evidences of Conversion, Winning Souls;* Elmer L. Towns, *The Christian Hall of Fame* (Grand Rapids: Baker Book House, 1975), pp. 110, 111.

EDWARDS, JONATHAN (1703–1758)

Born into the home of a minister in East Windsor, Connecticut, on October 5, 1703, Jonathan Edwards was the only son among 10 daughters. He entered Yale College in 1716 at age 13 and was converted to Christ shortly after graduating. He was ordained in February 1727 at Northampton while serving as an assistant to his grandfather, Solomon Stoddard. Upon Stoddard's death in 1729, Edwards became the sole pastor of one of the wealthiest and most influential churches in the colonies. Two years later, he published *God Glorified in the Word of Redemption by the Greatest of Man's Dependence Upon Him in the Whole of It.* It was the beginning of a lifelong battle against rationalism in New England theology.

Edwards is especially noted as a leader in the Great Awakening. His first revival began in 1734 at his Northampton church. He published an account of this revival in 1736, which was widely distributed throughout both England and the American colonies. In 1740, the colonies were engulfed in the Great Awakening revivalistic fervor of George Whitefield. However, not everyone was supportive of revival. Reactionary attitudes toward the revival and a conflict about his views of church membership resulted in Edwards being deposed by his Northampton church in 1750. That summer, he became a missionary to the remnants of the Mohican Indians living near Stockbridge, Massachusetts, while pastoring the village church. In 1758, he was invited to serve as president of the College of New Jersey (now Princeton University). Shortly after assuming the post, he died from complications associated with a smallpox vaccination.

References: Jonathan Edwards, *A Faithful Narrative of the Surprizing Work of God (1736)*; Elmer L. Towns, *The Christian Hall of Fame* (Grand Rapids: Baker Book House, 1975), pp. 70-73.

EGALITARIANISM

An approach to administration in missions that emphasizes equality in the distribution of resources. This approach tends to hinder church growth in responsive areas while ensuring support in nonresponsive areas.

Reference: See HARVEST PRINCIPLE.

EICOS PATTERN See OIKOS EVANGELISM

ELDER

(Lit. aged man). A technical term for a pastor of a local church—describing especially his qualification of maturity.

ELECTION

A doctrine emphasizing the sovereignty of God in

salvation, sometimes associated with Calvinism. From "before the foundation of the world" (1 Pet. 1:20), God had foreordained His plan to save people. Although His purpose was determined in eternity, His work is performed in time.

Evangelical Christians have a variety of perspectives on the doctrine of salvation. Some emphasize God working in salvation by choosing certain individuals and limiting the extent of Christ's atonement and the Holy Spirit's convicting ministry to this select group (2 Thess. 2:13,14). Others emphasize a broader offer of salvation to all people because Christ died for the sins of "the whole world" (1 John 2:2). A more biblical approach to the doctrine of salvation seeks to recognize both the sovereignty of God in providing salvation and the liberty of people to respond to God's gracious offer.

The doctrine of election is largely based on Paul's use of several terms describing God's sovereignty in salvation, including "predestinate," "foreknowledge," "chosen," "called," "the counsel of God," "God's will" and "God's good pleasure." These terms are used in Scripture in the context of God's programs, principles and plans that relate to salvation, sanctification and glorification. God has an elect and eternal plan of salvation for all who call upon him.

Reference: Elmer L. Towns, *What the Faith Is All About* (Wheaton, Ill.: Tyndale House Publishers, Inc., 1983), pp. 102-106.

ELECTRONIC CHURCH

A term used to describe evangelical television ministries, sometimes called "televangelism" or "pray TV."

Defenders of the electronic church argue it is only natural that an electronic age would produce an electronic church. Because Americans are conditioned to receive news, commentary, information and inspiration from electronic sources, churches should use the media to communicate to the masses. This enables leading evangelical spokespersons to communicate the gospel to large numbers quickly. Critics argue that the electronic church is unable to provide the body-life and accountability structure of a local community

of believers necessary for their maturity.

Both groups find biblical justification for their support or opposition to the electronic church. This apparent conflict is resolved only when it is agreed that the electronic church may have a significant role in quickly evangelizing large population centers, but is not intended to replace the ministry of local congregations. Many electronic churches have a policy of working together with local churches in discipling those converted through their radio and television outreach.

References: David Mainse with David Manuel, *100 Huntley Street* (Toronto, Canada: G. R. Welch Co., Ltd., 1979); Barry Siedell, *Gospel Radio* (Lincoln, Nebr.: Back to the Bible Broadcast, 1971).

ELLIOT, JIM (1927–1956)

Born into a Christian home in Portland, Oregon, Jim Elliot was himself converted at age six. Upon completing high school, Elliot enrolled at Wheaton College in 1945 with a goal of preparing for missionary service. Following a ministry trip to Mexico with a fellow student in the summer of 1947, he returned to college convinced God would have him serve as a missionary in Latin America.

During the 1948 Urbana Conference, Elliot became convinced his ministry would be among tribal people in South America. In 1952, he began his ministry in Ecuador. While there, he and four others formed a team to take the gospel to an unreached tribal group known as the Aucas. On Sunday, January 8, 1956, Elliot and his four fellow missionaries were killed by the tribe they were attempting to reach. News of their death is credited with motivating large numbers of North American college students to commit their lives to missionary work.

References: Elisabeth Elliot, *Through Gates of Splendor* (New York: HarperCollins, 1957); and *Shadow of the Almighty: The Life and Testament of Jim Elliot* (New York: HarperCollins, 1958).

ENCOURAGERS

A descriptive title given to those gifted in empathy

(Rom. 12:8) who use their gift in team evangelism to encourage absentees, the sick, shut-ins and those who have special needs. Their ministry of encouragement is patterned after that of Barnabas, who was effective in helping new converts mature and in edifying the Body. As part of the evangelism team, encouragers free up the time of evangelists, enabling them to reach others for Christ.

ENGEL SCALE

Evangelicals have recently begun speaking of conversion as an extended spiritual experience, in contrast with the historic evangelical view of conversion described by Moody and others as "sudden conversion." Previously, conversions were viewed as independent experiences in which a change took place in the life of a person independent of any process of change. For the past hundred years or so, evangelicals viewed conversion as a sudden change in the life of a sinner in which he or she repented of sin and placed saving faith in Christ for salvation.

The change in thinking from Moody's view of "sudden conversion" to the contemporary view of conversion as an extended spiritual experience is largely attributable to the development of the "Engel Scale" by Wheaton College Graduate School Professor of Communications Research, Dr. James F. Engel. C. Peter Wagner calls the Engel Scale "a remarkable instrument for helping to measure progress in the evangelistic process."[1]

The Engel Scale attempts to plot the progress of an individual in coming to Christ as Savior and beginning the Christian life. The scale assumes that the conversion experience is an extended

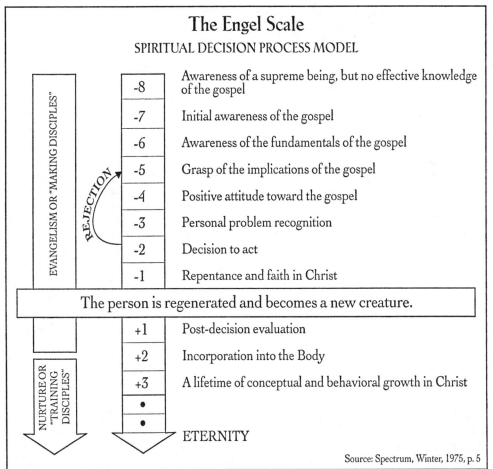

The Engel Scale — SPIRITUAL DECISION PROCESS MODEL

-8	Awareness of a supreme being, but no effective knowledge of the gospel
-7	Initial awareness of the gospel
-6	Awareness of the fundamentals of the gospel
-5	Grasp of the implications of the gospel
-4	Positive attitude toward the gospel
-3	Personal problem recognition
-2	Decision to act
-1	Repentance and faith in Christ

The person is regenerated and becomes a new creature.

+1	Post-decision evaluation
+2	Incorporation into the Body
+3	A lifetime of conceptual and behavioral growth in Christ
•	
•	ETERNITY

Source: Spectrum, Winter, 1975, p. 5

spiritual experience that includes an event similar to what Moody called "sudden conversion." Engel views the conversion experience as the next logical step in an experience in which the individual may have been involved for some time.

See The Engel Scale on the previous page.

Although Engel himself emphasizes the role of God in regenerating the individual, some modifications of the scale do not necessarily presuppose such an evangelical theology of regeneration. Without Engel's emphasis on the work of God in regeneration, the scale is little more than a practical expression of a view of conversion as a psychological experience.

There are differences between the Moody and Engel views of conversion, but those differences may not be as radical as they first appear. Moody anticipated and realized "sudden conversions" in his meetings, but the effect of evangelical revivals in the nineteenth century had apparently moved society as a whole to a -4 or -3 on the Engel Scale. Under the evangelistic preaching of Moody and others in that era, it was not unreasonable to expect members of the crowd to take the next step, moving to a -2. At that point, further steps to Christ along the Engel Scale would normally follow in rapid succession.

Reference: [1]C. Peter Wagner, *Strategies for Church Growth: Tools for Effective Mission and Evangelism* (Ventura, Calif.: Regal Books, 1987), p. 124.

ENROLLMENT, SUNDAY SCHOOL EVANGELISM BY

The contemporary Sunday School has lost a powerful means of growth. About 20 years ago, Sunday Schools stopped emphasizing enrollment and teachers stopped promoting the enrollment of new students for Bible study. If the Sunday Schools of the '90s would like to be strong and have a powerful outreach, they should return to an emphasis on enrollment as one powerful, yet forgotten, means to grow a Sunday School.

In the old days a teacher would say, "After you attend for three weeks, we will add your name to the roll." That was the teacher's way of challenging a student to be faithful so he or she would belong to the Sunday School class. Enrollment simply meant that a person was no longer a visitor, but a member of the "in group." The visitor now belonged to the other pupils and was one of the gang. Sunday School enrollment was considered less in privileges and requirements than church membership, but more than being just a visitor or stranger. Sunday School enrollment meant "submembership" to the local church.

Many times a businessman wanted to identify with a local church, but because of his lifestyle or dysfunctional belief, he would not be accepted into the membership of the church. So he would join the men's Bible class, which meant that his name was added to the roll. As a result, the man could make business contacts and move into the stability of the neighborhood. He had the privilege of church membership without meeting all the requirements. Although we do not condone all that this implies, we recognize the desire for people to associate with the positive benefits of the local church.

Sunday School enrollment is the "handshake" that welcomes the outsider into the fellowship of the class and makes that person an "insider." When people are enrolled in Sunday School, they no longer have a barrier to attending church services or to hearing the gospel. They network with other believers in a Bible study fellowship where they can learn from the Word of God.

Southern Baptists have long known the strength of enrolling people in Sunday School. Their formula indicates that 40 percent of Sunday School enrollment will be present in Sunday School attendance. As a result, they go out and ask people to enroll in the Sunday School. They ask, "May I enroll you in my Sunday School?"

Neil Jackson, a consultant with the Southern Baptist Sunday School Board, was eating in a Nashville restaurant. The waitress was obviously pregnant, almost nine months and ready to deliver. When the friendly waitress brought the food, Neil Jackson asked, "May I enroll your baby in Sunday School?"

"What do you mean?" she questioned.

Jackson replied, "The baby you are going to have ought to go to Sunday School where he can learn about God, learn to pray and get a purpose in life." Then he said to her, "God loves your baby."

When the waitress came back with the check she said, "Enroll my baby in your Sunday School. I am interested in anyone who is interested in my baby."

The waitress did not live near Three Rivers Baptist Church in Nashville where Neil attended. She lived on the other side of town. Jackson phoned a pastor friend who visited her that same afternoon and enrolled the baby, mother and father in Sunday School. When the baby was born, she was brought up in the house of God.

"Action Enrollment" is a relatively recent Southern Baptist program designed to provide growth in Sunday School attendance through increased Sunday School enrollment. Andy Anderson, while pastor of the Riverside Baptist Church of Fort Myers, Florida, came to realize that even given his best efforts or the efforts of others, his church would always average about 40 percent of its Sunday School enrollment. He devised a simple formula to depict the relationship between attendance and enrollment: $E = P + A$ (Enrollment = Present + Absent).

Briefly summarizing, the number of people present and the number absent will remain relatively constant in a ratio of 40 percent (attending) to 60 percent (absent). As enrollment rises, so does the number of those attending the class.

Southern Baptists are taking the positive approach and moving with renewed zeal toward building Sunday School through the "Action" method. This approach, interestingly, has demonstrated that of all persons enrolled by door-to-door canvasing, approximately 20 percent will never attend, 40 percent will come at least once but will not become active, while the remaining 40 percent will become active attenders.

How to Get New People to Enroll

The teacher must take the initiative to get new people to enroll in the Sunday School. However, this task can be delegated to an outreach class officer. The following are some ideas to get people to enroll in Bible study.

1. *Sponsor a "Join One Join All" campaign.* Initiate a campaign in your church so that when someone joins the church, that person also joins a Sunday School class. Assign someone in the class to enroll new members in the Sunday School class.

2. Contact those on the list who came to Vacation Bible School. They are excellent prospects to enroll in Sunday School.

3. Ask the youth to do a block survey in the neighborhood to determine those who are not church members or enrolled in Sunday School.

4. Request church members to identify neighbors who are unchurched.

5. Find unchurched parents who send their children to the church's day-care center.

6. Go through the visitor cards that have been turned in to the church in the last six months to identify those who can be enrolled.

7. Survey local newspapers for information on newlyweds.

8. Glean local newspapers for information on newborn babies.

9. Check the guest book in the church lobby to identify any visitors who have attended weddings, funerals and other meetings at the church.

10. Survey your church members to find the names of their friends who are prospects for Sunday School enrollment.

11. Subscribe to newcomer services for information on prospects such as hookups for gas, water and electricity.

12. Do a survey in the church foyer after a worship service. Ask each attendant to give you the names of those who would be good prospects for the Sunday School.

13. Ask the pastor to add the statement, Enroll Me, when making church announcements. The pastor can ask all those signing visitor cards on Sunday morning to add the phrase, Enroll Me, if they are interested in joining an adult Bible study. This small invitation seems trivial, yet prospects can be enrolled in Sunday School by showing an interest in them.

How to Get Enrollees to Attend Sunday School

Attach to each chair in the Sunday School room a card with the name of one person on your roll. Then, contact every class member and let them know his or her name will be attached to a chair for "Be There Sunday."

Another way to get enrollees is to write the names of all class members on a large card, large enough for everyone to read. Post the names on the wall and ask class members to call on anyone who is not attending regularly with the view of getting them in the Sunday School.

The Sunday School teacher can become the Saturday Night Caller. In less than an hour, a Sunday School teacher can phone everyone on his or her Sunday School roll, reminding them of Sunday School. The Saturday Night Caller can ask the class members, "I am trying to determine how many will be present Sunday. Will you be there?" If they are going out of town, do not put them on a guilt trip. Everyone needs time away for a vacation. Just say, "I'll see you in Sunday School when you get back." People want to know that you care about them, and your phone call tells them that. People do not care how much you know until they know how much you care.

Use "the big three" outreach tools: *phone, mail* and *visitation*. Go through the names of your Sunday School roll and contact every one of them three times.

Plan a double-your-enrollment-month. During a certain month, get everyone in your class to: (1) pray every day for every person on the roll; (2) take time out of class to write a postcard to five students, adding a personal note to nonattenders; (3) have everyone phone someone on the roll; and (4) have everyone visit someone on the roll. Although this is a gigantic task, it will pay gigantic results.

EQUIPPERS

Persons on the evangelism team who have the spiritual gift of teaching or shepherding. On visitation night, they are given names of those who have joined the church or have made a recent public profession of salvation. The equippers meet with a new convert to disciple that person in the faith. Equippers are not soul winners, though they may have some success in that area. They teach one-on-one, or two equippers meet with a couple. This discipling relationship exists for eight weeks, to make sure the new convert is grounded in the faith and "bonded" to the church. After an equipper has finished the eight-week lesson, he or she is given another new convert to teach.

ESSENTIAL ELEMENTS

A term used by the intelligence community when referring to the core of a given research assignment. For field workers, essential elements represent those informational gems that must be considered a success. —GOJR

ETERNALITY

The aspect of God's nature that means He is not limited by time (the sequence of events), has no beginning and will have no end (contrary to or other than "time").

ETHCLASS

A homogeneous unit of society determined by the dynamics of ethnicity on the one hand and social class on the other.

ETHICS OF CHURCH GROWTH

Like other movements before it, the Church Growth Movement has attracted both strong support and opposition within various quarters of the evangelical church. Many find significant value in this movement in its single-minded emphasis on mobilizing the whole church to reach the unreached peoples of the earth. Others challenge the validity of the movement. Most often, those who oppose the movement have difficulty with some of the ethical values apparently being promoted by church-growth leaders. In contrast, some church-growth pastors have questioned the ethics of those opposed to a church-growth emphasis.

The issue of ethics in the context of church growth is important because of the very nature of the Christian Church. The late Francis Schaeffer often described the Church as something of a counterculture intended to impact the culture as a whole. One of the unique features of the Christian counterculture historically has been its distinctive value system. If ethical values are important to the Christian Church, then questions about the ethics of certain segments of that Church need to be addressed.

The Ethical Foundation of the Church Growth Movement

Before looking at concerns that have been expressed about the direction of church growth, it should be noted that the movement itself views itself as ethical. Church-growth pastors would argue it is not ethical to fail to do all that can be done to reach people for whom Christ died. C. Peter Wagner argues that pragmatism is the foundational ethic of the movement. Commenting on McGavran's *The Bridges of God*, Wagner writes:

> The ethical issue is one of pragmatism. McGavran became alarmed when he saw all too many of God's resources—personnel and finances—being used without asking whether the kingdom of God was being advanced by the programs they were supporting. McGavran demanded more accountability in Christian stewardship. He wanted efforts evaluated by their results. His attitude reflects these words of Bishop Waskom Pickett, McGavran's mentor in the early years in India: "It is disturbing to read book after book about modern missions without finding so much as a hint about either what helped or what hindered church growth. In many books the author seems eager to prove that the missionaries have done everything according to God's leading and that if no church has come into being it means only that God's time for saving souls has not come: 'The disciples' duty is to sow the seed and leave it to God to produce.' How different this is from the command of Jesus, 'Make disciples of the nations!'"[1]

This pragmatic view is reflected in a different perspective toward evangelism and church growth from what was characteristic of the evangelical church in the middle of the twentieth century. This change is reflected in a change of nomenclature describing certain church-growth related activities. Perhaps the most startling example of this change is seen in the way church-growth pastors describe reaching lapsed members of other churches. Formerly, this practice was described by the somewhat pejorative term "sheep-stealing." Today, this practice is lauded as "finding lost sheep."

The example cited illustrates one of the points of tension between those inside and those outside of the Church Growth Movement. Often what is considered ethically right by church-growth pastors (i.e., "finding lost sheep") is perceived as unethical by those outside the movement (hence the term "sheep-stealing" remains in use). Still, even critics of the movement recognize this pragmatic approach to the Great Commission has brought value to the evangelical church. Os Guinness writes:

> Whatever criticisms of the movement need to be raised, the point is beyond dispute. The church-growth movement is extraordinarily influential and significant within American churches today. At its best, it needs to be applauded. But where it is not at its best, it requires criticism so that it might be. The church of Christ concerned for the glory of Christ needs more—not less—of the best of true church growth.[2]

Unfortunately, the strength of the Church Growth Movement—its pragmatic outlook—may also be the weakness that threatens to hinder its maturing. Too often, church growth has been viewed as the standard by which ethical decisions are made about new ideas and old values. The attitude has been, "If it works, it must be right." Thus, a pastor of a large church simply ignores the valid criticism made by the pastor of a smaller church. It is simply assumed that the pastor of the smaller church would be pastoring a larger church if his opinions were right. In extreme situations, this "logic" has been used to discern the validity of one's theological belief system.

The Church Growth Movement has to this point been concerned about church growth as a social science. The focus of the movement has been to discern factors that enhance growth as reflected in increased numbers of people coming to Christ for salvation and being assimilated into the church. Although it has not completely ignored theological and spiritual factors of growth, it would be fair to conclude that these have been apparently minimized (perhaps unintentionally) in the writings coming out of the movement. Most church-growth principles could be applied to a specific church and produce growth regardless of the theological and/or spiritual commitment of the church. Perhaps Guinness is not being too critical when he warns:

> The church-growth movement carries two potential dangers. They can be summed up simply in the words "no God" and "no grandchildren." ...In short, through its uncritical use of modernity, the church-growth movement is unleashing a deadly form of "practical atheism" in the churches. The result is a contemporary testament to the extraordinary power of religion that has no need for God.[3]

Ethical Concerns About the Direction of the Movement

Evaluations of the criticisms leveled at the Church Growth Movement tend to fall into three groups. First, valid and invalid criticisms are leveled against specific pastors or churches. These criticisms relate to broader issues that have no direct bearing on the movement itself. This would include views concerning such controversial issues as the ordination of women or divorced persons. There is no consensus on this and other issues facing the evangelical church either within or outside of the Church Growth Movement.

A second group of criticisms could be described as unfair. These are criticisms based on some leaders' extreme statements that do not accurately reflect the real values of the movement. Thus, in a particular seminar or in a book addressing an aspect of church growth, a statement might begin, "The single most important thing in your church is..." Depending on the topic of the book or seminar, that "single most important thing" may be the worship of God, a well-organized enrollment campaign, assimilat-

ing people into the church, keeping the services seeker-sensitive, having a large parking lot, having a well-staffed nursery, choices in adult Bible study groups or even the choice of colors in decorating the building. To criticize the movement on the basis of such statements is unfair. This kind of criticism simply reminds those who count themselves a part of the Church Growth Movement that they should be more careful in the words they use to express themselves.

A third group of criticisms leveled against the Church Growth Movement tends to demonstrate keen insights into the very nature of the movement by those who remain outside. Perhaps the distance from which these critics evaluate the movement enables them to see things missed by others more closely involved. Specifically, there are valid criticisms concerning the theology of church growth, the application of the principle of contextualization, the basic character of the Church, and the commitment of the movement to biblical authority.

Is there movement toward a theology? The Church Growth Movement is relatively young. It is not surprising, therefore, that a church-growth theology has not yet been written. Attempts have been made to write a theological basis for Church Growth itself, but to date the theological principles of Church Growth have not yet been assimilated into the broader field of systematic theology.

What one believes about Church Growth must be consistent with what one believes about God, the atonement, the work of the Holy Spirit, the nature of the Church, other spiritual beings, people, sin and eschatological expectations. When critics note this vacancy in the movement, they are right. But in fairness to the movement, it takes time for new ideas to be incorporated into theological systems.

But what may be viewed as a legitimate criticism of the movement in this area is the lack of movement toward developing a theology of Church Growth. Apart from a few isolated works, there does not appear to be a broadly based attempt to assimilate one's theological presuppositions and one's strategic ministry plans. Surely this is a point at which one's theology and church-growth principles should be tested and modified accordingly, yet there is little evidence of this taking place within the Church Growth Movement. Guinness accurately notes the extent to which this is being neglected in the following example.

Take the example of a well-known Christian magazine that is designed for pastors and deals with the problems of leadership in the church. A survey of the magazine showed that over the course of time, the magazine had examined almost every conceivable church problem in its pages. Yet, believe it or not, less than one percent of the articles had any reference to Scripture at all, or any serious theological component. In the form of the imperialistic genius of managerial and therapeutic insights, galloping secularization left theology in the dust.[4]

What about contextualization? A second area of valid criticism deals with applying the principle of contextualization. This principle is illustrated in Paul's desire to be all things to others, to more effectively reach them with the gospel (1 Cor. 9:19-22). Historically, the church has been adaptable to its culture to some measure, reaching people where they are and bringing them to faith in Christ. But being relevant to the world around you without a certain theological foundation tends to turn commonsense communication into compromise. According to Guinness:

The record of Scripture and Christian history is equally clear: identification is basic to communication. But without critical tension it is a recipe for compromise and capitulation. It is no accident that the charge of being "all things to all people" has become a popular synonym for compromise. Joining people where they are is only the first step in the process; clear persuasion and genuine conversion is the last step.[5]

The nature of the Church. The absence of theology coupled with an unbalanced emphasis on contextualization leads to a third problem in the movement: indecision about the essential nature and character of the Church. This is a particular-

ly stinging criticism. One would assume the Church Growth Movement would agree about the essential nature of the Church, yet, different church-growth strategies tend to emphasize different views. Jack Hayford's view of the Church as a worshiping body is radically different from Bill Hybels's seeker-service approach to ministry. These differences are more than different strategies. They involve radically different views of the Church itself and its purpose.

Without being firmly grounded in theology, where does the Church Growth Movement go to decide about the nature of the Church? Certainly, if Jesus is indeed the builder of the Church, His ideas concerning its nature and purpose should be considered as authoritative. But too often the emphasis on contextualization means the Church is defined more by the community in which it exists than by theological considerations. Indeed, the various attempts by church growth leaders to evaluate church types have been based almost exclusively on sociological rather than on theological typologies. Guinness writes:

When all is said and done, the church-growth movement will stand or fall by one question: In implementing its vision of church growth, is the church of Christ primarily guided and shaped by its own character and calling—or by considerations and circumstances alien to itself? Or, to put the question differently, is the church of Christ a social reality truly shaped by a theological cause, namely the Word and Spirit of God?[6]

What has just been stated concerning the nature of the Church also has a broader application in the area of the Church's commitment to biblical authority relating to other areas of concern. The same factors that influence how one defines the Church eventually define the message of that Church. Guinness is not too far off when he compares church growth to the World Council of Churches in this area.

Perhaps the most blatant example of this perverse bias toward compromise was the World Council of Churches' dictum in 1966: "The world must set the agenda for the church." Three decades later, it is hard to believe that such an advance warning of preemptive capitulation could have been trumpeted as a lofty and self-evident principle. But it is also worth checking to see whether similar inanities exist in the Church Growth Movement today. Take, for example, the current church growth infatuation with "marketing the church." Guinness also writes: "It is also critical that we keep in mind a fundamental principle of Christian communication: the audience, not the message, is sovereign."[7]

How important are these ethical concerns? The author knows many church growth pastors, writers and spokespersons personally and remains convinced they have a strong personal commitment to what might be described broadly as an evangelical theology. But the Church Growth Movement as a whole tends to neglect communicating that anchor to their disciples. It may be unfair to compare these evangelical pastors with the liberal theologians who lead organizations such as the World Council of Churches, but if this neglect of theology continues, the next generation of evangelical churches may have more in common with the liberal mainstream than we care to admit.

References: [1]C. Peter Wagner, *Church Growth: State of the Art* (Wheaton, Ill.: Tyndale House Publishers, Inc., 1989), p. 17. [2]Os Guinness, *Dining with the Devil: The Megachurch Movement Flirts with Modernity* (Grand Rapids: Baker Book House, 1993), p. 53. [3]Ibid. [4]Ibid., pp. 50, 51. [5]Ibid., p. 52. [6]Ibid. [7]Ibid., p. 62

ETHNE

The Greek word for "peoples" (also translated nations, tribes, people groups) used in the Great Commission, "Go therefore and make disciples of all the nations *[panta ta ethne]*" (Matt. 28:19).

ETHNIKITIS

Ethnikitis is one of the pathologies of church growth, representing an inbred allegiance to one ethnic group and a lack of adaptation or openness to other groups. This disease occurs when communities change their ethnic characters and churches fail to adapt to those changes.

Sometimes a symptom of ethnikitis is what has been called "white flight," where the traditional White Anglo-Saxon Protestant (WASP) churches move out of their communities as the ethnic character of the area changes.

In our growing nation, our churches must be multiethnic, reaching out to every new family or group of people moving into our neighborhoods. In one sense, the small neighborhood church is a homogeneous unit. But the growing church must have heterogeneous evangelistic strategies (having an open door to all people), yet made up of homogeneous cells (classes and cells that will attract and minister to each group within its neighborhood). Also, a church could plant a new church that is people-group sensitive to the gospel.

The church that suffers ethnikitis is, first, sinning against God; second, disobeying the Great Commission; and third, allowing a cancer to fester within its body.

How to Overcome *Ethnikitis*

1. Begin Bible classes or cells for new groups.
2. Hire staff members who represent the new groups moving into the neighborhood.
3. Begin a second-language preaching service.
4. If the church moves to another neighborhood, dedicate the present building that remains behind to spawn a continuing church.
5. New people from other ethnic groups do not automatically visit existing churches; they must be aggressively sought and brought into the church fellowship.

ETHNOCENTRICITY

The tendency to see everything in one's own cultural frame of reference, which has the overtone that other cultures are inferior.

EURICA

A term describing both Europe and America; the Western world.

Reference: See LATFRICASIA.

EVANGELICAL REVIVAL See GREAT AWAKENING, REVIVAL

EVANGELISM

Communicating the gospel in the power of the Holy Spirit to unconverted persons at their point of need with the intent of effecting conversions to bring them to repent of their sin and put their trust in God through Jesus Christ, accept Him as their Savior and serve Him as their Lord in the fellowship of His Church.

Evangelism is only effective when individuals are converted. Normally, those who are converted will identify not only with Christ, but with His Body—the Church—and will become active participants in the life of a local congregation of believers.

This view of evangelism identifies several essential elements. First, evangelism is a process of communication and is therefore not accomplished until the prospective convert has heard and understood the message of the gospel. Even when the message is rejected, it must first be heard and understood by the one choosing to reject it.

Second, evangelism may be described as vital in that its message produces spiritual life. It presupposes the work of the life-giving Spirit of God in regenerating the unregenerate.

Third, the target of all evangelistic activities is unconverted persons.

Fourth, evangelism is need-oriented in that it speaks to humanity's ultimate need—that of salvation from the consequences of sin.

Fifth, the intent of the evangelistic process is to effect conversions. Indeed, evangelism is only effective as persons are converted to Christ and His Church.

The Nature of Evangelism

Foundational to an evangelical understanding of evangelism and church growth is a correct understanding of the essential nature of evangelism. How people answer the question: What is evangelism? to a large extent determines how they approach the entire study of evangelism and church growth. A survey of the literature written in this field during the past two decades suggests

a significant difference of opinion about the nature of evangelism.

Admittedly, some of these differences find their roots in radical theological disagreements about the very nature of the Christian message. But the ongoing conflict between theological liberalism and a more conservative evangelical theology does not count for every distinction in the use of the term "evangelism." Evangelical church leaders themselves are divided in their understanding of the nature of evangelism. In an address to itinerant evangelists meeting in Amsterdam, The Netherlands, Billy Graham observed:

Today, the world church is not sure what evangelism is, and often the gift of the evangelist is neglected—evangelism is not taught in many of our Bible schools and seminaries. Today we have scores of definitions of what evangelism is, and what the evangelist is. Some think of evangelism simply in terms of getting more people to join the church. Others define evangelism as attempting to change the structures of society.[1]

Evangelism can be understood in at least six ways. These may be defined as (1) the theological approach, (2) the biblical approach, (3) the historical approach, (4) the homiletical approach, (5) the practical approach and (6) the sociological approach.

The theological approach to defining evangelism involves the methodology of systematic theology. Lewis Sperry Chafer defined this methodology as "the gathering, analyzing, arranging, displaying and defending of any and all facts, about God and His world."[2]

The biblical approach to defining evangelism is based on an exegetical study of the Great Commission. This Commission is repeated five times in the New Testament (Matt. 28:18-20; Mark 16:15; Luke 24:46-48; John 20:21; Acts 1:8).[3] Through a comparative analysis of these passages, an attempt is made to define evangelism as that which was intended in the Commission.

The historical approach to defining evangelism

looks to church history as its primary data source. This approach attempts to determine the nature of evangelism as practiced throughout church history.

The homiletical approach to defining evangelism represents an attempt to define evangelism in terms of preaching or proclamation. This approach distinguishes between three primary distinctions in the nature of evangelism as represented by C. Peter Wagner's P-1, P-2 and P-3 evangelism paradigms.[4]

The practical approach to defining evangelism represents an attempt to define evangelism in terms of eternal principles and contemporary methods that are effective in reaching people for Christ and incorporating them into the Church. This approach is to some extent representative of the Church Growth Movement as reflected in the writings of its modern father, Donald A. McGavran, and those influenced by him.[5]

The sociological approach to defining evangelism represents an attempt to describe it in its various manifestations. This is by far the most common way evangelism is described in popular evangelical literature on this subject. Hence, much that is written on evangelism tends to address a fairly restricted expression of evangelism such as soul winning[6] or bus evangelism.[7]

In addition to describing evangelism from these six perspectives, the term is also used with specific applications. First, evangelism involves presenting the gospel in an orderly way to others. Second, effective evangelism communicates the gospel across cultural barriers. Third, in that the Great Commission was given to the Church, churches ought to develop a local outreach strategy to accomplish this goal. Fourth, in that the Great Commission calls for discipling "all the nations" (*pante ta ethne*), evangelism also involves developing a regional outreach strategy.

References: [1]Billy Graham, "The Gift and Calling of an Evangelist" in *The Calling of an Evangelist: The Second International Congress for Itinerant Evangelists*, Amsterdam, The Netherlands, ed. J. D. Douglas (Minneapolis: World Wide Publications, 1987), pp. 15, 16. [2]Lewis Sperry Chafer, *Systematic Theology*, Vol. I (Dallas: Dallas Seminary Press, 1947), p. 4. [3]A few evangelical writers such as George W. Peters, *A Biblical Theology of Missions* (Chicago: Moody Press, 1972), p. 178, also include Acts 26:13-18 as a sixth biblical account of the Great Commission. The author is unconvinced that Paul's personal commission to ministry was a repetition of the Great Commission. There is widespread agreement among evangelicals that the five passages cited in the text are accounts of the Great Commission. [4]C. Peter Wagner, *Church Growth and the Whole Gospel: A Biblical Mandate* (New York: HarperCollins, 1981), pp. 55-57, and *Strategies for Church Growth: Tools for Effective Mission and Evangelism* (Ventura, Calif.: Regal Books, 1987), pp. 117-130. [5]Donald A. McGavran, *The Bridges of God* (New York: Friendship Press, 1955). [6]Jack Hyles, *Let's Go Soul Winning* (Murfreesboro, Tenn.: Sword of the Lord, 1962). [7]Gardiner Gentry, *Bus Them In* (Nashville: Church Growth Publications, 1973).

E-O EVANGELISM

The evangelism of unsaved members within the church congregation.

E-1 EVANGELISM

Evangelism that crosses barriers related to the church building or the perception of the Church in the minds of the unsaved. Evangelism at this level overcomes "the stained-glass barrier," which refers to popular perceptions of the Church that hinder the unsaved from becoming personally involved.

Reference: See STAINED GLASS BARRIER.

E-2 EVANGELISM

Evangelism that crosses ethnic, cultural and class barriers.

E-3 EVANGELISM

Evangelism that crosses linguistic barriers.

EVANGELISM: BIBLICAL DESCRIPTION

Although evangelical writers have used the term evangelism only during the past 150 years, the practice of evangelism may be traced to the Early

Church itself. The first generation of Christians quickly saturated the city of Jerusalem with their doctrine (Acts 5:28) and were accused of having turned their world upside down (17:6). Just how effective was the Early Church in evangelizing their world? Only 31 years after Jesus gave His disciples the Great Commission, Paul wrote to the Colossians of "the truth of the gospel, which has come to you, as it has also in all the world, and is bringing forth fruit, as it is also among you since the day you heard and knew the grace of God in truth" (Col. 1:5,6).

There is no biblical account of the Early Church's meeting to define the nature of that process we call "evangelism." Yet both the consistent involvement of the whole Church in the process and the significant results achieved within that first generation suggest the task before them was widely understood. They did not produce a definitive statement on the nature of evangelism, but they did use some 16 different Greek verbs to describe various aspects of evangelism.

New Testament Words Describing Evangelism		
English	Greek	Reference
Witnessing	martureo	Acts 1:8
Talking	laleo	Acts 4:1
Evangelizing	euangelizo	Acts 8:4
Confusing	suncheo	Acts 9:22
Explaining	dianoigo	Acts 17:3
Demonstrating	paratithemai	Acts 17:3
Teaching	didasko	Matt. 28:20
Reasoning	dialegomai	Acts 18:4
Discussing	suzeteo	Acts 6:9
Preaching	katangello	Acts 17:3
Announcing	kerusso	Acts 8:5
Declaring	gnorizo	1 Cor. 15:1
Winning	kerdaino	1 Pet. 3:1
Proving	sumbibazo	Acts 9:22
Discipling	matheteuo	Matt. 28:19
Persuading	peitho	2 Cor. 5:11

Taken together, these verbs produce a mosaic portrait of the ministry of evangelism. Just as no single tile in a mosaic contains the whole picture, so none of these terms contains a complete

description of evangelism. The true image is rather a composite of all its parts. In this section, we will examine the 16 parts that together are evangelism.

Martureo: Witnessing

The first verb describing the evangelistic process is "witnessing" (martureo). Jesus said, "You shall be witnesses to Me" (Acts 1:8). A witness shares what has been seen and heard. It is perhaps best understood in the legal context. As Michael Green explains:

It is primarily a legal term and was frequently used in Greek to denote a witness to facts and events on the one hand, and to truths vouched for on the other. In both cases, the personal involvement and assurance of the man making the witness was an important element.[1]

This Greek verb, which is related to the English word "martyr," implies both *being* a witness and *bearing* a witness. Christians are to witness, (1) what they have seen of Jesus Christ, (2) what they have heard concerning Jesus Christ and (3) what they have experienced. They are to tell how their lives were changed.

It was not uncommon for a defense of the faith to be included in one's witness. According to Gene Getz:

As you trace this word through the book of Acts it is obvious that in context it takes on a strong "apologetic" syndrome. Both Peter and Paul, the two apostles whose communication is described by this work, were attempting to convince their hearers that Jesus Christ was truly the Messiah promised in the Old Testament. They were not simply presenting the gospel, but were attesting and giving evidence from the Old Testament as well as from their personal experience that Jesus was the Christ.[2]

Laleo: Talking

The second verb describing the evangelistic process is "talking" (laleo). In Acts 4:1, the apostles "spoke to the people." Apostolic evangelism involved the transmission of words between the evangelist and the prospective convert. The verb *laleo* is used in the New Testament to describe this speaking or talking. This verb tends to emphasize "the words conveying the utterance," and is sometimes used to distinguish "the utterance, as opposed to silence."[3]

Euangelizo: Evangelizing

This process of evangelism is commonly described as "evangelizing" (*euangelizo*), or "preaching the word" (8:4). This verb emphasizes the idea of proclaiming the gospel. Concerning the use of this verb in Scripture, David Watson writes:

> The verb (*euangelizesthai*) is used fifty-two times in the New Testament, including twenty-five by Luke and twenty-one by Paul. Quite simply, "to evangelise" means to announce or proclaim or bring good news. In the Septuagint of the Old Testament it is used sometimes of a runner coming with the news of victory; in the Psalms it occurs twice in the sense of proclaiming God's faithfulness and salvation.[4]

Suncheo: Confusing

Some New Testament evangelism included "confounding" those who opposed the gospel as a pre-evangelism strategy (9:22). Luke used forms of the verb *suncheo* to describe this process. This verb literally means "to pour together" in the sense of mixing. It came to connote the idea of "confusing," in much the same way as the English idiom "mixed up." Of course, the early evangelists were not simply interested in "mixing people up," but in causing them to question and challenge their own preconceived notions of the Messiah. Concerning this verb, A. T. Robertson wrote:

> Confounded (*sunechunnen*). Imperfect active indicative of *sunchunno* (late form) of *suncheo*, to pour together, co-mingle, make confusion. The more Saul preached, the more the Jews were confused.[5]

This aspect of the evangelistic process finds its roots in the Jewish apologetic style of teaching.

The apostles apparently adopted this approach as part of their outreach to the Jews. They used it to confuse unconverted Jews about their preconceived wrong ideas about the Messiah as a preliminary step in presenting the Christian teaching on the subject.

Dianoigo: Explaining

The apostolic process of evangelism also involved explaining the gospel in a rational and systematic way. Luke used the verb "explaining" (*dianoigo*), to describe an aspect of Paul's usual evangelistic strategy (17:3). This word is also used by Luke to describe Jesus explaining the Scriptures to two disciples on the road to Emmaus (Luke 24:32).

But Luke's usage of this term implies more than just a rational explanation of the gospel. It is also used to describe the disciples' understanding being opened (v. 45) and the opening of Lydia's heart to the gospel (Acts 16:14). In both cases, this "opening" is attributed to the Lord. This term emphasizes both the divine and human aspects of the evangelistic process. In his study of this word, A. T. Robertson notes:

> Opening the Scriptures, Luke means, as made plain by the mission and message of Jesus, the same word (*dianoigo*) used by him of the interpretation of the Scriptures by Jesus (Luke 24:32) and of the opening of the mind of the disciples also by Jesus (Luke 24:45) and of the opening of Lydia's heart by the Lord (Acts 16:14). One cannot refrain from saying that such exposition of the Scriptures as Jesus and Paul gave would lead to more opening of mind and heart.[6]

When the gospel is explained, the speaker has communicated the message and the hearer understands the content of the gospel.

Paratithemai: Demonstrating

In describing the ministry of Paul in Thessalonica, Luke uses the expression "explaining and demonstrating" (*paratithemai*) in Acts 17:3. This suggests that Paul's exposition of the gospel was accompanied by the use of Scripture to demonstrate the accuracy and authority of his message. Although the apostle maintained that his gospel was given to him by revelation (Gal. 1:12), he also believed it was consistent with the rest of God's self-revelation in the Scriptures. The Greek verb *paratithemai* suggests that Paul lined up his message alongside of (*para*) the Scriptures to demonstrate that his message was compatible with the inspired writings. According to Robertson::

> Paul was not only "expounding" the Scriptures, he was also "propounding" (the old meaning of "allege") his doctrine or setting forth alongside the Scriptures (*paratithemenos*), quoting the Scripture to prove his contention which was made in much conflict (1 Thess. 2:2), probably in the midst of heated discussion by the opposing rabbis who were anything but convinced by Paul's powerful arguments, for the Cross was a stumbling-block to the Jews (1 Cor. 1:23).[7]

A further insight into the nature of evangelism may be gained by noting the context of this "demonstrating." It was done not in the relative calm of a theological seminary, but in a heated debate in a synagogue in which a significant number of individuals chose to be aggressively hostile to the gospel (Acts 17:13; 1 Thess. 2:2). The use of this term in the Thessalonian context suggests that Paul's explanation of the gospel was heavily integrated with Scripture.

Didasko: Teaching

Teaching was another part of the evangelistic process (Matt. 28:20). The verb *didasko* means "to give instruction" and tends to be used by Matthew as something distinct from preaching, another form of verbal communication (Matt. 4:23; 9:35). It describes a systematic explanation of the gospel intended to enable people to understand it better as a step toward believing it. The use of this verb to describe the evangelistic process suggests an emphasis on the content of the gospel communicated in evangelism.

Dialegomai: Reasoning

To use the word "reasoning" (*dialegomai*) to describe New Testament evangelism suggests the idea of coming together to discuss the gospel, and implies answering objections to it. Thus, Paul "reasoned in the synagogue" (Acts 18:4). The original word is composed of two Greek words, *lego*, meaning "to say" and *dia*, meaning "through." Although it was originally used to describe one "talking through" a matter within himself (i.e., pondering), it came to be commonly used to describe the act of one "getting through" to another (i.e., discussing, reasoning, etc). The use of this verb to describe the evangelism process implies that both the message of the gospel and the act of conversion are reasonable. According to Vine, the word "primarily denotes to ponder, resolve in one's mind (*dia*, through, *lego*, to say); then, to converse, dispute, discuss, discourse with; most frequently, to reason or dispute with."[8]

Suzeteo: Discussing

Luke uses the verb *suzeteo*—discuss—to describe the evangelistic ministry of both Stephen and Paul in hostile synagogues (Acts 6:9; 9:29). New Testament evangelism apparently included both formal and informal discussions, debates and disputes concerning the gospel. The Jewish synagogue lent itself to open debate and discussion of a wide variety of subjects. The early Christians apparently took advantage of this opportunity and often introduced their beliefs in Jesus as Messiah into the discussion.

Although Luke uses this same verb to describe the two disciples on the Emmaus road discussing the events of that Easter weekend together (Luke 24:15), the discussions of the gospel in the Acts engaged those who were angry enough to want to kill the messengers (Acts 7:59; 9:29). Commenting on the use of this verb in describing Stephen's ministry in the synagogue, A. T. Robertson writes:

> Present active participle of *suzeteo*, to question together as the two on the way to Emmaus did (Luke 24:15). Such interruptions were common with Jews. They give a skilled speaker great opportunity for reply if he is quick in repartee. Evidently Stephen was fully equipped for the emergency.[9]

Katangello: Preaching

The verb *katangello*—preaching—is another word used to describe New Testament evangelism (Acts 17:3). Implied in this verb is the idea of driving home or bringing forward an idea. It is most often used to describe the verbal proclamation of the gospel. The one notable exception is found in 1 Corinthians 11:26 where, according to Vine, "The verb makes clear that the partaking of the elements at the Lord's Supper is a proclamation (an evangel) of the Lord's death."[10] The description of this ordinance as an evangelistic activity suggests something of the primacy of preaching the gospel and the Lord's Supper as an act in the Early Church.

Kerusso: Announcing

The verb *kerusso*—announce—also emphasizes this proclamation aspect of the gospel; Philip the evangelist "preached Christ to them" (Acts 8:5). This verb suggests the idea of publicly announcing the gospel so that people can respond to it. The Greek verb is sometimes translated "heralding." It was used to describe the "heralding" of a message from a higher authority such as the king. Summarizing the usage of this word in its various related forms, Watson writes:

> "To proclaim" (*kerussein*), "proclamation" (*kerygma*), and "herald" (*kerux*). The verb, meaning "to preach" or "to proclaim," is used commonly as the verb "to evangelise," coming sixty-one times in the New Testament. The proclamation (*kerygma*) comes eight times, and the preacher (*keryx*) only three. The basic idea behind these words is that of a herald who delivers a message that has been given to him by the king.[11]

Gnorizo: Declaring

Paul said, "I declare [*gnorizo*] to you the gospel" (1 Cor. 15:1). Like several other proclamation verbs, this word also emphasizes the verbal communication of the gospel to others. But this verb differs from others in that it emphasizes the zeal with which the declaration was made. In writing both the Corinthians (1 Cor. 15:1) and the Galatians (Gal. 1:11), Paul expressed his zeal to emphatically make known the gospel. According to Harold J. Ockenga, "The word 'declare,' *gnorizo*, is used by St. Paul not only in 1 Corinthians 15:1, but also in Galatians 1:11 with the sense of certifying and means 'I make known emphatically.'"[12]

Kerdaino: Winning

The last four verbs in this list of terms used to describe New Testament evangelism differ from the others in that they directly imply success in securing conversions through evangelistic efforts. These verbs tend to be emphasized by those who adopt a P-3 Persuasion Evangelism view of evangelism.

The verb *kerdaino* is used by both Peter (1 Pet. 3:1) and Paul (1 Cor. 9:19,20 [twice], 21,22) in the sense of winning converts to the Christian faith. Both apostles use this term in a context that discusses a strategy by which others can be effectively evangelized. The use of this word by these two apostles suggests that those engaged in New Testament evangelism anticipated it would be effective in achieving its desired end.

Sumbibazo: Convincing

Part of winning converts involves convincing prospects of the truth of the gospel. The verb *sumbibazo* is used in the New Testament to describe this aspect of evangelism. Paul began his evangelistic ministry "proving that this Jesus is the Christ" (Acts 9:22). The verb *sumbibazo* literally means to coalesce or knit together. When used to describe evangelism, it pictures the apostle "knitting together" various aspects of the life of Jesus of Nazareth to convince others He was the anticipated Messiah. Commenting on this term, A. T. Robertson writes:

> Proving (*sumbibazon*). Present active participle of *sumbibazo*, old verb to make go together, to coalesce, to knit together. It is the very word that Luke used in [Acts] 16:10 of the conclusion reached at Troas concerning the vision of Paul. Here Paul took the various items in the life of Jesus of Nazareth and found in them the proof that he was in reality "the Messiah" (ho Christos). This method of argument Paul

continued to use with the Jews (Acts 17:13). It was an irresistible argument and spread consternation among the Jews. It was the most powerful piece of artillery in the Jewish camp that was suddenly turned round upon them.[13]

Matheteuo: Discipling

Jesus commanded His disciples, "Go therefore and make disciples" (*matheteuo*, Matt. 28:19). Making disciples involves bringing people to a conversion experience and enlisting them to follow Christ in the fellowship of His Church. A. T. Robertson explains that this "includes making disciples or learners (*matheteusate*) such as they were themselves...evangelism in the fullest sense and not merely revival meetings."[14] Jesus' use of this term may be the only use of the verb in the New Testament.

Peitho: Persuading

Paul "persuaded" (*peitho*) Jews and Greeks about Christ (Acts 18:4; 2 Cor. 5:11). According to Vine, this verb "signifies to apply persuasion, to prevail upon or win over, to persuade, bringing about a change of mind by the influence of reason or moral considerations."[15]

This verb suggests the apostles applied persuasion to convince people to change (i.e., convert). The nature of this persuasion appears to be on the basis of reasoning intellectually rather than the more negative connotations sometimes associated with the word "persuade." Although the apostles recognized each individual as a free moral agent, they did what they could to influence others to convert. As conversion is a voluntary act, coercion would not be an element in apostolic persuasion.

The use of these 16 Greek verbs to describe the evangelistic process reveals something of the plurality or mosaic of New Testament evangelism. Although it included both a genuine Christian presence and a clear proclamation of the gospel, it is evident it also assumed positive results would follow evangelistic efforts, including the conversion of some individuals.

These words show that evangelism starts with P-1 Presence Evangelism, but does not stop there. The evangelist must proclaim (P-2), but

his obligation is not finished until he persuades people to respond (P-3).[16] Preaching is different because the audience is different and the content is different.

References: [1]Michael Green, *Evangelism in the Early Church* (Grand Rapids: William B. Eerdmans, 1970, p. 70. [2]Gene A. Getz, *Sharpening the Focus of the Church* (Chicago: Moody Press, 1974), pp. 34, 35. [3]W. E. Vine, *An Expository Dictionary of New Testament Words*, Vol. 3 (Grand Rapids: Fleming H. Revell Company, 1981), p. 323. [4]David Watson, *I Believe in Evangelism* (London: Hodder and Stoughton, 1976), p. 26. [5]A. T. Robertson, *Word Pictures in the New Testament*, Vol. 3 (New York: HarperCollins, 1930), p. 123. [6]Ibid., pp. 267, 268. [7]Ibid., p. 268. [8]Vine, *An Expository Dictionary of New Testament Words*, Vol. 1, pp. 316, 317. [9]Robertson, *Word Pictures in the New Testament*, p. 76. [10]Vine, *An Expository Dictionary of New Testament Words*, Vol. 3, p. 216. [11]Watson, *I Believe in Evangelism*, p. 35, [12]Ralph G. Turnbull, ed., *Baker's Dictionary of Practical Theology* (Grand Rapids, Mich.: Baker Book House, 1967), in "The Pastor an Evangelist," by Harold J. Ockenga. [13]Robertson, *Word Pictures in the New Testament*, Vol. 3, p. 123. [14]Ibid., Vol. 1, p. 245. [15]Vine, *An Expository Dictionary of New Testament Words*, Vol. 4, p. 179. [16]This approach to defining the nature of evangelism is discussed more fully in the article EVANGELISM: P-1, P-2, P-3.

EVANGELISM EXPLOSION

The Evangelism Explosion plan suggests an introduction to lead people to Christ. Rather than beginning with accusing the person of being a sinner, it presents the results of sin. This presentation of the gospel begins with two questions: (1) Have you come to the place in your spiritual life where you know for certain that if you were to die tonight you would go to heaven? (2) Suppose you were to die tonight and stand before God and He were to say to you, "Why should I let you into My heaven?" What would you say?[1] The Evangelism Explosion puts the responsibility on the person to see that he or she does not deserve heaven and to be motivated to seek it. This then becomes the basis upon which the gospel is presented.

The Evangelism Explosion program was started by D. James Kennedy, pastor of Coral Ridge Presbyterian Church, Coral Ridge, Florida.

Reference: [1]D. James Kennedy, *Evangelism Explosion* (Wheaton, Ill.: Tyndale House Publishers, 1977), p. 51.

EVANGELISM, GIFT OF

The person who has the gift of evangelism (some call it the gift of evangelist) has the ability to lead people beyond their own natural sphere of influence to a saving knowledge of Jesus Christ. The person who has the gift of evangelism, or evangelist, is like a spiritual pediatrician who has discernment to know when the time is right, when the Holy Spirit is moving a person toward the new birth, and conversely, knows when to wait. In the exercise of this gift, the evangelist is the aggressive soul winner who seeks the lost. The strengths of this gift include (1) a consuming passion for lost souls, (2) a clear understanding of the gospel and what it can do in one's life, and (3) a desire to improve effectiveness through Scripture memory.

The common weaknesses of an evangelist include (1) a belief that everybody should be an evangelist, (2) a tendency to go after decisions even when people are not ready to respond and (3) a tendency to be confrontational in evangelism. Those who have this gift may fall into the danger of (1) pride and (2) becoming numbers oriented rather than people oriented.

Reference: Douglas Porter, *How to Develop and Use The Gift of Evangelism: A Practical Guide for the Layperson* (Lynchburg, Va: Church Growth Institute, 1992).

EVANGELISM: P-1, P-2, P-3

Various definitions of the term "evangelism" are offered today in an attempt to define its nature. One popular way of defining evangelism involves describing the input required in the evangelistic process. C. Peter Wagner suggests that contemporary definitions of evangelism may be classified in one of three representative views, which is "P-1"—Presence Evangelism, "P-2"—Proclamation Evangelism and "P-3"—Persuasion Evangelism.[1]

(Originally Wagner used the designation 1-P, 2-P and 3-P, but in time their use has been reversed to P-1, P-2 and P-3.) Each of these three approaches to evangelism deserves a closer look.

P-1 Presence Evangelism

The P-1 Presence Evangelism approach to evangelism tends to emphasize the social implications of Christianity independent of any attempt to identify Christian theological distinctives or suggest the superiority of a Christian worldview. In this approach to evangelism, acts of justice and mercy are performed as ends in themselves rather than as means to convince others to embrace Christianity. In this extreme expression, it is correct to conclude with Wagner that "this is not an evangelical point of view."[2] But a less radical form of this view of evangelism appears to be gaining recognition among some evangelicals. In the preface to his 1982 book on evangelism, Harvie M. Conn explains:

This book is not intended as a simple how-to-do-it manual on evangelism as traditionally known....Rather, this is an effort to look at the relation between evangelism and social questions as two sides of the same coin. Holistic evangelism has more recently been the term used to describe what I mean. Perhaps Lordship evangelism is easier to pronounce and understand. I want to speak of evangelism in context, of giving cups of cold water to the thirsty world, but giving them in the name of the Lord. I speak not of an easy truce between faith and works, not even a partnership. All partners may be equal but too frequently some are more equal than others. No, our goal is an interdependence that guards the integrity of both components and sees them constantly interacting.[3]

In a similar vein, Myron S. Augsburger suggests:

Evangelism is anything that makes faith in Jesus Christ a possibility for persons. It is the loving deed in the name of Christ as well as the loving word. Evangelism is sharing

```
        P-3
        Persuasion          Disciples Made

        P-2
        Proclamation        People Who Hear and Understand

        P-1
        Presence            People Helped
```

A. P-1 Presence evangelism

B. P-2 Proclamation evangelism
   Measure evangelism by how many hear and understand

C. P-3 Persuasion evangelism

Reprinted by permission from C. Peter Wagner

the joy of the new life in Christ in fellowship and friendship. It is inviting persons to open their lives to the lordship of Jesus.[4]

These statements by Conn and Augsburger concerning the nature of evangelism do not differ significantly from that of nonevangelical theologians such as Dom Helder Câmara, the archbishop of Recife in Brazil. According to Câmara:

Evangelization in the name of Christ...aims at humanization in the fullest sense. The boundary between the two fields is purely theoretical—with respect of course for the distinction from a theological point of view.[5]

The weakness of these definitions of evangelism is not so much what they state as what they leave unstated. Although the kind of positive expressions of Christianity called for by Conn, Augsburger and Câmara ought to be present in an evangelical life-style and witness, evangelism reaches beyond these acts of charity.

P-2 Proclamation Evangelism

A second and more popular way of defining evangelism by evangelicals is designated by Wagner as P-2 Proclamation Evangelism. Those who maintain this view argue that "evangelism is a proclamation of the Gospel which leaves men free to make their own decisions about it."[6] According to George W. Peters:

Evangelism is the announcement of a unique message. It concerns itself primarily with the proclamation of the gospel of God, the redemptive act of God in Christ Jesus....It is the announcement of good news to a world alienated from God, bound in sin, and under a sentence of condemnation.[7]

This view of evangelism may represent the predominant evangelical view of evangelism. According to Wagner:

This view of evangelism is very strong among evangelical Christians. I previously mentioned that many authors of books on evangelism simply assume a definition of evangelism. When they do, nine times out of 10 their definition is proclamation. They feel that it is so commonly accepted it needs no argument. Most evangelists and evangelistic associations that I am aware of also assume proclamation as their working definition of evangelism.[8]

Once again, the weakness of this view of evangelism is not found in what it states, but what it leaves unstated. Is it enough to "preach the gospel" without taking further steps to encourage a positive response to it on the part of the hearer? Some may agree it is enough. Others argue there must be something more.

J. I. Packer's book *Evangelism and the Sovereignty of God* advocates P-2 Evangelism. Packer, an Anglican minister, changed the Church of England's statement of evangelism to read, "To evangelize is to so present Christ Jesus in the power of the Holy Spirit that men may come to put their trust in God through Him, to accept Him as their Saviour, and serve Him as their King in the fellowship of His church."

Notice that the phrase "may come" leaves the obligation with the sinner. The previous phrase was "shall come," meaning that the minister has an obligation to get people to respond. At the Lausanne, Switzerland, conference on evangelism, John Stott said, "Not to preach so something will happen, but to preach whether anything happens or not." This is simply proclaiming the gospel (P-2) with no obligation to get results.

P-3 Persuasion Evangelism

A third view considers that evangelism has not been completed until a response (most understand this to be more than a decision, and incorporation into the Body) has been received from the unconverted. The growing popularity of this view of evangelism is probably attributable to the influence of the Church Growth Movement. According to Donald A. McGavran and Winfield C. Arn:

A Church Growth definition of evangelism is "to proclaim Jesus Christ as God and Savior, to persuade people to become his disciples and responsible members of his church."[9]

The idea that evangelism includes the concept of persuading individuals to respond positively to the gospel is older than the Church Growth Movement that promotes it. As early as 1918, the Archbishop's Committee of the Church of England framed the following definition of evangelism:

Evangelism is to so present Christ Jesus in the power of the Holy Spirit, that men shall come to put their trust in God through Him, to accept Him as their Saviour, and serve Him as their King in the fellowship of His Church.[10]

The British Archbishops were not the only pre-Church Growth Movement Christian leaders to conclude that evangelism presupposes a positive response to the message of the gospel. A committee of 30 Protestant ministers representing a variety of American denominations met in Columbus, Ohio, in 1946 and drafted the following definition of evangelism:

Evangelism is the presentation of the Good News of God in Jesus Christ, so that men are brought, through the power of the Holy Spirit, to put their trust in God; accept Jesus Christ as their Savior from the guilt and power of sin; to follow and serve him as their Lord in the fellowship of the church and in the vocations of the common life.[11]

This is apparently the preferred definition within the Church Growth Movement, in part because of its interpretation of the Great Commission as found in Matthew 28:18-20 as a strategy statement for both evangelism and church growth. According to Wagner:

This is the definition which best fits the understanding of the Great Commission.... To reiterate, the one imperative out of the four action verbs in Matthew 28:19-20 is "make disciples." "Go," "baptizing" and "teaching" are all participles in the original Greek. So far as measuring evangelistic results is concerned, the bottom line is how many disciples are made as the result of a given evangelistic effort, not how many people hear. And,...an acceptable criterion for knowing when a person who makes a decision is really turning out to be a disciple is that they become a responsible member of the Body of Christ in a local church.[12]

Although church-growth considerations no doubt have influenced some to accept this third view of evangelism, it is not without its own merit theologically, independent of a church growth agenda. In his book *Rethinking Evangelism: A Theological Approach*, Ben Campbell Johnson, a professor of evangelism, writes:

I suggest, as an initial working definition, that evangelism is "that particular task of the church to communicate the good news of God's love to persons so that they may understand the message, place their trust in Christ, become loyal members of his church, and fulfill his will as obedient disciples." This intentionally specific definition of evangelism focuses the vision and energy of the church on individuals and their relationship to Christ in the Christian community. It excludes corporate statements on national issues, ministry to the poor, the struggle for justice, and the various ministries of compassion, because these do not belong intrinsically to the evangelistic task of the church.[13]

Are These Conflicting or Complementary Views?

One of the most significant evangelical definitions of evangelism in the last quarter-century is that which came out of the International Congress of World Evangelization in Lausanne, Switzerland, in July 1974. Article 4 of The Lausanne Covenant recognizes the strengths of each of the previous definitions of evangelism and incorporates them into a hybrid evangelical view. The Lausanne Covenant affirms:

To evangelize is to spread the good news that Jesus Christ died for our sins and was raised from the dead according to the Scriptures, and that as the reigning Lord he now offers the forgiveness of sins and the liberating gift of the Spirit to all who repent and believe. Our Christian presence in the world is indispensable to evangelism, and so is that kind of dialogue whose purpose is

to listen sensitively in order to understand. But evangelism itself is the proclamation of the historical, biblical Christ as Saviour and Lord, with a view to persuading people to come to him personally and so be reconciled to God. In issuing the gospel invitation we have no liberty to conceal the cost of discipleship. Jesus still calls all who would follow him to deny themselves, take up their cross, and identify themselves with his new community. The results of evangelism include obedience to Christ, incorporation into his church, and responsible service in the world.[14]

One objective of the Lausanne Congress was to bring together various evangelicals committed to accomplishing the task of world evangelization. In such a broad gathering of evangelical leaders, developing a statement affirming common beliefs and commitments was not without its problems.[15] Nevertheless, the resulting statement about evangelism appears to be one that many evangelical leaders have chosen to support. One measure of the influence of the Lausanne Congress is seen in the following statement concerning the nature of evangelism offered by Billy Graham to those attending the Second International Congress for Itinerant Evangelists in Amsterdam.

The term "evangelism" encompasses every effort to declare the Good News of Jesus Christ, to the end that people may understand God's offer of salvation and respond in repentance, faith and discipleship. We must always make it clear that there is a "cost" to following Christ. There is the denial of self, and the taking up of a cross. Christ never offers cheap grace. He never lowers His standard for entrance to the kingdom of God.[16]

Evangelists must begin with Presence Evangelism (P-1) by "winning a hearing." They must have a good testimony and be interested in meeting the needs of the lost. The godly life of the soul winner will motivate some lost to seek Jesus Christ.

Next, ministers must proclaim (P-2) the gospel to the unsaved. Before people can be saved, they must hear the gospel (Rom. 10:14) and understand the message. Soul winners must not add works to the gospel nor dilute its obligation.

Finally, ministers must persuade (P-3) people to receive Christ. At times, Paul pleaded with great emotion (Rom. 9:2; 10:1); at other times, he persuaded with the rational arguments of a trial lawyer (Acts 13:43).

As we change our views of evangelism, that change may be reflective of other changes taking place in our lives, churches and/or our communities. Some ministers have experienced a gradual transformation from only P-3 evangelism to only P-2 evangelism. Perhaps they came to a place where they could not get results. Maybe it was a change in the culture of their neighborhoods without a change in their techniques. Maybe their sanctuaries got overcrowded and the unchurched stopped visiting the services. Or maybe the minister went through midlife burnout. Whatever the reason, when some ministers stop getting results, they change their evangelistic outlook from P-3 persuasion to P-2 proclamation.

Perhaps some ministers changed their theology of evangelism and the results were no longer a priority. Maybe it was spiritual pride when some ministers thought it was more sophisticated to be known as a pulpiteer than a soul winner.

Perhaps the erosion from P-3 to P-2 is part of an unseen but eternal decay that seems to attack Christianity. The tempter would do anything to destroy the effectiveness of the Church. When he cannot destroy it outwardly, he will attempt to blunt its effectiveness inwardly. It is a shame when the minister no longer weeps over lost souls and no longer pleads for sinners to receive Christ.

References: [1]C. Peter Wagner, *Church Growth and the Whole Gospel: A Biblical Mandate* (New York: HarperCollins, 1981), pp. 55-57, and *Strategies for Church Growth: Tools for Effective Mission and Evangelism* (Ventura, Calif.: Regal Books, 1987), pp. 117-30. [2]Wagner, *Strategies for Church Growth*, p. 119. [3]Harvie M Conn, *Evangelism: Doing Justice and Preaching Grace* (Grand Rapids: Academie Books, 1982), p. 9. [4]Myron S. Augsburger, *Evangelism as Discipling* (Scottdale, Pa.: Herald Press, 1983), p. 7. [5]Dom Helder Câmara, cited by Walter J. Hollenweger, *Evangelism Today* (Belfast: Christian Journals Limited, 1976), p. 45. [6]Douglas Webster, *What is Evangelism?* (London: The Highway Press, 1964), p.42. [7]George W. Peters, *Saturation Evangelism* (Grand Rapids: Zondervan Publishing House, 1971), p. 13. [8]Wagner, *Strategies for Church Growth*, p. 121, [9]Donald A. McGavran and Winfield C. Arn, *Ten Steps for Church Growth* (San Francisco: HarperSanFrancisco, 1977), p. 51. [10]Cited by Wagner, *Strategies for Church Growth*, p. 128. See also Charles Templeton, *Evangelism for Tomorrow*, p. 41. [11]Cited by Jess M. Bader, *Evangelism in a Changing America* (St. Louis: The Bethany Press, 1957), p. 15. [12]Wagner, *Strategies for Church Growth*, p. 122. [13]Ben Campbell Johnson, *Rethinking Evangelism: A Theological Approach* (Philadelphia: The Westminster Press, 1987), p. 12. [14]The Lausanne Covenant, 1974, Article 4, "The Nature of Evangelism," cited by Alfred C. Krass, *Evangelizing Neopagan North America: The Word That Frees* (Scottdale, Pa.: Herald Press, 1982), p. 191. [15]Wagner refers to this as it affects the definition of evangelism in his brief discussion of the resolution of a difference of opinion between himself and John Stott while working on the Lausanne Covenant (see *Strategies for Church Growth*, pp. 129ff.). See also Hollenweger's appraisal of the Lausanne Congress in *Evangelism Today: Good News or Bone of Contention*, pp. 6-9. [16]Billy Graham papers, *Lausanne Congress on Evangelism*, 1974, "The Gift and Calling of the Evangelist," p. 16.

EVANGELISM: PARADIGMS AND TECHNIQUES

For God so loved the unsaved, that He sent Christians to evangelize them. To most observers, evangelism is simple and straightforward; yet, great controversy swirls around soul winning. Some Christians go house-to-house attempting to win souls to Christ, yet other Christians criticize them. Some Christian magazines will not print the term "soul winning" because the term suggests manipulation or "arm twisting." They prefer the softer term "witnessing."

Some Christians emphasize the number of decisions or the number of baptisms recorded each year. Others disagree with emphasis on outward measurement of results; they claim the Holy Spirit works in hearts and that quality of character cannot be measured. They claim the Christian's duty is to proclaim the gospel whether or not there are results.

Some preachers speak intensely against sin to produce guilt or conviction so people will get saved. Other preachers disagree with emotional or revivalistic methods. They preach by using the overhead projector to help people understand the gospel. Some even claim that conversational preaching is the biblical model.

The controversy about results in evangelism continues. Those who emphasize quantitative results defend themselves by saying their attackers are jealous. Those who emphasize quality claim the other side worships success, and that the idea of measuring "souls" is "cultural," not scriptural.

Just as there are many kinds of growth, so there are many kinds of evangelism or evangelistic strategies used by churches to reach their communities. Traditionally, churches have engaged in front-door evangelism, also called "inviting evangelism" or "event evangelism." This is an attempt to win the lost by inviting them to come to an event, thus entering the church through the front door. More recently, side-door evangelism, which is networking the unchurched through nonevangelistic meetings, has become more common.

This article is not designed to train readers in evangelism nor to motivate them to win souls. It is designed to expose them to the kinds of evangelism that are available to today's church. One kind of evangelism should not be magnified over another. Evangelism, no matter what approach is used (Phil. 1:14-18), brings glory to God when a sinner comes to God. Some kinds of evangelism, however, are more effective in certain circumstances, while others are more effective at other times. Most churches use several expressions of evangelism, not just one expression. No matter what approach is taken, the church's mandate is to present the gospel so people will come to know Jesus Christ. The following summarizes several evangelism methodologies used by Christians today to reach others with the gospel.

1. Crusade evangelism. Churches conduct this method of evangelism by inviting an evangelist to come and conduct a series of meetings, usually called an evangelistic crusade. These have sometimes been presumptuously labeled "revival" meetings. Many times, however, there is no outpouring of the Holy Spirit, so there is no indication of revival. The meetings usually include special music (choir or soloist), an attempt to get the unsaved to attend, and organized prayer support. Historically, crusade evangelism in a church has attracted many unchurched people and has resulted in some of them coming to Christ.

Citywide crusades involve many churches in an area being responsible for attendance and financial and prayer support of an effort to evangelize an entire area. The rationale for a citywide crusade is that a larger arena could be constructed or rented and a well-known evangelist and singer known for results could be invited. Hence, the enterprise could be more successful than a crusade held in a single church. Dwight L. Moody, Billy Sunday, Billy Graham and Luis Palau are leading figures in the history of citywide crusades.

2. Mass media evangelism. The growth and influence of media has caused evangelists to use many aspects of it to preach the gospel to the masses. Radio evangelism has included broadcasting church services, Bible teaching programs and evangelistic programs such as the "Old Fashioned Revival Hour" by Charles E. Fuller. Also included are Christian radio stations that broadcast the gospel 24 hours a day. Most believe radio evangelism is more effective among the lost outside the United States, whereas in the United States, Christian radio is more effective among church members.

Television evangelism is similar to radio evangelism, except that it visually presents evangelistic crusades and apparently has a greater response from non-Christians than does radio evangelism.

Literature evangelism involves printing the gospel in tracts (usually for free distribution), magazines and books (usually for sale), and Bibles (both free and for sale). Many foreign mission agencies engage in colportage work, which is selling inexpensive Christian literature.

The media-coordinated evangelistic outreach of the I FOUND IT crusades of the mid-1970s combined a number of media—radio, television, billboards, newspaper advertisements and others.

The *Jesus* film might be one of the most influential expressions of mass media evangelism, considering the vast numbers of languages into which it has been translated, and the vast number of showings around the world in all kinds of situations and to all kinds of people groups.

3. Saturation evangelism. Originally developed by Ken Strachan, director of the Latin American Mission, saturation evangelism is a concept whereby a community is saturated with the gospel by Bible studies, visitation evangelism, media evangelism (usually Christian movies shown in public places), child evangelism and large crusade efforts to bring as many as possible to Christ. Strachan believed the efforts should not be tied to one evangelist, but rather should be the endeavors of the total church mobilizing its membership to use many avenues in evangelizing a community.

In 1971, Jerry Falwell, pastor of the Thomas Road Baptist Church in Lynchburg, Virginia, used the term "saturation evangelism" to mean "using every available means to reach every available person at every available time." Rather than applying it to citywide crusades, Falwell said media evangelism was a twentieth-century technique whereby one church could "capture its town for Christ." Hence, Falwell adopted the term for local church evangelism. In this context, Jerry Falwell added telephone evangelism, cassette evangelism and printing evangelism (every church purchasing a printing press and mailing its newspaper to its clientele). He also adopted the sociological principle of "synergism," which is using multiple agencies for maximum evangelistic outreach. Thus, Christian schools, homes for unwed mothers, deaf ministries, camps, bookstores and other local ministries are utilized to reach the church's "Jerusalem" by ministering to the various needs of individuals in the community.

The end product of Falwell's saturation evangelism was a large growing church that had multiple ministries, was located on a massive campus and became the focus of life for its members.

4. Superaggressive evangelism. This is a term the author coined to describe the attitudes of faith and optimistic fervor in evangelistic endeavors.

The Christians in Jerusalem were enthusiastic in making contact with every person, presenting them with the gospel (Acts 5:28) and persuading them to be saved (2 Cor. 5:11), realizing that through faith, the evangelist can accomplish unlimited results.[1]

5. Lifestyle evangelism. The Bible commands Christians to be witnesses (Acts 1:8)—technically, to be witnesses of the death and resurrection of Christ (5:30-32). Today, Christians share their faith with lost people by witnessing what they have heard, seen and experienced. Therefore, witnessing requires a Christian to have a good testimony so that he or she becomes an attractive advertisement to motivate lost people to want to have the same kind of life. When this is done, the Christian has built a bridge to the unsaved and has "won the right to be heard," or "earned the right to give the gospel."

Jim Peterson, author of *Evangelism as a Lifestyle*,[2] contends that many Americans cannot identify with Christianity because of their secular presuppositions. If they simply accept the verbal formulas of the plan of salvation, they will not get saved—they must experience the life of Jesus Christ. To do this, a lost person must have a role model to give meaning to the words of Christianity before he or she can make a meaningful decision for salvation. Hence, the testimony of a believer is foundational in evangelism.

6. Busing evangelism. The early 1970s experienced an explosion in soul-winning activity. Many churches got into the bus ministry and experienced growth in attendance, decisions and baptisms. As a result, new church buildings were built, staff members were added and ministries were multiplied. Busing evangelism includes canvasing a neighborhood (usually on Saturdays) to invite people to ride a bus to church (usually children). The worker is called a "bus pastor," and usually has a driver to assist him or her. It is the worker's job to care for the children who ride his or her bus and to try to win their families and friends to Christ. Usually a church has a bus director who organizes all the workers, the route and the equipment, and provides a program to motivate workers to be effective in soul winning.

During the late 1970s, many churches that got

into bus evangelism for the wrong reasons quickly got out when inflation caused the cost of gas, insurance and equipment to spiral. Also, many churches were nurture oriented, not evangelistically oriented, and could not handle the unruly children brought in by the buses. Finally, other churches constructed buildings to care for the additional children but got into financial trouble when they discovered the parents could not pay for the buildings. They got out of the bus ministry to stabilize themselves financially. In spite of the problems, many churches have continued a healthy evangelistic outreach through the use of buses.

7. *Front-door evangelism.* This expression describes all the efforts a church makes to attract people through its front door, where the lost will hear the gospel, respond and be converted. Front-door evangelism, also called "inviting evangelism," depends on the corporate church activities to reach and win people to Christ. It is not personal evangelism, media evangelism or any other phase of evangelism that attempts to win the unsaved outside the church, then gets them into church as a result of their conversion. A front-door evangelist attempts to personally invite lost people to church, where they will hear the gospel and be converted. This method is also called "event evangelism." Also included is the use of advertisements to make the unsaved aware of the church and to attract them to it.

Critics of front-door evangelism maintain the church is designed for worship or Bible teaching for the saints; it is not an evangelistic crusade. They maintain there is no command in Scripture to bring the lost into the house of God, nor is there an illustration of the unsaved coming into a church service. Yet, the church is to preach to all people (Mark 16:15), and most preaching takes place inside the front door of a church (1 Cor. 14:24,25).

8. *Side-door evangelism.* In contrast to front-door evangelism, side-door evangelism describes the route that many take in coming to salvation. They do not come through a church service, rather they are reached by other agencies or ministries of the church. People attend a group Bible study, a recreational program, or other kinds of fellowship where they are confronted with the gospel by lifestyle evangelism or personal evangelism or *oikos* (i.e., household, see the following listing) evangelism. Hence, they come to salvation through an agency of the church, but not a regular preaching service. Side-door evangelism is usually a result of Christians bringing their friends and relatives to Christ through a church ministry.

9. *Oikos evangelism.* Statistics reveal that most new converts are brought to Christ through the witness of those within their family or friendship network. The Greek word *oikos* is translated "family, kindred household (including servants), or (one's) own." Many in the New Testament who were brought to Christ were of the household of a new convert. Hence, oikos evangelism is when a new convert reaches friends and relatives for Christ and brings them to Christ through existing relationships. New Testament personalities associated with this form of evangelism include Lydia, the Philippian jailer, Matthew the tax collector, Zacchaeus and Cornelius. Hence, the first evangelistic priority of a person after being saved is reaching relatives and friends.

Oikos evangelism is also called "web evangelism." When applied to a church, it is the principle of the new convert reaching those closest to him or her. By working through web relationships, a church can evangelize its extended congregation (those who are responsive people) and guarantee a smaller dropout percentage of new converts and transfer members. This kind of outreach is also called "friendship evangelism," "relationship evangelism" and "F.R.A.N.gelism."

References: [1]Elmer L. Towns, *Church Aflame* (Nashville: Impact Books, 1971). [2]Jim Peterson, *Evangelism as a Lifestyle* (Colorado Springs: NavPress, 1980).

EVANGELISM: PROCESS AND EVENT

Salvation (the new birth) is an event. Jesus referred to salvation as a new birth experience (John 3:3,5). Peter also used the analogy of birth in reference to salvation (1 Pet. 1:23). John, in his first Epistle, indicated that salvation is a birth experience that begins with faith in Jesus Christ (1 John 5:1). Just as birth is an event, so salvation is an event.

Salvation is like a light bulb; it is either on or off. The lights may gradually become brighter or dimmer, but there is a point when they are turned on. So it is with salvation. Faith may gradually grow stronger, but the exercise of faith in which a person is saved is always instantaneous.

A birth is always an event. Look at any birth certificate. A person is not born at all hours of the day and night. The birth certificate may state "Born alive at 2:45 A.M," "Born alive at 5:18 P.M." or sometimes "Stillborn at 11:00 A.M." But it will never read "Born from 6:40 A.M. to 11:02 A.M." A birth happens at a point in time—it is an event.

Just as there are nine months of preparation before a birth, so a person is prepared for salvation before his or her conversion. This is called stair-stepping or pre-evangelism. The human life cycle begins with an event commonly referred to as conception. That event is then followed by a nine-month gestation period during which prenatal development takes place. That process leads up to the event of birth. After the event of birth, another process begins. This process—called postnatal—includes further growth, development, training and maturing. In reference to salvation, this is called "post-salvation." Some traditions call it "sanctification." McGavran called it "perfecting."

Salvation is therefore also a process. Each contact the church makes with a lost person should move him or her closer to acceptance. Just as there are nine months of prenatal growth before a baby is born, so there is usually a period of pre-conversion influence that brings a person to Christ. This is sometimes called "pre-evangelism," but in friendship evangelism, it is called "stair-stepping a person to the gospel."

Growing churches must not lose sight of the birth experience. Stair-stepping cannot be completed apart from the salvation of the unsaved. Salvation is neither the beginning nor the end of the process of evangelism, but without it there is no true evangelism. Like the human life cycle, evangelism is a process (pre-evangelism, conversion, post-evangelism) that consists of events.

EVANGELISM, TEAM

This approach to evangelism views it as a team ministry in which the conversion of the unsaved is achieved through the cooperative efforts of people who have various gifts and use their gifts to reach others. A program of team evangelism divides workers into five general tasks, representing five areas of spiritual gifts: (1) evangelists, (2) equippers, (3) encouragers, (4) helpers and (5) intercessors. Each of these tasks is discussed in separate articles in this book.

EVANGELISM, TYPES OF

Reaching the unbeliever with the gospel by employing every available means to bring people to Christ. The types include E-0 evangelism—bringing people to a commitment to Christ (new birth) who are already church members; E-1 "near-neighbor evangelism" of non-Christians whose language and customs are those of the Christian who is witnessing; E-2 evangelism across a relatively small ethnic, cultural or linguistic barrier; and E-3 evangelism across a relatively large linguistic barrier.

Reference: See E-0 EVANGELISM, E-1 EVANGELISM, E-2 EVANGELISM, E-3 EVANGELISM.

EVANGELIST, LOCAL CHURCH
See EVANGELISM, GIFT OF
and SOUL WINNERS

Evangelists are those on the evangelism team who have the spiritual gift of evangelism. On visitation night, they are given the names of prospects to visit that evening. Because they have the gift of evangelism, they want to meet strangers and do the work of winning others to Christ. They are usually effective in this ministry because it is their spiritual gift. Also, they probably have greater success than those who visit from other churches because they are going to see prospects who have visited the church. The prospects (receptive-responsive people) they go to see usually have a relationship with someone in the church. Hence, because they present the gospel to prospects with greater interest, they produce a higher number of decisions for Christ.

Evangelism is communicating the gospel in the power of the Holy Spirit to unconverted persons at their point of need with the intent of effecting conversions. It is perhaps the most exciting ministry in which you will ever be involved. There is a sense of personal fulfillment and inner joy experienced by Christians who effectively share their faith with others that cannot be experienced any other way. It is a ministry in which God wants all of us involved.

People picture a variety of things when they think of an evangelist. For some, an evangelist is a famous preacher who travels from city to city "preaching the gospel." Others think of the host or hostess of a popular religious television program. Still others think of those brave church members who go door-to-door to talk to strangers about the gospel. Too often we define effective evangelism according to our stereotyped pictures of an evangelistic ministry. But the real key to effective evangelism is not found in a program, but rather a person—the person who would be an evangelist.

Only one person was ever described as an "evangelist" in Scripture (Acts 21:8). Although Philip may have done many of the things we picture an evangelist doing, the context in which this evangelist is described suggests he was a fairly normal person who used his home to raise his family and entertain guests. Evangelism was something he and others did as part of the overflow of their Christian experiences (Acts 8:4,5).

How to Develop Credibility in Your Evangelism

Those who are most effective in their witness of the Christian faith tend to be people who have developed a lifestyle that lends credibility to what they say. When they share their faith with others, it seems like the most natural thing for them to do. And those who hear them share seem to be wanting to know more about how they, too, can experience a personal relationship with God.

What makes these people so unique? Are they born this way, or is it possible for us to become effective witnesses? The Bible has much to say about the kind of person who is effective in evangelism. The good news is that it is possible for us to develop a credible witness. We can do certain things to become more effective in evangelism.

The most effective witness is one that flows out of a maturing Christian life. As we grow into a deeper relationship with God by dealing with problems in our own lives, we will be more effective in sharing our faith with others (Ps. 51:10-13). People are going to be more responsive to a gospel they see working in your life than one that merely consists of abstract principles.

Part of that maturing process involves developing a genuine spiritual concern for others that keeps us faithful in sharing our faith with others (126:6). Certainly one of the keys to Paul's success in evangelism was his concern for those who did not know Christ as Savior (Rom. 9:1-3; 10:1).

Many Christians are effective in sharing their faith because they do so in response to a clear understanding of the love of God (2 Cor. 5:14). People do things for love they would not do for any other reason, and they do it differently than they might otherwise. As we begin to realize just how much God loves us, we will find ourselves naturally sharing His love with others (Rom 5:5; 1 John 4:9,19).

Perhaps it is their appreciation of God's love that produces a servant's heart toward others in many effective evangelists. They are willing to serve people even when no one expects it of them (1 Cor. 9:19). Their willingness to meet people where they are adds to their credibility as they share the gospel (v. 22).

The effective evangelist believes in the power of the gospel to make a positive difference in others' lives (Rom. 1:16). When people come to faith in Jesus Christ, they become a new creation (2 Cor. 5:17). The one who has personally experienced this change in his or her own life is more likely to recognize the life-changing potential of the gospel in the lives of others (1 Tim. 1:12-15).

People tend to listen to an evangelist when they have seen that difference in his or her lifestyle. This is especially true when they see the different way Christians respond to problems, with which everyone struggles in life. Peter reminded Christians to be prepared in the midst of their suffering to be ready to explain the gospel to those who ask (1 Pet. 3:14-17). He realized people would be attracted to Christianity when they saw the positive way Christians respond to problems. When unsaved family members see the consistent Christian witness of another in their home, they are often won to Christ without having the gospel explained to them (1 Pet. 3:1).

Those who are most effective in evangelism tend to exercise wisdom in the way they approach people and discuss their faith (Dan. 12:3). They have acquired a special insight from God that makes them more effective in dealing with people (Prov. 11:30). But this insight is also available to others. When we recognize a need for greater wisdom in our own lives, we can get what we need by asking God (Jas. 1:5). Also, as we make personal Bible study an ongoing spiritual discipline in our lives, we establish another means by which God provides us with His wisdom (Ps. 19:7).

Because effective evangelism is done in the power of the Holy Spirit, the effective evangelist is one who has acquired unique spiritual power through the fullness of the Holy Spirit (Eph. 5:18). In the New Testament, the consistent evidence of the fullness of the Holy Spirit was spiritual power for evangelism (Acts 1:8). We can obtain this spiritual power by (1) wanting to be filled with the Holy Spirit, (2) repenting of known sin in our lives, (3) receiving the fullness of the Holy Spirit through prayer and (4) trusting God to fill us and use us (John 7:37-39).

The same Holy Spirit who empowers us to be effective in evangelism also empowered the Scriptures to be effective in saving people (2 Tim. 3:15). One of the biblical expressions used to describe the Scriptures is "word of life" (Phil. 2:16), because it is the Word of God that produces spiritual life in others. Many effective evangelists commit the Scriptures to memory and use them when appropriate in their sharing because they recognize its power to effect conversions (Ps. 19:7). It is always easier to get a job done right when you have the right tools. In the work of evangelism, the Scriptures are the evangelist's tools.

Something about the ministry of evangelism is addictive. As we begin sharing our faith with others, something happens to us inside. Wanting to tell others about Jesus is the most natural response to this inner sense of fulfillment and joy that comes through evangelism. Before long, we find ourselves enjoying this ministry so much that we can barely conceive of not being involved in it (1 Cor. 9:16). What may seem intimidating today can by choice become a dominant part of your Christian life and ministry.

EVANGELIST: NEW TESTAMENT USAGE

The title "evangelist" is usually applied to anyone who travels from church to church or city to city conducting evangelistic crusades. Although some see this as only a spiritual gift, other denominational traditions call it an "office." The function, however, is different from the New Testament role of evangelist. The term "evangelist" is mentioned only three times in the New Testament. The first is in Acts 21:8 where Philip, chosen in Acts 6 to be a deacon, is named an evangelist. Philip was called an evangelist because he was carrying out the Great Commission by preaching the gospel and planting a church in Samaria (8:4), and winning the Ethiopian to Christ. The other references are 2 Timothy 4:5, where Timothy is told to do the work of an evangelist; and Ephesians 4:11, where the gift of an evangelist is listed.

The root meaning of the term "evangelist" comes from the word gospel (*euangellion*). The evangelist "gospelizes" or brings good tidings. The evangelist is tied to the gospel message. The evangelist usually goes to areas that have never been evangelized and preaches the gospel. Because of this designation, some denominational traditions call this person/office a "missionary." They view the evangelist as going to *people* and the missionary going to *people groups* to penetrate them with the gospel. When the gospel is presented as commanded in the Great Commission, the evangelist begins by announcing the good news, making disciples, baptizing and finally teaching converts to observe all things (Matt. 28:19,20). This process is the function of the church; hence, evangelists are implied as church planters, which is a description of the modern foreign missionary. Philip the evangelist carried out these tasks in both Samaria and with the Ethiopian eunuch in the desert.

In noting the gifts in the church, Paul lists the evangelist after the apostle and the prophet, but before the pastor-teacher (Eph. 4:11). This implies that the evangelist is sent forth by the first group and prepares the way for the second group. The evangelist is sent by the apostles and prophets who historically established the Church by writing Scripture, and prepares the way for the pastor who shepherds the flock after the church has been established. The evangelist uses his or her gift to plant churches. Today's foreign missionary fulfills the role of an evangelist more than the typical role filled by a citywide revivalist.

Some denominational traditions view the evangelist as an office while others do not. Most leaders view evangelism as a gift that implies a function. Therefore, many people may have the gift of evangelism who do not have the title evangelist. Because spiritual gifts are both qualitative and quantitative, this implies some are better than others at winning souls.

Philip is the classic example of the evangelist. He was a pioneer who went to unevangelized people. He preached the gospel in Samaria (Acts 8:5), Gaza (v. 26) and in his new home (v. 40). His ministry was an itinerant one. He went from place to place, even into the desert to talk with one man—the Ethiopian eunuch. Philip moved on when his work was finished and let others pastor those he won to Christ.

EVANGELISTIC MANDATE

Jesus' command to reach others in witness of the gospel; the mission and ministry of the Church as it is expressed in spiritual concerns.

Reference: See GREAT COMMISSION.

EVANGELISTIC MYOPIA

A common symptom of the disease of *koinonitis*— a fellowship that is limited to a church's self-concern rather than a concern to make disciples of all peoples.

Reference: See KOINONITIS.

EVENT EVANGELISM
See FRONT-DOOR EVANGELISM

EXCLUDED MIDDLE

A term derived from Paul Hiebert's observation that the worldview of most non-Westerners is three-tiered: on the top is the cosmic, transcendent world; in the middle are supernatural forces on earth; on the bottom rests the empirical world of our senses. The unique tendency of Western society has been to ignore the reality of the middle zone.—GOJR

EXHORTATION, GIFT OF

The person who has the gift of exhortation has the ability to stimulate faith in others and motivate others to a practical Christian life. The strengths of this gift include (1) a tendency to encourage another, (2) an excitement about practical principles of life, (3) a tendency to interpret personal experiences into principles and then validate them with Scripture, (4) a tendency to be comfortable ministering to both groups and individuals and (5) grief about sermons that are not practical.

Among the weaknesses of people who have this gift are (1) a tendency to give direction to those unwilling to receive it, (2) sometimes being accused of taking Scripture out of context and (3) a reluctance to win souls if follow-up is not assured. The person who has this gift needs to avoid the danger of (1) being discouraged with a lack of progress in listeners, (2) ministering for selfish purposes and (3) ministering to the symptoms rather than the real problems of a person.

EXPANSION GROWTH

Each congregation expands as it converts non-Christians and takes more of them into the same congregation. Growth by transfer is included also.

EXTENSION GROWTH

Each congregation plants daughter churches among its own kind of people in its neighborhood or region.

Reference: See CHURCH PLANTING.

EXTERNAL GROWTH

Numerical growth in attendance, offerings, membership or enrollment. This is growth that is observable, measurable and repeatable.

FACTORS OF GROWTH
See CONTEXTUAL FACTORS

FAITH

Saving faith is both simple and complex. Faith is as simple as a drowning man reaching for a rope, a child taking a step or a sinner looking to Jesus Christ. Faith is simple belief. On the other hand, saving faith is complex, setting in motion all the judicial machinery of heaven. The ultimate purpose of God is activated by faith; but eternal consequences are not received as easily as an impulsive purchase at the discount store. To be saved, a person must have proper knowledge, proper emotion and proper decision of the will in response to God who calls, convicts and converts.

"Faith" is one of those common words that is difficult to define specifically. Some have suggested that the concept of faith is actually beyond the ability of any human being to define. But we can recognize certain aspects of faith that make the idea more understandable. Leon Morris suggests:

Faith is clearly one of the most important concepts in the whole New Testament. Everywhere it is required and its importance insisted upon. Faith means abandoning all trust in one's own resources. Faith means casting oneself unreservedly on the mercy of God. Faith means laying hold on the promises of God for daily strength. Faith implies complete reliance on God and full obedience to God.[1]

The closest thing to a biblical definition of faith is "the substance of things hoped for, the evidence of things not seen" (Heb. 11:1). Its importance in the Christian experience is seen in that it is impossible to please God apart from faith (v. 6).

Faith is part of a person's response to God in the salvation experience. Some who have difficulty recognizing the human role in saving faith tend to identify faith as the gift of God. The *Heidelberg*

Catechism reflects the belief of Martin Luther: "The Holy Spirit works in me by the Gospel...."

(Faith) is not merely a certain knowledge, whereby I receive as true what God has revealed to us in His Word, but also a cordial trust, which the Holy Ghost works in me by the Gospel, that not only to others, but to me also, the forgiveness of sin, and everlasting righteousness and life are given by God out of pure grace, and only for the sake of Christ's merit.[2]

An error comes from not recognizing the role of the Gospel in producing faith in the individual. Scripture seems to express six separate uses of the term "faith." First, when faith is used with an article, as in *the faith*, it is a reference to the Scriptures or doctrinal faith. This is the source of the individual's faith and ultimately of the individual's regeneration.

Second, there is *saving faith*. Third, there is nonexperiential faith that is described as *justifying faith* (Rom. 3:27-31) that is imputed to the believer. The fourth is *indwelling faith*, which seems to be the active faith of Christ that indwells the believer and gives him or her the ability to trust in God (Mark. 11:22; Gal. 2:16,20). The fifth is the *daily faith* of the believer, which is living by the principles of God's Word (2 Cor. 5:7). The sixth is *the gift of faith*, a spiritual gift imparted to move obstacles that hinder the work of Christ (1 Cor. 12:9; 13:2). (See further under FAITH AND CHURCH GROWTH.)

Faith begins by knowing God and His plan. Intellectual faith has never saved anyone, but intellectual knowledge is the foundation for saving faith. It is the proper response to saving faith. Intellectual faith is measured by what a person knows about the historical facts of Christianity. It is not a matter of the emotions or the will, but simple knowledge of God.

Intellectual faith is the basis for volitional faith. In the first step, the person believes in the existence of God, that the Bible is God's Word, that Jesus shed His blood on the cross for the sins of humankind and that God will save those who call upon Him. This knowledge is not ultimate faith, but is the beginning.

There is a place for a person's intellect in faith. Someone once defined faith as "believing what ain't so." He was wrong. Saving faith is not a blind leap in the dark. It is based upon objective truth. As Morris notes:

The verb *pisteuo* is often followed by "that," indicating that faith is concerned with facts. This is important, as Jesus made clear to the Jews, "for if ye believe not that I am he, ye shall die in your sins" (John 8:24). But it is not all-important. James tells us that the devils believe "that there is one God," but this "faith" does not profit them (Jas. 2:19).[3]

Faith also involves *feelings*, as either a cause or effect. In mentioning the emotional aspect of faith, it should be added that faith is not an emotional feeling, nor does the intensity of our emotions make our faith efficacious. Yet emotions cannot be removed from the trust process that is complete, not partial, love from those who are joined to Him in salvation (Matt. 22:37-39).

Emotions are interwoven in faith, as good works are the natural outgrowth of faith. Just as a person's faith without works is dead, so a person's faith without the accompaniment of emotions is barren. Sometimes emotions drive people to the Word of God; in this sense, emotions bring people to faith. Other times, emotions are stirred by the Word of God and grow out of Scripture. In this sense, emotions are an integral part of faith. In Scripture, the emotions of joy and peace are both associated with faith (Rom. 15:13).

An irony comes into play when trying to combine the human will and faith. In one sense, the human will must act in faith. On the other hand, faith comes to those who cease self-effort. Some Christians emphasize the need to surrender or become passive. Others believe that their faith will move mountains if it is strong enough. The answer to this apparent contradiction is seen in a biblical understanding of faith. Morris examines the place for human will in the biblical idea of saving faith.

The characteristic construction for saving faith is that the verb *pisteuo* is followed by the preposition *eis*. Literally, this means "to believe into." It denotes a faith that, so to speak, takes people out of themselves, and puts them into Christ (cf. the expression frequently used of a Christian, being "in Christ"). This experience may also be referred to by the term "faith-union with Christ." It denotes not simply a belief that carries an intellectual assent, but one wherein believers cleave to the Savior with all their hearts. Those who believe in this sense abide in Christ and Christ in them (John 15:4). Faith is not accepting certain things as true, but trusting a Person; and that Person is Christ.[4]

When the Philippian jailer asked, "What must I do to be saved?" he was told, "Believe." Faith involves an act of the will on the part of the believer in that the believer surrenders to the will of God. In one sense, no person can ever surrender fully to Christ as Lord and Savior because humankind still has a sin nature. Yet, if people refuse consciously to surrender some part of their wills to Christ, they are not exercising faith.

References: [1]L. L. Morris, "Faith" *The New Bible Dictionary*, ed. J. D. Douglas (Grand Rapids: Wm. B. Eerdmans Pub. Co., 1977), p. 413. [2]*Heidelberg Catechism*, question 1. [3]Morris, *The New Bible Dictionary*, p. 411. [4]Ibid. Also see *Say-It-Faith*, Elmer L. Towns, (Wheaton, Ill.: Tyndale House Publishers, 1983).

FAITH AND CHURCH GROWTH

One of the leading causes of the growth of the world's largest and fastest-growing churches is the faith of the pastor-leader. When a church leader has a clear vision of what God wants to do through his or her church and effectively communicates that vision to the church, his or her faith results in significant church growth.

How to Increase Your Faith to Lead Your Church to Grow

As noted, the Scriptures describe six expressions of faith in the Christian life. These are expressions of the "one faith" that may be described as "affirming what God has said in His Word." This definition is expressed in the popular statement, "Faith is taking God at His Word." To have a great faith and move mountains, a person must move through all six expressions of faith.

1. Doctrinal faith. If we want faith, we must begin with a correct understanding of the Word of God. The more we know of the Bible, the more faith we can have; and the more correctly we know the Bible and the more we act on the promises of God in His Word, the more effective our faith will be.

Throughout the New Testament, the phrases "the faith" and "doctrine" are used interchangeably. When faith has an article preceding it, as in "the faith," it means "the statements of faith." Therefore, to have correct faith, we must have an accurate statement of doctrinal faith.

The apostle Paul certainly recognized the importance of correct doctrine. He constantly opposed those who sought to change the faith; perhaps he was concerned about accurate doctrine because of his own experience. When, as Saul of Tarsus, he was persecuting the church, he thought his doctrine was accurate and that he was serving God. Yet later when he met Christ on the Damascus road, he gained a living faith that changed what he believed and how he lived. Paul talked about those who "will depart from the faith" (1 Tim. 4:1) and those who had "denied the faith" (5:8). At the end of his life, the apostle was able to say, "I have kept the faith" (2 Tim. 4:7). Jude challenged his readers to "contend earnestly for the faith" (Jude 3).

If we want to have a growing biblical faith, we need to ground it upon a correct knowledge of God. A certain woman once heard someone compliment her great faith. "I have not a great faith," she responded, "I have a little faith in a great God."

Someone may ask, "How can I get more faith?" Paul wrote, "Faith comes by hearing, and hearing by the word of God" (Rom. 10:17). The gospel—meaning the good news of the message of Jesus Christ—is the source and foundation of all faith.

Doctrinal faith is both the beginning and the test of our Christianity. If our statement of faith is wrong, then our personal faith is misplaced. We must begin with a correct statement of faith and build saving faith thereupon. At this point, we are meeting some of the important conditions to correctly experience a life of faith and continue to learn about doctrinal faith.

2. Saving faith. A person becomes a Christian by faith. "For by grace you have been saved through faith" (Eph. 2:8). When the Philippian jailer was troubled about his salvation, he was exhorted to exercise belief—the verb expression of faith. "Believe on the Lord Jesus Christ, and you will be saved, you and your household" (Acts 16:31). When Nicodemus failed to understand how he could enter into a relationship with God, Jesus said, "For God so loved the world that He gave His only begotten Son, that whoever believes in Him should not perish but have everlasting life" (John 3:16). Apart from faith, personal salvation is impossible.

Personal salvation is experienced by the inner person. Because humans are composed of intellect, emotion and will, faith comes through a proper exercise of these three aspects of personality.

Our faith must be grounded on correct knowledge. People cannot put their trust in something they do not know about, nor can they honestly trust something that is proven false to them. People must first know the gospel, which means they have an intellectual knowledge of salvation. But this knowledge alone will not save them.

The Bible seems to make a distinction between "believe *that*" and "believe *in*." In the first place, people can believe that their teams will win or believe that their jobs are superior. The beliefs are opinion, but are not deep conviction (i.e., based on the object of their faith—Jesus Christ). When people "believe in," the beliefs are based on carefully weighing the evidence. When we say "believe in," we are speaking of a moral expression or a moral experience.

The Gospel of John uses the word "believe" 98 times and ties faith to the object of belief. We are exhorted to "believe in Jesus Christ." As a result, the important aspect of belief is *what* you believe, not just the measure of your belief. Therefore, to have saving faith, people must believe that God will punish sin (Rom. 6:23), and that Christ has made a provision for their salvation (Rom. 5:8). People must believe these truths, which means they accept them intellectually; but mere intellectual assent to biblical truth is not enough to save.

Our faith will have an emotional expression. Knowledge about God is the foundation of saving faith, but such faith will extend to the individual's emotional responses as well. Solomon wrote, "Trust in the Lord with all your heart, and lean not on your own understanding" (Prov. 3:5). Jesus repeated this truth, "You shall love the Lord your God with all your heart, with all your soul, and with all your mind" (Matt. 22:37). This means that intellectual belief is not enough. People cannot trust their own understanding about God. Although emotions are involved in faith, faith is more than emotional feeling. Our emotional response to the gospel must be founded upon an intellectual understanding of the Scriptures.

Your faith must be a volitional response. A third aspect of saving faith is an expression of volitional faith. People are saved as a result of an act of their wills whereby they rely on Christ as proclaimed in the gospel. Paul told the Roman Christians, "You obeyed from the heart that form of doctrine to which you were delivered" (Rom. 6:17). When people accept Jesus Christ as their Savior (John 1:12), it is a conscious act whereby they invite Him into their hearts (Eph. 3:16).

3. Justifying faith. Whereas saving faith is an experiential encounter with Jesus Christ, the next expression, "justifying faith" is nonexperiential. Justifying faith is belief that we have been justified or declared righteous. Justification is not something we feel with our senses. It is something that happens to our record in heaven. God is the One who performs the act of justification (Rom. 8:33). Humans are the ones who receive the action and are justified (Rom. 5:1). Justification is the judicial act of God whereby He justly declares righteousness to all those who believe in Jesus Christ.

Abraham was the first person in the Bible described as having been justified by faith (Gen. 15:6). This is not to say that he was the first person to become a child of God. God made a promise to Abraham that he accepted as possible, and God rewarded him for his faith.

Justification is an act whereby our legal position in heaven is changed. Being justified is similar to the act whereby the United States' government declares that aliens can become American citizens. Nothing happens to them internally the moment they are pronounced citizens. Their thought processes remain the same, as do their personalities and speech patterns. The only actual change is their legal standing. As they become aware of the benefits of being Americans, they may shout, cry or break into grins. These are simply emotional reactions to a legal action.

In the same way, justification changes our legal standing in heaven. We become children of God. In response to this new relationship, the new Christian may respond emotionally.

The basis of justifying faith is a double transference that happens at salvation. Our sin was transferred to Jesus Christ—He became our sin. In Paul's phrase "Christ died for us" (Rom. 5:8), the preposition "for" is the key word. It indicates that He gave His life for the Church (Eph. 5:25) and He gave Himself for the sins of the world (John 1:29).

The second transference is that the perfection of Jesus Christ was credited to our account. When God looks at us in judgment, He sees the righteousness of His son. "For He made Him who knew no sin to be sin for us [the first step of transference], that we might become the righteousness of God in Him [the second step of transference]" (2 Cor. 5:21).

4. Indwelling faith. The Bible teaches that people cannot overcome sin and sinful habits by themselves. Faith is the secret of the victorious Christian life. "This is the victory that has overcome the world—our faith" (1 John 5:4).

Even beyond living a triumphant life, a person can walk in moment-by-moment communion with God. A medieval monk described this victory as "practicing the presence of God." This life of victory and fellowship is made available by the indwelling of Jesus Christ. When people become Christians, Christ comes into their lives. Believers have union and communion with Christ (John 15:5).

Not only does Christ dwell within believers, but the power of Christ is also available to them. Paul testified, "Christ lives in me; and the life which I now live in the flesh I live by faith in the Son of God" (Gal. 2:20). The secret of victorious living is allowing the life of Jesus Christ to flow through us. Believers must surrender their fears and rebellions to Christ. In so doing, they find new faith to overcome their problems. Paul described this new faith that comes from Christ, "the promise by faith in Jesus Christ [that] might be given to those who believe" (3:22).

Every Christian has access to the faith of Jesus Christ. Yet many Christians are defeated and discouraged because they have not allowed Christ's power to flow out of their lives.

To get this victory, Christians must first recognize that faith comes from Christ; it is described as "Christ's faith" (Gal. 2:16; Eph. 3:12; Phil. 3:9). Second, Christians must yield (the nature of faith is trusting) and allow Christ to work through them. In addition, Christians must constantly obey the direction of the Word of God so that they can continually have power for victory.

5. *Daily faith.* When we live by faith, we are being set apart to God—this is the meaning of "sanctification." The Bible teaches that *positional* sanctification is a past action that was accomplished on calvary. *Progressive* sanctification is being carried out daily, and *future* sanctification will take place when we arrive in the presence of God. Daily sanctification requires an exercise of faith, "For we walk by faith, not by sight" (2 Cor. 5:7).

As we live by faith, God is able to use us and cause us to grow in grace. Sometimes daily growth seems minute or even nonexistent to a casual observer. We may sometimes become frustrated with the apparent lack of progress, not able to see the forest for the trees. It is good from time to time to look back and see how God has been working in our lives.

As bricklayers place one brick upon the other in building a large tower, they may feel their progress is insignificant. Yet the tower will be built one brick at a time. It is the same in our Christian lives. God makes the big changes through a series of little ones. We must learn to trust God for the little things so we can enjoy great growth. We must trust God daily so we can enjoy yearly gain. Like any other growing experience, living by faith is taking one step at a time.

We grow in faith through the Word of God. As we make the Word of God a part of our lives by reading, studying and memorizing, we begin to grow in faith (1 Pet. 2:2). Every Christian needs to hear the Word of God taught and preached regularly (Ps. 1:1-3).

We grow in faith by following biblical principles. A growing faith is an obedient faith. Usually, the exercise of faith will be rational in keeping with what God wants done. We must put complete trust in the principles of the Bible and not trust our feelings. Faith is not a blind leap into the dark; faith is following the light of God's Word.

We grow in faith through seeking the Lord. The doctrine of "seeking" the Lord is not usually emphasized, but it is biblical to search for God. "When You said, 'Seek My face,' my heart said to You, 'Your face, Lord, will I seek'" (27:8). Our faith will grow as we seek God. First, we will begin to recognize the issues that keep us from God. Then, as we search for a better relationship with the Savior, we will come to know God experientially.

We grow in faith through confessing our sins. No Christian will live a sinless life, but God is constantly cleansing us through the blood of His Son. "If we walk in the light as He is in the light, we have fellowship with one another, and the blood of Jesus Christ His Son cleanses us from all sin" (1 John 1:7). When we as Christians do sin, God will forgive and cleanse us if we confess our sins to Him (v. 9). Every time we recognize a sin in our lives and rid ourselves of its hindrance, we grow in faith.

We grow in faith by surrender. The Christian must constantly surrender to the Lordship of Christ. We do this once when we are saved, but there are also subsequent moments of surrender to Christ. As we yield our lives to the Lord, we are growing in grace (Gal. 3:3; Col. 2:6). Paul challenged the Romans to "present your bodies a living sacrifice, holy, acceptable to God, which is your reasonable service" (Rom. 12:1).

We grow in faith through constant communion. If we want a growing faith, we must have constant communion with Jesus Christ. As we spend time in prayer, Bible study and fellowship with Christ, we will develop our faith more fully. Jesus recognized that we would become like those with whom we spend time (Matt. 10:25). As we spend time with the Lord, we will become more Christlike in our faith.

We grow in faith through being tested by difficult experiences. Once we are saved, our faith is nurtured as we grow from victory to victory. Paul describes this as a movement "from faith to faith; as it is written, 'The just shall live by faith'" (Rom. 1:17). God wants us to have faith in Himself because that pleases and glorifies Him.

Living faith is not something we receive in the same way we take vitamin pills. The opportunity of taking a step of faith includes the risk of success or failure. When we successfully trust God, we should learn through the experience and grow thereby. Faith must come from a person's heart, which is governed by a free will. Therefore, to develop a person's faith, God will sometimes maneuver him or her into a corner so that the "creature" is forced to look at the Creator in faith. Through such experiences, we have the opportunity to grow in faith.

6. The gift of faith. The gift of faith is one of the gifts the Holy Spirit supernaturally gives believers to serve God (Rom. 12:7; 1 Cor. 12:9). This is more than saving faith, which is also called a gift. The gift of faith is considered to be a serving gift, or an ability whereby a person serves God by exercising faith. Paul explained that the gifts differ "according to the grace that is given to us" (Rom. 12:6). God has given some this special gift of faith to enable them to carry out their ministries in more effective ways. (See various views in the article FAITH, GIFT OF.)

If God has given us the gift of faith, we need to exercise it faithfully in keeping with well-balanced Christianity. Paul said, "Though I have all faith, so that I could remove mountains, but have not love, I am nothing" (1 Cor. 13:2).

The Bible teaches that the proper use of our gifts increases the effectiveness and usefulness of those gifts (Matt. 25:14-34). It also teaches that we can desire and pray for more gifts (1 Cor. 12:31). This could mean a greater variety of gifts for the local church body and applied to mean other gifts for individuals. Therefore, it is possible for us (individually or corporately) to have more faith to trust God for bigger opportunities for service than we have now. If we are faithful in small things, God will give us more faith. Note that Abraham grew from being weak in faith to one who was strong in faith (Rom. 4:19,20).

The ultimate human expression of Christianity is an act of faith. To the casual observer, faith is simply defined as "reliance, trust or dependence." But to the careful student of the Scriptures, faith has at least the six expressions we have defined.

FAITH: DOCTRINE
See DOCTRINAL FAITH

FAITH, GIFT OF
One of the enabling gifts of the Holy Spirit. It is a God-given ability to undertake a task for God and to sustain unwavering confidence that God will accomplish the task in spite of all obstacles. (See *6.* under "How to Increase Your Faith.")

The editor's study of the largest and fastest-growing churches in America has led him to the conviction that the faith of the pastor is one of the main contributing factors in the church's growth. Others have come to similar conclusions on the basis of their study of the pastors of the world's largest churches. Although these pastors all have different spiritual gifts through which they do ministry, they also possess a highly developed enabling gift of faith. Although much has been written about spiritual gifts in general or specific gifts such as speaking in other tongues, few books have been written that are devoted primarily to the gift of faith.

The gift of faith is a spiritual gift that is bestowed upon certain believers to edify the body of Christ and is employed to get extraordinary results. Although the spiritual gift of faith is often confused with saving faith, it is more than saving faith. It has been described as the faith of miracles, special faith, wonder-working faith, daring faith and the gift of prayer. Each of these expressions used to describe this gift indicate the special nature of the gift of faith.

Yet even when those who write about the gift of faith recognize that it is special, they do not generally agree on a definition. Perhaps their disagreement arises because (1) little is said of the gift of faith in Scripture, (2) the Church has largely ignored the gift of faith in its practice and (3) Christian writers have not researched the topic thoroughly.

Three approaches seem to be prevalent in

understanding and interpreting the gift of faith. First, some interpret the gift of faith as an instrument to be used in Christian service, as one would use the Bible, prayer or preaching to accomplish the work of God. The instrumental view appears to be the traditional or historical Christian view.

Second, the gift of faith is interpreted as insight or vision. The person who has the gift of faith discerns what God wants accomplished in a situation, then uses every resource available to accomplish that vision. This seems to be the recent interpretation and is maintained by most evangelical Christians who are now writing about spiritual gifts.

Third, the gift of faith is interpreted as the ability to move God by faith so that He divinely intervenes in a crisis that faces the believer or supernaturally intervenes in Christian service so that He accomplishes what the person with the gift believes will happen. This interventional interpretation is maintained primarily by Pentecostals, who believe that miracles are occurring in the work of God, and by non-Pentecostal pastors identified with large and dynamically growing churches. They may or may not believe the day of miracles has passed, but they believe they have experienced the intervention of God in their Christian service.

Perhaps the three interpretations of the gift of faith are not three exclusive interpretations, but three progressive steps in expressing the gift of faith. If this is true, the three views are different points on a continuum. Those who believe the first step have used faith as an instrument (Eph. 6:16), but they do not necessarily deny the work of God in the next two steps. They just have not continued to a higher level of usefulness. The same can be said of those who hold the second interpretation of the gift of faith, for they have used faith as a vision to see what God can accomplish. The third view does not interpret the gift of faith differently, but includes in it the first two aspects and then adds the interventional factor.

1. The gift of faith as an instrument. The gift of faith is interpreted by many to be the ability of the Christian to use the instruments of Christianity to carry out the work of God in a person or in a church. In Ephesians 6, Paul

describes other instruments that help the Christian fight the enemy: truth (6:14); righteousness—the knowledge of imputed perfection (6:14); the gospel (6:15); the helmet of salvation (6:17); and the sword of the Spirit—the Word of God (6:17). Christians also defend themselves with the shield of faith (6:16), which is an instrument.

The instrumental view of faith is more conformable to the historic Protestant view—that is, that the day of miracles has passed. This view believes that because miracles are viewed as a demonstration of authority to validate the message from God, there is no longer a need for miracles because the content of revelation is complete (Jude 3). This view implies that God does not supernaturally intervene in the Christian work, but works through the means of grace (the instruments, including faith) that He has already supplied. This view would regard the interventional gift of faith as having similar properties to a miracle—hence, not applicable to this age of grace.

The instrumental view takes a passive view of the person who has the gift of faith. As such, both the person and the gift are channels or vehicles used by God. God's power is within the Scriptures (Heb. 4:12; Jas. 1:17, 18; 2 Pet. 1:4) and the Holy Spirit (Acts 1:8). Power (including the instrumental gift of faith) is not resident within the person, for the person is an earthen vessel (2 Tim. 2:21)—the power is of God, not a human being. Christians accomplish the work of God through the Word of God by the Holy Spirit who indwells them. Only when they have the gift of faith are they instruments to accomplish what God has promised.

Perhaps those who hold the instrumental view see God controlling the destiny of this world (their extreme view of predestination has led to fatalism); therefore, they reject the interventional view because they believe humans cannot change the order of events by their faith. To them, faith is only instrumental, so it accomplishes only what God has predetermined. As such, they have not been aggressive (interventional) in changing the natural course of Christian service, but they surrender their initiative in the Word of God.

Others may view the gift of faith as passive because they relate the gift of faith to other ministries. They believe that spiritual gifts are given to persons such as preachers, teachers and evangelists (Eph. 4:11), and that God works through persons who are identified by their gifts (i.e., prophets have the gift of prophecy, teachers have the gift of teaching and so on). But no ministry—such as that of a "faither"—is identified with the gift of faith. Therefore, they see God working in the world through secondary sources, such as His laws, the influence of His Word, the Holy Spirit and the affairs of life. They do not see the gift of faith as an intervention by God in an active or direct role, but they see the gift of faith in an instrumental or indirect (secondary) role.

2. *The gift of faith as insight.* This view interprets the gift of faith as the Holy Spirit giving the Christian the ability to see what God desires to perform regarding a project. After Christians perceive what can be accomplished, they dedicate themselves to its accomplishment. The strength of this view of the gift of faith is in the Christian's ability to see what God can do in a given situation; hence, it is implied that the Christian must see God's nature and purpose, and these are understood only through His Word. (Some view this as similar to the gift of discernment, or the two gifts working together.)

The insight view recognizes that God is the source of all Christian work, but those who exercise faith sense their responsibility to carry out the project through their visions of the work. This view places a high degree of responsibility and accountability on the person. God is active in giving vision, but we are passive in receiving the vision; we allow God to work through us to accomplish the project. This view implies that the work of God is accomplished in relationship to the availability of the worker, including the worker's knowledge, wisdom, motivational powers, leadership ability and other human factors. Of course, God gave these abilities to people, but God gave them through secondary means, such as training, reading and role modeling, and works through the gifted person by secondary means.

Those who have the gift of faith may have the supernatural ability to determine what God will do in a church in the next 10 years or at any future date. (This is the gift of discernment or prophecy working together with faith.) As a result, those who have the gift of faith are growth oriented, goal oriented, optimistic and confident. Some people who have natural faith may display these four aspects and build a chain-store empire or a multimillion-dollar business. These characteristics can come from the power of positive thinking. The cause is the spiritual gift of faith or vision; the result is a confident attitude that usually produces results in the work of God. Because this gift has become such a strong conviction, some pastors who can communicate the vision to the congregation will work and sacrifice to accomplish the project.

Perhaps a problem with limiting the gift of faith to the insight view is that it makes it synonymous with vision, which might imply that faith is the passive ability to see what God wants done. Although faith seems to be active and is used by God to change circumstances, no one could honestly deny that vision is inherent in faith. In saving faith, people must see their sins, see God and see the remedy that God has provided in the gospel. In serving faith, people must incorporate the role of the seer-prophet (1 Sam. 9:9), which is seeing the need first, seeing farthest into the future, and seeing the greatest thing that God could accomplish in any situation. Perhaps the gift of faith not only incorporates vision, but also goes to the next aspect in which the man or woman of God intervenes in the circumstances of life.

3. *The gift of faith as intervention.* This view interprets the gift of faith as the ability to move God to divinely intervene in a crisis that is facing a project or to change the expected order of events so that the work of God goes forward. This view

THREE VIEWS OF THE GIFT OF FAITH

Name	Initiation	Vision	Power	Accomplishment	Availability
Instrumental	God	God	God	By God	To all
Insight	God	Person	God	By God	To chosen
Interventional	Person	Person	God	By God	To chosen

maintains that the gift of faith is active, the person is responsible, but God is the source of the gift and the source of accomplishment. Traditionally, it has been called the gift of miracles, and features divine intervention in a miraculous way. The person usually has a certainty that God will intervene (perhaps because of insight) and thus makes an expression of faith.

Interventional faith is the ability given by the Holy Spirit whereby a person overcomes problems in a normal ministry so that the work of God goes forward. Interventional faith is based on and grows out of using faith as a vision and as an instrument. Although the interventional view of faith is similar to the two previous positions, interventional faith is initiated by those who have the unique gift of faith. The three views of the spiritual faith indicate the differences in interpreting the biblical data. In all three, the power and the accomplishments come from God.

The chart on the previous page summarizes the foregoing discussion.

FAITH PROJECTION

A projected growth goal based on present growth patterns and a belief that God will increase the harvest. Faith projections are usually for a five-year period.

FAITH, SAVING

An experiential encounter with Jesus Christ whereby the person exercises the intellect to know the gospel, the emotions are stirred by conviction of sin and love of God, and the will responds in belief.

FAMILY ANALYSIS

An examination of the intricate network of blood and marriage relationships that tie communities together and have much to do with the inner life of any congregation.

FAMILY OF GOD

The spiritual kinship of all believers to each other and to God.

FASTING

Leaders and followers will fast when seeking spiritual power for evangelism. Although it is not *prescriptive* in the New Testament, its use is *descriptive* as a tool for outreach, power and communion with God. Its primary function is internal growth, but it also has implications for numerical growth.

How to Fast

As you approach your fast, prepare by making a list of things you want to accomplish during the fast. This list may include special reading projects such as a book of the Bible, Christian biography or book on the Christian life, special items for prayer or things to do for others. Then, tentatively arrange your schedule to avoid as much as possible things that might discourage your fast—meetings where food is served, grocery shopping or watching television. Until a person begins fasting, he or she often doesn't realize how many fast-food commercials are designed to make the viewer hungry.

Some people eat extra food before a fast, believing they will need the extra food energy. Actually, this makes fasting harder than if you eat a lighter meal. A meal of fruits or vegetables is advisable as you begin a fast.

As you begin fasting, reflect on your personal relationship with God. Like David, you can pray, "Cleanse me from secret faults. Keep back Your servant also from presumptuous sins; let them not have dominion over me" (Ps. 19:12,13).

Spend long periods of time in prayer during your fast. Pray for your pastor and the various ministries of your church. Then pray for the specific personal needs and prayer requests mentioned in your missionaries' prayer letters. Pray also for the needs of others in your congregation and those in your community you would like to see saved. Use the Lord's Prayer as your pattern for prayer during these extended prayer times.

Take time to read and memorize the Scriptures during your fast. The average person can read through one of the New Testament Epistles in about 20 minutes. You may wish to read several chapters in both the Old and New Testaments and meditate on them during your fast. You may want to memorize one of these special chapters or several other verses relating to a topic in which you are interested.

During your fast, you will abstain from eating solid foods, but not from drinking water. If you begin to feel hungry, drink a large glass of water. Most people find that drinking water as they begin to feel hungry at their usual mealtimes helps them avoid eating during their fast.

As you conclude your fast, take time to thank God for all you have learned and experienced during the fast. Breaking your fast with the observance of the Lord's Supper will help you focus on Christ and His sacrificial investment in your life. Take time to celebrate His gift of life to you and reaffirm your commitment to serve Him faithfully.

Be careful about concluding your fast with a large meal. Most people find it best to eat lightly the day they break their fast, and to return gradually to their usual eating habits. Some may use their fasting experience to make important changes in their dietary habits and adopt healthier lifestyles.

Reference: Bill Bright, *The Coming Revival* (Orlando, Fla.: Here's Life, 1995).

FELLOWSHIP

Fellowship groups within the church are also essential tools for effective outreach and external church growth. This article examines the role fellowship plays in church evangelism.

What Is Biblical Fellowship?
When the New Testament talks about fellowship, often the reference is to the believer's fellowship with God. This fellowship is foundational to a second dimension of fellowship identified in the New Testament Church—that of the believer with other believers. The concept of fellowship is identified in the New Testament by three Greek words.

Koinonia. This word is translated "communion" and "fellowship" in the New Testament. It has the idea of "sharing in common." It is derived from the noun *koinos*, which means "common." Early Christians used this term to communicate the

idea that they were together in a common cause.

Metoche. This word literally means "partnership." It conveys the idea of sharing in or partaking in something as one of the partners of the enterprise. New Testament Christians viewed themselves as partners in the faith.

Henotes. The idea of Christian fellowship is also conveyed in the affirmations of the unity of the Early Church. The Greek word *henotes*, meaning "unity" or "oneness," is used only twice in Scripture (Eph. 4:3,13), but the concept is emphasized in Acts by the expression "one accord" (Acts 1:14; 2:1; 4:24) and by statements concerning the church being "of one heart and one soul" (4:32).

FELLOWSHIP CIRCLE
See CONGREGATION

FELLOWSHIP INFLAMMATION

A symptom of koinonitis that represents an overemphasis on Christian fellowship.

Reference: See KOINONITIS.

FELLOWSHIP SATURATION

A symptom of koinonitis that results from a church's unwillingness to divide the congregation and cell structures when they reach beyond their respective tolerances of 80 and 12.

Reference: See KOINONITIS.

FELT NEED

The conscious wants and desires of a person; considered to be an opportunity for Christian evangelism that stimulates within the person a receptivity to the gospel.

FIELD TOTALS

The number of Christians in all congregations of a given denomination in a given field; may be a whole nation, a state, a province, a district or a part of a district.

FILLING OF THE SPIRIT
See FULLNESS OF THE SPIRIT

FINNEY, CHARLES GRANDISON
(1792–1875)

American evangelist during the Second Great Awakening.

Called "The Father of Modern Revivalism," Finney is one of the most significant evangelism leaders in American history. His *Autobiography* and *Lectures on Revival of Religion* are classics in the field of spiritual awakening.

In New York City and other places, Finney practiced an early version of what is now called "seeker services." Later, he became an ardent itinerant evangelist. Finney is best known for his "New Measures." These innovations to evangelism magnified his approach, which was more Arminian than Calvinistic. Such measures included "anxious seats" and "protracted meetings."

Finney attempted to point out historically that new measures occurred in every generation. In addition, he argued that he was merely recognizing and seeking new approaches that God was honoring. He was not merely seeking new techniques to be different. A study of Finney and his times can give a helpful perspective for those struggling with new, innovative approaches to evangelism and church growth today.

Finney is credited with providing the impetus for the shift from the work of God to the work of humans in revival and spiritual awakening. He has thus greatly influenced evangelical Christianity and evangelistic methods. The public invitation, protracted services (now often called "revival meetings" or simply "revivals"), and preparation for such meetings can be traced in large measure to Finney. He has been praised and condemned for this shift. In evaluating Finney, one must remember that he was reacting to the cold, lifeless, extreme version of Calvinism of his day. —ALR

FIRST GREAT AWAKENING

One of the first outbreaks of the revival that became known as "The First Great Awakening"

took place on Wednesday, August 13, 1727, on the estate of Count Nicolaus von Zinzendorf near Herrnhut, Germany. Prior to the outbreak of revival, the Moravian community had been troubled with a breakdown of interpersonal relationships and disputes about minor doctrinal issues. The revival came in part as a response to a reading of 1 John, and a concern about its emphasis on fellowship. According to J. Edwin Orr, "Through this Moravian Revival, German Pietism affected both the Evangelical Revival in Britain and the Great Awakening in the American Colonies."[1] According to Oswald J. Smith, the two most significant results of the Moravian revival were the composition of many hymns and a vision of worldwide missions.[2]

The Moravian commitment to missions resulted in their sending missionaries to establish other Moravian communities throughout both Europe and North America. Moravian influence was strongest among ethnic Germans who had settled in Pennsylvania, but its presence was felt throughout the Western world. One person influenced by Moravian missionaries to America was the Anglican missionary John Wesley, who had returned to England, having failed in his mission to Georgia.

Shortly after meeting these missionaries, John Wesley was converted at Aldersgate. Wesley became the driving force behind Methodism, which was essentially a lay-revival movement within the Anglican church. As Methodism grew and was increasingly opposed by the Anglican clergy, Methodism came to be viewed as a sect separate from the Church of England and became the soil out of which a number of holiness denominations have sprung. Wesley's Methodist beliefs might be viewed by some as an English expression of the same German pietism believed and practiced by the Moravians.

One of the outstanding preachers of this revival was George Whitefield. Whitefield pioneered open-air preaching to large crowds who would not usually gather in churches. He used this ministry effectively throughout both Britain and New England. Whitefield's second visit to America (1739) was marked by both revival and effective evangelism. J. Edwin Orr reports that

10 percent of the population of New England was converted and added to the churches between 1740 and 1742.[3]

The Great Awakening began in America long before Whitefield's visit. As early as 1727, Theodore Frelinghuysen was experiencing revival in New Jersey. One of the more remarkable expressions of this revival took place under the ministry of Jonathan Edwards in 1734 in Northhampton, Massachusetts.

The Great Awakening appears to have influenced both British and American society for nearly five decades. The original movement among the Moravians gave rise to a revival movement described as a prayer meeting that lasted 100 years. Commenting on the social effect of this revival in England, Martyn Lloyd-Jones suggested:

> Many secular historians are ready to agree that it was the evangelical awakening in the time of Whitefield and the Wesleys that probably saved this country from an experience such as they had in France and in the French Revolution. The Church was so filled with life and with power that the whole society was affected. Furthermore, the influence of that evangelical awakening upon the life of the last century is again something that is admitted freely by those who are aware of the facts. And, indeed, the same thing happened a hundred years ago in the revival to which I have been referring. And so it has happened in every revival.[4]

References: [1]J. Edwin Orr, *A Call for the Re-study of Revival and Revivalism* (Los Angeles: Oxford Association for Research in Revival, 1981), p. 1. [2]Oswald J. Smith, *The Enduement of Power* (Wheaton, Ill.: Crossway Books, 1987), pp. 104-108. [3]Orr, *A Call for the Re-study of Revival and Revivalism*, p. 6. [4]Martin Lloyd-Jones, *Revival* (Wheaton, Ill.: Crossway Books, 1987), p. 27.

FLUCTUATING RECEPTIVITY

The responsiveness of individuals and groups waxes and wanes because of the Spirit's peculiar activity in the hearts of people.

FOG

A term used by church-growth technicians to define inaccurate guesswork; uneducated opinions that are abundant regarding the growth and decline of the Church.

FOLDING

The process by which new Christians are assimilated into the local church. Also called bonding, assimilation and churching.

Reference: See BONDING PEOPLE TO THE CHURCH.

FOLLOW-UP GAP

The difference between the number of persons who make decisions for Christ in a given evangelistic effort and those who go on to become disciples.

FORGIVENESS OF SINS COMMITTED BEFORE THE CROSS

Many Christians have thought wrongly that the blood of lambs sacrificed in the Old Testament was the basis for forgiving sin. Some are just as wrong in thinking that when Jews attempted to keep the law, it was the basis of their sanctification. The truth is that in every dispensation, a person was saved by faith through grace. A person kept the law as an expression of obedience and fellowship to God, and on the same basis offered the blood sacrifice to God. "It is not possible that the blood of bulls and goats could take away sins" (Heb. 10:4).

The blood sacrifice of a lamb was a type that pictured the coming "Lamb of God who takes away the sin of the world!" (John 1:29). As a prefigure, it portrayed the coming sacrifice that atoned for the sin of the world. In one aspect, the sin was covered (the Old Testament word for atonement was *kaphar*—to cover) until Christ "takes away the sin" (v. 29).

Paul reminds us that "God set forth [Christ] as a propitiation by His blood, through faith, to demonstrate His righteousness, because in His forbearance God had passed over the sins that were previously committed" (Rom. 3:25). In this sense, Christ dealt with the sin that was committed before calvary.

A famous evangelist tells the story of taking a light tan suit on an ocean cruise. He planned to preach in the suit each evening. He spilled food on the suit the first night and the spot wouldn't come out. His wife used her talcum powder to cover the spot so he could wear the suit, but the powder came out. Each night he had to re-cover the spot with talcum powder. In the same way, the blood atonement covered the Old Testament sin and, because the sacrifice was not permanent, the saint had to bring a blood sacrifice continually. But "Christ was offered once to bear the sins of many. To those who eagerly wait for Him He will appear a second time, apart from sin, for salvation" (Heb. 9:28).

FOUR SPIRITUAL LAWS

A popular presentation of the gospel developed by Bill Bright and published by Campus Crusade for Christ. Translated and adapted for wide use internationally, this presentation begins with the question, Have you heard about the Four Spiritual Laws? The presenter then explains that just as the physical laws govern the physical universe, the spiritual laws govern our relationship with God.

Law One: *God loves you and offers a wonderful plan for your life.* "For God so loved the world that He gave His only begotten Son, that whoever believes in Him should not perish but have everlasting life" (John 3:16).

Law Two: *Man is sinful and separated from God.* Therefore, he cannot know and experience God's love and plan for his life. "For all have sinned and fall short of the glory of God" (Rom. 3:23).

Law Three: *Jesus Christ is God's only provision for man's sin. Through Him you can know and experience God's love and plan for your life.* "Christ died for our sins...he was buried,...he was raised on the third day according to the Scriptures,...he appeared to Peter, and then to the Twelve. After that, he

appeared to more than five hundred" (1 Cor. 15:3-6, *NIV*).

Law Four: *We must individually receive Jesus Christ as Savior and Lord; then we can know and experience God's love and plan for our lives.* "For by grace you have been saved through faith, and that not of yourselves; it is the gift of God, not of works, lest anyone should boast" (Eph. 2:8,9).

Reference: Bill Bright, *How to Experience and Share the Abundant Life in Christ* (San Bernardino, Calif.: Campus Crusade for Christ, 1971).

FOURTH WORLD

Peoples who have not yet become Christian.

FOX, GEORGE (1624–1691)

Founder of the Society of Friends (Quakers).

Born in Leicestershire, England, into a Puritan home, George Fox abandoned his Puritan heritage in 1643 when challenged by two other Puritans to a drinking bout. He began searching for a more meaningful religious experience, which he claimed in 1646. He began preaching about his mystical experience with God, and in 1652 organized the Society of Friends. In 1666, Fox introduced monthly meetings to provide order and encourage the good conduct of members of the movement. He traveled widely promoting the Quaker cause throughout England, Europe and North America. Fox died in London on January 13, 1691.

FRANS

An acrostic representing Friends, Relatives, Associates and Neighbors. These are receptive people that can be targeted for evangelistic outreach.

Reference: F.R.A.N.Tastic Days, an evangelistic program by Church Growth Institute, Lynchburg, Virginia.

FRELINGHUYSEN, THEODORE (1692–1747)

Pastor under whose ministry the Great

Awakening began in New England.

Theodore Frelinghuysen, a German educated under Pietist influence, served as pastor of a Dutch Reformed Church in New Jersey and urged his congregation to seek a deeper relationship with Christ during the 1720s. His ministry bore fruit as the Great Awakening began in his congregation in 1726. He continued to influence the progress of that revival primarily through his influence on Gilbert and William Tennent. One of Frelinghuysen's innovations in ministry, the prayer meeting, has become an integral part of the evangelical church in America.

FRIEND DAY

Friend Day is one of the most successful Sunday School attendance campaigns in the Church Growth Movement today. Historically, the Friend Day Campaign is attributed to Wendell Zimmerman at Kansas City (Missouri) Baptist Temple, who began using the idea in the late 1950s. Dr. Truman Dollar, who became pastor of the church, improved on the idea. The author further developed the idea, adding church-growth principles and turning it into a tool for all churches.

Friend Day is an evangelistic outreach involving the total membership in a strategy of church growth that uses existing human relationships to reach people. Its success lies in its simplicity—every church member brings a friend. Many churches have used this campaign to double their attendance on Friend Day. Using the campaign follow-up strategy, many churches have experienced a significant and sustained increase in attendance following Friend Day.

The strength of the Friend Day campaign is that it uses several principles of church growth, including: (1) identifying and reaching receptive-responsive people (quality prospects), (2) using existing social networks to reach others in the community, (3) using relationships to assimilate new converts to the church, (4) eliminating barriers and ministering to people at their felt needs, (5) utilizing people according to their spiritual gifts and (6) applying the results of church-growth research in a workable plan of evangelism.

FRIENDSHIP EVANGELISM

The principle of reaching others for Christ through natural relationships (i.e., one's friends, relatives, associates and neighbors). This is also called "web" evangelism—reaching people for Christ through the social "webs" to draw them into the church.

FRONT-DOOR EVANGELISM

Inviting people to an event at the church where they can hear the gospel and be saved. The method is often contrasted with "side-door" evangelism, which utilizes less direct means of evangelism.

Reference: See EVENT EVANGELISM

FULLER, CHARLES EDWARD (1887–1968)

Pioneer radio evangelist.

Born on April 25, 1887, Charles Fuller graduated from Pomona College in California and began a career in the fruit-packing business. In 1917, he was converted under the ministry of Paul Rader. The following year, Fuller traveled as an itinerant missionary in the Western states. Fuller launched his radio ministry "The Old-Fashioned Revival Hour" in 1925. During the 1940s, he also directed a large number of evangelists through the Fuller Evangelistic Association. At the time of his death in March 1968, "The Old-Fashioned Revival Hour" was heard on more than 500 stations around the world.

Fuller's contribution to evangelism extends beyond his own evangelistic ministry and those of the other evangelists in his association. The Fuller Theological Seminary and School of World Mission has been a center for research into evangelism and church growth, and a center from which the Church Growth Movement has developed.

FULLNESS OF THE SPIRIT

When a person is filled with the Holy Spirit, it is the source of power and effectiveness in evangelism and of church growth. The characteristics of the filling or fullness of the Holy Spirit include: (1) it is experiential in nature, (2) it relates to Christian living and service, (3) it is repeatable, (4) it involves yielding to God (i.e., not getting more of the Holy Spirit but the Holy Spirit getting more of you), (5) it is a postconversion experience with God and (6) all believers apparently do not take advantage of it.

Paul commanded the Ephesian Christians, "And do not be drunk with wine, in which is dissipation; but be filled with the Spirit" (Eph. 5:18). God has given men and women the opportunity to be continually filled with the Holy Spirit for effective service. Rather than allowing alcohol to control the mind of the Christian, it is God's desire that His Holy Spirit be in control. As we establish our fellowship with God through confession of sins (1 John 1:9) and yield to Him (Rom. 6:13), we can be filled with the Holy Spirit as commanded in Scripture. In the light of Paul's command, no Christian can claim to be in the will of God who is not constantly being filled with the Holy Spirit.

The Scriptures speak of "the law of the Spirit of life" (Rom. 8:2). Among other things, this suggests that certain eternal laws or principles govern the ministry of the Holy Spirit. These are the laws by which He gives power to those who serve Him. When these laws are understood, particularly as they relate to the fullness of the Holy Spirit, any and every believer can experience this fullness.

The human responsibility concerning the fullness of the Holy Spirit includes both yieldedness and faith. As people yield their wills to the Holy Spirit, they can by faith be filled with the Holy Spirit. Experiences associated with this fullness may vary with various personalities, but the eternal principles are unchanging. Bill Bright observes:

In like manner, and in different ways, sincere Christians are filled with the Spirit. It should be made clear at this point that to be "filled with the Spirit" does not mean that we receive more of the Holy Spirit, but that we give Him more of ourselves. As we yield our lives to the Holy Spirit and are filled with His presence, He has greater freedom to work in and through our lives to control us in order to better exalt and glorify Christ. God is too great to be placed in a man-made mold. However, there are certain spiritual laws that are inviolate. Since the Holy Spirit already dwells within every Christian, it is no longer necessary to "wait in Jerusalem" as Jesus instructed the disciples to do, except to make personal preparation for His empowering. The Holy Spirit will fill us with His power the moment we are fully yielded. It is possible for a man to be at a quiet retreat and become filled with the Holy Spirit. It is likewise possible for a man to be filled with the Holy Spirit while walking down a busy street in a great city....It is even possible for a man to be filled with the Holy Spirit and know something wonderful has happened, yet be completely ignorant at the time of what has actually taken place, provided he has a genuine desire to yield his will to the Lord Jesus Christ.[1]

Although yielding to God is one aspect of being filled with the Spirit, faith is another. The two are so closely related that it is questionable whether one can be experienced without the other. Some Christian leaders speak of it as "spiritual breathing." In this analogy, yielding to Christ by confessing sin is likened to exhaling, while appropriating the fullness of the Holy Spirit by faith is described as inhaling. Receiving the fullness of the Holy Spirit involves two expressions of faith—asking and accepting.

The Holy Spirit's fullness within us is primarily to produce the fruit of the Spirit (Gal. 5:22,23). In the book of Acts, the power to witness is evidence of the fullness of the Holy Spirit promised by Jesus (Acts 1:8). On some occasions (but not every occasion) when Christians were filled with the Holy Spirit, the building shook (4:31) or they spoke in tongues (10:44-46). But always the gospel was preached and people were saved. These occasional outward occurrences were often tools God used at that time to accomplish the main objective of witnessing. These outward signs were similar to the purpose that miracles had in the Early Church. They were objective authority for the message of God.

It is an undeniable fact that some Christian leaders have served God with greater effectiveness than others and in ways that cannot be explained by such factors as knowledge, personality or education. They experience the blessing of God in a unique way and appear to possess the power of God for effective service. Their deeper experiences with God are the result of their seeking God and surrendering their wills to Him. The experience these people have with God is available to some degree to all who are willing to seek His blessing and make themselves available for His service.

To seek God is to hunger and thirst after knowledge, love and fellowship. Those who were seeking after God were wanting (1) to know Him, (2) to know what He wanted them to do in a specific situation, (3) to draw closer to Him or (4) power to do God's will. It is similar to a young man seeking to be with the girl he loves so he can know her, love her and be loved in return.

Many abuses occur surrounding the doctrine of seeking God. Some monks have prayed in the snow, thinking that physical denial and/or abuse would lead them to know God or be blessed by God. Some have spent years in solitude in a monastery cell, or alone on a pole, as did Simon Stylites.

Although the deeper Christian life is described in various terms (the abiding life, the victorious life), it is ultimately a life characterized by seeking God and walking with Him. It is a life lived in relationship to God, and at the heart of this relationship is the believer seeking God or surrendering to God. Alexander MacLaren defined the essential nature of the Christian life: "The meaning of being a Christian is that in response for the gift of a whole Christ I give my whole self to Him."

Although this idea of surrendering the will is fundamental to the nature of the Christian life, the concept is verbalized much easier than it is realized. Terms such as revival, renewal and rededication exist in the Christian vocabulary to illustrate the difficulty with which this principle is applied. The constant struggle of the believer

with self and personal ambition means there tend to be times when the will is not surrendered to God and thus must be "revived, renewed, rededicated or recommitted."

Absolute Surrender

The two terms "surrender" and "seeking" go hand in glove. When Christians seek God, it is a process; when they surrender, it is the product. Seeking God is an action described with a transitive verb; being surrendered is a state of being, the result of seeking. Christians do not automatically surrender because they may not know what to surrender or how to surrender, or they may not have the ability to surrender. They just cannot give up their "sins" or "habits," or they cannot deny the flesh. So they pray, which is seeking God.

Christians seek God's help to surrender, or they seek to get rid of hidden sins or to affirm a Bible truth that will help them surrender. Seeking God usually comes before surrendering to God. However, seeking and surrendering usually hopscotch. Seeking leads to surrender, resulting in a deeper seeking that leads to a deeper level of surrender.

The biblical call to surrender is proclaimed throughout the pages of Scripture, but perhaps nowhere is it clearer than in Romans 12:1,2. Here the apostle Paul concludes a largely theological treatise by calling upon the readers to make practical applications by presenting themselves "a living sacrifice." The sacrifice of their lives is the same as surrendering to God:

> I beseech you therefore, brethren, by the mercies of God, that you present your bodies a living sacrifice, holy, acceptable to God, which is your reasonable service. And do not be conformed to this world, but be transformed by the renewing of your mind, that you may prove what is that good and acceptable and perfect will of God.

The apostle Paul used the term "beseech" (*parakaleo*) in his appeal to surrender rather than another term that might have had a greater degree of authority inherent in it. The term "beseech," however, is an appeal to a sentiment already existing in the heart. It calls for an emotional response. In Romans 12:1 it occurs alongside of "present" (*paristanai*), which in contrast is a technical term referring to the presentation of a sacrificial animal to God (cf. Luke 2:22). The term is here found in the aorist tense, suggesting the idea of presenting ourselves to God once and for all.

There are two aspects of surrendering to God. First is the initial surrender (once and for all). It is the surrender to the ownership of God. The second surrender is a daily surrender; it is surrender for daily guidance. This is illustrated in driving a car to a stop light. The once-and-for-all surrender signifies the drivers' attitudes when they make up their minds that they will obey all stop signs. They decide once and for all that they will stop at all red lights. They have surrendered to the authority of the laws. The daily surrender is illustrated when they approach a stop sign, and stop. They make a daily submission to the authority of the stop sign because they made a once-for-all submission.

Christians once-and-for-all surrender to the authority of Christ. They will not lie. When the temptation to lie faces them, they don't debate the pragmatics of what a lie will do for them. They make daily submissions to the authority of Christ. They tell the truth. Some have likened the once-for-all surrender to a big YES, and the daily surrender to a little yes.

Some commentators have stumbled over the apostle's use of the term "bodies" in Romans 12:1, but there is no reason to believe that Paul meant anything more than the presentation of the entire person. The word "body" is the comprehensive term for the whole person — body, soul and spirit (1 Thess. 5:23) — much as we might use the term "self" today. Paul probably used the word "body" in a desire to be consistent with the sacrificial theme in this statement.

The act of presenting one's self to God is foundational to sanctification. This assumes a continual growth in grace after a postconversion crisis in which the will or self is definitely and completely surrendered or yielded to God. This is the means whereby the believer enters into the deeper Christian life.

The surrender for which the apostle calls is

none other than the surrender of the will. In many respects, the sacrifices of wealth or influence might be easier for some to offer than to surrender to the will of God. This total surrender or absolute surrender is total to the Christian, but relative to God.

Christians dedicate their lives as completely as possible, but they are not perfect. They may search for secret sins and yield them to God. Even in the act of complete surrender, they have some hidden sins (hidden to them), that are unknown to them. Their levels of surrender move them closer to God. They rejoice in their dedication and new depth of fellowship with God, but they are not sinlessly perfect, nor are their acts of surrender perfect. Only after death or the rapture will they be sinless, a state also called glorification.

The image used by Paul in calling for this surrender of will is that of a living sacrifice. The use of this image naturally causes one to think in terms of the sacrificial system of Israel, particularly as the term is used in the context of a major discourse on Israel (Rom. 9–11). Of the five principal sacrifices of the Levitical system, the whole burnt offering is most likely the context in which this challenge should be understood.

In the context of the whole burnt offering, several significant principles illustrate the nature of this surrender to God. First, it is a call to sacrifice that which is most prized (Lev. 1:3,10). Second, the "faith" nature of this sacrifice is seen in the practice of laying on of hands (v. 4). Third, this act was usually accompanied by confession of sin to God. Fourth, the unique feature of the whole burnt offering was that it was completely consumed on the altar.

Seeking God

The abuses of some groups in the areas of "tarrying" and "seeking" (praying at the church altar) have influenced some conservative Christians to deny the biblical doctrine of seeking God both in faith and practice. Throughout the Scriptures, however, there are numerous commands, promises and illustrations that instruct a Christian to seek God. To neglect or ignore this doctrine is to neglect and ignore an important part of the revelation of God.

The various abuses of others necessitate first a clear identification of the meaning of "seeking God." To seek God means more than searching after a hidden God, because God is in all places present to reveal Himself to those who have eyes of faith to behold Him. Neither can the phrase "seeking God" be passed off as a meaningless idiom. Seeking God is the sincere attempt to reestablish deep communion and fellowship with God through intense prayer, concentrated Bible study and unswerving obedience to the revelation of God.

1. Conditions for seeking God. Several Scriptures identify the need to prepare the heart to seek God (1 Chron. 19:13). Among those conditions of the heart identified as prerequisite to seeking God are (1) repentance (Jer. 26:19), (2) brokenness (Jer. 50:4), (3) separation (Ezra 6:21), (4) humility, (2 Chron. 7:14; 33:12), (5) desire (Ps. 119:10), (6) faith (Rom. 9:32), (7) diligence (Heb. 11:6), (8) unity (Jer. 50:4), (9) rejoicing (1 Chron. 16:10), (10) fearing the Lord (Hosea 3:5) and (11) meekness (Zeph. 2:3).

2. Barriers to seeking God. The Bible suggests several reasons people do not seek God. Some do not seek Him because they do not know how, or they do not have an example of others seeking God, or they have never heard about it. Beyond these reasons, other excuses are given why people do not seek God. The Scriptures identify (1) sin (Ps. 119:155; Acts 17:30), (2) pride (Ps. 10:4; Hos. 7:10), (3) ignorance (Rom. 3:11; Acts 17:30), (4) security (Isa. 31:1), (5) faithlessness (Rom. 9:32), (6) failure to confess sin (Hos. 5:15) and (7) wrong doctrine (Acts 8:18-24) as barriers to seeking God.

3. Strategy for seeking God. The Scriptures record no directions about how to seek God, perhaps because it is an emotional experience that varies with the individual. Yet repeated examples in Scripture suggest various aspects of a biblical strategy before, during and after the effort of seeking God.

When people sought God in the Old Testament, they often prepared by stating their commitment to seek Him. This was expressed in (1) a covenant (2 Chron. 15:12), (2) an expression of desire (Ps. 19:10), (3) a willingness to continue (1 Chron. 16:10) or (4) a vow (2 Chron. 15:14).

The process by which they sought God included (1) the study of Scripture (Ps. 119:94), (2) prayer (Exod. 32:11; Ezra 8:23), (3) supplications (Dan. 9:3), (4) fasting (2 Sam. 12:16), (5) repentance (Jer. 26:19) and (6) responding to the Scriptures with obedience (Ezra 7:10).

Significant examples of seeking God in Scripture resulted in (1) building the Temple (1 Chron. 22:19), (2) keeping the Passover (2 Chron. 30:19) and (3) teaching the Law (Ezra 7:10).

Communion with Christ

Usually six acts in the experience of the believer are associated with entering into communion with Christ so a person may have power with Christ.

1. Knowledge. The first step in experiencing communion with Christ is knowledge. The apostle Paul often used the "do you not know" formula when introducing some aspect of the Christian experience (Rom. 6:3) For some, merely understanding aspects of the believer's togetherness with Christ—such as the person's position in Christ and full union with Him—is the beginning of a deeper communion with Christ. Truth cannot be fully appreciated unless it is at least partially understood intellectually.

2. Repentance. Repentance of known sin is the second aspect of entering into deeper communion. Repentance of sin is known by other words. It is called "turning from sin," "cleansing of sin" or "purging". All these phrases mean that the believer goes through the following actions: (1) searches the heart for sin that blocks fellowship with God, (2) sincerely begs forgiveness for sin (John 1:9), (3) asks God to forgive his or her sins by the blood of Jesus Christ (1 John 1:7) and (4) promises to learn lessons from the experience so it doesn't happen again.

Repentance is more than turning from known sin in our lives. It involves being aware of a lack of God-consciousness or communion with Christ. We must recognize we do not always seek God in prayer and we do not always try to walk by faith.

Repentance involves the confession of sin. During times of revival, sin is often confessed freely and publicly by those seeking the revival blessing. Often this practice of confession helps believers enter into the revival experience and encourages others to rejoice in what God is doing in their lives and to pray for them as they struggle with past sins. Also, the confession of one believer may lead others to honestly face sin in their lives and help initiate the process of revival in the lives of others.

Despite these positive results of the public confession of sin, at other times the confession of sin seems to hinder revival from taking place or leads to a waning of the revival experience in the church. Also, public confession of sin may sometimes embarrass or misrepresent others in the church and create a host of problems in that regard. In times of revival, public confession of sin may help or hinder the progress of the revival.

Confession of sin should be done in accordance with certain principles consistent with the teaching of Scripture. First, sin should be confessed to God because sin is essentially an offense against Him. Second, sin should be confessed only as publicly as the sin is known. If a man wrongs his wife in a minor way, he should confess that sin to God and his wife, but confessing it to a larger group may serve only to unnecessarily embarrass his wife. Third, a person should be careful in confessing not to include personal references to others who may have been involved. The purpose of confession is to cleanse the conscience and rebuild credibility, not to accuse others of faults.

Finally, there is a place for publicly confessing the corporate sin of a group when that sin is broadly practiced and is clearly offensive to God. When this is done, the person wording the confession should be prepared to so identify with the offenders as to experience personal guilt associated with that sin. Also, this kind of confession should be accompanied by intercessory prayer to God, asking for forgiveness and restoration. This was a common experience with several Old Testament prophets who called their people back to God.

3. Faith. Often, entering into communion with Christ is a matter of acting by faith on the Word of God. A person should appropriate the deeper life by faith just as one appropriates eternal life

by faith at salvation. Obviously, living by faith is an experience of the deeper life. Faith is more than a doctrinal statement of faith and more than the faith involved in initial salvation. It is also the basis of communion with Christ. It is possible for Christians to experience a faith greater than their own. Believers can live by the faith of Christ (Gal. 2:16,20).

How do believers enter the deeper life faith? First, faith is acting on the Word of God, so believers must obey the scriptural commands. Second, faith is applying the Word of God to their lives, so believers know what the Bible teaches about living in the power of "Christ's faith." Third, believers must let Christ control them so the power of Christ's faith can flow through them.

The deeper life of faith is the result of an intentional effort of believers to have communion with God. People do not accidentally stumble into spirituality, nor does it sneak up on them. The life of faith is an intentional walk with with God. No one aimlessly meanders through the Bible to find communion with God.

4. Yielding. The idea of surrendering or yielding to God is fundamental in virtually all deeper-life literature. Andrew Murray reflected this emphasis in calling a series of Keswick messages by the general title "Absolute Surrender." Phoebe Palmer, a leader among revivalistic Methodists in the nineteenth century, urged her hearers to place all on the altar and allow the altar to sanctify.

But when people yield their lives to God, it is more than becoming passive. They take control of their lives by deciding where they will obey. When they yield to God, they decide not to yield to their sinful natures or to the influences of ungodly friends. They decide not to yield to unbiblical demands on their lives. Yielding is both intentional and knowledgeable. First, you know what should not control your life (sin, temptation or harmful influence). Second, you know that God desires and is able to control your life. Third, you actively turn over the controls to Him.

There must be an initial yielding of your life to God. For some, this comes at salvation and remains an attitude for life. This person experiences constant communion with Christ. Others must yield constantly because they constantly stray from Christ. But each time they return to Him, they renew communion with Him.

Many things happen to your spiritual life when you yield your life to Christ. Yielding is a "neutral action" that is incorporated in several spiritual activities. These include (1) being filled with the Spirit, (2) understanding the Scriptures, (3) praying effectively, (4) living by faith and (5) being led by the Spirit. The action of yielding does not make you spiritual. The Person to whom you yield makes you spiritual. Christ is the measure of our spirituality.

5. *Obeying*. The attitude of yielding must be continued in the act of obedience. Some oppose the idea of a deeper life on the ground that it is inherently opposed to aggressive soul winning. In many cases, Christians claiming to have the deeper life have been guilty of a passive approach to Christian experience and evangelism. In fairness to the great deeper-life men of the past, they were great soul winners. During his 18 years as pastor of Moody Church in Chicago, Dr. H. A. Ironside saw public professions of faith in Christ on all but two Sundays. The reputation of many deeper-life missionaries such as J. Hudson Taylor is also well known.

6. *Crucifying self*. A final aspect of maintaining intimacy in communion with Christ is crucifying self or taking up one's cross. In deeper-life litera-ture, this often takes the form of a call to holiness. The Bible teaches that the old nature (old man, self, flesh) was crucified in the past act of Christ's death. Now, the believer must act on what has happened. The sin nature has been crucified. Believers cannot put their sinful urges to death out of their own power. Therefore, they must act on the power of calvary to crucify self.

Jesus identified bearing one's cross as a mark of discipleship (Luke 9:23; 14:27). This is not a reference to physically being crucified. Rather, the believer should (1) yield, (2) not seek sin, (3) obey and (4) claim the power over sin that comes from the accomplishments of the death of Christ. To take up one's cross is to apply the results of calvary to one's life.

References: [1]Bill Bright, *The Christian and the Holy Spirit* (Arrowhead Springs, Calif.: Campus Crusade for Christ, 1968), p. 16. Also see Elmer Towns, *Understanding the Deeper Life*, (Grand Rapids: Fleming Revell Co., 1988).

FUNDAMENTALS OF THE FAITH

The irreducible essence of Christianity that includes the verbal inspiration of Scripture, the deity of Christ (as reflected in the virgin birth), substitutionary atonement, physical resurrection and the bodily return of Jesus Christ.

G

Timothy apparently acquired giftedness similar to that of the apostle.

GARDINER, ALLEN FRANCIS (1794–1851)

Pioneer missionary to the native people of Latin America.

Following several unsuccessful attempts to begin missionary work in South Africa, former British naval officer Captain Allen Gardiner redirected his attention to Chile, then Tierra del Fuego. The native people resisted his efforts, and when supplies failed to arrive, Gardiner and his six companions starved to death. Although his attempts failed to achieve their desired goal, the South American Missionary Society he established survived him, eventually expanding into southern Chile and Paraguay. Gardiner's efforts represent the first Protestant effort to evangelize the native people of Latin America.

Gardiner's greatest contribution to evangelism came through his death. His example of heroism attracted both missionary candidates and financial resources to continue the work he began in evangelizing the native people of Latin America.

GHOST-TOWN DISEASE

A terminal church-growth condition occurring when the church community disintegrates as people leave the community and others do not move in. More common in remote and rural communities. Formerly known as "old age."

GIFT ASSIMILATION

The tendency of receptive people to assimilate the gift of those who minister to them. The biblical principle that "like produces like" suggests that people tend to assimilate the gifts of those with whom they are most closely associated (i.e., gifted teachers tend to produce their gifts in others). Some find a biblical basis for gift assimilation in Paul's exhortation to Timothy "to stir up the gift of God which is in you through the laying on of my hands" (2 Tim. 1:6). Through his prolonged association with Paul in ministry,

GIFT CONFIDENCE

A characteristic common to Christians who know and have accepted their unique giftedness. Gift confidence enables a person to use his or her gifts effectively in ministry without undue concern for ministry left undone that falls outside his or her area of giftedness. It also implies confidence in other members of the ministry team to use their gifts to accomplish ministry better performed by them. This approach to ministry effectively eliminates ministry motivated exclusively out of a sense of guilt or duty. Further, it suggests an approach to ministry that minimizes the possibility of such attitudes as jealousy and anxiety. The Christian characterized by gift confidence tends to find a place on the ministry team and work harmoniously with others toward accomplishing a common goal or task.

GIFT GRAVITATION

The tendency to be attracted to others who have a similar dominant gift or gift mix. Many times Christians are attracted to others who have the view of gift assimilation (i.e., becoming like their "role model"). As an illustration, some ministerial candidates who have the embryonic gift of teaching tend to apply to a seminary in which many faculty members are known as gifted teachers, while similar candidates gifted in evangelism tend to apply to seminaries whose faculty members are actively involved in evangelistic ministry.

In the context of a local church, gift gravitation tends to be one of the factors resulting in church types based on a certain strength of worship paradigms or ministry styles.

Reference: See TYPES OF CHURCH GROWTH, OR WORSHIP TYPES.

GIFT IGNORANCE

A condition experienced by some Christians who

are unsure of their spiritual gifts but seem to function well in ministry regardless. This condition apparently stands in contrast to the biblical injunction to know and understand one's giftedness (1 Cor. 12:1).

How to Overcome Gift Ignorance

Gift ignorance may be overcome through a study of spiritual gifts and going through the process of discovering one's personal giftedness. In recent years, a number of books have been written on the subject of spiritual gifts that may help one gain a better understanding of the subject. As one studies the characteristics of these gifts, he or she may be able to identify areas of commonality that suggest the probability of giftedness in a particular area. Often the counsel of those who know you and the subject of gifts can assist you in identifying your gift.

Many Christians find the use of a Spiritual Gift Inventory Questionnaire helpful in the process of discovery. These questionnaires guide the user to respond to selected attitudinal statements that tend to be characteristic of those gifted in various areas. The responses suggest probable areas of giftedness. When one's gift is used in ministry, maximum effectiveness is achieved with minimal effort.

References: Kay Arthur, *How to Discover Your Spiritual Gifts* (Chattanooga, Tenn.: Reach Out, Inc., 1977); Tim Blanchard, *A Practical Guide to Finding Your Spiritual Gifts* (Wheaton, Ill.: Tyndale House Publishers, Inc., 1979); Larry Gilbert, *Team Ministry: A Guide to Spiritual Gifts and Lay Involvement* (Lynchburg, Va.: Church Growth Institute, 1987); Leslie B. Flynn, *19 Gifts of the Spirit* (Wheaton, Ill.: Victor Books, 1983); The Sunday School Board of the Southern Baptist Convention, *Discovering Your Spiritual Gifts* (Nashville: The Sunday School Board of the Southern Baptist Convention, 1981); C. Peter Wagner, *Your Spiritual Gifts Can Help Your Church Grow* (Ventura, Calif.: Regal Books, 1979; revised edition, 1994). See SPIRITUAL GIFT INVENTORY.

GIFT IMITATION

The tendency of a person to imitate the giftedness of another respected Christian.

GIFT INTRUSION

The tendency of a person to compel others to fit a particular ministry mold based on one's unique gift mix.

GIFT MANIPULATION

The tendency of a person to attempt to use gifts he or she does not actually possess to accomplish ministry.

GIFT MIX

The unique blending of the spiritual gifts of an individual Christian or group of Christians.

Reference: See SPIRITUAL GIFT INVENTORY.

GIVING, GIFT OF

One of the task-oriented gifts of the Holy Spirit; the ability to invest material resources in other persons and ministries to further the purpose of God. The strengths of this gift include (1) the ability to organize one's personal life to make money, (2) the desire to give quietly and secretly, (3) a tendency to give out of a sense of need, (4) a sincere desire to see a ministry grow, (5) sensitivity to quality, (6) personal involvement with giving and (7) a tendency to become a positive role model for others.

Among the problems of this gift are: (1) others may feel a person gives for an outward impression, (2) others may feel a person overemphasizes money and (3) may be perceived as being selfish. The individual who has this gift needs to avoid the danger of (1) pride, (2) measuring others' spirituality by his or her prosperity or (3) insensitivity to the needs of others because of his or her apparent lack of personal discipline.

GOAL SETTING

The process of targeting numerical and other forms of growth by faith over a specific period of time.

How to Set Goals

Several kinds of goals should be considered when setting ministry goals. Be careful about devoting all your energy toward the accomplishment of a single goal, no matter how worthy that goal may be. A church that sets a goal to baptize 200 converts in one year may only baptize 187, falling short of its goal by 13. But if the goal of baptizing 200 was accompanied by other goals relating to outreach efforts, church attendance and conversions, that church can rejoice in God's blessing upon its ministry. Setting several goals will create momentum and excitement in the church. A church should set several ministry goals and several kinds of goals to give direction to its ministry.

Attendance goals. Usually, a church will not grow unless it aims to grow. First, set a long-range attendance goal. How many people would you like to see attending church in the next 5 to 10 years? Next, set an annual goal. This goal will keep your vision lifted and a challenge before the people. Then set a goal for a high day in the spring and/or fall.

Output goals. Now that goals have been discussed, they need to be refined. Among the goals you set, you will need some output goals. These are the "bottom line" of expected results. In computer terminology, "output" is the result of what you put into the computer.

Input goals. These are steps that need to be taken to reach a goal. Just as certain causes lead to effects, so input goals include the things you need to do to reach your output goals. Input goals deal with such factors as the number of new prospects enrolled, the number of visits made and the number of phone calls made.

The next step in goal setting involves communication. Educate your people so they know and can work toward accomplishing the goals. Advertising the goals will help people identify with them and help build excitement and enthusiasm. Unless everyone accepts the goal, it will not achieve its objective. Remember, goals must be bought and owned or they will not motivate church members to work for growth.

Be sure to set reachable goals. Goals that are unreachable discourage people and kill momentum. A missed goal is like a broken bone in the body—it takes a long time to heal. When you set an unreachable goal and fail to reach it, church members will be reluctant to support a reachable goal the next time. Set SMART goals when you set goals—those that are Specific, Measurable, Attainable, Reachable and on a Time Table.

SMART GOALS
Specific
Measurable
Attainable
Reachable
Time Table

Know the strengths and weaknesses of your church before setting your goals. If members have a wide personal sphere of influence outside the church, you will have a larger prospect base with which to work. Conversely, if the church is inbred and has few contacts outside the church, it will be more difficult to find the needed prospects.

Sometimes a church has problems and it is not the time to reach out. If someone is experiencing a death or crisis, the members are preoccupied with the problems and are not mentally ready to reach out for growth. Knowing your strengths will help you feel the pulse of your group. Also, if the church has gone through a split, financial crisis, leadership problems or other major setback, it should evaluate carefully when would be the best time for an outreach campaign. Just as there are times when the sick need to go to bed to recuperate, so there is a time for church inreach instead of outreach.

Examine past statistics to determine the best time to plan an outreach day, the day you want people to bring their friends, relatives, associates and neighbors to church. Generally, the best-attended Sunday in the fall of the year tends to be the last Sunday in October (time-change Sunday). The largest attended day in the spring traditionally is Easter. The second largest attended Sunday in the spring is Mother's Day.

Pray for God's guidance in setting your goals. Set a goal to do what you believe God wants you to do. Long before you set an attendance goal or choose an outreach campaign, add the item to your prayer list. (1) Ask God to give you wisdom in setting goals and campaigns. (2) Pray about them until you feel comfortable about the goal or campaign. (3) Consider the problems and barriers before publicly announcing the task. (4) When you finally make a decision by prayer, then get off your knees and make it work out in reality.

One of the unique features of the leaders of growing churches around the world is that they are people of faith. Setting goals is an expression of faith. When a church sets a goal, it is expressing what it believes God wants to do in its fellowship. Refusing to set goals is not characteristic of spirituality. Sometimes it is more reflective of a church's unwillingness to trust God.

Make sure your goals are biblical (i.e., are consistent with biblical principles). Prooftexting is not enough; goals should grow out of Bible study and be in harmony with the Scriptures. This is always a good procedure when attempting to discern the will of God.

References: Truman Brown, *Church Planning a Year at a Time* (Nashville: Convention Press, 1991); Ted Engstrom, *Ministry Planning and Goal Setting* (Lynchburg, Va.: Church Growth Institute, 1992). See FAITH PROJECTION.

GOD

The Creator, Sustainer, Judge and One in whose image humans are made. The nature of God includes: (1) Spirit, (2) Person, (3) Life, (4) Self-Existence, (5) Immutability, (6) Unlimited by time and space and (7) Unity, which means God is one God. God is spirit, infinite, eternal and unchangeable in His being, wisdom, power, holiness, justice, goodness and truth.

GORDON, ADONIRAM JUDSON (1846–1895)

Pastor, missionary executive and educator.

Born in New Hampton, New Hampshire, on April 13, 1846, A. J. Gordon was converted to Christ at about age 15. Sensing the call of God upon his life about a year later, Gordon trained at the New London Academy, Brown University and Newton Theological Seminary. In 1863, he became a pastor of a Baptist church at Jamaica Plain, near Boston, Massachusetts. Six years

later, he was called to the Clarendon Street Baptist Church, where he remained pastor for more than 25 years.

While at Clarendon Street Baptist Church, he began editing a monthly magazine named *Watchword* (1878), became chairman of the Executive Committee of the American Baptist Missionary Union (1888) and founded the Boston Missionary Training School (1889), which has since become Gordon College and Divinity School. Gordon was one of the more prominent speakers in Moody's Northfield Conventions. He also wrote several books and hymns. He died on February 2, 1895.

A. J. Gordon's greatest contribution to evangelism came through his establishing a school to train missionaries, a school that continues today. His personal ministry also motivated and encouraged missionaries. He also provided leadership for his denominational missionary efforts.

GOSPEL: DEFINITION

(Greek *euggelion*, i.e., good news). The content of what a person must believe for salvation—Christ died for our sins according to the Scriptures, and that He was buried, and that He rose again the third day, according to the Scriptures (1 Cor. 15:1-5). The gospel is both a proposition and a person. The proposition is the death, burial and resurrection of Jesus Christ. The Person is Jesus Christ Himself, the object of belief.

GOSPEL: DESCRIPTION

The word "gospel" comes from an Anglo-Saxon term meaning "good news." The term originated from the New Testament word *euangelion*, "good news, message."

The gospel is succinctly stated by the apostle Paul in 1 Corinthians 15:1-5. Thus, the gospel message is the heart of Christianity. It was central to the evangelistic work of the Early Church.

The term "gospel" also refers to the four New Testament books (Matthew, Mark, Luke, John), which record the life and teachings and the death, burial and resurrection of Jesus. The central message of the gospel summarized in 1 Corinthians 15:1-5—the death, burial and resurrection of

Jesus—is given in much more detail in the Gospel accounts in the New Testament.—ALR

GRACE

Unmerited favor.

Paul described "the grace of God that brings salvation" (Titus 2:11). Because people cannot save themselves, grace is the necessary basis and motivation that brings the experience of salvation to them. Then, revealing the progressive nature of salvation, believers are expected to "grow in grace" as part of their experience of sanctification. As such, grace becomes an important part of the doctrine of salvation.

The Greek noun *charis* originally came from a verb that meant to make a gift, including the idea of forgiving a debt or wrong. It came to include the forgiveness of sin. Commenting on this word as it occurs in Ephesians 2:8, W. Curtis Vaughan notes:

The phrase by grace, which has the place of emphasis in verse 8, expresses the means by which men are saved—not by weeping, not by their own willing, not through their own works or efforts, but by sovereign grace. But what is grace? The word is used more than one hundred fifty times in the New Testament (almost a hundred times by Paul alone) and with a wide variety of meanings. But its basic meaning is that of "favor shown to the utterly undeserving." The words by grace assert that God was under no obligation to save man, that salvation is a bounty from God, not a reward for merit.[1]

The source of grace begins with God, and is more than His response to the human's request for salvation. Grace is an attribute of God that permits Him to save sinful humankind. Grace is an extension of the goodness of God toward humanity. According to Tozer:

Grace is the good pleasure of God that inclines Him to bestow benefits upon the undeserving. It is a self-existent principle inherent in the divine nature and appears to us as a self-caused propensity to pity the wretched, spare the guilty, welcome the outcast, and bring into favor those who were before under just disapprobation. Its use to us sinful men is to save us and make us sit together in heavenly places to demonstrate to the ages the exceeding riches of God's kindness to us in Christ Jesus.[2]

The concept of grace in the Scriptures is not limited exclusively to the New Testament. It is true that Jesus Christ is the Revealer of grace (John 1:17), but it is also true that grace characterized God and His actions in the Old Testament. The Hebrew word for grace is *hen*. Defining this Old Testament term, J. H. Stringer notes:

This is not a covenant word and not two-way. It is used of the action of a superior, human or divine, to an inferior. It speaks of undeserved favor, and it is translated "grace" (38 times) and "favor" (26 times)....No one can show *hen* to God (as no one can show *hesed*), for no one can do Him a favor.[3]

Salvation never has or will exist apart from the grace of God. Conservative Christians agree that salvation is all of grace and not of works. Most Christians would wholeheartedly agree with the following observation of Tozer:

No one was ever saved other than by grace, from Abel to the present moment. Since mankind was banished from the eastward Garden, no one has ever returned to the divine favor except through the sheer goodness of God. And wherever grace found any man it was always by Jesus Christ. Grace indeed came by Jesus Christ, but it did not wait for his birth in the manger or his death on the cross before it became operative. Christ is the Lamb slain from the foundation of the world. The first man in human history to be reinstated in the fellowship of God came through faith in Christ. In olden times men looked forward to Christ's redeeming work, in later times they gazed back on it but always they came and they came by grace, through faith.[4]

References: [1]W. Curtis Vaughan, *The Letter of the Ephesians* (Nashville: Convention Press, 1963). [2]Aiden Wilson Tozer, *The Knowledge of the Holy: The Attributes of God: Their Meaning in the Christian Life* (New York: HarperCollins, 1961), p. 100. [3]J. H. Stringer, "Grace" *The New Bible Dictionary*, ed. J. D. Douglas (Grand Rapids: Wm. B. Eerdmans Publishing Co., 1977), p. 491. [4]Tozer, *The Knowledge of the Holy: The Attributes of God: Their Meaning in the Christian Life*, p. 102.

GRAHAM, WILLIAM (BILLY) FRANKLIN, JR. (1918-)

International evangelist.

Billy Graham was born near Charlotte, North Carolina, and was raised in a Christian home atmosphere by church-going parents. At age 16, Graham was converted to Christ during an evangelistic campaign led by Mordecai F. Ham, a tent evangelist. In 1936, Graham began classes at Bob Jones University, but transferred to Florida Bible Institute in Tampa in 1937. He struggled with a call to a preaching ministry. One evening in March 1938, on a golf course near the Bible Institute, Graham surrendered himself to a life of gospel preaching.

From 1940-1943, Graham attended Wheaton College in Wheaton, Illinois. There he met and married Ruth Bell, the daughter of Dr. and Mrs. Nelson Bell, Presbyterian missionaries to China. Graham became an evangelist for Youth for Christ in 1944 and made two evangelistic trips to England. He also served as the president of Northwestern Bible College in Minneapolis, Minnesota, (1947-1951).

Graham's evangelistic efforts in Los Angeles in 1949 brought him national attention. Before the crusade at Forest Home, a Christian conference center in California founded by Henrietta Mears, Graham committed himself completely to the lordship of Christ and to preach the Word of God on the authority of God. Thereafter, he became even more determined to preach what "the Bible says."

As a result of the success of the Los Angeles Crusade, William Randolph Hearst gave the order to his newspaper people to "puff Graham." Suddenly, his crusades were the subject of many newspaper articles, and Graham appeared on the front pages of *Time*, *Newsweek* and *Life* magazines.

In 1950, Graham founded the Billy Graham Evangelistic Association, and "The Hour of Decision" radio program went on the air on November 5 of that year. Graham continued to preach, and each crusade grew larger until he conducted the largest crusades in the world. In 1954, the Graham team ministered in England and had remarkable results. This crusade ushered Graham into the international arena. In those years he published an important book— *Peace With God* (1953). In 1956, he was a major force in establishing the publication *Christianity Today*. Graham's stature in American society led him to become an unofficial spiritual advisor and confidant to many United States presidents, beginning with Dwight D. Eisenhower and continuing through Bill Clinton.

Criticism began to mount regarding the evangelist's positive stance on cooperative evangelism—meaning Graham's policy of working cooperatively with nonevangelical, mainline churches. This criticism came to a head in the summer of 1957 in the wake of the New York Crusade—one of the first nationally televised crusades. A number of fundamentalists broke with Graham because they believed that "decision cards" were not necessarily going to conservative churches for the follow-up of converts. They also charged that unconverted pastors were invited to sit on Graham's platform.

Other critics found fault with Graham's theological techniques. Reinhold Niebuhr believed that Graham oversimplifies moral issues to the detriment of his goal. Graham declares, "Every human problem can be solved and every hunger satisfied and every potential can be fulfilled when a man encounters Jesus Christ and comes in vital relation to God in him."

Graham accepts criticism and praise with equal composure, although he believes the majority of Christians support his cause. "Some of the extreme fundamentalists are among my most vocal critics," says Graham, "and extreme liberals think I'm too fundamentalist. But I think the vast majority of people support me."

Graham became involved in launching several important congresses on evangelism: Berlin (1966), Lausanne (1974) and Itinerant

Evangelist (1983, 1986). These congresses focused on world evangelism.

GRAPHS OF GROWTH

Charts mapping out the rise and fall of church membership and or attendance over a decade, used for diagnostic purposes. The most common are a 10-year line graph of composite membership and a 10-year bar graph of annual growth rates.

GREAT AWAKENING See FIRST GREAT AWAKENING and SECOND GREAT AWAKENING

GREAT COMMISSION

Evangelism may be described as including those activities whose primary purpose is that of fulfilling the mandate expressed in the Great Commission. This Commission has been called "the evangelistic mandate of the Church." In many respects, one's view of evangelism is dependent upon one's emphasis in interpreting this Commission. It is therefore reasonable to assume that an adequate view of evangelism is dependent upon a complete understanding of this Commission.

The Great Commission was given at five different times in separate locations. On each occasion, the Lord added to the previous command, and the reader must see the total picture to understand the full implication of the Great Commission.

The Great Commission was initially given on the afternoon of the Resurrection to 10 disciples. Jesus said, "As the Father has sent Me, I also send You" (John 20:21). Jesus was simply giving His perplexed disciples a Commission to represent Him. Here, Jesus compares His sending out of the apostles with the Father's sending of Jesus to the world. At this place, the message, destination and task were not given to them. Perhaps they were not ready to receive it. Commenting on the Commission that resulted in the Incarnation, Gottfried Osei-Mensah notes:

To whom was Jesus sent? He was sent by the Father to a lost humanity; to men and

women spiritually dead in sin (John 3:16). Jesus identified completely with those to whom He was sent. To them He brought God's message of salvation and the offer of eternal life to all who would believe in Him (John 17:2,3). The world did not receive Him kindly. It was openly hostile....We have the same Gospel to share, which we have received ourselves (1 Corinthians 15:3-5). The Lord has already warned us that the world will be hostile to us, as it was to Him (John 17:14,15). Nevertheless we should seek to love and care for those to whom we are sent, without losing our Christian identity.[1]

A week later in the Upper Room, Thomas was present—now counting 11 disciples. Jesus told them, "Go into all the world and preach the gospel to every creature" (Mark 16:15). Two aspects were added to the Commission. First, they were not just to minister to Israel, but also to the world. Second, they were to preach the gospel to every person in the world.

Mark's account of the Great Commission is found in a disputed passage of the Gospel. Although Mark 16:9-20 is absent in both Codex Sinaiticus and Codex Vaticanus, the author believes its presence in nearly all other manuscript copies of the Gospel suggests the likelihood of its authenticity. This account of the Commission stresses the role of preaching the gospel in evangelism. According to Gottfried Osei-Mensah:

The preaching of the Gospel is an awesome responsibility. The eternal destiny of the hearers is at stake. Mark emphasizes the response of men and women to the Gospel. Wherever it is faithfully preached, the Gospel always divides mankind into two groups. Those who believe in the Savior and submit to Him in baptism are saved. Those who disbelieve and reject His offer of forgiveness and new life must ultimately face His judgment and condemnation. Nevertheless, the Gospel is "Good News" and we must always preach for decision, earnestly seeking to persuade our hearers to turn to the Savior in personal faith and repentance (2 Corinthians 2:15,16).[2]

As noted, our understanding of the Great Commission tends to influence our view of evangelism. Evangelist Billy Graham tends to stress this version of the Commission in his ministry of evangelism. Commenting on the motives of the evangelist in an address to other evangelists, Graham noted:

But our primary motive, in my view, is the command of our commander-in-chief, the Lord Jesus Christ. We engage in evangelism today not because we want to, or because we choose to, or because we like to, but because we have been told to. We are under orders. Our Lord has commanded us to go, to preach, to make disciples— and that should be enough for us. Evangelistic inactivity is disobedience.[3]

The next time the Great Commission was repeated was at least two weeks later. The disciples were no longer in Jerusalem, but on a mountain in Galilee along with more than 500 brethren (1 Cor. 15:6). This Commission is given in a context that recognizes the unique authority of Christ in both heaven and earth. He assumed they would eventually obey, for He used the participle "as you are going" (Matt. 28:19, literal translation). On this basis, Jesus sends out His followers to "make disciples of all the nations" (v. 19). This task of disciple making is essential to the work of evangelism, according to Kassoum Keita, pastor of the Evangelical Church in Bomako, Mali. Addressing the Second International Congress for Itinerant Evangelists in Amsterdam, he said:

Evangelism which does not make disciples does not conform to the New Testament model. Conversion must lead to service. The New Birth must lead to a new life of communion with Christ and of service to Christ.[4]

Indeed, this is the only imperative verb in Matthew's account of the Commission. The verbs "go," "baptizing" and "teaching" are all secondary to the primary verb "make disciples."

According to Robert Culver:

In this commission there is one dominant and controlling imperative, while all the other verb forms are participles. In the original Greek the central verb is formed on the noun for "disciple" and should be translated "make disciples" as it is in the American Standard Version. It is a first aorist imperative, second person plural. The word translated "go" is a participle and could be translated "going" or "as ye go." Likewise the words translated "baptizing" and "teaching" are participles. While these participles are immensely important the imperative "make disciples" is of superlative importance.[5]

The scope of this Commission is universal. The Greek word *ethne*, translated "nations," originally meant "a multitude" and is used in the New Testament to identify an ethnic group such as the Jews (cf. Luke 7:5; 23:2). Matthew himself seems to use this term in a way that suggests he was thinking of other than a political entity (cf. Matt. 24:7). Although the popular interpretation of this passage as a call to disciple the nations of the world is not outside the implied meaning, Matthew's use of this term may suggest that the Commission is to disciple the distinct people groups of the world.

Before one can effectively make disciples, it is necessary to determine the nature of a disciple. Clearly, this verb implies more than mere conversion, although conversion is included in this process. George Peters suggests a number of characteristics of a disciple, of which faith might be considered foundational. According to Peters:

A disciple of Christ is a believing person:
1. living a life of conscious and constant identification with Christ
   a. in life, death and resurrection
   b. in words, behavior, attitudes, motives and purposes
2. fully realizing Christ's absolute ownership of his life
3. joyfully embracing the saviorhood of Christ
4. delighting in the lordship of Christ
5. living by the abiding, indwelling resources of Christ

6. according to the imprinted pattern and purpose of Christ

7. for the chief end of glorifying his Lord and Saviour.[6]

The fourth giving of the Great Commission (Luke 24:46-48) stated that the gospel message must include repentance and belief. The Lucian account stresses the content of the message declared in the effort to evangelize the world. This emphasis is in harmony with Luke's stated purpose to write for Theophilus "that you may know the certainty of those things in which you were instructed" (Luke 1:4). The need for this emphasis is evidenced even today in the tendency of some committed to the fulfillment of the Commission to wander from the primary task of communicating the message of the gospel. According to Oswald Chambers:

It is easy to forget that the first duty of the missionary is not to uplift the heathen, not to heal the sick, not to civilize savage races, because all that sounds so rational and so human, and it is easy to arouse interest in it and get funds for it. The primary duty of the missionary is to preach "repentance and remission of sins in his name."[7]

In Luke's account, the emphasis of Jesus was "that repentance and remission of sins should be preached in His name to all nations, beginning at Jerusalem" (24:47). As in Matthew's account, this message is to be communicated "to all nations." It is significant that an urban area is mentioned in two of the three Lucian accounts of the Commission (Acts 1:8). Gottfried Osei-Mensah summarizes the strategies implied in this Commission as it relates to the preaching of repentance and forgiveness, noting:

How should we proclaim repentance? We need to emphasize that it was on account of my sins that Jesus died. My sins crucified Him. God commands me as a sinner to repent. Christ forgives each repentant sinner, but He will judge the unrepentant. Christ has broken sin's power for me, so I can live in righteousness for Him. How

should we encourage the assurance of forgiveness? By emphasizing that God lifts the crushing load of guilt from those He forgives. He washes away the stain of sin. He restores the repentant sinner to His favor because of Christ's death on the Cross. God's forgiveness brings inner joy and peace, and a fresh desire to love and serve Him. Blessed is the man whose sin is forgiven.[8]

The last reiteration of the Great Commission was given the same day at the Ascension. This account is unique in two respects. First, it includes a reference to the power of the Holy Spirit mentioned in the first account. Second, Christ calls on His disciples to be witnesses of Him in four distinct areas: Jerusalem, Judea, Samaria and "the end of the earth" (Acts 1:8).

These accounts of the Great Commission provide a theological foundation for the practice of evangelism. This foundation is summarized by Peters, who writes:

The Great Commission is more than just one commission among many commands of Christ. It is lifted out because of its singularity as a command of the risen Lord and of its restatement in one form or another by the four evangelists, each presenting it from his own point of view and with his own unique emphasis.[9]

Most significant, however, is the theological comprehensiveness of the Great Commission. It establishes the following facts:

1. The sovereignty of the Lord of the Christian gospel—"All authority has been given to Me" (Matt. 28:18; cf. Phil 2:9-11; Rev 3:7).
2. The imperative of the Christian gospel (Matt. 28:18-20; Mark 16:15,16; Luke 24:44-47).
3. The universality of the Christian gospel (Matt. 28:18-20; Mark 16:15,16; Luke 24:44-47; Acts 1:8).
4. The nature of the Christian gospel (Luke 24:46,47; John 20:23; Acts 26:15-23; cf. 1 Cor. 15:1-3).
5. The human instrumentality in the procla-

mation of the Christian gospel (Matt. 16:15,16; Luke 24:48; Acts 1:8; 26:16).

6. The need for spiritual equipment to minister successfully in the Christian gospel (Luke 24:49; John 20:22; Acts 1:8).

Thus, the Great Commission is made dynamic by a great theological substructure.

References: [1]Gottfried Osei-Mensah, "The Evangelist and the Great Commission" in *The Calling of an Evangelist* (Papers from The Lausanne Congress on Evangelism, 1974), p. 224. [2]Ibid., p. 223. [3]Billy Graham, "The Gift and Calling of the Evangelist" (Papers from The Lausanne Congress on Evangelism, 1974), p. 17. [4]Kassoum Keita, "The Evangelist's Goal: Making Disciples" in *The Calling of an Evangelist* (Papers from The Lausanne Congress on Evangelism, 1974), p. 211. [5]Robert D. Culver, "What Is the Church's Commission," *Bibliotheca Sacra* (July 1968): 244. [6]George W. Peters, *A Biblical Theology of Missions* (Chicago: Moody Press, 1972), p. 188. [7]Oswald Chambers, *So Send I You: A Series of Missionary Studies* (Fort Washington, Pa.: Oswald Chambers Publications Association and Christian Literature Crusade, 1975), p. 142. [8]Osei-Mensah, "The Evangelist and the Great Commission," p. 223. [9]Peters, *A Biblical Theology of Missions*, p. 176.

GREGORY (THAUMATURGUS)
(d. A.D. 270)

"Power" evangelist, primarily responsible for the evangelization of Pontus.

Born in Pontus into a pagan but wealthy and prominent home, Gregory was sent to Palestine for part of his education. There he studied philosophy under Origen and was converted to Christianity. Returning to Pontus in 240, he was made bishop of his city. Gregory used miracles as part of his evangelistic strategy to reach Pontus with the gospel, earning him the title "Thaumaturgus," meaning "miracle worker" or "worker of wonders." It is reported that only 17 Christians resided in Pontus when he became bishop, but through his efforts, only 17 pagans resided in Pontus at the time of his death.

Gregory is viewed by some as a third-century example of the evangelistic strategy known as "power evangelism" because he used Christian miracles to counteract the miracles claimed by pagan priests and demonstrate the superiority of Christianity.

GREGORY THE GREAT
(A.D. 540–640)

Pope of the Roman Catholic Church who launched missionary activity to England.

Born into a noble and affluent family of Rome, Gregory was given a legal education and pursued a career in government service that climaxed in his being appointed prefect of Rome in A.D. 573. Soon after that appointment, he used the fortune he had inherited from his father to establish seven monasteries in Rome and became a monk himself. From 579 to 585, he served as the Vatican ambassador to Constantinople. Upon his return to Rome, he became the abbot of St. Andrew's monastery. Upon the death of Pope Pelagius in 590, Gregory was chosen as the new Pope. He used that office to expand the influence of the Roman church, launching an aggressive missionary outreach to England. His expertise in administration resulted in the bishopric of Rome becoming one of the wealthiest in the Church of his day.

Gregory's greatest contribution to evangelism was his emphasis on missions, especially in his mission to England. During his reign, he extended the influence of Rome and is regarded by many historians as the first of the medieval Popes.

Gregory also introduced the Gregorian chant into the worship style of the Roman Catholic church, expanded the influence of Rome and shaped the theology of the medieval church.

Reference: Jonathan Scott, Albert Hyma and Arthur H. Noyes, *Readings in Medieval History* (New York: Appleton-Century-Crofts, Inc., 1933), pp. 88-94.

GREGORY THE ILLUMINATOR
(c. 240–c.332)

Pioneer missionary to Armenia in the third century.

Born into the Armenian aristocracy, Gregory was converted to Christianity while in exile in Caesarea in Cappadocia. Returning to his homeland, he preached the gospel throughout

Armenia. Although initially persecuted, Gregory eventually was able to count the king of Armenia among his early converts. The conversion of the king and support of the nobles resulted in a significant people movement, and Armenia became the first Christian nation in history. He has been described by the title "The Illuminator" because of his successful evangelization of Armenia.

GREIG, GARY S.

Dr. Gary S. Greig is Associate Professor of Hebrew and Old Testament in the School of Divinity at Regent University in Virginia Beach, Virginia. He is the former senior editor of Gospel Light Publications, Ventura, California, and former Adjunct Assistant Professor of Hebrew, Fuller Theological Seminary, Pasadena, California. He received a B.A. (Archaeology and Egyptology, 1983) from the Hebrew University, Jerusalem, Israel, did graduate study in the School of Theology at Fuller Seminary (1982-1983), Pasadena, California, and received an M.A. and Ph.D. (Near Eastern Languages and Civilizations, 1990) from the University of Chicago, Oriental Institute. He has published articles in scholarly publications and journals. In 1993, he and Kevin N. Springer coedited *The Kingdom and the Power* (Regal Books).

GRID MAPPING

The systematic notation of relevant research sites within a given community. In urban settings, this process generally involves identifying centers associated with spiritual quests and social bondage within six-square-block grids. — GOJR

GROUND-LEVEL SPIRITUAL WARFARE

A term coined by C. Peter Wagner to connote ministry activity that is associated with individual bondage and deliverance. — GOJR

GROWTH, MEASURING

The practice of identifying and evaluating the net church growth experienced over a specified period of time. Growth may be measured by the following criterion:

1. Attendance
2. Enrollment
3. Financial income
4. Physical facilities
5. Programs and services.

GROWTH, TRADITIONAL LAWS OF SUNDAY SCHOOL

A statement of church growth principles developed and used by Southern Baptists to administer growth in their Sunday Schools. They may be stated as follows:

1. Sunday Schools grow in proportion to their workers at a ratio of 10:1.
2. Sunday Schools grow when they have adequate facilities.
3. New units will produce more workers and growth than old units; therefore, there must be a continual dividing of units for multiplied growth.
4. Sunday Schools must grade by ages for growth.
5. Sunday School growth is directly tied to visitation.

References: J. N. Barnette, *The Pull of the People* (Nashville: Convention Press, 1956); Arthur Flake, *Building a Standard Sunday School* (Nashville: Convention Press, 1922).

GUTZLAFF, KARL (1803–1851)

Pioneer missionary to China and Thailand.

Dr. Karl Gutzlaff was one of the first two missionaries to Thailand in 1828. In a three-year period, he completed a draft translation of the whole Bible in the Thai language. The death of his wife and infant son, together with his own serious illness, resulted in his leaving his field of service never to return again.

Gutzlaff's greatest contribution to evangelism was his translation of the Bible into the Thai language.

HALDANE BROTHERS

James (1768-1851) Robert (1764-1842)
Two brothers, Robert and James Alexander, who were prominent leaders in the mid-nineteenth century revival. They served as effective revivalists in their native Scotland and also in Switzerland. Their disciples carried the revival to North America.

HAM, MORDECAI (1878-1959)

American evangelist.
Mordecai Ham was an effective citywide evangelist in the southern United States during the first half of the twentieth century. It is estimated he saw more than 33,000 conversions during his first year of ministry alone. More than 300,000 additions to Baptist churches throughout the south followed his citywide crusades. His strong stand against the use of alcoholic beverages earned him a reputation in the prohibition movement similar to that of Billy Sunday.

Ham's greatest contribution to evangelism was not the large crowds reached through his extensive ministry, but rather one convert in particular who responded during the invitation in his Charlotte, North Carolina, crusade: Billy Graham was converted under Mordecai Ham's preaching.

Reference: Edward E. Ham, *50 Years on the Battle Front with Christ: A Biography of Mordecai F. Ham* (Louisville: The Old Kentucky Home Revivalist, 1950).

HARVEST PRINCIPLE

The strategy of concentrating the maximum resources to reaching receptive people without bypassing more resistant people.

Reference: See RESISTANCE-RECEPTIVITY AXIS.

HARVEST THEOLOGY

The communication of the gospel that results in nonbelievers deciding to follow Jesus Christ as Savior and Lord.

Reference: See SEARCH THEOLOGY.

HEART

The heart figuratively is the center of the immaterial man, the seat of the conscious life in its moral, intellectual, volitional and emotional aspects.

HEART LANGUAGE

The mother tongue, the language used in most intimate communication. The language that is most effective in evangelism.

HELPERS

Members of the evangelism team gifted in the areas of ministry and/or administration responsible for record keeping and administration in team evangelism. Some members may be involved in more service-oriented ministry such as preparing meeting rooms or catering the fellowship meal.

Reference: See EVANGELISM, TEAM.

HIDDEN PEOPLE

A people group lacking a viable church capable of completing the evangelistic task through E-1 Evangelism. An unreached people group.

References: See E-1 EVANGELISM; PEOPLE GROUP.

HIGH PLACES

Specific locations where a community or its leaders pay obeisance to tutelary deities and/or idolatrous philosophies. In biblical contexts, the term is applied to literal mountains or towers that were elevated over the surrounding terrain.—GOJR

HISTORY OF EVANGELISM: SURVEY

"Evangelism" is a relatively new word in the

vocabulary of English-speaking Christians. It was apparently first used in print in the middle of the nineteenth century. By the beginning of the twentieth century, it was widely used by evangelicals to describe the work of making disciples. According to Charles McKay:

> In 1850, Charles Adams authored a book entitled *Evangelism In The Middle Of The Nineteenth Century*. Another in 1888 was written by Arthur T. Pierson under the title, *Evangelistic Work In Principle And Practice*. Since that time the term has come to indicate the major thrust of New Testament churches.[1]

Although the English word itself is of comparatively recent origin, the work of evangelism has been with the Church since Peter stood to address those who had gathered in Jerusalem for Pentecost. What happened that day, and in the days following, has continued in various forms until this present day. Evangelism is the means by which the Church of Jesus Christ has continued to communicate the message of the gospel from generation to generation.

Some students of evangelism recognize the existence of this ministry prior to establishing the Church on Pentecost. In the Old Testament, God chose Israel as a unique people in part to be "a light to the Gentiles" (Isa. 42:6). The Greek word translated "evangelist" in the New Testament is used in the *Septuagint* to describe the people of Jerusalem as those "who bring good tidings" (Isa. 40:9). Although God's intent for Israel was that they be engaged in the evangelism of the world, little evidence can be found of significant evangelistic outreach on the part of the nation. The most notable exception to this rule, Jonah, was himself hesitant to fulfill his mission and disappointed with the success of his ministry.

The Early Church

In the New Testament, the work of evangelism became the responsibility of the Church. On a mountain in Galilee, Jesus gave the embryonic church, a gathering of about 500 people (1 Cor. 15:6), the responsibility of making disciples "of

all the nations" (Matt. 28:19). At His ascension into heaven, Jesus suggested a geographic pattern of outreach (Jerusalem, Judea, Samaria, the end of the earth — Acts 1:8), which served as a pattern by which the Church did, in fact, reach its world for Christ.

The evangelistic activity of the apostles and the Early Church emphasized persuasive preaching of the gospel and establishing churches that conserved the results. A distinct urban missions emphasis was placed in that apostolic strategy and they established churches in the principal cities of their world (e.g., Jerusalem, Antioch, Ephesus, Corinth, Rome, etc.). This does not mean less urban areas were neglected. Rather, the churches established in these urban centers apparently became the means by which other communities were reached with the gospel and churches established in those settlements.

In many cities in Judea, churches were presumably established by people converted through the ministry of the Jerusalem church. Although Paul taught for two years in the school of Tyrannus at Ephesus, "All who dwelt in Asia heard the word of the Lord Jesus, both Jews and Greeks" (Acts 19:10). It is generally assumed this was accomplished through the church-planting efforts of Paul's students in other Asian communities rather than through apostolic ministry tours. It may also be reasonable to assume the church at Cenchrea was the result of an extension ministry of the church at Corinth.

The evangelistic activities of the Early Church were such that the enemies of the gospel accused it of having "filled Jerusalem with your doctrine" (Acts 5:28) and "turned the world upside down" (Acts 17:6). These charges are consistent with the apostolic evaluation of their own success in evangelism. Paul reminded the Colossians of the gospel, "Which has come to you, as it has also in all the world, and is bearing forth fruit, as it is also among you since the day you heard and knew the grace of God in truth" (Col. 1:6).

Evangelism continued throughout the patristic period of church history. Evidence of the success of the evangelistic efforts of the Early Church is seen not only in the continuation of the Christian faith in a generally hostile age, but also in the increased numbers of known churches in the world. Among the church fathers, several are remembered for their evangelistic ministry, including Tertullian, a Christian apologist, and John Chrysostom, considered the golden-mouthed preacher. Much of the writings of the church fathers dealt more directly with church problems than with evangelistic appeals. This does not mean, however, that they were not concerned about or involved in evangelism. Much of the apostolic literature also deals directly with church life, but Acts records their aggressive evangelistic outreach missions. It is unlikely Christianity would ever have risen to the position of being a contender as a state religion by the time of Constantine without a continued evangelistic emphasis during the patristic period.

Medieval Movements

After the Church and State united under Constantine, the character of the Church experienced a significant change. In the context of the Holy Roman Empire, all peoples of the empire were considered Christians, both members of the Church and citizens of the State. This fact, coupled with the limited data available from that period of history, makes it difficult to continue tracing the progress of evangelism by the Church. It is reasonable to assume some evangelism did take place within the established State Church, and genuine conversions were experienced in that context. But two other indicators prove the existence of significant evangelistic activity during this medieval period of history.

First, the existence of medieval evangelical sects, to some degree distinct from the established Church, suggests evidence of evangelism being carried on throughout this age. These sects are identified by various names and existed at different times in diverse places throughout the empire. Some have supposed a direct relationship between these sects can be traced from the apostolic church until this present day, but the lack of verifiable data makes it difficult to arrive at that conclusion. Rather, it is likely these sects represent isolated attempts to reestablish the evangelical character of the Church. Although what is known of their beliefs suggests some may have been viewed as cultic in a contemporary

context, many placed a strong emphasis on conversion through faith in Christ. These were Bernard of Clairvaux, Savana Rola and John Huss.

The second indicator of evangelism in the medieval period is the monastic movement. These movements are usually seen by church historians as an attempt to escape the corruption of the established church, a sort of introspective holiness movement. Although that may have been a significant factor in their continuity, the founders of these movements established their respective orders through an itinerant preaching ministry. These monastic orders also provided candidates to take their message to unevangelized areas such as Ireland and Scandinavia. Although specific doctrinal beliefs held by some of these orders may be inconsistent with contemporary evangelical theology, many of them showed concern in helping others live a simpler life of faith.

The Reformed Church

On October 31, 1517, Martin Luther posted his 95 Theses and launched a reformation of the Church that would have significant influence on the Church. The Protestant Reformation was a reaction against the obvious corruption of the established Church, and was a call to a simpler faith in Christ as the basis of a new religious order. The Reformation was established on the rediscovery of the doctrines of justification by faith alone and biblical authority over church cannons—two doctrines that remain foundational to much of today's evangelism by evangelical churches.

The success of the reformers in establishing reformed churches was as much a political as a religious accomplishment in many states. By supporting the reformers' efforts to break from the established church at Rome, political leaders also won their independence from church authority. Following the pattern set by the Holy Roman Empire, the reformed churches tended to identify with particular states (e.g., Lutheran Church (Germany), Evangelical Church (Switzerland), Reformed Church (Holland), Presbyterian Church (Scotland), Anglican Church (England). Because of their state affiliations, it is difficult to measure the evangelistic success of the Reformation. It is known, however, that the reform message was evangelical and had an emphasis on personal conversion. It can only be assumed that many within the reformed church were converted.

As a result of the increased interest in studying the Scriptures that accompanied the Reformation, the Bible was translated into the language of the people and widely read. Previously, the Scriptures had been available only to church leaders, many of whom could not read. But, because the Bible was viewed as the source of the Reformation itself, it was thought important to translate the Bible so the common people could read it for themselves. Martin Luther himself translated the Bible into German; the students of Erasmus took his Greek text and translated it into English and other languages. The availability of the Scriptures gave rise to more distinct evangelical sects during this period.

Some thought the reforms had not gone far enough and urged a return to a more simple faith as reflected in the apostolic church. Most notable of these were the Anabaptists of north and central Europe and the Lollards of England. These movements taught the Scriptures to the common people by using a strong evangelical emphasis. So effective were these groups that they were actively opposed by the established churches of their area. In Switzerland, the Swiss Brethren were drowned in mockery of their belief in believer's baptism. In Holland, Menno Simons evangelized the lowlands, giving birth to the Mennonite church. In England, these groups tended to be identified simply as nonconformists. Because of their emphasis on a regenerate church membership, the growth of the Anabaptist churches is a reasonable indicator of their evangelistic success.

The establishment of the reformed churches caused the lethargy that had characterized the Church prior to the Reformation to quickly set into the newer state churches. Perhaps the most significant evangelical response to this problem was the movement known as Pietism. Indeed, some observers see Pietism as the root of all contemporary evangelistic endeavors. Like other movements before it, Pietism called the Church back to a simpler life of faith. Though largely based in Germany, it quickly influenced the Church throughout Europe and North America.

The Evangelical Revival

The most significant factor in the history of evangelism since the Reformation has been the repeated outpourings of the Holy Spirit during the past 300 years. The first of these worldwide movements began in Germany, among a pietistic sect known as the Moravians. On August 13, 1727, an outpouring of the Holy Spirit occurred among the Moravian Brethren at Herrnhut, Germany. One of the unique features of that revival was a prayer meeting that continued uninterrupted for 100 years. This revival, which ran parallel with the Great Awakening in America (Jonathan Edwards), also gave rise to missionary interest among the members of the colony, resulting in establishing Moravian colonies in various parts of the world.

One of the indirect consequences of the Moravian Revival was the Evangelical Revival under the Wesleys and others. It was through the witness of Moravian missionaries that both Charles and John Wesley were first awakened to their need for personal salvation. The explosive growth of the Sunday School and the rise of the Methodist Church during this period are indicators of the evangelistic successes experienced during this revival. Church planting was a direct result of the evangelistic outreach of this period as both Sunday Schools and Methodist societies, or classes, grew into churches.

During this period of revivals, cross-cultural evangelism once again came into prominence in the outreach ministries of the Church. William Carey, the father of modern missions, took the gospel to India. Later, the Church sent others to various parts of the world to preach the gospel and to establish the Church in a variety of cultures. During this period of English dominance in the world, the city of London became a center of Christianity from which the entire world was being evangelized.

The Rise of the Evangelist

In America, the success of Charles Finney's "new measures" introduced a new feature into the evangelistic activities of the Church. The itinerant preacher was well established in the more evangelical Methodist Church prior to Finney, but Finney legitimized the role of the evangelist by using creative means to effect conversion within the more Calvinistic churches. By the end of the nineteenth century, Dwight L. Moody had taken Finney's rural evangelism to the city and used citywide united crusades to reach the cities for Christ.

The influence of Finney and Moody on evangelism was not the creation of a new outreach strategy, but rather the adaptation of an existing outreach strategy to more effectively reach people for Christ. Many pastors during this period, and prior to that, were evangelistic and churches had previously held special meetings in an attempt to effect conversions. But before Finney and Moody came along, most of these special meetings were conducted by the pastor of the church or by a visiting pastor from another church. By the time of Moody's death in 1899, the itinerant evangelist was viewed as having a legitimate place in the evangelistic ministry of the Church.

The evangelical church also began to change its perspective of evangelism during this period. Prior to the publication of Finney's *Lectures on Revivals of Religion*, it was widely believed that "harvest seasons" took place from time to time as God was pleased to give them to His Church. Finney challenged this thinking, arguing on the basis of the law of sowing and reaping that "revivals" could happen whenever people or churches were prepared to take specific actions to that end. So revolutionary were Finney's ideas in his day, that more than a century and a half later evangelicals of a more extreme Calvinistic persuasion are still disputing their legitimacy.

The rise of the itinerant evangelist caused the popular evangelical view of conversion to also be changed. Moody began talking about "instantaneous salvation," emphasizing the independence of the moment of actual conversion from the process of which it was formerly viewed a part. Along with this change in understanding the nature of conversion came a parallel change in the nature of evangelism. The more confrontational approach to personal evangelism advocated by Trumble in *Taking Men Alive* and by R. A. Torrey in *How to Bring Men to Christ* set the normal pattern for much evangelistic ministry throughout the twentieth century.

As the Church approached the twentieth century, world evangelism received renewed optimism. To equip ministerial candidates to take the gospel to other cities and cultures, Christians began establishing Bible Institutes. Spurgeon established his Pastor's College in London, and through his students established Baptist churches throughout England. A. B. Simpson established a school in Nyack, New York, which continues to train candidates for ministry among the Christian and Missionary Alliance. Perhaps the best known of the Bible Institutes established during this period is Moody Bible Institute (MBI). Until recently, the curriculum plan established by R. A. Torrey at MBI served as a model for similar schools in other centers.

The initial success of these turn-of-the-century evangelistic efforts was quickly interrupted by the introduction of liberal theology into leading seminaries. Indeed, the growth of the Bible Institutes in this century was to some degree a conservative response to liberalism in theological seminaries. Early in the twentieth century, evangelicalism came to be expressed in two diverse movements: fundamentalism and Pentecostalism. Although both movements advocated certain distinctive doctrines as essential to their faith, both were evangelistic and continued to experience growth through conversions in their churches while failing to grasp control of the major denominations.

The rise of the dynamic evangelist Billy Sunday and the introduction of prohibition in America perhaps marked fundamentalism's climax in influencing American society. Sunday, and the fundamentalists who identified with him, preached the gospel by having an emphasis on both repentance and faith to effect conversions. It was widely held that genuine conversions would effect significant visible lifestyle changes. In the context of American society in the early twentieth century, this change usually involved abstinence from alcoholic beverages. The successful repeal of prohibition caused American evangelicals to see themselves as ineffective in effecting lasting social change and they began de-emphasizing that aspect of their message. They continued to preach the gospel, but without the social import of previous generations.

Things changed in the middle of the twentieth century after Billy Graham had back-to-back successes in crusades in Los Angeles and in New England. Shortly after his spectacular crusades in the United States, Graham conducted successful crusades in Europe and established himself as the world-class evangelist for the latter half of the twentieth century. Particularly during the 1950s and early 1960s, evangelism was largely synonymous with the Billy Graham Evangelistic Crusade in the minds of many evangelical Christians. Other evangelists were also effective during this period (e.g., Percy Crawford, Jack Wrytzen and John R. Rice), but Graham's success gave him an audience outside of the evangelical community.

Cross-Cultural Evangelism

About the time of Billy Graham's initial successes in crusade evangelism, an increased interest in missions also occurred. Existing denominations were slow to respond to this interest and this, together with the growing ecumenical nature of the evangelical community, gave rise to the interdenominational faith missions. Some of these missions tended to target specific groups within North American society (e.g., youth, college students, military personnel, native peoples).

Some organizations looked to other cultures, especially tribal groups (e.g., New Tribes Mission, Regions Beyond Missionary Union, Unevangelized Fields Mission). Some missions organizations were established to take the gospel to particular regions (e.g., Latin America Mission, Sudan Interior Mission, Africa Inland Mission). Some of the interfaith missions that had existed prior to the 1940s and 1950s also experienced significant growth during this period and were able to expand their ministry (e.g., Africa Evangelical Fellowship, World Wide Evangelization Crusade).

Initially, missionaries took not only the gospel, but also Western culture with them as they sought to evangelize those in other countries. In some cases, the churches established by mission-

aries were led by missionaries. This system tended to make the churches scatter when the missionaries returned to their home church. Recognizing the failure of this approach to missions, mission leaders began studying the problem to arrive at a workable solution. This gave rise to a greater understanding of the principles of cross-cultural evangelism. One of the first expressions of this new approach to evangelism was the emphasis on establishing indigenous churches and using native leadership.

Once again, this was not a new idea. J. Hudson Taylor had understood and applied this principle in his work in China in the nineteenth century, as had David Livingstone in Africa. But not until the last half of the twentieth century was cross-cultural evangelism again practiced and the indigenous church once again established as the primary goal of missions.

The Church Growth Movement

During the late 1960s, certain churches began experiencing significant growth through evangelistic outreach based on their Sunday School ministry. When the author began listing America's largest and fastest-growing Sunday Schools, enthusiasm and renewed interest in evangelism and church growth spread throughout the evangelical church in North America. The author's book *The Ten Largest Churches*, is viewed by many church-growth authorities as the beginning of the study of church growth in the context of the American church.

The United States was not the only place where significant church growth was being experienced. Donald McGavran, the father of the Church Growth Movement, had for some time been a student of evangelism and church growth, particularly in the context of the church in India and other two-thirds world countries. He was first challenged to think of the means by which significant church growth was effected through the writings of Bishop Pickett.[2] By his own admission, McGavran "lit his candle at Pickett's flame."

In 1950, McGavran was concerned that the various ways the term "evangelism" was being used tended to diminish the term of its special meaning. He believed the term was picking up excess baggage in some circles and used in reference to other areas of ministry in certain places. He looked for an alternate term he could use with greater confidence to define evangelism, not in terms of input (e.g., spirit-filled life, activities), but in output. He began using the phrase "Church Growth" as an expression of the normal output of effective evangelism.[3]

Through writing on the subject and by teaching church-growth principles derived from his studies, McGavran had a significant influence on evangelical missions and gave birth to the Church Growth Movement. McGavran's work was the original influence on evangelical thinking, primarily through the influence of the School of World Mission at Fuller Theological Seminary. In a very real sense, the Church Growth Movement is perhaps the most recent of many historic attempts to prompt the Church to return to its first calling, that of making disciples of all nations.

References: [1]Charles L. McKay, *Five Simple Keys to Effective Evangelism: You Too Can Do It* (Washington, D.C.: University Press of America, 1978), p. 4. [2]Jarrell Waskom Pickett, *Christian Mass Movements in India* (Lucknow, U. P., India: Lucknow Publishing House, 1933). [3]Donald A. McGavran, "Address to the North American Society for Church Growth" Pasadena, Calif., November 20, 1985.

HOLINESS

(Lit. to cut off; it is a condition of separateness.) That aspect of God's nature that makes Him separate from sin because He is pure and undefiled.

HOLY SPIRIT: HIS WORKING

The third person of the Trinity. Before salvation, the Holy Spirit convicts of sin and brings the person to Christ. At salvation, the Holy Spirit works in the person's heart to regenerate this sinner and to give a new nature so that the believer experiences new life. The Holy Spirit indwells those who yield to God. The Spirit works through the Christian by means of spiritual gifts to produce the fruit of the Spirit. The Christian receives new standing in Christ from the Holy

Spirit and is sealed with the guarantee of eternal life. He lives in every Christian and His presence becomes the channel through which God makes the Christian holy and spiritual—is active in restraining the power of sin in the world.

HOMESTEADERS

Families who move into a community and begin attending an established church, lacking a first-hand knowledge of the pioneering era of the church. Second-generation church growth.

Reference: See PIONEERS.

HOMOGENEOUS UNIT
See PEOPLE MOVEMENT

A social group in which all members have common characteristics. A homogeneous unit is a social group in which old members have *enough* common characteristics to experience an affinity with one another.

Reference: See PEOPLE GROUP.

HOMOGENEOUS UNIT: BIBLICAL

Matthew 24:14 describes the end time. It is a teleological conclusion set in eschatological discussion. In that reference, Jesus speaks about the end and the coming of the end, and He says that this gospel must be preached to *panta ta ethne* and then the end will come. The obvious question is: If all it takes is to proclaim the gospel to different *nations*, then why hasn't the end come? Where is Jesus? The gospel has been published and proclaimed in all the nations. In one way or another, if the word "nations" is understood as geographical political entities, it absolutely makes no sense. However, if *panta ta ethne* means people groups, then the people-group approach makes sense and there's significant reason why the Lord has not returned yet.

The same words, *panta ta ethne are* included in the Great Commission, Matthew 28:19,20. They are further repeated in Paul's summary statement in Romans 16:26 and elsewhere. The real key to interpretation of this evangelistic strategy is to allow Scripture to interpret itself. Looking ahead at the completion of the fulfillment of the Great Commission, reflected in Revelation 5:9 where the words panta ta ethne are not used, but in fulfillment of the Great Commission, a commentary about the use of God's evangelistic strategy is clearly given. The people that are gathered as a result of the Great Commission are people from every tribe, language, nation and race — that is, the world is segmented in a far greater and sophisticated way than geopolitical entities such as "nations."

This clearly identifies an evangelistic strategy that is sensitive to different people groups who have a cultural affinity with one another. This means that the average church that wants to obey and fulfill the Great Commission will look at its community and develop evangelistic strategies that are people-group sensitive. — KRH

HOMOGENEOUS UNIT AND PEOPLE MOVEMENTS

Donald McGavran's often repeated statement recognizes and is sensitive to people groups. "People like to become Christians without having to cross racial, linguistic, or class barriers." The *Bridges of God* concept in reaching people was to be sensitive to barriers and to honor them, but to reach them by cross-cultural evangelism. Perhaps a no more significant and at the same time controversial principle comes out of McGavran's writings. According to C. Peter Wagner:

In 1979 I published my doctoral dissertation under the title *Our Kind of People* (John Knox). I included a chapter entitled "Church Growth in the New Testament Mosaic," in which I reexamined biblical evidence and found that New Testament church growth generally followed homogeneous unit lines. Because I used a phenomenonologically-informed hermeneutical methodology, my conclusions were unacceptable to the traditionalists. They called "foul!" and accused me of practicing eisegesis rather than exegesis. They told me I should stick to sociology and leave the theology to them. One was so incensed that he wrote an article-length review in *Soujourners* under the headlines, "Evangelism without the Gospel."[1]

In other contexts, primarily in the Third World, the homogeneous unit principle has been consistently applied (often without understanding the principle itself) and has resulted in a phenomena identified as a people movement. McGavran described a people movement, suggesting:

A people movement results from the joint decision of a number of individuals — whether five or five hundred — all from the same people, which enables them to become Christians without social dislocation, while remaining in full contact with their non-Christian relatives, thus enabling other groups of that people, across the years, after suitable instruction, to come to similar decisions and form Christian churches made up exclusively of members of that people.[2]

Some evangelical Christian leaders have expressed concern about a people-movement approach to evangelism and conversion, in part, on theological grounds. To them, it appears the conversion of a group is contradictory to their understanding of conversion as an individual experience. Alan R. Tippett and Donald A. McGavran argue that this objection to people movements is based on a misunderstanding of the nature of a people movement. In his study of people movements in Southern Polynesia, Tippett notes:

The term *mass movement* is a bad one. It envisages a fearful hysterical crowd acting as an irrational mass. Any figure of speech implying irrationality fails to meet the requirements of the phenomenon we are investigating. They have been called *people movements*, and *peoples' movements*, the former suggesting the multi-individual character, and the latter the structural entity. The former is valuable for describing the conversion of a village or a family, the latter for differentiating between, say, the Tongan and Maori movements. In this work I have spoken of people movements and I imply that they have specific structures, that the groups involved comprise individuals who have specific places and rights.[3]

Similarly, McGavran explains the nature of a people movement, noting:

> What really happens is *multi-individual, mutually interdependent* conversion, which is a very different thing. These exact terms are important. One should learn to use them correctly and easily....
>
> ...What I am affirming is that conversion does not have to be the decision of a solitary individual taken in the face of family disapproval. On the contrary, it is better conversion when it is the decision of many individuals taken in mutual affection. *Multi-individual* means that many people participate in the act. Each individual makes up his mind. He hears about Jesus Christ. He debates with himself and others whether it is a good thing to become a Christian. He believes or does not believe. If he believes, he joins those who are becoming Christian. If he does not believe, he joins those who are not becoming Christian....
>
> *Mutually interdependent* means that all those taking the decision are intimately known to each other and *take the step in view of what the other is going to do.* This is not only natural; it is moral. Indeed, it is immoral, as a rule, to decide what one is going to do regardless of what others do. Churchmen ought frequently to say to inquirers, "Since Jesus Christ is the Savior, the pearl of great price which you have found, and since you are a loyal member of your family, you do not want to enjoy salvation secretly all by yourself. The first thing you want to do is to share your new-found treasure with your loved ones. The person who loves the Lord most will try most to bring his intimates to Him. Andrew went and found his brother Simon. You do the same."
>
> In a people movement—whether in Berlin or Bombay—members of the close-knit group seek to persuade their loved ones of the great desirability of believing on Jesus Christ and becoming Christians. Often they will defer their own decision in order to be baptized together. A husband waits six months for an unbelieving wife. A brother labors for two years so that his other three brothers and their wives will all confess Christ together—the conversion made sweeter because it is shared with the people who supremely matter to him. A wise man deciding to become Christian leads many of his fellows to promise that they will accept Christ the same day he does.
>
> Conversion means participation in a genuine decision for Christ, a sincere turning from the old gods and evil spirits, and a determinated purpose to live as Christ would have men live. The individual decisions within a people movement exhibit all these marks. It is a series of multi-individual, mutually interdependent conversion.[4]

Several things may be implied from this rather lengthy description of a people movement. First, a people movement should not be viewed as a denial of the essentially individual nature of conversion. Second, a people movement results when several members of a group make that individual decision to convert by understanding that a similar decision is being made by others in the group. Third, a people movement involves a genuine decision for Christ as described in McGavran's discussion of the nature of conversion. Fourth, the unique feature of a people movement is that a series of these conversions occur within a limited time frame, thus giving the impression of a group, rather than a group of individuals, coming to Christ.

Are People Movements Biblical?

The New Testament describes conversion in a group context when it refers to the conversion of the *oikos*. The Greek word *oikos* is translated "home," "house" or "household" in the New Testament, and may refer to both the immediate family of a particular person and that person's broader sphere of influence, including household servants and slaves. Both Peter and Paul used the word *oikos* in discussing the conversion of a particular person and that of a larger group of people closely associated with the primary convert (Acts 11:14; 16:31). The New Testament records several *oikos* conversions, including that of Cornelius's household (Acts 10:7, 24), Lydia's household (Acts 16:15), the Philippian jailer's family (Acts 16:33), the household of Crispus (Acts 18:8) and the household of Stephanas (1 Cor. 1:16). According to McGavran:

> In the New Testament we repeatedly come upon the conversion of households — *eikoi* in Greek. The *eicos* pattern, once seen, is a noteworthy feature of New Testament church growth. Christians of the Baptist persuasion have been slow to recognize this, lest it endanger their position that *believers only* should be immersed. Yet the *eicos* pattern really has nothing to do with who is baptized. Family by family, men became Christian — this is what is affirmed. At what stage they are baptized is another question. The truer we are to the New Testament, the more we shall welcome *eicos* and other multi-individual conversions. Both East and West, winning families is a good goal.[5]

The biblical example of household conversions is the basis of what Leonard Tuggy describes as "family evangelism." Tuggy defines family evangelism when he states:

> Family evangelism is a strategy of evangelization which specifically aims at winning whole families to Christ and His Church as they respond to the Gospel through mutually interdependent decisions.[6]

Tippett explains the conversions of groups in a cultural way, noting that limits on individual freedoms in some societies mean that converting to Christ must involve a decision of the group rather than that of an individual. He explains:

> The group does not exist as a living organism unless the individuals act and interact,

each according to his specific role and rights. Biblically the church is conceived in the same terms as a body. The total group is really the decision-making body, although it may be for one individual to make the pronouncement as the representative of all. In many communal societies there is no decision without unanimity in the village or tribal councils. The decision-making group may be a family or a village, or a lineage, or a caste. This is a basic determinant in people movements.[7]

Wagner apparently agrees with Tippett's conclusion. He writes:

> This kind of conversion seems strange to many of us who have been raised in Western society where individualism is valued. Western culture gives permission to individuals to make important decisions such as who to marry, what job to take, where to live and whether to accept Christ with a minimal involvement of parents and grandparents, aunts and uncles, brothers and sisters or close friends. Most cultures of the two-thirds world know nothing of such individualistic decisions, and the group rejects them almost by a reflex action when they occur.[8]

A further biblical concept that appears to justify the idea of conversion in a people-movement context is that of the evangelism of the *ethnos*. The Greek word *ethnos* originally meant "multitude," but came to be used to identify a distinct nation or people group. It is often used in the New Testament to identify the Jews as distinct from other ethnic groups and in the plural to refer to the Gentiles as a whole. The English word "ethnic" is derived from this term and suggests the Greek and English words have similar meanings.

The biblical teaching concerning the conversion of the *oikos* and the evangelization of the *ethnos* supports the idea of conversions in a people-movement context. In light of this, and other biblical research in people movements, a growing number of missiologists are apparently convinced this approach to conversion is consistent with biblical teaching. McGavran concludes:

> The people movement to Christ is a thoroughly biblical way of coming to salvation. It was the way the Jews, the Samaritans, and the synagogue communities around the Great Sea came to Christian conviction. It should be systematically taught in all seminaries, so that every pastor, priest, and minister of the Gospel knows how these movements develop, has eyes open to discern responsive peoples, and knows how to shepherd a people movement when God gives him one.[9]

Are People Movements Practical?

Notwithstanding biblical support for the concept of a people movement, the question remains: Is it valid to anticipate the conversion of entire people groups today? If societies are going to be converted today, it is almost certain that people movements will be involved. McGavran is careful to point out, however, that a people movement itself does not require the conversion of large numbers of people. According to McGavran:

> It is helpful to observe what a people movement is not. It is not large numbers becoming Christians. Most people movements consist of a series of small groups coming to a decision. At any one time only one group makes the decision, is instructed, and is baptized. A people movement does not involve careless accessions or hurried baptizing.[10]

Although McGavran correctly argues that a people movement does not necessarily involve the conversion of large numbers, the practical results of a people movement over time is the conversion of a large group of people. This is implied by McGavran himself when he notes:

> At least two-thirds of all converts in Asia, Africa, and Oceania have come to Christian faith through people movements. In many provinces, nine-tenths of all those

who first moved out of non-Christian faiths to Christianity came in people movements. Most Christians in Asia and Africa today are descendants of people-movement converts. But for people movements, the Churches on those continents would be very different and very much weaker than they are. People-movement growth has accounted for considerable ingathering in Latin America also.[11]

The nature of a people movement suggests the likelihood of people groups being converted when such movements are significant. If the people movement involves a significant part of the tribe or caste, it will theoretically change the culture of that tribe or caste. This logical conclusion of the nature of a people movement has been demonstrated repeatedly in the historical record of the conversion of primitive societies. Many cases of significant people movements that have reached entire tribes suggest this is more than an exception. The conversion of these societies suggests the possibility of other societies being converted, at least among the more primitive tribal groups. But can people movements be effective in a more urban context?

Although only 13 percent of the world's population lived in urban centers at the beginning of the twentieth century, it is estimated that only 13 percent of the world will live outside urban centers by the end of the century. The twentieth century began with only one world-class city (a city consisting of one million or more people and having some world influence) but will likely end with 500 such cities.

The history of the evangelization of the city of London demonstrates the possibility of people movements being effective in evangelizing significant urban areas. The successful conversion of London in the eighteenth and nineteenth centuries is generally attributed to the influence of the evangelical revival under the Wesleys and others. This claim is so commonly made that it is rarely called into question. What was at the birth of Wesley a city known for its baseness became the center of evangelical activity, spreading throughout the entire world.

The effective evangelization of London suggests the possibility of an urban society being converted. Some observers believe this may already be happening in other world-class cities, such as Seoul, South Korea. A century ago, Christianity was just being introduced to Korea. Today, many evangelical churches in Seoul average more than 10,000 people attending each week. Many other churches are also serving the evangelical needs of that city.

References: [1]C. Peter Wagner, *Church Growth: State of the Art* (Wheaton, Ill.: Tyndale House Publishers, Inc., 1989), p. 34. [2]Donald A. McGavran, *Understanding Church Growth* (Grand Rapids: William B. Eerdmans Publishing Company, 1980) p. 335. [3]Alan R. Tippett, *People Movements in Southern Polynesia: Studies in the Dynamics of Church-planting and Growth in Tahiti, New Zealand, Tonga, and Samoa* (Chicago: Moody Press, 1971), p. 199. [4]McGavran, *Understanding Church Growth*, pp. 340, 341. [5]Ibid., p. 348. [6]A. Leonard Tuggy, "You and Your Household" in *Church Growth in the Third World*, ed. Roger E. Hedlund (Bombay: Gospel Literature Service, 1977), p. 244. Tuggy's use of the plural pronoun in describing the family's response to the gospel tends to minimize the individualistic nature of conversion. In the biblical context, a family is only converted when individual members of that family are converted. [7]Tippett, *People Movements in Southern Polynesia*, pp. 199, 200. Tippett's comments are made in the context of a study of people movements in primitive cultures that tend to be communal. The existence of people movements in noncommunal societies suggests an entire group does not need to be involved in a people movement nor is it necessarily impossible or immoral for an individual to make a decision apart from the group. [8]C. Peter Wagner, *Strategies for Church Growth* (Ventura, Calif.: Regal Books, 1989), p. 187. [9]Donald A. McGavran, *Ethnic Realities and the Church: Lessons from India* (South Pasadena, Calif.: William Carey Library, 1979), p. 232. [10]McGavran, *Understanding Church Growth*, pp. 334, 335. [11]Ibid., p. 336.

HOMOGENEOUS UNIT CHURCH

A church composed exclusively of members of a single homogeneous unit.

HOMOGENEOUS UNIT PRINCIPLE

A foundational principle of church growth

expressed by Donald McGavran as follows: *People like to become Christians without having to cross racial, linguistic or class barriers.* The homogeneous unit principle leads to evangelistic strategies that are sensitive to people groups.

HOMOGENEOUS UNIT PRINCIPLE: APPLICATION

Perhaps the single most significant action taken by a church to improve its evangelistic effectiveness involves recognizing existing cultural structures within its target community. In the early 1980s, Donald McGavran called on North American churches to do this. He wrote:

Today we must identify the social realities of our industrial urban society. Let us observe the complex social systems and behavior patterns of our congregations. Let us take advantage of the insights of the sociologists and management experts so abundantly available. Let us take seriously the social structure of small groups and the dynamics which create change in small groups and harness these to the spread of the gospel and the multiplication of churches....

Nongrowing congregations and denominations refuse to see social realities. The fact of the matter is that the majority of their members are better educated, better off, live in the suburbs, and are employed in professional and administrative positions. We have somewhat class-bound churches which have less and less contact with the native born white dweller, the private tenant, and the white proletariat in general. The existing Church has little ability to reproduce in the "low" sector of society. Its desire to evangelize these people is even less. Nongrowing churches do not recognize social realities.[1]

When churches follow McGavran's advice and begin looking at existing cultural structures as a basis for developing an evangelism strategy, the end product will differ from community to community. These differences are to a large extent because of the diverse characteristics of the people groups being targeted. In tightly knit tribal societies, relatively few existing social networks will be in place, but they will tend to be strong. In more urban societies, more networks will be in existence, but each will be less influential.[2]

An increasing number of evangelical church leaders are calling for a new approach to evangelism based on understanding the principles of networking and stair-stepping people to Christ. One of these leaders, George Hunter, suggests five steps to implement this approach to evangelism in the local church.

1. Secure the names of all undiscipled persons within the social webs of your active credible Christians. Have some member of your evangelism committee visit, with each active member, the undiscipled persons he or she has listed.
2. As you win some of those target persons, secure the names of their undiscipled relatives and friends. Have an evangelism committee member visit, with the new believer, these people to be reached.
3. Survey each member each season to get the names of new undiscipled prospects. This will continually reveal a fertile harvest field for your church—undiscipled persons who are already linked to one or more persons in your congregation.
4. As you reach out, do not in every case attempt to gather Christ's prepared harvest in just one visit or conversation. Be prepared to visit with persons a half-dozen more times to help them work through what their response to the invitation might be.
5. As some of your people begin serving as new bridges for others, reinforce this action through appropriate public recognition. For instance when you receive new members into the church, invite members who served as bridges for them to stand with them, and pray both for new disciples and their human bridges.[3]

This strategy of evangelism, as old as Andrew bringing his brother Simon Peter to Christ, is being revitalized and applied in churches across the nation. The program itself is a tool by which church members reach the unchurched by reaching those in their circles of concern or spheres of influence.

Evangelism is designed to involve all people and all spiritual gifts in the evangelistic outreach of the local church. The key to the success of this program is found in using people where they are useable. Some are best used as "evangelists" who present the gospel to the unsaved in their homes. Others are employed as "equippers" or "educators" who disciple the new converts into the church. Also used are the "encouragers" who have the gift of showing mercy. These people encourage others to be faithful and are ready to help them resolve their problems. Helpers and intercessors support the outreach program in prayer and by caring for details behind the scenes. These people run the program and ensure its success.

Two Fundamental Principles

Two foundational principles that make evangelism work are expressed in "the law of three hearings" and "the law of seven touches." These two principles refer to the results of research into the successful evangelistic strategy of growing churches.

The law of three hearings. Research shows that the average visitor to the church does not decide to accept Christ or join the church the first time he or she visits a church. A person will usually attend a church 3.4 times before making a meaningful decision to become a Christian and to unite with the church. It is similar to a person purchasing a new suit: the more significant the purchase, the longer it takes to make a decision. This does not mean some are not saved the first time they visit a gospel-preaching church. The time it takes for someone to be saved depends on the person's receptivity to the gospel and the responsiveness to the church. The 3.4 figure is a statistical average and implies that those who make a permanent decision for Christ usually attend church about three times before deciding to be saved.

The law of seven touches. It takes more than three hearings, however, to get a permanent response to the gospel. The unsaved must be networked into the church if they will remain true to the decision they make for Christ. This means "the law of the seven touches" must also be put into practice. Research shows that people are more likely to return for the second and third visit if they are contacted seven times after their first visit. These contacts, or touches, can be initiated by the church through letters, phone calls, visits or other personal contacts. These seven touches also include times the prospects see the church message in the Yellow Pages, billboards, advertisements, flyers or the church newsletter. The obvious conclusion is that the church that contacts the most people the most times will probably have the greatest results. Evangelistic results never depend on only one aspect, however, such as the number of contacts a church makes with a prospect or the number of hearings given to the gospel. But when all aspects of evangelism are followed—including the laws of the three hearings and the seven touches—the more likely a person will be to respond to the gospel.

Ideally, evangelism should target "receptive-responsive" people. The old term for unsaved people was the word "prospects"; the new term is "receptive-responsive" people. A prospect was usually identified as an unchurched family. Just because they are not identified with a church does not mean they can be reached with the gospel. Soul winners visiting from house to house to witness for Jesus Christ are usually not invited into homes, although some people may be pleasant enough to them. Some are hostile because of the church represented, or some other reason, and a few may be hostile to the gospel.

The ideal candidate for salvation is "receptive" to the soul winner and "responsive" to the gospel. Every once in a while someone is receptive and the soul winner is invited into the home. This receptiveness prepares the way for the soul winner to present the gospel and for the prospect to then receive Christ as Savior. Thus, the new Christian is prepared to attend the church, be baptized and go on to serve Christ.

If soul winners knew which people were receptive to them and responsive to the gospel, they could give priority time to them—the people that used to be called "prospects." Unfortunately, not everyone fits into this "receptive-responsive" category. When Jesus told the Parable of the Soil, only one part of the field was receptive to the seed; that was the place where the crop grew and a harvest was possible.

The Church should evangelize all its "Jerusalem" by using as many means as possible. But the Church should also invest its priority time reaching those who are receptive-responsive people because: time is short, resources are limited, it follows the biblical example, and through discipleship it produces greater results.

Why should the Church place priority on visiting those who are receptive and responsive? Because emphasizing receptive-responsive people is: trying to be as fruitful as possible for Christ; winning the winnable while they are winnable, before their receptivity cools; growing the Church faster and larger; and being a good steward of time and resources.

Because time and resources are limited, stewardship of these factors should be considered in every aspect of life, including evangelism. Jesus Himself clearly taught that evangelistic efforts should reach all people (Mark 16:15), but it is best to concentrate on those who are receptive and responsive (Matt. 10:14; 28:19). This principle brought about a turning point in the apostle Paul's ministry (Acts 13:46).

Because the homogeneous unit principle demands a strategy to reach the unreached people group in a church's neighborhood, the church should employ diagnostic tools and techniques to "bridge" the gospel to them, plant a church to reach them and develop strategies to reach them.

The churches that are growing through evangelism are: finding those in their communities who are most receptive to the gospel; establishing relationships with them; presenting the gospel to them; and helping those who are less receptive to become more receptive to Christ.

Evangelism is reaching the reachable while they are reachable and winning the winnable while they are winnable. Two key components in this strategy are a program of stair-stepping people to Christ and a program of bonding people to the Church.

References: [1]Donald A. McGavran, "Why Some American Churches Are Growing and Some Are Not" in *The Complete Book of Church Growth* by Elmer L. Towns, John N. Vaughan, and David J. Seifert (Wheaton,

Ill.: Tyndale House Publishers, 1981), pp. 290, 292.
[2]Donald A. McGavran, *Understanding Church Growth*
(Grand Rapids: Eerdmans, 1980), pp. 403, 404.
[3]George G. Hunter, *Finding the Way Forward* (Nashville:
Discipleship Resources, 1980); and "The Bridges of
Contagious Evangelism" in *Church Growth: State of the
Art*, pp. 74, 75.

HOUTS QUESTIONNAIRE

A document containing 125 questions designed
to help Christians begin the process of discovering their spiritual gift(s). Also known as the
Wagner-Modified Houts Questionnaire.

Reference: Richard F. Houts, *Houts Inventory of Spiritual
Gifts* (Pasadena, CA: Charles E. Fuller Institute of
Evangelism and Church Growth, 1985).

HUBMAIER, BALTHASAR (1481–1528)

Early Anabaptist leader.

Balthasar Hubmaier studied at the University
of Ingolstadt under John Eck, who opposed
Martin Luther earning his Doctor of Theology
degree. He pastored at Waldshut near the Swiss
border, where he came under the influence of the
Swiss Brethren. In 1525, he and 300 followers
were baptized. He went to Zurich to escape
Austrian authorities and was then banished to
Moravia. He became the leader of other exiles as
well as thousands of Moravian converts. In 1528,
he was burned at the stake for his beliefs.

Hubmaier's greatest contribution to evangelism was in providing significant leadership in the
early days of the Anabaptist movement. His insis-
tence upon the separation of Church and State,
biblical authority and believers' baptism established core values that continue to be practiced by
the various evangelical denominations that trace
their spiritual roots to the Swiss Brethren.

Reference: Henry C. Vedder, *Balthasar Hubmaier* (New
York: G. P. Putman's Sons, 1905).

HUNTER, KENT R.

Dr. Kent R. Hunter (born in 1940) is president
of the Church Growth Center in Corunna,

Indiana, and director of the Consultation
Division of the Center, Creative Consultation
Services. He is founder of HarvestSearch, the
research arm of the Center and the Great
Commission Bookstore, a resource center and
publishing arm of the ministry. Hunter is heard
on Christian radio as The Church Doctor™.

He received his education from Concordia
Seminary, St. Louis, Missouri (M.Div.), Lutheran
School of Theology in Chicago, Illinois (S.T.D.)
and Fuller Theological Seminary, Pasadena,
California (D.Min. in Church Growth).

An ordained minister of the Lutheran Church
Missouri Synod, Kent has served churches in
Michigan, Indiana and South Australia from
1972 to 1986. Kent is senior editor of *Strategies for
Today's Leader* magazine, a quarterly formerly
named *Global Church Growth* magazine and
Church Growth Bulletin. Kent became senior editor
in 1986 at the request of Donald McGavran who
started the magazine in 1964. The quarterly has
subscribers in 65 countries.

As a consultant, Kent has worked with
churches and Christian agencies from 37 denominations in the United States, and many other
groups on several continents. His articles have
appeared in *Christianity Today, Leadership,
Lutheran Education, Global Church Growth/Strategies
for Today's Leader, Ministries Magazine, Church
Growth, Growing Churches* and *Ministry Advantage*.
He served as a feature writer for *World
Evangelization*, the periodical of the Lausanne
Committee for World Evangelization.

Kent's books include *Launching Growth in the
Local Congregation* (Church Growth Analysis and
Learning Center, 1980); *Great Commissioning the
Christian Teacher* (Church Growth Analysis and
Learning Center, 1980); *Facing the Facts for Church
Growth* (coauthored with Diane Barber) (Church
Growth Analysis and Learning Center, 1980);
*Your Church Has Doors: How to Open the Front and
Close the Back* (Church Growth Analysis and
Learning Center, 1982); *Gifted for Growth: An
Implementation Guide for Mobilizing the Laity*
(Church Growth Analysis and Learning Center,
1983); *Six Faces of the Christian Church: How to Light
a Fire in a Lukewarm Church* (Church Growth
Analysis and Learning Center, 1983); *Your Church
Has Personality* (Abingdon, 1985); *The Road to*

Church Growth (Church Growth Analysis and Learning Center, 1985); *Moving the Church into Action* (Concordia Publishing House, 1989); *Courageous Churches: Refusing Decline/Inviting Growth* (coauthored with David Luecke and Paul Heinecke) (Concordia Publishing House, 1992); *The Lord's Harvest and the Rural Church* (Beacon Hill Press, 1993); *Foundations for Church Growth: Biblical Basics for the Local Church* (Church Growth Analysis and Learning Center, 1994); and *Confessions of a Church Growth Enthusiast* (book project pending).

HUSS, JOHN (c.1369–1415)

Forerunner of the Reformation.

John Huss studied at the University of Prague and became rector of the school in 1402. He became convinced of Wycliffe's open approach to the Scriptures and began teaching them. The popularity of Huss's preaching coincided with the rise of Bohemian nationalism, making Huss both a religious and national leader. Huss's calls for reform within the Roman Catholic church resulted in his being called before church officials at the Council of Constance. Although Huss was promised safe conduct, the promise was not honored. When he refused to recant, Huss was condemned to be burned at the stake.

Huss's greatest contribution to evangelism was his teaching of evangelical principles in Bohemia. The movement he began is better known in one of its unique expressions, the Moravian Brethren.

HUTTER, JACOB (d. 1536)

Founder of the Hutterites, or Hutterian Brethren, an Anabaptist sect that practiced community of goods. Like many early Anabaptist leaders, Hutter was tortured and burned at the stake for his religious beliefs.

HYDE, JOHN (1865–1912)

Missionary to India and a prayer warrior.

Born in Carrollton, Illinois, into the home of a Presbyterian minister, John Hyde was educated at Carthage College and at the Presbyterian Seminary in Chicago. In October 1893, he sailed for India as a missionary. During the next 20 years, his significant prayer life became legendary, earning him the title "Praying Hyde." His ministry in Indian villages was extremely effective, resulting in as many as 4 to 10 converts daily for many years. Hyde was also instrumental in establishing the Sialkot Conference, an annual deeper life conference for missionary and national workers. He died on February 17, 1912.

Hyde's greatest contribution to evangelism grew out of the testimony of his prayer life. His example has inspired others to develop spiritual disciplines (especially in the area of prayer) in their pursuit of a deeper relationship with God and a more effective ministry.

Reference: Norman P. Grubb, *Praying Hyde* (Fort Washington, Pa.: Christian Literature Crusade).

HYPERCOOPERATIVISM

A pathology of church growth resulting from making interchurch cooperation an end in itself, thus moving churches from the priority of evangelism.

HYPOTHESIS OF THE 10 PERCENT

The hypothesis that about 10 percent of those attending an average evangelical church have the gift of evangelism.

Reference: See PROBLEM OF THE 9.5.

IDEOLOGICAL EXPORT CENTER

A specific location, most commonly a city, that serves as a recognized distribution point for adverse moral and philosophical influences.— GOJR

ILLUMINATION

The ministry of the Holy Spirit that causes the believer to understand and apply the spiritual message of the Scriptures.

IMAGE OF GOD

Used primarily in reference to humans—something that is similar, with the same properties, but not necessarily identical (reflection).

INCARNATION

Jesus became flesh—the God man. The miracle of God becoming fully human, yet remaining fully God. This theological truth becomes the driving evangelistic focus that requires the gospel to be presented in the heart language of the hearers, because it is the ultimate expression of God's love to us that Jesus came in the flesh to die for the sins of the world.

INDWELLING OF THE SPIRIT

When people become Christians, the Holy Spirit comes into their lives, gives them a new nature, eternal life and guarantees the promise of God to them.

INERRANCY

That which God revealed and inspired (the Bible) is accurate, reliable, authoritative and without error.

INSPIRATION

The supernatural guidance of the writers of Scripture by the Spirit of God, whereby what they wrote became the divine Word of God, transcribed accurately, reliably and without error in the original manuscripts (impetus behind, superintendence over).

INTERCESSION

The foundation of evangelism and church growth is prayer, but not just any kind of prayer. It must be intercessory prayer—prayer for the lost to be saved, for conviction of sin, for the growth of the church and for power in preaching the gospel.

Communion, Petition and Intercession

To understand the nature of intercessory prayer, it needs to be seen in relationship to the three basic kinds of prayer. The first kind of prayer is *communion*. Communion means the kind of prayer that is essentially an expression of intimacy or fellowship with God. Communion prayers are "talking with God" about things of common concern, but not necessarily making specific requests for divine intervention. Many of the psalms represent this form of prayer at its best.

The second basic kind of prayer may be described as *petition*. Petition prayers are "asking or requesting" prayers. This is the essential idea behind the biblical idea of prayer and may be the most common form of prayer practiced by Christians today. In the model prayer Jesus taught His disciples, petition is preceded by communion. If communion raises us into an awareness of the presence of God, petition brings God down to an involvement and intervention in our needs.

Intercession is the third kind of prayer and is an outgrowth of communion and petition. People cannot be intercessors until they have an intimacy in their relationship with God expressed in communion prayer. The intercessor is also comfortable making requests of God, as is characteristic of petition prayer. According to S. D. Gordon, intercession prayer rests on the foundation of communion and petition.

True prayer never stops with petition for one's self. It reaches out to others. The very word intercession implies a reaching out for someone else. It is standing as a go-between, a mutual friend, between God and someone who is either out of touch with Him, or is needing special help. Intercession is the climax of prayer. It is the outward drive of prayer. It is the effective end of prayer outward. Communion and petition are upward and downward. Intercession rests upon these two as its foundation. Communion and petition store the life with the power of God; intercession lets it out on behalf of others. The first two are necessarily for self; this third is for others. They ally a man fully with God: it makes use of that alliance for others. Intercession is the full-bloomed plant whose roots and strength lie back and down in the other two forms. It is the form of prayer that helps God in His great love-plan for winning a planet back to its true sphere. It will help through these talks to keep this simple analysis of prayer in mind. For much that will be said will deal chiefly with this third form, intercession, the outward movement of prayer.[1]

Identification, Agony and Authority

Although intercession is related to other aspects of prayer, it is different from what might be referred to as normal, or the usual, prayer expressions of the Christian. In his biography of Rees Howells, Norman Grubb explained this difference in terms of identification, agony and authority.

> Perhaps believers in general have regarded intercession as just some form of rather intensified prayer. It is, so long as there is great emphasis on the word "intensified"; for there are three things to be seen in an intercessor, which are not necessarily found in ordinary prayer: identification, agony, and authority.[2]

Howells taught that intercessors must first come to identify themselves with the one for whom they are praying, just as Jesus numbered Himself among the transgressors. Second, intercessors must agonize in prayer as Jesus agonized

in the garden of Gethsemane. Third, Howells saw intercessors as those who prayed with authority in that they knew they could and would influence God with their prayers. True intercessors never doubt that God has heard and will soon make the answer to their prayers evident to others.

Howells himself earned the reputation of being an intercessor during his lifetime and used prayer during his ministry to win many spiritual victories. These victories included securing finances and facilities for ministry, and converting people who expressed a hardened response to the gospel. During World War II, Howells turned his attention and prayers to world events, and together with a small group of followers prayed intensely for England and the Allies in their battle against Nazi Germany. Howells often emerged from prayer meetings during the war and issued public statements that God was, or soon would, intervene in the war effort on behalf of England and that Hitler and other leading Nazis would be destroyed. His biographer claims the prayers of Howells and his associates were effective in the war effort and a major contributing factor to the eventual victory of Britain and the allies over Germany.[3]

Intercession as Redemptive

Many biblical references to intercessory prayer appear to emphasize the redemptive quality of this kind of prayer (i.e., that it is born out of a desire to effect deliverance from some impending danger). One of these is the prayer of Moses for Israel when he came down off the mountain (Exod. 32:31, 32). The effectiveness of this prayer is later acknowledged by the psalmist. "Therefore He said that He would destroy them, had not Moses His chosen one stood before Him in the breach, to turn away His wrath, lest He destroy them" (Ps. 106:23).

The next example of intercessory prayer that emphasizes this redemptive quality is that of Jesus in His high priestly prayer (John 17). This prayer was redemptive in the purest sense in that it was followed by Christ's offering of Himself as the ultimate sacrifice for sin. Summarizing Christ's intercession as our Great High Priest, the writer of Hebrews notes, "Who, in the days of His flesh, when He had offered up prayers and supplications, with vehement cries and tears to Him who was able to save Him from death, and was heard because of His godly fear, though He was a Son, yet He learned obedience by the things which He suffered. And having been perfected, He became the author of eternal salvation to all who obey Him" (Heb. 5:7-9).

Paul also expressed something of the redemptive nature of intercessory prayer when he confessed, "For I could wish that I myself were accursed from Christ for my brethren, my kinsmen according to the flesh" (Rom. 9:3). In the Old Testament, Ezekiel suggested the destruction of Jerusalem may have been averted through intercessory prayer (Ezek. 22:30). Abraham's intercessory prayer for Sodom was essentially redemptive in nature as well (Gen. 18:16-33). In this context, it is understandable that in the midst of his catastrophe Job cried out, "Oh, that one might plead for a man with God, as a man pleads for his neighbor!" (Job 16:21).

Intercession as Christian Service

The late Oswald J. Smith often claimed intercessory prayer was "the highest form of Christian service," and urged those in his audiences and those reading his books to engage in this ministry on behalf of missionaries and national Christian workers on the mission field. Smith was not alone in his conviction that intercession was a legitimate form of Christian service. Many other Christian leaders of various backgrounds throughout history have agreed with men such as S. D. Gordon that intercession is not only a form of Christian service, but also perhaps the highest form of Christian service.

It helps greatly to remember that intercession is service: the chief service of a life on God's plan. It is unlike all other forms of service, and superior to them in this: that it has fewer limitations. In all other service we are constantly limited by space, bodily strength, equipment, material obstacles, difficulties involved in the peculiar differences of personality. Prayer knows no such limitations. It ignores space. It may be free of expenditure of bodily strength, where rightly prac-

ticed, and one's powers are under proper control. It goes directly by the telegraphy of spirit, into men's hearts, quietly passes through walls and past locks unhindered, and comes into most direct touch with the inner heart and will to be affected.[4]

Praying for the Pastor

In leading people into the ministry of intercession, wise pastors will first urge people to pray for them, as Paul asked those in churches he ministered to pray for him (Col. 4:2-4). When Paul asked people to pray for him, he asked that two specific requests be made. First, he was desirous that God would open doors of opportunity to him. Second, he asked people to pray that he would effectively communicate the gospel as he had the opportunity. These are two requests all pastors could share with their people. Pastors who enlist their people in the ministry of intercession on their behalf will have a more effective ministry in their churches.

The ministry of intercession has a very large place in connection with carrying the gospel to a lost world. Far more is accomplished in secret than Christians generally realize. The preachers who have been most widely used have been men of prayer. Not only have they prayed themselves, but it will generally be found that others were linked with them in this precious service, and many of these prayer-evangelists have never been brought to public notice. Theirs are not the gifts that attract the attention of the throngs, but they are mighty men and women of prayer prevailing against the unseen enemy in the heavenlies, and by their intercession bringing down power from heaven and blessing upon the public ministry of the Word through others. An Epaphras always laboring fervently in prayer is as important in the work of evangelization as a Paul carrying the glad tidings to the regions beyond.[5]

It is absolutely necessary for the preacher to pray. It is an absolute necessity that the preacher be prayed for. These two propositions are wedded into a union which ought never to know any divorce: the preacher must pray; the preacher must be prayed for. It will take all the praying he can do, and all the praying he can get done, to meet the fearful responsibilities and gain the largest, truest success in his great work. The true preacher, next to the cultivation of the spirit and fact of prayer in himself, in their intensest form, covets with a great covetousness the prayers of God's people.[6]

Praying for the Unsaved

As intercessors pray for evangelistic opportunities for their pastors, they should also pray specifically for unsaved friends, relatives, associates and neighbors. Jesus prayed for contemporary believers in His intercession prior to their trusting Him as Savior (John 17:20). The prayers of a praying mother for unsaved children have become legendary in the testimonies of many Christian leaders and are the subject of several contemporary gospel songs. If God is not willing that any should perish, Christians should pray in accordance with the will of God for the salvation of specific people when God gives them a burden to pray for them.

Can the salvation of specific people be ensured through intercession on their behalf? The answer is twofold. First, people must make their own decisions for Christ and nothing can be done to force God to act contrary to their will in saving them. But when prayers for the unsaved are offered, the Holy Spirit is invited to work in people's lives to make them more receptive and responsive to the gospel. It is doubtful if many people have ever been saved without someone, a parent, pastor, Sunday School teacher, evangelist or a Christian friend first praying for their salvation.

Praying for Missions

If praying for the pastor leads to a more effective ministry, the same results can be anticipated when Christians pray for the missionary outreach of their churches. In his classic on prayer, *The Power of Prayer and the Prayer of Power*, R. A. Torrey suggested seven specific areas of requests when praying for missions.

But what shall we pray for in connection with foreign missions? First of all we should pray, just as the words of our Lord Jesus we are studying command us to pray, for men and women....In the second place, we should pray for the missionaries who have already gone out....In the third place, we should pray for the outpouring of the Spirit on different fields....In the fourth place, we should pray for the native converts....In the fifth place, we should pray for the native churches....In the sixth place, we should pray for the secretaries and official members of the various boards here at home....In the seventh place and finally, we should pray for money.[7]

Intercession as Christian Experience

The ministry of intercession is an aspect of Christian experience in that a person is engaged in an activity with God in a rather unique sense. Both Jesus and the Holy Spirit are identified in Scripture as currently being active in this ministry (Rom. 8:26; Heb. 7:25). Oswald J. Smith viewed intercessory prayer as the summit of the mountain of Christian experience because Christ on His throne chose to engage in it constantly.

Intercessory prayer is the high-water mark of Spiritual experience. There are many who boast of wonderful supernatural manifestations who are not intercessors. It is possible to have some of the gifts of the Spirit, and yet not to be an intercessor. To fail here is to fail everywhere, but to thus enter into fellowship with Christ is the greatest of all blessings.

You can never get higher than the throne-life. When Jesus Christ returned to the right hand of His father it was to engage in the great ministry of intercession on behalf of His Church. For nineteen hundred years now He has been occupied in this way. In His estimation at least it is the most important work that He has to do. The throne-life is the high-water mark. To engage in this same ministry is to do down here what Christ is doing up there.[8]

Intercession and Revival

The ministry of intercession is also instrumental in introducing others to various dimensions of Christian experience, not the least of which is revival. It is doubtful that a revival has ever taken place that has not been preceded by the intercession of one or more people longing for revival. Prayer calls on God to do what only God can do, and although steps can be taken to establish conditions favorable to promoting revival, God usually sends the outpouring of the Holy Spirit in response to prayer.

Intercessory prayer is God's all powerful agency for the outpouring of the Spirit. No revival has ever yet been given apart from this ministry. Someone has prayed. Go, if you will, to the records of the great awakenings for years past and you will find that the secret, the source, has been prayer. God has burdened a little group here and there, sometimes only two or three in number, but these have so given themselves to intercessory prayer that the result has been a mighty outpouring of the Holy Spirit.[9]

There are two kinds of means requisite to promote a revival: the one to influence men, the other to influence God. Prayer is an essential link in the chain of causes that lead to a revival, as much so as truth is. Some have zealously used truth to convert men, and laid very little stress on prayer. They have preached, and talked, and distributed tracts with great zeal, and then wondered that they had so little success. And the reason was that they forgot to use the other branch of the means, effectual prayer. They overlooked the fact that truth, by itself, will never produce the effect, without the Spirit of God, and that the Spirit is given in answer to prayer.[10]

How to Engage in Intercessory Prayer

Now I want to mention some things which it is necessary to remember if we are to engage in this, the highest form of Christian service. First of all, it means that we must be standing on praying ground. That is to say, we must be certain that everything is right between us and God. Unless this is the case it is useless to even attempt to pray....In the second place, intercessory prayer means that we have prayed beyond ourselves, our needs and problems, and that we are in a place and position spiritually to enter into this blessed ministry with Jesus Christ, taking upon us the burden for others in a real soul-travail, and allowing the Holy Spirit to pray through us in the will of God.[11]

As noted by Oswald Smith, those who engage in the ministry of intercession should be certain they have a proper relationship with God so their prayer is not hindered. Second, they must develop an "others" attitude and emphasis in their prayers. In his discussion of intercessory prayer, Smith later alludes to a third condition necessary if people are to be effective in this ministry. They must have an enduring faith that not only is prepared to believe God for an answer, but also endure and continue in prayer until that answer is realized. Those engaging in this ministry are unlikely to escape the notice of Satan and should be prepared for unusual spiritual warfare.

Now I want to go on and say that intercessory prayer is without doubt not only the highest form of Christian service, but also the hardest kind of work. To the person who is not an intercessor such a statement seems absurd. Prayer to most people is looked upon as an easy occupation. Difficulties are unknown. But that is because they know nothing at all of the ministry of intercession....But the Christian who enters upon the ministry of intercession will pass through a very different experience. Satan will do everything in his power to hinder and obstruct. There will be a conscious realization of his presence and opposition. Then, too, discouragement will cross our pathway. Again and again we will feel like giving up....Then, when all else has failed, he will burden us with work. Satan would rather have us work than pray any time. Full well he knows that prayerless work will be powerless and fruitless. Hence if he can only keep us busy so that we do not have time to pray he will have accomplished his purpose.[12]

References: [1]S. D. Gordon, *Quiet Talks on Prayer* (New York: Grosset & Dunlap Publishers, 1904), pp. 39, 40. [2]Norman P. Grubb, *Rees Howells Intercessor* (Fort Washington, Pa.: Christian Literature Crusade, 1980), p. 86. [3]Ibid., p. 262. [4]Gordon, *Quiet Talks on Prayer*, p. 18. [5]H. A. Ironside, *Praying in the Holy Spirit* (New York: Loizeaux Brothers, 1946), p. 56. [6]E. M. Bounds, *Power through Prayer* (Grand Rapids: Baker Book House, 1973), p. 109. [7]R. A. Torrey, *The Power of Prayer and the Prayer of Power* (Grand Rapids: Zondervan Publishing House, 1980), pp. 52-54. [8]Oswald J. Smith, *The Man God Uses* (London: Marshall, Morgan & Scott, 1977), p. 115. [9]Ibid., p. 117. [10]Charles Grandison Finney, *Revivals of Religion* (Grand Rapids: Fleming H. Revell Co., n.d.), p. 49. [11]Smith, *The Man God Uses*, pp. 109, 110. [12]Ibid., pp. 111, 112.

INTERCESSORS

Members of the evangelism team who undergird the evangelistic outreach of the church primarily through the ministry of prayer. While others are making evangelistic visits, intercessors pray together in small groups for specific prospects, new converts and those who have special needs.

INTERCESSORY PRAYER

Petitions, entreaties and thanksgivings made on behalf of another. Intercession also involves the act of standing between the object of prayer and spiritual forces. In the case of God, the positioning is taken in order to submit requests; in the case of the devil, it is to deflect his attacks. —GOJR

INTERCESSORY UNITY

A spiritual mapping-team cell that is dedicated to petitioning God for guidance, favor and protection. Members will carefully record specific promptings, warnings and confirmations gleaned in the place of prayer. —GOJR

INTERNAL CHURCH GROWTH See QUALITATIVE GROWTH.

INVERTED DISCIPLESHIP

The tendency of missions to invest increasingly more significant resources to maturing the converted while investing decreasing resources in the evangelism of the unconverted.

IRVING, EDWARD (1792–1834)

Forerunner of modern Pentecostalism.

Edward Irving was a Scottish Presbyterian minister who became convinced the church should experience the "charismatic" gifts of the Holy Spirit. About 1842, he established the Catholic Apostolic Church. Irving's followers emphasized "speaking in tongues" and believed in the imminent return of Christ. He is widely regarded today as "the forerunner of modern Pentecostalism." —RC

JACKSON, SHELDON (1834–1909)

Presbyterian missionary in frontier America.

Born in New York, Sheldon Jackson served as a Presbyterian missionary to American native people in Oklahoma and developed Presbyterian churches in Minnesota. As the Superintendent of Missions for Western Iowa, Nebraska, Dakota, Montana, Wyoming and Utah, he traveled throughout the region starting churches and enlisting others in church-planting ministries. He concluded his ministry as a missionary to the native people of Alaska.

Jackson's greatest contribution to evangelism was his emphasis on church planting in the western United States.

While serving in Alaska, Jackson introduced Siberian reindeer to Alaska to provide food for the Eskimos.

JEHOVAH

The name for the Lord that indicates His self-existent nature and covenant-keeping relationship to humans (Lit. "I am that I am" from the verb "to be").

JOHN OF ANTIOCH
See CHRYSOSTOM

JOHN OF MONTE CORVINO (c. 1247–1330)

Franciscan monk, missionary to China.

John of Monte Corvino was the first Franciscan missionary to China. He arrived in 1294, the year Kublai Khan died. The Franciscan mission experienced growth in spite of the opposition of the Nestorians who preceded them. Much that was accomplished through this mission was lost when the Chinese overthrew the Mongol Dynasty in 1364.

JONES, ROBERT REYNOLDS (1883–1968)

American evangelist and educator.

Born on October 30, 1883, in Shipperville, Alabama, Bob Jones was converted to Christ at age 11, ordained to preach by a Methodist church at age 15 and began preaching almost immediately. His preaching ministry continued to grow, and at one time Jones was the leading citywide evangelist in America. In 1926, he established Bob Jones College near Panama City, Florida (now Bob Jones University of Greenville, South Carolina).

Jones's greatest contribution to evangelism was achieved in starting Bob Jones University, which has prepared students for ministry around the world.

JONES, SAMUEL PORTER (1847–1906)

American evangelist.

Born in Oak Bowrey, Alabama, Sam Jones studied and practiced law in Georgia. At his father's deathbed, he was converted to Christ and began preaching a week later. He served several pastorates but is best known for his evangelistic crusade ministry in some of America's largest cities. It is estimated over a half million people were converted to Christ in his meetings.

JUDSON, ADONIRAM (1788–1850)

Pioneer missionary to Burma.

Adoniram Judson was among the first missionaries sent out by the American Board of Commissioners for Foreign Missions to India in 1812. On the voyage to India, he became convinced of the Baptist view of baptism and was baptized in India by William Carey. He broke with the mission and launched his own mission to Burma through the support of American Baptists.

Reference: S. R. Warburton, *Eastward: The Story of Adoniram Judson* (New York: Round Table Press, 1937).

JUSTIFICATION

One of the most important questions ever asked in the history of humankind is, "How then can man be justified with God?" (Job 9:2; 25:4,

KJV). This question becomes more crucial as humans seek to understand their relationship to God.

Justification is an act whereby people's legal standing in heaven is changed and they are given a new standing before God. Being declared justified is similar to the act whereby a government declares that aliens are citizens. The moment people are pronounced citizens nothing happens to them physically. Their thought processes remain the same, as do their personalities and patterns of speech. The only actual change is their legal standing, but as they become aware of their new legal standing, they may shout, cry or break into a grin. The emotional reaction has no organic connection to their changed legal status, but they surely have a cognitive awareness of their new advantages. In the same way, justification changes people's legal papers in heaven; they become children of God. In response to this new relationship they may cry, rejoice or worship God in silent gratitude.

Justification is an act of God in the unique experience of salvation and has been so defined by religious writers throughout the years. According to the *Westminster Catechism*, justification is: "An act of God's free grace, wherein He pardoneth all our sins, and accepteth us as righteous in his sight, only for the righteousness of Christ imputed to us, and received by faith alone."[1]

According to Strong:

> By justification we mean that judicial act of God by which, on account of Christ, to whom the sinner is united by faith, he declares that sinner to be no longer exposed to the penalty of the law, but to be restored to his favor. Or, to give an alternative definition from which all metaphor is excluded: Justification is the reversal of God's attitude toward the sinner, because of the sinner's new relation to Christ. God did condemn; he now acquits. He did repel; he now admits to favor.[2]

Justification is the act whereby God declares a person righteous when that person accepts God's Word. Hence, justification teaches that a rela-

tionship between God and humans can exist. Justification makes humans perfect in God's sight. It is a declarative act of God. It is not that humans have become perfect, only that God has declared them righteous and therefore they stand perfect in the sight of God.

That justification is a declarative act of God is evident in the meaning of the words translated "justify" and "justification" in the Scriptures. Commenting on the use of these four Greek terms in the *Septuagint* and New Testament, Augustus H. Strong suggests:

> (a) uniformly, or with only a single exception, signifies, not to make righteous, but to declare just, or free from guilt and exposure to punishment. The only O. T. passage where this meaning is questionable is Dan. 12:3. But even here the proper translation is, in all probability, not "they that turn many to righteousness," but "they that justify many," i.e., cause many to be justified.... (b) is the act, in process, of declaring a man just, that is, acquitted from guilt and restored to the divine favor (Rom. 4:25; 5:18)... (c) is the act, as already accomplished, or declaring a man just, that is, no longer exposed to penalty, but restored to God's favor (Rom. 5:16, 18; cf. 1 Tim. 3:16)... (d) is the state of one justified, or declared just (Rom. 8:10; 1 Cor. 1:30).[3]

Abraham is the first person in the Bible described as having been justified by faith. This is not saying he was the first person to be a child of God, only that he is the first recorded person of whom this expression is used and applied. "He [Abraham] believed in the Lord, and He [God] accounted it to him [Abraham] for righteousness" (Gen. 15:6). God made a promise to Abraham that he accepted as possible and trusted in God as though it were actual. The "believing" by Abraham constituted an act of declaration. In return, God made His declaration.

Some have noted the apparent contradiction of Paul and James in writing on justification. Justification in Paul's view is clearly by faith without works. Yet in James 2:14-26, James appears to connect works to justification.

Actually, both Paul and James agree on the nature of justification. Paul, using the expression in its technical sense, emphasizes the means whereby God justifies. James, using the term in a more popular way, emphasizes the evidence that a person has, in fact, been justified by faith. As J. I. Packer notes:

> James quotes Gn. xv 6 for the same purpose as Paul does—to show that it was faith that secured Abraham's acceptance. But now, he argues, this statement was "fulfilled" (confirmed, shown to be true, and brought to its appointed completion by events) thirty years later, when "Abraham (was) justified by works, in that he offered up Isaac" (2:21). By this his faith was "made perfect," i.e., brought to due expression in applying appropriate actions; thus he was shown to be a true believer.[4]

References: [1]*Westminster Catechism*, Chapter 1.5. [2]Augustus Hopkins Strong, *Systematic Theology: A Compendium Designed for the Use of Theological Students* (Grand Rapids: Fleming H. Revell Company, 1970), p. 849. [3]Ibid., pp. 850-52. [4]J. I. Packer, "Justification" *The New Bible Dictionary*, ed. J. D. Douglas (Grand Rapids: Wm. B. Eerdmans Publishing Co., 1977), p. 686.

KELLY, CHARLES S., JR.

Dr. Charles S. Kelly (born in 1952) is director of the Center of Evangelism and Church Growth, located in the influential New Orleans Baptist Theological Seminary. This is the second-largest seminary in the United States, where more than 3,000 students are preparing for the ministry. He also is chairman of the Division of Pastoral Ministries and the Roland Q. Leavell Professor of Evangelism.

Dr. Kelly grew up in Southern Baptist churches and has been involved in the Southern Baptist movement. He has been a member of the powerful Committee on Boards and a member of the Committee on Resolutions. He graduated from Baylor University in 1974 and received the M.Div. degree from New Orleans Baptist Theological Seminary in 1978 and the Th.D. degree in 1983.

Dr. Kelly has written *How They Did It: The Story of Southern Baptist Evangelism* and *Show Me the Way*, published by Convention Press (SBC). In addition, he has written a number of articles on evangelism for Southern Baptist publications and prepared training materials on evangelism for Southern Baptist agencies.

KENNEDY, D. JAMES (1930-)

D. James Kennedy was born November 3, 1930, in Augusta, Georgia, and was educated at the University of Tampa (B.A. 1958), Columbia Theological Seminary, (B.D. 1959) and was ordained in the gospel ministry of the Presbyterian church. He also received a Ph.D. degree from New York University.

Kennedy leads Coral Ridge Presbyterian Church, Ft. Lauderdale, Florida, in growth so that it has become one of the largest congregations in America. He is recognized for his television ministry across America and around the world.

Kennedy wrote the book *Evangelism Explosion* (Tyndale House, 1970), which taught personal evangelism by presenting Jesus Christ to people.

He organized the concept of personal evangelism into a corporation, Evangelism Explosion, Inc., and the program has been taught in seminaries, colleges and churches throughout the United States and beyond.

KENOSIS

(Lit. to empty oneself). When Christ became a man, He veiled His glory, subjected Himself to human limitation, and voluntarily gave up the independent use of His absolute attributes.

KERYGMA

The term *kerygma*[1] is a transliteration of the Greek word for proclamation or preaching. It refers literally to the proclamation of a herald; in the New Testament a herald is sent by God. Paul said, "It pleased God by the foolishness of preaching *[kerygma]* to save them that believe" (1 Cor. 1:21, *KJV*).

C. H. Dodd has given the classical argument that the Early Church gave the heart of the message of Christianity with great clarity and consistency. Whereas the Church gave attention also to *didache*, or ethical teaching, *paraklesis*, or exhortation and homilia, the informal dialogue about aspects of the Christian life, people became Christians through *kerygma*. As Dodd has noted:

> For the early Church, then, to preach the Gospel was by no means the same thing as to deliver moral instruction or exhortation. While the Church was concerned to hand on the teaching of the Lord, it was not by this that it made converts. It was kerygma, says Paul, not by didache, that it pleased God to save men.[2]

The consistent message of the Early Church is seen throughout the New Testament. It is most clearly seen, however, in the actual sermons recorded in the Acts of the Apostles, including these features:

- The age of fulfillment has dawned (Acts 2:17; 3:18,24).
- This has occurred through the ministry,

death, and resurrection of Jesus (2:22, 30-31; 3:22).

- Jesus has been exalted at the right hand of God (2:33-36; 3:13; 5:31).
- The Holy Spirit in the Church is the sign of Christ's power and glory (2:33).
- The Messianic Age will be consummated with the return of Christ (3:21).
- An appeal is given for repentance and the promise of salvation (2:38-39; 3:19; 4:12).[3]

The *kerygma* has much significance for contemporary evangelism and church growth. Although the Church must constantly discover new methods and approaches to present the gospel, the message, consistently delivered by the first Christians, must never be diluted or compromised. Growing churches must continually evaluate their purpose and practice by the timeless message of the cross. —ALR

References: [1]William F. Arndt and F. Wilbur Gingrich, *A Greek-English Lexicon of the New Testament* (Chicago: University of Chicago Press, 1957), *Kerygma*, p. 432. [2]C. H. Dodd, *The Apostolic Preaching and Its Developments* (New York: HarperCollins, 1964), p.8. [3]Ibid., pp. 21-23.

KINSHIP CIRCLE See CELL.

KOINONITIS

A pathology of church growth caused by an overemphasis on fellowship, resulting in an inward-focused church that loses sight of those who need to be reached in the community.

KOREAN PENTECOST (1905) See TWENTIETH-CENTURY AWAKENING.

KRAPF, J. LUDWIG (1810–1881)

Pioneer missionary explorer in East Africa.

In addition to his work as a missionary, Krapf was involved in exploring East Africa and is credited with discovering Mounts Kenya and Kilimanjaro as part of his extensive exploration of the region.

LATFRICASIA See AFRICASIA.

LAW OF GOD (NATURAL)

The laws of the universe were established by God as an extension of His presence and purpose and are the means by which He maintains order.

LEADERSHIP CLASSES

Leadership classes are the typology by which Christian workers are designated into one of five classifications on the basis of the nature and focus of their work.

How to Identify the Various Leadership Classes

Five leadership classes can be identified, based on the nature and focus of a person's ministry. Class I Leaders include those whose energies are primarily focused on servicing existing Christians and church structures. Class II Leaders include those whose energies are primarily focused on outreach-oriented ministries designed to reach people and to incorporate them into the church. Class III Leaders include those who pastor new small churches. They are usually part-time or bivocational kinds of workers. Class IV Leaders include the full-time professional staff of ongoing churches. Class V Leaders include denominational and interdenominational leaders.

LEADERSHIP DESCRIPTIONS

Although God is the undisputed leader of His Church, He continues to use human instrumentality to accomplish His work. Following are some of the descriptions of positive influential leaders.

Poise. Poise is not a "front" or a mask. Poise results when leaders know their subjects and the age group to whom they minister. Poise comes from relying on the indwelling presence and aid of the Holy Spirit. Thus, the leader's outer manner reflects inward faith and assurance.

Bearing. The leader's bearing further reflects an inner attitude through posture and walk. Although the head is raised in confidence, it is not tilted with pride. Although the leader walks with an air of assurance, it is not a strut of vanity. Leaders may be recognized by the pleasure and assurance with which they approach a task—the attitudes, again, born of faith, as well as preparation.

Projection. Leaders have eye contact and heart contact with those they lead. They reach out to their listeners with an interest and concern evident in their words and tone. They know what they are going to say without having to read it to an audience, so their eyes constantly scan the faces of their hearers and note their reactions. They know enough about the subject to be able to present additional facts if the listeners register lack of comprehension or unrest.

Sharing. Leaders do not attempt to perform all the functions in their given sphere of activity. If, for example, the leader is the general superintendent of the Sunday School, the leader's function is to share personal knowledge and give direction for others to follow. The leader does not constantly push from behind, saying, "You must do this or that." Rather, a leader shares personal knowledge of how to do it and sets an example through performance.

Humility. Probably this quality differentiates the real leader from the self-styled "big shot." The true leader in God's work has the qualification listed by the Lord Jesus Christ, "If anyone desires to be first, he shall be last of all and servant of all" (Mark 9:35). Faithful, willing service commends a person for consideration for leadership posts. Although some people seem to have inborn leadership qualities, study and practice can improve this ability. Giving of self in service to Christ and His church develops a servant of God. True leaders recognize their constant dependence upon the wisdom, direction and strength imparted by the Holy Spirit who appointed them to their task.

Followship. The leader is essentially a follower—of the leadership of the Holy Spirit of God. The Spirit's direction may be extended through the process of open and shut doors, realization of need in a specific area, or a vision of possibilities in a particular field through a message or a book.

Example. The qualities of spiritual devotion a church has a right to expect from any Christian will be exemplified by the leader. The leader's strength and courage and vision will come from fellowship with God through prayer and Bible study, as well as through service. A leader has self-discipline and goes the second mile in unselfish effort. A leader's enthusiasm and other attitudes are contagious. In short, those who look up to the leader are going to emulate the leader's qualities, which, therefore, must be the highest and finest.

Leadership Characteristics

Successful leaders have a variety of personality types, however, they usually have the following characteristics:

Vision. A leader projects into the future, seeing ahead. The first law of leadership is the law of vision/dreams. When people buy into leaders' vision, they buy into their leadership.

Commitment. This age of tension—nuclear war, social revolution, population explosion, automation, moral crises, materialism and mobility—breeds ruthlessness, lack of identification, alienation and meaninglessness. Leaders who have found the purpose of God in Christ should be able to express their convictions in commitment.

Involvement. Leaders don't just talk about commitment, they do something about commitment. Involvement means concern for life as it is, not what they wish it to be. Leaders must have a willingness to help solve society's problems.

Positive concept. Leaders are realistic about their self-image. They can assess themselves objectively, neither being deceived or discouraged by their limitations nor puffed up by their potentialities. They are not overly self-centered or self-concerned. They admit mistakes, but feel competent despite them.

Acceptance. Leaders believe others are of worth and are supportive, encouraging, helpful and empathetic. They cooperate, rather than compete. Believing other people are worthwhile, they are apt to think their efforts are worthwhile. They find it difficult to say no when asked to assist in a worthy cause. They are giving people.

Perception. Leaders are aware of people, circumstances, ideas, attitudes and the world outside themselves. They see the world in shades of gray, rather than black and white.

Tolerance. Leaders tolerate ambiguities and uncertainties. They do not jump to conclusions or insist upon immediate action. They may appear to be indecisive, "middle-of-the-roaders," but they are in reality suspending judgment, knowing that there is a time for waiting and a time for action.

Creativity. Leaders must be creative for the outworking of their unique selves. To be creative is to be authentic, original and insightful, rather than imitative.

Interdependence. Leaders relate to others and recognize dependence upon them. Other people's individuality and uniqueness make leaders' own lives fuller and more productive. They know that real strength comes from contacts with others. When they accept and support others, they strengthen themselves. Leaders' relationships are not characterized by domination or submission, aggression or appeasement; they are magnanimous and forgiving.

Communication. Leaders are open; they do not wear masks. They listen to others and do not dismiss an idea simply because of its source. They are not as concerned with having people agree with them, as with being understood. In striving to be understood, they may try to "get through" the defensive psychological mechanisms of others by couching their own ideas in nonthreatening terms. This is not compromise, for they are tenacious and vigorous in presenting their beliefs when necessary.

LEADERSHIP, GIFT OF
See ADMINISTRATION, GIFT OF

LEADERSHIP TRAINING

Leadership is one of the differences between a healthy and a sick church, between a growing and a stagnant church. Dr. Lee Robertson once said, "Everything rises and falls on leadership." By this statement, he meant that a person can make a difference in the face of insurmountable odds, difficult circumstances and limited resources. Leadership makes a difference, and the greatest need in today's church is leadership.

Why Leadership Training?

Everyone has some leadership responsibility. We wrongly think the pastor does the work of the church. This results in developing Christians who only watch, or listen to, the pastor's ministry. The Bible teaches that everyone has a ministry (Eph. 4:16). Thus, because everyone has a responsibility to minister to others, everyone is a leader to some degree. Therefore, leadership training is needed to equip everyone to minister in the Body.

People can lead other people. Everyone is a potential leader. Young girls may grow up to be mothers who lead their children. Young boys and young girls may grow up to be Sunday School teachers, deacons or a foreman on a job. They may supervise a typing pool, or lead a boy scout troop. No matter how far down the totem pole in age, rank or education, everyone is a potential leader. Therefore, we ought to train everyone to reach his or her potential leadership.

People can be trained to do their jobs better. Everyone is in the process of change, either for making things better or for causing things to deteriorate. People can be molded, thus we should train them to become leaders to serve Jesus Christ. Because they can be leaders, and they are changing, they need to be trained to do a better job for Christ.

Leadership training utilizes unused talent and untapped ability in the church. Some have noted that in the average church, 85 percent of the people are spectators and 15 percent do the necessary jobs. A realistic goal is to enlist and train 50 percent of the people in every church for service in their churches.

Train others to carry out the Great Commission. Pastors cannot carry out the Great Commission by themselves. They must challenge, recruit, train and employ others to be leaders. These new leaders will then help pastors reach the lost. The average pastor does not need to work harder, but to delegate the ministry to others. Why do the work of seven people? Instead, get seven people to work for Christ.

How to Train Leaders

Strategies to develop personal leadership abili-

ties and to help others attain them include the following:

Orientation. Proper orientation helps a worker do a job better. The first few weeks on the job will be decisive in determining the attitudes and habits of work. Supervisory relationships are best established early.

Job descriptions. A job description is a useful tool for orientation and supervision. It needs to be flexible but should spell out duties, relationships, available assistance and expectations.

Observation. Trainees should have opportunities to observe experienced workers. Observing the leader in a teaching-learning situation and having a chance to discuss the session is helpful to both the observer and the teacher-leader.

Supervisory conference. Workers should have the privilege of reviewing their stewardship of teaching with a qualified supervisor. Evaluation and plans for future emphasis should be discussed.

Workers' conference. A regularly scheduled conference of workers provides face-to-face interchange of viewpoints in a group setting. The conference can be an effective vehicle for focusing on spiritual concerns, providing specialized training, discussing business items that affect the entire group and providing fellowship.

Guided reading, listening and seeing. Church, public and personal libraries contain valuable information, including a growing supply of audiovisual training aids. Workers can study these materials at their own pace. Suggested materials can be circulated among church workers, and later shared and evaluated.

Visits from specialists. Guest lecturers and discussion leaders can meet with your workers and share from their experiences and studies.

Delegates to conferences. Arrange for representatives to attend gatherings that discuss relevant matters and allow them to report back to the group.

Courses of study. Formal courses of study are a useful means of personal improvement for workers. Because the courses involve a well-trained leader, required attendance and prescribed reading, they are a valuable feature of your leadership training program. Some churches require their leaders to attend these improvement sessions.

Apprenticeship. This ancient method of learning

is valuable for contemporary leaders. Observing, discussing, attempting, receiving correction and encouragement is an effective way to learn.

Team teaching and consultation. In a team teaching setup, members of the team discuss objectives, evaluate experiences and prepare strategy. Leadership is shared according to the skills of the team members. Consultation is especially valuable at the beginning of a team experience.

LEFT–END PEOPLES

People groups and individuals that tend to be resistant to the gospel; so named because they tend to be plotted to the left on the Resistance-Receptivity Axis.

References: See RESISTANCE-RECEPTIVITY AXIS; RIGHT-END PEOPLES.

LEY LINES

Geographic continuums of spiritual power that are established—or at least recognized—by the early inhabitants of an area (whereas European Freemasons offer a good example of the former, the animistically inclined Inca merely acknowledged a preexisting power nexus when founding the mountain stronghold of Machu Picchu). Depending on the culture in which they are found, ley lines may be viewed either as conduits through which spiritual power is transmitted, or as demarcation lines for spiritual authority.—GOJR

LIFE–SAVING STATION: ILLUSTRATION OF CHURCH PURPOSE

"On a dangerous seacoast where shipwrecks often occur, there was once a crude little life-saving station. The building was just a hut and there was only one boat, but the few devoted members kept a constant watch over the sea; and with no thought for themselves they went out day or night tirelessly searching for the lost. Many lives were saved by this wonderful little station, so that it became famous. Some of those who were saved, and various others in the surrounding area, wanted to associate and give their time and money. New boats were bought and new crews were trained. The little life-saving station grew.

"Some of the new members of the life-saving station were unhappy that the building was so crude and so poorly equipped. They felt that a more comfortable place should be provided as the first refuge of those saved from the sea. So they replaced the emergency cots with beds and put better furniture in an enlarged building. Now the life-saving station became a popular gathering place for its members, and they redecorated it beautifully and furnished it exquisitely. Fewer members were now interested in going on life-saving missions, so they hired lifeboat crews. The life-saving motif still prevailed in the club decoration and there was a liturgical life-saving boat in the meeting room. About this time, a large ship was wrecked off the coast, and the hired crews brought in boatloads of cold, wet and half-drowned people. They were dirty and sick and some of them had yellow skin. The beautiful new club was considerably messed up. So the property committee immediately had a shower house built outside the club where victims of shipwreck could be cleaned up before coming inside.

"At the next meeting, there was a split in the club membership. Most of the members wanted to stop the club's life-saving activities as being unpleasant and a hindrance to the normal social life of the club. Some members insisted upon lifesaving as their primary purpose and pointed out that they were still called a life-saving station. But they were finally voted down and told that if they wanted to save lives of all the various kinds of people who were shipwrecked in those waters, they could begin their own life-saving station down the coast. They did.

"As the years went by, the new station experienced the same changes that had occurred in the old. It evolved into a club, and yet another life-saving station was founded. History continued to repeat itself, and today you will find a number of exclusive clubs along that shore. Shipwrecks are still frequent in those waters, but most of the people drown!"[1]

Reference: [1]Rev. T. O. Wedel, Warden, College of Preachers, Washington Cathedral, Washington, D.C.

LIFESTYLE EVANGELISM

An approach to evangelism that emphasizes believers being role models of Christianity for non-Christians. In this approach, Christians establish credibility to the gospel and lead non-Christians to become more receptive to Christ and to salvation. Lifestyle evangelism is rooted in the belief that every Christian's lifestyle should bear witness for Jesus Christ (Acts 1:8). The strengths of this approach to evangelism are its emphasis on: (1) the use of a nonverbal testimony to build bridges and to establish redemptive relationships, (2) a nonconfrontational approach to sharing the gospel and (3) evangelism within existing social networks. The primary weakness of lifestyle evangelism is its tendency to be nonchurch related, sometimes resulting in failure to incorporate new converts into the life of a church.

Reference: Joe Aldrich, *Life-style Evangelism.* (Sisters, Oreg.: Multnomah Books, 1984).

LIVINGSTONE, DAVID (1813-1873)

Pioneer missionary explorer to Africa.

David Livingstone was born near Glasgow, Scotland, and studied medicine and theology at the University of Glasgow in preparation for missionary service in China. The Opium War in China closed that door and Livingstone was influenced to consider inland Africa by Robert Moffat. Livingstone joined Moffat in Africa and later established a new mission base at Mabosta, about 200 miles inland. Throughout his life, Livingstone continued to explore the African continent to open new fields for missionary service. He died in Africa, but his body was returned and buried in Westminster Abbey. News of his death inspired a significant number of new missionaries and explorers to enter the once dark continent.

Livingstone's greatest contribution to evangelism came through his explorations of the African continent. As he shared his discoveries in England, new missionary societies were established to evangelize the people of various African regions. His example of committed service also inspired many to follow in his footsteps.

In addition to his missionary accomplishments, Livingstone is best remembered as the explorer and geographer responsible for opening the continent of Africa.

References: W. G. Blaikie, *The Personal Life of David Livingstone* (Grand Rapids: Fleming H. Revell Co., 1880); R. J. Campbell, *Livingstone* (New York: Dodd, Mead & Co., 1930); George Seaver, *David Livingstone* (New York: McGraw-Hill Inc., 1962).

LORD'S SUPPER

Jesus initiated this church ordinance at the Passover meal eaten with His disciples on His final night on earth before His crucifixion. To many, this ordinance, symbolized by the cup that represents His blood and the loaf that represents His body, provides an opportunity for self-examination. Some Protestant traditions see the Lord's Supper as a sacred act (sacrament) in which Christ's body and blood are present and in which the recipient receives forgiveness of sins if truly repentant.

LOYOLA, IGNATIUS (c.1491-1556)

Founder of the Roman Catholic order of the Society of Jesus (Jesuits).

Born into a noble family in Guipuzcoa, Ignatius Loyola served for a time in the military. As he was recovering from a battle wound, he read a book on the life of Christ and another book on the lives of the saints. These books made an impression on Loyola, causing him to renounce his past lifestyle and to join a Benedictine monastery. He traveled to Jerusalem, intending to be a missionary to the Muslims, but was forbidden to do so by the Franciscans in that city. On August 15, 1534, he formed the Society of Jesus with only seven followers, but it became a major institution, extending the influence of the Roman Catholic Church around the world. By the time of his death, his new society had more than 1,000 members.

Ignatius Loyola was instrumental in extending the influence of the Roman Catholic Church through the Jesuit order.

References: P. Dudon, *St. Ignatius of Loyola* (Milwaukee: The Bruce Publishing Co., 1949); H. D. Sedgwick,

Ignatius Loyola (Indianapolis: Macmillan Publishing, 1923).

LULL, RAMON (c.1232–1315)

Pioneer missionary to the Muslims and an advocate of reaching unreached people groups.

Born into an aristocratic home on the island of Majorca, Ramon Lull was converted to Christ as a result of a recurring vision of Christ on the cross. Upon his conversion, he made provision for his wife and family and gave most of his wealth to the poor. He studied religion and traveled widely, advocating the establishment of monasteries to train missionaries to go to unreached people groups. He also developed a system of presenting the gospel to non-Christian peoples, which he believed could be effective in converting Muslims. He made three trips to North Africa to test his theories. His initial success infuriated Muslim leaders, who expelled him from their country. His third missionary journey ended in his martyrdom.

Lull's greatest contribution to evangelism was his deep vision to reach unreached people groups. He also established a precedent in preaching the gospel to Muslims.

References: E. A. Peers, *Ramon Lull: A Biography* (London: Society for Promoting Christian Knowledge, 1929); *A Fool for Love: The Life of Ramon Lull* (London: Student Christian Movement Press, 1946).

LUTHER, MARTIN (1483–1546)

Father of the Protestant Reformation.

Martin Luther was born on November 10, 1483, in Eisleben, Saxony, studied at the University of Erfurt and began pursuing a career in the legal profession. These plans were halted when in a thunderstorm he prayed to St. Anne and promised he would become a monk if she kept him safe. Luther was protected, became a monk, was ordained in 1507 and began teaching at the University of Wittenberg the following year. Through his study of the Psalms and Romans, Luther became convinced of the doctrine of justification by grace through faith alone. On October 31, 1517, Luther posted his Ninety-Five Theses on the door of the Wittenberg Church, the first act of the Protestant Reformation. Luther attempted to reform the Roman Catholic Church but opposition to his teaching resulted in his excommunication in 1521. Luther translated the Bible into German and published commentaries and catechisms that reflected his Protestant beliefs.

Luther's great contribution to evangelism was his recovery of the principle of justification by grace through faith alone. The Protestant churches of the Reformation carried that doctrine throughout the world.

References: Roland Bainton, *Here I Stand* (Nashville: Abingdon Press, 1950); Vivian H. H. Green, *Luther and the Reformation* (New York: The Putman Berkley Group Inc., 1964); Arthur C. McGiffert, *Martin Luther: The Man and His Work* (London: T. Fisher Unwins, 1911); Earnest G. Schwiebert, *Luther and His Times* (St. Louis: Concordia Publishing House, 1950); Preserved Smith, *The Life and Letters of Martin Luther* (Boston: Houghton Mifflin Co., 1911).

M

MAKEMIE, FRANCIS (1658-1708)

The father of American Presbyterianism.
Born in Ireland, Francis Makemie emigrated to the American colonies in 1683. By 1706, he had organized a presbytery in Philadelphia, and 10 years later the first synod of the colonies was held. In 1729, the American Presbyterians adopted the Westminster Confession as their doctrinal standard. By the time of the American revolution, Presbyterians were among the four largest denominations in America.

MANCHURIAN REVIVAL (1906) See TWENTIETH CENTURY AWAKENING

MANDATE FOR EVANGELISM See GREAT COMMISSION

MARSDEN, SAMUEL (d. 1838)

Pioneer missionary to New Zealand.
Sent to Australia as a chaplain in 1793, Samuel Marsden became interested in the native Maori people of the region. His interest led him to establish the first mission on the north island of New Zealand in 1822. By 1854, it was estimated that all but about 1 percent of the Maoris were nominally Christian.

MARTIN, T. T. (1862-1939)

American evangelist.
Born in Smith County, Mississippi, on April 28, 1862, T. T. Martin was raised amid the poverty of the postwar South. After graduating from Mississippi College, he sensed the call of God to preach and prepared for ministry at Southern Baptist Theological Seminary in Louisville, Kentucky, graduating in 1891. His plans to serve as a missionary were thwarted by a near fatal attack of food poisoning. After several years of pastoral ministry, Martin entered full-time evangelistic work in 1900. The success of his ministry caused him to begin erecting tents for his meetings because most churches were too small to handle the crowds. Also, he directed other evangelists to preach at meetings he was unable to conduct. Martin died on May 23, 1939.

In addition to his own evangelistic ministry, Martin contributed to the cause of evangelism by forming an evangelistic association in which relatively unknown evangelists were given an opportunity to conduct crusades. Some of these evangelists later had their own highly successful ministries.

MARTYN, HENRY (1781-1812)

Pioneer missionary to India.
Henry Martyn went to India as the chaplain of the East India Company in 1806. During the next six years, he had an extensive preaching mission to both Hindus and Moslems and translated the New Testament into three languages while fulfilling his duties as chaplain. His zeal for missions is best reflected in his diary entry when he arrived in India, "Now let me burn out for God."

MASS EVANGELISM

The presentation of the gospel to more than one person, or a mass of people. Traditionally, mass evangelism refers to local church or areawide campaigns and has the purpose of evangelizing the lost. Beyond the usual practice of evangelistic campaigns, mass evangelism also refers to any attempt to present the gospel to a group. This includes musical concerts, drama and other special events.

MASS MOVEMENT

An archaic term for people movement.

Reference: See PEOPLE MOVEMENT.

MASSES

The majority or bulk of society that lives in submission to the classes—the proletariat.

Reference: See CLASSES.

MASTERING THE BIBLE

The Bible is the most indispensable instrument for a Christian. The Bible brought you into the Christian world; it will cause you to grow and will prepare you for heaven. As has been said, "The Bible will keep you from sin, or sin will keep you from the Bible." The Bible deserves our best efforts to master it, because it:

1. Keeps you from sin by its instructional power. "Your word have I hidden in my heart, that I might not sin against You" (Ps. 119:11).

2. Teaches the correct way of life. "Your word is a lamp to my feet and a light to my path" (v. 105). Arnold Toynbee, the historian, noted that the Bible "pierces through the intellect and plays directly upon my heart."

3. Is like a vaccination, protecting you by cleansing your conscience (John 15:3).

4. Gives joy (Jer. 15:16).

5. Corrects wrong teaching that would allow deviation (2 Tim. 3:16).

6. Produces a "hedge" against sin in your life (Heb. 4:12).

7. Is the only source of the message of salvation. "And that from childhood you have known the Holy Scriptures, which are able to make you wise for salvation through faith which is in Christ Jesus" (2 Tim. 3:15).

8. Gives you assurance of your salvation. "These things have I written to you who believe in the name of the Son of God, that you may know that you have eternal life" (1 John 5:13).

9. Enables you to grow in Christian character. "As newborn babes, desire the pure milk of the word, that you may grow thereby" (1 Pet. 2:2). It is (a) milk for the body (1 Pet. 2:2), (b) meat for the growing Christian (Heb. 5:12,14), (c) bread for the hungry (John 6:51) and (d) honey for satisfaction (Ps. 19:10).

10. Brings peace when your heart is troubled.

11. Imparts the characteristics of Jesus Christ as you study it. "But we all, with unveiled face, beholding as in a mirror the glory of the Lord, are being transformed into the same image from glory to glory" (2 Cor. 3:18).

12. Is filled with promises we can depend on. "By which have been given to us exceedingly great and precious promises, that through these you may be partakers of the divine nature" (2 Pet. 1:4).

How to Master the Bible

1. Read the Bible daily.

2. Bible study is more than reading Scripture. Begin your study by asking these questions:

a. What is it saying? Don't read your thoughts into the verse. Ask what the author meant. Interpret each verse in its context.

b. Where else does God say this? Use the center column reference in your Bible to find other places teaching the same truth. You may have to use a concordance to find a parallel passage. Comparing Scripture with Scripture will expand your knowledge of the Bible (2 Pet. 1:20,21).

c. What are the problems in the passage?

d. What does it mean to me? Here you apply the Scripture to your life. Think of the ways you could apply these verses to your life. Then write out the principles so you have a clear understanding of the practical application.

e. Analyze words. Look up their meaning in a dictionary. Then look up the words in a concordance to see how they are used in other references. In-depth word study is an excellent way to grasp biblical doctrine.

3. Memorize special passages. The psalmist declared, "Your word have I hidden in mine heart, that I might not sin against You" (Ps. 119:11). Memorize Scripture by first marking the verse in your Bible. Underline the verse so it will stand out the next time you study the passage. Next, write or type the verse on a small card. Carry the cards with you for review in your free time. Plan a systematic way to review the verses you have already memorized. Without review, you can't remember the exact words you memorize. You may even forget the whole verse. But you will grow in the process of applying diligent effort to master the verse and its meaning.

4. Meditate on what you have studied. "Blessed is the man who walks not in the counsel of the ungodly, nor stands in the path of sinners, nor sits in the seat of the scornful; but his delight is in the law of the Lord, and in His law he meditates day and night" (1:1,2).

MAYHEW FAMILY (1642–1806)

Family devoted to the evangelism of native Americans.

When the Mayhew family received their land grant, it included Martha's Vineyard and Nantucket Island, which was already home to many native people. They believed they had an evangelistic responsibility to reach their neighbors, and began doing so with the efforts of Thomas Mayhew. When he was lost at sea, his father became involved in continuing the mission to the native Americans. Ultimately, five generations of this one family became actively involved in the evangelism of native people.

McCHEYNE, ROBERT MURRAY (1813–1843)

Scottish revivalist and missionary leader.

Born in Edinburgh, Scotland, May 21, 1813, Robert Murray McCheyne proved himself a distinguished student in his studies at Edinburgh University. He served as the pastor of St. Peter's Church in Dundee for all of his brief ministry. The Dundee revival that had begun under his predecessor, William C. Burns, continued throughout McCheyne's ministry, having as many as 39 prayer meetings conducted weekly in his church. At age 24, he joined others in advocating Jewish evangelism and traveled to Palestine to investigate the best means to achieve that goal. McCheyne died of typhus on March 25, 1843.

McCheyne's greatest contribution to evangelism was his role in encouraging Jewish evangelism. He is best known today in the context of pastoral ministry. His published sermons are still widely read today by those in ministry.

McGAVRAN, DONALD A. (1897–1990)

As a third-generation missionary, McGavran served with the United Christian Missionary Society (Disciples of Christ) in India from 1923–1955. This service followed the completion of undergraduate training at Butler University, Indianapolis, Indiana, (Ph.D., 1933). His doc-

toral dissertation was a statistical analysis of the influence of Christian schools on the religious beliefs of students from Hindu families.

A significantly new era unfolded for Dr. McGavran from 1934–1935 through the influence of Bishop J. Waskom Pickett, a Methodist observer of "people movements" in India. Donald H. Gill notes, "This led McGavran to further research which indicated many of the reasons why the church in 136 districts had grown by 11 percent in 10 years while in 11 other districts it had grown by some 200 percent in the same period."[1]

Prior to his experience with Bishop Pickett, McGavran considered the individualistic "one-by-one" approach to evangelism as the most biblically based and pragmatically fruitful. He had heard of large groups of "peoples" claiming to have undergone Christian conversion and baptism, but viewed them as suspect. His term for this was "half-baked mission work"! In an interview with John K. Branner for *Evangelical Mission Quarterly*, he confided:

In 1934–35 I began to see that what we had heard was quite wrong. What we had deemed "unsound, half-baked work" was really one great way in which the church was growing quite effectively. God was blessing that way of growth. They were becoming better churches than ours. It was heresy to say that in 1935.[2]

In the same interview, Dr. McGavran shared that these concepts germinated in his mind. Earlier, in 1930, he had written *How to Teach Religion in Mission Schools*, and now in 1936 he collaborated with Pickett and Singh in writing the early classic on people movements, *The Mass Movement Survey of Mid-India*. This title was revised in 1958 to *Church Growth and Group Conversion*.

Resigning his position as executive secretary of the United Christian Missionary Society (UCMS) in 1937, he spent three years as a researcher in Chattisgarh and served as principal of mission schools as well as superintendent of the leprosy home and hospital.

According to Donald Hill, another cornerstone event occurred in 1953 when McGavran and his wife agreed that she would manage the mission while he absented himself for a month to a retreat site about 25 miles away to compile research notes and write *The Bridges of God*. Furlough time, scheduled to begin in 1954, allowed him to share his manuscript with Sir Kenneth Grubb in London. As a result, World Dominion Press published both this book and *How Churches Grow* (1959).

These were difficult days for what proved to be a message rejected by many mission leaders. Dr. McGavran writes, "In 1959, a profound discouragement seized me, and I was at the point of quitting. What I had to say had not caught fire and my efforts seemed futile."[3]

Opinions changed rapidly, however, when colonial empires began to take measures for self-government during the 1950s. Revolutionary movements destroyed or seized missionary properties, and McGavran says, "Missions wallowed in a twenty-year trough, which reached its lowest point around 1968." Pessimism then began to turn into optimism as mission leaders searched for new approaches to world evangelism. These forces led to a moral relativism that strongly opposed the Church Growth Movement's priority of evangelism.

A major revival of obedience to the Great Commission occurred in 1966. The Congress on the Church's Worldwide Mission assembled at Wheaton, Illinois, in April. In late October, 1,200 delegates assembled in Berlin for the two-week World Congress on Evangelism. McGavran and his team of missiologists had much influence on the Wheaton congress, but less in Berlin. Receptivity by evangelicals for church-growth concepts was heightened by the 1970 publication of *Understanding Church Growth* by McGavran, *Church Growth and the Word of God* by Dr. Alan Tippett, an Australian missiologist, and *The 25 Unbelievable Years: 1945-1969* by Dr. Ralph Winter, a Fuller missiologist. Articles on the movement would soon follow in both *Eternity* and *Christianity Today* magazines (1972).

During the 1960s, four other events of magnitude occurred. First, almost obscured by the slopes of the Cascade Mountains, just a hundred miles south of Portland, Oregon, the Northwest

Christian College (Disciples of Christ) employed Dr. Donald McGavran to begin the Institute of Church Growth in 1961. Second, the *Church Growth Bulletin* was published just three years later in 1964 under Dr. McGavran's leadership and Norman Cumming's initiative in offering Overseas Crusade's printing and mailing sponsorship.

Third, the dream of Dr. Charles Fuller became reality when Dr. McGavran accepted the invitation to establish the Fuller School of World Mission and Institute of Church Growth at Fuller Theological Seminary in Pasadena, California (1965). At that time, a faculty of missiologists began to be assembled.

Finally, North American interest in church growth was awakened to the abundance of superchurches in the United States, as researched by Dr. Elmer Towns's best-seller *The Ten Largest Sunday Schools* (1969), and the annual listing of the largest evangelical and fundamentalist churches in his articles for *Christian Life* magazine.

Dr. C. Peter Wagner reminds us of Dr. McGavran's earlier plans in 1963 "to add to the Institute of Church Growth at Eugene an American Division headed by an American minister of church growth convictions, but the plan did not mature."[4] Wagner also notes: McGavran's "*How Churches Grow* [1959] did attempt to address church growth in America. One of its chapters was reprinted as a booklet under the title *Do Churches Grow?* It sold thousands of copies among American church leaders, but failed to light any fires. The time was not yet ripe."[5]

Yet McGavran always had the long view. He said, "We stand in the sunrise of missions." His greatest influence beyond his writings are the thousands of missionaries, educators and denominational officials who have been trained at Fuller Seminary. They have gone around the world to "make disciples of all nations." In a tribute to McGavran, C. Peter Wagner wrote:

Donald McGavran was born of missionary parents in India before the turn of the century. His grandparents had also been missionaries to India, sailing around Africa's

Cape of Good Hope to get there. He is a graduate of Yale and Columbia. He has climbed the Himalayas. He has produced motion pictures. He was the director of a missionary agency. He managed a leprosarium and supervised a school system. He went one-on-one with a wounded tiger and met a wild boar in combat. He is fluent in Hindi and Chattisqarhee. He stopped a cholera epidemic. He was the founding dean of a prestigious missiological institution. He has written twenty-three books on missions and church growth. His travels have taken him to virtually every nation of the world.

When, one or two generations from now, historians of religion look back to the twentieth century, McGavran will most likely be remembered chiefly as the father of the Church Growth Movement....

Having laid the conceptual groundwork for the Church Growth Movement in the 1950s, McGavran's crowning achievement was the establishment of the institution which was to become his base of operations. In 1961 he started an Institute of Church Growth at Northwest Christian College in Eugene, Oregon. In 1965 he moved the Institute to Fuller Seminary and became the founding dean of the Fuller School of World Mission and Institute of Church Growth. Although he stopped teaching at the age of eighty-three, McGavran continued an active schedule of research, writing, traveling, and speaking, and works in his seminary office daily when he is in town. His school is the foremost institution of missiological training with a resident faculty of twelve full-time and thirty part-time members and a student body of over 500.

With over three billion of the world's people yet to believe in Jesus Christ, Donald McGavran sees the golden years of missions yet ahead. Resources for completing the task have never been greater. Missiological research and knowledge have never been so advanced. Peoples around the world have never been more open to

the gospel. God is on the throne. Jesus said, "I will build my church," and he continues to do it. No wonder that Donald McGavran, with a twinkle in his eye and determination on his lips, says today with more verve than ever, "We stand in the sunrise of missions."[6]

References: [1]Donald H. Gill, "Apostle of Church Growth," *World Vision* 12, no. 7 (September 1968): 11. [2]John K. Branner, "McGavran Speaks on Roland Allen," *Evangelical Mission Quarterly* 8, no. 3 (Spring 1972): p. 173. [3]Donald A. McGavran and Win Arn, *Ten Steps for Church Growth* (San Francisco: HarperCollins, 1987), p. 5. [4]C. Peter Wagner, *Your Church Can Grow* (Ventura, Calif.: Regal Books, 1976), p. 14. [5]Ibid, p. 13. [6]C. Peter Wagner, ed. *Church Growth: State of the Art* (Wheaton, Ill.: Tyndale House, 1986), pp. 15, 17, 18.

McINTOSH, GARY L.

Dr. Gary L. McIntosh is the Director of the Doctor of Ministry program at Talbot School of Theology, Biola University in La Mirada, California, where he also serves as Associate Professor of Practical Theology, teaching courses in the field of church growth. He received his education from Rockmont College, Denver, Colorado (B.A. in Biblical Studies), Western Conservative Baptist Seminary, Portland, Oregon (M.Div. in Pastoral Studies) and Fuller Theological Seminary, Pasadena, California (D.Min. in Church Growth Studies).

An ordained minister in the Conservative Baptist Association, Gary served several churches as a youth pastor, Christian education director and senior pastor in Colorado, Oregon and California from 1968 to 1983. From 1983 through 1986, Gary was vice president of Consulting Services for the influential Institute for American Church Growth (later Church Growth, Inc.) in Pasadena, California. He was primarily responsible for church consulting and direction of the Church Growth Associate program, training more than 90 people as church consultants in a three-year period.

Gary is editor of the popular *Church Growth Network* newsletter, and has authored *How to Develop a Pastoral Compensation Plan* (Church Growth Institute, 1991), *How to Develop a Policy*

Manual (Church Growth Institute, 1992), *How to Start a Small Group Ministry* (Church Growth Institute, 1991, with Dr. Rodney Dean), *Finding Them, Keeping Them* (Broadman Press, 1992, with Dr. Glen S. Martin) and *The Issachar Factor: Understanding Trends That Confront Your Church and Designing a Strategy for Success* (Broadman & Holman, 1994, also with Dr. Glen S. Martin). One of McIntosh's prevailing interests focuses on generational change in the Church, and his newest book, *Three Generations: Riding the Waves of Generational Change in Your Church* (Revell, 1995), speaks directly to that interest.

Gary's articles have appeared in *Global Church Growth, Net Results, The Win Arn Growth Report, Leadership Church Growth: America, Growing Churches* and many denominational publications. He is a contributor to *The Pastor's Church Growth Handbook Vol. II,* edited by Dr. Win Arn (1982) and *The Leadership Handbooks of Practical Theology, Volume Two: Outreach and Care,* edited by James D. Berkley (1994).

MEDIA EVANGELISM
See SATURATION EVANGELISM

MELTING-POT THEORY

A point of view that people of differing cultural backgrounds will automatically develop a commonness and oneness because they are in geographic proximity.

MEMBERSHIP, CHURCH
The doctrine of church membership is linked to evangelism and church growth because it is the end result of the evangelistic process. In some churches, gospel invitations are given to "come forward" for salvation or church membership. In some, people join the church after going through a church-membership class or a catechism class. In some denominations, the names of children are added to a "list" when they are born into families of members. Therefore, a study of membership in local churches is necessary to determine its scriptural position and how, if at all, to implement it into our evangelistic outreach.

What Is Church Membership?
We like to think of church membership as an expression of belonging. When people join a church, they are telling others they feel at home there and want to be a full participant in the life of the church. Therefore, church membership involves more than just adding a name to the roll. It is an expression of a desire to be enfolded into the church family. It provides the opportunity to be involved in the lives of others.

Why Join a Church?
Church membership has lost its meaning for many. The Bible teaches that every Christian is "baptized into one body" (1 Cor. 12:13). This refers to the baptism of the Holy Spirit by which all Christians are one in Christ. The Bible also uses the expression "body of Christ" to describe the local church (v. 27). Therefore, when Christians are baptized by water and join a church, they are demonstrating outwardly what has already happened inwardly in their lives. Because they become a part of the Body of Christ by receiving Him as Savior (John 1:12), they want to become an active member of a local church, which is a local expression of the Body of Christ.

When moving into a community and worshiping there, it is only natural that you would want to take steps to transfer membership there. The Bible describes everyone as an individual part of the corporate Body (1 Cor. 12:14-27). This means the Body is incomplete without everyone! It also implies that you are incomplete without the Body. When Christians understand this principle, they want to determine where they fit into the Body and thus become valuable members of the church.

Joining a church places a person under the discipline of the Scriptures—the Word of God. God gave us the Bible to aid in spiritual growth (1 Pet. 2:2), help obtain victory over sin (Ps. 119:9-11), enable our prayers to be answered (John 15:7), help us develop a strong character (1 Cor. 3:3) and grow in the ability to believe God (Rom. 10:17). As we hear the Word of God preached and study the Scriptures with others, we can begin to experience these benefits in our own lives.

God made us to need relationships with others. Becoming a part of a church provides us with the opportunity to encourage others and to be encouraged by others (Heb. 10:25). In the New Testament, those who received Christ as Savior quickly chose to become part of the church (Acts 2:41). As they interacted with each other on a regular basis, they were able to build steadfastness into their lives in various spiritual disciplines (v. 42). Becoming active in the life of a church is one way of ensuring personal success in the Christian life.

When to Leave a Church?

It is not uncommon for Christians who are dissatisfied with their churches to begin looking for new church homes. Just as God moves pastors from one church to another, He may also intervene and lead a person from one church to another. But take time to be sure God is indeed leading in this step.

Sometimes Christians choose to leave a church rather than face a difficult situation that has developed. No one likes the discomfort associated with interpersonal conflict, but leaving the church is not always the right answer. The Scriptures offer specific guidelines for dealing with conflict. It is important to take these steps before making a decision about a church home.

When a conflict arises, we are expected to identify our personal contribution to the conflict and deal with it (Matt. 5:23,24). Only then do we have the right to confront others who have offended us (18:15). In confronting another person about a problem, we need to do it gently (Gal. 6:1) in an attempt to reconcile our differences (Luke 17:3). This involves both using the right words (Prov. 25:11,12) and having the right attitude as those words are spoken (15:1). If there is no response, others in your church may need to be involved in helping resolve the problem (Matt. 18:16,17).

One of the marks of the New Testament church was the members' spirit of unity (Acts 2:46). God wants members of His family to get along with others in the family (Ps. 133:1). Even if other factors are involved in a decision to leave a church, it is always best to reconcile differences quickly (Prov. 17:14). People who habitually fail

to deal with conflict often become the source of conflict themselves (15:18). In contrast, as we mature in our Christian lives, God can use us to help others resolve their conflicts (16:7).

Sometimes the problem is the unreasonable expectations a Christian may have for his or her church. Although church members ought to live up to their calling as Christians (Eph. 4:1), often we don't. All of us still struggle with our sin natures (1 John 1:8). When thinking of leaving a church because the people there are not perfect, be aware that you, too, must struggle to overcome the old nature.

Basis for Church Membership

In the New Testament, church membership was related to four conditions. First, people did not join the church until they had first received Christ as personal Savior (Acts 5:13,14). Second, Christians were baptized as a profession of their faith prior to joining a church (2:41). Third, Christians remained members of a church only as long as they remained in agreement with the church's doctrinal beliefs (Titus 3:10). Fourth, church members were responsible for living moral lives so as not to hinder the corporate testimony of the church (1 Cor. 6:9-11).

Responsibilities as a Member

Just as the parts of the body work together in harmony to enable the body to function, so church members need to work together to enable the church to accomplish its ministry (12:27). Church members invest in their local church in several ways. First, they make a special effort to give time to church services and ministry projects (Eph. 5:16). Second, they use their spiritual gifts as ministry tools in the church (4:12). Third, their consistent financial giving to the church helps underwrite the costs associated with the church's ministry (1 Cor. 16:2). Fourth, they help build up others in the church (Heb. 10:25). Fifth, they use their influence to help others receive Christ as Savior and become a part of church life (Acts 8:4).

Joining the church is more than adding a name to the membership list. As people join a church, they are indicating they want to be involved in the life of the church, and want others in the church to become involved in their lives. They are becoming part of a family. As such, they are entitled to all the privileges associated with family life, as well as assuming the responsibility of making that family work.

MEMCON

Memorandum of conversation. A printed record of an interview or discussion held in connection with a spiritual-mapping research project. — GOJR

MERCY, GIFT OF See SHOWING MERCY, GIFT OF

METHODIUS (d. c.885)

Missionary of the Eastern church to the Khazars and Moravians.

Born into the home of an army officer and prominent citizen of Salonika, Methodius was well educated and may have been a civic official before entering the monastery. He served as a missionary to the Khazars and Moravians and was involved in translating the Scriptures and other religious books into the Slavonic language. His work was opposed by the German clergy who argued that the Eucharist could only be conducted in Latin, Greek or Hebrew, rather than the common language of the people that was the custom of the Eastern Church. He traveled to Rome in 868 to raise the matter with Pope Hadrian II. The Pope apparently permitted the practice of using Slavonic in the Eucharist, a decision that was later reversed by Pope John VIII. John later changed his earlier position and made Methodius archbishop and head of the hierarchy for the Moravians. Methodius died about 885.

METHODS, EVANGELISTIC

Evangelistic methods refer to those approaches or techniques that seek to present the timeless gospel to a given culture. Although biblical principles and the essential message (see KERYGMA, GOSPEL) must be constant, methods must be changed to reach various cul-

tures and eras in history. Examples from history illustrate this.

The Apostle Paul
Paul used the following methods:

1. Personal evangelism. This timeless method was used often by Paul (e.g., Acts 16:25-32).

2. Urban evangelism. Paul focused on the great cities of his day. He knew the gospel would spread from these centers to surrounding areas.

3. Reaching those with common interests. Although called to be apostle to the Gentiles, Paul always began by witnessing to the Jews, with whom he had much in common.

4. Church planting. Paul planted churches, which continued the spread of the gospel.

The Eighteenth Century
Examples of methods in the eighteenth century include:

1. Field preaching. Preaching the gospel outdoors to common people was begun by Whitefield and Wesley during the Evangelical Awakening in England.

2. Small-group evangelism. A basis for Wesley's small-group development was to gather persons who desired to "flee from the wrath to come."

3. Itinerant preaching. Whitefield and Wesley, along with others, resurrected the practice of preaching from town to town.

4. Lay preachers. In the First Great Awakening, John Wesley and Theodore Frelinghuysen used lay preachers to assist in ministry.

The Nineteenth Century
1. Camp meetings. These gatherings began in Kentucky in the Second Great Awakening at the turn of the nineteenth century, and continued to be an effective method for generations.

2. New Measures of Charles Finney. See FINNEY.

3. Evangelistic literature. The American Tract Society, evangelistic music attractions, citywide crusades, the public invitation and evangelistic Sunday Schools all depended on literature distribution.

4. The "faith" mission movement. This was an organization of interdenominational foreign mission boards who sent missionaries. These missionaries raised their own financial support apart from denominational resources, hence the name "faith."

5. *The Rescue Mission movement.* These missions were established in growing urban areas to evangelize homeless people (primarily men).

The Twentieth Century

More recent methods include the use of television and radio in evangelism, seeker services and special-event evangelism. It should be noted that the most effective methods in history were born out of revival or renewal. This fact should cause sincere believers to avoid merely secular approaches in developing methods. The best methods are born in the heart of God and are utilized by Christian leaders. -ALR

MEYER, FREDERICK BROTHERTON (1847–1929)

British evangelist and Bible teacher.

Born in London and educated at Brighton College, F. B. Meyer had several successful pastorates between 1870 and 1895. In 1872, he met Dwight L. Moody and was instrumental in introducing the evangelist to British churches. Following a term as president of the National Federation of Free Churches (1904–1905), Meyer served as an evangelist with that group, conducting missions in South Africa and the Far East. For many years, he was closely associated with the Keswick Conferences.

Meyer's greatest contribution to evangelism was introducing D. L. Moody to the British churches. He is best remembered for his various books on the Christian life.

MILLS, SAMUEL JOHN (1783–1818)

Pioneer American missionary statesman.

When the American Board of Commissioners for Foreign Missions sent out its first group of missionaries in 1812, Samuel J. Mills remained in America to stimulate interest in missions among American churches. He encouraged interest in both foreign and home missions. Among his accomplishments were the establishment of a New England school to train America's native people, Asians and people from the Pacific

islands as missionaries to their own people; the formation of the American Bible Society and the formation of the American Colonization Society, which returned freed slaves to Liberia. Mills died at sea during a return voyage from Liberia.

Mills's greatest contribution to evangelism was his involvement in establishing a school to train indigenous Christian workers.

MINISTRY

Ministry is defined as communicating the gospel to people at their point of need. It is not something restricted to pastors and other church officers. Rather, ministry is something in which every Christian can and should be involved. The key to effective ministry involves using one's spiritual gifts to meet needs in the lives of others.

The definition of ministry contains three parts: First, ministry involves communication. The word "communication" means to make common. Second, the gospel is being communicated in ministry. The gospel may be viewed as propositional truth such as the death, burial and resurrection of Jesus Christ (1 Cor. 15:3,4) and personal truth (i.e., the person of Jesus Christ Himself) (Mark 1:1). Third, ministry is concerned with meeting needs. Ministry meets people at their felt needs and takes them to their ultimate need of Christ and salvation. All these needs can and should be met through the communication of the gospel.

MINISTRY, GIFT OF HELPS

The person who has the gift of ministry or helps has the ability to serve God by ministering to the physical and spiritual needs of others. Often those in the office of a deacon (*diakonos*) have the gift of ministry or helps (*diakonia*). But many have the gift who do not have the office. The strengths of this gift include: (1) enjoys manual projects or practical service, (2) serves without fanfare, but needs to be appreciated, (3) senses physical and financial needs of others, (4) works for immediate goals and (5) gets satisfaction out of completing projects.

Among the weaknesses of this gift are: (1) may tend to be too practically oriented, to the exclusion of understanding the biblical motive for doing a task, (2) insensitive to the lack of involvement by prophets or teachers in practical projects and (3) others wrongly interpret their good works. The person who has this gift needs to avoid the danger of (1) pride, (2) being critical of nonpractical church leaders, (3) becoming bitter if not recognized and (4) being critical of steps of faith that appear unpractical.

MISSIOLOGY

The study of cross-cultural communication of the Christian faith.

MISSION

The task for which God sends His people into the world. Mission includes the evangelistic mandate and the cultural mandate.

References: See EVANGELISTIC MANDATE; CULTURAL MANDATE.

MISSION STRUCTURES
See SODALITY

MISSIONS EDUCATION FOR A CHURCH

Why are there not enough volunteers to fill the openings on the various mission fields? Certainly it is because young people are not being faced with the challenge of giving themselves in missionary service. If they do not belong to a special missionary organization, many Sunday School pupils—young or old—do not receive specific information on missions.

The logical place for Sunday School members to learn about missions is the Sunday School.

1. Have a plan. Unless missions teaching is incorporated in the regular curriculum of a denomination or church, a definite plan must be implemented to include it regularly. What is left to hit-or-miss will be missed.

a. Appoint a person within each department (class) to be responsible for the missionary teaching.

b. Choose a regular time—weekly or monthly—when the missionary story or facts will be presented.

c. Choose specific mission fields for study to be sure the teaching is thorough, rather than presenting sketchy information about many places and people.

2. Have a program. Suggest that the missionary chairman select others to serve as a committee to build a definite program.

a. Select the fields for study.

b. Find books, pictures, maps, filmstrips and other necessary materials on those fields.

c. Have pictures available of the missionaries on those fields for the pupils to "meet" during the study.

d. Plan songs or games and occasionally a food typical of the land being studied.

e. Use the national costume during presentation of the material, if possible.

f. Display articles from the land under study.

3. Develop missionary projects.

a. Let the students work on a missionary map. Some who are artistic can enlarge a map of the area being studied. Let students add the names of towns, using the small map as a guide. From time to time (weekly or monthly), let a small representative picture be placed on the map at the location discussed in class.

b. Prepare a missionary box. Fill the box with pictures, books, games or puzzles missionaries can use in their teaching. Missionaries find Sunday School paper pictures useful as awards to boys and girls who otherwise would never see such a picture. Classes may prepare scrapbooks of Bible pictures and stories for the missionaries. Adult classes may make garments to send to hospitals for new babies, or supply other medical needs.

c. Make a class scrapbook. Although all the students may contribute pictures and write articles to place into the scrapbook, organize a committee that is responsible for planning and arranging the contents.

d. Write to missionaries. Appoint a committee of students to correspond with boys and girls on the mission field. Letters from the missionaries may be added to the scrapbook.

e. Make teaching devices for missionaries.

Classes of juniors through adults can make object lessons, posters, puppets, charts, story wheels and other aids to use in teaching. Such aids are expensive to take in a missionary's luggage and hard to make from materials available on the mission field.

f. Have a systematic missionary offering. Students often give with more concern to those with whom they are acquainted. Although the church may have a missionary budget, students will feel more personally involved in giving if an occasional special offering is received for missionaries about whom they have studied.

4. Extend the missionary challenge. After a missionary presentation, opportunity should be given for students to make a definite commitment to service, if God has laid it on their hearts. A public acknowledgment of dedication increases the responsibility of the student making the decision.

MOBILE UNIT

A spiritual-mapping team cell that extracts useful information from primary research sources with a community. A mobile unit will typically gather this information through observation and interviews. —GOJR

MODALITY

The vertical structure of churches into which people are born and raised; the local church, district denomination or congregational structure.

Reference: See SODALITY.

MODEL CHURCH APPROACH

A recent method of leadership training for church growth in which a rapidly growing church becomes a model for others. Normally, such a church will host conferences at its headquarters to demonstrate and explain how it grew. Willow Creek Community Church in South Barrington, Illinois, is perhaps the best example of this method.

The strength of this approach is in the adage, "evangelism [or church growth] is more caught than taught." The experience of seeing the results of what is taught can be beneficial. The weakness, however, is in the danger of copying the methods of one church in one cultural context and attempting to apply the same techniques in a different setting. Principles and encouragement can be learned from this approach; specific methods should be followed with great care. — ALR

MODERNITY

The prevailing cultural system that is produced by the forces of development and modernization in the present world, especially as it influences the Church. More than modernism (i.e., the liberalization of conservative doctrine), modernity is the influence on biblical Christianity of capitalism, industrialization, technology, telecommunications and marketing. Although these facts may enhance life, they may also assault the humanness of all people, and Christians in particular.

One of the particular concerns of those who accuse The Church Growth Movement of giving into modernity is that evangelism has uncritically used strategies borrowed from the human sciences, advertising, television and marketing—in essence, "selling Jesus."

MOFFAT, ROBERT (1795–1883)

Pioneer missionary to Africa.

Born in Ormiston, Scotland, Robert Moffat was converted to Christ through the efforts of Wesleyan Methodists. He sensed the call of God to missions during a missionary conference in Manchester, England. He was accepted by the London Missionary Society and at age 21 set sail to South Africa. During his ministry, Robert Moffat translated the Bible into major tribal languages of South Africa. Following the death of his wife in 1871, Moffat traveled widely to promote the cause of world missions. One of those challenged to missionary service by Moffat became his son-in-law and perhaps the most famous missionary to Africa in history—David Livingstone.

Moffat's greatest contribution to evangelism was to lay the foundation upon which future African evangelism would take place.

MOODY, DWIGHT L. (1832–1899)

An evangelist who, it is said, "shook two continents for God."

The foundation for Moody's worldwide ministry came through Sunday School. As a young man, his Sunday School teacher came into the shoe store where Moody was working and led him to Jesus Christ. After that, Moody moved to Chicago and joined the Plymouth Congregational Church. He rented five pews and filled them with young boys he brought in off the street. But he realized he could do more to reach Chicago for Christ. Moody started a Sunday School in a former saloon in the vice-ridden section of Chicago called "little hell." When this small room could not accommodate the students, Moody moved it to North Market Street and it eventually became the largest Sunday School in Chicago.

Moody spread enthusiasm through the Illinois Sunday School conventions between 1859–1864. At the Sunday School Convention in Springfield, Illinois, he remarked, "This thing [the convention] so far has been a dead failure." He began a prayer meeting along with a few other people, and within a few days the entire convention experienced revival. Sunday School delegates returned home to revive Sunday Schools across Illinois. Out of that convention came the great Sunday School leaders Jacobs, Eggleston, Tyng, P. B. Bliss, Wannamaker and others.

Because of his passion for education, Moody founded other educational endeavors for Christ, such as Northfield Schools. Next he founded the Moody Bible Institute in 1882, one of the first Bible Institutes in America. Out of Moody Bible Institute came the Moody Colportage Series, an organization that provided inexpensive Christian literature: *Moody* magazine and Moody Press. Today, the organization founded by Moody offers extensive ministries around the world.

Moody eventually went into citywide evangelistic crusades that brought hundreds of thousands to Jesus Christ.

MORAVIAN REVIVAL (1727) See GREAT AWAKENING

MORRISON, HENRY CLAY (1857–1942)

American evangelist and educator.

Born in Barren County, Kentucky, Henry Clay Morrison was raised by his grandfather following the death of his parents. At about age 11, he was converted to Christ and sensed the call of God to ministry. He began preaching as a circuit rider and station pastor about eight years later, eventually becoming the pastor of a respected Methodist church in Kentucky. In 1890, he left the pastorate to devote himself more fully to evangelism—primarily through camp meetings. He twice served as president of Asbury College (1910–1925; 1933–1940) and was instrumental in establishing Asbury Theological Seminary (1923).

MORRISON, ROBERT (1782–1834)

Pioneer missionary to China.

Robert Morrison was sent to China by the London Missionary Society in 1807, and for much of his ministry was the sole Protestant missionary in China. He overcame cultural obstacles and studied the Chinese language, producing a Chinese dictionary and grammar. His linguistic efforts culminated in the translation of the Bible into Chinese.

MOSAIC

The variety of cultural, ethnic, economic, educational and linguistic groupings of people found in a city, country, state or nation.

MOTIVATION FOR EVANGELISM AND CHURCH GROWTH

Flavil R. Yeakley, in his 1976 Ph.D. dissertation in Speech Communication (University of Illinois), conducted research to compare churches with high, medium and low growth rates and the differences among converts, dropouts and nonconverts.

A mail survey was conducted among 2,000 randomly selected congregations of the Church of Christ throughout the United States. One thousand and nine questionnaires were returned and a follow-up study was conducted among 250 of the nonresponding congregations. Using this data, 48 congregations were selected for in-depth study. Selection was made on the basis of net growth rate. Sixteen local churches were selected in each of three groups: the top, middle and bottom 20 percent relating to net growth rate.

The in-depth studies in these 48 congregations included: data collection from church records; interviews with the 48 pulpit ministers; interviews with 240 converts, 240 dropouts and 240 nonconverts; and interviews with 513 members of those congregations who were identified as being the ones primarily involved in the effort to persuade the 720 subjects to become members of the church. Much of the information gathered in this survey was used in other parts of a broader study of persuasion in religious conversion, but several major parts of this survey focused directly on the relation of theory, practice, perception and results in religious communication.

Three Paradigms of Evangelism/Communication

Yeakley identified three types of evangelism/communication.

1. The Manipulative Monologue Model. This is the "salesman preacher." In this model, the messenger sends the message (stimulus) that elicits a response. The right presentation produces the right response. The message is information based. The appeal may be emotional, conditional or otherwise persuasive. Religion is sold like a soft drink to a prospect, not a person. The converts are viewed passively because God is active, or because the soul winner is active. Hearers are treated as objects to be manipulated, not as people who have the power of choice.

2. The Information Transmission Model. This is the teaching preacher. Plato argued that "ignorance causes evil"; therefore, "if all men had the knowledge of truth, all men would be good." The preacher motivated in this way believes that if the hearer is fed the correct information, the correct response will be given. The control belongs to the sender. When people who are exposed to correct religious data refuse to respond, the speaker blames him or herself. The listeners

become mechanical receivers, not persons. Authentic communication authenticates personhood (i.e., develops Christian selfhood).

3. The Nonmanipulative Dialogue. This is the friend or relational preacher. This preacher believes no two persons ever see things the same way. This speaker attempts to look at things from the perspective of the other person and seeks to share his or her faith and understanding. Nonmanipulative dialogue does not rule out possessing strong convictions and sharing strong convictions, but respects the free choice and individuality of the other person. Nonmanipulative dialogue recognizes that conversion is not effective if the other person does not internally respond from his or her power of choice and personhood.

Yeakley compiled statistics relating these models to several aspects of church growth. The first of these looked at the minister's view of evangelism. In high-growth churches, all ministers accepted the Nonmanipulative model. In medium-growth churches, 94 percent of the ministers accepted the Manipulative model. In low-growth churches, 87 percent of ministers accepted the Information Transmission model.

Yeakley also looked at the preaching style of ministers. In high-growth churches, 87 percent were perceived as positive. In medium-growth churches, 81 percent were perceived as negative. In low-growth churches, 75 percent were perceived as negative. Eighty percent of the ministers who accepted Information Transmission were negative. Ninety percent of the ministers who accepted Manipulative Monologue were negative. All ministers who accepted Nonmanipulative Dialogue were positive.

It was possible to distinguish the converts', dropouts' and nonconverts' views of the evangelist. In this study, a convert was one who stayed in the church at least a full year, a nonconvert was one who did not respond, and a dropout was one who left the church within two weeks. Seventy percent of the converts were contacted by nonmanipulative dialogue. Eighty-seven percent of the nonconverts were contacted by Information-Transmission. Seventy-five percent of the dropouts were contacted by manipulative monologue.

How did the subject of these evangelistic efforts view the evangelist? Seventy-one percent of converts saw the evangelist as a friend (Nonmanipulative Dialogue). Eighty-five percent of the dropouts saw the evangelist as a salesperson (Manipulative monologue). Eighty-seven percent of the nonconverts saw the evangelist as a teacher (Information Transmission).

Conversion and the Seasons of the Soul

The subjects were asked whether or not they were satisfied with their lifestyles before the church attempted to influence them. Eight percent of the converts and 50 percent of the dropouts and nonconverts had no concerns. This part of the study suggests that people who have appropriate concern are those who are most likely for conversion or church membership.

The degree of change the 720 subjects had recently experienced was measured by the Thomas H. Holmes' psychological stress scale. The more change in a person's life, the more likely he or she is to be converted to Christianity or change church membership. A big change was observed among subjects in high school through age 30. Those in the ranges of 45-50 and 60-65 also experienced a degree of change. Other age groups were fairly stable.

Yeakley's research is the basis for several general conclusions. First, growing churches use 8.6 different methods of contact. This is the basis for the "law of seven touches." Medium-growth churches used 6.9 different methods. Low-growth churches used only 3.3 different methods. Robert Schuller argues that a church should make five contacts in five different ways. New converts who stay in the church are exposed to a variety of evangelistic contacts.

Also, this research suggests that new converts who stay in the church develop a meaningful relationship with someone in the church before conversion. New converts who stay in the church may also develop relationships with members of the congregation after conversion, but they must develop within two weeks. They tend to join a primary group with whom they can closely identify.

Further, this research suggests a convert will remain in the church if he or she has an area of harmony with those already in the church. High-growth churches had a 2.9-year difference in age. Medium growth churches had a 7.7-year difference in age. Low growth churches had an 11.1-year age difference. This is a strong argument for the age-graded Sunday School. Also, high-growth churches were composed of people in a socioeconomic group a half step above the convert. In low-growth churches, the spread was two steps away.

Developing a Strategy for Growth

To develop a strategy for growth in a local church, consider the findings in this research. Each of the three models of evangelism-communication were effective in reaching certain kinds of people. Therefore, plan outreach strategy to target the people who are most "reachable." Target those whom your church is most likely to reach, and let other churches reach those they are most likely to reach. This will result in better stewardship of the energy expended in the ministry of evangelism.

A second important principle coming out of this research should extend one's view of evangelism. In a growing church, evangelism is viewed as both presenting the gospel and incorporating new converts into the church. If assimilating new converts into the church is the goal of evangelism, this bonding process should be a part of your evangelism strategy. The way a convert is bonded in the preconversion phase of evangelism is reflective of their bonding in the postconversion phase of evangelism.

MOTIVES FOR EVANGELISM

Evangelism is an imperative for all Christians. Although this is true, it is also a privilege and an honor. The apostle Paul calls us "Ambassadors for Christ." The reasons for evangelism include (1) it is commanded by Christ (Matt. 28:19; Mark 16:15); (2) the needs of people for salvation (Rom. 3:10,23); (3) our love for Christ (2 Cor. 5:14); (4) our love for others (John 1:41); (5) the example of Christ and His disciples as soul winners; (6) our Christian obligation as stewards (1 Cor. 4:1); (7) our desire to bring glory to God (John 15:8); (8) the ongoing lack of workers in the harvest field (Matt. 9:37); and (9) the promise of rewards (Ruth 2:12).

MOTT, JOHN RALEIGH (1865–1955)

Early leader in the Student Volunteer Movement for Foreign Missions.

Born in 1865, John Raleigh Mott was challenged to consider missions as a college student through the influence of C. T. Studd. Mott traveled widely around the world, first as an evangelist and later organizing student movements. He became an influential leader in Protestant missions. This was reflected in the major role Mott played in the World Missionary Conference held in Edinburgh, Scotland, in 1910, and his appointment as the first chairman of the International Missionary Council.

MULTICONGREGATIONAL MODEL

A church structure in which each homogeneous unit forms its own congregation and worships in its own language and/or style, yet the churches are all under the umbrella structure of one larger church. This is an option for a church that serves a pluralistic community. Frequently the various churches share the same facilities.

MULTI-INDIVIDUAL DECISION

A decision for conversion to Christianity made by a community rather than an individualistic decision-making process. After discussing the pros and cons of salvation, the entire group decides to follow Jesus.

MULTIRACIAL OR MULTIETHNIC CHURCH

A church composed of different peoples from different cultures.

Reference: See CONGLOMERATE CONGREGATION.

MUSIC, EVANGELISTIC

"The Christian Church was born in song."[1] In recent centuries, music has increasingly become central to the evangelistic ministry of the Church. During the Middle Ages, the fervency of singing alluded to by the apostle Paul (Eph. 5:19; Col. 3:16,17) was lost because of the rise and emphasis upon the institutionalized Church and the liturgical centrality of the Eucharist, and away from a personal encounter with Christ. During the Reformation, Martin Luther gave both the Bible and the hymnbook back to the people, introducing hymns that had familiar tunes and were written in the language of the people.

The Pietists of the late seventeenth and early eighteenth centuries began writing subjective hymns, reflecting their emphasis on "religion of the heart." At the same time, English dissenters, most clearly represented by Isaac Watts (called "the father of English hymnody"), began writing hymns that flourished in Congregational, Baptist and Presbyterian circles.

The modern era of evangelistic music directly parallels the era of the Great Awakenings. The roots of music used for evangelistic purposes can be most clearly traced to the Wesleyan Revival of John and Charles Wesley. The hymns of Charles Wesley, who wrote more than 6,000 hymns, were crucial to the theology of early Methodism. John preached in a practical, application-oriented manner to which Charles wed hymns by utilizing secular tunes. This was not unlike the practice of the German Reformation. As Donald P. Hustad commented, "Worthy lyrics sanctify the secular melody."[2]

The camp meetings of the Second Great Awakening were characterized by simple emotional hymns, many of them having evangelistic appeals. The influence of Charles Finney upon composer Thomas Hastings led to the first published songbook specifically for protracted revival services. Finney used the hymns of Hastings and others during his altar calls.

The first "music evangelist" to be widely recognized was Ira D. Sankey (1837–1899), who teamed with evangelist Dwight L. Moody. Sankey led congregational songs and sang solos. He was followed by scores of others, including Charles Alexander, who traveled with R. A. Torrey and J. Wilbur Chapman and "brought the 'gospel choir' to its nadir"[3]; Homer Rodeheaver, who teamed with Billy Sunday; and more recently, Cliff Barrows of the Billy Graham team.

Also in the twentieth century, music broadcast on radio, such as Stamps-Baxter gospel quartet music and revivalistic southern hymns have added to evangelistic music. More recent times have seen contemporary Christian music become a significant evangelistic tool. Artists who sing evangelistic songs are followed by gospel invitations in their concerts. We have also seen the rise of contemporary Christian radio stations and the use of such music in churches.

Evangelistic music is characterized by simplicity, joy and excitement, employing secular tunes and instruments, and a focus on a personal relationship with Christ. For the past 200 years, each generation of evangelicals has found a style of music that presents the gospel through music to that generation. Interestingly, each generation is always concerned about the use of secular tunes. —ALR

References: [1]Ralph P. Martin, *Worship in the Early Church* (Grand Rapids: Wm. B. Eerdmans, 1964), 39. [2]Donald R. Hustad, *Jubilate!* (Carol Stream, Ill.: Hope Publishing Co., 1981), p. 127. [3]Ibid., 134.

NATHANAEL See BARTHOLOMEW

NATURAL REVELATION

The self-revelation of God through His creation (the cosmological, teleological, anthropological and ontological arguments).

NEAR-NEIGHBOR EVANGELISM

Denotes evangelistic efforts to those who have the same language and culture.

References: See EVANGELISM, TYPES OF; E-1 EVANGELISM.

NEESIMA, JOSEPH HARDY (1843–1890)

Japanese educator and evangelist.

Born into the samurai class in his native Japan, Joseph Hardy Neesima was educated in America, where he was also converted to Christianity. With assistance from American Christians, he returned to Japan and established Doshisha University in Kyoto. Neesima's strategy was to reach his nation through educating the upper classes. Although he experienced some success during his lifetime, the goal of reaching the entire nation of Japan was not achieved.

NETWORKING EVANGELISM

This has a twofold definition. First, it is the principle of establishing and building redemptive friendships for the purposes of evangelism. Second, it is reaching and winning people to Christ through existing relationships.

NEVIUS, JOHN L. (1829–1893)

Presbyterian missionary to China and advocate of the indigenous church principle.

As a missionary to China, John L. Nevius published a series of articles on "The Planting and Development of Missionary Churches,"

which would have a profound effect on church planting in Korea. Missionaries in Korea sympathetic to Nevius's ideas invited him to Korea in 1890 to explain his principles more fully. "The Nevius Plan" stressed five principles of missionary work, including: (1) missionary evangelism should be done through extensive itinerant ministry, (2) the national church should be self-propagating, (3) the national church should be self-governing, (4) the national believers should underwrite the costs of their own buildings and contribute to the support of national workers and (5) every national believer should be involved in systematic Bible study in a small-group ministry.

The Nevius Plan, with its emphasis on developing strong indigenous churches, was Nevius's most significant contribution to the cause of world evangelism.

NEW MEASURES

This expression was coined by Charles Grandison Finney during his ministry, which involved measures not previously used by evangelical preachers to encourage a positive response to the gospel. Finney recognized that certain means of evangelism appeared to be effective in achieving the desired results even though they may not have been used previously. In a more contemporary appeal to use "new measures" in effectively evangelizing the masses during times of revival, Donald McGavran writes:

Revivals in conglomerate congregations at towns have more chance of issuing in reproductive conversions outside the existing church if...Churches and missions form their policies in the light of whatever means the Holy Spirit has already used to multiply churches in their kind of societies.[1]

One problem with the new measures approach to evangelism is that measures are new for only a brief period of time. What may have been an effective tool of evangelism at one point will not necessarily be effective in the same context a decade later. The monthly lecture was a new measure during the Great Awakening that has failed to be as effective since. Some new measures appear to be revived old measures. The evangelistic crusade may be considered a new measure of both the mid-nineteenth century revival and the mid-twentieth century revival.

A second problem with new measures is that some are so tied to a specific culture that they may not be easily adaptable to other contexts. Adult-education strategies of evangelism utilized with some degree of effectiveness in a Western urban context may not prove as effective in a Third World village where illiteracy is high. Continual research needs to be done to identify those new measures that appear to be effective in various contexts. In some cases, communication networks may also need to be established among evangelicals to communicate these findings.

How can an evangelical church take best advantage of the new measures approach to evangelism? Charles L. Chaney and Ron S. Lewis suggest the following:

> One secret of spontaneous growth is to find out what God is doing in the world and then join him in his work. God only blesses with fantastic effectiveness what he initi-

ates himself. These three steps can help us discover what he is doing.

1. Find out what he is blessing.
2. Evaluate that method in the light of your church and the unchurched community.
3. Seek the guidance of the Holy Spirit in adapting methods to your church.[2]

References: [1]Donald A. McGavran, *Understanding Church Growth* (Grand Rapids: Wm. B. Eerdmans, 1990) p. 202. [2]Charles L. Chaney and Ron S. Lewis, *Design for Church Growth* (Nashville: Broadman & Holman, 1978) pp. 83, 84.

NOMINALITY

A term used to describe those for whom the Christian faith and life are in name only. They participate in the church through a sense of habit or social tradition, and have little or no commitment to Christ and the Body of Christ.

NONGROWTH EXCUSES

Rationalizations of failure to grow, often used as justification for nongrowth.

OIKOS EVANGELISM

The conversion of whole households and the spread of the gospel along natural lines of relationship.

Reference: See WEB MOVEMENTS.

OLD AGE See GHOST-TOWN DISEASE

OMNIPOTENCE

The ability of God to do everything that is in harmony with His nature and perfection.

OMNIPRESENCE

The presence of God everywhere in creation at the same time in His fullness, without extension.

OMNISCIENCE

The perfect knowledge of God of all things, actual and potential.

ONE-BY-ONE CONVERSION

Also called Christianization by abstraction — a mode of conversion that pries people out of their social matrix and leads them to become Christians against the tide of society.

ONE HUNDRED BARRIER TO SUNDAY SCHOOL GROWTH

The first plateau of Sunday School growth comes when attendance reaches beyond the average attendance of 66 and stops growing at 100 to 150. This kind of Sunday School is called the "one-room" Sunday School or the "Class" Sunday School. It is called that because everything is organized around individual classes, or they meet in the auditorium (one room) for opening exercises or opening worship. Just as a houseplant will outgrow the pot in which it was planted as it grows, so the number of students will outgrow the facilities and organizational structure as it grows. If the Sunday School is not reorganized to take care of more students, both the plant and the Sunday School will become "root bound" and begin to die without growth. A root-bound plant chokes on its own roots.

Why do Sunday Schools get root bound at the 100 to 150 plateau? Here are three primary reasons. First, they simply run out of space or classrooms. New classes cannot be started for growth because they have no space.

The second reason for this natural plateau in growth is related to the basic management principle of span and direction. One manager should never have more than seven people reporting to him or her. A superintendent cannot give effective direction, nor take responsibility for more than this amount of workers. By the time the class Sunday School has reached 100 to 150, the Sunday School superintendent is probably trying to manage 10 to 15 teachers and everyone begins to wonder why so many details are falling between the cracks.

A third reason for this danger level of 100 to 150 is that when the average Sunday School reaches this level, the leaders usually cannot think of other new classes to develop. These Sunday Schools tend to have developed about 15 classes, one or two for each grouping in a departmental Sunday School.

This danger level is perhaps the most serious, simply because it is the one that so many churches face in their present situation. Several steps can be attempted to break the "100" danger level. The Sunday School could consider changing its organizational structure to a departmentally organized Sunday School. The church may also need to find more room to grow. But the real key to breaking this danger level is to begin new classes.

How to Break the 100 Barrier
1. Begin new classes.
2. Find additional administrators.
3. Find additional space for new classrooms (perhaps off campus).
4. Consider going to a split-level Sunday School.

5. Change large classes taught by one teacher into a team-teaching situation and have several teachers.

6. Organize large classes or team-taught classes into a department.

7. Appoint one teacher as a departmental superintendent to supervise/coordinate the other teachers.

ONE-ROOM SUNDAY SCHOOL
See CLASS SUNDAY SCHOOL

OPS

Abbreviation for operators—those persons equipped to manage an organization once it is established and organized.

References: See CATS; ORGS.

ORDINANCES (CHURCH)

Protestant traditions in the low church tend to interpret ordinances as the Lord's Table and baptism (some include foot washing and/or the love feast). These are symbolic rites that reflect the sacrifice of Christ for the sinner that have no saving or sanctifying merit in themselves, but when exercised the believer is obedient to God, thus grows in Christian experience. The liturgical tradition, sometimes called the high church, would tend to call them sacraments and interpret them differently. Sacramental traditions see the Lord's Supper as a sacred act (sacrament) in which Christ's body and blood are present and in which the recipient does receive forgiveness of sins, if truly repentant.

ORGANIC GROWTH

The development of the infrastructure of the church; the boards, committees, activities, training programs and small groups.

References: See CONGREGATION; CELL.

ORGANIZATION

Organization means breaking down group responsibility into smaller parts that can be assigned to individuals or small groups of people. Organization assures orderly planning, work and problem solving. It will help a church carry out the plan and purpose of the Church—presenting the message of Christ to the world in the most effective way. The church must be properly organized for an effective spiritual thrust into its community.

Why Should a Church Be Organized?
Organization will contribute to the church in six important areas: (1) makes planning possible, (2) identifies areas of responsibilities, (3) identifies problems, (4) charts the future, (5) provides a channel of communication and (6) facilitates cohesiveness.

Basic Guidelines to Organization
Denominations differ in their patterns of organization; even churches within a denomination differ in some details. Some basic principles for church organization, however, are clear. First, the pastor is the head of the Church as Christ's representative. He or she is the shepherd of the flock. Second, each church department should have goals to meet specific needs. Third, organizations should be directed and supervised by duly-elected officials, all being members of the church. The various boards should be coordinated into an executive board of the church. Church boards should at specified times also report their activities to the general membership, as they are ultimately responsible for the congregation.

As a church grows, the pastor and church board will also need help in coordinating the educational program. One means of accomplishing this task it to establish a board of Christian education to help ensure the continued growth and efficiency of the church.

ORGANIZATION AND CHURCH GROWTH

Most people who want to build a New Testament Church pay attention to the spiritual growth principles in the Word of God but neglect the natural factors of good organization and good techniques in operating a church.

These principles built on common sense cannot be ignored. The natural and spiritual factors fit hand in glove. It is possible to accomplish numerical growth by utilizing circuses or a clown to attract people to the church, for example. This is not biblical, although the end result can be church growth and people making decisions for Christ. Leaders in each church will have to prayerfully consider the means to the end.

ORGS

Abbreviation for organizers, or those people equipped to set in place the organizational structure needed to undergird a new organization.

References: See CATS; OPS.

OUTPOURING OF THE HOLY SPIRIT

Solomon Stoddard wrote in 1713: "There are some special Seasons wherein God doth in a remarkable Manner revive Religion among his People." Stoddard had five such "seasons" in his ministry, which he also called "harvests" because of the large numbers of people converted to Christ. Later, his grandson Jonathan Edwards was also involved in a great "harvest" during a season of revival.

Throughout history, evangelical revivals have energized Christians in their outreach ministries, resulting in great harvest seasons for the Church. This phenomenon is best understood in the context of what the Scriptures call "the outpouring of the Holy Spirit." When God pours out His Spirit, Christians are revitalized in their spiritual lives and the unsaved in the community are awakened to their need of Christ. This combination normally results in a significant harvest season for the Church and for the reformation of society.

A survey of all the biblical references to the outpouring of the Holy Spirit suggests seven revival-friendly conditions that tend to encourage the process of revival and its resulting effects. These include (1) a desire to experience the blessing of God, (2) interventional prayer, (3) repentance of known and practiced sin, (4) yielding to God and recognizing His authority over all of life, (5) restoration of fractured relationships between Christians, (6) the worship of God and (7) significant giving to God.

Reference: Douglas Porter, "An Analysis of Evangelical Revivals with Suggestions for Encouraging and Maximizing the Effects of an Outpouring of the Holy Spirit in Evangelism" (D.Min. Thesis Project, Liberty Baptist Theological Seminary, Lynchburg, Va., 1991).

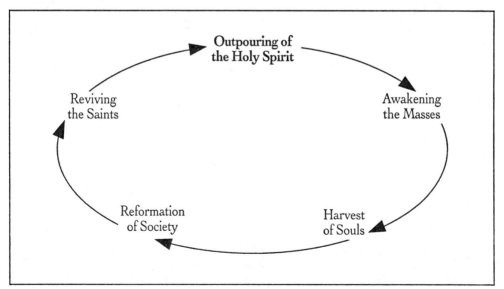

PANTA TA ETHNE See ETHNE

PARALLELISM

A missions methodology whose adherents consciously or unconsciously believe that all the many activities carried on by missions are of equal value and should therefore receive parallel thrust and priority.

Reference: See EGALITARIANISM.

PARTICIPATORY ACTIVITIES

Direct involvement with questionable spiritual rituals or objects, and/or deliberate exposure to "how to" techniques in books dealing with occult subjects. Such things are forbidden to Christians even in the name of research.—OJR

PASTORAL LEADERSHIP TRANSITION

The role of pastors who plant churches changes as the churches grow in size and structure. The change in roles causes the pastor's self-perception also to change. When the church is first planted, pastors do it all, but as churches grow pastors must make the transition to a stage in which they work through boards, assistant ministers and superintendents—through the organizations they have built. Some of the founding pastor's original authority is relinquished, but hoping it is without losing the influence of pastoral leadership.

When discussing a change in pioneer-pastors, it is really growth we are describing. The pastor who has a long successful ministry will be a growing Christian, and must grow in status as the church grows in size and influence. The pastor's capacity, ability and compassion must grow as the problems of a larger congregation become more complex.

This role shift is not unique to churches. Leadership roles also change in the military. The lieutenant who leads an attack up a hill becomes

the general who plans strategy behind the lines. Pastors who lay concrete blocks with their people become the leaders of multi-million dollar corporations. What was once a high-structural management changes to a shared-management concept of leadership.

In business, the field of management recognizes the need for a strong personality at the inception of a business. Called high-structural management, or downward cycle, the entrepreneur or businessperson is the pioneer, personnel manager, visiting fire fighter and motivator all wrapped up in one person. The aims, motivations and evaluations reside in the person. The owners and the businesses are inseparable; they are the company. Usually, the employees work for the boss and have a direct relationship with that person.

After the company has existed for a length of time and has grown large, new needs arise that demand a different kind of management. Employees lose contact with the boss, and bureaucracy settles over the organization with its accompanying apathy and sometimes atrophy. Shared management, goal setting and an upward cycle of change is necessary for business prosperity.

The typical American church uses a low structural management, especially when a new pastor arrives. Typically, the new leader attempts to introduce change from the bottom. By using this method, a training program communicates new knowledge that is supposed to change the attitudes of the employees, thus modifying individual behavior and ultimately changing group behavior. This is the upward cycle of leadership, where management is shared with employees following the route of "indigenous leadership." The employee is given reasons, motivation and training to improve his or her performance in the company. As the employee improves, of course, production improves and profits rise. This is often called an upward cycle in management. It tends to result in improved *esprit de corps* among all employees and to curb deteriorating employee-employer relationships.

High-structured management begins at the top and forces change downward through the system. The manager sets standards for the entire group regarding production goals, dress codes, regulations concerning behavior and so on. The theory of high-structured management is: (1) group behavior is the result of individual conformity to group standards, (2) individual behavior is slowly internalized, (3) the individual begins to assume the attitudes of the corporation and those who work around him or her; and (4) the individual takes on the knowledge needed to improve him or herself and ultimately the company.

Sometimes a young pastor comes into an existing church with great zeal, but, lacking experience, uses a high-structured management style, trying to enforce group behavior on all church members. This usually results in (1) a split congregation, (2) the loss of certain members or (3) the firing of the pastor.

The pastor who begins the church must begin with a high-structured leadership because there is no existing organization. There must be a downward cycle because the pastor usually personifies the standards of behavior and service in the church. The new church does not have group behavior, so it must be set by the pioneer-pastor. Dr. David Stoffer of Calvary Christian Temple, St. Louis, Missouri, justified this style by explaining, "I had a new church with unstructured Christians. I could not let them determine the standards of the church, so I had to crack the whip with love." Stoffer, who understands business management, also said, "I enforced a coercive style of management, realizing I was causing a volatile reaction among some people, but there was no other way to get the church started." Some came and left the young church. Stoffer ultimately wants to reverse the cycle of planned change from a downward-management style to an upward style.

PASTORAL MINISTRY PARADIGMS

The Church, like any other organization, needs human leaders. Even in the early stages of church history, the Church was organized through human instrumentality. Initially, the twelve (Acts 1:26) gave leadership to establishing the Church. As the Church grew, the needs of the ministry demanded the appointment of seven men to serve as deacons (Acts 6:1-7). By the time the church at Jerusalem hosted the Jerusalem Conference, James had clearly risen to be the chief elder or pastor of the church (Acts 15:2,13). By the time the apostle Paul traveled among various cities of Asia Minor and Europe to start churches, it was generally recognized that two leadership offices—pastors and deacons—were to be established in the church, (1 Tim. 3:1,8). Because the growth and strength of a church reflects the stature of its leaders, we should study their biblical qualifications, first to understand their roles and then to understand the strength and direction of our own churches.

Every church is led by Christ if it is a New Testament church. "He is the head of the body, the church, who is the beginning, the firstborn from the dead, that in all things He may have the pre-eminence" (Col. 1:18). When the presence of Christ leaves a church and He is no longer the ruler, we may *call* the organization a church but it is not an organic church according to the biblical use of the term.

The final seat of authority in church government rests in the congregation as the people are led by the Spirit of Christ. The apostle Paul encouraged the Philippian believers to continue in and strengthen their unity as a church (Phil. 2:1,2) and pleaded with the Corinthians that they do everything within their power to correct and prevent divisions that existed in their church (1 Cor. 1:10). Because the Holy Spirit works through believers, He is able to freely lead a church when the members are yielded to His direction.

The pastor is the human individual responsible before God for the spiritual welfare of the church (Acts 20:28). At the return of Christ, He will judge and reward pastors according to their faithfulness in leading the church to accomplish the will of God (1 Pet. 5:4). In one sense, everything a church is and does is an extension of the pastor's personal ministry—so much so that the prophet Isaiah identifies the similarity between the leader and followers, "As with the people, so with the priest" (Isa. 24:2).

The office of the pastor is identified by various titles in different denominations. The pastor is called reverend, pastor, bishop, minister, elder, doctor or some other title. It is sometimes awkward for a person of one church to address the pastor of another denomination because of uncertainty how to address that pastor. This problem has been complicated throughout church history when terms readily understood in a culture have been applied to a church office, only to remain after the culture has changed. Some denominations use the title bishop to identify the person who supervises many churches in a large area, whereas the New Testament apparently applied it to the leader(s) of one church.

Biblical Terms for Leaders

At least seven different terms are used to identify people who fill the office of pastor in New Testament churches. Each of these words contributes toward a fuller understanding of the nature of the pastor's office.

Why are so many different terms used to describe the pastoral ministry? First, leaders differ in spiritual gifts that are reflected in different ministry styles. Second, different needs demand leaders who will sharpen their skills to meet those needs, thus creating new roles for the pastor. Third, the phenomenon of gift colonization brings together similarly gifted pastors and people. Also, the chronological and spiritual growth of the leader may affect the pastor's giftedness (1 Cor. 12:31). Fifth, younger pastors have their heroes who motivate them to develop strength in different areas and dream different kinds of dreams.

The Bible implies at least seven of these roles.

Church Leadership Roles

Term	Trait Emphasized
Elder	Character
Bishop	Administration
Shepherd	Giftedness
Preacher	Exhortation/motivation
Teacher	Communication
Servant	Ministry to needs
Messenger	Spiritual direction

Elder

The first term used especially in the Jerusalem church was elder (Acts 11:30). The term "elder"

appears more than 20 additional times in the New Testament. Perhaps it was brought over from the Old Testament synagogue as a term describing those who were respected for their maturity and wisdom. The book of Proverbs gives admonition to heed those who can make wise decisions. Although chronological age was certainly a consideration in identifying a man as an elder, the real emphasis was on wisdom and spiritual maturity. It is not advisable to place a young convert, even if saved late in life, in a position of leadership without that person first being given the opportunity to gain spiritual maturity. In listing the qualifications of a pastor, the apostle Paul warned, "Not a novice, lest being puffed up with pride he fall into the same condemnation as the devil" (1 Tim. 3:6).

The term "elder" is often used in the plural (Acts 20:17; Titus 1:5; Jas. 5:14; 1 Pet. 5:1), supporting the idea of a plurality of elders in a single local church. In many contemporary churches, there are senior ministers, youth pastors, ministers of music and directors of Christian education, all considered pastors. In the New Testament, even where many elders existed in one church, there seems to be a hierarchy of elders. There were many elders in the church at Jerusalem, but James was recognized above the others as spokesman. He apparently had more authority than the apostles (Acts 15:2,13,22). There were many elders at the Ephesian church (Acts 20:17), but Jesus addressed His comments to a single leader of that church (Rev. 2:1). Presumably, this leader was recognized by other pastors as the leader among leaders.

The elder leads by role modeling and example. The pastor who wants to be a good elder-leader should be a godly person. The pastor uses insight and knowledge to make decisions and wisdom to solve problems. The elder also dreams dreams and leads others by personal dreams. The elder is both a ruler and teacher (1 Tim. 5:17).

Bishop

The term "bishop" is also used to describe the office of pastor and the man who fills it. The term is translated "overseer" in Acts 20:28 and is used in four other places where it is translated "bishop" (Phil. 1:1; 1 Tim. 3:2; Titus 1:7; 1 Pet. 2:25,

KJV). The emphasis of the word "bishop" seems to be "one who takes the oversight of a church," or the office of manager, superintendent or chief executive officer of the church. It is largely an administrative term used to identify the work of this church leader.

The pastor is to lead the church (Heb. 13:7,17). The term "bishop" was used in Greek culture to identify the agent of the central government who was sent out to inspect the subject-states and govern them. As the apostles used this term to identify the pastor, members of the church would have understood what was implied. Whereas the term "elder" implied the character of the pastor, the term "bishop" implies the ability to organize and administer the church.

The pastor-leader should not do the work of 10 people, but rather get 10 people to work. This means the pastor-leader needs to learn how to delegate. As an administrator, the pastor-leader is responsible for putting the right person in the right place, to do the right thing, in the right way, with the right tools, at the right time, for the right purpose. Only four things in life need to be managed: (1) people, (2) money, (3) time and (4) resources. The bishop manages these through both long- and short-range planning.

Pastor

The term "pastor" is probably the most common title used today by conservative Christians to identify their church leaders. The term "pastor," however, is rarely used in the New Testament. This does not mean that the title of pastor is unimportant. In contrast, it reflects one of the chief aspects of a pastor's ministry. This is the same word that could be translated "shepherd." As the shepherd of the flock is responsible for the care of the sheep, so the pastor is responsible for the care of the flock (Acts 20:29; 1 Pet. 5:3).

First, the pastor-shepherd is instructed to "take heed to yourselves and to all the flock" (Acts 20:28). This makes the pastor responsible for watching over others to meet their needs. Sometimes a church member will become discouraged or backslidden. The pastor is the person best able to encourage that person so he or she remains faithful or comes back into fellowship with the Lord.

Three times Jesus reminded Peter of his pastoral shepherding responsibility to feed the flock (John 21:15,16,17). This second responsibility mainly involves the teaching ministry of the pastor. To better accomplish this task, many pastors give leadership to such programs as Sunday School, youth clubs or Bible study groups. Even when the pastor has delegated the ministry in part to others, the pastor remains responsible before God for feeding the flock (Acts 20:28).

In the third place, pastors should also protect their flocks. The apostle Paul recognized that "savage wolves" would come from the outside and gain control in the Church if the flock were not carefully guarded (Acts 20:29). Sometimes good people in the church may change and thus become dangerous to its security (Acts 20:30). In both cases, the chief responsibility of protecting the flock falls on the pastor. Many times a pastor may be misunderstood when insisting upon certain spiritual standards or certain emphasis in special music or guest preachers. Actually, the pastor may be attempting to protect those Christians who do not understand the total ministry that may be best for the church.

Most conservative churches use the term "pastor" to identify their church leaders for cultural reasons. Often, the pastor who is a recent graduate is younger than the deacons, so the title "elder" seems inappropriate. The term "bishop" has come to refer to a nonbiblical ecclesiastical hierarchy, thus becoming unsuitable for popular use in a Bible-believing church.

The terms "elder" and "bishop" are used interchangeably in 1 Peter 5:1-4 and Acts 20:17-28, implying that these are two functions of the same office. A person grows into becoming an elder, but learns how to function as a bishop.

	Acts 20:17-31	1 Peter 5:1-4
Elder	20:17 shepherd	5:2 shepherd
Bishop	20:28 overseer	5:2 taking oversight
Pastor	20:28 to feed	5:2 feed the flock

The strength of the pastor's leadership is ministry. Ministry is communicating the gospel to people at their point of need. Also, the pastor-shepherd leads through personal strength in relationships and networking.

Preacher

The term "preacher" implies the public proclamation of the gospel. Noah was the first to preach (1 Pet. 2:5), although Enoch's prophesying may also have involved preaching (Jude 14). Preaching is often defined as "the communication of the Word of God with persuasion through the personality." The pastor is the person God has called to proclaim His message in the Church, and this is accomplished through preaching. "But he who prophesies speaks edification and exhortation and comfort to men" (1 Cor. 14:3).

The preacher leads his people by motivation. If the preacher is gifted in prophecy, the emphasis of motivation will tend to be negative. If the preacher is gifted in exhortation, the emphasis of motivation will tend to be positive. Both emphases are needed to build a growing church, although the pastors of growing churches tend to be twice as strong in positive motivation than negative motivation.

Two laws of leadership relate to motivation. First, that which gets inspected gets done (prophet). Second, that which gets rewarded gets done (exhortation). In both cases, the preacher tends to lead best through the ministry of preaching.

Teacher

The teaching ministry is referred to some 97 times in the New Testament. The pastor was given the dual gift of shepherding-teacher (Eph. 4:11). There is no Greek word in Ephesians 4:11 for "and," implying that all pastors also had the gift of teaching. This gift was exercised in the Church from its beginning (Acts 2:42). Note that Jesus left His disciples with a "teaching" commission (Matt. 28:19,20). Their obedient response is seen in the biblical record. "And daily in the temple, and in every house, they did not cease teaching and preaching Jesus as the Christ" (Acts 5:42).

The teacher leads through communicating the truth. The teacher often acts as a role model, helping the people become better students of the Bible. The teacher is a model of biblical knowledge and wisdom. This is the pastor who devotes most of the week to sermon preparation. This pastor communicates (1) biblical content, (2) biblical attitudes, (3) ministry skills and (4) understanding and insight into life.

Servant

The Greek term *doulos*, usually translated "servant," might better be translated "slave." Usually this term is used to refer to deacons, but it is also used in connection with pastors (1 Pet. 2:16; 5:3). Pastors are to be the servants of the congregation. A pastor must keep sensitive to the poor, downtrodden and underprivileged in the flock to remain effective. As a slave of God, the pastor is the servant of the Church because the assembly is indwelt by Christ and is His Body. Jesus used the slave-master relationship to illustrate our duty to Him. "So likewise you, when you have done all those things which you are commanded, say, 'We are unprofitable servants. We have done what was our duty to do'" (Luke 17:10).

The servant tends to lead through role modeling, and is often gifted in the area of helps and showing mercy. Because the character of the pastor is often reflected in the life of the people, the humble servant-pastor is often reflected in a revived people.

The biblical term "servant" (*doulos*) is usually brought over into the contemporary title of "minister," which may be one of the more frequent titles for pastors. It carries the aspect of helping, serving or caring for sheep (i.e., the flock of God).

Messenger

When Jesus addressed the pastors of the seven churches of Asia, He used the Greek word *angelos*, which may be translated "angel" or "messenger." There were many "elders" in Ephesus (Acts 20:17), but apparently only one messenger. There were many pastors in the church, but one apparently determined the ministry emphasis of that church (i.e., its message).

In light of the different words used to describe the pastoral ministry, it is important that we be tolerant of those who may choose to express ministry differently. Each ministry style will reach people who may not be reached by another ministry style. Rather than looking at the weaknesses of each style, we should focus on the strengths and build on them.

PATHOLOGY OF CHURCH GROWTH

The pathology of church growth is the study of the growth-inhibiting diseases of churches, the characteristics and symptoms of those diseases and the prescriptions to deal with them to achieve the goals of church health and growth.

References: C. Peter Wagner, *Your Church Can Be Healthy* (Nashville: Abingdon Press, 1979). A list of the eight major growth-inhibiting diseases in American churches. Also see ARRESTED SPIRITUAL DEVELOPMENT; ETHNIKITIS; KOINONITIS; OLD AGE; PEOPLE BLINDNESS; SOCIOLOGICAL STRANGULATION; ST. JOHN'S SYNDROME; HYPERCOOPERATIVISM.

PATON, JOHN GIBSON (1824–1907)

Pioneer missionary to the New Hebrides Islands.

Born near Dumfries, Scotland, John Paton was 30 years old when he responded to an opportunity to be a missionary of the Reformed Church of Scotland in the New Hebrides Islands. Paton began his ministry on the island of Tanna, but eventually established his headquarters on the island of Aniwa, where the entire island was converted under his ministry. When his translation of the New Testament into Aniwa was published in 1899, missionaries were living on 25 of the 30 New Hebrides Islands.

Paton's chief contribution to evangelism was the translation of the New Testament into Aniwa for the young church established under his ministry.

PATRICK (389–461)

Pioneer missionary to Ireland.

Patrick, the son of a deacon in Britain or Gaul, was captured by raiders when he was 16 and taken to Ireland, where he remained for six years before escaping. When he was converted to Christ, Patrick had a vision and concluded he should return to Ireland as a missionary. He established churches and baptized thousands of converts on the Emerald Isle.

Patrick's greatest contribution to evangelism was achieved in establishing Christianity in Ireland. The Irish church proved to be instrumental in the evangelization of the rest of the British Isles and parts of northern Europe.

As a political move to gain control of the Irish churches, Patrick was later canonized by the Roman Catholic church.

PATTERSON, PAIGE

Dr. Paige Patterson, president of Southeastern Baptist Theological Seminary in Wake Forest, North Carolina, is one of the leading men in the Southern Baptist Convention because of his leadership at Criswell College, 1975-1982; his presidency of Southeastern Baptist Theological Seminary, Wake Forest, North Carolina; and his role in the conservative "turnaround" of the Southern Baptist Convention beginning in the mid-1970s until most of the boards and seminaries of the Southern Baptist Convention were restructured according to the historic roots of Baptists.

Paige Patterson received his B.A. from Hardin Simmons University in 1965, and his Th.M. and Th.D. from New Orleans Baptist Theological Seminary in 1973.

Patterson has been pastor of churches in Rotan, Texas; Abilene, Texas; New Orleans, Louisiana; Fayetteville, Arkansas; and was associate pastor of First Baptist Church, Dallas, Texas from 1975-1993.

Patterson has served on several committees throughout the Southern Baptist Convention, including being a member of the Foreign Missions Board and the Christian Ethics Study Commission of World Baptist Alliance. He has also been a member of the Board of Governors, the Council for National Policy, the International Policy Forum, the Executive Council and the International Council on Biblical Inherency.

Patterson was the managing editor for the *Criswell Study Bible*, Thomas Nelson, Nashville, 1979, and the managing editor for *The Believer's Study Bible*, Thomas Nelson, Nashville, 1991.

Patterson is known for being a powerful preacher of the Word of God, for conducting evangelistic crusades and revivals throughout the Southern Baptist Convention, for his scholarship, passion for the unsaved and commitment to the fundamentals of the faith.

PAXON, STEPHEN (1808–1881)

One of the greatest American pioneers, Stephen Paxon did not search for land, rivers or natural resources, but for lost souls. During his lifetime, he founded 1,314 new Sunday Schools having an enrollment of 83,000 students.

Paxon was born with a speech impediment and later was nicknamed "stuttering Stephen." He was also lame, but these difficulties did not prohibit him from doing the work of God.

Paxon first became involved in Sunday School when his little daughter begged him to attend so she could win a prize. When Paxon got there, he was asked to teach a class of boys. Teaching involved listening to the boys read the Scriptures, and Paxon simply correcting them when they made mistakes. "Let's go home," he said when they finished the lesson. "You are supposed to ask us questions out of the little book," the boys told him.

Paxon was so embarrassed that he did not know the Scriptures that he took a Bible home and read it carefully. He became a Christian by reading the Scriptures and ultimately volunteered his life as a missionary for the American Sunday School Union.

He named his horse Robert Raikes, after the English founder of the Sunday School. The horse was so well trained that it never passed a child, but waited for Paxon to stop and give out the gospel.

Paxon was a well-known speaker on the East Coast, raising money for Sunday School libraries. He made the sophisticated audiences laugh and cry, but more important, he made them give money. They could see beyond his grammatical mistakes to the great vision he had for pioneering the West with the Word of God. As a result, Paxon began Sunday Schools in cabins, tobacco barns, taverns and dance halls.

Stephen Paxon retired to a St. Louis office, and died in 1881. He is remembered as the spirit of Sunday School because of his great enthusiasm and commitment for the movement.

PENTECOST, DAY OF

The outpouring of the Holy Spirit in Jerusalem on the Day of Pentecost is generally acknowledged as the first revivalistic movement involving the Christian Church. It is also noted as the birth of the Christian Church, or the first physical manifestation of the local church. Therefore, it also serves as a model by which all other such outpourings can be identified and evaluated. According to Lloyd-Jones:

It is a truism to say that every revival of religion that the Church has ever known has been, in a sense, a kind of repetition of what has happened on the day of Pentecost, that it has been a return to that origin, to that beginning, that it has been a reviving.[1]

The tendency to consider the Pentecost outpouring of the Holy Spirit as a prototype of evangelical revivals illustrates the significance of this event in the history of revival. J. Edwin Orr has summarized the events associated with this outpouring of the Holy Spirit on several occasions. He writes:

It is more than interesting to compare the characteristics of the Awakenings of various decades with the prototype of evangelical revivals in the Acts of the Apostles, a perennial textbook for such movements.

Our Lord told His disciples: "It is not for you to know the times or seasons which the Father has fixed by His own authority. But you shall receive power when the Holy Spirit has come upon you; and you shall be My witnesses...to the end of the earth." Thus was an outpouring of the Spirit predicted, and soon fulfilled.

Then began extraordinary praying among the disciples in the upper room. Who knows what self-judgment and confession and reconciliation went on? There were occasions for such. But, when they were all together in one place, there suddenly came from heaven a sound like the rush of a mighty wind and it filled all the house....

The Apostle Peter averred that the outpouring fulfilled the prophecy of Joel, which predicted the prophesying of young men and maidens, the seeing of visions and dreams by young and old. He preached the death and resurrection of Jesus Christ. What was the response? The hearers were pierced, stabbed, stung, stunned, smitten — these are the synonyms of a rare verb which Homer used to signify being drummed to earth. It was no ordinary feeling; nor was the response a mild request for advice. It was more likely an uproar of entreaty, the agonizing cry of a multitude.

Those who responded to the Apostle's call for repentance confessed their faith publicly in the apostolic way. About three thousand were added to the church. Then followed apostolic teaching, fellowship, communion and prayers....

The Apostles continued to urge their hearers to change and turn to God, which they did by the thousands. And no hostile power seemed for the moment able to hinder them. Persecution followed, but the work of God advanced.[2]

References: [1]Martin Lloyd-Jones, *Revival* (Wheaton, Ill.: Crossway Books, 1987), p. 199. [2]J. Edwin Orr, *The Flaming Tongue: Evangelical Awakenings, 1900* (Chicago: Moody Press, 1975), pp. vii, viii.

PEOPLE APPROACH

Strategizing the evangelistic and missionary task by first identifying the unreached people groups in a given geographic area and tailoring the approach to each group according to its culture and felt needs.

Reference: See PEOPLE GROUP.

PEOPLE BLINDNESS

The inability of the Church to see the spiritual, cultural, social and community needs of a people. People blindness is the Church's inability or unwillingness to identify and distinguish people groups and then reach out to them in cross-cultural evangelism. The key to an effective, grow-

ing ministry may be summarized in the expression "find a hurt and heal it." Hence, a church must have a "vision" of a community's needs, then develop a program to meet them. Some churches have begun a worship service for those of another culture and/or language. A church that has a food service for the poor will attract and minister to the poor. Some churches have ministries for the hearing impaired (sign-language interpreting), classes for the mentally retarded, single-parent families, widowed or newly married. Other churches have planted a church among a group of people different from themselves. The church that is sensitive to the aches and pains of each people group within its neighborhood will always have a ministry.

How to Solve People Blindness

1. Create a task force of members to brainstorm the potential community needs not being met by the church.

2. Have the task force brainstorm possible programs to meet these needs.

3. Study the "philosophy of ministry" in churches similar to yours that minister in neighborhoods similar to yours.

4. Plan special Sunday School classes or Bible studies for "need" groups.

5. Have the pastor preach on the definition of ministry as "communicating the gospel to people at their point of need."

6. Begin a church (service) in your facilities for those of a different people group.

7. Plant a church and evangelize those of a different people group within your community.

Reference: See PEOPLE VISION.

PEOPLE FLOW

A term designating the movement of people into the church, how they enter, what kind of people they are and in what quantity.

PEOPLE GROUP

A significantly large grouping of individuals who perceive themselves as having a common affinity for one another.

Reference: See HOMOGENEOUS UNIT.

PEOPLE MOVEMENT See HOMO-GENEOUS UNIT PRINCIPLE

A joint decision of a number of individuals from the same people group that enables them to become Christians without social dislocation or isolation, while remaining in full contact with their non-Christian relatives. This enables other segments of that people group, across the years, to come to similar decisions and form Christian churches made up primarily of members of that people group.

Types of People Movements
The following five classifications represent the most common people movements.
1. Lystran movement—a part of the people become Christian, while the rest become hostile to the Christian religion.
2. Lyddic movement—the entire community becomes Christian.
3. Laodicean movement—the movement slows down and stagnates.
4. Ephesian movement—people who desire to become Christians but simply do not know how are provided with the necessary knowledge.
5. Web movement—the gospel spreads through natural friendship and kinship ties. This happens when the gospel is communicated to each people group, and allows those within a people group to evangelize others in that group.

PEOPLE VISION

In contrast to people blindness, the ability to discern and respect the many significant differences among social groups.

Reference: See PEOPLE BLINDNESS.

PERFECTING

The process of nurturing and development (following discipling) that is required to take believers from their initial acceptance of Jesus Christ to mature faith and obedience—sanctification.

References: See DISCIPLING; DICIPLING-PERFECTING.

PERSONAL SIN

A sinful act committed by a person (as opposed to the sin nature and imputed sin). It may be an act or attitude, a sin of commission or of omission.

PERSUASION EVANGELISM

Evangelism in which the goal is perceived to be making disciples, stressing the importance of not separating evangelism and follow-up. The goal is incorporating people into the Body of Christ. Designated P-3 evangelism.

Reference: See EVANGELISM, P-3.

PHILIP THE EVANGELIST

Philip stands out in that he is the only person Scripture designates as an evangelist (Acts 21:8), although the office of evangelist apparently existed in other churches (Eph. 4:11), and Timothy is exhorted to do the work of an evangelist (2 Tim. 4:5). Philip's ministry represents a unique model in that it apparently did not rely on existing church authority for ministry (cf. Acts 8:14,26).

Philip's ministry as an evangelist is described in the context of ministry in Samaria and the conversion of the Ethiopian eunuch (Acts 8:5-39). In both cases, Philip preached Christ to them (Acts 8:5,35) and baptized those who believed (Acts 8:12,38). Philip's baptizing of converts suggests a preliminary step in the organization of a church. In this sense, Philip's model of evangelism may be the biblical precedent for the contemporary church-planting missionary.

PHILOSOPHY OF MINISTRY

A statement of purpose, priorities, emphases and style that identifies how one church is unique and different from others; a reflection of the church's identity and image.

References: Kent R. Hunter, *Your Church Has Personality*

(Nashville: Abingdon Press, 1985); Harold J. Westing, *Create and Celebrate Your Church's Uniqueness: Designing a Church Philosophy of Ministry* (Grand Rapids: Kregel Publications, 1993).

PIETISM

A renewal movement that began in the late seventeenth century among Protestants in Europe. The movement was transdenominational, although its origin is normally traced to the work of a Lutheran—Philip Jacob Spener's *Pia Desideria*, or "Pious Desires," in 1675.

The Pietists sought to bring renewal to the dead ritualism of its day through individual devotion to God, belief in the authority of Scripture, concerted Bible study, an "experimental piety" in which a person's commitment to Christ was obvious and a desire to affect society's ills through the love of God.

Key Pietists include Spener (1635–1705), whose *Pia Desideria* continues to be a classic on church renewal. Johann Arndt (1555–1621) is considered by some to be the father of Pietism. His devotional work *True Christianity* influenced generations. A. H. Francke (1663–1727) came to the new University of Halle and quickly led it to be a nerve center for the Pietist revival. Count Nicolaus Ludwig von Zinzendorf (1700–1760), born into German nobility, was influenced at a young age by Pietism. He inherited an estate, and Hussites (followers of John Huss's teachings) came there to escape persecution. Zinzendorf was truly ecumenical and evangelistic. Through his influence, the Moravians and the 100-year Moravian prayer movement were born, resulting in missionaries being sent around the world decades before Carey became a missionary.

Pietists have been criticized for their emphasis on the individual Christian as opposed to the organized church, as well as their focus on emotional or sentimental aspects of the spiritual life.—ALR

PILGRIMAGES OF REPENTANCE

Journeys undertaken that have the intent of identifying with past sin and subsequent suffering through repentance. These pilgrimages are often public events that retrace the movements of displaced peoples back to a point of origin.— GOJR

PIONEERS

The founding members or the old-timers who, by virtue of fighting the early battles in the formation of a church, become a tightly knit fellowship. Contrast with homesteaders, or late-comers— pioneers tend to exclude them.

Reference: See HOMESTEADERS.

PLANNED PARENTHOOD

Intentional church planting. A congregation decides to become a mother church, and plants a daughter church.

PLATEAUING

When a growing church ceases to grow and remains about the same year after year.

PLUTSCHAU, HENRY

Priest-missionary to India.

At the request of the King of Denmark, Henry Plutschau accompanied Bartholomew Ziegenbalg as the first Protestant missionaries to India in 1706. Together, these two Germans established the Danish-Halle Mission.

POST-DENOMINATIONAL CHURCHES

Churches that have no organic connection with historic Christian denominations. The form many of the most vital churches are taking today is different from the likes of D. L. Moody, Charles Spurgeon or A. B. Simpson, each of whom was identified with a particular denomination. Probably not since the Protestant Reformation has there been such widespread change in the sights and sounds (paradigms) of Christian churches in all parts of the world.

By far, the most rapidly growing segment of

Christianity on all seven continents is a kind of church that does not fit traditional categories or classifications. Missiologists have recognized its presence for some time, but it is such a recent phenomenon that they have not yet agreed on a name for it. In almost any metropolitan area, the largest Christian church will probably be one of these new post-denominational churches.

In Lagos, Nigeria, it would be the Deeper Life Bible Church, pastored by William Kumuyi. On a recent Sunday, 74,000 adults worshiped together, and 40,000 children met in a separate building across the street.

In Buenos Aires, Argentina, the Waves of Love and Peace Church is less than 10 years old and already counting a membership of 150,000. Pastor Hector Gimenez and his staff conduct 13 hours of services each weekday and 23 hours on Saturdays and Sundays in a converted motion picture theater that seats 2,500 people.

In Colorado Springs, Colorado, at the New Life Church, pastor Ted Haggard leads worship for 4,000 in a building designed by the architects for Wal-Mart. Full-sized flags from every nation in the world hang from the ceiling.

In Kathmandu, Nepal, where vital Christianity is just getting a start, a 2,000-seat worship center is currently being constructed to house Bethel Church. The congregation is pastored by Lok Bhandari, who narrowly escaped joining the distinguished ranks of Christian martyrs a decade ago.

Whether large, small or in between, these churches represent the cutting edge of the kingdom of God today. Sample names such as "Waves of Love and Peace," "Deeper Life Bible Church" or "Vision Christian Fellowship" do not appear in the Yearbook of American and Canadian Churches or the membership directory of the World Council of Churches.

Mike Berg and Paul Pretiz have done pioneer research on these congregations in Latin America, calling them "fifth wave" churches. Their view of the first four waves are (1) the immigrant churches, (2) the mainline denominations, (3) the faith missions and (4) the new denominations. Berg and Pretiz recognize that these new churches are significantly different from churches in the past four waves.

Although the term "fifth wave" might describe Latin American churches, it does not work as well for their counterparts in China, the United States and elsewhere. Unlike Latin America, the history of Roman Catholic/European colonization is not a determining factor in many other parts of the world where very similar churches are multiplying.

Some call the new churches "independent." Typically, however, they are not independent but *inter*dependent churches because they often link with other likeminded churches in networks or associations. The relationship between such churches is seen as a spiritual bond rather than the legal or organizational bond found in the bureaucratic structures of older denominations.

Terms such as "interdenominational" or "non-denominational" do not describe these churches as well as we might think. Although the new churches are sociologically a type of denomination, they are not essentially mixtures or crosses of denominations as these terms imply.

Are these churches "charismatic"? In parts of the Third World, if we were to ask the leaders of these churches, "Are you charismatic or non-charismatic?"" they wouldn't even understand the question. Lines that have been so important in the West are surprisingly insignificant to many vital churches on this cutting edge.

They might answer, "We're just trying to be as biblical as we can be." As a result, on the surface they would tend to look quite "charismatic." Because this is a nonissue to them, the term may not be the most adequate description.

Besides, not all of these groups look charismatic. For example, the largest church in the Chicago area is Willow Creek Community Church—very much a part of this new phenomenon, but not explicitly charismatic according to our traditional categories.

Because no other generic term seems to fit the suggestions, "post-denominational" seems to be the most appropriate expression. This term is technically valid because of the new leaders' attempts to distinguish themselves from recognized denominational structures. Also, they often form their own interdependent apostolic networks.

Characteristics of the Post-Denominational Church

Indigenous Leadership

Post-denominational pastors are more frequently than not those who have never been under the direct influence of Western missionaries or Western institutions. Many of these gifted leaders have been converted as mature adults, nurtured by fellow national Christians and released by them into the ministry.

Ordination requirements are not as complex as is often the case. Surprisingly, this does not seem to diminish the quality and depth of those who are leading the post-denominational churches. In many cases the pastors leading these churches are more successful than missionaries have been in the past.

Apostolic Networks

In most cases, the local post-denominational churches are autonomous, own their own property, make their own decisions and raise and spend their own money. Often, however, they are closely networked under the leadership of a recognized apostolic figure.

These apostles (some prefer titles such as "elder," "bishop," "superintendent" or something similar) exercise a remarkable degree of authority. But it is seen as spiritual authority, delegated by the Holy Spirit Himself rather than derived from a position or an election. Post-denominational pastors who belong to such networks can withdraw at will, but they seldom do. To many, withdrawal from the apostolic network would seem a lot like willful disobedience to God.

An example familiar to many in the United States is the Association of Vineyard Churches under John Wimber, one who prefers not to refer to himself by the term "apostle." I previously mentioned William Kumuyi of Nigeria who, besides pastoring a local church of nearly 100,000, is also the general superintendent of 4,500 other churches in Nigeria as well as churches in 35 African nations.

Contemporary Worship

These post-denominational churches have a worship style that would be unrecognizable to Charles Wesley or Martin Luther. It has three major characteristics:

A musical idiom. Pipe organs, choirs and hymnals are out. Keyboards, guitars, drums, worship teams and overhead projectors are in. Praise and worship in Guatemala, Kenya or elsewhere may be indigenous, the songs not being more than a few months old; nevertheless, the same sound is emerging all over the world. It is apparently a sovereign move of the Holy Spirit, perhaps unprecedented in church history.

A song heard recently in Malaysia says it well:

There is a sound coming out of Zion
That's stirring up the church for war,
And in her midst there's celebration,
Such music we've never heard before!

Some of this music is spontaneous. At such times, individuals will begin to sing their own praises to God, as heavenly tones and harmonies flow over the congregation. It often sounds, curiously enough, like the Gregorian chants of yesteryear!

Body language. Today's worship lifts traditional inhibitions on body language. Some people sit, some stand, some kneel, some even dance! Arms are in the air, and hands clap to the rhythm. This is not choreographed by a leader. It is spontaneous and freewheeling, and a notable lack of self-consciousness is observable on the part of individual worshipers.

Applause. Worship sessions, particularly between songs, are punctuated by enthusiastic applause, even cheering. This boisterous demonstration is explicitly directed not at performers but at the triune God as a form of worship.

Concert Prayer

Another factor that tends to unify post-denominational churches is "concert prayer." Not to be confused with the Concerts of Prayer, which is a specific design for interchurch prayer meetings, concert prayer occurs when participants all pray aloud at the same time.

The pattern for this may have originated in Korea or in the early camp meetings of the

Appalachians in the United States (the term "concert prayer" was used in Pentecostal denominations and early Baptist churches). In the last few years, concert prayer has become universal. It may sound strange to those of us accustomed to more sedate praying, but this is the only kind of prayer ever heard in church by a growing number of contemporary Christians.

The noise level may be extremely high. In Korea, it is stopped by a bell on the pulpit.

Power Ministries

A fifth characteristic of most post-denominational churches is the acceptance of power ministries. In the book *The Gospel People* (MARC), Mike Berg and Paul Pretiz say, "North Americans may dismiss all this as nonsense, but most Gospel People take the spirit world seriously." Unlike some of their traditional counterparts, most post-denominational Christians "will believe that the local fortune-teller or witch doctor does manipulate demonic spirits as they are described biblically."

Healings, demonic deliverance and miracles are commonplace. Battling demonic principalities and powers in "strategic-level" spiritual warfare is not a matter of theological debate—it is an issue of survival in many post-denominational churches of the Third World.

Asian Outreach's David Wang says of Chinese churches: "They rely very heavily upon the extraordinary signs and the work of the Holy Spirit, for nowhere is there a denominational headquarters where one can get directions. The Holy Spirit is our headquarters."

These seem to be the strategic similarities of post-denominational churches. Although differences exist in tactics and peripheral doctrinal points, they all agree on the major tenets of Christianity as reflected in such historic statements as the Apostolic Creed.—CPW

POWER ENCOUNTER

A visible, practical demonstration that Jesus Christ is more powerful than the spirits, powers or false gods worshiped or feared by the members of a given society or people group.—GOJR

POWER EVANGELISM

Spreading the gospel by using accompanying supernatural signs and wonders.

POWER IN EVANGELISM See ANOINTED PREACHING; FILLING OF THE SPIRIT

POWER POINTS

Specific natural or man-made locations that are widely regarded as bridges or crossover points to the supernatural world. Such sites are often made numinous by the investments of faith offered over time by large numbers of people.

PRAGMATISM

The principle that demands results from biblically sound strategies; when no results are recorded, the strategy is changed to another one that is equally sound theologically.

PRAYER EXPEDITIONS

Long-distance, transterritorial prayerwalks along strategically developed routes. Intercession is offered for entire countries and regions.—GOJR

PRAYER JOURNEYS

Intentional prayerwalking in cities other than one's own. Sites often include capitals and ideological export centers.—GOJR

PRAYER REVIVAL OF 1857–1858

The Prayer Revival, or Layman's Prayer Revival, is normally remembered for the union prayer meetings in New York City begun by Jeremiah Lanphier. Lanphier began prayer meetings in September 1857 as a lay missionary for the old North Dutch Reformed Church. Only a handful attended the first meeting, but the enthusiasm for prayer soon spread until 50,000 were meeting daily to pray in New York alone. The prayer meetings spread to Philadelphia and across the Midwest.

At the Jayne's Hall in Philadelphia, as many as 6,000 met daily for prayer. At this meeting, George Duffield Jr. wrote the hymn "Stand Up, Stand Up for Jesus."[1] Estimates stated that 10,000 were converted in that city in one year. At the same time, powerful church revivals, a Presbyterian conference that called the denomination to prayer, Sunday School outreach efforts and a national financial panic contributed to the spread of revival fires.

This awakening was somewhat unique in that it produced no major controversy and no major personalities served as leaders. The revival did powerfully affect a young man named D. L. Moody.[2] J. Edwin Orr stated that 1 million people were converted through this awakening. —ALR

References: [1]Harold A. Fischer, *Reviving Revivals* (Springfield, Mo.: The Gospel Publishing House, 1950), p. 172. [2]William R. Moody, *The Life of D. L. Moody* (Chicago: Fleming H. Revell, 1900), p. 41.

PRAYERWALKING

The practice of on-site, street-level community intercession. Prayers are offered in response both to immediate observations and researched targets. It is sometimes designated as praying on-site with insight. —OJR

PREDESTINATION

(Lit. to mark off or choose). The doctrine that God chooses those who will participate in His plan of salvation.

PRESENCE EVANGELISM

A definition of evangelism for which the goal is perceived as getting next to people and helping them; doing good in the world; designated P-1 evangelism.

PRIESTHOOD OF BELIEVERS

The doctrine that every Christian has direct access to God through Jesus Christ.

PRIMARY SOURCES

Uninterpreted information sources such as artifacts, census reports, original writings and human subjects of direct interviews. —OJR

PRINCIPALITIES AND POWERS

Demonic agents and structures that exert deceptive control over coconspiratorial human political kingdoms and systems (see Eph. 6:12). —GOJR

PRIORITIES

Items that have more importance and, therefore, require attention prior to other items. The priority of evangelism is primary for church growth.

Reference: See THREE PRIORITIES.

PROBLEM OF THE 9.5

Whereas it is hypothesized that up to 10 percent of the members of the average congregation have the gift of evangelism or evangelist, only 0.5 percent of the members in the average congregation are actively using their gift for regular, structured evangelism ministry, leaving 9.5 percent who have the gift but who need to discover, develop and use it.

Reference: See HYPOTHESIS OF THE 10 PERCENT.

PROCLAMATION EVANGELISM

Evangelism for which the goal is perceived as presenting the gospel. The death and resurrection of Christ is communicated, and people can hear and can respond; designated P-2 evangelism.

PROPHECY, GIFT OF

The person in the contemporary church (the Old Testament office is not discussed in this article) who has the gift of prophecy has the ability to proclaim a message that God has brought spontaneously to mind. The ability to predict the future (1 Sam. 9:9) and to be a channel of revelation (Eph. 2:20) is not operative today according to some evangelicals, but others believe in the use of the miraculous gift.

In the exercise of this gift, the prophet "speaks edification and exhortation and comfort to men" (1 Cor. 14:3). The strengths of this gift include (1) sensitivity to the reputation of God, (2) the ability to quickly perceive and denounce sin, (3) an understanding of the sinful motive of humans and intolerance of hypocrisy, (4) directness and frankness in communication, (5) desire for apparent evidence of conviction and (6) discernment of people before considering the message.

The common weaknesses of a prophet include (1) an apparent lack of care for individuals, (2) viewed as being harsh, (3) uncomfortable in a discussion session, (4) difficulty in adjusting to others and (5) a tendency to be crowd oriented. Those who have this gift may fall into the danger of (1) being dependent on the proclaimed message for ministry, (2) overlooking the needs of others or (3) pride.

PROPITIATION

The act of Christ in satisfying, by His death, the demands of God's offended holiness.

"Propitiation properly signifies the turning away of wrath by an offering. In the New Testament this idea is conveyed by the use of *hilaskomai* (Heb. 2:17), *hilasterion* (Rom. 3:25), and *hilasmos* (1 John 2:2; 4:10)."[1]

The biblical terms for propitiation denote the fact that satisfaction was made for the sins of the world by Christ's death. The justice of God had been offended by the sin of humankind. The sin could not be retracted and the nature of God could not forgive the sinner without a payment of satisfaction. The price of satisfaction was the blood of Jesus Christ, and the act of satisfaction is propitiation. The Bible teaches that Jesus is the propitiation for the world. "He Himself is the propitiation for our sins, and not for ours only but also for the whole world" (1 John 2:2; cf. Luke 18:13; Rom. 3:25; Heb. 9:5; 1 John 4:10).

Redemption contemplates our bondage and is the provision of grace to release us from our bondage. Propitiation contemplates our liability to the wrath of God and is the provision of grace whereby we may be freed from that wrath.[2]

The concept of propitiation involves satisfying God's just wrath against sin by the holiness of Jesus Christ's death. Romans 3:25,26 declares the mercy, forbearance and righteous justice of God in His setting forth Christ to be our propitiation. God gave His Son for our sin. Christ did more than die for us; He gave Himself up for God's wrath. This is the ultimate in love in that Christ, being God, went against His nature for us.

The necessity of propitiation is found in the holiness of God and the sinfulness of humans. A holy God cannot look on sin. Neither can sin stand in the presence of God. ("Our God is a consuming fire," Heb. 12:29.) The death of Jesus Christ satisfies the justice of God that must be poured upon sin. The coordinate reason for propitiation is the love of God as proclaimed in 1 John 4:10. A holy God could justly consign all sinners to hopeless condemnation, but because of His love He provided a propitiation.

Hebrews 9:2-5 describes briefly the Old Testament tabernacle and its furnishings. Verse 5 speaks of the "mercy seat," which was a lid on the ark of the covenant. The term "mercy seat" (*hilasterion*) and "propitiation" are synonymous. (Other verses that amplify this doctrine are Rom. 3:25; 1 John 2:2 and 1 John 4:10.)

In Luke 18:13, the praying publican realized that the Law could never satisfy the demands of a holy God. Therefore, he prayed "God, be merciful to me, a sinner!" The term "merciful" is *hilastheti* and the verse may be translated properly, "God be propitious (satisfied) to me a sinner." Today, we would pray the publican's prayer: "Lord, look upon me as Thou would look upon the mercy seat of Christ's death, and be satisfied."

References: [1]Everett F. Harrison, *Baker's Dictionary of Theology* (Grand Rapids: Baker Book house), pp. 424-425. [2]John Murray, *Epistle to the Romans, The New International Commentary on the New Testament* (Grand Rapids: Wm. B. Eerdmans Publishing Co., 1973), p. 116.

PROSPECT

Someone who is receptive to the Church and responsive to the message of the gospel. Another term is "candidate." This is someone who could be reached by your presentation of the gospel. A Southern Baptist definition used in its evangelistic Sunday School enrollment campaign is: "Anyone in driving distance of the church who is unsaved and unchurched."

Where to Find Prospects for Your Class

One key to building a growing church is finding prospects. These prospects can be found in several ways. (1) Prospects discovered during visitation should be recorded and systematically followed-up. (2) Anyone who visits one Sunday or attends a special function may be considered a prime prospect. (3) As members report newcomers to the community, names and addresses should be recorded for future contacts. Other facts can be added to the record following other visits. (4) The friends and associates of your church are among the best prospects you may have for your class.

PROVIDING ADDITIONAL SPACE

Additional space is a crucial factor in church expansion. One of the diseases of the Church Growth Movement is sociological strangulation, which happens when the physical facilities of a church are not able to provide space for growth (i.e., new members). Attendance in many growing churches has leveled off because the building was inadequate. When additional room is not available, growth usually stops.

Lack of Sunday School space halts attendance growth for many reasons. First, you cannot organize new ministries for growth if there is no place to put people. Just as a farmer needs additional acreage to harvest a larger crop, so a church needs room to expand its ministry.

Second, attendance levels off, then begins to decline, when so many people are packed into rooms that efficient ministry is hindered. The farmer knows that planting corn too close together will ruin the crop. In a similar way, overcrowded facilities ultimately stymies growth.

Third, lack of facilities thwarts initiative. When the facilities are overcrowded, there is little incentive to get more students, even when exhorted to "go out and reach the lost."

An auditorium-sanctuary is filled when it reaches 80 percent capacity. The tendency of people not to touch others and not to want others in their spaces makes it difficult to use all of the space in pews. The fringe people are pushed out and lost first. That includes those who do not have a commitment to the Body of Christ.

When the auditorium is filled past 80 percent, overcrowding also influences the parking lot, rest rooms, hallways and Sunday School classrooms.

The Bible does not give a blueprint for local church facilities, nor does it contain an organizational chart on how to arrange people in groups. The Bible, however, does tell Christians to gather as a congregation (Heb. 10:25), to teach (Matt. 28:20) and to preach (2 Tim. 4:2). These functions can be carried out only as people congregate. This usually has to happen in a specially designed building because most homes are too small. But what happens when the church building is too small? The gospel is preached, but people do not commit their lives to Jesus because they do not return, and in many cases, do not return to any church, alienating them from an opportunity to respond to God.

Congregations have resolved this problem in a variety of ways. Some churches are able to secure nearby buildings that can be easily renovated to provide the needed space for classes. Others may elect to use their Sunday School buses as Sunday School classrooms. Still others have changed their approach to teaching, moving from small classes to a master-teacher plan.

Another response is to begin a second Sunday School at an alternate time to handle the growth. Other churches have moved to a unified service by moving youth and adult classes into the service, thus freeing that space for additional children's classes. A strategy used by some churches is to begin a mission Sunday School in another part of town—sometimes in a building formerly used for other purposes.

PYRAMID PRINCIPLE

The idea that if a church wishes to serve more people, it must first expand its base of organization, ministry and leadership.

QUALITATIVE GROWTH

The collective improvement in Christian commitment and ministry among the members of a given local church.

Reference: See INTERNAL CHURCH GROWTH.

QUANTITATIVE GROWTH

An increase in membership and worship attendance in a given local church.

QUESNEL, PASQUIER (1634–1719)

Forerunner of the Jansenist Catholic Church (Holland).

Pasquier Quesnel followed Blaise Pascal as the leader of the Jansenists, a puritan movement within the Roman Catholic church that emphasized Augustinian theology and a deeper experience of communion with God. Strongly opposed by Louis XIV and the Jesuits, Quesnel was forced to flee to Holland in 1710. Three years later, Quesnel's writings were condemned by a papal bull. The first Jansenist Catholic church was organized in Holland in 1723 by the followers of Quesnel.

QUID PRO QUO CONTRACT

An arrangement whereby individuals or communities offer long-term allegiance to spiritual powers in exchange for deliverance from immediate traumatic circumstances. —GOJR

RADER, PAUL (1879–1938)

American evangelist and pastor.

Born in Denver, Colorado, the son of a Methodist minister, Paul Rader studied at the University of Denver, the University of Colorado and Harvard University. He adopted liberal ideas about the Bible and theology and began a career as a businessman.

Following his conversion in New York City, Rader left business and entered the ministry, eventually serving pastorates in Boston, Massachusetts, Pittsburgh, Pennsylvania, Chicago, Illinois, and Fort Wayne, Indiana. He was a pioneer in the Tabernacle movement, building large "tabernacles" that drew large crowds and had little church organization. Rader served as president of The Christian and Missionary Alliance denomination (1921–1923) and preached the gospel over the CBS radio network.

Rader's greatest contribution to evangelism was achieved through those he influenced to enter the ministry and the missionaries he helped send to countries throughout the world.

RAIKES, ROBERT (1736–1811)

Robert Raikes became a newspaper editor at age 22, taking over *The Gloucester Journal* in Gloucester, England, from his father in 1757. He spent Sunday afternoons reading the Bible to young men in prison. He became convinced that a vice could be better prevented than cured. When the publisher went to the rough slum district one afternoon in search of a gardener, he was jostled by a gang of ragged boys. He determined to do something about the condition of the children. Raikes took the problem to the Reverend Thomas Stock, the rector of the district, who collected names of 90 children, and together the two men conducted a strenuous visitation campaign. They gathered a class into the kitchen of a Christian lady, Mrs. Meredith, who at first did the teaching.

The first Sunday Schools were serious educational ventures and had secular and religious content. The material was administered with painful discipline, but instilled a deeply conscious religious atmosphere. Raikes wrote four of the early textbooks used in Sunday School.

Next Raikes began a Sunday School in his parish near his home. Several other schools sprang up around Gloucester. Not until three years later did Raikes use his newspaper as a platform to report and publicize Sunday School. Raikes maintained that starting with children, the lives of the slum dwellers could be improved. His enthusiastic report caught the attention of Christian leaders working in other vice-ridden areas. They responded to his plea and started Sunday Schools throughout England.

At first, Sunday School began at 10 o'clock in the morning. At noon they had a break, then returned for another lesson. Then it was time for a whole group to be taken to church. This was as disagreeable to the parishioners as the students who were forced to attend church, then herded back to Sunday School. At first only boys were enrolled, but almost immediately both boys and girls were accepted. Raikes made three necessary conditions for his scholars to observe: They must come to school with "clean hands, clean faces and their hair combed." A ragged child, however, would not be turned away.

Teachers were originally paid for their services and the use of their kitchens. Robert Raikes, however, suggested that instructors as well as monitors should be volunteers.

In 1785, the Society for the Support and Encouragement of Sunday Schools Throughout the British Dominions (understandably shortened to "The Sunday School Society") was founded and became responsible for the rapid expansion of the movement. It financed and founded the new Sunday Schools.

When Robert Raikes died in 1811, 250,000 students were enrolled in Sunday School. By the time a statue was erected in his memory in 1831, Sunday Schools in Great Britain were ministering weekly to 1,250,000 children, approximately 25 percent of the population.

RAINER, THOM S.

Dr. Thom S. Rainer, born in 1955, is the founding dean of the Billy Graham School of Missions, Evangelism and Church Growth at the Southern Baptist Theological Seminary in Louisville, Kentucky. He is one of fewer than 30 people who hold a Ph.D. in evangelism. His dissertation is considered one of the most significant research projects about the Church Growth Movement from the Fuller perspective: "An Analysis of C. Peter Wagner's Contributions to the Theology of Church Growth."

In addition to serving on the editorial board for this book, Rainer has authored or edited five other books. *Evangelism in the Twenty-first Century* (Harold Shaw Publishers, 1989) is a collection of 21 essays about evangelism from some of the most significant leaders in the field. *The Book of Church Growth: History, Theology, and Principles* (Broadman and Holman, 1993) has been hailed as the first true textbook of the Church Growth Movement. It has been used in at least 40 educational institutions.

Eating the Elephant (Broadman and Holman, 1994) is considered by many to be one of the first leadership and church-growth books written specifically for leaders of established, traditional churches. *God Gave...Evangelists* (World Wide Publications, 1995) is a book commissioned by the Billy Graham Evangelistic Association for itinerant evangelists. Rainer and three other evangelism leaders authored this book.

Giant Awakenings: Nine Surprising Trends for the Church (Broadman and Holman, 1995) traces nine unexpected trends for the Church in the twenty-first century.

In addition to writing books, Rainer has written many articles and reviews. He is a regular contributor to *Global Church Growth* and *Growing Churches* magazines.

Thom Rainer came to the Southern Baptist Theological Seminary as dean of the Billy

Graham School after serving as senior pastor of four growing churches. The last church he served grew to nearly 2,000 in membership during his tenure there. In addition to serving in these churches, Rainer also served adjunctively at Tampa Bay Theological Seminary in Holiday, Florida, and the Beeson Divinity School of Samford University in Birmingham, Alabama.

A popular speaker, Rainer has developed church growth and evangelism seminars designed to challenge churches for the twenty-first century. Some of his topics include: developing vision in traditional churches, amazing trends in churches, developing a spiritual-gifts based ministry in the church, new methodologies for outreach, and new developments in church planting. He has been the plenary speaker for both the Academy for Evangelism in Theological Education and the American Society for Church Growth.

The Billy Graham School of Missions, Evangelism and Church Growth at Southern Seminary, where Rainer is dean, is one of only five graduate schools in the nation that specializes in Great Commission Studies. Since Rainer began leading the school, it has begun offering several degree programs: the Master of Divinity, the Master of Theology, and the Doctor of Missiology, the Doctor of Ministry and the Doctor of Philosophy, all in specific areas of Great Commission Studies. The Graham School has become one of the fastest-growing and most reputable schools in its field.

Rainer is married to the former Nellie Jo King. They have three sons: Sam, Art and Jess.

RAMABAI, PANDITA (1858–1922)

Christian leader among Indian women.

Born into India's highest caste (Brahman), Ramabai was given an education, contrary to the usual custom of that day. After the death of her parents, scholars in Bengal were so impressed with her learning that they gave her the title "Pandita." Disillusioned with Hinduism, Ramabai was eventually converted to Christianity. She established homes for widows and orphans and worked to improve the status of womanhood in India.

REACHING PEOPLE FOR CHRIST

The process of making contact with a person and motivating him or her to give an honest hearing to the gospel. The biblical foundation for the doctrine of reaching is found in 1 Corinthians 9:19-23. This is sometimes called "pre-evangelism."

Reference: Elmer L. Towns, *How to Grow an Effective Sunday School* (Denver: Accent Books, 1979), pp. 43-55.

RECEPTIVITY

The state of being open to evangelism, the gospel and the communicator of the message.

Receptive people are those who are positive toward the gospel message as a result of social dislocation, personal crisis or internal working of the Holy Spirit. They are open to hearing and obeying the gospel of Jesus Christ. The lost who are related to the church are among the most receptive-responsive people a church can reach with the gospel. This includes both those who do and do not attend the church, but have never made a personal commitment to Christ. It also includes those who do not attend the church but are influenced positively by friends, relatives, associates and neighbors who are faithful members. This group is receptive to the church because they have friends in the church, and they may be responsive to the gospel because they have viewed the positive effects of the gospel in the lives of others.

The church should evangelize all its "Jerusalem" by using as many means as possible. But the church should also invest its priority time reaching those who are receptive-responsive people because (1) it follows the biblical example, (2) time is short, (3) resources are limited and (4) through discipleship it produces greater results.

If a person (layperson or pastor) can make only five evangelistic visits during a given time period, it would seem wise to give priority to visiting those who are receptive and responsive. Why? Because emphasizing receptive-responsive people is (1) trying to be as fruitful as possible for Christ, (2) winning the winnable while they are winnable, before their receptivity cools, (3) growing the church faster and larger and (4) being a good steward of one's time and resources.

Time and resources are limited. Therefore, there should be a stewardship of these factors in every aspect of life, including evangelism. Jesus Himself clearly taught that evangelistic efforts would reach all (Mark 16:15), but to concentrate on those who are receptive and responsive (Matt. 10:14). This principle brought about the turning point in the apostle Paul's ministry (Acts 13:46).

Reference: See RESISTANCE-RECEPTIVITY AXIS.

RECEPTIVITY: HOW TO CULTIVATE

Some people are already receptive and responsive. Most friends of believers are open to the gospel because of their relationship, yet each one has a different degree of receptivity. You must recognize this receptivity if you want to be successful in reaching them.

"FRANs" (friends, relatives and neighbors) are usually receptive-responsive people. These people are already within our sphere of influence. Usually, an initial contact has already been made because a relationship has been established. If the relationship is positive, trust has been built. They are already receptive to the messenger because they are close enough to us to be familiar with the Christian lifestyle. In most cases, they should already have some knowledge of the gospel.

A second group of receptive-responsive people are those who have visited the church, but it is not limited to them only. They may feel a need for change. These are people in whom the Holy Spirit has already been working to bring conviction because they heard the gospel in church. Their hearts are softened to the gospel because of Christian influence. They may have no idea what their real needs are, but they are aware that needs exist.

The third group consists of those who are experiencing external changes. God works through circumstances to make them receptive. Some event of joy or sorrow may force them to reevaluate their lives. Things such as graduation, marriage, the birth of a child, separation or divorce, a move across country, the death of a friend or loved one may be used by God to make them aware of their need for God.

Many of those receptive-responsive people may not be within the sphere of influence of any Christian. A community search, sometimes referred to as a community census, can help locate such people. The process is simple. It involves going door-to-door throughout the community to locate those who seem to be receptive to the gospel.

Receptivity can be cultivated in others. The process of cultivating receptivity begins by winning people to yourself. Remember, the citizens of Nazareth refused to hear the message of Christ because they rejected Him and His claims to deity. Therefore, before people will hear the gospel from your lips, you must establish credibility by winning them to yourself. You must take the initiative to contact them and begin building a friendship. Paul clearly taught that Christians can contact people for the gospel's sake (1 Cor. 9:20-23).

Once you have won an individual to yourself, you must then win a hearing for the message. That means two things. First, you must demonstrate through your life that Jesus Christ is meeting your needs (2 Cor. 9:8). Second, you must point out that Jesus Christ is also sufficient to meet their felt needs.

Share with them the sufficiency of Christ by both victorious Christian living and verbal testimony. If you are not victorious, it will be difficult to convince others that such a victory is available to them. Be open and transparent with the people you are trying to influence for Christ. Allow them to see that you have problems and burdens just as they do, but that God helps you through them (Phil. 4:19). Share with them how God is meeting your needs and lifting your burdens.

Showing others how Christ can meet their needs will require some knowledge of their needs. This can be gained by observation and listening. Once you know their needs, you can show them how Christ can help them.

The Word of God is the final key. Whether you are dealing with unsaved people—trying to stairstep them to the gospel—or with Christians—trying to help them become more mature—the Word of God is essential to the process. Faith in Jesus

Christ and Christian growth comes through the Word of God (Rom. 10:17; 1 Pet. 2:2).

The church that is growing through evangelism is (1) locating those in its community who are most receptive to the gospel, (2) establishing relationships with them, (3) presenting the gospel to them and (4) moving those who are less receptive to become more receptive to Christ.

Receptivity Rating Scale

Rating	Event
100	Death of spouse
73	Divorce
65	Marital separation
63	Jail term
63	Death of close family member
53	Personal injury or illness
50	Marriage
47	Fired from work
45	Marital reconciliation
45	Retirement
44	Change in family member's health
40	Pregnancy
39	Sex difficulties
39	Addition to family
39	Business readjustment
38	Change in financial status
37	Death of close friend
35	Change in number of marital arguments
31	Mortgage or loan over $10,000
30	Foreclosure of mortgage or loan
29	Change in work responsibilities
29	Son or daughter leaving home
29	Trouble with in-laws
28	Outstanding personal achievement
26	Spouse starts work
26	Starting or finishing school
25	Change in living conditions
24	Revision of personal habits
23	Trouble with boss
20	Change in work hours conditions
20	Change in residence
20	Change in schools
19	Change in recreational habits
18	Change in social activities
18	Mortgage or loan under $10,000
17	Easter season
16	Change in sleeping habits
15	Change in number of family gatherings
13	Vacation
12	Christmas season
11	Minor violation of the law

Reprinted by permission of Dr. Win Arn, ed., *The Pastor's Church Growth Handbook* (Pasadena, Calif.: Church Growth Press, The Institute for American Church Growth, 1979).

RECEPTIVE-RESPONSIVE PEOPLE
See PROSPECT

A term used to designate prospects who are receptive to the gospel messenger and responsive to the message of the gospel.

Some people want to evangelize house to house, but they cannot get into most homes because the residents are not receptive to them.

There is a place for house-to-house outreach, but the most effective evangelism is when Christians share Christ with their Friends, Relatives, Associates and Neighbors (FRANs). These people are usually receptive to their friends and are responsive to the gospel. This article will give the reasons we should focus our evangelistic attention on winning those with whom we have relationships.

The church should evangelize all people in its "Jerusalem" by using as many means as possible. This involves spreading the gospel through the use of radio, TV, newspapers, flyers, tract distribution and so on.

We should invest our high-priority time reaching those who are responsive-receptive people because (1) it follows the biblical example, (2) time is short, (3) resources are limited and (4) through discipleship it produces greater results.

In light of their stewardship, Christians must establish priorities for evangelism. They must be interested in reaching all, but they also must determine where their evangelistic efforts are likely to be most productive, and give that area attention. That does not mean Christians can forget or ignore the rest of the world. It does mean, however, that they should determine which people are likely to be most receptive and responsive to them, then concentrate their efforts on them. (See RECEPTIVITY.)

1. Who is a prospect? (The term "candidate" is also used by some.) At one time, a church considered a prospect anyone in its neighborhood who was not its member, a member of another church, or a professing Christian. So a neighborhood canvass was conducted to determine who fit the above parameters, and those who did were identified as prospects.

A community canvass is still useful as a first step in identifying receptive-responsive people. However, some who are identified as prospects are not receptive to the gospel messenger, or being saved. They have been hardened to the Church or the gospel. The canvass identifies them as prospects because they have no church affiliation, but they are not responsive-receptive people. Therefore, we must be careful when using the word "prospect," for many times it simply means a nonchurch member.

A technical definition of a prospect is one who is "a likely or potential candidate." That definition points to two distinct groups of people: potential candidates and likely candidates. The potential candidates are those unsaved persons who might possibly become Christians. Likely candidates are those whose conversion seems probable because they are more receptive to the witness and/or to the gospel message.

2. Potential candidates. For purposes of evangelism, every unsaved person is commonly thought of as a prospect, and rightly so. Every unsaved person is a sinner who needs salvation; there are no exceptions (Rom. 5:12). When Christ died on the cross, He made a provision sufficient for all (1 Tim. 2:6; 4:10; 1 John 2:2), and it is not the will of God that any should perish (1 Tim. 2:4; 2 Pet. 3:9). Therefore, every unsaved person is a potential or possible candidate for salvation, and the Church is commissioned to take the gospel to every unsaved person (Mark 16:15).

3. Likely candidates. Likely candidates are those who are receptive and responsive to both the messenger and the message. Because they are receptive and responsive, they have a far greater probability of being stair-stepped through the process to trust Christ as Savior. In other words, they are likely to be ready to be saved. Therefore, a responsive-receptive person has the greatest possibility of success.

Likely candidates are those who are already in the believer's sphere of influence, or could be brought into that sphere. Because everyone has a different sphere of influence, every believer has a different group of likely candidates for evangelism.

Targeting receptive-responsive people knows no racial, economic or social barriers. It does not imply any respect of persons, but, rather, simply stresses winning the winnable while they are winnable.

References: Elmer L. Towns, *Winning the Winnable* (Lynchburg, Va.: Church Leadership Institute, 1986), pp. 27-33; *154 Steps to Revitalize Your Sunday School and Keep Your Church Growing* (Wheaton, Ill.: Victor Books, 1988), pp. 76-81.

RECONCILIATION

The result of the death of Christ that makes humans savable because God looks favorably on them since His wrath has been propitiated.

REDEMPTION: DOCTRINE

Literally, being redeemed or "bought back"; in Scripture usually referring to salvation.

Because the law is eternal, unchangeable and applicable to everyone, no one can escape the demands of the law. Because a degree of criminality is attached to every violation of the law, and because God will punish according to the degree of criminality (Luke 10:10-15; 12:47,48), every violation of the law will be punished according to a predetermined standard. Moreover, all people have violated the law and will suffer its consequences, and nothing in them can help them escape the criminality of their actions. God cannot treat the violations as though they never occurred, nor forgive any violations arbitrarily. Because the law was an extension of the Person of God, breaking the law is offending God, and He must be compensated before the person is saved.

God has two opposing, yet eternal, desires within His nature. First, God wants to let humans go free. Hence, in redemption, He is satisfying His desire to be good or loving. On the other hand, God must punish every violation of a crime, to the degree of its criminality, to satisfy His sense of justice. Both desires in God were satisfied when He found another person to suffer the punishment of criminality, allowing humans to go free (Gen. 22:8).

To carry out this transaction, God's Son, Jesus Christ, satisfied the human's violation of God's law. Christ was born without sin, lived a perfect life, neither breaking the Law nor deserving its criminality. Christ took upon Himself the criminality that had been accumulated by all people, suffering in their place. Because punishment must be eternal and complete, Christ suffered ultimately for all criminality. This act, called the vicarious substitutionary atonement, means that Christ suffered in the place of the sinner (vicarious), and that the death of Christ was the substitute for sin and satisfaction of the law.

The symbol of this transaction was the actual blood of Jesus Christ, which is a symbol of His substitutionary death. "It is shed blood which has always been required for deliverance, and thus it was in the type and the antitype, Christ in His crucifixion."[1]

Yet the symbol of the blood was not introduced on the cross of Jesus Christ, but goes back into the pages of the Old Testament. There, God required a blood sacrifice as the righteous ground for the remission of sin.[2] When Adam and Eve sinned, the Bible says, "Then the eyes of both of them were opened, and they knew that they were naked; and they sewed fig leaves together and made themselves coverings" (Gen. 3:7). Adam and Eve experienced guilt that came from breaking the law of God. God did not punish them on the spot, for that would mean eternal death and separation from God. God knew that one day His Son would die for all people, including Adam and Eve. Christ is "the Lamb slain from the foundation of the world" (Rev. 13:8). Peter also tells us that the symbolic price of this transaction was "the precious blood of Christ, as of a lamb without blemish and without spot" (1 Pet. 1:19). Therefore, God chose an animal as the symbol of redemption—most likely a sheep, for later, God's Son would be called "The Lamb of God who takes away the sin of the world!" (John 1:29).

Although the account in the Garden of Eden does not include the word "blood," the skins of the animals were given as a symbolic covering for their nakedness (Gen. 3:21). Because of their criminality, they deserved the wrath of God. Yet they watched God put an animal to death, shedding innocent blood. As such, God was providing His sovereign grace to point them to calvary where the Lamb of God would die for their sins.

Adam and Eve left the garden realizing that "without shedding of blood there is no remission" (Heb. 9:22). This was a type of salvation without works. Nothing Adam and Eve did deserved salvation. The animal had shed its blood in Eden to provide a covering for their nakedness; even so the blood of Jesus Christ, the Lamb of God, covers the criminality of all who believe in Him, and robes them in His righteousness (Rom. 3:24,25).

Cain and Abel, sons of Adam and Eve, brought their sacrifices to God. Both brothers recognized the existence and the demands of God in their lives. Both brothers brought an offering to God, but only one offering was acceptable to God. Cain brought the fruit of the field, representing what he had done in raising food. It was a symbolic gift of hard work. Cain's offering was rejected. It was not as though Cain rejected God, nor did he refuse to bring something to God. Cain actually attempted to satisfy God by bringing the results of his work; he rejected the use of a blood sacrifice. Throughout Scripture, Cain is represented as a type of salvation by works.

Regardless of how hard humans work to save themselves, it is not acceptable to God. The Bible calls the religion of good works "a form of godliness but denying its power" (2 Tim. 3:5). Humans are always saved by grace through faith, not of works (Eph. 2:8).

In contrast, Abel brought an animal sacrifice that was predictive of the blood of Jesus Christ that would be offered in the future. "By faith Abel offered to God a more excellent sacrifice than Cain, through which he obtained witness that he was righteous" (Heb. 11:4).

When God's people were in bondage in Egypt, God brought a series of plagues upon the nation to motivate Pharaoh to free them. After nine plagues, the Lord finally said to Moses, "I will bring one more plague on Pharaoh and on Egypt" (Exod. 11:1). The last plague was the death of the firstborn of each family. God told His people in Egypt that they were to take a lamb and kill it; hereby God instituted the first Passover.

The New Testament calls Jesus Christ our Passover Lamb (1 Cor. 5:7). Moses instructed Israel to choose a lamb "without blemish, a male of the first year" (Exod. 12:5). This was a type of Jesus Christ "who knew no sin" (2 Cor. 5:21); hence, Jesus Christ fulfilled the type of being without blemish. The Jews were instructed to separate the Passover lamb from the rest of the flock to make certain it was without blemish. In type, Jesus Christ was "holy, harmless, undefiled, separate from sinners, and has become higher than the heavens" (Heb. 7:26).

The Passover lamb was killed and its blood was sprinkled on the sides and tops of the doors of the Israelites. God commanded, "The blood shall be a sign for you on the house where you are. And when I see the blood, I will pass over you" (Exod. 12:13). When the death angel came to Egypt to punish every home, he passed over the home that was protected by the blood. From then on, Israel celebrated the Passover each year by the slaying of a lamb as a type of Jesus Christ.

Israel also recognized the blood atonement on the tenth day of the seventh month each year. The high priest took the blood of a slain lamb and went into the Holy of Holies to offer atonement. This was repeated once each year for the sins of the nation. This included any sins that were committed intentionally or in ignorance (Lev. 4:1-35). The high priest went into the Holy of Holies and sprinkled the blood of the sacrificial animal on the mercy seat to atone for the sins of the people (Lev. 16:14-19).

The argument, therefore, is that the Scriptures expressly declare that these sacrifices were made for the expiation of sin. This idea is expressed by the *Septuagint* (the early Greek translation of the Old Testament) in terms such as "to hide from view," "to blot out" and "to expiate." Hence, the Septuagint means "that which delivers from punishment or evil." It is the common word for an atonement, but it also is used for a ransom, because it is rendered "to secure deliverance."[3]

This is a type of Christ, our High Priest who "entered into heaven" after the death on the cross. The high priest, also a type of Jesus Christ, was the mediator between God and man. Christ fulfilled that priestly office: "He is the Mediator of the new covenant, by means of death" (Heb. 9:15). In another place Paul tells us, "For there is one God and one Mediator between God and men, the Man Christ Jesus" (1 Tim. 2:5).

The word "redemption" (Gr. *apolutrosis*) comes

from a word that means "to buy back." Christ gave His blood a ransom for sin, hence redeeming the lost (1 Pet. 1:18-20). The price of redemption is blood that is paid for the remission of sins (Heb. 9:12,22). The Greek words for "redeemed" are applied to purchasing servants in the ancient slave market. The biblical use of the terms reveals the extent of redemption to all people.

First, the Bible teaches that Christ purchased the sinner in the marketplace. *Agorazo* is the verb that means to go to the marketplace (*agora*) and pay the price for the slave. The verb is "Common in deeds of sale,"[4] and generally meant paying a price for a group of slaves. Those who were "sold under sin" are redeemed (Gal. 3:10). In each of the following Scriptures the term *agorazo* is used. Revelation 14:3, 4 speaks of the 144,000 as those redeemed from the earth. Revelation 5:9 notes that Christ's blood was the price paid for redemption and 2 Peter 2:1 shows that Christ redeemed (paid the price for) not only the saved, but also the false Christians. *Agorazo* speaks of the aspect of redemption that is simply paying the purchase price—in this case, the blood of Christ.

The next word used of redemption in the Bible is *ekagorazo* (*ek*, out, plus *agorazo*, to buy out or from). This term refers to the fact that Christ paid the price with His blood and bought the slave "out of the marketplace" (*ekagorazo*). The slave was never again exposed to sale (Gal. 3:13). Galatians 4:5 also shows that when Christ took humans out from under the Law, He placed them in a different relationship with God by providing for them the opportunity to become the adopted sons of God. *Ekagorazo* emphasizes the removal of the curse of the Law (Gal. 3:13; 4:5).

The third word that refers to redemption is *lutroo*. This word means to pay the price for the slave and release him or her (Gal. 4:5). It emphasizes the freedom Christ makes available to those He redeemed. In Titus 2:14, the use of *lutroo* (redeem) shows that Christ wants to separate us from sin completely.

A consideration of each of these terms and the verses in which they appear demonstrates clearly that Jesus Christ has provided redemption for all people, including false teachers, if they repent (2 Pet. 2:1), by shedding His own blood (Heb. 9:12).

References: [1]Lewis Sperry Chafer, *Systematic Theology* (Dallas: Dallas Seminary Press, 1962), Vol. VII, p. 53. [2]Ibid. [3]Charles Hodge, *Systematic Theology* (Grand Rapids: Wm. B. Eerdmans Publishing Co., 1975) Vol. II, p. 502. [4]James Hope Moulton and George Milligan, *The Vocabulary of the Greek New Testament* (Grand Rapids: Wm. B. Eerdmans Publishing Co., 1972), p. 6.

REDEMPTION AND LIFT

A phenomenon that occurs when a person or group becomes Christian and thereby is lifted out of his (its) former environment and separated from it in social and economic respects. This causes a gap between the new Christian(s) and unsaved friends.

REDEMPTIVE GIFT

A distinct characteristic or facet of every city's life and/or history that can be seized upon by God to demonstrate divine blessing and truth.—GOJR

REGENERATION

The work of the Holy Spirit in the salvation experience that produces new life in the believer. It is used only once in Scripture, where Paul speaks of "the washing of regeneration" (Titus 3:5). The concept is communicated in Scripture through other expressions, particularly the idea of being "born again." According to Edgar Mullins:

Regeneration may be defined as the change wrought by the Spirit of God, by the use of truth as a means in which the moral disposition of the soul is renewed in the image of Christ. All definitions come short of reality. But the above contains the essential points. It is a change wrought by the Holy Spirit. It is accomplished through the instrumentality of the truth. It is a radical change of the moral and spiritual disposition. It is a challenge in which the soul is recreated in the image of Christ.[1]

Augustus Strong notes:

Regeneration is that act of God by which the governing disposition of the soul is made holy, and by which through the truth as means, the first exercise of this disposition is secured. Regeneration, or the new birth, is the divine side of that change of life which, viewed from the human side, we call conversion.[2]

Regeneration is the work of God through the Holy Spirit, of placing in one who has faith a new nature capable of doing the will of God. Regeneration results in more than eternal life. It gives the believer new desires to do the will of God (a new nature) and gives him or her the life of God. Also, it makes possible sanctification. Through an act of God, a person is not entirely passive in the results of regeneration. As M. R. Gordon states:

The initiative in regeneration is ascribed to God (Jn. i. 13); It is from above (Jn. iii. 3, 7) and of the Spirit (Jn. iii. 5, 8). The same idea occurs in Eph. ii. 4, 5; 1 Jn. ii. 29; iv. 7; etc. This divine act is decisive and once for all. Aorists are used in i. 3, ii. 3, 5, 7. The use of perfects indicates that this single, initial act carries with it far-reaching effects as in 1 Jn. ii. 29, iii. 9, iv. 7, v. 1, 4, 18. The abiding results given in these passages are doing righteousness, not committing sin, loving one another, believing that Jesus is the Christ, and overcoming the world. These results indicate that in spiritual matters man is not altogether passive. He is passive in the new birth; God acts on him. But the result of such an act is far-reaching activity; he actively repents, believes in Christ, and henceforth walks in newness of life.[3]

Regeneration is an act of God. Only God can save a soul. Jonah recognized that "Salvation is of the Lord" (Jon. 2:9). Salvation is called "the gift of God" (Rom. 6:23; Eph. 2:8). No one but God can forgive sin and save a soul (Mark 2:7).

When a person receives Jesus Christ, he or she becomes a new creature; but this does not mean the sin nature is eliminated or diminished in any way. While on earth, a Christian will struggle with the desires of the old nature. But in regeneration, the Christian receives a new nature with new power and new attitudes. Strong emphasizes this truth, noting:

Regeneration is not a physical change. There is no physical seed or germ implanted in man's nature. Regeneration does not add to, or subtract from, the number of man's intellectual, emotional, or voluntary faculties. But regeneration is the giving of a new direction or tendency to powers of affection which man possessed before. Man had the faculty of love before, but his love was supremely set on self. In regeneration the direction of that faculty is changed, and his love is now set supremely upon God.[4]

The Agent of Regeneration. The Holy Spirit is the Person who grants eternal life to the repentant sinner. He is the divine Workman who regenerates the individual. He works in the heart to convict the sinner of sin, then He draws the sinner to the Savior. Next, the Holy Spirit effects the work that Paul describes: "Put on the new man who is renewed in knowledge according to the image of Him who created him" (Col. 3:10). Paul also affirmed that "the Spirit of God dwells in you" (Rom. 8:9). After the Spirit is in our hearts, He witnesses to our conversion. "The Spirit Himself bears witness with our spirit that we are children of God" (v. 16). Henry Thiessen comments on the work of the Holy Spirit in regeneration, noting, "The real efficient Agent in regeneration is the Holy Spirit (Jn. 3:5, 6; Tit. 3:5). Truth does not itself constrain the will; besides, the unregenerate heart hates the truth until it is wrought upon by the Holy Spirit."[5]

The Instrument of Regeneration. The Word of God is the instrument God uses in an individual's regeneration. Just as a workman uses tools to get his job done, so God uses His Word as a tool to deposit spiritual life in the believer. We are "born again, not of corruptible seed but incorruptible, through the word of God which lives and abides forever" (1 Pet. 1:23). The Word of God convicts of sin (John 16:8-11), gives a new nature (2 Pet. 1:4) and becomes the basis of spiritual power to overcome sin (Ps. 119:9,11).

The Word of God contains an interesting promise concerning its power: "So shall My word be that goes forth from My mouth; it shall not return to Me void, but it shall accomplish what I please, and it shall prosper in the thing for which I sent it" (Isa. 55:11).

References: [1]Edgar Young Mullins, *The Christian Religion in Its Doctrinal Expression* (Philadelphia: Roger Williams Press, 1917, p. 365. [2]Augustus Hopkins Strong, *Systematic Theology: A Compendium Designed for the Use of Theological Students* (Grand Rapids: Fleming H. Revell Company, 1970), p. 809. [3]M. R. Gordon, "Regeneration," *The New Bible Dictionary*, ed. J. D. Douglas (Grand Rapids: Wm. B. Eerdmans Publishing Co., 1974), p. 58. [4]Strong, *Systematic Theology: A Compendium Designed for the Use of Theological Students*, p. 823. [5]Henry Clarence Thiessen, *Lectures in Systematic Theology* (Grand Rapids: Wm. B. Eerdmans Publishing Company, 1951), p. 344.

REID, ALVIN L.

Alvin L. Reid (born 1959) is the Associate Professor of Evangelism and holds the Bailey Smith Chair of Evangelism at Southeastern Baptist Theological Seminary in Wake Forest, North Carolina. Reid was the founding John R. Bisagno Chair of Evangelism at Houston Baptist University in Houston, Texas, prior to his coming to Southeastern. He taught adjunctively for Southwestern Seminary, Boyce Bible School of Southern Seminary and Oklahoma Baptist University.

Reid served as Director of Evangelism-Stewardship for the State Convention of Baptists in Indiana. In that position, he directed the Crossover Indianapolis evangelistic effort in conjunction with the 1992 Southern Baptist Convention. He also served as a missionary commissioned by the Home Mission Board. He was a pastor or staff member of churches in Alabama and Texas.

Reid holds a Ph.D. with a major in evangelism from Southwestern Baptist Theological Seminary, where he also received an M.Div. Reid graduated from Samford University with a B.A. in 1981. While at Samford, Reid met and married his wife, Michelle. The Reids have two

children, son Joshua, and daughter Hannah.

Reid has spoken in churches across the country and directed training events on evangelism, prayer and spiritual awakening, and church growth in hundreds of churches. He has served on many committees related to evangelism in the Southern Baptist Convention. A personal focus of study for Reid has been the subject of spiritual awakenings. He teaches a seminar that focuses on the implications of spiritual awakening on evangelism and church growth.

Reid's publications include (coeditor with Tim Beougher) *Evangelism for a Changing World* (Harold Shaw Publishers, 1995); *Experiencing God in Revival: Brownwood, Fort Worth, Wheaton and Beyond* (coeditor with John Avant and Malcolm McDow) (Broadman and Holman, 1996); "Witnessing Without Fear," sermon in *Fifty Great Soul-Winning Motivational Sermons* (Atlanta: Home Mission Board, 1994).

Reid is a member of the Academy of Evangelism in Theological Education, the American Society for Church Growth, the Evangelical Theological Society and Theta Alpha Kappa. He was recently selected to *Who's Who Among America's Teachers*. He was formerly a trustee of the Stewardship Commission of the Southern Baptist Convention.

RELATIONSHIP EVANGELISM

Winning a person to Christ through existing relationships, or cultivating receptivity by forming relationships. Christianity is a reflection of relationships.

People's problems are not of being maladjusted, irreligious, nonworshipers or slothful church attenders. People's problems are sin. People are alienated from God (Eph. 4:17,18; Col. 1:21). The unsaved person has no relationship with God, and until such a relationship is established, has no hope of salvation (Eph. 2:12,13). A relationship between Christians and unsaved people has proved to be the most effective means of influencing unsaved people to get saved.

Working through existing relationships was used effectively during the earthly life and ministry of Christ. John the Baptist introduced Andrew, one of his own disciples, to Jesus (John

1:35,36), then Andrew immediately introduced his brother, Simon Peter to Christ (vv. 41,42). The day following, Jesus found Philip (v. 43) a resident of the same town as Andrew and Simon Peter (v. 44). Friendships played a part in Philip's meeting the Savior. Philip applied the principle of networking by immediately finding his friend Nathanael and introducing him to Jesus (vv. 45,46).

In retrospect, three things become clear. (1) A relationship with God is the foundation to the Christian faith. (2) Human relationships are the most effective way of opening the door to reach people for Christ. (3) Working through existing relationships or networking people for the gospel is a biblical approach to evangelism.

Bonding newcomers to the church through networking. Getting new converts or members to join a group is the glue that keeps them in the church. Newcomers who become actively involved in Sunday School classes and feel they are needed and vital parts of the classes are usually permanently bonded to the church. Research shows that new converts and members who do not become involved in cell groups are often lost to other churches, or they abandon church completely. Because the cell (Sunday School class, Bible study) is the glue that holds groups of people to the church, what is the glue that holds individuals to the cell? The answer is meaningful interpersonal relationships. Cell groups are small enough to allow interaction between members and newcomers. This interaction cultivates friendships and bonds newcomers to the cell and to the church.

REMNANT THEOLOGY

In a misapplication of a biblical theme, the glorification of littleness in which to be small is to be holy. Slow growth is adjudged good growth. The position is supposedly based on the biblical teaching that God will save a faithful remnant even though a majority of His people are unfaithful.

RENEWING ALLEGIANCES

Steps taken by contemporary generations and communities to reaffirm spiritual pacts and practices initiated by their predecessors. In many instances, these steps are linked to traditions involving specific rituals, festivals and pilgrimages.—GOJR

REPENTANCE

A change of mind relating to one's actions or attitudes, rather than a change of character or nature. It may be reflected in sorrow or remorse.

RESISTANCE-RECEPTIVITY AXIS

A measurement scale by which people are designated according to their openness to the gospel.

References: See RIGHT-END PEOPLES; LEFT-END PEOPLES; HARVEST PRINCIPLE.

RESURRECTION OF CHRIST

The coming to life of the physical body of Christ; the reuniting of His body with His spirit. In Christ's resurrection, death was subjected to Him and He was given a new position and a transfigured body. His mortality took on immortality.

RETARDATION, MENTAL

Can the retarded be saved?

Although the theological implications of the question have been argued pro and con by church leaders through the centuries, teachers of the mentally retarded have found that the trainable as well as the educable usually have a sense of right and wrong. They feel the need for God. Because their understanding is childlike, the gospel must be presented to them as to a very small child. They can be shown that "all have sinned" (Rom. 3:23); that "the wages of sin is death, but the gift of God is eternal life in Christ Jesus our Lord" (6:23); and that "Christ died for us" (5:8). Some may not understand the way of salvation, but all should be given the opportunity of a careful, clear explanation.

REVELATION

The act of God whereby He gives knowledge about Himself and His creation.

Theologians often speak of two categories— *general revelation*, the knowledge of God available through the wonders of His creation and the universal moral sense (see Rom. 1:19,20); and *special revelation*, the knowledge of the way of salvation through the Word.

REVERSION

The decline of church membership attributed to those who renounce the Christian faith or become delinquent members of the church. Reversion also includes those who move away or do not transfer to a new church, and are thus dropped or purged from membership rolls, often because their whereabouts are unknown.

Reference: See ROLL PURGING.

REVIVAL See AWAKENING; FIRST GREAT AWAKENING

An extraordinary work of God in which Christians tend to repent of their sins as they become intensely aware of His presence in their midst, and manifest a positive response to Him in renewed obedience to His known will. Genuine revival results in both a deepening of individual and corporate experience of God and an increased concern for both their own spiritual welfare and that of others within their communities.

This definition recognizes several distinctives of revival. An "extraordinary work of God" should be differentiated from the more ordinary work of God in the life of the believer. The realization of the unique presence of God during times of revival is consistently reported in the testimonies of the revived. Although evangelicals universally believe in the omnipresence of God, the realization of that theological principle during a revival has a threefold result in the life of the revived. First, the response of the revived in revival is renewed obedience to the known will of God. Second, revival tends to draw individuals into a deeper Christian life experience with God. Third, the revived tend to develop a deeper concern for the spiritual condition of others. In a growth-oriented environment, this concern tends to be expressed in terms of evangelistic activity. In an environment where revival is viewed as an end in itself, this concern tends to be expressed in terms of activities designed to encourage reviving others.

The popular definition of revival is "the outpouring of God on His people." This definition is the preferred term in America and among groups influenced by Americans. Outside the United States, the preferred term is "awakenings," a term generally used in church history (i.e., The First Awakening, the Second Awakening and so on).

Americans have sometimes used the term "revival meeting" when they mean an evangelistic meeting. Although evangelism usually happens in a New Testament revival, much more than soul winning is occurring. "Atmospheric revival" is evident by two criteria. (1) It occurs when emotional and volitional expressions of believers flow from meeting the conditions of revival, and (2) there is a supernatural manifestation of God's presence (more than His omnipresence) in conviction of sin, joy, burden for evangelism, assurance and the leadership of the Holy Spirit.

RICCI, MATTEO (1552–1610)

Pioneer Jesuit missionary to China.

Matteo Ricci overcame Chinese contempt of outsiders and became the first Jesuit missionary to Peking in 1601. He studied both the Chinese language and Confucianism to understand the people of China, and sought to express Christianity using titles of God borrowed from Confucian literature. His message proved to be a mix of Confucian teaching, ancestor worship and Roman Catholicism.

During his lifetime, many prominent members of Chinese society, including a prince, converted to Catholicism. Ricci's willingness to incorporate Confucian teaching and ancestor worship became the focus of a major controversy within the Catholic church in the eighteenth century, first being rejected by the Pope and later adopted.

Ricci's greatest contribution to the extension of the influence of the Roman Catholic church was his success in establishing the basis of the Roman Catholic church in China.

Reference: K. S. Latourette, *A History of Christian Missions in China* (New York: The Macmillan Co., 1929).

RIGHT-END PEOPLES

People who are receptive to the gospel; those who fall on the right end of the resistance-receptivity axis.

References: See RESISTANCE-RECEPTIVITY AXIS; LEFT-END PEOPLES.

RIPE FIELDS

Groups of people who are receptive to the gospel and who will accept it when it is communicated to them.

References: See HARVEST PRINCIPLE; RECEPTIVE PEOPLE.

ROBERTS, EVAN (1878–1950)

Leader in the Welsh revival.

Evan Roberts burned himself out through extensive ministry during the Welsh revival of 1904–1905. Although his public ministry was brief, it was effective in promoting revival throughout Wales.

ROBINSON, REUBEN (1860–1942)

American evangelist.

Born in a log cabin in Tennessee, "Uncle Bud" Robinson was converted to Christ at age 20 in a Texas camp meeting and immediately sensed God's call upon his life to preach. Although he stuttered and had no formal education, about 300 people were converted in his first year of ministry. Robinson traveled more than 2 million miles during his ministry, preached more than 33,000 sermons, brought about more than 100,000 conversions and wrote 14 books.

ROLL PADDING

The practice of adding inactive names to church membership records or receiving into membership those who have no intention of being active members of a church. It also includes the habit of leaving on the rolls those who are obviously inactive, have moved away, or their whereabouts are unknown, and those who have died. It is a useless and dishonest practice.

ROLL PURGING

A process by which the church reflects its actual membership by removing the names of those who no longer belong on the records because of inactivity, death, transfer to another church or moving away. Roll purging results in "reversions."

ROMAN ROAD

A popular plan for presenting salvation by utilizing key verses in the Epistle to the Romans. People must follow God's road to heaven, just as the travelers followed the Roman roads during the time of Christ. The Roman Road of salvation is often used to illustrate this fact.

How to Present Salvation Using the Roman Road

Step 1—Know your need. "For all have sinned and fall short of the glory of God" (Rom. 3:23). It makes little difference how good we are. Even if we were almost perfect, we still fall short of God's holy standard of perfection. The teacher should quickly clarify that he or she, also, is included, for all have sinned.

Step 2—Know the penalty of sin. "For the wages of sin is death, but the gift of God is eternal life in Christ Jesus our Lord" (6:23). This refers to both physical and spiritual death. Physical death occurs upon the separation of the body and the spirit of humans (Jas. 2:26). Spiritual death occurs when one is eternally separated from God.

Step 3—Know God's provision. "But God demonstrates His own love toward us, in that while we were still sinners, Christ died for us" (Rom. 5:8). Although the wages for sin is death, Christ died in people's stead. He died for our sins because we could not pay the price or atone for them. This provision gives the sinner the option to receive or reject God's gift of eternal life.

Step 4—Know how to respond. "That if you confess with your mouth the Lord Jesus and believe in your heart that God has raised Him from the dead, you will be saved" (10:9). To believe in Christ is the same as receiving Him. "But as many as received Him, to them He gave the right to become children of God, even to those who believe in His name" (John 1:12).

Step 5—Bringing to decision. After explaining salvation, a person should not be left with mere head knowledge. An opportunity for decision should be given. Ask the person to pray simply for Christ to come into his or her life.

RULES OF INTERPRETATION

The fundamental principles for determining the accuracy and relevancy of research data. Important guidelines include contextual analysis, integrity of source, level of confirmation, and scriptural validation. —GOJR

SALVATION

The most common biblical expression to identify the change wrought in the life of one who by faith obtains the benefits of the atonement of Christ.

The term "salvation" appears in both Old and New Testaments, implying the ideas of deliverance, safety, preservation, healing and soundness. In a sermon based on Acts 16:31, American evangelist Billy Sunday observed:

Salvation means "to be brought from a state or condition not favorable to our welfare or happiness into a condition which is favorable." The salvation of the sick would mean their health, but the salvation mentioned here is from sin.[1]

Although Billy Sunday was not known as a systematic theologian, his simple definition of the term communicates the contemporary usage of the biblical expression. In a more technical definition of the biblical term, G. Walters observes:

The English term used in A.V. is derived from Latin *salvare*, "to save" and *salus*, "health," "help"; and translates Hebrew *yesua* and cognates ("breath," "ease," "safety") and Greek *soteria* and cognates ("cure," "recovery," "redemption," "remedy," "reserve," "welfare"). It means the action or result of deliverance or preservation from danger or disease, implying safety, health, and prosperity.[2]

As with many other theological expressions, this term has a more specialized meaning when brought from the exegetical to the contemporary theological arena. It "denotes the whole process by which a man is delivered from all that would prevent his attaining to the highest good that God has prepared for him."[3] Lewis Chafer observes:

According to its largest meaning as used in the Scripture, the word "salvation" represents the whole work of God by which He rescues man from the eternal ruin and doom of sin and bestows on him the riches of grace, even eternal life now and eternal glory in heaven. "Salvation is of the Lord" (Jonah 2:9). Therefore, it is in every aspect a work of God in behalf of man, and is in no sense a work of man in behalf of God.[4]

Salvation is both an instantaneous event and a progressive experience in the life of the believer. The verb appears in Scripture in three tenses: past, present and future. As noted in *The Scofield Reference Bible:*

Salvation is in three tenses: (1) the Christian has been saved from the guilt and penalty of sin (Lk. 7:50; 1 Cor. 1:18; 2 Cor. 2:15; Eph. 2:5, 8; 2 Tim. 1:9) and is safe. (2) The Christian is being saved from the habit and dominion of sin (Rom. 6:14; 8:2; 2 Cor. 3:18; Gal. 2:19, 20; Phil. 1:19; 2:12-13; 2 Thess. 2:13). And (3) the Christian will be saved at the Lord's return, from all the bodily infirmities that are the result of sin and God's curse upon the sinful world (Rom. 8:18-23; 1 Cor. 15:42-44), and brought into entire conformity to Christ (Rom. 13:11; Heb. 10:36; 1 Pet. 1:51; 1 Jn. 3:2).[5]

The progressive nature of salvation does not in any way minimize the importance of an experience whereby the individual "is saved," but rather reveals what it means to be saved, including the understanding that the initial experience was the beginning, not the end, of the work of Christ in the life of the believer. As Burton Easton notes:

Salvation is both a present and future matter for us. The full realization of all that God has in store will not be ours until the end of human history (if, indeed, there will not be opened infinite possibilities of eternal growth), but the enjoyment of these blessings depends on conditions fulfilled in and by us now.[6]

This future aspect of salvation does not by any means imply the possibility of an incomplete salvation in the present. Those who maintain that salvation in some way depends upon a person's obedience of faithfulness believe that those who do not "stick to it" will fail to acquire the benefits of their future salvation. But as Lewis Chafer writes:

> The fact that some aspects of salvation are yet to be accomplished for the one who believes does not imply that there is ground for doubt as to its ultimate completion; for it is nowhere taught that any feature of salvation depends upon the faithfulness of man. God is faithful, and having begun a good work, He will perform it until the day of Jesus Christ (Phil. 1:6).[7]

References: [1]William Ashley Sunday, *Wonderful and Other Sermons* (Grand Rapids: Zondervan Publishing House, n.d.), p. 27. [2]G. Walters, "Salvation," *The New Bible Dictionary*, ed. J. D. Douglas (Grand Rapids: Wm. B. Eerdmans Publishing Co., 1977), p. 1126. [3]Burton Scott Easton, "Salvation," *The International Standard Bible Encyclopedia*, ed. James Orr (Grand Rapids: Wm. B. Eerdmans Publishing Co., 1974), p. 2665. [4]Lewis Sperry Chafer, *Major Bible Themes* (Chicago: Moody Press, 1926), p. 154. [5]*The New Scofield Reference Edition* (1967), p. 1211, f.n. 1. [6]Easton, "Salvation," *The International Standard Bible Encyclopedia*, p. 2670. [7]Chafer, *Major Bible Themes*, p. 155.

SALVATION, PLAN OF

At some point in the process by which people are evangelized, the gospel must be presented in a clear and understandable manner that enables people to make a decision in response. This involves explaining the essential principles of the gospel, having a plan by which that is done, and understanding the process by which people are converted to Christ and experience salvation.

Explaining the Gospel

To be saved, a person must know the gospel. There is only one gospel (Gal. 1:9), but it contains two sides of the same truth. Just as a door has two sides, so the gospel is both propositional truth and personal truth. It is propositional truth in that it is a formula that is accurate. The gospel is the account of the death of Christ for our sins, His burial and resurrection from the dead on the third day (1 Cor. 15:1-4). Only Jesus could provide salvation for us. "But God demonstrates His own love toward us, in that while we were still sinners, Christ died for us" (Rom. 5:8).

The gospel is also personal truth. When Paul came to Corinth to preach the gospel, he "determined not to know anything among you except Jesus Christ and Him crucified" (1 Cor. 2:2). The gospel is not complete in its presentation until it focuses attention on the Person of Christ. Jesus said, "And as Moses lifted up the serpent in the wilderness, even so must the Son of Man be lifted up, that whoever believes in Him should not perish but have eternal life" (John 3:14,15). If a person does not trust in Christ, that person is not saved. To be converted, it is important that we know both the content (doctrine) and the Person (Jesus Christ) of the gospel.

Knowing the propositional truth of salvation is knowing God's plan of salvation. A person who wishes to become a chess master must learn the rules of the game and be disciplined to play by them. A person who wishes to be a Christian must follow God's plan. People must know they are lost, that the penalty of sin is eternal separation from God, that the gospel reveals God's provision to save them as a free gift and that they must respond in faith to Him. (See ROMAN ROAD.)

Leading a Person to Christ

Many local churches and Bible colleges offer a course entitled "personal evangelism," whereby students are given techniques, approaches, verses and answers to objections so that they may win souls to Christ. Evangelical churches tend to label this as "evangelism," whereas fundamental churches call it "soul winning." A high degree of motivation is included in personal evangelism classes.

The Roman Road of Salvation	
Human Need	Romans 3:23
Sin's Penalty	Romans 6:23
God's Provision	Romans 5:8
The Person's Response	Romans 10:9

Many churches and Bible colleges teach the "Roman Road" as a means of leading a person to Christ (see chart and ROMAN ROAD). Others use "The Four Spiritual Laws" developed by Campus Crusade International. This approach does not begin with an emphasis on sin, but the overriding motive is God's love. The thought is that soul winners must have the same motive as God has if they are going to reach people for Christ. (See FOUR SPIRITUAL LAWS.)

The Four Spiritual Laws
• God loves you and has a wonderful plan for your life.
• Man is sinful and separate from God; thus, he cannot know and experience God's plan for his life.
• Jesus Christ is God's only provision for man's sin. Through Him, you can know and experience God's love and plan for your life.
• We must individually receive Him as Savior and Lord. Then we can know and experience God's love and plan for our lives.

Evangelism Explosion, developed by Dr. James Kennedy, is used in many churches. Teams of three are sent out to present the gospel. Their approach begins with an assumption that the person knows he or she will die and appear before God. The next step is to ask why God should allow the person to enter heaven. The lost person is then faced with the fact that he or she has not made preparation to enter into the presence of God:

Evangelism Explosion
1. Have you come to a place in your spiritual life where you can say for certain that if you were to die today you would go to heaven?
2. Suppose that you were to die tonight and stand before God and He were to say to you, "Why should I let you into My heaven?" What would you say?[1]

The Bible teaches personal evangelism by the example of Jesus (the woman at the well, Nicodemus, Zacchaeus) and Philip (the Ethiopian eunuch). Actually, each occasion of one person leading another to Christ is a clear example of personal evangelism. The examples

of Paul evangelizing the Philippian jailer and Sergius Paulus grew out of situations where other circumstances drew the persons to Christ.

In personal evangelism, the soul winner makes an intentional effort to bring the unsaved person to Christ. Technically, personal evangelism is not a by-product of casual relationships, nor is it leading people to Christ after they respond to a public invitation.

Certain congregations are characterized as "soul-winning churches" because they plan programs for the intentional evangelization of the lost. This program of personal evangelism is carried out at a regular time. Sometimes this is done by visiting those whose names are supplied on a card, or by visiting all the homes in a neighborhood. The evangelist goes door to door to witness for Christ (Acts 5:42). Sometimes the evangelist goes to a public place such as a bus station having a view of attempting to win people to Christ. This is sometimes called "the fisherman's club" or "soul-winning visitation."

Reference: [1] D. James Kennedy, *Evangelism Explosion* (Wheaton, Ill.: Tyndale House Publishers, 1977), p. 51.

SANCTIFICATION

The action of God in setting apart as holy a person, institution or thing.

In *past* sanctification, the saved person was positionally set apart. In *present* sanctification, the person is becoming set apart in his experience. In *future* sanctification, the person will become perfect when he or she is glorified.

SANCTIFICATION (PRACTICAL)

A continual process beginning with conversion and finally accomplished at the coming of Christ, which involves the Christian becoming Christlike by struggling in the present life with sin, and appropriating the divine and biblical means of overcoming it.

SANCTIFICATION (PROSPECTIVE)

The final glorified state of a person set apart to God without sin at the rapture.

SANCTIFICATION GAP

A symptom of *koinonitis* that occurs when a church, turned inward on itself, demonstrates a high degree of visual piety, which in turn causes a new Christian to feel uncomfortable and often unwanted among the people of that church.

Reference: See KOINONITIS.

SATELLITE PRINCIPLE

The strategy of planting churches in which the daughter churches are semiautonomous, relating organically to the mother church and each other.

SATURATION EVANGELISM

This term grew out of the In-depth Evangelism movement given impetus in Central and South America by Kenneth Strachan, when entire nations were evangelized by total mobilization. Jerry Falwell heard the term when visiting in Latin America and applied it to local church outreach. Falwell described it as "using every available means, to reach every available person, at every available time." It included crusade evangelism, personal evangelism, bus evangelism and so on. Saturation evangelism also involves the use of methods such as radio, television, tracts and newspaper advertisements.

Falwell based his definition on Acts 5:28: "You have filled Jerusalem with your doctrine." He preached that a church should fill its local "Jerusalem" with the gospel by every means possible. He explained that conviction of sin continued in a person's life even when the church doors were not open and a soul winner present. Therefore, something should be present at all times to communicate the gospel in a person's hour of need.

SAVONAROLA, GIROLAMO (1452–1498)

Pre-Reformation reformer.

Born in Ferrara, Italy, Girolamo Savonarola was the leader of the Florentine Revival. He originally trained in medicine but became a Dominican monk in 1474 in response to a sermon by an Augustinian friar. In 1481, he began preaching in Florence. Savonarola attempted to reform the Church, preaching against the sinful lifestyle of the pope and other perceived evils within the church. Pope Alexander VI offered to make Savonarola a cardinal if he would end his preaching against the church. Savonarola refused the honor. Opposition to his ministry continued to grow, culminating with his hanging and burning on May 23, 1498.

Savonarola's greatest contribution to evangelism was in exposing the corruption of the Roman Catholic church. Although he was unsuccessful in achieving the reform he desired, he was among those who prepared the way for a future generation that would prove more responsive to reform.

SCHMIDT, GEORGE (1709–1785)

Pioneer missionary to the Hottentots of South Africa.

When George Schmidt, a Moravian missionary, arrived at the Dutch colony at the Cape of Good Hope, Africa, in 1737 to begin evangelizing the native people of that region, few settlers saw much potential of success. Their only dealing with the native Hottentots was that of capturing them for the slave trade. When Schmidt began baptizing converts, the settlers actively opposed his work and forced him to leave the colony about six years later.

Schmidt's greatest contribution to evangelism was that of evangelizing the native people of southern Africa in an age in which they were being enslaved by non-Africans.

SCHWARTZ, CHRISTIAN FREDERICK (1726–1798)

Notable missionary and evangelist of the Danish-Halle Mission.

Christian Frederick Schwartz traveled widely as an effective missionary evangelist throughout the Danish colony in India from 1750 to 1798.

SCOFIELD, CYRUS INGERSOLL
(1843–1921)

Bible scholar and missionary leader.

Born August 19, 1843, in Lenawee County, Michigan, C. I. Scofield moved with his family to Tennessee as a young boy. His college education was delayed by the Civil War. He served as an orderly in the Confederate Army and was awarded the Confederate Cross of Honor. Following the war, he studied law in St. Louis and for a time served as the United States District Attorney for Kansas.

When Scofield was later converted to Christ, he immediately became actively involved in Christian work. He was ordained in Dallas, Texas, in October 1883 when he began his ministry as the pastor of First Congregational Church. Influenced through private conversations with Hudson Taylor, Scofield led his church to adopt a greater missionary emphasis, which resulted in establishing the Central American Mission in 1890. In 1907, he completed work on a study Bible that was published by the Oxford University Press in January 1909. He died on Sunday morning, July 24, 1921, in Douglaston, Long Island.

Scofield's greatest contribution to evangelism was achieved through founding the Central American Mission. He is best remembered today for *The Scofield Reference Bible*, which has been widely used by conservative evangelical Christians throughout this century.

SCUDDER, JOHN (1793–1855)

First medical missionary.

Although many missionaries before him had some basic medical training, Dr. John Scudder became the first fully qualified medical missionary when he was sent out by an American missionary agency to India in 1819. Since then, providing medical services has been an important part of missionary strategy throughout the Third World. Scudder's granddaughter, Dr. Ida Scudder, was later instrumental in establishing a medical school at Vellore, South India.

Scudder's greatest contribution to evangelism was in pioneering a new evangelistic strategy around providing health care.

SEARCH THEOLOGY

A theological justification of the practice of continuing to use a given evangelistic methodology even though it does not result in making disciples.

SECOND GREAT AWAKENING

Toward the end of the eighteenth century, a second great awakening was experienced throughout the evangelical world. According to J. Edwin Orr, this awakening "began in the industrial cities of Yorkshire in late 1791."[1] Revival was also experienced throughout the British Isles during that decade, and throughout Europe beginning about the turn of the century. One of the results of the revival in England was the abolition of slavery in the British commonwealth.

The Second Great Awakening in America touched colleges and spread through the West through camp meetings, the rise of the American Sunday School Union and the mission societies. Whereas the First Great Awakening in America was identified with the preaching of Jonathan Edwards, the Second Great Awakening was identified with the preaching of Charles Finney.—ALR

Reference: [1] J. Edwin Orr, *A Call for the Re-study of Revival and Revivalism* (Pasadena, Calif.: School of World Mission, 1981), p. 11.

SECONDARY SOURCES

Information sources such as books, articles and dissertations that are generally interpretive in nature.—GOJR

SEEKER SERVICE

A church service designed for the comfort of an unsaved person who is honestly seeking knowledge and experience about God, barriers to reach the person are removed, and an approach is used especially to reach secular people with the gospel.

The seeker service helps people come to Christ without crossing too many cultural or "man-made" barriers. One pastor said, "I don't ask unsaved people to pray the Lord's Prayer because they can't pray, 'Our Father.'" The pastor went on to say, "I'm not an expositional preacher because the unsaved will not listen to Bible lectures." A seeker service features contemporary Christian music and drama and is issues oriented to meet the needs of modern secular people.

A seeker-driven service is a contemporary evangelistic church service that is designed to reach the unsaved who do not have a church tradition and do not understand the activities in a traditional worship service.

There is a difference between a seeker-driven church service (the purpose is to reach unsaved secular people) and the seeker-sensitive church service (the service is designed for believers but is sensitive to the needs and limitations of secular people without a church background).

SENILITY

A pathology of church growth describing a church lacking a workable growth strategy.

SETTING PERSONAL GOALS IN EVANGELISM

Understanding the Goal of Evangelism

The vast majority of Christians think of evangelism as a confrontational event. They have the impression that evangelistic success can only be measured in terms of decisions for Christ. If their efforts do not produce a decision as quickly as expected, they experience a sense of failure. The perception of failure then breeds discouragement, and believers may give up on witnessing to their most promising friends before the task is completed. Some become completely disillusioned and stop all efforts to reach the unsaved. A proper understanding of goals and of "stair-stepping" people to Christ can eliminate much of this problem.

1. "Stair-stepping" as a goal. Without question, the success of evangelism is the decision of the unsaved to trust Jesus Christ as their personal Savior. But there are many levels of successes in the process of sharing Christ with a friend. This can be referred to as stair-stepping toward conversion.

A young man chooses boxing because he sees an Olympic gold medal as the height of success. However, there must be many successes before he achieves the Olympic gold. Before he can even compete in the Olympics, he must first win the local competition, the state, the regional, the national and ultimately the Olympic trials.

Success—whether in sports or evangelism—is reaching goals that stair-step people toward the ultimate objective. When initial contact is made with unbelievers, the ultimate goal is to see them become mature Christians. But the immediate goal is to see them move one step closer to salvation. Each time they progress from one step to the next, there is success.

2. Making realistic witnessing goals. The ultimate objective of introducing the unsaved to Jesus Christ must be broken down into realistic goals. The Christian must exercise patience to stair-step the unsaved toward faith in Christ in steps small enough that the unsaved are able to follow them (Isa. 28:10). Too often the Christian tries to bring every unsaved friend to Christ in a single leap. If the person is not a responsive-receptive prospect, Christians think they have failed because no decision was made for Christ. Instead of feeling used of God because they were able to share their faith, they become discouraged because no decisions were recorded. Remember that although an adult can easily climb two or three steps at a time, small children must learn to take them one step at a time.

3. Measuring success as moving people closer. Any progress in moving people closer to making a decision for Christ is the achievement of a goal. Understanding the nature of success and setting realistic goals provides a means of constantly evaluating the process of evangelism. Each time a goal is reached, success can be measured in terms of the progress that has been made toward the ultimate goal of bringing a person to Christ.

Stair-stepping enables Christians to concentrate their efforts on winning the winnable while they are winnable. They are either sharing their faith, which makes some more receptive, or they are bringing a prepared person to a decision of salvation. In either case, they are making progress.

SEVEN TOUCHES, LAW OF

The principle of networking unsaved people with several approaches designed to lead them to Christ and enable them to remain true to their commitments.

Research shows that people are more likely to return for second and third visits if they are contacted seven times after their first visits—hence the Law of Seven Touches. These contacts can be initiated by the church through letters, phone calls, visits or other personal contacts. The obvious conclusion is that the church that contacts the most people the most times will probably have the greatest evangelistic results. Long-term evangelistic results are rarely realized by making only one contact. But when all aspects of evangelism are followed—including the laws of the Three Hearings and the Seven Touches—people are more likely to respond and remain faithful to the gospel.

Suggested Follow-up Bonding Strategy for Your Church

When people visit the church on a Sunday morning (usually the most common time for people to make a first visit to a new church), they should be immediately followed up in accordance with the Law of Seven Touches. The most important immediate concern of the church should be to get those visitors back the second and third time (see THREE HEARINGS, LAW OF). To do this, the visitors should be contacted seven times before the next Sunday. The following is a suggested outline to apply seven touches:

The first of these seven contacts or touches can be Sunday afternoon. The pastor or teacher should phone the visitors and thank them for visiting with them. The phone call should establish three things. First, the callers should offer to help the family in any way they can. Second, they will want to mention the special "Friendship Packet" the church has prepared for them, and that someone would like to deliver the packet to their homes. Third, the visitors should be told the church secretary will phone for an appointment to bring the packet to the home.

The next of the seven touches occurs Sunday evening. The pastor or Sunday School teacher should write a letter covering much of what was said during the phone call. This could be a standard form letter that comes off a home computer and goes out to visitors, but if so, each letter should be personalized to the recipient.

Suggest a time for the visit to their home during the phone call and/or follow-up letter that can later be confirmed by the secretary. Because it is important to win the winnable while they are winnable and reach the reachable while they are reachable, many churches find Tuesday evening a good time for this second phone call. When suggesting a time, be approximate so as to give you liberty to stay longer or leave earlier on other visits you may make that evening. You might suggest you could drop by around 7:00 P.M. on Tuesday evening.

After the Tuesday evening phone call, write a letter to the prospect confirming the time of the visit. (Although some letters arrive after the visit because of delays in postal service, it is part of the accumulative effect of Follow-up.) Again express your interest in being of service to them and their families, and assure them that they are welcome to visit the church services as often as they can.

On Wednesday or Thursday evening, someone from the church or Sunday School class they would be involved in should visit them. Ideally, this should be the teacher, but if a number of people need follow up, it is better that another class officer or member make the visit rather than putting it off several weeks until the teacher can make the call.

During the visit, the teacher should tell the prospect about the class and how he or she could fit into the class. The teacher will also want to be familiar with the rest of the church program that might be of interest to others in the family (e.g., children's and youth ministries). The primary reason for visiting the home is to present Jesus Christ to the person, so the pastor/teacher should be alert to sharing the gospel with the prospect if the opportunity arises. Beyond this, the visitor should be alert to any other needs in the home.

The pastor/teacher should immediately take the time to write a letter to the prospect outlining the next spiritual step he or she should take. After the visit, the pastor/teacher should know if the person needs to accept Christ, rededicate himself, join the church, or whatever. The letter should clearly outline what is expected. The letter should also thank the prospect for letting the pastor/teacher visit, and again extend the invitation to visit the appropriate Sunday School class the next Sunday.

An informal follow up with a phone call on Saturday inviting the prospect to the Sunday School class or service the next day provides the finishing touches to a week of following up a receptive, responsive person. By the end of the week, the casual visitor has met several people from the church and recognizes that the church is interested in him or her. Unless there is some particular reason why they cannot, it is very likely that the visitors will return the following week to the church where they know they are welcome and accepted.

SHEEP STEALING

A term used to describe the phenomenon of a person in one church being encouraged to join another. Some consider this sheep "finding" rather than stealing, based on the premise that active members who are a part of a church cannot be persuaded to leave it unless their needs are not being met.

SHEPHERDING

The ministry of pastoral care in a small-group setting involving the threefold responsibility of (1) providing direction and leadership, (2) guiding people into meaningful Bible study and growth and (3) protecting them from harmful influences. Some call this the gift of pastor or pastoring.

SHEPHERDING, GIFT OF

One of the task-oriented gifts of the Holy Spirit; the supernatural ability to serve God by overseeing, training and caring for the needs of a group of Christians. The strengths of this gift include (1) a burden to see others learn and grow, (2) a high sense of empathy and sensitivity and (3) a strong others orientation in ministry.

Among the weaknesses of this gift are (1) a tendency to become overinvolved in ministry, (2) a failure to involve others and (3) a tendency to become overprotective of people. A person who has this gift needs to avoid the danger of (1) discouragement, (2) pride and (3) selfishness.

SHIELDS, THOMAS TODHUNTER (1873–1955)

Fundamentalist leader.

Born in Bristol, England, T. T. Shields was converted to Christ as a child in a revival meeting in his father's church. He began his ministry in his native England, but accepted a call to pastor the Jarvis Street Baptist Church in Toronto, Ontario, Canada, in 1910, a position he held until his death 45 years later. From that influential pulpit and through his publication, *The Gospel Witness*, Shields became a leading voice in the fundamentalist controversy in both Canada and the United States. In 1927, Shields established the Toronto Baptist Seminary to train evangelical Baptist pastors and missionaries. Much of his ministry was patterned after Charles Haddon Spurgeon, and Shields was often called "the Spurgeon of Canada" by his supporters.

Shields's greatest contribution to evangelism was achieved through establishing Toronto Baptist Seminary, a school that continues to train evangelical Baptist pastors and missionaries to this day.

Reference: Leslie K. Tarr, *Shields of Canada* (Grand Rapids: Baker Book House, 1967).

SHOWING MERCY, GIFT OF

One of the task-oriented gifts of the Holy Spirit; the supernatural ability to locate those in distress and express sympathy to give spiritual help.

The strengths of this gift include (1) the ability to empathize with those who have problems that affect their spirituality so that they desire the healing that is available, (2) placing greater emphasis on emotional or spiritual needs than the physical needs and (3) having rapport and identifying with individuals or groups.

Among the weaknesses of this gift are (1)

being perceived as offering help when it is not wanted, (2) being perceived as being too intimate with people to whom the person is ministering and (3) a tendency to attract to him or herself those who have emotional problems, the mentally deficient, the handicapped and socially dysfunctional. A person who has this gift needs to avoid the danger of (1) lacking firmness in dealing with people, (2) basing his or her life on personal emotions or feeling, or (3) resenting others who are not sensitive to inner needs.

SIDE-DOOR EVANGELISM

An approach to evangelism through nonevangelistic events such as networking people to Christ.

Side-door evangelism is bringing people into the church's events such as recreation programs, fellowship events, service to their needs and so on. This approach usually involves three steps. First, the unsaved in the community are networked to church members. Then they are networked into specific church activities and ministries that address their felt needs. Ultimately, they are networked to the person of Jesus Christ through their relationships with other Christians and involvement in these ministries.

Side-door evangelism seeks to establish readiness to hear and responsiveness to accept the message of the gospel prior to calling on people to make a personal commitment to Christ. Sometimes this is called stair-stepping people to Christ.

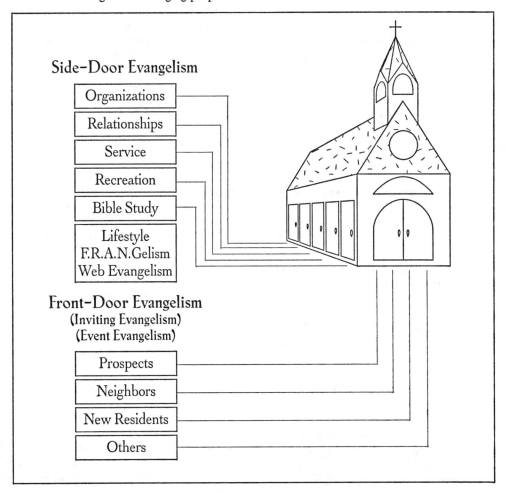

Side-Door Evangelism

- Organizations
- Relationships
- Service
- Recreation
- Bible Study
- Lifestyle
- F.R.A.N.Gelism
- Web Evangelism

Front-Door Evangelism
(Inviting Evangelism)
(Event Evangelism)

- Prospects
- Neighbors
- New Residents
- Others

SIGNS AND WONDERS: BIBLICAL OVERVIEW

(NOTE: Verses in this article are taken from the NIV *Bible; italics in the verses are added by the author.)*

Together with certain other related words, the phrase "signs and wonders" comprises the lexical field of "Power" in New Testament Greek.[1] This lexical field is comprised of *dunamis* "power" and its synonyms, which include the word "signs (*semeia*)"; the phrase "signs and wonders (*semeia kai terata*)"; "power, miracle (*dunamis*)"; "acts of power, miracles (*dunameis*)"; *erga*, denoting "miraculous works"; "wonders (*thaumata, thaumasia*)"; "wonderful thing (*paradoxon*)"; "power in exercise, energy[2] (*energeia*)"; "force, violent power (*bia*)"; "strength, especially physical (*ischus*)"; "might, manifested power (*kratos*)"; and "authority, liberty of action (*exousia*)."[3]

Within this lexical field, the words and phrases "signs and wonders (*semeia kai terata*)," "signs (*semeia*)," "miracles (*dunameis*)" and "miraculous works (*erga*)" all denote healing and deliverance from demons[4] (otherwise denoted by *therapeuo* "cure, heal," *iaomai* "heal" and *sozo* "save, heal").[5] The phrase "signs and wonders" and the words "sign" and "miracle" are also often associated with, and may denote, the gifts of the Holy Spirit. Though the word "sign" (*semeion*) does not always denote miraculous events (e.g., Matt. 26:48; Luke 2:12; Rom. 4:11; 2 Thess. 3:17),[6] the majority of occurrences in the New Testament denote miraculous events of one sort or another.[7]

The following passages show that "signs, wonders and miracles" denote healing, deliverance from demons and spiritual gifts in the New Testament:

1. "Signs"[8] and "signs and wonders" denote healing and deliverance from demonic oppression according to Mark 16:17,20; John 4:48,54; 6:2; 9:16; 12:17,18; Acts 4:9,16,22 (cf. 3:18); 5:12,15,16; 8:6,7,13; 14:3 (compared with 14:8-10).
2. "Signs" and "signs and wonders" are related to, and can denote, the gifts of the Spirit according to Mark 16:17,18,20; 1 Corinthians 14:22; Hebrews 2:3,4.
3. "Signs" and "signs and wonders" are synony-mous with "miracles" in denoting healing and deliverance from demonic oppression according to Acts 2:22; 8:6,7, 13; 19:11,12; 2 Corinthians 12:12; Hebrews 2:3,4.
4. "Signs, wonders and miracles" of healing and deliverance are worked through the power of the Holy Spirit according to Romans 15:18,19 (cf. 1 Cor. 2:4,5; 12:9-11; 2 Cor. 12:12); Galatians 3:5 associates God's Spirit with the working of miracles.

"Signs, Wonders and Miracles" Are Not Restricted to the Apostles

"Signs, wonders and miracles" are not restricted to the apostles, as some have claimed in the past. Although the magnitude of miracles, signs and wonders worked by the apostles was greater, according to New Testament evidence, miracles, signs and wonders were also worked by non-apostles and lay believers in the Early Church. The words "signs" and "signs and wonders" and the miracles of healing and deliverance that they denote were also worked by such laymen as Stephen, Philip and Ananias according to Acts 6:8; 8:5-7,13; 9:11,12; 22:12,13.

Furthermore, Romans 12:6-8, 1 Corinthians 12-14, Galatians 3:5, Ephesians 4:11, 1 Thessalonians 5:20, James 5:14-16, 1 Peter 4:10 and other passages throughout the New Testament suggest that the congregations of the Early Church continued to experience the gifts of the Spirit, miracles and signs and wonders quite apart from the apostles. The relevant biblical evidence shows that what "signs and wonders" denote—healing, deliverance from demons and spiritual gifts—were practiced by all believers throughout the Early Church according to the New Testament. The Corinthians (1 Cor. 12-14) ministered with gifts of healing, miraculous powers, tongues and prophecy—all "signs"[9] according to Mark 16:17,18 and 1 Corinthians 14:22.[10] The Galatians saw God's Spirit work miracles regularly according to Galatians 3:5. The Ephesians and Thessalonians ministered with gifts of prophetic revelation according to Ephesians 4:11 and 1 Thessalonians 5:20. Philip's daughters regularly prophesied in the church of Caesarea according to Acts 21:9. The churches in Asia Minor were fully conversant with all the gifts of the Spirit according to 1 Peter 4:10.

Hebrews 6:1-5 includes "the laying on of hands" among the "elementary teachings" of the churches addressed by that letter. Besides bestowing the Holy Spirit and spiritual gifts[11], the "laying on of hands," mentioned in the list of elementary teachings, is one of the principal means of prayer for healing in the New Testament (Matt. 9:29; Mark 1:41; 5:23; 6:5; 7:32; 16:18; Luke 4:40; 13:13; Acts 9:17; 28:8; Jas. 5:14 "let them pray over [*epi*] him").[12] It follows that prayer for healing and prayer to convey the power and gifts of the Spirit were included in the "elementary teachings" of the Early Church and were not just the practice of the apostles.

James 5:14,15 affirms that through the prayer of the elders of the churches, the Lord will "make the sick person well." And all the lay believers of the congregations are addressed by James 5:16: "Therefore confess your sins to each other and pray for each other so that you may be healed."

Certain New Testament passages also suggest that the Lord Jesus and the apostles are to be viewed as models for all Christians in *every aspect*, including what signs and wonders denote—healing ministry and gift-based ministry. Clearly Paul had an all-embracing view of discipleship in 1 Corinthians 11:1 ("Follow my example, as I follow the example of Christ"); Philippians 4:9 ("Whatever you have learned or *received* or heard from me, or *seen in me*—put it into practice"); 1 Thessalonians 1:5,6 ("Our gospel came to you not simply with words, but also with power....*You became imitators of us and of the Lord*"). Philippians 4:9 seems rather all inclusive. Paul does not say, "Whatever you have learned or...seen in me except for signs and wonders, healing and spiritual gifts."

The cumulative evidence from the New Testament shows, then, that Christians throughout the early churches also imitated the way the apostles exercised spiritual gifts, proclaimed the gospel and preached the Word with signs and wonders—healing and gift-based ministry: Acts 6:8; 8:5-7,13; 9:11,12 (22:12,13); 19:5,6; 21:9; Romans 12:6ff.; 1 Corinthians 12:8-10,28 and 14:1,5,13-15,18f.; Galatians 3:5; Ephesians 4:7-11; 1 Thessalonians 5:20; James 5:14-16; and 1 Peter 4:10.

Signs, Wonders and Miracles Encouraging Belief and Deepening Faith in Christ.

One function of signs, wonders and miracles in the ministry of Jesus and the Early Church was to awaken and encourage faith in the gospel being preached. This is why the Early Church prayed prayers such as the one in Acts 4:29,30, asking God for signs and wonders of healing to accompany its evangelism. God obviously granted such requests in the Early Church (e.g., Acts 5:12-16; 6:8; 8:4-8,12,13,26-39; 9:17,18,32-42, etc.).

Jesus more than once challenged His listeners to believe His Word on the basis of His miraculous works (Matt. 9:6; Mark 2:10: Luke 5:24; John 10:37,38; 14:11). In his Gospel, John calls all of Jesus' works of miraculous healing "signs" (*semeia*, John 4:54; 6:2; 9:16: 12:17,18)—e.g., John 6:2: "They saw the miraculous signs he had performed on the sick."[13] The miraculous healings of Jesus are also called "works" (*erga*) in John's Gospel.[14] Jesus provided abundant "signs" of miraculous healing to those who were open and seeking God, as every one of the Gospel accounts show. John then said of the signs: "These are written *that you may believe* that Jesus is the Christ, the Son of God" (John 20:31). In His condemnation of Korazin and Bethsaida's lack of repentance and faith, Jesus indicates that His miraculous works were intended to produce repentance and faith in Him (Matt. 11:21 and Luke 10:13).

Paul expected to proclaim the gospel "by the power of signs and wonders through the power of the Spirit" (Rom. 15:18,19; cf. 1 Cor. 1:6,7; 2:4,5; 2 Cor. 12:12; 1 Thess. 1:5), and he expected God to continue to distribute spiritual gifts and work miracles among the churches to confirm the gospel and build up and encourage the Church (Rom. 12:6-8; 1 Cor. 1:7; 12:1—14:30; Gal. 3:5; Eph. 4:7-13; 1 Thess. 5:19-22; 1 Tim. 4:14; 2 Tim. 1:6,7). Paul says that the gift of prophecy is a sign "for believers" (1 Cor. 14:22).[15] As a sign it encourages and builds up the church in its faith (1 Cor. 14:1-5). Through it God gives supernatural insight into the secrets of people's hearts ("the secrets of his heart will be laid bare" 1 Cor. 14:25),[16] and thus it demonstrates that "God is really among you!" (1 Cor. 14:24,25).

Signs and Wonders Emphasizing Both Christ and His Power

Paul affirms in 1 Corinthians 2:4,5 that our faith in Christ is strengthened in a unique way by demonstrations of His Spirit's power. Paul makes clear that it is not a question of *either* trusting *or* experiencing God's power, but that both work together. Experiencing God's work and power are an illustration of the truth and person of Christ in whom we have put our trust. Faith, Paul says, is reinforced when we see Christ doing what His Word says He does:

> **1 Corinthians 2:4,5**—My message and my preaching were not with wise and persuasive words, but with a demonstration of the Spirit's power [*en apodeixei pneumatos kai dunameos*], so that your faith might not rest on men's wisdom, but on God's power.

The use of "Spirit" and "power" in this passage shows that the "demonstration" referred not only to conveying spiritual gifts (explicitly referred to in 1 Cor. 1:6,7),[17] but also to the signs, wonders and miracles characteristic of Paul's ministry in Corinth (2 Cor. 12:12) and linked by him to the power of the Spirit in Romans 15:18,19. Thus, Paul teaches that *both* the object of our faith—Christ, the message of the Truth—*and* God demonstrating the truth by His power in our lives strengthen and reinforce our faith.

This same principle mentioned in 1 Corinthians 2:4,5 is also evident in Paul's own conversion. Paul himself was not converted by a presentation of rational evidence (although Acts 9:19b-20 suggests this came later) but by a demonstration of God's power through the appearance of Christ to him on the road to Damascus (Acts 9:3ff.,20,22). This experience of the manifest power of God obviously forced him to take another look at the gospel and reevaluate his understanding of Scripture, the Messiah and the life and work of Jesus of Nazareth (Acts 9:20). His faith was in the *content of the gospel*, but it was born out of his conversion experience of the gospel's power in the risen Christ. When Paul was converted, he not only read of Christ in the Scriptures and heard of Christ from the community of believers in Damascus (Acts 9:19b), but he also *saw* the gospel's power in the risen Christ on the road to Damascus and also when he was healed of his blindness and filled with the Spirit through Ananias's prayer (Acts 9:10-12,17,18; 22:13).

Signs, Wonders and Miracles Illustrating God's Grace in the Gospel

The New Testament shows that signs, wonders and miracles function to glorify Christ and to illustrate God's grace in the gospel. Romans 15:17-20 shows that both preaching and working signs and wonders were to "glory in Christ" (Rom. 15:17) for Paul. Both word and miraculous deed were to "fully proclaim [*pleroo*] the gospel of Christ" and to "preach the gospel where Christ was not known" (Rom. 15:20):

> **Romans 15:17-20**—Therefore *I glory in Christ Jesus* in my service to God. I will not venture to speak of anything except what Christ has accomplished through me in leading the Gentiles to obey God by what I have *said* and *done*—by the *power of signs and wonders and miracles*, through the *power of the Spirit*. So from Jerusalem all the way around to Illyricum, I have *fully proclaimed* [*peplerokenai*] *the gospel of Christ*. It has always been my ambition to *preach the gospel where Christ was not known*, so that I would not be building on someone else's foundation.

Signs and wonders functioned in this way to illustrate God's grace in the gospel throughout the book of Acts: when Peter said to Aeneas, "Jesus Christ heals you. Get up and take care of your mat" (Acts 9:34) and then won the inhabitants of Lydda and Sharon to the Lord; when Philip "proclaimed the Christ" in Samaria (Acts 8:5) by healing the lame and demonized, along with his preaching (Acts 8:6,7); when Paul preached the gospel at Lystra (Acts 14:7,9) and healed the man who had been lame from birth (Acts 14:10); when Paul performed "the signs of an apostle"[18] with great perseverance, along with "signs, wonders and miracles" (2 Cor. 12:12) as part of his ministry there of preaching "nothing...except Jesus Christ and him crucified" (1 Cor. 2:2,4).

Signs and Wonders Bearing Witness to the Risen Christ and His Power to Save Sinners

The New Testament evidence suggests that signs and wonders bear witness to the risen Lord and His power to save sinners. Peter's words in the Temple show that ongoing works of miraculous healing in Christ's name glorify Christ and bear witness to His resurrection (Acts 2:22; 3:13):

> **Acts 3:12,13,15,16**—When Peter saw this, he said to them: "Men of Israel, why does this surprise you? *Why do you stare at us as if by our own power or godliness we had made this man walk?* The God of Abraham, Isaac and Jacob, the God of our fathers, *has glorified his servant Jesus*....You killed the author of life, but *God raised him from the dead. We are witnesses of this.* By faith in the name of Jesus, this man whom you see and know was made strong. *It is Jesus' name and the faith that comes through him that has given this complete healing to him,* as you all can see."

Discussing this passage, Dr. Cyril Powell quotes F. F. Bruce and notes that "by the 'power of God manifested in mighty works' (F. F. Bruce), the Apostles went on giving this testimony."[19] Dr. Alan Richardson notes that "the New Testament...sees in the miracles of the Lord a revelation of the power and of the saving purpose of God." He goes on to point out that "the miracle-stories do not constitute a secondary *stratum* of the Gospel tradition which is somehow foreign to the *ethos* of the Gospel in its primary sense."[20] Professor Walter Grundmann stresses that the power of God, which is the power of salvation in the New Testament's view, is expressed in miraculous healing in Christ's name on the one hand and in proclaiming the gospel on the other: "This *dunamis* ['power'] is expressed in proclamation on the one side (Acts 6:10) and miracles on the other (Acts 6:8)."[21]

Signs and Wonders and Proclaiming the Gospel in Word and Deed

In Romans 15:18,19, Paul uses the word *pleroo* "fill, fulfill, bring to full expression"[22] to state that he brought the gospel to full expression:[23] *peplero-*

kenai to euaggelion tou christou literally, "to have fully proclaimed the gospel of Christ." Paul says he proclaimed the gospel not only in word (*logo*), but also in deed (*ergo*). The deeds that proclaimed the gospel were obviously "signs and wonders, through the power of the Spirit" (Rom. 15:19). This passage shows, then, that the gospel is also revealed and given expression through signs and wonders that act as a symbol of God's grace and God's power to save sinners through the gospel.

Similarly, Paul explicitly says the gospel came to the Thessalonians "not only in word" (*ouk egenethe eis humas en logo monon* 1 Thess. 1:5). The gospel also came to them and was revealed to them "in power [*en dunamei*] and in the Holy Spirit [*en pneumati hagio*]" (1 Thess. 1:5). The association of "power" (*dunamis*) and "the Spirit" (*pneuma*) with signs, wonders and miracles of healing and deliverance throughout the New Testament[24] suggests that what is being referred to in 1 Thessalonians 1:5 are the miraculous deeds of the Spirit's power through which the gospel was manifested alongside Paul's preaching.[25] Although the concept of God's "power" in such passages is not restricted to miracles, it clearly includes them as a basic element of the notion of God's "power." Dr. Karl Gatzweiler points out that "for the reader, who already knows that the apostle worked miracles alongside the proclamation of the gospel [cf. 2 Cor. 12:12; Rom. 15:18,19], it suggests miraculous events also be understood as self-evident among the notions of 'might' and 'power' which accompany the proclamation of the gospel."[26]

Signs and Wonders as Illustrations of God's Kingdom Rule in Christ

Mainstream New Testament scholars cited in the notes following appear to be unanimous regarding the New Testament evidence. In the New Testament's view, the healings accompanying the preaching of Jesus, the apostles and the Early Church were symbols, illustrations and demonstrations of the presence of God's kingdom— God's grace and forgiveness of sin through Christ. Such passages as Matthew 12:25-37, Mark 3:22-30 and Luke 11:17-23 show that signs, wonders and miracles are evidence that the kingdom of God has drawn near. A clear connection between miraculous healing and proclaiming the gospel of the Kingdom is established by such passages as Matthew 10:7,8; Mark 6:7-13; Luke 9:1,2; and 10:9 (cf. Acts 8:4-7,12 as well as 3:6,12; 4:29,30; 5:12-16,20,21,28,42; 6:8,10; 9:17,18 [cf. 22:13], 34,35; 14:3,8-10,15ff.; 15:12,36; 18:5,11 [cf. 2 Cor. 12:12; 1 Cor. 2:4,5]; 19:8-12; Rom. 15:18,19; 1 Cor. 2:4,5; 11:1; 12:1-11,28-31; 2 Cor. 12:12; Gal. 3:5; 1 Thess. 1:5,6; Heb. 2:3,4).

Many New Testament scholars, such as Hunter, Powell, Richardson and others have pointed out that in the New Testament's view, the signs and wonders of miraculous healing in Jesus' ministry, which were continued by the apostles and the Early Church, show the coming of the kingdom of God, God's reign in Christ.[27] They are tokens of God's grace and illustrations of the forgiveness of sin accomplished by Christ's cross. In Hunter's words, "The miracles are tokens of the coming of God's Reign in Jesus. They are the Kingdom of God in action—God's sovereign grace and forgiveness operative in Christ."[28] Richardson adds, "The connexion between healing and salvation (in the religious sense) is a characteristic feature of the Gospel tradition. Miracles of healing are, as it were, symbolic demonstrations of God's forgiveness in action."[29]

The New Testament evidence clearly shows that God desires to heal the sick as a sign of His kingdom reign and His grace in Christ toward His people (Matt. 12:28; cf. Isa. 33:22,24). Jesus healed the sick.[30] The apostles and Early Church laity healed the sick (Stephen, Philip, Ananias, the Corinthians, Galatians, Jewish Christian churches, etc.).[31] God gave the Church gifts of healing (1 Cor. 12:9,28,29), and He commands the Church to pray for the sick (Jas. 5:14-16).

Some scholars also point out that although God desires to heal as a sign of His kingdom, healing, like the kingdom, will only be experienced in part in this age.[32] In spite of the many signs and wonders recorded in the New Testament, the evidence also shows that in some cases Christians apparently did not experience immediate or complete healing.[33] In 1 Corinthians 13, Paul says that in this age the Church will only experience spiritual gifts, which include healing, "in part" (*ek merous*) until the second coming of Christ: "For we know in part and we prophesy in part" (1 Cor. 13:9; cf. 1 Cor. 1:6,7 and 13:8-10,12; 1 John 3:2; Rev. 22:4).[34] James 5:15 nonetheless seems to state the general rule for healing ministry in the Church: "The prayer offered in faith will make the sick person well; the Lord will raise him up."

Signs and Wonders Versus "The Sign from Heaven"

A clear distinction is made in the New Testament between the signs and wonders of miraculous healing in the ministry of Jesus and the Early Church and the "sign from heaven" demanded by the Pharisees that Jesus refused to give. Jesus did not condemn ordinary people for seeking signs and wonders (*plural*) in His healing ministry in Matthew 12:38-40; 16:1-4; Mark 8:11,12; Luke 11:16; and John 6:30f. Rather, He condemned stubborn, unbelieving religious leaders (Matt. 12:38; 16:1; Mark 8:11) for demanding a "sign [singular] from heaven" (Mark 8:11; Luke 11:16; cf. Matt. 16:1; John 6:30f.). (Even in the so-called "rebuke" of John 4:48, Jesus granted the "sign," healing the royal official's son, and this led to the conversion of the official and his family [John 4:53,54].)

The religious leaders were calling demonic the signs of Jesus' healing ministry (Matt. 12:24; Mark 3:22; Luke 11:15). They were asking for a prophetic sign from heaven, beyond those of Jesus' healing ministry, like those performed by prophets such as Moses, Elijah or Isaiah—manna from heaven (John 6:30-31); plagues of the Exodus, which were "signs" (Exod. 7:3; 8:23; 10:1,2; Num. 14:23; Deut. 6:22; 11:3f.; 7:19; 26:8; 29:3; 34:11; Josh. 24:17); drought, which was a "sign" (Deut. 28:22-24,46; cf. 1 Kings 17:1ff.); the retreating shadow of the sun, which was a "sign" (2 Kings 20:9).[35]

The New Testament shows that Jesus gave abundant signs of God's kingdom in His healing ministry, as did the apostles and the Early Church in their evangelism. But Jesus provided no sensational sign from heaven to those who were unbelieving and remained closed to His teaching, and its basis in Scripture (Matt. 5:17-20; cf. John 3:10,11). Such an attitude refused to ask God for guidance about Jesus and His teaching (John 5:39,40; 6:45; 7:17).

The New Testament shows that the Early Church asked God for signs and wonders to accompany its evangelism in prayers, as found in Acts 4:29,30: "Now, Lord, consider their threats and enable your servants to speak your word with great boldness. Stretch out your hand to *heal* and *perform miraculous signs and wonders* through the name of your holy servant Jesus." God obviously granted such requests to the Early Church on a regular basis (e.g., Acts 5:12-16; 6:8; 8:5,6,26-40; 9:17,18; etc.). Paul likewise expected to proclaim the gospel "in the power of signs and wonders" (Rom. 15:18,19; 2 Cor. 12:12); he expected God to continue to work miracles among the Galatians (Gal. 3:5); and he told the Corinthians to seek the gift of prophecy, which he said is a "sign" for believers (1 Cor. 14:1,22).[36]

According to the evidence presented, the New Testament shows that signs, wonders and miraculous healing worked by God in Christ's name glorify Christ and testify to His resurrection. They demonstrate in a special way God's rule in Christ and God's presence among His people, the Church. They illustrate the grace and power of God, which saves sinners through the Cross of Christ, and they confirm the proclamation of the gospel and the Word of God. Finally, they show the power of God's Word—Scripture—and teach us the importance of simply taking God at His Word.—GSG

References: [1]Professor C. F. D. Moule of Cambridge referred to the group of words comprising this lexical field in NT Greek as "a vocabulary denoting *significant manifestations of power*...signs of God at work" (C. F. D. Moule, "The Vocabulary of Miracle," in Moule, ed., *Miracles. Cambridge Studies in Their Philosophy and History* [London: A. R. Mowbray & Co., 1965], p. 238). [2]For translating *energeia* as "energy," see G. Bertram, *"energeo,"* in G. Kittel, ed., *Theological Dictionary of the New Testament* [hereafter *TDNT*] (Grand Rapids: Eerdmans, 1964-74), vol. 2, p. 652; C. H. Powell, *The Biblical Concept of Power* (London: Epworth Press, 1963), p. 136. [3]H. Hendrickx, *The Miracle Stories of the Synoptic Gospels* (San Francisco: HarperSanFrancisco, 1987), p. 10 and nn. 3-4; A. Richardson, *The Miracle-*

Stories of the Gospels (London: SCM Press, 1941), pp. 6-7. [4]That the phrase "signs and wonders" and the word "sign" denote healing and deliverance from demons is noted by Professor Karl H. Rengstorf, in Kittel, *TDNT,* VII, pp. 239-240. [5]The same lexical field (group of words) includes other terms denoting manifestations of God's power in healing and deliverance, such as *hugies* "whole," *iasis* "healing," *megaleios* "mighty deed," *endoxos* "glorious deed," *paradoxos* "wonderful thing," *thaumasios* "wonderful thing," according to R. C. Trench, *Synonyms of the New Testament* (London: Macmillan, 1894), p. 339. [6]W.Bauer, W. F. Arndt, W. F. Gingrich, and F. W. Danker, *A Greek-English Lexicon of the New Testament and Other Early Christian Literature* [hereafter *BAGD*] (Chicago: University of Chicago Press, 1979), pp. 747-748 *"semeion"* (1). [7]Ibid., p. 748, *"semeion"* (2). [8]That the word "sign" (*semeion*)" and the phrase "signs and wonders (*semeia kai terata*)" are synonymous and interchangeable was noted in a linguistic study of the Greek terms by McCasland, "Signs and Wonders," *Journal of Biblical Literature* 76 (1957): 151. The following passages demonstrate this point: John 4:48,54 ; Acts 4:16,22,30; compare the phrase "signs and miracles" in Acts 8:13 with the phrase "miracles, wonders and signs" in Acts 2:22, "signs and wonders and miracles" in 2 Corinthians 12:12, and "signs, wonders and...miracles" in Hebrews 2:4. [9]Compare John 4:48,54 (healing a fever is a "sign"); 6:2 (healing of the sick is called "signs"); 9:6,7,16 (healing blindness is one of "such signs"); 12:17,18 (raising the dead is a "sign"); Acts 4:16,22 (healing a lame man is an "obvious sign"); 5:12-16 (healing the sick and demonized is called "signs and wonders"); 8:5-7,13 (healing the sick and demonized is called "signs and miracles"). [10]The grammatical structure of 1 Corinthians 14:22 cannot be understood any other way: the elliptical clause *he de propheteia ou tois apistois alla tois pisteuousin* depends on the preceding clause for its full grammatical and lexical meaning; see Fee, *The First Epistle to the Corinthians* (*NICNT*, ed., F. F. Bruce, [Grand Rapids: Eerdmans, 1987]), p. 682 and n. 38; Wayne Grudem, *The Gift of Prophecy in I Corinthians* (Washington, 1982), pp. 193-194; id., *The Gift of Prophecy in the New Testament and Today* (Wheaton, Ill.: Crossway, 1988), pp. 173f. and n. 68. [11]*Laying on of hands to bestow the Holy Spirit and spiritual gifts*: Acts 8:17; 19:15f.; 1 Timothy 4:14; 5:22; 2 Timothy 1:6. Related to this, laying on of hands *to commission for a task*: Acts 6:6; 13:3; *to bestow blessing*: Matthew 19:13-15; Mark 10:16. [12]See E. Lohse, *"cheir,"* in Kittel, *TDNT,* vol 9, pp. 431-432. [13]Rengstorf, in Kittel, *TDNT,* vol. 7, p. 246. [14]For *erga,* denoting "miraculous works" when referring to Jesus and God in the Gospel of John: *BAGD,* p. 308; G. Bertram, *"ergon," TDNT,* vol. 2, p. 642; K. H. Rengstorf, *"se — meion," TDNT,* vol. 7, pp. 247-248. [15]See note 11. [16]See the remarks of Grudem, *The Gift of Prophecy,* pp. 136-137; A. Oepke, in Kittel, *TDNT,* vol. 3, p. 976 and n. 42. [17]See Fee, *The First Epistle to the Corinthians,* p. 95, n. 2. The context of "weakness" in 1 Corinthians 1—2 that Fee mentions does not make it less likely that 1 Corinthians 2:4b refers to the "signs, wonders and miracles" of 2 Corinthians 12:12 than the spiritual gifts mentioned in 1 Corinthians 1:6,7, because in the very context of mentioning his own weakness Paul alludes to the signs and wonders of his ministry in 2 Corinthians 12:12 (compare 2 Corinthians 12:7-10,21; 13:4b,8 and 2 Corinthians 12:12). [18]On the "signs of an apostle" in 2 Corinthians 12:12 not being equivalent to signs, wonders and miracles, but referring to Christlike ministry, selfless lifestyle, endurance of hardship, ministering without demanding money in return, see Wayne Grudem, in G. S. Greig and K. N. Springer, *The Kingdom and the Power* (Ventura, Calif.: Regal, 1993), pp. 63-67. [19]Powell, *The Biblical Concept of Power,* p. 136; Justin Martyr similarly argued in the second century A.D. that Jesus' healings are a witness of how Jesus would restore the whole body at the resurrection of all those who are in Christ (H. van der Loos, *The Miracles of Jesus* [Supplements to Novum Testamentum, vol. 8, Leiden: E. J. Brill, 1965], p. 248, n. 1). [20]Richardson, *The Miracle-Stories of the Gospels,* p. 17. [21]W. Grundmann, *"dunamai/dunamis,"* in Kittel, *TDNT,* vol. 2, pp. 309-311. [22]*BAGD,* pp. 670ff. [23]The use of *pleroo* "bring (the gospel) to full expression" in Romans 15:19 cannot mean that Paul *finished* preaching the gospel, because he was still planning to visit Rome and preach the gospel further in Spain (Rom. 1:13,15; 15:23f.). Nor can it mean that he *said everything* there was to say about the gospel, as Murray points out: "He says he 'fully preached' the gospel. This means that he had 'fulfilled' the gospel (cf. Col. 1:25) and does not reflect on the fulness with which he set forth the gospel (cf. Acts 20:20, 27)....Neither does 'fully preached' imply that he had preached the gospel in every locality and to every person in these territories" (J. Murray, *The Epistle to the Romans* [NICNT; Grand Rapids: Eerdmans, 1968], vol. 2, p. 214). But, as G. Friedrich points out, it means that Paul proclaimed the gospel in the way he described in Romans 15:18,19, *"in word and deed, by the power of signs and won-*

ders, by the power of the Spirit": "Again, Romans 15:19...does not mean that Paul has concluded his missionary work, but that the Gospel is fulfilled when it has taken full effect. In the preaching of Paul Christ has shown Himself effective in word and sign and miracle (v. 18). Hence the Gospel has been brought to fulfillment from Jerusalem to Illyricum and Christ is named in the communities (v. 20)" (G. Friedrich, in Kittel, *TDNT,* vol. 2, p. 732). [24]E.g., Matthew 12:28; Mark 5:30; Luke 5:17; 6:18,19; 8:46; Acts 3:12; 10:38; Romans 15:19; 1 Corinthians 12:4,9,10; Galatians 3:5; Hebrews 2:4; etc.; See Grundmann, *"dunamai/dunamis,"* in Kittel, *TDNT,* vol. 2, p. 311 and n. 91; E. Schweizer, in Kittel, *TDNT,* vol. 6, p. 398. [25]See K. Gatzweiler, "Der Paulinische Wunderbegriff," in A. Suhl, ed., *Der Wunderbegriff im Neuen Testament* (Darmstadt: Wissenschaftliche Buchgesellschaft, 1980), p. 403 and n. 52; Grundmann, in Kittel, *TDNT,* vol. 2, p. 311; Ellis, *Prophecy and Hermeneutic in Early Christianity: New Testament Essays,* p. 65; Hofius, *NIDNTT,* vol. II, p. 632. [26]Gatzweiler, "Der Paulinische Wunderbegriff," pp. 403-405, n. 52: "Für den Leser, der schon weiss, dass der Apostel bei der Verkündigung des Evangeliums Wunder gewirkt hat (vgl. 2 Kor. 12, 12; Röm. 15, 18-19), liegt es nahe, wie selbstverständlich unter den begriffen 'Macht' und 'Kraft,' die die Verkündigung des Evangeliums begleiten, auch Wunderereignisse zu verstehen." [27]Richardson, *The Miracle-Stories of the Gospels,* pp. 38, 41-42, 44-45; A. M. Hunter, *The Work and the Words of Jesus* (London: 1950), p. 55; Powell, *The Biblical Concept of Power,* pp. 82, 114. Similarly, van der Loos, *The Miracles of Jesus,* pp. 223-224; Hendrickx, *The Miracle Stories of the Synoptic Gospels,* pp. 11-12. [28]A. M. Hunter, *The Work and the Words of Jesus* (London: 1950), p. 55; Powell, *The Biblical Concept of Power,* pp. 82, 114 and n. 35. Similarly, Powell, *The Biblical Concept of Power,* p. 82: "The Kingdom comes chiefly, not as claim and decision, but as saving *dynamis,* as redeeming power, to set free a world lying in the clutches of Satan...." [29]Richardson, *The Miracle-Stories of the Gospels,* pp. 61-62. [30]E.g., Matthew 4:23; 9:35,36; 10:1,7,8; 11:5; 12:15,18; 15:30; 19:2 (cf. Mark 10:1); 21:14 (cf. Luke 21:37). Mark 1:38,39; 2:2,11; 3:14,15; 6:12,13; 10:1 (cf. Matt. 19:2). Luke 4:18; 5:17,24; 6:6-11,17,18; 7:22; 9:1,2; 10:9,13; 13:10-13,22,32; 14:4,7ff.; 21:37 (cf. Matt. 21:14); 16:15-18,20. John 3:2; 7:14,15,21-23,31,38; 10:25,32,38; 12:37,49; 14:10,12. Acts 1:1; 2:22; 10:38. [31]E.g., Acts 3:6,12; 4:29,30; 5:12-16,20,21,28,42; 6:8,10; 8:4-7,12; 9:17,18 (cf. 22:13),

34,35; 14:3,8-10,15ff.; 15:12,36; 18:5,11 (cf. 2 Cor. 12:12; 1 Cor. 2:4,5); 19:8-12. Romans 15:18,19. 1 Corinthians 2:4,5; 11:1; 12:1-11,28-31. 2 Corinthians 12:12. Galatians 3:5. Philippians 4:9. 1 Thessalonians 1:5,6. Hebrews 2:3,4; 6:1,2. James 5:13-16. [32]Hendrickx, *The Miracle Stories of the Synoptic Gospels*, pp. 14-15. [33]In Ephesians 6:18, Paul commands us to "pray in the Spirit on all occasions with all kinds of prayers and requests" (cf. 1 Thess. 5:17; Col. 4:2). Yet, Paul was ill in Galatia for a long enough period that it "was a trial" to the Galatians (Gal. 4:14); Epaphroditus did not experience immediate healing from illness and almost died according to Philippians 2:27; Timothy had chronic illnesses involving his stomach, which were not completely healed according to 1 Timothy 5:23; and Paul had to leave Trophimus sick in Miletus, apparently seeing no healing in response to prayer (2 Tim. 4:20). [34]On experiencing healing of illness as a "gift of grace" (1 Cor. 12:9,28,29) experienced only in part in the Early Church according to the New Testament, see Oepke, "*iaomai*," in Kittel, *TDNT*, vol. 3, p. 214; on experiencing spiritual gifts in this age only "in part (*ek merous* 1 Cor. 13:9)," see Fee, *The First Epistle to the Corinthians*, p. 644 and n. 21; Schneider, in Kittel, *TDNT*, vol. 4, p. 596. [35]Bruce, *The Hard Sayings of Jesus*, pp. 94-97. Similarly, Hendrickx, *The Miracle Stories of the Synoptic Gospels*, p. 17; Richardson, *The Miracle-Stories of the Gospels*, p. 47: "St. Mark leaves us in no doubt that, although He refused to show a sign to the Pharisees, Jesus nevertheless regarded His miracles as 'signs.'" [36]See note 11.

SIGNS AND WONDERS: DEFINITION

The linguistic evidence related to the phrase "signs and wonders" (*semeia kai terata*) in the New Testament shows that it largely denotes miraculous healing of the sick, deliverance from demons and the gifts of the Spirit. Long ago, in a linguistic study of the evidence, S. V. McCasland noted that the phrase "signs and wonders" in the New Testament largely denotes "ordinary deeds of healing performed by faith" rather than "grandiose phenomena" as it denotes in the *Septuagint*, the Greek translation of the Old Testament.[1] —GSG

Reference: [1]S. V. McCasland, "Signs and Wonders," *Journal of Biblical Literature* 76 (1957): 151.

SIGNS AND WONDERS MOVEMENT

The signs and wonders movement is only one expression, though a leading expression, of the wider Third Wave renewal around the world. The signs and wonders movement was sparked by John Wimber, founder of the Vineyard Christian Fellowship church movement, and others, in the late 1970s and early 1980s. The signs and wonders movement stimulated an increasing amount of research on power evangelism—the biblical and practical relationship of signs and wonders to the growth and multiplication of Christian churches and the biblical and practical relationship of healing and the miraculous work and gifts of the Spirit to evangelism.

Though there are few exceptions, evidence from around the world suggests that "the growth and multiplication of churches in which healings, deliverances, prophecies, and other miraculous works of the Holy Spirit are normative components of ministry is substantially greater than in the churches in which they are not."[1] —GSG

References: [1]C. Peter Wagner, "Church Growth," in S. M. Burgess et al., eds., *Dictionary of Pentecostal and Charismatic Movements* (Grand Rapids: Zondervan, 1988), p. 184. See THIRD WAVE MOVEMENT.

SIMONS, MENNO (1496–1561)

Founder of the Mennonites.

Menno Simons studied both Latin and Greek in preparation for life as a Roman Catholic priest, and was ordained to that office in 1524. Within a year of his ordination, Simons began to have doubts about the efficacy of the Mass and was troubled by the persecution and execution of Anabaptists in his area. Simons responded by studying the Scriptures and eventually adopting Anabaptist beliefs. On January 30, 1536, Simons renounced his priesthood and soon afterward was baptized by Obbe Phillips. Simons quickly became a leader among Anabaptists, traveling widely throughout Holland, Germany and Denmark. He also wrote extensively. By the time of his death, Anabaptists were probably the majority among Protestant groups in Holland. After his death, many of his followers adopted the name "Mennonites" to describe their movement.

Simons's greatest contributions to evangelism was achieved through his itinerant preaching and extensive writing ministry.

References: H. S. Bender, *Menno Simons' Life and Writings* (Scottdale, Pa.: Mennonite Publishing House, 1936); J. Horsh, *Menno Simons: His Life, Labors and Teachings* (Scottdale, Pa.: Mennonite Publishing House, 1942).

SIMPSON, ALBERT BENJAMIN (1844–1919)

Founder of The Christian and Missionary Alliance.

Born December 15, 1844, in Cavendish, Prince Edward Island, Canada, A. B. Simpson entered Knox College at the University of Toronto, Ontario, in 1861 and worked his way through college by teaching and preaching. He was ordained September 12, 1865, and became the pastor of Knox Church in Hamilton, Ontario. From there he went to the Chestnut Street Presbyterian Church in Louisville, Kentucky. Both churches experienced significant growth under his ministry. In 1881, Simpson founded an independent Gospel Tabernacle in New York. The next year he founded the Nyack Missionary College. He began publishing the *Alliance Weekly* and preaching in various conventions, activities that led to the formation of The Christian and Missionary Alliance. He also authored 70 books about Christian living. Simpson died October 29, 1919.

Simpson's greatest contribution to evangelism was achieved through founding the Nyack Missionary College and organization of the Christian and Missionary Alliance.

Reference: A. E. Thompson, *A. B. Simpson: His Life and Work* (Camp Hill, Pa.: Christian Publications, Inc., 1960).

SIN

Anything that is opposed to the character and will of God. The New Testament word for sin (*hamartia*) means literally "missing the mark." Sin can be defined as an attitude, a volitional act or falling short of God's standard. The three basic kinds of sin are personal, the sin nature and imputed sin.

The Effects of Sin

1. People are cut off from God. When Satan tempted Adam in the garden, he had the ability to make a moral choice, but fell into sin. Sin cut him off from God.

Not only Adam and Eve, but everyone from that time forth was cut off from God's presence. The Scriptures teach, "For all have sinned and fall short of the glory of God" (Rom. 3:23).

Humans are sinners in three ways. First, anything less than God's perfect holiness is sin. Sin is similar to an arrow falling short of the target. It did not attain to the perfect standard. So every person born into the world does not measure up to God's perfect standard. The sin of omission is not doing what is required or demanded.

Second, rebellion is sin, usually translated "transgression." Sin is breaking God's law, either volitionally or ignorantly.

The third way people sin is by inherent wickedness or moral impurity. This is described as filth or uncleanness and is abhorred by God, who is pure and holy.

The result of sin is that it blinds sinners (2 Cor. 4:3,3; Eph 4:17). Usually people do not recognize they are sinners and cut off from God. Therefore, sinners need the law communicated to them to reveal that they are sinners.

2. People become their own point of reference. When Satan promised Eve, "You will be like God" (Gen. 3:5), he somewhat fulfilled that promise. As a result, people in the world today are their own standards of measurements. They have all become the focus of the circles in which they live. The fall of humans has created an upside-down condition. Instead of humans placing God on the throne of their lives, they sit there in supreme ignorance that they have usurped the place of God. And like God, they *know* the difference between good and evil.

3. People suffer alienation and isolation. Sin is not just punishment after death. People also suffer the consequences of sin in this life. Sin results in isolation or alienation from God. Spiritual death is the ultimate form of isolation from God. As a result of people's sin, they need eternal salvation to bring them into fellowship with God.

4. Sin cuts people off from one another. People are social animals who need relationships to keep themselves healthy. Recluses who hate people and mystics who separate themselves from people in their search for spirituality do not reflect the God who created humans to fellowship with Him. Friendship Evangelism strikes at the core of this problem. Soul winners use their relationships with friends, relatives, associates and neighbors (FRANS) to bring them to Christ.

The answer to isolation is that God took the initiative to have fellowship with humans. "When the fullness of the time had come, God sent forth His Son" (Gal. 4:4). And again, "God,...has in these last days spoken to us by His Son" (Heb. 1:1,2).

5. Sin fills people with anxiety. Any life that is separated from authority and purpose is like a boat without an anchor; it is drifting. People may be anxious because they do not have all the answers to the questions raised by others, or even the questions asked in their own hearts. All people have basic needs within their hearts. They know that something is missing, but they usually refuse to identify it as God. They look for answers and find none. The vacuum created by God's absence produces anxiety. "Anxiety" is another word for fear, depression, jealousy or any other condition that keeps people in emotional disequilibrium.

6. Sin robs people of meaning and purpose. Because people are isolated and affected by sin, they usually lack meaning in life. Those who are slaves to drugs know that narcotics do not lead to happiness or meaning. The same can be said for wealth, fame or even success. Some people do not know where to go or how to get where they want to go—but they want to go somewhere. They have not found the secret in life. They need the God that gives purposes for which humans should live.

7. Sin leads to spiritual death. People march inevitably toward death. Thousands die annually of some form of cancer, and that frightens most. We experience the same fear when a friend is killed or we hear of a tragic accident. The threat of death is all about us. Within our decaying bodies we realize that death is our enemy. We want to rise above the limitations of our bodies. Yet we see dimly because our eyes are wearing out. Our arms ache because of arthritis. Even the 30-year-old feels the inevitable rising tide of age when a younger person takes his or her place on the team.

Not everyone realizes that our ultimate enemy is spiritual death. The Bible teaches that "the wages of sin is death" (Rom. 6:23), and the ultimate need of a person is an explanation for death. A little boy standing next to his father asked, "Does everyone have to die?"

"Yes," the father replied.

The young son pondered, then blurted out, "Even if they're lucky?"

Sin has influenced individuals, societies and the physical world itself. To see the remedy for sin, consult the articles about Redemption, Salvation and Conversion.

SIN OF COMMISSION

Any intentional act that is prohibited.

SIN (IMPUTED)

The sin of Adam being charged to the account of each person, resulting in physical death (Rom. 5:12).

SIN (OMISSION)

Neglecting to do what is required.

SIN (PERSONAL)

May be a sin of commission (an intentional act), or a sin of omission (neglecting to perform). Personal sin may express itself as an act, an attitude or neglect.

SIN NATURE

The inborn desires of humans that drive them to act contrary to the law of God.

SINGLE-CELL CHURCH See CELL CHURCHES; FOUR PARADIGMS

SMALL SUNDAY SCHOOLS

Generally, Sunday Schools with attendance below 66.

Although much is written about the large Sunday Schools in America and around the world, the average church in the United States has about 87 in worship attendance, and 66 in Sunday School attendance. These churches do not need to think they can only have a "second-rate" ministry. Instead, they can build on their strengths. Although larger churches tend to have citywide outreaches, the smaller church can have a greater impact on a local neighborhood or a people group. Also, a smaller church can provide personal pastoral care more easily to the members of the congregation. The educational program of a smaller church can be built on the greater interaction of its members, which should result in better learning. Also, because everyone tends to be responsible for some aspect of ministry in a smaller church, this could lead to greater individual spiritual growth.

Though all agree that a church must begin small, not all agree that it should remain small, nor is there agreement about how large a church should grow. Problems in the smaller church can be resolved as the church grows. This growth can be best realized by building on the strengths as a small church and being willing to adapt to the changes experienced as the church begins growing.

Reference: See CHURCH GROWTH JUSTIFICA-
TION.

SOCIAL ACTION

Christian involvement to alleviate the needs of the poor and oppressed (i.e., to minister to them in a physical *and* spiritual manner). Social justice is changing the structures of society to help the poor and oppressed.

References: See SOCIAL SERVICE; CULTURAL MANDATE.

SOCIAL BONDAGE SITES

Strongholds of community suffering, destabilizing social values and/or destructive vices. Specific examples might include crack houses,

nightclubs, gang hideouts, abortion clinics and porno theaters. —GOJR

SOCIAL SERVICE

Christian and social involvement designed to meet the immediate and long-term needs of the poor and oppressed. Also called "relief" and "development."

References: See SOCIAL ACTION; CULTURAL MANDATE.

SOCIOLOGICAL STRANGULATION

A condition in which limited space becomes the primary factor hindering the continued growth of a church and/or specific church ministry. Normally, churches in the United States experience sociological strangulation when they reach 80 percent of their capacity in their auditorium/sanctuary and have no immediate plans for expanding their facilities. The 80 percent rule also influences parking, rest rooms, classrooms, hallways and so on.

SOCIOLOGICAL TISSUE REJECTION

A Christian group's rejection of persons of another culture or class.

Just as in physical organ transplants in which the blood type may match, but the skin tissue rejects the new organ, so some Christian groups reject a new believer because of his or her difference. This is the sociological phenomenon in which some people would prefer the death of their own social group rather than see it infiltrated with people of another homogeneous unit—a characteristic not always changed by becoming a Christian.

SODALITY

A task-oriented organization that draws people from various modalities; not in itself a church, sometimes called a parachurch; requiring a second decision to join, a decision beyond a person's decision to be a Christian.

Reference: See MODALITY.

SOIL TESTING

An evangelistic strategy that seeks out those people who are open to receiving the gospel at the present time.

References: See HARVEST PRINCIPLE; RECEP-
TIVE-RESPONSIVE PEOPLE.

SOUL

The life principle within human beings. "Man became a living soul" (Gen. 2:7, *KJV*).

SOVEREIGNTY OF GOD AND CHURCH GROWTH See CHURCH GROWTH: SOCIAL SCIENCE

"If God wants to save the heathen, He can do it without the help of Mr. William Carey." From the very beginning of the modern missionary movement, there has been an ongoing tension between the sovereignty of God as defined by some Christians and the work of evangelizing large numbers of people. It is believed by some that the very work of evangelism is an infringement into an area under the complete control of God. Those who maintain this view tend to identify themselves as Calvinists.

In fairness to John Calvin, it should be noted that there is some question whether this expression of "Calvinism" accurately represents his real position. Although the early editions of *The Institutes* tend to emphasize predestination, his later commentaries place greater emphasis on human responsibility. Commenting on 1 John 2:2, Calvin himself wrote:

Christ suffered for the sins of the whole world, and in the goodness of God is offered unto all men without distinction, His blood being shed, not for a part of the world only, but for the whole human race; for although in the world nothing is found worthy of the favor of God, yet He holds out the propitiation to the whole world, since without exception He summons all to the faith of Christ, which is nothing else than the door unto hope.[1]

Just as it is disputable that John Calvin was a "Calvinist" in its most extreme expression, so is the belief that only Calvinists believe in the sovereignty of God. Few would consider John Wesley a Calvinist (he is usually described as an Arminian in theology), yet his journal entries and sermons on the character of God and prayer demonstrate a deep commitment to the belief that God is sovereign in the affairs of people. Sovereignty, defined as God's ultimate control over all things, is recognized by many who would choose not to identify themselves as Calvinists.

An Extreme Calvinistic View of the Sovereignty of God

The problem between one's view of the sovereignty of God and evangelism is to some extent based on how one defines the will of God. Extreme Calvinists tend to define sovereignty in an active sense with specific application in the lives of individuals. Others view sovereignty in a more passive sense with broad application in the world setting in which individuals find themselves. This becomes especially apparent in the way one looks at aspects of soteriology.

All evangelicals agree that "Salvation is of the Lord" (Jon. 2:9), but not all agree what that means specifically. Extreme Calvinists tend to explain that statement in what has become known as the TULIP formula (Total depravity, Unconditional election, Limited atonement, Irresistible grace, Perseverance of the saints). Others argue that such a view involves a denial of human freedom, a concept also taught in the Scriptures.

In an extreme Calvinist approach to salvation, the theologian begins with the presupposition that only God can be active in the saving process. Therefore, the expression "total depravity" is used to define the human condition. But this depravity differs from that taught in Scripture, in that people are viewed as incapable of any actions including repentance and faith without a particular manifestation of grace. It is argued that God gives this grace exclusively to those He has for His own reasons chosen to be saved (unconditional election). It is for these individuals alone that Christ died (limited atonement). It is also these individuals whom God calls to salvation with an irresistible grace or effectual calling. Further, it is maintained that those who are chosen, for whom Christ died, and who are called to salvation will persevere to the end and be found faithful.

Because of their unique view of divine sovereignty, Calvinists believe that all for whom Christ died will be saved. Therefore, they conclude that those who are not saved were never chosen for salvation, never had salvation provided for them in the atonement, and were never called to salvation by the Holy Spirit. In its most extreme expression, Calvinism does not recognize an active role for the human will in the salvation experience. Many view this as perhaps the greatest weakness in its theological system.

This view of sovereignty stands in contrast to the apparent teaching of the Scriptures in several areas. First, the Bible teaches that people are made in the image and likeness of God and may be held responsible for decisions they make. Second, various biblical expressions seem to indicate a much broader view of the atonement than that held by extreme Calvinists (2 Cor. 5:19; 2 Pet. 2:1; 1 John 2:2). Third, the Bible cites specific examples of people and people groups who did resist divine grace (Acts 26:28; Rom. 9:1; 10:1).

A Biblical Approach to the Sovereignty of God

The Bible uses such phrases as "chosen in Him," "predestinated unto the adoption of children" and "elect according to the foreknowledge of God." But this does not mean the terms reinforce the position of an extreme Calvinistic view to the exclusion of another position. These are biblical terms that must be interpreted properly.

First, election in the Bible is applied broadly. Election must always be interpreted within its context. The term "elect" is related to the Church, or to all believers, or those who have already accepted Christ. It is not applied to an unsaved person, even if he is a candidate for salvation. As such, it relates to God's plan of salvation because He has elected salvation and those in salvation are identified as elect. When taken in

light of the nature of salvation, we understand that Jesus Christ made atonement for all. Those who respond to His plan of salvation are characterized as elect.

Second, to say that God has chosen some and passed over others is to breach the nature of God. God is One, which means He is unity and acts in perfect harmony with His nature. Every part of God influences every other attribute of God. One attribute can never act in isolation from the others, hence God cannot be guilty of acting ignorantly or with a double mind. The nature of God expresses His love, as well as His justice. The Bible teaches that God so loves the world, hence this emotion is constant to all creatures at all times. An extreme Calvinist's view of unconditional election implies that God chooses some out of His nature, but not others, thus breaching the unity of God. Also, the love of God is breached because He is not able to love all equally. If God chooses (elects) some, it must proceed out of pure motives from His total person. The election of some and passing over of others divides the unity of God, implying duplicity, ignorance or partiality in God.

Evangelism/Church Growth and the Will of God

Perhaps the real problem in attempting to harmonize evangelism and church growth with the sovereignty of God is related to which side of the equation we are attempting to understand. Most who address this subject tend to focus on sovereignty from the perspective of that which God does independently. But can even the best of us understand that which God does independently? One of the acknowledged limitations of all theological systems is the certain failure of finite human minds to completely understand the eternal and infinite mind of God. In any theological system there must always be an element of mystery in this area.

Another aspect of sovereignty can be understood. That aspect involves a human response to the clearly revealed will of God. The will of God concerning the salvation of the lost is expressed in both positive and negative terms in the New Testament (1 Tim. 2:4; 1 Pet. 3:9). In giving the Great Commission to His Church,

Jesus began with a reminder of His authority over all things in both heaven and earth (Matt. 28:18). When we know God wills the salvation of people and has directed His Church to be actively involved in accomplishing that goal, those who recognize the sovereignty of God at a practical level will respond with obedience and use the resources available to them to accomplish that goal.

Sovereignty not only teaches us something about God—it also teaches us something about people. If God is indeed sovereign (Prov. 21:1), then we as people created and redeemed by that sovereign God are accountable to Him for our actions (1 Cor. 4:1,2). In light of that, one might ask, "Who really believes in sovereignty?" If the evangelical church professes belief in a sovereign God, it should promote the work of evangelism given to them by Him.

Reference: [1]John Calvin, *Commentary on First John*, s.v.

SPAN AND CONTROL, LAW OF

A widely accepted management principle suggesting that an administrator is most effective in management when his or her managerial responsibilities are limited to seven people.

SPECIAL REVELATION

The self-revelation of God through Scripture, finalized in Jesus Christ, and relating to God's plan of salvation. (See REVELATION.)

SPIRITUAL GIFT INVENTORY

A tool that has been developed to help Christians identify their spiritual gift(s). This approach normally includes a questionnaire completed by the candidate that tends to identify areas of interest that suggest the possibility of giftedness in various areas.

References: The Team Spiritual Gift Inventory, The Wagner-Modified Houts Questionnaire, Wesley Spiritual Gifts Questionnaire, Houts Inventory of Spiritual Gifts, Spiritual Gifts Discovery Survey and Scoring Sheet and Trenton Spiritual Gifts Analysis.

SPIRITUAL GIFTS

Supernatural abilities given by God through the Holy Spirit to His people that enable them to effectively minister in different areas and in different ways. When people use their gifts in ministry, they establish the basis upon which they help others.

Spiritual gifts have an important role in church growth. In the business community, managers have for some time been concerned with workforce economics. In the context of church ministry, workforce economics refers to the idea of using people where they are most usable (i.e., using people according to their spiritual gifts or abilities).

We are living in the midst of an awakening of spiritual gifts. During the 1950s, a few scholars began identifying spiritual gifts. Then with the rise of the charismatic renewal movement in the '60s and '70s, pastors began to study spiritual gifts. Today, laypeople in the church are becoming aware of their spiritual gifts and developing and using them in ministry.

Biblical Definition of Spiritual Gifts

The first question to be answered in understanding the relationship between spiritual gifts and church growth is: What is a spiritual gift? Leslie B. Flynn suggests "a gift is a Spirit-given ability for Christian service."[1]

Chuck Swindoll expands on that description, describing a spiritual gift as "a skill or ability that enables each Christian to perform a function in the body of Christ with ease and effectiveness."[2]

Five terms are used interchangeably or explicitly in Scripture to identify spiritual gifts. Each of these terms occurs in the introduction to the discussion of spiritual gifts in 1 Corinthians 12. An understanding of these terms will give insight into spiritual gifts and lead to a workable definition.

What Is a Spiritual Gift?
Pneumatikon—spiritual in character
Charismata—freely and graciously given
Diakonia—opportunity to minister
Energema—energy of God to activate
Phanerosis—an evident work of God

Paul advised the Christians in Corinth, "Now concerning spiritual gifts, brethren, I do not want you to be ignorant" (1 Cor. 12:1). The word "gifts" is not in the original text, but is supplied in the English translation, perhaps because the term appears in verse 4. The word *pneumatika* is also found in 1 Corinthians 14:1 and again the word "gifts" is added to the term "spiritual." *Pneumatika* is an adjective that gives meaning to the thing or person that possesses it. Hence, the word emphasizes the spiritual nature of the gift. Therefore, the Holy Spirit, who is the source of a Christian's spirituality and who also dispenses the gift, makes the gift spiritual.

The term *charismata* is found in 1 Corinthians 12:4 and is translated "gifts." The root of the word comes from *charis*, which means "grace." Grace is freely given at salvation (Eph. 2:8,9), and when the word is used with spiritual gifts it implies that they are freely and graciously given. Hence, a spiritual gift is that which is not sought or earned by human initiative, but is bestowed by the Spirit.

The word *diakonia* is translated "ministries" or "administrations," but is also a reference to spiritual gifts (1 Cor. 12:5). A gift is a ministry that is given by the Lord. When this word is used in the context of spiritual gifts, it implies that spiritual gifts are in fact spiritual ministries. Therefore, gifts are for a purpose—to be used in ministry. The verb form, *diakoneo*, means to be a servant, to serve or wait upon another person, particularly to wait on tables by serving food to guests. Hence, those who are given a spiritual gift should receive it with the purpose in mind of serving other people, not ministering primarily to oneself. A spiritual gift is given to serve others.

The word *energemata* is translated "operations" in 1 Corinthians 12:6 (*KJV*). Paul uses this term to denote spiritual gifts as the activity produced by God's enduements of people for service. The word is derived from the verb *energeo*, from which we get the English term "energy." It implies the power or energy of God to activate or set something in motion. Hence, a spiritual gift is not the natural ability of the individual but is a ministry empowered by God.

The fifth term, *phanerosis*, is translated "manifestation" in 1 Corinthians 12:7. A spiritual gift is a manifestation of the Holy Spirit. The word *phanerosis* comes from the verb *phaneroo*, which means "to make visible or clear." A spiritual gift is identified as clearly residing in the believer. When a Christian exercises a spiritual gift, it should be an evident work of the Holy Spirit.

Therefore, a spiritual gift is spiritual in character (*pneumatikos*), sovereignly given by God the Holy Spirit (*charismata*), to minister to others (*diakonia*), in the power of God (*energma*), with an evident manifestation of the Holy Spirit through the Christian as he or she serves God (*phanerosis*). Spiritual gifts are the various abilities given sovereignly to believers by the Holy Spirit so that when they faithfully serve the Lord there are spiritual results and the believer grows in effectiveness and/or develops other spiritual abilities of service.

Spiritual Gifts
Source: From the Holy Spirit *Bestowed:* To all believers *Purpose:* For Christian service *Nature:* Spiritual ability *Discovery:* By a proper relationship to the Holy Spirit *Responsibility:* To be exercised by believers *Number:* Plural *Identification:* Gifts are persons

Types of Spiritual Gifts

Although the apostle Paul discusses gifts at length in his Epistles, no complete listing of them is given in any of these discussions. Rather, the gifts of which Paul speaks must be collected to gain a complete listing. (See Rom. 12:6-8; 1 Cor. 12:4-11,28; Eph. 4:11.) When this is done, it is quickly apparent that there are different kinds of spiritual gifts. Larry Gilbert describes the three kinds of spiritual gifts as "miraculous gifts, enabling gifts, and team gifts."[3]

The miraculous gifts refer to those gifts more commonly thought of as "signs and wonders."

Four spiritual gifts—faith, discernment, wisdom and knowledge—may be described as enabling gifts. Like a chemical catalyst in a solution, these are the gifts that tend to energize and activate the task-oriented spiritual gifts. Standing alone, these four spiritual gifts tend not to accomplish much for God, but when they are applied to the exercise of the task-oriented gifts, they enhance one's effectiveness in ministry. Enabling spiritual gifts may be viewed as qualities possessed rather than activities to be performed. Every Christian has the ability to develop each of these gifts.

Faith is described as "being fully convinced that what He [God] had promised He was also able to perform" (Rom. 4:21). We can grow in faith through the Word of God (10:17) and as a result of our growing faith experience with God (Heb. 11:8-19).

Discernment is the ability to distinguish between that which is of God's Spirit and that which is of Satan, that which is real and false, and to set priorities based on that which is good, better and best. People who work in banks learn to identify counterfeit money by handling the real thing. Likewise, Christians tend to become more discerning as they gain a better understanding of the Scriptures that are described as truth (John 17:17).

Wisdom is understanding things from God's point of view. If we sense a need for greater wisdom in our lives, we can develop this gift by asking God for wisdom (Jas. 1:5); and by studying the Bible, which is able to make us wise (Ps. 19:7).

Knowledge is imparted by God through this gift. Christians who want to grow in their ministry effectiveness need to study the Scriptures as a prospector might search for mineral wealth (Prov. 2:1-5). This approach to Bible study was characteristic of Christians in Berea (Acts 17:11).

Developing Your Spiritual Gifts

There are two ways to develop one's ministry potential in the context of spiritual gifts. First, one can use his or her task-oriented gift in ministry and develop that gift for greater ministry. Second, one can strengthen the enabling gifts that make spiritual gifts more effective.

Several excellent spiritual gift inventories/surveys are available to help Christians locate and/or discover their spiritual abilities. The number of gifts differ and their designations/definitions also differ. The differences perhaps exist because of differences in doctrinal orientation to church ministry. Although differences exist, there is a common core of similarities that make it possible to discuss them all together.

The greatest differences are between including the miraculous gifts or not including them in a spiritual gift inventory/survey. The following paragraphs identify only the nonmiraculous gifts, also called the serving or ministering gifts. This list is not complete and does not use the same titles that all people would use. This list is only suggestive and brief.

The gift of evangelism is the Spirit-given capacity and desire to serve God by leading people, beyond their natural sphere of influence, to the saving knowledge of Jesus Christ. Those who have this gift may be described as aggressive soul winners who seek the lost.

The gift of prophecy is the Spirit-given capacity and desire to serve God by proclaiming a message from God. A person so gifted may be the hellfire-and-brimstone preacher who points out sin.

The gift of teaching is the Spirit-given capacity and desire to serve God by making clear to others the truth of the Word of God with accuracy and simplicity. The scholar making clear the doctrine and teachings of the Bible may have this gift.

The gift of exhortation or encouragement is the Spirit-given capacity and desire to serve God by motivating others to action by urging them to pursue a course of conduct. A person who has this gift may be described as the "how-to" teacher, giving the application of the Word of God.

The gift of shepherding is the Spirit-given capacity and desire to serve God by overseeing, training and caring for the needs of a group of Christians. The person illustrating this gift is the shepherd who leads and feeds, or the coach of the "team." This is the gift most desirable for Sunday School teachers who are the extension of pastoral ministry in the life of their classes.

The gift of showing mercy is the Spirit-given capacity and desire to serve God by identifying with and comforting those who are in distress. A person gifted in this way understands and comforts fellow Christians.

The gift of serving or helps is the Spirit-given capacity and desire to serve God by rendering practical help in both physical and spiritual matters. People who have this gift are able to meet the practical needs of others. They tend to be the Marthas in the Church who assume everybody needs to be doing something practical to get the job done.

The gift of giving is the Spirit-given capacity and desire to serve God by giving of one's material resources, far beyond the tithe, to further the work of God. This gifted person meets the financial needs of others.

The gift of administration is the Spirit-given capacity and desire to serve God by organizing, administering and promoting the various affairs of the church. People who lead the church and its ministries need to have the gift of administration.

The miraculous gifts are called "sign gifts" by some. See Signs and Wonders article.

Spiritual Gift Abuse

Although spiritual gifts may be viewed primarily as tools for ministry, they can be abused in ways that hinder the church's ministry effectiveness and hence slow growth. Kenneth Gangel describes three problems faced by those enlisting others in ministry. He writes:

> We face three basic problems in utilizing people in the service of Christ through the church: misuse, disuse, and abuse. The first is a reference to the employing of unqualified teachers and workers; the second, to the many uninvolved Christians that throng our church pews; and the last, to the problem of over-burdened workers in the church.[4]

An understanding of the role of spiritual gifts in ministry should motivate one to exercise caution to avoid certain common abuses of spiritual gifts. These include (1) gift ignorance, (2) gift blindness, (3) gift imposing, (4) gift gravitation, (5) gift colonization, (6) gift coveting and (7) gift assimilation.

Gift ignorance refers to one's lack of knowledge concerning the possession of spiritual gifts and their functions. Paul wrote to the Corinthians, "Now concerning spiritual gifts, brethren, I do not want you to be ignorant" (1 Cor. 12:1). We can overcome gift ignorance by learning about spiritual gifts and identifying our own gifts.

Gift blindness is a condition that results from gift ignorance and renders the victims incapable of recognizing their own spiritual gifts and their influence upon their own lives and ministries.

Gift imposing is the act of forcing one's spiritual gift upon another and attempting to compel them to perform as though it is God's gift to them as well.

Gift gravitation identifies the tendency among Christians to attract and be attracted to other Christians who have similar spiritual gifts.

Gift colonization is the direct and inescapable result of unrestrained gift gravitation. It is building "colonies" of a certain gift. This tends to happen more commonly in individual churches, but may also extend to interdenominational movements and denominations.

Gift coveting is desiring a gift of another person, other than that which God has given. There is a sense, however, in which we should "earnestly desire the best gifts" (v. 31) and we may be able to develop gifts from God that we do not presently have.

Gift assimilation refers to the tendency of acquiring the gifts of those with whom we are closely associated in ministry. Timothy received gifts through his association with Paul (2 Tim. 1:6), much as pastoral candidates today may assimilate the dominant gifts of a teacher or pastor with whom they have close associations.

Spiritual Gift Utilization

Spiritual gifts are the primary channels through which we minister (1 Cor. 7:7). They are supernatural capacities and desires that can be used as tools to make us more effective in ministry. Using one's spiritual gift can be a source of both joy and energy in the Christian life. Our spiritual gifts are closely related to God's calling upon our lives and our responsibilities in ministry. Gifts may be viewed as the building blocks of the church. Stressing the need for Christians to use their gifts in ministry, Juan Carlos Ortiz notes:

> Each believer needs to know his place in the body. Most church congregations are not a spiritual building, but a mountain of bricks. There is a difference. However good the

materials may be, if they are not situated in their right place and correctly related to one another, there is no building. Each member of the congregation is a brick. The evangelists are continually bringing in new bricks. The pastor encourages this, even teaching classes on soul winning. Bring in more bricks, he urges. But bricks are not a building. Instead of a builder, the pastor now becomes a caretaker of bricks.[5]

As pastors lead their churches, they should endeavor to avoid the abuses and misuses of gifts by teaching their correct usage. They should also avoid making impulsive decisions. Helping people find meaningful ministry is as important as helping them identify spiritual gifts. Also, avoid gift obsession. Don't be obsessed with the theology of gifts but rather be obsessed with the function of what you can do well. Also, be careful not to substitute a gift emphasis in ministry for a deeper walk with God.

Many Christians are reluctant to begin using their gifts in ministry because they lack self-confidence. This is especially true when they are asked to accept responsibility for an entire aspect of ministry. Some churches find it easier to enlist people onto ministry teams than to specific ministry positions. To some degree, this marks a return to a more biblical pattern of ministry. Commenting on the use of ministry teams in the New Testament, one writer notes:

The apostles continued ministering as a team in the early days of the church. They were recognized as a distinct group within the church and together were involved in the ministries of evangelism (Acts 2:14; 5:42), teaching (Acts 2:42; 5:25), miracles (Acts 2:43; 5:12), prayer (Acts 3:1; 4:24), and administration (Acts 4:37; 6:2). They chose to appoint ministry teams to solve problems whether those problems were as common and everyday as feeding widows (Acts 6:3) or as major as confirming the authenticity of a reported new ministry (Acts 8:14).[6]

When an individual's unique spiritual gifts are considered as a part of the enlistment process, those involved in ministry are likely to experience greater fulfillment through ministry and prove more effective in the long term. When gifted Christians are teamed together for ministry, they can serve to complement one another so they can better meet the needs of others. Without training and enlisting gifted laymen and laywomen in ministry, it is unlikely that a church will experience prolonged growth.

References: [1]Leslie B. Flynn, *19 Gifts of the Spirit* (Wheaton, Ill.: Victor Books, 1976), p. 21. [2]Charles R. Swindoll, *He Gave Gifts* (Pasadena, Calif.: Insight for Living, 1992). [3]Larry Gilbert, *Team Ministry: A Guide to Spiritual Gifts and Lay Involvement* (Lynchburg, Va.: Church Growth Institute, 1987), p. 63. [4]Kenneth O. Gangel, *Leadership for Church Education* (Chicago: Moody Press, 1970), p. 42. [5]Juan Carlos Ortiz, *Call to Discipleship* (Plainfield, N.J.: Logos International, 1975), p. 14. [6]Douglas Porter, *How to Develop and Use The Gift of Evangelism: A Practical Guide for the Layperson* (Lynchburg, Va.: Church Growth Institute, 1992), p. 89. Also see C. Peter Wagner, *Your Spiritual Gifts Can Help Your Church Grow* (Ventura, Calif.: Regal Books, 1979; revised edition, 1994); Kent R. Hunter, *Gifted for Growth: An Implementation Guide for Mobilizing the Laity* (Detroit: Church Growth Analysis and Learning Center, 1985).

SPIRITUAL MAPPING

The discipline of diagnosing and responding to the spiritual dynamics at work in a given community. By combining fervent prayer and diligent research, practitioners are afforded a compass with which to measure the landscape of the spiritual dimension and to discern moral gateways between it and the material world. — GOJR

SPIRITUAL QUEST SITES

Any natural or manmade location that facilitates spiritual investigation, ritual or worship. — GOJR

SPIRITUAL TERRITORIALITY

Relating to the fact that spiritual powers routinely forge strategies that are linked uniquely to specific cultures and geography. — GOJR

SPIRITUAL STRONGHOLDS

Ideological fortresses that exist in the mind and objective territorial locations. Manifesting both defensive and offensive characteristics, archetypal strongholds simultaneously repel light and export darkness.—GOJR

SPIRITUAL WARFARE

Conflicts with demonic strongholds and moral deception that require noncarnal weaponry and spiritual armor (Eph. 6).—GOJR

SPONTANEOUS GROWTH

Sudden growth in church membership, apparently unrelated to conscious planning.

SPURGEON, CHARLES HADDON (1834–1892)

British pastor.

Born in Kelvedon, Essex, on June 19, 1834, Charles Haddon Spurgeon was converted to Christ at age 16 and began preaching immediately. In 1854, he was invited to pastor a small church in south London. The church immediately began experiencing significant growth under their new pastor, and after moving several times to accommodate the crowds, the church built the Metropolitan Tabernacle, which would seat 6,000 people.

Spurgeon's popularity continued to increase as crowds gathered to hear him preach and others purchased his sermons, which were published weekly beginning in 1855. In 1865, he began editing the monthly *Sword and Trowel*. He established a training college for pastors and various other benevolent institutions. Before his death in 1892, he had published more than 2,000 sermons and 49 other volumes, including *The Treasury of David*, an extensive commentary on the Psalms, and various lectures on the ministry.

Spurgeon's greatest contribution to evangelism was achieved through the wide distribution of his sermons and the ministry of those trained at his college. His example of a church-based approach to training pastors has been widely copied by other Baptist pastors during the century since his death.

During his lifetime, Spurgeon was widely regarded as a leader among evangelical Christians in Britain and throughout the English-speaking world. He has been called the greatest preacher since the apostle Paul. His sermons, commentaries and books about the ministry con-

Analysis of St. John's Syndrome

Time ⟶

First Generation — Second Generation

PEOPLE

First Generation	Second Generation
High Commitment	Follow the Crowd
Strong Camaraderie	Cog in Bureaucratic Machine
Informal Association	Defined Status
Ad Hoc Process	Rationalized Rules
Charismatic Leader	Bureaucratic Leader
Personal Relationships	Impersonal Relationships
Unity Based on Trust	Written Confession of Faith

INSTITUTION

First Generation	Second Generation
Vision	Tradition
Goal Orientation	Self-Maintenance
Flexibility	Rigidity
People	Program
We Control Institution	Institution Controls Us
Growth	Nominality

tinue to be widely read and studied by evangelical pastors and Christian workers today.

References: Lewis Drummond, *Spurgeon: Prince of Preachers* (Grand Rapids: Kregel Publications, 1992); W. Y. Fullerton, *C. H. Spurgeon: A Biography* (London: Williams and Norgate, 1920).

ST. JOHN'S SYNDROME

A pathology of church growth describing a church in transition from first-generation Christians to second- and third-generation Christians characterized by a diminished love for God and declining zeal for evangelism and other outreach ministries. The title "St. John's Syndrome" derives from Revelation 2:4, "you have left your first love." It describes a church that was guilty of leaving is first generation commitment to Christ. Because the apostle John wrote The Revelation, early church-growth leaders ascribed the principle to his name.

STAINED-GLASS BARRIER

"Stained glass" reflects more than windows or church sanctuaries. It is a symbolic word for barriers that stand between those on the outside of the church and getting them to come inside to hear the gospel. These barriers include areas of organized Christianity and Christian practices. These barriers make it difficult for a person to attend a Sunday School or church service, or to continue to attend. The stained-glass barrier includes such things as poor location, inadequate parking, and unkept or poorly maintained facilities.

It is a barrier for a visitor to have to find a parking place in the street when the parking lot is full. Some, however, think that adequate parking or eliminating other barriers will cause church growth. No! There must be a dynamic that draws people to Jesus Christ. The church must have warm services and the pastor must preach with power. A barrier just makes it harder, not impossible, to reach people, and eliminating barriers makes it easier to reach people.

Stained-glass barriers also include perceptions, such as a lost person's dislike for a denomination's name or what an unchurched person remembers about a particular church. Some

have had a bad experience with a church member from a certain denomination, hence the church name is a barrier. A church split becomes a barrier to the neighborhood, making it harder for both halves to reach people for Christ.

STAIR-STEPPING

A systematic and natural approach to bringing people to Christ and salvation. It allows the Christian to keep the ultimate objective in clear focus and, at the same time, see where the candidate is in the process of evangelism. The unique quality of stair-stepping is that it takes the guesswork out of evangelism and provides an objective means of measuring progress.

The entire church undershepherding team must be aware of the stair-stepping goal. The team will come in contact with people on different steps. Its aim is to network people into the church and stair-step them to a meaningful decision for Christ. Barriers must be removed. The

STAIR-STEPPING MODEL
8. Conversion/Salvation.
7. Repent/Receive Christ.
6. I am willing to be saved.
5. I recognize I am reconciled to God through Christ.
4. I realize sin has alienated me from God.
3. I realize I am a sinner.
2. I know I am responsible to God.
1. I know there is a God.

unsaved must hear the gospel often so they will become more receptive to it.

Stair-stepping is a holistic approach to the task of evangelism or disciple making. It includes all that is involved in reaching the unsaved where they are and bringing them to Christ. It is moving people through a process, which is accomplished one step at a time.

The following chart illustrates the entire process.

Stair-Stepping to a Decision

1. The process of evangelism. Stair-stepping includes all that is involved in reaching the unsaved where they are and influencing them to accept Christ. It is moving people through a process, which is accomplished one step at a time. The initial contact could be made with a person at any level. An unsaved person is not required to begin on the first step. Therefore, stair-stepping can begin or end with any of the various steps in the process.

2. Stair-stepping is both supernatural and natural. Many things bring a person to Christ, such as the power of the gospel, the convicting work of the Holy Spirit and the drawing of the Father. The power of God that brings salvation resides in the gospel, not in any human program or humanly devised scheme (Rom. 1:16). Only the Holy Spirit can convict the sinner (John 16:8ff), and every possible precaution must be taken to see that no conscious or unconscious attempt is made to replace spiritual conviction with psychological pressure or human manipulation. Regardless of human effort, only God can draw sinners to Himself (John 6:44).

At the same time, it is neither logical nor biblical to expect a "God hater" to be saved without taking some intermediate steps in that person's understanding and acceptance of the person of God. Before the person can exercise faith in Christ, he or she must understand the provision Christ has made for his or her redemption (Heb. 11:6).

In evangelism, the decision to trust Jesus Christ by faith is usually preceded by many other decisions. Some of those decisions may be subconscious, or they may come so early in life that the person has forgotten that he or she made them. Unsaved people do not repent and trust Christ until they see their need for the gospel. Looking at the stair-stepping process, it is obvious that each step is dependent upon the one before it. Stair-stepping is natural to Friendship Evangelism.

3. Entry level to stair-stepping. The first step of an individual toward God is determined by personal need. As previously stated, that could be on step five, six or even seven of the stair-stepping process. The important thing is that the process begin at the level of the sinner's understanding of the gospel. Then the person must proceed to salvation.

Most of the time, the process begins when a friend contacts a lost person. Usually the believer has some general biblical knowledge, understands the implications of the gospel and has a positive attitude toward both the gospel and the Christian faith. If the lost person believes in the existence of God, the believer must begin farther up the stairs toward conversion because the person is ready to take the next step.

Contractors beginning construction of a 30-story skyscraper begin work with the foundation, and then move up one floor at a time. It would be foolish to consider building even the first floor without the foundation. That would be similar to the foolish man who built his house upon the sand (Matt. 7:26,27). If, however, the contractor goes bankrupt after having completed only 20 floors, and the bonding company employs another builder to complete the structure, the new contractor does not go back and lay the foundation again. Rather, the crews continue work on the twentieth floor.

Stair-Stepping People to the Gospel

Obviously, anyone can be saved the first time he or she hears the gospel, as were the Philippian jailer and Zacchaeus. When God has prepared the heart, we must lead a person to Christ. But our research tells us a person hears the gospel 3.4 times (the Law of Three Hearings) before receiving Christ. Usually the person is stepping closer to salvation each time the gospel is heard.

When people are stair-stepped toward the gospel, it is not presented with a "now or never" ultimatum. Usually, the gospel is presented with such finality that the prospects do not accept Christ. As a result, sometimes the prospects leave church farther away from God than when they entered. Prospects should be stair-stepped toward the gospel. Similar to helping a young baby walk, every step that prospects take toward God should be supported.

Evangelism is too often viewed as an isolated activity. You, the soul winner, confront the unsaved person with the gospel, which means proclaiming the gospel and trying to persuade that person to respond. Every contact with the person is viewed as a separate, isolated activity. Evangelism should be seen as an on-going process that includes pre-evangelism and poste-vangelism.

The Scriptures refer to evangelism in terms of "making disciples." Evangelism is not painted as a fragmented picture. The biblical approach of making disciples is neither haphazard nor piece-meal. God has clearly given an ongoing approach to the task of disciple making, one that begins with relating to the unsaved where they are, and is not complete until they become mature, productive and reproducing members of the Body of Christ.

Reference: See SETTING PERSONAL GOALS IN EVANGELISM.

STATIC CHURCHES

Churches in which growth has ceased and a decline in enrollment is imminent.

STEW POT

America's ethnic reality in which many cultural groups are enriched by others without losing their own identity and integrity. Contrast this concept with the "melting pot" theory, which implies the loss of separate identity.

STEWARDSHIP CAMPAIGN

An organized program presenting the financial needs of a church to the congregation by having a view of soliciting their involvement in the total work of the church. Although finances are usually the focus, a proper stewardship campaign does not just aim at finances. Stewardship is defined as managing one's resources (time, talent and treasure) for the glory of God. Therefore, the total stewardship of a believer is the focus of a stewardship campaign, even though money seems to get most of the attention.

During this campaign, attention is focused on educating people about biblical stewardship. Usually Sunday School lessons emphasize the Christian's stewardship for God. Then letters are mailed from the church reminding people about the church budget, the stewardship theme of the year, such as "God Is Able" or "Tithing Is Christian," and the person's responsibility to tithe. The pastor usually preaches a series of sermons on stewardship. Then laypeople are asked to present testimonies in the church service about why they tithe. The intent is to get every person in church to be aware of his or her responsibility to God and to be obedient in giving through the church.

Stewardship campaigns are biblical. Just as a church has a campaign for soul winning, foreign missions or to especially emphasize Bible reading, so a church ought to emphasize stewardship during a designated time of the year. Most churches set aside January as stewardship month. The biblical basis is that whatever God has commanded His people to do, the pastor and church ought to motivate the congregation to perform. A stewardship campaign is an organized program to educate and motivate everyone to faithfulness.

Many mistakenly think that stewardship is just fund-raising. They often think that a stewardship program in a local church is raising money much as a community agency raises money. Although money is raised during a stewardship campaign for the church budget, that is not the bottom line. Stewardship is not talking people out of their money. It is teaching people how to use their money properly. Stewardship is a biblical concept: Jesus taught the importance of being a good steward in Luke 16:2.

A steward was usually a servant who managed the household for the owner of the house or the farm, managing the money, time, resources and personnel. Jesus used the illustration of good stewards and bad stewards to teach how we should be stewards for Him.

Christians should manage their time (schedule), talent and money for God. Part of a stewardship campaign is to teach that all money belongs to God, not just 10 percent (the tithe), because God wants all of our money to glorify

Him. Christians should spend all of their money wisely, find more bargains and get more out of life; but first give 10 percent to God automatically.

A stewardship campaign is not to acquire money for the church but to teach believers how to live the abundant life. When Christians obey the financial principles of the Bible, their lives will be lived more abundantly and God's work will be financed.

Why a Stewardship Campaign?

1. To help strengthen Christians. The purpose of stewardship is to strengthen every believer in the local church. Little children should be taught how to handle money—although they may receive small allowances—as well as a person who may receive a small retirement income, thus has little to give.

Stewardship emphasizes that all money belongs to God. If we realize we do not own our money, it is easier to give it back to God. To illustrate, if we drive a company car we know that it is not our car, but is to be used for business. God wants us to treat our possessions with that attitude. God is letting us use the money He gives to us for His business. A Christian's business is God's business. Just as a company gives a salesperson rules and limits on how the company car is to be used, God has instructed us on how to use our time, talent and treasures. Therefore, a stewardship program should educate church members about how to manage their time, talent and treasures for the glory of God.

A Christian is called to be a disciple, which means to live a disciplined life. Because stewardship is management or discipleship, it is an expression of the Christian life. Stewardship does not just involve money, it involves something deeper. It involves our discipleship to Jesus Christ that can be expressed in the way we use our money.

2. To help all Christians become obedient. During the stewardship campaign, letters should be mailed to every person in the congregation because some marginal members will not attend church to hear the stewardship sermons and see the stewardship posters. Also, a phoning campaign is initiated to contact every person in the congregation. Why? Not just to acquire money, but to help everyone to obey God and become stewards of His resources.

A Christian cannot become spiritual without being obedient. Therefore, a stewardship campaign cannot be viewed as something carnal merely because it involves money. The campaign should be viewed as the highest expression of spiritual ministry in the Sunday School year. If conducted properly, more people will obey Jesus Christ and follow His Lordship.

3. To identify and help backsliders. During a stewardship campaign, every person in the church is contacted. One hardened church member once complained, "The only time you contact me is during a stewardship campaign." Although the visitors or those who make the telephone contacts should do more than talk about money, the man complaining should be grateful that someone was concerned about his spirituality. Lax church members are contacted for that reason—because they are lax. Too often the faithful are exhorted to give money and they are already doing it. In a stewardship campaign, those who need to become faithful are exhorted to become stewards.

4. To share our blessings. God does not ask those who have nothing to give to Him, nor does God ask for a fixed amount. God only asks for stewardship after He has given to us. In the parables of the vineyard, the landowner came for his share after there was fruit on the vine. The workers were expected to manage a vineyard for the owner. But once there was a harvest, the owner wanted his share of the harvest. As Christians, we are the workers and God is the owner. Our stewardship is to manage the vineyard for Him. Everything in this world belongs to God who created it and redeemed us.

The psalmist recognized the source of all of his benefits and responded, "I will praise You, for I am fearfully and wonderfully made; marvelous are Your works, and that my soul knows very well" (Ps. 139:14). When Christians see how much God has given to them, it is embarrassing to see how little they return to Him. Good stewards will manage their resources for their master's best interest.

5. To reveal our hearts. The problem with possessions is that they possess us, rather than our possessing them. A stewardship campaign reveals the hearts of all the members because they are brought to the place where they must account for the way God has blessed them during the past year. It is a time of self-evaluation, commitment to God and potentially a time for revival.

6. To give to God. Like any investment-oriented businessman, God expects a good return on His resources. He has placed Christians in control of His business (i.e., His ministry in the world). Surveying the parables of Jesus, it is significant that whenever the master went on a long journey, he always came back looking for a return from his farm. In application, God created us in His image and likeness. He has given us a good mind, strong wills and the opportunities to make something of our lives for His glory. God now comes and wants us to use our gifts and abilities for Him.

During a stewardship campaign, all Christians should be reminded that they should return finances to God so that the work of God may prosper.

7. To teach judgment. Christians should know that they will be judged, and that judgment is based on stewardship. In Jesus' parables on this subject, the landowners judged their managers based on their faithfulness. Because the owner delegated the vineyard to someone else does not mean that they owned it. Even though the workers might develop an emotional attachment to the vines and the vineyard, the farm still did not belong to them. Yet the workers always treated the farm as if it were their own. The issue is always ownership. Who owned the vineyard?

Once a year during the stewardship campaign, all Christians need to be reminded of "who owns the vineyard." That means they are reminded of who owns their houses, their bodies and their investment portfolios. If God is the owner of all things, and He allows Christians to manage them for His glory, then a judgment day is coming.

God will judge Christians not on the basis of what they did not have, but for what they have done with what they have been given. Some sit in a pew and think that God doesn't need their possessions. That is not the issue. Others think that we need to give God some money to see the church through the week. Some Christians treat the church as though it were an automobile. They put enough money in the offering plate to buy gas and to get God through this week, then they will help Him out again next Sunday. We do not give money to God to help Him out. He owns our resources; we manage them for Him. We give back to God what is His.

There are always those who complain and say, "The church is after money." We must be careful to deal with the problem of criticism before it turns into the poison of bitterness. When a person is cut and injured, pain is associated with the wound. We never doubt the wisdom of the doctor who inflicts more pain on the already sore area by applying iodine or an antiseptic to the wound. The doctor doesn't do it to hurt needlessly, but to help in the healing process. Without the medication, there would be the risk of infection. Without the teaching on stewardship, Christians risk the infection of selfishness, materialism, and worldliness.

Five "Pockets" of Stewardship

Money that people give to Christian institutions usually comes from five sources. Obviously, these are not actual pockets, but are symbolic pictures to represent the five major motives of church members in giving to their church. When church leaders understand the nature and source of their financial income, they can better plan a strategy for outreach and growth.

First, the money in this pocket is earmarked for "lighting and heating bills." This represents the desire to contribute to the general fund. Members are motivated out of concern to give for the operating expenses of the church. "The light and heat" pocket represent salaries, supplies, utilities and general maintenance.

The second pocket has money for "missions." Certain members want most of their money to go to foreign missions, and often members want at least some money to go to outreach, usually out of their concern for the Great Commission.

The third pocket has money to buy "ivy walls." Because some church members value higher education, they direct their money to build college classrooms, libraries or to equip science laboratories.

The fourth pocket contains money for the "cup of cold water." These members have compassion for the needs of their hurting brothers and sisters. They give to feeding projects and hospitals, and provide housing and emergency relief.

The last pocket contains money for "brick and mortar." This money is specially earmarked for church buildings. Some will give large amounts here and some will fund no other project. Almost all members, however, want to give something for their church's building project.

Some church leaders hesitate to enter a building campaign because things are tight in the "light and heat" pocket. A church's inability to properly meet its operational needs is not a proper reason to hold back a building campaign. Understanding the following principle, however, should overcome that heresy.

First, money in one pocket usually will not go for projects of another pocket. Just because a church has no excess finances to pay bills does not mean it cannot raise excess money for a new sanctuary, missions or its denominational college. The emotional or spiritual commitment of members usually does not transfer from one project to another.

Second, money in the "brick and mortar pocket" that is not collected will be lost to the church. Finances that are not given to local church members will usually go to an interdenominational or humanitarian agency. Therefore, to postpone a capital fund project means the church is losing money it could otherwise use.

Third, church leaders are not aware of what members have in their pockets until the members are presented with a financial challenge. People give in response to a challenge and their preference is unknown until they give. Therefore, a capital stewardship campaign may be a step of faith because there is no history of giving to a building fund, but it is a step of faith based on the fact that Christians have "brick and mortar pockets."

Fourth, once a member's pocket is opened, he or she will give again from that same pocket with the same motivation to the same kind of need. Just as members give their tithes and offerings regularly for the ongoing church expense, so those who have "brick and mortar pockets" will continue to give because that preference fulfills their needs.

In conclusion, knowledge of giving habits by church members will help church leaders plan a healthy and continuous strategy for financial enlargement that will provide for church growth.

STRATEGIC-LEVEL SPIRITUAL WARFARE

Pertains to intercessory confrontations with demonic power that is concentrated over given cities, cultures and peoples. —GOJR

STRATEGY

A mutually agreed upon plan of action to achieve the goals that have been determined by a particular group.

Strategy to Reach One's Friends

What is the best way to reach our friends for Christ? In one sense, there is no wrong way to reach people for Christ. But different people respond to different approaches. Most people come to faith in Christ through the faithful witness of a Christian with whom they have a meaningful relationship. This may partly be because of a friend's understanding of them and how best to share the gospel in the context of their unique needs.

As we pray for our friends and try to reach them for Christ, our concern is to discern the best way to share the gospel. This article is designed to help you better understand your friend, relative, associate and/or neighbor, and develop an outreach strategy that is most likely to be effective in reaching him or her.

As we begin, write your friend's name on a piece of paper and list as much information as you can about him or her. Include such things as the spouse's name, wedding anniversary, birthday, address, phone number, workplace, hobbies, special interests and the names of any children.

Perhaps in completing this information, you realized some things you do not know about your friend. During the next several weeks, make it your goal to get to know your friend better. Remember, people don't care how much you know until they know how much you care. That's why demonstrating your Christian love for them through acts of kindness is an important first step in designing an outreach strategy. Based upon your friend's unique interests and situation in life, list a dozen things you could do in the next three months that he or she would appreciate.

People develop meaningful relationships when they do things together. What kind of things does your friend enjoy doing? Which of these could you do with your friend to develop your relationship and use it as a means of reaching your friend for Christ? In light of your friend's unique personality and interests, list half a dozen events he or she might enjoy doing with you in the next six months. Some of these events may be church outreach events that present the gospel in a way that may appeal to your friend in a special way (e.g., through drama, music, recreation and so on).

Remember, your ultimate goal is to help your friend come to personal faith in Jesus Christ as his or her Lord and Savior. The Bible explains, "So then faith comes by hearing, and hearing by the word of God" (Rom. 10:17). Most people need to hear and consider the gospel three or four times before they are prepared to make a personal commitment. How could you share your faith with your friend in a way that he or she would find nonoffensive and give an honest consideration to the gospel? These witness opportunities may vary from talking about your faith over coffee or a meal, to sharing gospel literature or other media (video, audiocassette tape and so on) with your friend, to involving your friend in an outreach event with others.

As you worked through the process of designing a personal outreach strategy, you identified the things that will probably be most effective in communicating your concern and faith to your friend. This is likely the means by which your friend will come to personal faith in Christ as his or her Lord and Savior. Don't become discouraged if your friend does not make a decision for Christ quickly. When Jesus talked to the Samaritan woman, she was witnessing to her friends about her newfound faith in Christ before the end of the day (John 4). Earlier, He

also talked to Nicodemus, a ruler of the Jews (ch. 3). Nicodemus did not come to faith in Jesus until later, but his conversion was just as significant as that of the Samaritan woman.

One way to fight the tendency to become discouraged is to look for signs of progress in your friend's movement toward salvation. Most people take several little steps toward faith in Christ before taking the giant step of becoming Christians. Look for changing attitudes about Christianity and increased interest in the gospel as evidences of the Holy Spirit's working in your friend's life. Then continue praying for your unsaved friend and remain faithful in demonstrating and sharing God's love for him or her.

Of course, the best evangelistic strategy is ineffective unless it is implemented. Don't wait for a better time to begin witnessing to your friend. Begin today. As you faithfully demonstrate and share God's love with your friend, may God bless your efforts and give you the joy of seeing your friend trust Christ personally.

STUDD, CHARLES T. (1860–1931)
Missionary to China, India and Africa.

Born into a wealthy British home, C. T. Studd achieved fame early in life through his athletic ability, becoming captain of the school's cricket team at Eton at age 19. He was converted to Christ through the preaching of D. L. Moody. Soon afterward, he sensed God's call upon his life for missions, and in 1885 sailed to China to work with Hudson Taylor. Poor health caused him to return to England and he devoted his energies to raising funds for missions. He served six years as a missionary to India before again returning to England. In 1912, Studd went to his third field of service—Africa. After completing his original two-year term of service, Studd returned for another five-year term.

C. T. Studd's greatest contribution to evangelism was the establishment of the World Wide Evangelization Crusade, which became the world's largest interdenominational faith mission.

Reference: Norman P. Grubb, *C. T. Studd: Athlete and Pioneer* (Grand Rapids: Zondervan Publishing House, 1937).

SUNDAY, WILLIAM (BILLY) ASHLEY
(1862–1935)

American evangelist.

Born in Ames, Iowa, on November 19, 1862, Billy Sunday was raised in an orphanage because his father died before the child was a year old. In 1883, he began a professional baseball career with the Chicago White Sox and was converted three years later after stumbling into a meeting at the Pacific Garden Mission in Chicago. In 1891, he gave up his baseball career and began working with evangelist J. Wilbur Chapman. Three years later, Sunday launched his own evangelistic ministry. His flamboyant style and strong preaching against the use of alcohol drew large crowds to his meetings and pushed him into the forefront of the prohibition movement. By the time of his death on November 6, 1935, it is estimated he had reached a million people with the gospel.

Sunday's greatest contribution to evangelism was achieved in his citywide crusades. His preaching was characterized by a strong emphasis on both the gospel and the social/moral issues of his day.

Sunday is best remembered for his flamboyant preaching style and his practice of building tabernacles for his crusades. The tabernacle floors were covered with sawdust, engendering the expression "hitting the sawdust trail" to refer to the response at the public invitation. Sunday worked with music evangelist Homer Rodeheaver. His preaching style was described as follows:

> Sunday skipped, ran, walked, bounced, slid and gyrated on the platform....He would, in a rage against the Devil, pick up the simple kitchen chair which stood behind the reading desk and smash it to kindling....He would impersonate a sinner trying to reach heaven like a ball player sliding for home — and illustrate by running and sliding the length of the improvised tabernacle stage.[1]

Sunday was controversial and often criticized, but was nevertheless an effective evangelist in the early twentieth century.—ALR

Reference: [1]Bernard A. Weisberger, *They Gathered at the River: The Stories of the Great Revivalists and Their Impact Upon Religion in America* (New York: Little, Brown and Company, 1958), p. 247.

SUNDAY SCHOOL

A lay evangelism and educational ministry and movement that has proved foundational in the church-growth strategies of many denominations through the last 200 years. Sunday School has been described historically as "the reaching, teaching, winning, maturing arm of the church."

References: J. N. Barnette, *The Pull of the People* (Nashville: Convention Press, 1956); Elmer L. Towns, *How to Grow an Effective Sunday School* (Denver: Accent Books, 1979), pp. 5-16. See EVANGELISM IN THE SUNDAY SCHOOL.

SUPERAGGRESSIVE EVANGELISM

The attitude of energetic zeal and innovation in communicating the gospel to others.

SUPERCHURCH

A church that has demonstrated a strong desire and ability to grow, has many agencies for growth (synergistic approach to evangelism), is located on a large church campus and has a varied staff of professionals. Although a superchurch usually numbers members in the thousands, it is known more for its aggressive attitude in outreach than its actual size.

SYMPATHIZERS

People who, distinct from adherents, simply possess an interest in the church. Sympathizers attend the evangelical teaching but do not join the church. They are favorable to Protestants and aid evangelicals when they are persecuted.

SYNAGOGUE: RELATIONSHIP TO THE CHURCH

Gatherings of Jews for the purpose of the reading and exposition of Scripture, developed in the period between the Testaments.

The Old Testament Tabernacle, and later the Temple, was set up by God, but the synagogue does not appear on the pages of the Old Testament. Yet in the New Testament the synagogue is fully developed. Obviously, the synagogue was developed by Jews in the dispersion who were unable or unwilling to travel regularly to Jerusalem to worship in the Temple (Deut. 16:16). This does not imply that they were wrong in setting up and using the synagogue, which became the place of teaching and the instrument to perpetuate Jewish religious culture.

Some have wrongly taught that the synagogue was the blueprint for the Church. To imply this seems to deny that the Church came by revelation. Rather, the Jews who originated the idea of the synagogue followed natural social organizational patterns. Because these truths had their source in God, as does all truth, it is only natural to expect Him to follow these principles in establishing His church.

To organize a synagogue, it was necessary to have at least 10 available men. The elders of the congregation selected a ruler (or several of them). The ruler was responsible for synagogue services and properties. He often designated others to conduct the expressions of praise, prayers, reading of the Law and prophets, and the giving of exhortations. Several assistants carried out menial duties, administered corporal punishment or otherwise disciplined members, and dispensed alms received from the members.

New Testament believers, therefore, had a model for church leadership and organization. It is not to be inferred that they followed this synagogue pattern rigidly, however. The point is that the early believers were aware of basic ways and means for conducting corporate spiritual life and business.[1]

The Church belongs to Jesus, while the synagogue belonged to the Jews. Jesus clearly said, "I will build My church" (Matt. 16:18). No such statement is made of the Jewish synagogue. We can thus understand also how the Christian community in the midst of Israel could be simply designated *ekklesia* (church) without being confounded with the Jewish community, the synagogue (Acts 2:47).[2]

The Church is a symbol of victory—the gates of hell could not stand against it—while the synagogue was a symbol of defeat. The Church is pictured by Christ on the offensive, not the defensive. Even from the Jewish perspective, the synagogue reveals no sacrifices or Levites—the essentials of the Jewish faith were not present.

The synagogue was primarily a place of learning. Later, the synagogue furnished a meeting place for the Church (Acts 19). Basically, the synagogue was similar to a religious civic center owned by the Jews and open to all Jews. In no way is the Church a continuation of the synagogue.

References: [1]David J. Hesselgrave, *Planting Churches Cross-Culturally* (Grand Rapids: Baker Book House, 1980), p. 351. [2]Hermann Cremer, *Biblico-Theological Lexicon of New Testament Greek* (New York: Charles Scribner's Sons, 1895), pp. 333-334.

SYSTEMATIC THEOLOGY

Collecting, arranging, comparing, exhibiting and defending all facts from any and every source concerning God and His works, especially as focused in the Scriptures.

TAYLOR, JAMES HUDSON
(1832–1905)

Pioneer missionary to inland China, founder of the China Inland Mission.

Born in Barnsley, England, May 21, 1832, into the home of a Methodist minister, James Hudson Taylor was trained by his parents, and early adopted his father's dream of going to China as a missionary. He was converted to Christ at age 17 and after studying medicine and theology, went to China in 1854 under the auspices of the China Evangelization Society. Taylor differed with the missionary strategy of his day, choosing to identify as fully as possible with the Chinese in their culture and dress. He also had concerns about the mission's practice of deficit spending to support its missionaries.

In 1860, Taylor returned to England, where he completed the translation of the Bible into the Ningpo dialect. In 1865, he established the China Inland Mission, which became the prototype of the independent "faith" missions that followed. In the next 40 years, Taylor's new mission established 205 mission stations and enrolled 849 missionaries and 125,000 Chinese Christians in the work of evangelizing China. He died in Changsha, China, in 1905.

Taylor's greatest contribution to evangelism was achieved through the establishment of the China Inland Mission. Not only was this mission effective in reaching people for Christ, but also in representing a new ministry paradigm that has been widely copied by other evangelical faith missions reaching other parts of the world.

Taylor's emphasis on the deeper Christian life and living by faith has helped many Christians who have read books by or about him.

Reference: Howard and Geraldine Taylor, *Hudson Taylor's Spiritual Secret* (Chicago: Moody Press, 1932).

TEACHING, GIFT OF

The person who has the gift of teaching has the ability to accurately make clear God's truth so all can understand it. The strengths of this gift include (1) a desire to study and classify truth, (2) a feeling that this gift is foundational to others, (3) a tendency to present truth systematically, (4) concern about learning, (5) concern with the accurate communication of Scripture and lack of tolerance for its misinterpretation, (6) a tendency to listen to those who have correct knowledge and (7) a sensitivity for using biblical illustrations in teaching.

Among the common weaknesses associated with this gift are (1) a greater interest in interpretation than application and (2) the absence of practical faith. Those who have this gift may fall into the danger of (1) pride over knowledge, (2) concentrating on details rather than the broader issues of life or (3) having a greater concern for truth than for individuals.

TENNENT, GILBERT (1703–1764)

Leader in the Great Awakening among Presbyterians in the middle colonies.

TENNENT, WILLIAM, JR. (1673–1746)

Leader in the Great Awakening among Presbyterians in the middle colonies.

TERRITORIAL SPIRITS

Demonic powers that have been given controlling influence of specific sites, peoples and areas. The belief in such hierarchical arrangements is culturally widespread and often involves protective deities linked to homes, temples, clans, cities, valleys and nations. —GOJR

TERTULLIAN, QUINTUS FLORENS
(C. A.D. 160–220)

Early church father and apologist.

Born into the home of a Roman centurion stationed in Carthage, Tertullian was trained in both Greek and Latin. He practiced law and taught public speaking in Rome prior to his conversion to Christianity. He opposed the formalism beginning to characterize some parts of the church, and chose to join the Montanists about

A.D. 202. In A.D. 197, he wrote *Apologeticum*, an attempt to convince a Roman governor of the loyalty of Christians to the Empire and of the failure of efforts to destroy the church by persecution. His conclusion that "the blood of the martyrs is the seed of the church" has been proved accurate throughout the history of evangelism.

Tertullian's greatest contribution to evangelism was his effort to defend Christianity for Roman authorities.

TESTIMONY

Christians verbally sharing what they have seen, heard and experienced in Jesus Christ—their lives reflecting the inner reality of their faith.

TESTIMONY EVANGELISM

Sharing our experience in Jesus Christ with other people so that they, too, will want to experience what we have in Christ.

Testimony evangelism can be used in a side-door approach to evangelism. This is verbal evangelism in which believers share their experiences. Some Christians cannot present the plan of salvation to a lost person, thinking that this is preaching or salesmanship. But everyone can tell what has happened to them personally.

1. Witnesses should share *what they have seen* about Jesus Christ. "That which was from the beginning,...which we have seen with our eyes, which we have looked upon" (1 John 1:1). First, we want to share what we have seen in Jesus Christ. The two disciples on the road to Emmaus were at first blinded to Christ, but He gave them spiritual sight. The Bible says "their eyes were opened" (Luke 24:31) and they knew Him. When we know Christ, we want to share Him with our friends. Second, we see a difference in our lives—how our desires have changed and the difference that has made in our lives. Then we want to share with our friends what Christ has done for us.

2. Witnesses should share *what they have heard* about Jesus Christ. When Peter and John were called to the Sanhedrin for their preaching, they confessed, "For we cannot but speak the things which we have seen and heard" (Acts 4:20). When people are called as witnesses in legal trials, judges will not permit their opinions, but only what they have seen, heard or experienced.

3. Witnesses should share *what they have experienced* in their relationships with Jesus Christ. In Acts 4:1-20, a healed man who had been lame from birth stood with Peter and John. He gave his testimony about what had happened to him, "And seeing the man who had been healed standing with them, they could say nothing against it" (v. 14).

Testimony evangelism is an effective evangelistic strategy because it gives credibility to the message.

Preparing Your Personal Testimony

Our testimonies may be our most effective evangelistic tools. Some people will not give the gospel a second thought until they see the change it has made in our lives. But even if they see a change, they may not know what caused it until you take time to share your testimony.

A testimony is our expression of what God has done in our lives. Normally, it focuses on our conversion experience, although it is not uncommon also to refer to what God has been doing in our lives subsequent to conversion. The content of our testimonies depends upon what we are trying to accomplish with our testimonies. If we are using our testimonies in evangelism, it is best to talk about our conversions. If we are using our testimonies to encourage another Christian in the Christian life, then a testimony concerning God's continued work in our lives would be more effective.

Sometimes our testimonies may be one of several steps in the extended process of bringing others to Christ and salvation. At other times it may be effective in opening the door to an evangelistic discussion. On yet other occasions we may use our testimonies to help someone make a decision to receive Christ as Savior. In each case, our testimonies can be important tools in reaching others for Christ.

In former times, people might listen to an hour-long sermon and consider everything that was said. Not so today. We are more likely to listen to a three-minute song on the radio than a three-hour rendition of Handel's *Messiah*. It is not surprising, therefore, that a 3-minute testimony may prove more effective in evangelism than a 30-minute sermon.

As you write your testimony, begin by praying for wisdom (Jas. 1:5,6). Although we can and should do certain things in the evangelistic process, only God can perform the miracle of regeneration. We need to work with Him rather than against Him. Therefore, ask God to help you view your testimony from His perspective and in the context of how He can use it to draw others to Himself.

On three occasions in Acts, the apostle Paul gave his personal testimony (Acts 22:1-21; 24:10-11; 26:2-23). Comparing these accounts reveals that Paul had a plan for presenting his testimony. He began by briefly describing his life before his conversion. Then he told his listeners how he was converted. Finally he described the difference his conversion had made in his life. That three-point outline is a good guide for preparing your personal testimony.

Be positive as you prepare your testimony. You can do this by emphasizing the change in your new life rather than the failings of your old life. Also, emphasize the good things you have in Christ rather than the things you lost or gave up in becoming a Christian. Every life change involves gains and losses, but the life change that occurs at conversion has far more gains than losses. Therefore, emphasize the gains and use your testimony to affirm the positive character of the Christian life.

It is best to focus on a single theme in your testimony rather than addressing several topics. When you describe your experience in the context of loneliness, forgiveness, a pursuit of happiness or a search for personal fulfillment, people who have similar needs will readily identify with your experience. If you try to identify all of the more than 100 things God does when He saves us, your testimony might confuse others and cause them to put off making a decision for Christ.

As you describe your life before conversion, your purpose is to build a bridge between yourself and the listener. Include enough detail to enable the other person to readily identify with your experience, but be careful not to glamorize a sordid past. Some testimonies unwittingly leave the impression that life without Christ is far more exciting than the Christian life. In actual fact, the abundant life is found only in Christ (John 10:10).

If you are using your testimony as part of a larger gospel presentation, use it to build interest in the gospel that effected the change in your life. If your testimony is standing alone, be sure to explain clearly how you repented and believed the gospel to be converted.

The climax of your testimony should answer the question: What does Christ mean to you today? You could say many things to answer that question, but for the purpose of your testimony, it is best to mention only two or three things that are most significant. Emphasize that which is most meaningful in your life without sounding like a soap or shampoo commercial. Your testimony is an expression of what God has done in your life. It doesn't have to be exciting, but it should be interesting.

When you have finished writing the body of your testimony, write the introduction and conclusion. Take time to work on an opening statement that is likely to capture the interest of the listener and is consistent with the rest of your testimony. You may wish to include one or two significant Scripture references in your testimony. If you do this, do it in a way that flows with your speech. Be careful not to turn your testimony into a Bible lesson.

When you complete the first draft of your testimony, go back over it and make it better. Look at it critically from the perspective of the listener. Are you using clichés, negative statements, stereotypes or words that have connotations you don't want to communicate? Is your testimony graphic enough that others can identify with you? Is there continuity in your presentation that naturally flows from one paragraph to the next? If you used humor in your testimony, would it be offensive to some people or appear frivolous to others? Although it is *your* testimony and should communicate who you are, remember you will only communicate what others can hear.

Check the length of your testimony by counting the number of words you use. The typical newscaster reads the news at a rate of 160 words a minute. This means a 300- to 500-word testimony would take two to three minutes to share.

Before using your testimony in a witness situation, share it with two or three friends who will help you make it better. Ask them to critique you as you share your testimony. Then, when you have committed a final draft of your testimony to memory, ask them to critique you on the way you share your testimony. Avoid speaking softly, sounding preachy or adopting a "ministerial" tone in your speech.

We all know the value of the saying "practice makes perfect." Practice saying your testimony until it flows naturally and loses that "canned" sensation. Then practice saying it in front of a mirror so you can see how you say it. You may be surprised at what you see. Remember, you also communicate through body language. Therefore, practice good posture and watch for nervous physical habits that may distract from what you say.

Like any other tool, your personal testimony is only effective if it is used. Therefore, be alert to opportunities to introduce it naturally into your conversation as part of your personal strategy of evangelism.

THIRD WAVE MOVEMENT See SIGNS AND WONDERS

The Third Wave renewal movement is a worldwide renewal movement in which evangelicals and other Christians who, unrelated to the teachings and practices of Pentecostalism or the charismatic movement, testify to an ongoing experience of being filled, empowered and energized by the Holy Spirit for evangelism, Christian life and ministry. The term "Third Wave" was coined by C. Peter Wagner in 1983.[1] Anglican researcher and statistician Dr. David Barrett has estimated that 33 million believers worldwide are a part of the Third Wave movement, which, together with the Pentecostal and charismatic movements, make up approximately 25 percent of organized global Christianity.[2] The term "Third Wave" refers to the third wave of the power and renewal of the Holy Spirit experienced in the Body of Christ in the twentieth cen-

tury. The first wave is seen as the Pentecostal movement, starting at the beginning of this century, and the second wave is seen as the charismatic movement dating back to 1960. The Third Wave does not replace the other two waves but is simply seen as a different expression of the same kind of renewal in the Holy Spirit.[3]

The Third Wave movement is a diverse renewal movement. Many evangelicals in the movement come from reformed and dispensational backgrounds. Although Third Wavers applaud the work of the Holy Spirit in the first two waves, they perceive themselves as having certain important differences with Pentecostal and charismatic terminology, teachings and practices.[4] They testify to experiencing the Spirit's supernatural and miraculous ministry, though usually without recognizing a baptism in the Spirit separate from conversion (1 Cor. 12:13). At the same time, they acknowledge the need to be filled and empowered by the Holy Spirit more than once after conversion (Acts 4:8,31; 7:55; 13:9,52; Eph. 5:18). They exercise the miraculous gifts of the Spirit with much less emphasis on the gift of tongues. They emphasize lay ministry and the potential of all Christians, not just specially gifted people, to minister healing and to minister with all the miraculous gifts (Matt. 7:7-11; John 14:12; 1 Cor. 12:7; 14:1,5,12,13,24,31). They also emphasize power evangelism—the strategic place of signs and wonders, healing ministry, miraculous gifts, and power encounters in evangelism and church planting.[5]

Those in the Third Wave generally do not identify themselves as either Pentecostal or charismatic and have either remained in their non-Pentecostal, noncharismatic mainline denominational church traditions or have formed independent church movements unrelated to any denomination—"post-denominational" churches according to C. Peter Wagner[6] (e.g., the Vineyard Christian Fellowship movement in North America and abroad, Nepal Christian Fellowship churches in Nepal, Deeper Life Bible Churches in Nigeria and throughout Africa, the Chinese house-church movement).

The Third Wave movement is not the result of the intersecting ministries of C. Peter Wagner and John Wimber, though Wagner and Wimber along with many others (Charles H. Kraft, John White, Wayne Grudem, David Pytches, Don Williams, Ken Blue, George Mallone) have articulated the distinctive theological views and practices shared by many in the Third Wave movement around the world. Many evangelical church leaders, including those just named, underwent paradigm shifts in their thinking, attitudes and ministry in which the signs and wonders recorded in the Gospels and Acts were no longer regarded as occurring only on the mission field or in the past. These leaders began to see God's miraculous work and signs and wonders as relevant to evangelism and church growth today in North America as well as around the world.

The leadership of John Wimber and the Vineyard Christian Fellowship has been a major factor in stimulating such a paradigm shift among traditional evangelicals. Wimber underwent his own paradigm shifts around 1978 when he founded the Vineyard Christian Fellowship of Anaheim, which rapidly developed from a home Bible study into one of America's most outstanding megachurches. Wimber systematized his teaching on power evangelism, the work of the Holy Spirit, spiritual gifts and healing, by teaching for several years the much-publicized Fuller Seminary course "MC510: Signs, Wonders, and Church Growth" and by publishing books on these subjects.[7] During Wimber's years of teaching at Fuller, Professor C. Peter Wagner, a Congregationalist, and Professor Charles Kraft of the Evangelical Covenant Church became overt proponents of Wimber's teaching and ministry models, and they wrote books of their own.[8] Wagner began to research and write on the relationship of signs and wonders to church growth in the early 1970s and 1980s. More recently, Wagner is researching and writing on the relationship of prayer and spiritual warfare to evangelism and church growth.[9]

The Third Wave movement is not simply a North American phenomenon. The movement embraces a worldwide renewal characterized by the Holy Spirit's miraculous work in the spread of the gospel and in day-to-day church ministry without direct ties to the Pentecostal or charismatic movements. It includes a spectrum of the

Body of Christ as diverse as the Southern Baptist Fullness Movement (2,000 pastors);[10] the Chinese house-church movement; the "Mekane Yesus" Lutheran Church (750,000 members in 1986) in Ethiopia; some of the largest Baptist, Methodist and Presbyterian churches in the world located in South Korea; many Baptist churches in Northeast India; the Nepal Christian Fellowship association of churches (60,000 members); and the Deeper Life Bible Church in Lagos, Nigeria (nearly 100,000 members with 4,500 satellite churches throughout Africa).

The Third Wave movement is comprised of evangelicals whom Michael Cassidy of African Enterprise described as those who "live in that theological twilight between a rather rigid evangelicalism and a full-blown Pentecostalism."[11] Anglican Canon James Wong of Singapore described the same renewal movement not "as a charismatic force" but as a "new wave of the Holy Spirit" and "a tremendous revival and awakening of spiritual hunger in the hearts of people when they see the Holy Spirit working sovereignly with signs and wonders."[12]

Thus, the Third Wave movement embraces part of the unprecedented growth of evangelical Christianity attended by the miraculous work of the Spirit, healing, and signs and wonders in the latter half of the twentieth century around the world in such places as China, South Korea, Latin America (most recently Argentina and Brazil), West and East Africa, Sudan and Nepal. In China, David Wang, International Director of Asian Outreach, which ministers in 20 Asian nations, has given first-hand reports since the early 1980s of multitudes of simple Chinese people coming to Christ through signs and wonders, healing and miraculous demonstrations of Christ's power. Current estimates, according to Wagner and Wang, are that 35,000 Chinese are becoming Christians every day as a result of the miraculous work of the Spirit confirming the gospel there.[13]

In Ethiopia, the "Mekane Yesus" Lutheran church grew from 140,000 members in 1970 to 750,000 members in several congregations in 1986. Signs and wonders—expulsion of evil spirits, healings, power encounters—were a major factor of growth according to 60 to 80 percent of the members interviewed in the satellite congregations.[14] In Korea, the Sung Rak Baptist Church in Seoul, which has 40,000 members, is pastored by Ki Dong Kim and has its roots in the U. S. Southern Baptist Convention. The signs and wonders attending evangelism and ministry that have been reported by Ki Dong Kim include raising people from the dead, expelling demons, and many being healed who were once totally crippled but who now walk. The two largest Methodist churches in the world are located in Inchon and Seoul, South Korea. Both have 20 to 30,000 members and report that signs and wonders are a normal component of their evangelism and ministry.[15]

In northeast India, Baptist churches report that signs and wonders, healings and expulsion of demons are a frequent and normal part of evangelism and ministry.[16] Paul Eschleman of the Jesus Film Project (Campus Crusade) reports that in such places as Thailand, India and the Solomon Islands, signs and wonders, healings and demon expulsions have followed and confirmed the preaching of the gospel among new converts to Christ and in the newly formed home-fellowship groups spawned by the influence of the *Jesus* film. Third World converts seem to take literally the message of the Gospel of Luke in the *Jesus* film and believe that Jesus heals and casts out demons today.[17]

In 1976, Nepal had only 500 baptized believers. By 1986, the Nepal Christian Fellowship counted 60,000 converts to Christ. Today, the Bethel Church, pastored by Lok Bhandari, one of the largest churches in Nepal, has a 2,000-seat worship center. The Nepal Christian Fellowship association of churches does not identify itself as Pentecostal or charismatic, but reports that signs and wonders, healings and deliverances are a normal part of evangelism and ministry in their churches.[18]

In 1949-1950, China had only 1 million Protestant believers. By the mid-1980s, conservative estimates put the number at 50 million converts to Christ. The Chinese house churches are not affiliated with the Pentecostal or charismatic movements, but it is well known that signs and wonders, prophecies, healings, demon expulsions, tongues and miraculous ministries are a normal part of evangelism and ministry in a majority of the house churches. The miraculous work of the Holy Spirit is simply considered by the Chinese believers to be a normal part of Christian experience and is almost taken for granted.[19]

Indigenous post-denominational churches, such as evangelical, Bible-centered examples of African independent churches and Latin American independent churches, can be included here among churches that are unaffiliated with the Pentecostal or charismatic movements but where signs and wonders, healings and demon expulsions are a normal part of evangelism and church life. Pastor William Kumuyi's Deeper Life Bible Church in Lagos, Nigeria, for example, has nearly 100,000 baptized believers and has planted 4,500 other churches in Nigeria and 35 other African nations. The "Waves of Love and Peace Church" founded by Hector Gimenez has 150,000 members in Buenos Aires, Argentina, and has planted numerous satellite churches.[20] —GSG

References: [1]C. Peter Wagner, "A Third Wave?" *Pastoral Renewal* 8/1 (July-August, 1983): 1-6; id., "The Third Wave," *Christian Life* (Sept., 1984):90; id., *The Third Wave of the Holy Spirit* (Ann Arbor: Servant, 1988); id., *How to Have a Healing Ministry in Any Church* (Ventura, Calif.: Regal, 1988). [2]D. B. Barrett, "Statistics, Global," in Burgess et al., eds., *Dictionary of Pentecostal and Charismatic Movements* (Grand Rapids: Zondervan, 1988), pp. 810, 812-813. [3]C. P. Wagner, "Third Wave," in S. M. Burgess et al., eds., *Dictionary of Pentecostal and Charismatic Movements* (Grand Rapids: Zondervan, 1988), p. 843f. [4]Ibid.; D. B. Barrett, "The Twentieth-Century Pentecostal/Charismatic Renewal in the Holy Spirit, with Its Goal of World Evangelization," *International Bulletin of Missionary Research* (July, 1988): 7; id., "Statistics, Global," in S. M. Burgess et al., eds., *Dictionary of Pentecostal and Charismatic Movements* (Grand Rapids: Zondervan, 1988), p. 820f. [5]A leading expression of Third Wave theology and practice has been articulated by John Wimber and Kevin Springer as well as C. Peter Wagner and Charles H. Kraft, with various contributions by Wayne Grudem, David Pytches, Don Williams, Ken Blue, George Mallone and others: John Wimber and Kevin Springer, *Power Points: Your Action Plan to Hear God's Voice, Believe God's*

Word, Seek the Father, Submit to Christ, Take Up the Cross, Depend on the Holy Spirit, Fulfill the Great Commission (San Francisco: HarperSanFrancisco, 1991); id., *Power Evangelism*, 2nd revised and expanded ed. (San Francisco: HarperSanFrancisco, 1992); id., *Power Healing* (San Francisco: HarperSanFrancisco, 1987); Kevin Springer, ed., *Power Encounters Among Christians in the Western World* (San Francisco: HarperSanFrancisco, 1988); C. Peter Wagner, *The Third Wave of the Holy Spirit* (Ann Arbor: Servant, 1988); id., *How to Have a Healing Ministry in Any Church* (Ventura, Calif.: Regal, 1988); Charles H. Kraft, *Christianity with Power: Your Worldview and Your Experience of the Supernatural* (Ann Arbor: Servant, 1989); id., *Defeating Dark Angels* (Ann Arbor: Servant, 1992); Ken Blue, *Authority to Heal* (Downers Grove, Ill.: InterVarsity, 1987); Wayne Grudem, *The Gift of Prophecy in the New Testament and Today* (Wheaton, Ill.: Crossway, 1988); George Mallone, *Those Controversial Gifts* (Downers Grove, Ill.: InterVarsity, 1983); id., *Arming for Spiritual Warfare* (Downers Grove, Ill.: InterVarsity, 1991); David Pytches, *Come, Holy Spirit* (London: Hodder & Stoughton, 1985) —published in North America as *Spiritual Gifts in the Local Church* (Minneapolis: Bethany, 1985); Don Williams, *Signs, Wonders, and the Kingdom of God* (Ann Arbor: Servant, 1989); id., "Following Christ's Example: A Biblical View of Discipleship," in G. S. Greig and K. N. Springer, *The Kingdom and the Power* (Ventura, Calif.: Regal, 1993), pp. 175-196. [6]C. P. Wagner, "Those Amazing Post-denominational Churches," *Ministries Today* 7-8 (1994): 49ff. [7]See note 5. [8]See note 5. [9]C. P. Wagner, *Engaging the Enemy* (Ventura, Calif.: Regal, 1991); id., *Warfare Prayer* (Ventura, Calif.: Regal, 1992); id., *Prayer Shield: How to Intercede for Pastors* (Ventura, Calif.: Regal, 1992); id., *Breaking Strongholds in Your City* (Ventura, Calif.: Regal, 1993); id., *Churches That Pray* (Ventura, Calif.: Regal, 1993). [10]Barrett, "Statistics, Global," in S. M. Burgess et al., eds., *Dictionary of Pentecostal and Charismatic Movements* (Grand Rapids: Zondervan, 1988), p. 827. [11]Michael Cassidy, *Bursting the Wineskins* (Wheaton, Ill.: Harold Shaw, 1983), p. 11. [12]James Wong, "Reaching the Unreached," *The Courier* (March-April, 1984): 6. [13]Wagner, "Post-denominational Churches," p. 53. [14]C. P. Wagner, "Church Growth," in S. M. Burgess et al., eds., *Dictionary of Pentecostal and Charismatic Movements* (Grand Rapids: Zondervan, 1988), p. 189. [15]Ibid., p. 190. [16]Ibid. [17]Ibid. [18]Ibid., David Wang, *Prayer Track News (AD 2000 Prayer Track)* 1/3 (1992):2. [19]Wagner, "Church Growth," p. 190; id., *How to Have a Healing Ministry*, p. 80; Sharon

Mumper, "Where in the World Is the Church Growing?" *Christianity Today* (July 11, 1986): 17; Karen M. Feaver, "Chinese Lessons: What Chinese Christians Taught a U. S. Congressional Delegation," *Christianity Today* (May 16, 1994): 33-34. [20]Wagner, "Post-denominational Churches," pp. 49, 52.

THOMAS

One of the 12 apostles.

Thomas's reluctance to believe in the resurrection of Jesus has earned him the nickname "doubting Thomas." Actually, he was the first of the disciples to indicate a willingness to die for Christ (John 11:16). His ministry after Pentecost is not detailed in the Scriptures, but it is widely believed that he carried the gospel as far east as India.

References: William Barclay, *The Master's Men* (Nashville: Abingdon, 1976); Leslie B. Flynn, *The Twelve* (Wheaton, Ill.: Victor Books, 1985); William Steuart McBirnie, *The Search for the Twelve Apostles* (Wheaton, Ill.: Tyndale House Publishers, 1973).

THOMSON, JAMES (?–1850)

First Protestant missionary to Latin America.

A native of Scotland, James Thomson became the first Protestant missionary to Latin America when he arrived in Argentina in 1818. Recognizing the need for schools and the lack of qualified teachers, Thomson established Lancastrian Schools throughout the country, a system whereby the teacher "hears" the lessons read to him or her by the older students, then the older students listen to, and correct, the younger students as they read the lessons. Using the Lancastrian System of education, more students could be taught by using a minimal number of certified teachers. As a representative of the British and Foreign Bible Society, Thomson incorporated the Bible as the primary textbook in his schools. His success resulted in his being made an honorary citizen of Argentina and invitations to extend his ministry in Chile and Colombia.

Thomson's greatest contribution to evangelism was the development of education and Bible distribution as effective evangelistic strategies.

THREE BATTLEGROUNDS

A term popularized by Francis Frangipane that deals with the three arenas of spiritual warfare—the mind, the church and the heavenly places. (Dean Sherman employs the same term in reference to the mind, the heart and the mouth).—GOJR

THREE HEARINGS, THE LAW OF
See SEVEN TOUCHES

The conclusion, based on research, that first-time visitors to a church usually attend an average of 3.4 times before deciding to accept Christ or join the church.

The phenomenon is similar to a person purchasing a new suit: the more significant the purchase, the longer it takes some people to make up their minds. This does not mean that some are not saved the first time they visit a gospel-preaching church. The time it takes to get someone saved depends on the person's receptivity to the gospel and responsiveness to the church. The figure 3.4 is a statistical average and implies those who make permanent decisions for Christ usually attend church about three times before they decide to be saved.

THREE PRIORITIES

(1) Commitment to Jesus Christ, (2) commitment to the body of Christ and (3) commitment to the work of Christ in the world.

TORREY, REUBEN ARCHER
(1856–1928)

American evangelist and educator.

Born on January 28, 1856, in Hoboken, New Jersey, R. A. Torrey graduated from Yale as well as universities in Germany. In 1889, he became the pastor of Moody Memorial Church and supervisor of the Moody Bible Institute, positions he held until 1908. He also pastored the Chicago Avenue Church.

From 1912–1924, he pastored the Church of the Open Door in Los Angeles and was dean of the Bible Institute of Los Angeles (Biola College). Among his many books, *How to Pray* was apparently effective in bringing revival to many churches and communities where it was read. He was also a key leader in developing the 12-volume work opposing modernism called *The Fundamentals*.

Torrey is best known as an evangelist and is credited with causing 100,000 professions of faith to be made through his ministry. D. L. Moody often relied on Torrey to prepare churches for his citywide crusades. Torrey also had a prominent role in the widespread revivals in the first decade of the twentieth century. Torrey conducted evangelistic campaigns around the world, many along with music evangelist Charles Alexander. Torrey's sermons appealed to the intellect, but he also emphasized the power of the Holy Spirit in the Christian life. He was also a skilled personal evangelist, and believed in the importance of evangelism. He wrote, "It is a great privilege to preach the Gospel, but this world can be reached and evangelized far more quickly and thoroughly by personal work than by public preaching."

Torrey's writings continue to be read widely, particularly his books about the work of the Holy Spirit and revival. He died on October 26, 1928.

Torrey contributed to evangelism on three fronts. As an evangelist, he was directly involved in the conversion of 100,000 people. As a revivalist, his preaching and books brought revival to churches and communities. As an educator, he helped shape the character of two schools that continue to train missionaries and Christian workers today.

References: R. A. Torrey, *How to Work for Christ* (Grand Rapids: Fleming H. Revell, n.d.); *The Baptism With the Holy Spirit* (Grand Rapids: Fleming H. Revell, 1897); *How to Promote and Conduct a Successful Revival* (Grand Rapids: Fleming H. Revell, 1901); *How to Obtain the Fullness of Power* ((Grand Rapids: Fleming H. Revell, 1897).

TOTAL DEPRAVITY

The doctrine that sin has influence of every aspect of a person, and that a person can do nothing to save him- or herself or gain merit before the Lord. It is also called "original sin" and/or "pollution." Total depravity is one's condition from birth, and influences what one does.

TOUR QUESTIONS

Questions designed to encourage respondents to provide an interviewer with full descriptions of particular places or experiences. — GOJR

TOWNS, ELMER L.

Dr. Elmer Towns, born in 1932 in Savannah, Georgia, made his first significant contribution to church growth with the research and publication of *The Ten Largest Sunday Schools and What Made Them Grow* (Baker, 1969, 10 editions). C. Peter Wagner calls this book the first study on church growth in the United States. The findings had a significant influence for several reasons. First, Towns developed a sociological modeling research tool that inducted principles of ministry and church growth from growing churches. Second, these churches in turn became models that motivated many churches to grow (during a period when media reflected a downward trend in church growth). Third, Towns used his position as Sunday School editor of *Christian Life* magazine to popularize the results of his study, especially in the annual listing of the 100 largest Sunday Schools.

Towns wrote five other books that modeled growing churches: *Church Aflame* (Impact Books, 1971); *Capturing a Town for Christ* (Fleming H. Revell, 1973); *America's Fastest Growing Churches* (Impact Books, 1972); *The World's Largest Sunday School* (Thomas Nelson, 1974); and *Great Soul-Winning Churches* (The Sword of the Lord, 1973). Towns compiled the list of the 100 largest Sunday Schools for 10 years, 1967-1976 (*Christian Life*), and the list of the fastest growing Sunday Schools for 10 years, 1973-1982 (*Christian Life* and *Moody* magazine). *The Complete Book of Church Growth* (Tyndale House Publishers, 1981) concluded that there were seven church types that were catalysts for growth.

Towns has never left his Sunday School roots. He was first brought to Sunday School as a five-

year-old boy to the Eastern Heights Presbyterian Church, Savannah, Georgia, and there he earned 14 years of Sunday School pins for perfect attendance. His first pastorate was the Westminster Presbyterian Church, Savannah, Georgia, 1952-1953. While doing research on the phenomenal growth of Thomas Road Baptist Church, Lynchburg, Virginia, 1971-1973, he also served as Sunday School superintendent of that church to implement the laws of growth he had discovered in his research of the largest Sunday Schools.

Although Towns is presently known in the field of church growth, his original professional contribution was in religious education. He was associate professor of Christian Education, Midwest Bible College, St. Louis, Missouri, 1958-1961; professor of Christian Education, Winnipeg Bible College, Winnipeg, Manitoba, Canada, 1961-1965 (he was also president of the college); and associate professor of Christian Education, Trinity Evangelical Divinity School, Deerfield, Illinois, 1965-1971. During this time, he wrote *Successful Lesson Preparation* (Baker Book House, 1968); *Successful Ministry to Single Adults* (Regal Books, 1967); *The History of Religious Educators* (Baker Book House, 1975); *Team Teaching with Success* (Standard Publishing, 1971); *Teaching Teens* (Baker Book House, 1967).

Towns was a member of the advisory board for the Evangelical Teacher Training Association for whom he wrote two teacher manuals and the textbook *Evangelize Through Christian Education*, 1970. He also wrote for the Accent Teacher Training Series, *How to Grow an Effective Sunday School* (Accent Books, 1979, translated into three languages).

Finally, in the field of Sunday School, Towns wrote *The Successful Sunday School and Teacher's Guide Book* (Creation House, 1975) and *Towns' Sunday School Encyclopedia* (Tyndale House Publishers, 1991).

Towns attended Fuller Theological Seminary in Pasadena, California, to earn a D.Min. degree in church growth in 1982. In his dissertation, he examined the spiritual gift of faith as it is related to church growth. He surveyed the Liberty Baptist Fellowship for church planting and determined that Jerry Falwell's primary strength in church growth was the gift of faith, and this has been communicated to his students. Towns had each pastor measure the intensity of his faith on a scale of 1 to 10 and then showed a correlation between those who had the fastest church growth and those who had the highest assessment of faith. This sociological assessment of the role of faith in church growth is published in *Stepping Out on Faith* (Tyndale House Publishers, 1984).

Towns was converted to Christ on July 15, 1950, at a small Presbyterian mission in Bonnabella, Georgia. He attended Columbia Bible College, South Carolina, 1950-1953, where he met his wife, Ruth Forbes. He graduated from Northwestern College, Minneapolis, Minnesota, in 1954. The next four years were spent at Dallas Theological Seminary where he became a Baptist under the preaching of Dr. W. A. Criswell, pastor of First Baptist Church. There he developed a love for large growing churches. While in Dallas, he attended Southern Methodist University and earned his M.A. in education in 1958. He also received a Th.M. from Dallas Seminary the same year.

Towns taught at the small Midwest Bible College, St. Louis, Missouri, from 1958 to 1961, where Christian education was his main field, but he also taught theology, Bible, evangelism and philosophy. Most importantly, he was secretary to the national committee that brought the National Sunday School Convention to St. Louis in 1960. Because of his research in Thomas Road Baptist Church, Towns was asked to be cofounder of Liberty Baptist College, Lynchburg, Virginia. This gave him an opportunity to train pastors to produce church growth.

Towns presently serves as dean of Liberty University School of Religion. During his ministry, Towns has presented lectures at more than 50 colleges and seminaries in this country and abroad. He and his wife have three children—two daughters and a son.

TRADITION BEARERS

A term developed by folklife scholars to describe individuals whose good memories, unique roles, performance skills and/or long lives make them especially well qualified to provide information about a given community. —GOJR

TRANSFER CHURCH GROWTH

The increase of certain congregations when members transfer from one church to another, and are accepted into the receiving church by a letter of recommendation from the sending church.

TROTTER, MELVIN ERNEST (1870–1940)

The "Bishop of the Bowery."

Born in Orangeville, Illinois into the home of a godly mother and an alcoholic father, Mel Trotter chose to follow the example of his father. After years in a destructive lifestyle, Trotter stumbled into the Pacific Garden Mission in Chicago and was converted to Christ. Later, he was ordained as a Presbyterian minister and was called to be the superintendent of a rescue mission in Grand Rapids, Michigan. His zeal for that ministry resulted in his establishing 67 rescue missions across America.

Although Trotter also saw some success in evangelistic crusades, his greatest contribution to evangelism was achieved through establishing rescue missions in major American centers.

TRUETT, GEORGE W. (1867–1944)

Longtime pastor of the world's largest church.

Born on May 6, 1867, in Hayesville, North Carolina, George Truett was converted to Christ at age 19. He was ordained to the gospel ministry in 1890 and graduated from Baylor University in 1897. In September of that year, he was called as the pastor of First Baptist Church in Dallas, Texas, and remained there for 47 years. Under his leadership, there were 18,124 additions to the church, including 5,337 baptisms. Sunday School attendance reached 4,000, and First Baptist in Dallas became the world's largest church. Truett's influence extended beyond his church. He served as president of both the Southern Baptist Convention (1927–1929) and

Baptist World Alliance (1934–1939).

Truett's greatest contribution to evangelism was achieved in establishing a strong church that continues to be influential today.

TWENTIETH-CENTURY AWAKENING

Early in this present century, another worldwide outpouring of the Holy Spirit occurred. Significant regional revivals were reported in Australia and New Zealand (1902), Wales (1904), Korea (1905), Manchuria (1906) and other places. Describing the scope of this revival, J. Edwin Orr writes:

> It was the most extensive evangelical awakening of all time, reviving Anglican, Baptists, Congregational, Disciple, Lutheran, Methodist, Presbyterian and Reformed churches and other evangelical bodies throughout Europe and North America, Australia and South Africa, and their daughter churches and missionary causes throughout Asia, Africa, and Latin America, winning more than five million folk to an evangelical faith in the two years of greatest impact in each country. In the wake of the revival, there arose the Pentecostal denominations.[1]

Although isolated revivals have continued to be experienced throughout this century, the worldwide influence of the early twentieth-century revival came to an end with the outbreak of world conflict in 1914. Neither the postwar economic boom nor the Great Depression appeared to encourage revival in Western churches, nor did the advent of World War II (1939–1945). Evangelical energies that might have been devoted to revival and evangelism were expended in the fundamentalist/modernist controversy and the prohibition movement. There were exceptions to this rule, but they tended to be short lived and lacked the effectiveness of previous revivals.

Reference: [1] J. Edwin Orr, *A Call for the Re-study of Revival and Revivalism*, p. 41.

TWO-HUMPED CAMEL, LAW OF

A growing Sunday School will have an attendance chart that looks like a two-humped camel. Growth is experienced in the spring and fall, and attendance dips in the summer and winter (unless the area is affected by holidays or vacations). Because these are seasons when Sunday Schools grow, attendance goals should be set and outreach campaigns conducted in the growth seasons, not at other times of the year.

There are 36 to 37 weeks in the Sunday School growth year (the Sunday after Labor Day until the Sunday before Memorial Day weekend). Plan growth in the fall and spring, the primary growth weeks in the Sunday School.

TWO HUNDRED BARRIER

The most formidable numerical barrier to church growth. This represents a range of 150–250 reasonably active adults in attendance. In a context emphasizing church growth through Sunday School expansion, this is called the Class Sunday School or One-Room Sunday School.

Reference: Bill Sullivan *Ten Steps to Break the 200 Barrier* (Kansas City, Mo.: Nazarene Publishing House, 1992).

TYNDALE, WILLIAM (C.1494–1536)

Bible translator.

Ordained to the priesthood in 1521, William Tyndale broke with the Roman Catholic church and pursued his dream of making the Scriptures available to the ploughboys of England. His break with the Church forced him to leave England and pursue his dream in Europe. In 1525, his translation of the New Testament became the first printed English New Testament. Tyndale also translated much of the Old Testament before he was betrayed by a friend and arrested in Brussels, Belgium. He was condemned as a heretic, strangled, and his body burned. His last words were reported to be, "Lord, open the King of England's eyes." Less than a century later, the *King James Version* of the

Bible (1611) was published, using about 60 percent of Tyndale's translation.

Tyndale's greatest contribution to the cause of evangelism was achieved through his translation of the Scriptures into English.

TYPES OF CHURCH GROWTH, OR WORSHIP TYPES

Originally identified by the author in *The Complete Book of Church Growth* and since modified to more accurately reflect the unique church types, these six primary typologies are based on worship and ministry styles. They include:

1. The evangelistic church, characterized by organized evangelistic outreach (soul winning, networking according to a plan) with individual religious response, pastor-led churches, evangelistic preaching (revival, seeker sensitive), and emphasis on numerical growth as evidence of divine endorsement.

2. The body-life church, characterized as unified bodies, controlled by love as a lifestyle, servant leadership and ministering laity. This church does most of its ministry through small groups and emphasizes the New Testament ministry of *koinonia* (fellowship). Church growth is initiated by personal concern (never organized or manipulative).

3. The renewal church, has an emphasis on the presence of God in its meetings, sharply altered lifestyles based on spiritual giftedness, enthusiasm and an emphasis on organism rather than the organization of the church. Those attending a renewal church expect the touch of God as in a revival. These churches may be conservative (Keswick churches) or charismatic in theology (charismatic movement).

4. The expositional Bible church, characterized by strong expository Bible teaching in the worship service and emphasis on the edification of believers. The pastor equips the saints to do the task of evangelization, spiritual leaders are disciplined, an intense caring spirit is manifested and it usually has a plurality of godly leaders.

5. The congregational church. This is a church of the people, featuring informal services, high involvement by the people, sermons of exhortation and a well-rounded program for all types of ministries to all ages and needs of its members.

6. The liturgical church, characterized by an emphasis on liturgical (traditional or "high church") worship, nurture of members, service outreach and attention to internal programs. This church is usually not evangelistic in the worship service, but centers on worshiping God (i.e., giving "worthship" to God).

UNIVERSALISM

Claims that all people are born the children of God, hence denies the necessity of Christ's dying for sin. It teaches that all religions lead to the same destination. Also holds the belief that there is no eternal punishment for sin, hence there is no need for salvation.

UNREACHED PEOPLE GROUP

A people group among which there is no indigenous community of believing Christians with adequate numbers and resources to evangelize its people.

How to Identify Unreached People Groups in Your Community

Some Christians struggle with the reality of unreached people groups living within their communities. This is especially true of second- and third-generation Christians attending stable evangelical churches located in communities in transition.

Two significant sociological factors have influenced many communities, resulting in the presence of unreached people groups. First, a steady decline has been occurring in the influence of Christian values on American society. Second, immigration patterns have resulted in large numbers of people from other countries moving to North American cities and significantly changing the demographics of those cities. Some cities, such as Toronto and Philadelphia, are becoming increasingly more cosmopolitan as they become home to people from a variety of nations. Others such as Vancouver and Miami are actually being transformed culturally as significant numbers of Asians and Latinos begin calling these cities home.

Regardless of the source of unreached people groups in your community, your presence alongside them suggests God may want you to develop cross-cultural evangelism strategies to reach them with the gospel. The first step in accomplishing this goal involves identifying specific groups to reach. Many churches do this through conducting a demographic survey of their communities. The article in this encyclopedia about demographic studies includes specific suggestions for conducting such a survey.

Some churches fail to recognize an unreached people group because they don't know how. As you evaluate your data, seek to group people in a variety of ways. Some people groups are distinguished by a common ethnic or racial background. Others are held together by a common language. Remember that the variety of dialects within a language reminds us of the variety of people groups within a larger linguistic group. People from Australia, Canada, England and the United States all speak dialects of English, but each group has a distinct cultural identity.

Other sociological factors may be used to group people, including economic status, marital and/or family status and place of origin. Factory workers, yuppies and the unemployed all have different needs and interests that both bind them together as a people group and make them distinctive from other groups. Likewise, a single parent on social assistance has little in common with a recently married couple who have professional careers. Significant differences can exist between former Texans, Georgians and Floridians who live in the same California community.

Once you have identified the various people groups living in your community, the next step is to determine which of those may be classified as unreached. As noted in our previously given definition, a community of people is considered unreached when there is no indigenous church in their midst. Therefore, determine the kind of people who attend the churches in your area. Most evangelical churches in a given community tend to focus their ministries on reaching the historically dominant people group in their communities. Therefore, you may find most of the churches in your community targeting the same people group. Those groups that are neglected because no specific ministry is targeting that group (e.g., ethnic church, Bible study group, outreach mission and so on) should be considered unreached.

How to Evangelize Unreached People Groups in Your Community

As you survey your list of unreached people groups, divide the list into two groups. Some unreached people groups may be part of the extended social network of existing church members, or could easily become a part of that network. The second group includes people groups that have no apparent ties to your church or individual members in the church.

When a church already has members tied to an unreached people group, these church members are key to bridging the church to the community and evangelizing the group. When an evangelical church in a largely White Anglo-Saxon Protestant (WASP) community identified Italian Roman Catholics living in their town as an unreached people group, members of the WASP church who had an Italian background were organized into Bible study groups in an attempt to reach other Italians. Other churches have used a similar approach to reach professional groups.

People groups that are not already linked to your church can also be reached through a strategy of cross-cultural evangelism. After identifying a specific people group, begin praying for them. Ask God to work in the life of that people group to make them responsive to the gospel and receptive to the church. As you pray, ask God to give a person or small group a burden for that people group. That person or small group will become the key to reaching the unreached.

Those who become burdened for the people group should begin studying the unique culture of the group. They should listen to their music to get a feel for the heart of the culture. Some people groups are vastly different (e.g., they speak another language, have different social customs, eat different food and so on). Other groups differ in more subtle ways (e.g., they speak with a slightly different accent, have different values that may not be readily apparent in their lifestyles and so on). To reach an unreached people group, you need to learn to think like a member of that people group.

By having a basic understanding of the people group and its culture, an attempt should be made to make contact and develop relationships through repeated acts of kindness. Your church needs to be a friend to those you are trying to reach. By addressing their felt needs, you can develop a relationship that will enable you to address their ultimate need for Christ and salvation. When a retired English teacher wanted to help her church reach Hispanic farm workers, she volunteered her services through a local school board to tutor students in remedial English. Her interest in the children was appreciated and she and her husband established a social relationship with three Mexican families in an area trailer park. These families later became part of a Spanish mission established by her church.

The key to reaching people groups is through networking them to your church through side-door ministries. You may already have some side-door ministries that could be used to reach unreached people groups (e.g., children's clubs, youth ministry and so on), but you may want to begin others as a part of your outreach strategy (e.g., English as a Second Language classes, an inner-city athletic league and so on). The specific ministries that will be most effective in your church will depend on the felt needs of your target group. The goal of side-door ministries is to provide a setting in which members of the target group are most likely to meet and relate to other caring Christians in a nonthreatening environment.

As individual members of the unreached people group are converted, care should be taken to encourage them to network others in their personal sphere of influence to Christ. Just as the woman Jesus reached at the well in Samaria in turn reached her entire city, so the few members of the people group you reach for Christ will be more effective in reaching other members of that group with the gospel. Avoid the tendency to have people break ties with their indigenous people group and become a part of your own church culture. When this happens, your unreached people group will remain unreached.

Reference: *Global Church Growth* (This magazine's issue focusing on People Group Approach to world evangelization), XXVII, no. 1, (January-March, 1990).

URBANA CONFERENCE

An international student missionary convention sponsored by InterVarsity Christian Fellowship.

This convention, which has been held every three years since 1942 on the campus of the University of Illinois in Urbana/Champaign, Illinois, is primarily directed at motivating university students to consider their involvement in world evangelism. It has proved effective in motivating thousands of students to enlist in short-term and/or career missionary service. The conference is conducted at the end of the year to coincide with the Christmas/New Year's break from university studies.

VACATION BIBLE SCHOOL

Vacation Bible School (VBS) has been described as "Everyday Sunday School."

VBS offers an unequaled opportunity to supplement the Sunday School coverage of Bible subjects. VBS is usually conducted during the morning, afternoon or evening for one or two weeks during the summer months when the public school is dismissed for vacation. VBS is correlated with the Sunday School in that it continues studies of subjects, characters or passages that strengthen the foundation laid in Sunday School.

How to Conserve the Results of Your VBS

In many churches, VBS is announced and open to boys and girls from any church or no church at all. It is viewed as a missionary opportunity. Often these churches may reach a large number of children not involved in a Sunday School. Several things can be done to conserve the results of a VBS outreach and increase the attendance in Sunday School.

If the children are not enrolled in a Sunday School when they come to Vacation Bible School, their names and addresses should be provided to the proper department superintendent or teacher. If children accept Christ or dedicate their lives for service during VBS, this fact should be passed on to their teachers. A home visit may be needed before a child joins the church and is baptized.

The Sunday School teacher should follow up on the new children in VBS by visiting in the homes. Interest thus expressed may result in a family won for Christ. The Sunday School teacher should learn and use the new songs taught during VBS and refer to the characters and stories studied in VBS to aid in bridging the Sunday School and VBS in the minds of the children. Sunday School and VBS should be complementary rather than competing ministries of the church.

VAUGHAN, JOHN

Dr. John Vaughan is author of the *The World's*

Twenty Largest Churches (Baker Book House, 1984), *The Large Church: A Twentieth Century Expression of the First Century Church* (Baker Book House, 1985), and is coauthor of *The Complete Book of Church Growth* (Tyndale House Publishers, 1981) with Elmer Towns and David Seifert. Vaughan and Elmer Towns together published the only comprehensive listing of the 100 largest congregations in the United States.

Vaughan has personally visited most of the world's largest churches and has actively served as a church growth consultant to churches in several states.

Born in 1941, Vaughan's early years were spent in Baptist and Presbyterian churches. Most of his early education was received in Catholic schools. At the age of 16, he made his public profession of faith in Christ in the growing 1,600-member Berclair Baptist Church of Memphis, Tennessee. In 1962, five years later, he married the former Joanne Wooten, and they have a son, John, and a daughter, Johnna, both born in Iowa City, Iowa.

A doctoral graduate in church growth from Fuller Theological Seminary, Pasadena, California, Vaughan's dissertation is titled *Satellite Groups: Valid Church Growth Strategy*. This study analyzes the presuppositions, definitions, illustrations through Christian history and the use of small groups in the large churches of the world. Special attention is given to the use of small groups meeting outside the main campuses of the Jotabeche Methodist Pentecostal Church of Santiago, Chile, Yoido Full Gospel Church of Seoul, Korea and Young Nak Presbyterian Church of Seoul, Korea.

Vaughan has also earned an M.Div. from Southwestern Baptist Theological Seminary and a B.A. in Sociology and History from Memphis State University, Memphis, Tennessee.

VIRGIN BIRTH

The supernatural conception of Jesus Christ in the womb of Mary without the seed of man. The miraculous birth was verified by the statement that she was a virgin, having had no sexual relations with a man.

VISITATION PROGRAM

An organized outreach on the part of a church to contact nonmembers or unsaved persons with a view of getting them to join the church or become Christians. Some churches include other kinds of visits in an organized program, such as visiting absentees, the sick and those who are shut-ins.

Those who visit on behalf of a church are usually trained in personal evangelism. They go to contact prospects that have been supplied to them, or they go home-to-home to contact people for Jesus Christ. Visitation is the one area of church ministry in which it may be said that "everybody's job is nobody's job." Experiments in hit-or-miss visitation compared with an organized plan have proven that a planned program reaches the most people.

Who Visits?

1. The pastor. Just as pastors must set the spiritual pace in other areas of church life, they set the pace for the visitation program by their own examples of regular visitations. Some churches believe they have hired a professional church visitor when they pay the pastor's salary. Visitation is only one of the pastor's many responsibilities and it should be shared with others. Some large churches employ full-time ministers who focus on visitation for evangelism and/or hospital visits.

2. Sunday School workers. Teachers best show their interest and concern when they visit in the home of every student. In a very large class, the responsibility may be shared with assistants. There is no substitute for a home visit to help a teacher become really acquainted with the background and the interests, hopes and fears of the students, whether they are young or old. Until something of the spiritual status and needs of the family is known, there cannot be effective ministry.

Not only should a teacher visit those on the attendance record, but special visits should be made to students confined to the home or a hospital with an extended illness. The teacher also should visit homes of new church attenders who have children of his or her class's age level.

3. The elders/deacons. These usually represent the church rather than the Sunday School when they visit. They should be interested in the Sunday School to the extent that they will encourage attendance on the part of any who may be lax.

4. Other church officers. Paid or unpaid workers in the church should visit absentees and prospects, particularly non-Christians in the Sunday School or in the community.

5. All members. Any Christian should be willing to express interest in an absentee by making a visit. All Christians should be willing to go to the homes of newcomers and extend invitations to the worship service. Older Christians will seek to win the lost to Christ during such visitation, as the Lord opens the way and reveals the need.

When to Visit?

1. At a designated time. Set aside a night or afternoon when all visitors meet at the church to pray and to receive visitation assignments. It encourages all present to see that others are concerned.

2. Whenever possible. Sometimes employment schedules do not allow some teachers or members to visit at the time set by the church. Their visits at another time may be even more fruitful.

3. At times of special need. Bereavement or illness in a family may not coincide with the visitation program. Visits at those times are usually opportunities to extend the greatest help because hearts are the most open to the Word of God. Also, visits should be made to those who are shut-in, in the hospital and/or other institutions.

4. In case of absence. When students are absent, phone them and let them know they are missed. Everyone likes to know someone cares. When a class member is absent two Sundays, visit in the home. After the student is absent three Sundays, the departmental superintendent should visit in the home. If the person is absent four Sundays, the Sunday School superintendent and pastor should do all they can to solve the problem and to reach this family for Christ. Prayer for the person and the family should increase with each absence.

5. Tele-shepherding. In our modern world, the role of "tele-shepherding" is a growing method of visitation (i.e., contacting people by way of the telephone and/or internet computer communication).

Where to Visit?

The answer at first glance would seem to be in the immediate area around the church. The outlook of most churches, however, has changed regarding this practice. A long time ago a church could say: This is my territory. Now, in the age of communication and transportation, the church family is scattered widely.

References: Dale Galloway, *Tele-Shepherding Kit; Tele-Care System: How to Unlock the Power in Prime Time Phone Ministry* (available through New Hope Community Church, Portland, Oreg.); Kent R. Hunter, *Tele-Shepherding: Feeding Sheep in an Electronic World* (Corunna, Ind.: Church Growth Analysis and Learning Center, 1993).

VITAL SIGNS OF A HEALTHY CHURCH

The normal signs of life that are found in healthy and growing churches. Seven vital signs are commonly recognized: (1) the pastor, (2) the people of the church, (3) church size, (4) structure and functions, (5) homogeneous unit, (6) methods and (7) priorities.

WAGNER, C. PETER

Dr. C. Peter Wagner is the Donald A. McGavran Professor of Church Growth at Fuller Theological Seminary of World Mission in Pasadena, California. The School of World Mission became a part of Fuller Seminary in 1965 when Donald McGavran, father of the Church Growth Movement, moved his nonacademic Institute of Church Growth to Pasadena from Northwest Christian College in Eugene, Oregon.

Since that time, Fuller Seminary has been the institutional base for the Church Growth Movement, first in its global expression and later in its North American expression. The faculty of missiology, which McGavran founded, now numbers 12 full-time professors and serves more than 700 students annually from 60 to 70 different countries. Studies in church growth are required for graduation in all the degree programs, from M.A. and Th.M. to D.Miss. and Ph.D.

McGavran founded the School of World Mission with the intention of serving students who ministered in the Third World. The scope broadened, however, when Peter Wagner joined the faculty in 1971. Previously Wagner served as a missionary in Bolivia for 16 years. He did evangelistic work, church planting, Bible school and seminary teaching, and also directed the mission, which is now the Andean field of SIM International. During his furlough of 1967-1968, Wagner enrolled as a student at Fuller Seminary (where he received his M.Div. in 1955) and studied under Donald McGavran. McGavran invited him to become a faculty member in 1968, but prior commitments made it impossible at that time. Wagner flew to Pasadena frequently to teach as an adjunct professor, then moved back to the United States with his family in 1971.

Under Peter Wagner's leadership, the field of American church growth developed along two lines: the theoretical and the practical. The theoretical began with an experimental course taught for American pastors in the fall of 1972. Wagner invited McGavran to team teach with him, and the course was a success. Among its students was Win Arn, who almost immediately stepped out in faith and established the Institute for American Church Growth, also located in Pasadena. Both Wagner and McGavran were members of the founding board of directors. For two decades, Arn gave brilliant leadership to the Institute for American Church Growth and ranks as the premier communicator of the Church Growth Movement in North America.

In 1975, the Fuller School of Theology began a new Doctor of Ministry program, and Peter Wagner was asked to teach a church growth course. A second course was soon added. Now students can take up to 80 percent of their D.Min. work in church growth. A helpful feature is that all classes are two weeks long, and only three two-week sessions are needed for the program. Auditors as well as credit students are admitted. As of this writing, more than 1,500 pastors and denominational executives have received church-growth training in the Fuller Doctor of Ministry program.

Wagner's practical contribution to the Church Growth Movement was related to his position as executive director of the Fuller Evangelistic Association, which he assumed simultaneously with his professorship at the seminary. Recognizing the need for professional church growth consultation, in 1975 he invited John Wimber to become the founding director of what is now the Charles E. Fuller Institute of Evangelism and Church Growth. Wimber got the Institute off to an excellent start, then left to become the founding pastor of Vineyard Christian Fellowship of Anaheim and Vineyard Ministries International. Carl George replaced Wimber, and the Fuller Institute has since become a leader in providing church growth consultation for both churches and denominations.

In addition to his two degrees from Fuller Seminary, Wagner holds a Th.M. from Princeton Seminary and a Ph.D. from the University of Southern California. He did his undergraduate work at Rutgers University.

Peter Wagner is a prolific author and has written more than three dozen books about missions and church growth. His best-selling book is *Your Spiritual Gifts Can Help Your Church Grow* (Regal Books, 1976; rev. ed. 1994), which has almost 200,000 copies in print. Closely following is *Your Church Can Grow* (Regal Books, 1974; rev. ed. 1984). More recently, he has been researching and writing about the relationship of prayer and spiritual warfare to church growth. His Prayer Warrior Series, published by Regal Books, comprises *Warfare Prayer* (1992), *Prayer Shield* (1992), *Breaking Strongholds in Your City* (1993) and *Churches That Pray* (1993).

Wagner has just completed writing a three-volume commentary about the book of Acts, which, more than other commentaries, highlights the dimensions of missiology and power evangelism associated with the earliest church growth. The commentary, also published by Regal Books, comprises the following three books: *Spreading the Fire* (Book 1, 1994); *Lighting the World* (Book 2, 1995); *Blazing the Way* (Book 3, 1995).

Wagner was instrumental in organizing the American Society for Church Growth, and became its founding president in 1984. In the same year he was honored by Fuller Seminary with the Donald A. McGavran Chair of Church Growth. He serves as international coordinator of the United Prayer Track of the A.D. 2000 and Beyond Movement.

Wagner lives in Altadena, California, with his wife, Doris, who is executive director of Global Harvest Ministries and the A.D. 2000 United Prayer Track. The Wagners have three daughters and six grandchildren.

WAGNER-MODIFIED HOUTS QUESTIONNAIRE
See HOUTS QUESTIONNAIRE

WALDO, PETER (d. 1217)

Founder of the Waldensians.

About 1176, Peter Waldo of Lyons, France was converted to Christ through reading the New Testament. He sold his possessions, keeping only enough to care for his family. He then began organizing a group he called "Poor in Spirit." This movement emphasized lay preaching, something that was forbidden by the Church at that time.

In 1184, Waldo and his followers were excommunicated from the Catholic church. The movement continued emphasizing many values that would later characterize the Protestant Reformers. The movement had a strong emphasis on biblical authority and simplicity in lifestyle. Waldo continued to lead the movement until his death in 1217. Despite intense persecution through the centuries, a small band of Waldensians exists today across the mountains from Lyons, in northern Italy.

Waldo's greatest contribution to evangelism was in establishing a movement of lay preachers during the middle ages.

Reference: E. Comba, *Waldo and the Waldensians Before the Reformation* (New York: Robert Carter & Brothers, 1880).

WARFARE PRAYER

The application of strategic-level spiritual warfare to evangelistic efforts. An uprooting of prevailing spiritual strongholds that hinders the gospel. —GOJR

WEB MOVEMENTS

Movements through natural ties of friends and family to compel many to come to Christ.

How to Identify Your Personal Sphere of Influence

The Great Commission calls the Church to be actively involved in the process of making disciples (Matt. 28:19). As we understand this mandate, it means that each of us needs to be involved in the process of bringing people to faith in Christ, assimilating them into the life of the Church, and discipling them in their Christian life and witness.

Sometimes we make the mistake of thinking the Great Commission is meant for missionaries serving in some pagan mission field. But the really exciting thing is that God has already placed you in a unique mission field of your own. He has given each of us a unique sphere of influence composed of our friends, relatives, associates and neighbors (FRANs).

Research into what influences people to come to faith in Christ consistently suggests they are most likely to be reached through the witness of a Christian with whom they have developed a meaningful relationship. By taking a few minutes to survey your personal sphere of influence, you can identify those you are most likely to be effective in reaching for Christ.

Begin your survey of your personal sphere of influence with your family. As you think of your extended family, list those who are related to you by blood and marriage who, to the best of your knowledge, do not have a personal relationship with our Lord Jesus Christ.

Next, consider your associates. Associates include those with whom we rub shoulders on a fairly regular basis. Your list might include people you associate with in a workplace or school setting, people you regularly meet through routine activities such as commuting, shopping or working out, and people you know through mutual involvement in various community activities. List all those you know by name who, to the best of your knowledge, are not Christians.

Add to this list your neighbors. As you consider those you know by name living in your immediate community, list each who, to the best of your knowledge, is not a Christian. Of course, you do not want to forget your friends. Some people who may be important to you may not fit into one of the three groups already surveyed. As you consider these friends, list each one who, to the best of your knowledge, is not a Christian.

As you complete this survey, you are identifying those God has placed in your personal sphere of influence. Research in the field of evangelism and church growth suggests that you are the most likely person to be effective in reaching these people for Christ. Use this list as a prayer guide and begin looking for opportunities to communicate the gospel to those who are closest to you.

References: Win Arn, *The Master Plan of Evangelism* (Pasadena, Calif.: Church Growth Press, 1982); Larry Gilbert, *Team Evangelism: Giving New Meaning to Lay*

Evangelism (Lynchburg, Va.: Church Growth Institute, 1991); Elmer L. Towns, *Winning the Winnable: Friendship Evangelism* (Lynchburg, Va.: Church Growth Institute, 1986). See OIKOS EVANGELISM.

WELSH REVIVAL (1904–1906) See TWENTIETH CENTURY AWAKENING

WESLEY, JOHN (1703–1791)

Founder of the Methodists.

Born in Epworth, England, the 15th of 19 children, John Wesley narrowly escaped death when the Wesley home was burned in 1709. He studied at Oxford in 1720 on a scholarship, and was ordained as a priest in the Anglican Church in 1728. In 1735, Wesley traveled with his brother Charles to Savannah, Georgia, to minister to the Indians, but his position against slavery alienated the colonists and he returned to England three years later.

Before his return voyage, Wesley met two Moravian missionaries who talked to him about the new birth. Realizing that he lacked a personal sense of salvation, he became troubled in spirit. Finally, on May 24, 1738, while reading the preface to Luther's *Commentary on Romans* at a meeting in Aldersgate St., London, he was converted, leading to his later reflection that "I felt my heart strangely warmed."

Attempting to share his experience and to revitalize the churches, Wesley found many of them closed to his ideas. He continued to be strongly influenced by the Moravians and borrowed many of their ideas as he organized Bible study and fellowship groups that came to be called Methodist societies.

Wesley's small groups were predictive of the Sunday School that was to come later. Some of his followers in Savannah claimed that he began the first Sunday School in their city in 1736. Careful study, however, shows that Wesley taught the catechism to the children of his parish on Saturday and Sunday afternoons. Although this religious exercise does not fit the technical description of a Sunday School, his desire to reach all children with the gospel was later manifested in the Sunday School movement.

Wesley wrote more than 300 books in his lifetime aimed at helping lay preachers give out the Word of God, again, predictive of the Sunday Schools that provided literature for the lay public. Wesley also worked with the masses outside the established Church. During his lifetime, he traveled about 250,000 miles on horseback throughout the British Isles, and preached 42,000 sermons. He became a champion of the Sunday School movement, incorporating it into the life of the Methodist church, and is widely regarded as a leading revivalist of his day. Although much of his ministry was limited to England, he directed others in the worldwide expansion of Methodism.

Wesley's greatest contribution to evangelism was his organization of Methodist societies to conserve the results of revival and evangelism. Church historians trace the contemporary emphasis on small-group ministry to the influence of Wesley and the early Methodist missionaries to Korea.

Reference: F. J. McConnell, *John Wesley* (Nashville: Abingdon Press, 1939).

WESLEYAN REVIVAL See GREAT AWAKENING

WHITE FLIGHT See ETHNIKITIS

WHITEFIELD, GEORGE (1714–1770)

A major leader in the Great Awakening in both England and the American colonies.

Whitefield was born in Gloucester and was converted while at Oxford University. Whitefield was one of John and Charles Wesley's companions in the "Holy Club" while the three were students at Oxford. Whitefield continued to associate with John Wesley, although serious differences developed between Whitefield's Calvinism and Wesley's Arminian views. Whitefield encouraged the Wesleys to begin the new method of field preaching.

Whitefield came to the colonies on seven visits, and his itinerant ministry is credited with fanning the embers of revival into the flame of the Great Awakening. He developed friendships with many church leaders, including Jonathan

Edwards. He also established the Bethesda orphanage in Georgia.

Whitefield is considered one of the greatest orators in the history of preaching. His influence on American preaching is significant. His simplicity, use of gestures and illustrations, and extemporaneous style was emulated by many. Benjamin Franklin admired Whitefield, reporting on the evangelist's ministry in his paper and hearing him often. Franklin estimated one of Whitefield's open-air crowds at 30,000, a testimony to his unusual oratorical gifts.—ALR

Resources: Harry S. Stout, *The Divine Dramatist: George Whitefield and the Rise of Modern Evangelicalism* (Grand Rapids: William B. Eerdmans, 1991); Arnold Dallimore, *George Whitefield: God's Anointed Servant in the Great Revival of the Eighteenth Century* (Wheaton, Ill.: Crossway Books, 1990).

WILFRID (634–709)

Early English bishop and pioneer missionary to Friesland in the northern Netherlands.

Bishop Wilfrid is credited with reaching the South Saxons and people of the Isle of Wight with the gospel. He also introduced the gospel to Friesland in the winter of 678–679 as a result of being shipwrecked on the coast. His initial success ended following the death of the king who had been supportive of his cause. The people lapsed back into their pagan beliefs until they were later evangelized by Willibrord. Wilfrid completed the evangelization of England and introduced the gospel to Friesland.

WILLIAMS, GEORGE (1821–1905)

Founder of the Young Men's Christian Association (YMCA).

George Williams established the first YMCA in England in 1844. The first American YMCA was established in 1851. In its early years, the YMCA was a center of evangelism. Many citywide evangelists began their careers as YMCA secretaries.

WILLIAMS, JOHN (1796–1839)

Pioneer missionary to the South Pacific islands.

John Williams traveled widely within a 2,000-mile radius of Tahiti from 1817 to 1839, seeking to bring the gospel to the native people of the South Pacific islands. On a trip to the New Hebrides in Melanesia, he and his missionary companion were clubbed to death and eaten by cannibals. Since then, the London Missionary Society has named its mission ships in the South Pacific in his honor.

Williams's greatest contribution to evangelism was in evangelizing the South Pacific islands and establishing a firm foundation upon which future missionary work was developed.

WILLIBRORD (657–738)

Pioneer missionary to Friesland in the northern Netherlands.

Born into a devout English home, Willibrord trained in a monastery at Ripon, which had been established by Wilfrid (see Wilfrid entry). At age 20 he went to Ireland. In 690 he and 11 companions traveled to Utrecht to establish a base for the evangelism of Friesland. He continued in this ministry for nearly half a century. By the time of his death, Christianity had been firmly established in Friesland.

Although other evangelistic missions had been launched before his, Willibrord succeeded in establishing Christianity in Friesland. Also, he was a mentor of Boniface, who also engaged in effective missionary activity.

WINNABLE PEOPLE

Those who are considered receptive to the gospel; those who will respond.

References: See HARVEST PRINCIPLE; RESISTANCE-RECEPTIVITY AXIS.

WINNING, SOUL

Communicating the gospel in an understandable manner and motivating a person to respond.

WORD OF GOD

The record of God's self-revelation to humans and the communication of good news to people at their points of need. As such, the Word is rational and logical. The inspired Word of God is the ultimate revelation of Jesus Christ, who is the incarnate Word of God.

WORDLESS BOOK

The Wordless Book has been used for many years by teachers to present the plan of salvation. It is easy and quick for the teacher to make such a book from construction paper. Obviously, there are no words in the Wordless Book. The teacher should explain each colored page and its spiritual meaning as the pages are shared with the students.

Page 1—black. This black page is used to show the students the blackness of sin in their hearts (Prov. 4:19). Talk about the things we do wrong in making our hearts black with sin. The punishment of this sin is death (Rom. 6:23).

Page 2—red. The red page tells how God made a way for you to have your sins forgiven. Explain that the blood of Jesus Christ—God's Son—cleanses from all sin (1 John 1:7).

Page 3—white. Explain to the students that their hearts can be white as snow when Christ takes away their sins (Isa. 1:18).

Page 4—green. Green represents growth. When we receive Jesus Christ, we shall have everlasting life (John 3:36).

Page 5—gold. Explain that gold represents the streets of heaven where we shall all spend eternity (Rev. 21:18).

WORLD RULERS OF DARKNESS

Demonic forces involved in deceptive and destructive manipulation of natural elements and systems.—GOJR

WORLDVIEW

A philosophical paradigm. The perspective adopted by a given individual or culture about the world that surrounds them.

One's worldview influences what is accepted as truth. For example, if a person's worldview rules out miracles, it is difficult to accept the miracles in the Bible.

We often hear modern people scoff at what they call Scripture's "three-story worldview." They suppose that the Bible's writers believed in an ethereal heaven above a flat earth, hell literally being below the earth's surface. The fact is, the Bible speaks of "the circle of the earth" (Isa. 40:22), and heaven and hell are realities not confined to a geographical worldview.

WORSHIP

Acts and thoughts that ascribe "worthship" or worthiness to the divine. The fact of worship is found from the beginning of Scripture, when Cain and Abel brought offerings to the Lord.

Humans were created for worship. According to the *Westminster Shorter Catechism*, "The chief end of man is to glorify God and to enjoy Him forever." The 24 elders in heaven affirm to God, "You are worthy, O Lord, to receive glory and honor and power; for You created all things, and by Your will they exist and were created" (Rev. 4:11).

Worship demands that fallen humans offer sacrifice. Although God desires obedience over sacrifice (1 Sam. 15:22), the worship of fallen humans always involves some measure of sacrifice. Most Old Testament sacrifices involved shedding blood, which represented the life of the sacrificial animal. In practice, the sacrifice involved giving up of life.

Under the New Covenant, God himself offered the supreme sacrifice—His Son Jesus Christ—in our behalf. Yet Christians still worship by sacrificing to God something pertaining to life (e.g., time, talents, financial resources and influence), and in that way offer sacrifices. In the New Testament Epistle that so clearly explains why the offering of blood sacrifices is not necessary today, the author urges his readers, "Therefore by Him let us continually offer the sacrifice of praise to God, that is, the fruit of our lips, giving thanks to His name" (Heb. 13:15).

Definition from New Testament Words

Worship in the New Testament is perhaps best understood in the context of four principal verbs used to identify various aspects of worship.

1. Latreuo. This word means to serve or render religious service or homage. Although it is often translated "worship" in the New Testament, it is most often translated "serve." The word tends to emphasize worship as a service to God on the part of the worshiper. Anna the prophetess "served God with fasting and prayers" (Luke 2:37). God must get something out of our worship as we minister to Him and serve Him. Hence, some call the church's assemblies the "worship service."

2. Proskuneo. The Greek word *proskuneo* is a compound composed of *pros* meaning "toward" and *kuneo* meaning "to kiss." The word means to make obeisance or do reverence to, and is most often simply translated "worship" in the New Testament. J. N. Darby used the expression "do homage" when translating this term in his English translation of the Bible.

3. Sebomai/sebazomai. These words are related terms conveying the idea of revering God, having an emphasis on a feeling of awe or devotion often associated with worship. This sense of awe or devotion is so strongly implied in these words that four times in the New Testament the word *sebomai* is translated to be "devout" (Acts 13:43,50; 17:4,17).

4. Eusebeo. The fourth verb used in the New Testament to describe worship is *eusebeo*, meaning "to act piously toward." The apostle Paul claimed the Athenians "worshiped" the Unknown God in this way when addressing them on Mars Hill (17:23). The same Greek word is also used by Paul to identify the obligation of children and grandchildren toward their widowed mother or grandmother (1 Tim.5:4). The root idea of this word in both places seems to be that of showing honor toward one who should be honored.

Worship and the Total Person

Worship should be an emotional, intellectual, volitional and moral response to God. Worship is a face-to-face involvement with a living God, based on a regeneration experience, prompted by the Holy Spirit and resulting in the exaltation of God's glory.

Because of this, worship is a growing thing and is a dynamic entity. Worship is personal. True worship cannot be divorced from the worshiper. Worship, we might say, is an earnest effort to recreate the conditions and experiences that have been found to deepen the human's relationship to God.

Worship is not just an intellectual process; it involves more than knowledge and fact. Worship must stir the emotions and result in activity. It begins with a knowledge of the Word of God. The heart moves upon biblical facts to recreate a fundamental experience simply and dramatically, to help the person gain a personal understanding of the Lord. Then the person can give back to God and magnify Him for what He is.

The roots of worship are knowledge, emotions and will. Worship is not a mystical experience; it is at best a spiritual experience. People do not automatically worship because they have Christian knowledge. Worship must be learned, and some people never have the stirring experience of genuine worship of God. Because worship not only affects God, but also the worshiper, this means the person is missing out on an important dimension of the Christian life.

Psychology teaches us that emotions or inner drives control our lives. Only as we display every emotion of love in approbation to God do we truly worship. As a volitional process, worship focuses all of our ideas, actions and feelings in effective tones on a specific center, which is God Himself. All our thinking and action must be wrapped up in worship. Worship can be said to be an emotional and volitional response to an intellectual evaluation.

Too often worship is neglected because it is not understood. We ought to distinguish between worshiping, the worship service and learning to worship. People need to learn how to worship God so they may participate in the actual act of worship. The worship service is often the place where people are most likely to learn worship.

To this point, we have considered worship as an affirmation of God's worthiness in both His person and acts; but worship is more than this. Worship also invites the very power and presence of God to be manifested in the presence of the worshiper or worshiping group. Although one may and should worship God privately, a special uniqueness is involved in corporate worship.

What Is a Worship Service?

Christianity is concerned not only with the end (worship experience and transformed life), but also with the means to an end (media of worship). There are scriptural patterns for both the manner and the instruments of worship. Some organizations claim they worship God, but their practice does not observe the New Testament means of worship. Only an emotional subjective experience is felt and if a change in the life results, it is a self-inflicted change. God invades the life through divinely set instruments and means. Among the common means by which believers worship God today is the worship service.

Our service to God in worship. In the worship service, we first serve God and offer praise to Him. This involves several things. First, we must assemble ourselves together (Heb. 10:25). Then we worship God corporately through such activities as singing unto the Lord (Ps. 96:1), continuing in prayer, the Lord's Supper and sharing the apostle's doctrine (Acts 2:42). This was the essence of the worship service of the Early Church.

Meeting people's needs through worship. Worship not only serves God, but it also meets the needs of those who worship. This is because of the nature of worship in that it invites the very presence of God in the midst of the worshiping body. Although most human needs can be met in a variety of ways, they can be best met in God (i.e., through both His presence and His ministry in our lives).

How to Worship God

The worship of God is a spiritual exercise that involves our total being as we express our praise and service to Him. Worship involves our spirit, our emotions, our will and even our physical being.

1. We worship God with our regenerated spirits. Speaking to the woman at the well, Jesus said, "The hour is coming, and now is, when the true worshipers will worship the Father in spirit and truth; for the Father is seeking such to worship Him" (John 4:23). As we come to worship God, it must first be spiritual in character. This means we worship God with that part of our being that was "made alive" at our conversion. The spiritual character of worship may be one reason worship is restricted to spiritual beings (i.e., angels, or beings with a spirit—e.g., people).

2. We worship God with our renewed minds. Worship is also expressed to God through our renewed minds. The believer should have the mind of Christ (Phil. 2:5), which is also called a renewed mind (Rom. 12:2). The Scriptures link functions of the intellect such as understanding with both prayer (1 Cor. 14:15) and praise (Ps. 47:6,7).

3. We worship God with our revived emotions. God created humans as emotional beings, and He expects that part of our personalities to be involved in the worship of God. "And whatever you do, do it heartily, as to the Lord and not to men" (Col. 3:23). Sometimes the emotions are expressed publicly as we rejoice in the Lord (Ps. 100:1). At other times, our emotions may appear less prominent to others as we are silent before the Lord (46:10).

4. We worship God with our ready wills. The will is also a part of the human personality that must be involved in worship. As noted, among the verbs translated "worship" in the New Testament is the word *latreuo*, which means to serve or render religious service. This can only occur as we exercise our wills, which have been surrendered to the will of God.

5. We worship God with our rededicated bodies. When Paul called on the Romans to "present [their] bodies a living sacrifice" (Rom. 12:1), he did so in language that described the act of worship by a priest offering the whole burnt offering. God wants our bodies surrendered to Him so that we may worship Him. Physical expressions of worship in the Scriptures include kneeling (Phil. 2:9,10), bowing the head (Mic. 6:6-8), raising hands (Ps. 63:3,4) and dancing (Ps. 149:3). Although these and other physical expressions of worship may or may not be appropriate in some circumstances and on some occasions, they illustrate that our physical bodies must also be involved in the worship experience.

Keeping Worship Worshipful

One of the most difficult tasks in leading the worship service is ensuring that it is a service of worship and not just the repetition of a religious ritual of another time. What is meaningful to

people today may not be appropriate next month. A particular song that leads people to worship God will lose its effectiveness when overused. To keep worship "worthy," several principles must be remembered and applied.

1. Preparation. When a speaker addresses a congregation, this is not worship. Worship must include involvement by the people. People, however, may worship God during a sermon if the Lord is lifted up and magnified in the hearts of the people. When the hearts of hearers are correctly prepared for 5 minutes, a 50-minute message may be effective. Preparation is essential to worship.

2. Examination. Sincere worship begins by examining the heart's motives. Why am I attending church? What am I looking for in this service? Am I content with myself? What do I need? How can the Lord speak to me? What do I owe God? As we examine our own hearts' needs before the Lord, we see ourselves as we really are. As we objectify our needs, the Lord can meet these needs.

Note several worship experiences in the Bible in which people examined themselves before worshiping God. When Isaiah was worshiping in the Temple (Isa. 6:1-13) and saw the holiness of God he cried out, "Woe is me, for I am undone! Because I am a man of unclean lips" (v. 5). Note that the praise of the greatness of God is tied to the humility of examining the heart.

In Exodus 3:1-17, God met Moses at the burning bush. After a revelation of the holiness of God in the midst of the bush that burned with fire and was not consumed, Moses examined himself. He cried out, "Who am I that I should go to Pharaoh?" (v. 11). In God's challenge to service, Moses saw his own uselessness.

Worshipers should examine themselves at the communion table. Whether the service is simple or elaborate, the element of examination should be there. When Jesus instituted the Lord's Supper, the question rang out from the hearts of the disciples, "Master, is it I?" (Matt. 26:25, *KJV*). Later, the apostle Paul exhorted those who would worship through the Lord's table, "Let a man examine himself, and so let him eat" (1 Cor. 11:28). When believers participate in the Lord's Supper, it is a time when their hearts in true worship and praise can render unto God the glory and adoration that are due to Him.

Finally, Paul's experience on the Damascus road (Acts 9:1-9) shows that self-examination is at the heart of worship. This experience contained the elements of worship, although it was a time of intense emotion. Here was a man zealously following his conviction—persecuting Christians—when suddenly his whole life is threatened. Paul meets God. In the light of a true revelation of God, Paul falls to his face and examines himself. "Who are You, Lord?...Lord, what do You want me to do?" (v. 5,6) were his responses, just as they may be ours today.

3. *Expectation.* The psalmist said, "My soul, wait silently for God alone, for my expectation is from Him" (Ps. 62:5). Only as people come expecting to meet God can they have true worship experiences. The human spirit inevitably reaches out to the Lord. The pastor can help create an atmosphere of expectancy. God does not need the apostle Paul to speak to people. But when a person endures a worship service where needs are ignored or denied, he or she will not come to the next worship service expecting to meet God. God needs open, expectant hearts among His people. Then they can respond and meet Him. Expectation is a vital element of faith, and faith is needed in a worship experience.

4. *Appropriation.* Worship is a form of human activity. Active people need activity in worship. A person does not participate in a meal unless he or she eats. Likewise, a person doesn't participate in worship unless he or she appropriates the presence of God.

One of the faults in much of Christian worship today is that we do not appropriate what is offered. We do not take what God gives. Worship is not overcoming the acquiescence of God. Worship is laying hold of His willingness. The Father makes available all we need in worship; yet we often do not worship because we have not taken what He has offered.

5. *Meditation.* True worship involves quietness, meditation and thinking. A person receives understanding only by exerting mental effort. Therefore, it takes work to worship. Worship is not coming to an end of activity and effort. It is not just quietness, but quietness that is filled with

reflection, interpretation and integration that produces a spiritual dynamic in the life.

6. *Consummation.* Just as a mountain must have a peak, so the worship experience must come to an end, but not merely through the benediction or closing prayer. The worship service must end in a complete and fitting close. The peak of the worship experience is a dedicated life. The revelation of God demands a response in the worshiper's life. God has revealed truth to produce an experience. Worship is the deepest experience in life. If this worship experience does not overhaul one's thinking and change his or her life, it is meaningless and empty.

7. *Transformation.* Believers must have more than just dedicated lives. They can be dedicated to causes but without strength and ability to carry out the demands of the cause. The enemy, the nature of this world and sin are all against having them living for Christ. Therefore, they need supernatural transformation. Worship should minister to the believers' divine enablement to help them live their lives for the glory of God.

In a true worship experience, believers examine themselves in light of meeting with God. They expect that God can do for them what only God can do. They then appropriate the power and person of the Lord for their lives. Through deep meditation, they dedicate their lives as the result of this experience. With these dedicated lives, they can go out and live for God. Their lives are transformed.

Moses was in the presence of God on the top of Mount Sinai. From this experience he walked again among the people. The people saw the presence of God in his life: "The children of Israel saw the face of Moses, that the skin of Moses' face shone" (Exod. 34:35). Thus, true worship will meet needs and transform lives.

WORSHIP SERVICE: BEGINNING ANOTHER

One of the most frequently asked questions by pastors of growing churches is, "How can I begin another worship service?" They realize that this is the path to growth. In the past, they have usually thought first of a larger auditorium. But a new auditorium may involve other problems such as higher interest payments on borrowed money, unavailable ground, additional parking and so on. Today, the first step to growth is inaugurating multiple worship services.

Some have objected that a second service divides the church into two congregations. Multiple services, however, produce a larger attendance and have a greater evangelistic outreach. Most churches cannot get past the barrier of 100 to 150 in attendance. They are single-cell churches. Adding a second worship service puts the church into a multiple-cell church category. The church body grows by the addition of cells.

A second objection is that by having two worship services, members think they won't know everyone. Statistics have proved, however, that the average church attender is on a first-name basis with only 59.7 people, no matter how large the attendance. So the threat of not having intimacy because of two worship services is not valid. Many who enjoy the intimacy of a small church should realize they will not lose intimacy with friends. A second service provides a larger outreach, and those in the other worship service will have relationships with those who belong in that fellowship. Remember, the purpose of a church is not that everyone know everyone, but that the church carry out the Great Commission.

The innovation of multiple services was first introduced by Roman Catholics as early Mass. Later, mainline churches began using multiple services, especially in metropolitan areas. Now churches throughout America are beginning to use multiple services on Sunday morning to expand their outreach, solve crowded conditions, meet the scheduling problems of their people and amortize their financial overhead for better stewardship per person.

As you prepare to begin a second service, you need to ask and answer seven questions. This will help you know what to expect as you begin. Also, knowing these answers will defuse potentially explosive issues before they arise in the church.

1. Why begin a second service? The greatest purpose is to reach unchurched and unsaved people who are not presently being reached because of the limitations of time, space, money and so

forth. Most churches begin a second worship service because it provides auditorium space and additional parking for church growth. Some begin a second worship service because of convenience to worshipers, and others want to provide other forms of worship. When a church has two worship services, it turns the church into a multiple-cell church so that each worship service is a source of ministry and growth. The church that offers two services is no longer a single-cell church that cannot grow. Both the physical body and the church, which is a spiritual body, grows by the division of cells.

2. Who will come to an earlier service? Usually senior saints enjoy an earlier service as well as young singles who are not married and do not have children. Families that have children usually don't attend the earlier service, so a nursery is not mandatory when first beginning an additional service.

3. What time of the year should it begin? Begin an additional worship service in early September or early spring when secular culture gives energy to the church schedule. The principle of the two-humped camel (see article) indicates that attendance will grow at this time of year and contribute to the success of the additional service.

4. Should the new worship service be identical to the existing one? Some pastors have begun a second service to introduce a different type of worship experience (for example, a formal liturgical service or an informal praise service with audience participation). Most pastors, however, will lead both services from their hearts, which means they will follow one form of worship. Even then the services will not be identical. The pastor will preach the same sermon, but the expression will not be identical.

5. Should the same choir be used twice? No, because it tends to diminish their effectiveness. Use other singing groups or solos for special music in the earlier service. Using a variety of groups or individuals will double the number of people serving the Lord through music. Each worship service ought to be treated as a separate congregation.

6. Should the same ushers or workers be used? No, involve more members in serving the Lord.

7. What if the auditorium is not filled? Sometimes space is not the problem that prohibits growth. It could be a lack of excitement, outreach or limited vision that puts a cap on attendance. A new worship service can provide a step of faith, or break the fear barrier.

Do not begin a new worship service in an auditorium that is already too large, however, because the people will rattle like small stones in a box. Use a marriage or prayer chapel that will provide intimacy. If one is not available, redecorate a Sunday School room into a prayer chapel. The renovated room will contribute to church excitement.

References: Kent R. Hunter, *How to Start an Alternative Worship Service Without Shooting Yourself in the Foot* (Corunna, Ind.: Church Growth Center, 1992); Elmer L. Towns, *How to Go to Two Services* (Lynchburg, Va.: Church Growth Institute, 1989).

WYCLIFFE, JOHN (c. 1328–1384)

The "morning star" of the Reformation.

John Wycliffe studied and taught at Oxford, and until 1378 worked at reforming the Roman Catholic church by removing immoral clergy and reducing the wealth of the church. After 1378, he began challenging aspects of Catholic doctrine, including papal authority and the Catholic view of the Mass.

By 1382, Wycliffe completed the first English translation of the New Testament. When official opposition to his views forced him to retire in 1382, Wycliffe organized a group of lay preachers who became known as Lollards. They took Wycliffe's teaching throughout England. Among those influenced by his writings was John Huss, who adopted a similar approach in Bohemia. This movement continued in England until the British Parliament passed a law against preaching Lollard ideas in 1401, making the act punishable by death. Although Wycliffe's teachings were condemned, he died a natural death. Later, however, a Church council ordered his bones to be dug up and burned.

John Wycliffe's greatest contribution to evangelism was achieved in England, where he translated the Bible into the language of the people, and in Bohemia as he sowed the seeds that would yield their fullest fruit during the Reformation.

XAVIER, FRANCIS (1506–1552)

Founding member of the Society of Jesus (Jesuits) and Roman Catholic missionary to Asia.

Described as "one of the greatest missionaries of all time," Francis Xavier was instrumental in establishing Jesuit missions throughout south and east Asia, including India, Malacca, the East Indies and Japan. He died in the east while preparing to open China as a new field for Jesuit ministry. His ministry established the foundation of Roman Catholicism, which persists to this day in those countries where he ministered.

Xavier was widely recognized for his missionary success even by those who objected to his Roman Catholic theology. He extended the influence of the Roman Catholic church into the Far East. Although the Jesuits came into frequent disfavor with various Popes, Xavier was canonized after his death and is today recognized by Catholics as a saint.

References: A. Brou, *Saint Francis Xavier, 1506-1548* (Paris: Gabriel Beauchesne & Co. 1912); H.J. Coleridge, *The Life and Letters of Francis Xavier* (London: Burns, Oates & Washbourne, 1872); E. A. Robertson, *Francis Xavier* (London: Student Christian Movement, 1930).

YOUTH EVANGELISM

The vast potential and the unique problems locked up in youth challenge every church leader. Adolescent years are the years of decision. The span of time from the ages of 12-18 is a comparatively small portion of the total life expectancy, but this is a time when many accept the Lord. Although adolescence is a period of doubts and honest questions, teens are spiritually sensitive and religious awakening is evident.

Many Christian movements challenge youth, requiring the dedication and sacrifice of adult leaders. If you can give yourself to this service you can be the instrument of many young people giving themselves to Christ and the challenge of being obedient to Him.

At times, young people seem to have a cynical attitude toward life. However, this is only a veneer. Underneath is a tenderness to life and a need for love that only Christ can provide. In the record of the conversation between Jesus and the rich young ruler, Mark comments on the fact that "Jesus...loved him" (Mark 10:21). Christ's attitude toward all youth in all generations is love. If we are going to reach young people, we also must love them. At times it is difficult for adults to love youth, because teens frustrate or seem to threaten them. As long as the adults in a group outnumber the young people present and thus maintain control, there is no problem. But when youth outnumber adults, many older persons forget love, and barriers arise that become hindrances to effective witness for Christ.

Young people represent a restless and troublesome segment of our society. Today's youth are caught in the midst of pressures. On one side, they face pressure from their teen companions, and on the other side from adults. There is tension between peer demands and church doctrines. Conflicting demands bombard youth. The result is rebellion and conflict.

Adolescence is in a no-man's-land, a buffer zone between childhood and adulthood. Adolescents want to be treated as mature people. They do not want others to decide for them, but want to find out for themselves. However, they lack the judgment and insight of adulthood. They do not understand their own behaviors and are unable to predict their own conducts. It is these young people, facing pressures from the outside as well as pressures from within, who need Christ.

Adolescence—An Age of Changes

Physical change. In the early teens, a physical change introduces adolescence. Teens enter a new experience. The physical change of puberty usually takes approximately 13 months. Although today's teens experience puberty earlier than did their parents, this period of the half-child/half-adult often is extended into high school. During puberty, the skeletal frame grows and an adolescent's interest in sex becomes active.

Social change. Society has pushed children to grow up. They are encouraged to date before they are ready, and to act like adults while still children. Perhaps the title of an article in a popular women's magazine is a fitting commentary on these changing times: "Mascara on My Lollipop." Social pressure has resulted in problems for youth that can best be faced with a sense of security and inner spiritual stability.

Psychological change. During adolescence, there is a new interest in physical appearance. Prior to this stage, youth generally give little thought to their appearances. Then self-awareness comes suddenly. "Am I normal?" the teen may ask. "What's happening to me?" Sometimes these physical changes trigger psychological problems. How teens think they look and how they feel about their looks are important and affect their attitudes and relationships.

Teens must understand that their physical forms and development come from God. Scriptural attitudes concerning their bodies must be presented. They should be made aware that God wants their bodies to be used for worship and service.

Intellectual change. Youth is the age of doubts. These generally center about self, God and family. Why do they doubt? Their self-awareness is focusing for the first time in their lives. Without a variety of experiences to temper them, they tend to be idealistic. Teens often expect the best, the ultimate and the perfect, so they are critical. Critical thinking can lead to creative thinking,

however, if it is guided by a teacher dedicated to thoughtful consideration of life.

Habit change. Youth styles and fads change. They intend to create a world all their own. Most teens fall into line with fads to symbolize their identity with their youth subculture. To others, fads are a way of rebelling against adult authority. Fighting teen fads may hinder communication and opportunity for witness. Unless they are immoral, most fads can be ignored. The gulf between youth and adult worlds must be bridged by the youth communicator if he or she is to reach young people. Youth workers must provide a ministry that is definitely pointed at the conversion experience even if indirect in message. They must always be ready to give information, interpretation and example, so as to help develop Christian attitudes.

"Who Am I?"—Stepping Stone to Conversion

Young people seek identity. "Who am I?" is their inner question. In the past few years, there has been a rising emphasis on self-identification psychology. Psychologists are finding that youth go through an identity crisis as they develop. They want to be accepted as persons. They are bombarded with the "Who am I?" question at school, in teen literature and other forms of media. The Bible has an answer for this, and the evangelist can move from the self-identity need into communicating the gospel. Following are some biblical answers to the question: Who am I?

A sinner. Whether subjectively felt or not, youth are sinners. This sinful nature must be viewed and interpreted for what it is—rebellion against God. In seeing themselves as sinners, youth are on the road to understanding salvation.

A person who is loved. No single additional factor can contribute so much to youth's sense of self-esteem as to be loved unconditionally (John 3:16). God in love has a plan for each life that is in the best interest of that person, and in love He will enable a young person to fulfill that plan.

A deciding person. During childhood, most major decisions were made for young people. But as they approach the end of adolescence, they must choose mates, careers and roles in their lives that will bring personal satisfaction. They alone must make these choices. To choose too early is to run the risk of detoured lives. To choose too late is to run the danger of missing God's best.

Youth desire to be self-determining individuals. They demand the right to choose their own clothes, their own friends and their own means of happiness. Their greatest choice concerns heaven and hell. They must make that choice for themselves. In this grave responsibility of choice between life and death, however, young people need mature people to guide them, to answer their honest doubts honestly and to lead them to right decisions by accepting Jesus Christ as Savior and Lord. Youth need to be challenged with the acceptance of salvation.

An accepted person. Teens are concerned about being accepted by peers and adults. They should also be concerned about being "accepted in the Beloved" (Eph. 1:6). Teens should realize, "I am one who has been accepted by God, because I know Jesus Christ." The youth worker must face youth with the obligation of responding to God's provision of salvation before they can be accepted by others.

Each young person must make meaningful relationships, for the depth of life's meaning is found in friends. If they will become friends with Christ and receive Him, they will establish a relationship with God. Then they can branch out into in-depth relationships with other members of God's family.

Christian youth need not remain with their conflicts indefinitely unresolved. Although it is true that no one can extricate him or herself from sin and problems, God, through the Holy Spirit, can and does produce a transformed nature in the new birth.

Evangelizing Through Bible Study

The evangelist must recognize teenage doubts and build a ministry on an intelligent interpretation of the Bible. The teacher should never laugh at the teens' questions, but teach them the difference between criticism and evaluation. When they ask questions the evangelist can't answer, he or she must be willing to say, "I don't know." Youth won't listen to someone who thinks he or she knows everything.

One of the ways youth can find answers to their problems is through Bible study. Here they find the answers to life's needs—the Lord Jesus Christ. The lives of young people can be changed if they learn to dig intelligently, thoroughly and systematically into the Word of God. The following are some factors in a successful Bible study for youth.

Assumptions. The Word of God is the final authority. It is revelation from God that demands a response. Therefore, the youth worker must teach for a decision and encourage teens to respond to the Word. Teenagers should realize that God's Word is not optional; it is essential. The Bible brings conviction of sin and leads to transformation of life. Therefore, Bible study is basic for evangelism.

Attitudes. The whole Bible must be taught and applied to the whole life. Bible study can be meaningful and purposeful only when directed to the life of the students.

All of life is sacred in the sense that Christ is to be at the center. The Bible has principles for all of life and should be related to every need. The Word of God is truth (John 17:17), so life must be molded according to God's Word.

Approach. The task of the evangelist is to guide youth in exploring the Scriptures. Young people should bring the Bible with them to church because it is used in class. Direct involvement is a necessity in Bible teaching. Teaching can be just as evangelistic as a preaching service. Any method that brings lost teens into contact with the message of the Scriptures is evangelistic. A direct study of the Bible is a vital element in all successful evangelistic teaching.

Participation in Bible study involves mental and emotional responses. Because youth have the capacity for critical thinking, every session of the class should be thought provoking. It is not necessary to resort to sensationalism or startling remarks to get youth to think, for nothing is more powerful than an idea. Learning takes place when a student is actively engaged in considering, discussing, analyzing, interpreting and applying ideas to meet a need in life. In so doing, youth are not only learning facts, they are also building up intellectual and emotional attitudes that will help them make decisions for Christ.

Atmosphere. Teaching is most effective when participation takes place. In an informal situation, the teacher can make it possible for any class member to ask questions and to become involved in the teaching-learning situation. The teacher must welcome questions from the students. A question may be the one thing keeping youth from accepting Christ. Questions are evidence of interest. Therefore, questions should be answered from the Word. The true teacher will join youth in the quest for truth. A willingness to learn with the student will prove to be a great asset in motivating the young person to receive Jesus Christ.

Bringing Youth to Decisions

"Reaching youth in time provides them with firm anchorage and steady rudder."[1] The young person may need to experience a crisis in life to realize he or she is a rebel against God. Sverre Norberg expresses this realization of rebellion strongly: "There must be a sin-experience, sin-feeling, sin-despair, and sin-deliverance."[2]

As presented in the plan of salvation in the book of Romans, the evangelist must explain the need of salvation (Rom. 3:23), the penalty of sin (6:23), God's provision (5:8) and the necessity of a person's response (10:9,10).

It must be made clear to the young person that conversion is an experience involving all three elements of the personality—the intellect, the emotions and the will. Conversion involves a voluntary turning away from sin called "repentance." This involves (1) a recognition of sin as the individual's personal sin and rebellion (Ps. 51:3,7,11); (2) a change of feeling (i.e., a heart sorrow for sin and love for God); and (3) inward turning from sin, the renunciation of sin and sinful ways (Ps. 51: 5,7,10; Jer. 25:5).

But conversion also involves saving faith—a change in the sinner in which he or she turns to Christ. This involves (1) acceptance of the Scripture and what it teaches about the provision of Christ's death on the cross; (2) a personal assent to the power and grace of God as revealed in Christ Jesus, trusting Him as the only Savior from sin; and (3) a dedication of the soul to Christ as expressed in the positive act of receiving and appropriating Christ as the only source of pardon and spiritual life.

Using Youth to Reach Youth

Youth need to be evangelized, and youth need to be involved in evangelism. A Christian teen needs to be grounded in the Word of God if he or she is to mature. Some will accept Christ and return to a home where nothing is known about Christ. Church leaders will need to assume some responsibility in nurturing this young person and grounding him or her in the Word.

One of the best ways to win youth to the Lord is through the witness of other Christian youth. Youth should be involved in the church's evangelistic thrust. Youth can be mobilized in many ways to reach their peers for Christ. Youth have been challenged to prepare and then teach Vacation Bible School during the summer. They have also been effective in "five-day backyard" Bible clubs. Youth will respond to a challenge when it is sufficiently challenging.

Leading young people to Christ is a privilege and an obligation. Youth thus won to Christ have a foundation for right living and a set of goals toward which to strive. The teacher can help settle their convictions and loyalties and guide them in life's quest. The church must reach, teach and win youth to Christ. The church must use youth to reach youth.

References: [1]Ted W. Engstrom, "All Out for Youth" *Moody* magazine, LVII:25 (July 1957). [2]Sverre Norberg, *The Varieties of Christian Experience* (Minneapolis: Augsburg Publishing House, 1937), p. 137. Lawrence O. Richards, *Youth Ministry* (Grand Rapids: Zondervan Publishing House, 1972). Fritz Ridenour, *Tell It Like It Is* (Ventura, Calif.: Regal Books, 1968). Roy Zuck and Warren Benson, *Youth Education in the Church* (Chicago: Moody Press, 1978).

Z

ZEISBERGER, DAVID (1745–1808)

Moravian missionary to the native people of America.

At a time of widely held prejudice against America's native people, David Zeisberger earned the respect of the native people of Delaware and won many converts. Unfortunately, settlers refused to believe the "praying Indians" were converted and forced them to move as far inland as Ohio. The prejudice of that era resulted in settlers slaughtering many native people who had converted to Christianity because of doubts about the reality of their conversion.

ZELOTES, SIMON

One of the 12 apostles.

Simon was a member of a radical nationalistic Jewish organization called the Zealots prior to becoming a disciple of Jesus. The Scriptures say very little about Simon or his ministry, but some traditions credit him with taking the gospel to Britain and Persia during the first century.

References: William Barclay, *The Master's Men* (Nashville: Abingdon, 1976). Leslie B. Flynn, *The Twelve* (Wheaton, Ill.: Victor Books, 1985); William Steuart McBirnie, *The Search for the Twelve Apostles* (Wheaton, Ill.: Tyndale House Publishers, 1973).

ZERO GROWTH

The condition in a church that realizes no annual net growth.

How to Lead a Zero Growth Church into Evangelism

In some situations, sociological conditions of which the church has no control will result in stabilizing growth or decline in membership. Other causes, however, are usually involved in zero growth. It is estimated that up to 85 percent of all evangelical churches have pla-

teaued or are declining in attendance. This includes many churches in rapidly growing communities where people may be receptive to the gospel.

Zero growth is often the natural result of a nongrowth emphasis among the leadership of the church. Therefore, the first step in leading a zero growth church into evangelism is to effectively communicate the mission of the church, which is "making disciples." Also, the church should be evaluated to determine what pathologies of church growth are hindering its ability to reach and incorporate new people into its membership.

Having laid a foundation for growth and corrected pathological conditions that might hinder growth, church leadership should then begin modeling a networking approach to evangelism that can be utilized widely in the church family. As people begin seeing others practicing evangelism in a nonthreatening environment, they will be more receptive to becoming involved themselves.

Many church leaders have used a Friend Day Campaign to introduce this approach to evangelism in the church. To ensure that networking is most effective, church leaders should identify and train gifted evangelists in basic skills relating to explaining the gospel and leading others to make personal commitments to Christ. As these evangelists become more proficient, they should be encouraged both to do the work of evangelism and train others in strategic aspects of this ministry.

References: See FRIEND DAY; PATHOLOGY OF CHURCH GROWTH; NETWORKING EVANGELISM.

ZIEGENBALG, BARTHOLOMEW (1682–1719)

Priest-missionary to India.

At the request of the King of Denmark, Bartholomew Ziegenbalg accompanied Henry Plutschau as the first Protestant missionaries to India in 1706. Together, these two Germans established the Danish-Halle Mission. In the course of his ministry, Ziegenbalg translated the Bible into the Tamil language.

ZINZENDORF, COUNT NICOLAUS LUDWIG, VON (1700–1760)

Leader in the Moravian Revival.

Born into a Pietist home in 1700 and educated at Halle, Germany, Count Nicholas Ludwig von Zinzendorf developed at an early age a deep passion for Christ and a zeal to spread Christianity throughout the world. The focus of his Pietism was expressed in the statement, "I have one passion, 'tis He" (i.e., Christ).

In 1722, persecuted Protestants from Bohemia and Moravia settled on his estate near Berthelsdorf, about 70 miles from Dresden. He founded the village of Herrnhut on his land and became bishop of its church. The Moravian Revival began there at a communion service on Wednesday, August 13, 1727.

Under the influence of Zinzendorf, the revived Moravian community sent missionaries to establish Moravian communities throughout Asia, Europe and North America. Moravian missionaries were also sent to the West Indies (1732) and the Dutch possessions on the north coast of South America (1735), as well as parts of Africa. Moravian missionaries were also influential in bringing John Wesley to personal faith in Christ. Shortly after his conversion, Wesley traveled to Herrnhut to meet Zinzendorf and incorporated many Moravian ideas into his Methodist movement.

Zinzendorf's greatest contribution to evangelism was achieved through the missionary work of the Moravians and the influence of the Moravians on John Wesley.

References: Kenneth Scott Latourette, *A History of Christianity* (New York: HarperCollins, 1953), p. 897; Oswald J. Smith, "The Outpouring on the Moravians," in *The Enduement of Power* (London: Marshall, Morgan & Scott, 1974), pp. 95-108. See MORAVIAN REVIVAL; PIETISM.

ZWEMER, SAMUEL M. (1867–1952)

Missionary to the Muslims.

In 1889, Samuel M. Zwemer was one of the founders of the Arabian Mission, a mission committed to evangelizing the Muslims of Arabia. Zwemer's work among Muslims earned him the reputation of being the most effective missionary to Muslims of his day.

ZWINGLI, ULRICH (Or HULDREICH) (1484–1531)

Swiss reformer.

Born January 1, 1484 in Switzerland into a prosperous peasant home, Huldreich Zwingli was educated for the priesthood by his family in both Austria and Switzerland. He studied Latin and Greek and was influenced by the writings of both Augustine and Erasmus. His interest in Erasmus resulted in his memorizing much of the Greek text of the New Testament.

Zwingli began his ministry as a chaplain with Swiss mercenaries stationed in Italy. After ministry in both France and Switzerland, he became the people's priest of Great Minster Church (Zurich) in 1519. Zwingli himself fell victim to a plague that struck the city that year, and prayed for divine assistance. He attributed his recovery to divine intervention, and thereafter worked closely with civic officials to lead his church away from Rome.

In 1520, he surrendered his Papal pension, and formalized his break with Rome two years later. That break was completed in 1525 when he replaced the Roman Catholic Mass with the first Reformed communion service in his church. His reforms included removing all images, relics and organs from the church, breaking with the practice of praying to the saints, and restructuring the worship service around the sermon.

Like the other Reformers, Zwingli believed in salvation by grace alone through faith, arguing that "it is perfected when a man wholly casts himself off and prostrates himself before the mercy of God alone, but in such fashion as to have entire trust in it because of Christ who was given for us." From his pulpit in Zurich, he was instrumental in spreading reform throughout the Swiss cantons. Not above using military force to advance his reform cause, Zwingli himself died October 11, 1531, in the Battle of Kappel when he was fighting neighboring Roman Catholic cantons.

Zwingli's greatest contribution to evangelism

was achieved in establishing Zurich as a Reformed city from which the message of the Reformation would spread throughout Europe.

References: C. M. Dent, "Zwingli," in *The Study of Spirituality*, ed. Chesley Jones, Geoffrey Wainwright, and Edward Yarnold (Oxford: Oxford University Press, 1986), pp. 346-349; Kenneth Scott Latourette, *A History of Christianity* (New York: HarperCollins, 1953), pp. 747-749; Elmer L. Towns, *The Christian Hall of Faith* (Grand Rapids: Baker Book House, 1975), pp. 40, 41

Bibliography

Allen, Roland. *Essential Missionary Principles*. New York: Revell, 1913.

Amberson, Talmadge, ed. *The Birth of Churches: A Biblical Basis for Church Planting*. Nashville: Broadman, 1979.

Anderson, Andy, with Linda Lawson. *Effective Methods of Church Growth*. Nashville: Broadman, 1985.

Anderson, Leith. *Dying for Change*. Minneapolis: Bethany, 1990.

Annan Nelson. *More People! Is Church Growth Worth It?* Wheaton, Ill.: Harold Shaw, 1987.

Appleby, Jerry. *Missions Have Come Home to America*. Kansas City, Mo.: Beacon Hill, 1986.

Arn, Win. *Church Growth Ratio Book*. Pasadena: Church Growth, 1979.

Arn, Win, ed. *The Pastor's Church Growth Handbook*. Pasadena: Church Growth, 1979.

———. *The Pastor's Church Growth Handbook Volume II*. Pasadena: Church Growth, 1982.

Arn, Win, and Charles Arn. *The Master's Plan for Making Disciples*. Pasadena: Church Growth, 1979.

Arn, Win, and Donald McGavran. *Back to Basics in Church Growth*. Wheaton, Ill.: Tyndale, 1981.

Arn, Win, Carol Nyquist, and Charles Arn. *Who Cares About Love?* Pasadena: Church Growth, 1986.

Arnold, Jeffrey. *The Big Book on Small Groups*. Downers Grove, Ill.: InterVarsity, 1992.

Barna, George. *Marketing the Church*. Colorado Springs: NavPress, 1988.

———. *The Frog in the Kettle*. Ventura, Calif.: Regal, 1990.

———. *The Power of Vision*. Ventura, Calif.: Regal, 1992.

———. *User Friendly Churches*. Ventura, Calif.: Regal, 1991.

———. *What Americans Believe*. Ventura, Calif.: Regal, 1991.

———. *Without a Vision, the People Perish*. Glendale: Barna Research, 1991.

Bartel, Floyd. *A New Look at Church Growth*. Scottdale, Pa.: Faith and Life, 1979.

Bassham, Rodger. *Mission Theology: 1948-1975, Years of Worldwide Creative Tension: Ecumenical, Evangelical, and Roman Catholic*. Pasadena: William Carey, 1979.

Beasley-Murray, Paul, and Alan Wilkinson. *Turning the Tide: An Assessment of Baptist Church Growth in England*. Swindon, England: British Bible, 1981.

Belew, M. Wendell. *Churches and How They Grow*. Nashville: Broadman, 1971.

Benjamin, Paul. *The Growing Congregation*. Lincoln, Ill.: Lincoln Christian College, 1972.

Bontrager, Edwin, and Nathan Showalter. *It Can Happen Today! Principles of Church Growth from the Book of Acts*. Scottdale, Pa.: Herald, 1986.

Brock, Charles. *The Principles and Practices of Indigenous Church Planting*. Nashville: Broadman, 1981.

Brown, J. Truman, Jr. ed. *Visionary Leadership for Church Growth*. Nashville: Convention, 1991.

Brown, Lowell. *Your Sunday School Can Grow*. Ventura, Calif.: Regal, 1974.

Callahan, Kennon. *Twelve Keys to an Effective Church*. San Francisco: HarperSanFrancisco, 1977.

Chandler, Russell. *The Kennedy Explosion*. Elgin, Ill., David C. Cook, 1972.

———. *Racing Toward 2001: The Forces Shaping America's Religious Future*. Grand Rapids: Zondervan and Harper, 1992.

Chaney, Charles L., and Ron S. Lewis. *Design for Church Growth*. Nashville: Broadman, 1977.

Cho, Paul. *More Than Numbers*. Dallas: Word, 1984.

Clemmons, William, and Harvey Hester. *Growth Through Groups*. Nashville: Broadman, 1974.

Conn, Harvie. *Theological Perspectives of Church Growth*. Phillipsburg, N.J.: Presbyterian and Reformed, 1976.

Cook, Harold. *Historic Patterns of Church Growth*.

Chicago: Moody, 1971.

Costas, Orlando. *The Church and Its Mission: A Shattering Critique from the Third World.* Wheaton, Ill.: Tyndale, 1974.

Crawford, Dan. *Church Growth Words From the Risen Lord.* Nashville: Broadman, 1990.

Dale, Robert. *To Dream Again.* Nashville: Broadman, 1981.

Dodd, C. H. *The Apostolic Preaching and Its Developments.* Grand Rapids: Baker, 1980.

Drummond, Lewis. *The Awakening That Must Come.* Nashville: Broadman, 1978.

DuBose, Francis. *How Churches Grow in an Urban World.* Nashville: Broadman, 1978.

Dudley, Carl S. *Where Have All Our People Gone?* New York: Pilgrim, 1979.

———. *Making the Small Church Effective.* Nashville: Abingdon, 1978.

Dudley, Roger L., and Des Cummings, Jr. *Adventures in Church Growth.* Washington, D.C.: Review and Herald, 1983.

Easum, William. *The Church Growth Handbook.* Nashville: Abingdon, 1990.

Elliot, Ralph. *Church Growth That Counts.* Valley Forge, Pa.: Judson, 1982.

Ellis, Joe. *The Church on Target: Achieving Your Congregation's Highest Potential.* Cincinnati: Standard, 1986.

Engel, James F., and Wilbert H. Norton. *What's Gone Wrong with the Harvest? A Communication Strategy for the Church and World Evangelism.* Grand Rapids: Zondervan, 1975.

Exman, Gary W. *Get Ready...Get Set...Grow! Church Growth for Town and Country Congregations.* Lima, Ohio: CSS, 1987.

Faircloth, Samuel D. *Church Planting for Reproduction.* Grand Rapids: Baker, 1991.

Falwell, Jerry, and Elmer Towns. *Church Aflame.* Nashville: Impact Books, 1971.

———. *Stepping Out on Faith.* Wheaton, Ill.: Tyndale, 1984.

Fickett, Harold. *Hope for Your Church.* Ventura, Calif.: Regal, 1972.

George, Carl F. *Prepare Your Church for the Future.* Grand Rapids: Revell, 1991.

George, Carl F., and Robert E. Logan. *Leading and Managing Your Church.* Grand Rapids: Revell, 1987.

Gerber, Vergil. *God's Way to Keep a Church Going and Growing.* Ventura, Calif.: Regal, 1973.

Gibbs, Eddie. *I Believe in Church Growth.* London: Hodder & Stoughton, 1985.

———. *Ten Growing Churches.* London: MARC Europe, 1984.

Glasser, Arthur F., and Donald McGavran. *Contemporary Theologies of Missions.* Grand Rapids: Baker, 1983.

Green, Hollis. *Why Churches Die.* Minneapolis: Bethany, 1972.

Griswold, Roland E. *The Winning Church.* Wheaton, Ill.: Victor, 1986.

Hadaway, C. Kirk. *Church Growth Principles: Separating Fact from Fiction.* Nashville: Broadman, 1991.

———. *What Can We Do About Church Dropouts?* Nashville: Abingdon, 1990.

Hale, J. Russell. *The Unchurched: Who They Are and Why They Stay Away.* San Francisco: HarperSanFrancisco, 1980.

Hemphill, Ken. *The Bonsai Theory of Church Growth.* Nashville: Broadman, 1991.

Hemphill, Ken, and R. Wayne Jones. *Growing an Evangelistic Sunday School.* Nashville: Broadman, 1989.

Hesselgrave, David J. *Planting Churches Cross-Culturally: A Guide for Home and Foreign Missions.* Grand Rapids: Baker, 1980.

Hoge, Dean R., and David A. Roozen, ed. *Understanding Church Growth and Decline 1950-1978.* New York: The Pilgrim Press, 1979.

Horton, Michael Scott, ed. *Power Religion: Selling Out of the Evangelical Church?* Chicago: Moody, 1992.

Hundnut, Robert K. *Church Growth Is Not the Point.* New York: HarperCollins, 1975.

Hunter, III, George G. *The Contagious Congregation: Frontiers in Evangelism and Church Growth.* Nashville: Abingdon, 1979.

———. *To Spread Power: Church Growth in the Wesleyan Spirit.* Nashville: Abingdon, 1987.

Hunter, Kent R. *Foundation For Church Growth.* Corunna, Ind.: Leader, 1983.

———. *The Road to Church Growth.* Corunna, Ind.: Church Growth, 1986.

———. *Your Church Has Doors: How to Open the Front and Close the Back.* Corunna, Ind.: Leader, 1983.

Jackson, Neil, Jr. *100 Great Growth Ideas.*

Nashville: Broadman, 1990.

Jenson, Ron, and Jim Stevens. *Dynamics of Church Growth*. Grand Rapids: Baker, 1982.

Johnson, Douglas W. *Vitality Means Church Growth*. Nashville: Abingdon, 1989.

Jones, R. Wayne. *Overcoming Barriers to Sunday School Growth*. Nashville: Broadman, 1987.

Kane, J. Herbert. *Understanding Christian Missions*. Grand Rapids: Baker, 1978.

Kelley, Dean M. *Why Conservative Churches Are Growing*. New York: HarperCollins, 1977.

Kraus, C. Norman, ed. *Missions, Evangelism, and Church Growth*. Scottdale, Pa.: Herald, 1980.

Lawson, E. LeRoy, and Tetsunao Yamamori. *Church Growth: Everybody's Business*. Cincinnati: New Life, n.d.

Lewis, Larry L. *Organize to Evangelize*. Nashville: Broadman, 1977.

Logan, Robert E. *Beyond Church Growth*. Grand Rapids: Revell, 1989.

Martin, Glen, and Gary McIntosh. *The Issachar Factor*. Nashville: Broadman and Holman, 1994.

McCall, Emmanuel L. *Black Church Lifestyles*. Nashville: Broadman Press, 1986.

McCoury, D.G., and Bill May. *The Southern Baptist Church Growth Plan*. Nashville: Convention, 1991.

McGavran, Donald A. *The Bridges of God*. rev. ed. New York: Friendship, 1981.

———. *Church Growth and Group Conversion*. Pasadena: William Carey, 1973.

———. *Church Growth Bulletin: Second Consolidated Volume*. Pasadena: William Carey, 1977.

———. *Effective Evangelism: A Theological Mandate*. Phillipsburg, N.J.: Presbyterian and Reformed, 1988.

———. *How Churches Grow*. London: World Dominion, 1959.

———. *Understanding Church Growth*. 2nd rev. ed. by C. Peter Wagner. Grand Rapids: Eerdmans, 1990.

McGavran, Donald A, ed. *Church Growth and Christian Mission*. Pasadena: William Carey, 1976.

———. *Church Growth Bulletin: First Consolidated Volume*. Palo Alto, Calif.: Overseas Crusades, 1969.

McGavran, Donald A., and Win Arn. *How to Grow a Church*. Ventura: Regal, 1973.

McGavran, Donald, and George C. Hunter III. *Church Growth: Strategies That Work*. Nashville: Abingdon, 1980.

McIntosh, Gary, and Glen Martin. *Finding Them, Keeping Them: Effective Strategies for Evangelism and Assimilation in the Local Church*. Nashville: Broadman, 1992.

McQuilkin, J. Robertson. *Measuring the Church Growth Movement: How Biblical Is It?* Chicago: Moody, 1974.

Miles, Delos. *Church Growth: A Mighty River*. Nashville: Abingdon, 1987.

Murren, Doug. *The Baby Boomerang*. Ventura, Calif.: Regal, 1990.

Mylander, Charles. *Secrets for Growing Churches*. San Francisco: HarperSanFrancisco, 1979.

Neighbour, Ralph W. *Where Do We Go From Here? A Guidebook for the Cell Group Church*. Houston: Touch, 1990.

Ogden, Greg. *The New Reformation*. Grand Rapids: Zondervan, 1990.

Padilla, C. Rene, ed. *The New Face of Evangelicalism: An International Symposium on the Lausanne Covenant*. Downers Grove, Ill.: InterVarsity, 1976.

Palmer, Donald C. *Explosion of People Evangelism*. Chicago: Moody, 1974.

Paton, David, and Charles H. Long, ed. *A Roland Allen Reader: The Compulsion of the Spirit*. Grand Rapids: Eerdmans, 1983.

Peace, Richard. *Small Group Evangelism*. Downers Grove, Ill.: InterVarsity, 1985.

Pentecost, Edward C. *Reaching the Unreached*. Pasadena: William Carey, 1974.

Peters, George W. *A Theology of Church Growth*. Grand Rapids: Zondervan, 1981.

Peterson, Jim. *Church Without Walls*. Colorado Springs: NavPress, 1992.

Pickett, J. Waskom. *Christian Mass Movements in India*. New York: Abingdon, 1933.

———. *The Dynamics of Church Growth*. Nashville: Abingdon, 1963.

Piland, Harry M., and Arthur D. Burcham. *Evangelism Through the Sunday School*. Nashville: Convention, 1981.

Poloma, Margaret M. *The Assemblies of God at the Crossroads: Charisma and Institutional Dilemmas*. Knoxville, Tenn.: The University of Tennessee

Press, 1989.

Powell, Paul W. *The Nuts and Bolts of Church Growth*. Nashville: Broadman, 1982.

Ratz, Calvin, Frank Tillapaugh, and Myron Augsburger. *Mastering Outreach and Evangelism*. Portland, Oreg.: *Christianity Today* and Multnomah, 1990.

Rainer, Thom, ed. *Evangelism in the Twenty-First Century*. Wheaton, Ill.: Harold Shaw, 1989.

Rainer, Thom. *The Book of Church Growth*. Nashville: Broadman, 1993.

Redford, Jack. *Planting New Churches*. Nashville: Broadman, 1978.

Roozen, David A., and C. Kirk Hadaway, ed. *Denominational Growth*. Nashville: Abingdon, 1993.

Schaller, Lyle E. *Assimilating New Members*. Nashville: Abingdon, 1978.

———. *Growing Plans*. Nashville: Abingdon, 1983.

———. *Hey That's Our Church!* Nashville: Abingdon, 1975.

———. *It's a Different World*. Nashville: Abingdon, 1987.

———. *Looking in the Mirror*. Nashville: Abingdon, 1984.

———. *The Middle-Sized Church*. Nashville: Abingdon, 1985.

Schuller, Robert H. *Your Church Has Real Possibilities*. Ventura, Calif.: Regal, 1975.

Slocum, Robert E. *Maximize Your Ministry*. Colorado Springs: NavPress, 1990.

Spader, Dan, and Gary Mayes. *Growing a Healthy Church*. Chicago: Moody, 1991.

Sullivan, Bill M. *Ten Steps to Breaking the 200 Barrier*. Kansas City, Mo.: Beacon Hill, 1988.

Tillapaugh, Frank R. *The Church Unleashed*. Ventura, Calif.: Regal, 1982.

Towns, Elmer. *The Single Adult and the Church*. Ventura. Calif.: Regal, 1967.

———. *Evangelize Through Christian Education*. Wheaton, Ill.: ETTA, 1970.

———. *America's Fastest Growing Churches*. Nashville: Impact, 1972.

———. *Great Soul-Winning Churches*. Murfreesboro, Tenn.: Sword of the Lord, 1973.

———. *Is the Day of the Denomination Dead?* Nashville: Thomas Nelson, 1973.

———. *World's Largest Sunday School*. Nashville: Thomas Nelson, 1974.

———. *Getting a Church Started*. Nashville: Impact, 1975.

———. *Say-it-Faith*. Wheaton, Ill.: Tyndale, 1983.

———. *How to Grow an Effective Sunday School*. Lynchburg, Va.: Church Growth Institute, 1987.

———. *154 Steps to Revitalize Your Sunday School*. Wheaton, Ill.: Victor, 1988.

———. *Ten of Today's Most Innovative Churches*. Ventura, Calif.: Regal, 1990.

———. *Ten Sunday Schools That Dared To Change*. Ventura, Calif.: Regal, 1993.

———. *Winning the Winnable—Friendship Evangelism*. Lynchburg, Va.: Church Leadership Institute, 1986.

Towns, Elmer, John Vaughan, and David Seifert. *The Complete Book of Church Growth*. Wheaton, Ill.: Tyndale, 1981.

Vaughan, John. *The Large Church: A Twentieth Century Expression of the First Century Church*. Grand Rapids: Baker, 1984.

Vines, Jerry. *Wanted: Church Growers*. Nashville: Broadman, 1990.

Wagner, C. Peter. *What Are We Missing?* (formerly *Look Out! The Pentecostals Are Coming*). Lake Mary, Fla.: Creation House, 1973.

———. *Church Growth and the Whole Gospel: A Biblical Mandate*. San Francisco: HarperSan Francisco, 1981.

———. *Church Planting for a Greater Harvest*. Ventura, Calif.: Regal, 1990.

———. *Engaging the Enemy*. Ventura, Calif.: Regal, 1991.

———. *Frontiers in Missionary Strategy*. Chicago: Moody, 1971.

———. *How to Have a Healing Ministry in Any Church* (formerly *How to Have a Healing Ministry Without Making Your Church Sick*). Ventura, Calif.: Regal, 1988.

———. *Leading Your Church to Growth*. Ventura, Calif.: Regal, 1984.

———. *On the Crest of the Wave*. Ventura, Calif.: Regal, 1983.

———. *Stop the World! I Want to Get On*. Ventura, Calif.: Regal, 1974.

———. *Strategies for Church Growth*. Ventura, Calif.: Regal, 1987.

———. *Warfare Prayer*. Ventura, Calif.: Regal,

1992.

———. *Our Kind of People: The Ethical Dimensions of Church Growth in America*. Atlanta: John Knox, 1979.

———. *Your Spiritual Gifts Can Help Your Church Grow*. Ventura, Calif.: Regal, 1979; rev. ed. 1994.

Wagner, C. Peter. ed., with Win Arn, and Elmer Towns, *Church Growth: State of the Art*. Wheaton, Ill.: Tyndale, 1986.

Wagner, C. Peter, and F. Douglas Pennoyer, ed. *Wrestling with Dark Angels*. Ventura, Calif.: Regal, 1990.

Waymire, Bob, and C. Peter Wagner. *The Church Growth Survey Handbook*. Santa Clara, Calif.:

Global Church Growth Bulletin, 1980.

Wimber, John, with Kevin Springer. *Power Evangelism*. San Francisco: HarperSanFrancisco, 1986.

———. *Power Healing*. San Francisco: HarperSanFrancisco, 1987.

———. *Power Points*. San Francisco: HarperSanFrancisco, 1991.

Yeakley, Flavil R., Jr. *Why Churches Grow*. Nashville: Anderson's, 1977.

Zunkel, C. Wayne. *Church Growth Under Fire*. Scottdale, Pa.: Herald, 1987.

Zunkel, C. Wayne. *Strategies for Growing Your Church*. Elgin, Ill.: David C. Cook, 1986.

Resources from Elmer Towns